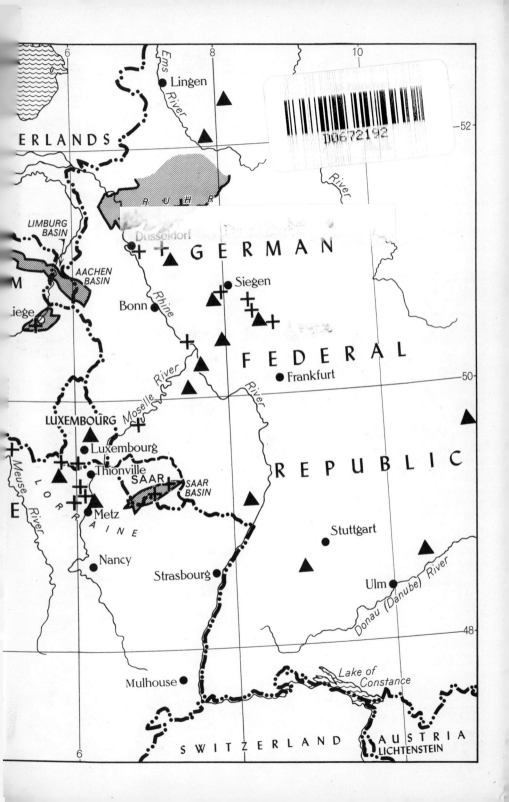

THE SCHUMAN PLAN

A Study in Economic Cooperation

1950-1959

THE
SCHUMAN PLAN

A Study in Economic Cooperation
1950–1959

by WILLIAM DIEBOLD, JR.

Published for the
COUNCIL ON FOREIGN RELATIONS
by
FREDERICK A. PRAEGER
New York
1959

THE SCHUMAN PLAN:
A STUDY IN ECONOMIC COOPERATION, *1950-1959*

Copyright, © *1959, by Council on Foreign Relations, Inc.*
Printed in the United States of America

All rights reserved, including the right to reproduce
this book or any portion thereof in any form.

For information, address Council on Foreign Relations,
58 East 68th Street, New York 21

FIRST EDITION

The Colonial Press Inc., Clinton, Mass.

Library of Congress catalog card number: LC 58-11204

Published in Great Britain and the British
Commonwealth, excluding Canada, by
London: Oxford University Press

COUNCIL ON FOREIGN RELATIONS

4147

PREFACE

SEVEN YEARS ago I finished a book called *Trade and Payments in Western Europe: A Study in Economic Cooperation, 1947-51* (New York: Harper, for the Council on Foreign Relations, 1952). In it I was incautious enough to speak of another volume that would discuss several issues left out of the first, especially the efforts "to unify certain Western European industries, . . . reaching their highest peak in the Schuman Plan." My intention was good and my material largely in hand but my foresight was clouded. While other duties delayed the writing, European cooperation moved into a new phase. OEEC and EPU extended their valuable work, activity continued in other spheres, but increasingly my attention was drawn to what was going on in the European Coal and Steel Community. Here was something really new, a serious effort to integrate the coal and steel industries of six countries by methods going beyond intergovernmental cooperation and the traditional attack on trade barriers. To combine the ever-growing story of the Schuman Plan with the omissions from the previous book—manpower, transportation, the futile efforts to coordinate national investment programs—would produce a strange, lopsided volume, something falling into the class of *biblia a-biblia*, books that are not books. So at the cost of some broken promises, which I regret, this book is devoted entirely to the Schuman Plan. In part it is a sequel to the earlier volume; more importantly, it is an investigation of a new form of international economic cooperation that differs in many ways from the process examined in the book on trade and payments. While this study was being completed Europe moved into yet a third major phase of economic cooperation with the opening of a wider common market, the creation of Euratom, and the negotiations for a possible free trade area. This phase will differ from

vii

the one dominated by the Schuman Plan, but the experience of the first years of the European Coal and Steel Community is relevant to it, and is itself an important part of a continuing story.

In the years I have been writing on this subject my indebtedness for many kinds of help has mounted beyond any possibility of adequate acknowledgment. Bibliography and footnotes suggest something of what I owe to those who have written in this field but my obligations are also very great to the many people, in Europe and the United States, who have been willing to talk at length with me about matters which I could not adequately have understood from reading alone. Only a few of them can be mentioned here, along with others whose help in many forms made this book possible.

The Council on Foreign Relations permitted me to devote a substantial amount of time over a number of years to this study. The Committee on Studies and its chairman, Henry M. Wriston, and the Council's Executive Directors, Walter H. Mallory and George S. Franklin, Jr., have been patient and helpful. My colleagues Philip E. Mosely and John C. Campbell have been wise advisers on many matters and have taken on themselves much of our common burden to free my time to complete this book. Ruth Savord and her library staff have been of vital help in obtaining much material. Though we departed from the Council's usual practice and did not organize a study group to consider in detail the issues examined in this book, I have had the benefit of the work of a number of Council groups during the time I was carrying on this study. I have gained much from the knowledge and experience of visiting research fellows; Ben T. Moore, for instance, has a long acquaintance with Schuman Plan matters and was carrying on a closely related study. I have a special debt to a number of Council members closely acquainted with matters discussed in this book who have always been most generous of their time and their experience in helping me. As always, I have benefited in many ways from the advice and encouragement of Percy W. Bidwell.

During two trips to Europe I was able to talk with a large number of people concerned with the Schuman Plan. I was helped by scholars and journalists, officials of governments and international organizations, politicians and labor union officers, men in the coal and steel business and in consuming industries. National experts and those in the ECE and the OEEC were most helpful but I have a special debt to the officials of the Coal and Steel Community. I have talked, often at length, with a number of members of the High Authority, including all three chairmen, and with several dozen members of their staff and those of other Community organs. They were all most helpful, and several have made major contributions to my understanding by their frank talk, but since they are international civil servants it is perhaps best to adhere to the tradition of anonymity. An exception may be in order for two who are no longer with the Community. Max Kohnstamm, formerly Secretary of the High Authority, was always most kind and did much to improve my understanding of Community problems. I have a very great obligation to François Duchêne, then on the High Authority's staff, who took me in hand when I first went to Luxembourg. He was a most important guide who not only made it possible for me to see the people who would be most helpful to me but also gave me his own highly informed analysis of Community problems and policies. Elsewhere, as in the past, I was very greatly assisted by my good friends connected with institutes of international affairs with which the Council has long-established cooperative relations. I am particularly grateful to Margaret Cleeve in London, Gerolamo Bassani in Milan, Emmanuel Coppieters in Brussels, Wilhelm Cornides in Frankfurt, John Goormaghtigh in Geneva, Jacques Vernant in Paris, and B. H. M. Vlekke in The Hague.

In the United States, too, I have debts to government officials, former government officials, people in the coal and steel industries, and others. George Ball who has been close to Community affairs since the summer of 1950 has often talked with me about Community problems and opened many doors to me in Luxembourg and Paris. Leonard

Tennyson who represents the Community in Washington has been helpful to me in many ways over the years. Willard Thorp was kind enough to invite me to the Merrill Center for Economics where two weeks of discussions about labor costs and international trade did much to clarify my mind on several issues. American officials abroad were always ready to give me the benefit of their experience and observation. I was also helped by many Americans whose private activities abroad gave them insight into the problems with which I was concerned.

John H. Williams read the manuscript of this book for the Council's Committee on Studies and encouraged me greatly by what he said. Others who have read parts of the manuscript are: Robert Bowie, Pierre Gerbet, Ernst B. Haas, John J. McCloy, W. Brian Reddaway, and Raymond Vernon. None of these people has any responsibility for what I have said, especially since I did not take all the good advice they offered me.

For material, published and unpublished, I am grateful to a number of those already mentioned (especially to Ernst Haas and Leonard Tennyson), to some who are referred to in the bibliography, and to Hermann Abs, André Armengaud, Bruno Calabi, J. K. Evans, Jacques Ferry, Thomas Farmer, Hans Gottfurcht, Fritz Hellwig, W. H. Johnstone, Nathaniel Samuels, Lucien Sermon, and Fernand Spaak.

My other obligations are numerous. A generous grant from the Alfred P. Sloan Foundation made an important contribution to the Council's support of this study. Andrew Leith gave me permission to quote from an unpublished paper by his father. Louis Lister, who is preparing a study of the Schuman Plan for the Twentieth Century Fund, cleared up some points for me. E. D. Weldon drew the map and William D. Schlutow the charts. My daughter Barbara made first drafts of the graphs and worked on the index. My son John calculated the area of the "great triangle." My wife Ruth gave me editorial advice on many parts of the manuscript (not all of which I took) and above all carried the burdens that go with seemingly interminable writing that occupies nights, weekends and summers.

It would not have been possible to write this book without the constant loyal and efficient work of a series of helpers. When I began the book Lorna Brennan was my secretary and she did much digging and typing on the first stages. Then Alice Yoakum worked through at least one draft of most of the chapters and made a thorough analysis of the French Assembly's treaty debates. Her successor Jean Pearce must have typed the whole book twice, did much of the work on the galleys and looked up a thousand facts. She was my mainstay during the hardest part of the work. Evangeline Tsirkas arrived at a late stage but there was still a great deal to be done. Helena Stalson, economist on the Council's staff, was also heavily involved in the last stages of the work, providing editorial, bibliographical, and statistical assistance as well as general advice. These two also prepared the index.

Considering how many people have talked very frankly with me, I should add to the usual disclaimer of responsibility for them a word about the kind of book this is. I have made no attempt to tell an "inside story." Though my observation has been enlightened by these conversations, and much of what I say about points of view rests on them, this book is essentially an analysis from the outside, written primarily from the public record. I have probably made mistakes of fact; my analysis of some matters undoubtedly overlooks relevant points. In trying to cover the main elements of the Community's history during the transitional period I have surrendered the possibility of going as deeply into some issues as I should have liked. If the result provides a setting for more specialized work by others I shall be satisfied. Finally there is the time factor. My emphasis has been on the transitional period, ending February 1958, but I have been able to take account of major events through February 1959. My aim in doing this was not primarily to keep up to date, which is impossible in a book like this, but to show how the Community dealt with problems it had not faced before. Though I have had to give much attention to what went on during this period my objective has been a broader one than to chronicle the Community's early years. I have tried to use these data to show the nature of this new kind of international economic cooperation and to suggest the problems that it will encounter for some time to come.

As an American I have been concerned with the meaning of the European Coal and Steel Community for the United States. Parts of several chapters consider specific policy issues in some detail. It seems clear to me, however, that the most important implications of the Schuman Plan for the United States go beyond these questions. They lie in the effect of the Community on Europe and in what we can learn about the processes of international cooperation and economic integration from this remarkable and novel effort.

March 6, 1959   W.D.Jr.

CONTENTS

PART TWO
THE COMMUNITY IN ACTION

Tables

Figures

PART I

FROM PLAN TO TREATY

ONE

MAY 9, 1950

". . . The French Government proposes that the entire French-German production of coal and steel be placed under a common High Authority, in an organization open to the participation of the other countries of Europe."

With these words, Robert Schuman, the French Minister of Foreign Affairs, startled the world on the afternoon of May 9, 1950, and gave his name to a most ambitious, most drastic, and most novel venture in international economic cooperation.

The coal-steel pool, Schuman said, would immediately provide a common basis for economic development, "the first step in the federation of Europe. . . ." It would "make it plain that any war between France and Germany becomes, not merely unthinkable, but materially impossible." The word "supranational" which was to play so great a part in the subsequent discussion of the Schuman Plan did not occur in the initial statement, but Schuman touched its essence when he spoke of "a new High Authority, whose decisions will bind France, Germany and other member countries. . . ." The task of the High Authority, he said, would be to secure: "the modernization of production and the improvement of its quality; the supply of coal and steel on identical terms to the French and to the German markets as well as to the markets of other member countries; the development of common exports to other countries; the equalization through improvement of the living conditions of the workers in these industries." Transitional measures to adapt industries to the new circumstances would be necessary, but at the very outset customs

I

barriers and discriminatory transport rates would be eliminated. Unlike a cartel, the new organization would "ensure the fusion of markets and the expansion of production." As time passed, "Conditions will gradually develop that will spontaneously provide the most rational distribution of production at the highest level of productivity."

In a few paragraphs the French foreign minister brought Europe face to face with extraordinary new prospects. He was suggesting, officially and with full solemnity, measures that would touch the heart of Western Europe's political and economic life. France was proposing partnership with the hereditary enemy; what is more, the partnership was to rest on the creation of a common interest in basic industries, the sinews of war and the mainsprings of the economy of peace. France, one of the birthplaces of modern nationalism, was suggesting that national sovereignty be given up in matters that by any reasonable definition could be called "vital interests." The heavy industry of Western Europe, notorious for its history of concentrated private power, interlocking connections, restrictive practices, and cartels, and marked by conflicts of private and public interest, was to be placed under international public supervision and dedicated to the expansion of production, the merging of markets, and the increase of living standards. The industrial and mining complex of Lorraine, the Ruhr, the Saar, Belgium, Luxembourg, and northern France, was to be restored to the "natural unity" that had scarcely existed except in the mind's eye since the advent of the modern steel industry in the last decades of the 19th century.

These were "high astounding terms" indeed, like those that Marlowe put in the mouth of Tamburlaine. But the Asian had been threatening Europe while the Frenchman who had grown up in Lorraine when the Kaiser ruled that province was promising, or at least holding out hope. But could these things be? If Schuman's sketch were filled in, if his words were carried into practice and the main principles he proposed adhered to, it would mean the creation of a wholly new economic and political entity in Western Europe. The basic industries of the region would gain new strength from their operation in a larger area than before; resources that had been separated by national barriers would be brought fruitfully together; the impact on the economic life of the whole area, including the parts not covered by the new plan, would be immense. Or so it seemed.

If Schuman's ideas were carried out, France and Germany would have created a community of political interest that would put major new limits on the possibilities of separate national action. That step could hardly fail to spread until the interests of the two nations fused over a much wider range. Defeated Germany would be brought back to virtually equal status in the comity of nations and would be linked almost indissolubly with its western neighbors who for generations had feared its might and now would in some sense share it. An unprecedented degree of political and economic integration would have been achieved in an historical trouble spot. One of the Western world's weakest points would have been turned inside out to become a major source of strength. This at least was the promise.

Such vast vistas inevitably provoked vast skepticism. Were these words not intended to shock and stimulate, to gain a psychological advantage for France, rather than to presage real agreement? Was this not a statement of ultimate desiderata that would at best produce some small practical gains, moving a modest inch toward a more rational use of Western Europe's resources? Who would actually agree to such drastic propositions? Would not the technical rendering of these ideas in a detailed agreement empty them of their radical content? And if the agreement were not detailed, would it not prove to be a cloak for "business as usual"—public and private? Even if the initial drive were real, how could one maintain *élan* during the years of negotiation and adjustment that would have to pass before the new order came to be? And without *élan*, would not habitual attitudes and traditional interests reassert their dominance? What signs had Europe given that it was ready to revolutionize itself in this fashion? Anyone could see the obstacles; well-entrenched private interests would fight the proposals and could almost certainly draw on deep-set political attitudes to block their realization. Governments would be no readier to surrender so much power in such critical fields. The world had heard many fine words before. Few, if any, of the postwar plans and organizations had lived up to their initial fanfares. Would it not be the same old story with the fine, new Schuman Plan?

Time has given part of the answer to some of these questions. There have been long negotiations, active opposition, technical difficulties. But the initial result was true to the first statement of principles. Six nations ratified a fifty-year treaty embodying Schuman's main proposals. They removed trade barriers, gave real powers over the coal and steel industries to supranational bodies, agreed on rules covering a wide range of activities, set forth aspirations, named specific objectives, and established procedures for working toward them. The first obstacles were overcome. Since 1952 the European Coal and Steel Community has been a reality. In February 1958 it emerged from its "transitional period," a kind of initiation into its major problems. Problems remain. New ones have appeared. The significance of what has been done is not altogether clear. Every turn of events creates uncertainty. Skepticism, too, remains and is justified. But undoubtedly something new exists in Western Europe; actions have been taken that have changed circumstances; some kind of a future lies ahead for the coal and steel pool, whether it is a fuller realization of momentous potentialities, a drab routine, or failure, plain or fancy.

THE PLAN OF THE BOOK

The purpose of this book is to contribute to the understanding of the European Coal and Steel Community. It comprises a rather mixed bundle of elements. The Community deals primarily with economic problems, so that is where the main emphasis of the book lies. This does not rule out politics, otherwise one could understand neither the problems nor the Community; but the book does not pursue political questions as far as it does the economic ones. My central purpose is analytical, but I have had to give much space to description and narration, without which the analysis might seem thin and arbitrary. Where familiar issues are involved, such as the tariff, much can be taken for granted about what the reader will know. In dealing with problems on which only specialists are likely to have much information, such as transportation, I have thought it wise to describe issues at somewhat greater length. For this and other reasons, the importance of a subject cannot be judged by the space given to it in this book. While some sections are quite detailed, their purpose is to contribute to broad judgments. Often it is only the details that show what the real issues are. This book looks forward to the future, but to do so it must give primary attention to the past.

The life of the Community has many facets. To examine all problems in a single perspective is to ignore part of the Community's character. To examine every issue in all its aspects would be impossible in a single volume. Therefore, to convey some sense of the complexity of the Community, the chapters that follow vary in emphasis or focus. Sometimes the relation of the High Authority to the governments, or to industry, or to the Assembly, provides the thread of the argument; sometimes a broader narrative of events or a direct analytical attack on a problem is employed. When one element is stressed the others are apt to be ignored, but they were not absent. Each should be read into every situation in some reasonable degree.

Naturally, the book provides only part of the story. Legal issues, administration, personalities, and day-to-day politics are almost entirely left out. I have avoided digesting reports, reproducing statistics, describing negotiations, or listing all the steps in a process, except to the extent necessary to explain central issues. There are limits, too, resulting from ignorance, or the practical difficulty of using all the available material or of considering the analyses made by others. The Critical Bibliography calls attention to some of the material not dealt with, and takes the place of extensive acknowledgments in footnotes of the work of others. Above all, to understand its limitations, one must bear in mind that this is a book about the Community and not primarily a study of the coal and steel industries; it therefore often stops short on the brink of some very interesting problems, because their exploration would require a different kind of analysis or an excursion of impracticable length.

The book has four main parts. The remaining chapters of this opening section tell something of the background of the Schuman Plan and sketch the process by which the French foreign minister's words of May 9, 1950, were translated into the physical reality of the High Authority's first meeting in Luxembourg on August 10, 1952. This history is not recited for its intrinsic interest, great as that is, but to show the issues that the Schuman Plan raised and the hopes and fears it generated; these are guides to the understanding of what happened when the Community got under way. Part II examines the Community's experience during the transitional period. More intertwined than their titles may indicate, these ten chapters provide the data and the piece-by-piece analysis on which the broad evaluation of the Community must rest. Part II is largely inward-looking; it concerns the effort to put the Treaty into practice within the six countries. Part III deals more briefly with the Community's external relations and includes a chapter on American interests and policies (matters which are considered elsewhere in the text as well). The final section of the book fits all these pieces together in a broad evaluation of the Community. These chapters deal with its economic impact, what it has meant to each participating country and to outsiders, the character of the coal and steel economy that has emerged, the kind of entity the Community has turned out to be, its relation to other measures of European integration, the consequences of "partial integration," and, at the end, the problems for the future.

The emphasis of the book is on the transitional period. Most of the writing was completed by the summer of 1958 but in dealing with some subjects I have been able to take account of events up to the beginning of 1959. In the nature of things, this book can be only an interim appraisal. The Community has not completed all of its initial tasks. Major problems lie ahead—some of them quite different from those of the past. Still, much has happened and the appraisal of the transitional experience is the best basis we have for understanding what the Community is and what it may become.

TWO

BEHIND THE SCHUMAN PLAN

WHY DID Schuman make his remarkable statement of May 9, 1950? Why was France reversing its policy toward Germany in a way that would break the historic mold of national power and responsibility? Why was heavy industry chosen as the starting place for a drive toward European union? And why was this decided in the spring of 1950, and not a year before or afterward? We need at least rough answers to these questions to understand some of the forces that shaped the Treaty and the Community.

The elements of the immediate story were dramatic and rather bizarre: a businessman and banker turned public servant who, while guiding the reconstruction of the French economy, dreamed a common-enough dream of United Europe in an intensely personal fashion, complete with political strategy; a foreign minister who took a major foreign policy initiative with little or no consultation with his own ministry; a rapid elaboration of the final version of the plan in great secrecy by a tiny group of people; only the briefest discussion before the Cabinet—which had just heard of the proposal—endorsed a measure that went well beyond foreign policy and would have a major effect on the defense and the economy of France; almost immediate public announcement with only the shortest notice to allies and others on whose assent success would depend. This is surely one of the most singular examples of foreign policy-making in modern times, and an even more remarkable origin for an elaborate structure that became a practical reality true to the principles of the original announcement and even to its main concrete proposals.

8

Interesting as the episode and its implications are,[1] our concern is with the broader circumstances that help explain why a serious French initiative could come out of so unlikely a sequence of events.

"THE GERMAN QUESTION"

Foreign Minister Schuman made his historic statement on the eve of a conference with Dean Acheson, the American Secretary of State, and Ernest Bevin, the British Foreign Secretary. A meeting of the Council of the North Atlantic Treaty Organization followed immediately. No specific item on the agenda of either of these meetings seems likely to have elicited the French proposal, nor does it appear that the new initiative greatly influenced the course of discussion at the two conferences. Indeed, Schuman's statement came so suddenly that the representatives of other governments may well have shied away from talking about it until they could fathom its meaning. Schuman gained honor and a psychological advantage by his bold proposal, but its very boldness—and particularly its apparent reversal of traditional French policy toward Germany—inevitably generated skepticism and the suspicion that the French move was only a *beau geste*.

The relative importance of these events is now much clearer. We are familiar with the process set in motion by Schuman's statement, but we have to scrabble among books and papers to recall what else was discussed in the week of conferences that followed. And then we can see that it is not the particular circumstances of those conferences but the process of which they were a part that is important in understanding the Schuman Plan.

Not so many years before, citizens of the Western powers had confidently imagined that defeated Germany would remain disarmed and perhaps occupied for a generation. By 1950 it was plain that Western Germany was moving toward the resumption of an independent role in the

---

[1] The complete story has not been told. The best account is Pierre Gerbet, "La Genèse du Plan Schuman," *Revue Française de Science Politique*, Jl.-Sept. 1956, pp. 525-553.

comity of the free world. Occupation continued but controls had been removed or loosened, one after another. The
policy of keeping Germany militarily weak by holding
down its industrial activity had been abandoned. The German economy was reviving. A German government sat in
Bonn at the head of the newly created *Bundesrepublik*.
The victors retained some powers under the Occupation
Statute, but the spirit of their action was to hold a watching
brief while giving the Germans increasing autonomy.

Officially there were no public proposals to arm Germany, but people were talking about that step privately
and publicly, particularly in the United States and Britain.
The logic was simple. NATO was a defensive alliance
against possible Soviet aggression; with American help
Europe was rearming but remained weak; a major political
aim was to keep Germany tied to the West; for political
and military reasons Germany had to be defended; at the
same time Germany had a military potential that was not
being used. Clearly events were moving toward increased
independence, strength, and eventually rearmament, for
Germany.

This was a difficult situation for France. The French
government had gone along reluctantly with American and
British measures relaxing controls on Germany. Many
Frenchmen thought the process much too fast. The International Ruhr Authority, once looked on as a means of
continuing control, showed no signs of being a lasting
bulwark. The prospect of Boches with guns was hideous to
the average Frenchman and spelled death, in another sense,
to French governments. The compulsion some Frenchmen
felt to reiterate that France was still a great power seemed
itself a frenetic sign of weakness. The war in Indochina
was a serious drain on French economic and military
strength; North Africa was sporadically troubled. The
French economy showed good recovery in many respects
but was subject to heavy and chronic inflationary pressure.
Governments continued to show great parliamentary weakness. The French were acutely sensitive to the fact that in
spite of ritual references to Lafayette and "our oldest ally,"

many rather vocal Americans were more impressed with the sturdy virtues they thought they discerned in the Teuton than with the way the democratic and military traditions of France were manifesting themselves.

In these circumstances the French had only a few choices. They could continue backwards along the route they had followed since the end of the war, delaying where they could and hoping something would turn up to divert the course of events and make German revival and the prospect of rearmament less dangerous. This course was not very promising; the most likely benefit—if it was a benefit—was only delay. The consequences of saying an everlasting "no" to the United States and Britain might be serious, and might even lead them to feel that they had, in some sense, to "choose" between France and Germany. The pursuit of some form of neutralism was another unpromising course. Alternatively, France could find a new approach to the German problem. That was what Schuman seemed to be doing. He was proposing a merger of French and German interests to replace the rivalry and friction of the past. Schuman was saying, in effect, "We shall deal directly with the Germans and offer them equal status in return for mutual safeguards, not on paper but in the mines and factories of the Ruhr and Lorraine."

This was a drastic change in the direction of French policy. It caught foreigners and Frenchmen by surprise. Such speed, in contrast to the long and slow exchanges of views, mulling, and cautious drafting that normally precede major shifts in policy, inevitably raised questions about motive, sincerity, and feasibility. No one could say how far the Assembly and the French people would back the foreign minister, even if foreign governments—for whom the implications were also drastic—proved responsive. Yet there was a clear, basic logic. France could not prevent the growth of German strength; to try to delay that growth would weaken France's position; the possibility that remained was to find a new framework within which German development could proceed along channels that were not only less worrisome for France but that promised positive

benefits to both countries; to serve mutual interests France
would have to make concessions and treat Germany as an
equal.

The thought was not entirely new. The desire to provide
a constructive way of dealing with the perennial "German
question," in a sense to "contain" Germany, had been one
of the many elements going into the movement toward
closer cooperation, perhaps even union, in Western Europe.
The logic had never been carried as far as in the proposal
for a coal and steel pool. This time, said Schuman as he introduced his formal statement, "it is no longer a question of
vain words, but of an act, a bold act, a constructive act."

EUROPEAN INTEGRATION

There was more to the movement toward European integration than a desire to counter or contain Germany. The
main elements are well known: the need for strength, the
desire to end old conflicts and rivalries, the sense that only
in combination could the countries of Europe carry a
weight in world affairs even approaching that of the
United States and the Soviet Union. Economically the
case for greater integration rested on a string of familiar
propositions about the advantages of removing national
trade barriers and creating a large market, increasing competition, improving the allocation of resources, and improving Western Europe's trade and payments position in the
world.

French political leaders, including Schuman, had been in
the forefront of the movement for European political integration. They had played an important part in setting up
the Council of Europe (which Germany was invited to join
in March 1950). Many French spokesmen professed to want
more rapid progress toward closer political association, with
less emphasis on national veto powers. British unwillingness
to come into anything resembling a European federation
was widely blamed, especially in France, for the slow progress toward political union. French opinion on the desirability of pushing ahead toward some kind of Continental
federation without Britain was divided. A potent factor in

the calculations was the implication of having to face Germany alone, or almost alone, in a closer political union. But so long as Britain provided the obstacle the French never had to face the hard political decisions involved in surrendering sovereignty; they could endorse the principle of union and say that one must *faire l'Europe* without having to accept the consequences of that position.

Those who really wanted European integration were rather frustrated. They had been disappointed in the limited scope and accomplishments of the Council of Europe where action seemed blocked by governments. They did not believe that the Organization for European Economic Cooperation with its unanimity rule could create a real union. They were divided in their views as to whether a basic political union or a piecemeal approach via concrete measures of limited cooperation was the more promising. Whichever view one took, nothing that was happening held out the hope of important progress toward European unity. It was to these people that Schuman was speaking when he called the proposal he was about to make "the first decisive act in building Europe." From the outset, he and Monnet stressed the point that the Schuman Plan was a step toward a larger political union. "The pooling of coal and steel production," said the original statement, "will immediately assure the setting up of common foundations of economic development, the first step in the federation of Europe . . . ."

Though political aims dominated, the Schuman Plan was also part of the process of economic cooperation. In this perspective, too, it was novel and drastic. France had played an active part in Western European economic cooperation, but it had not been a leader in devising major projects that worked in practice. Indeed, French economic difficulties had been a recurrent source of trouble for the process of cooperation. Inflation and a heavy demand for imports coupled with difficulties in expanding exports produced chronic deficits in France's foreign accounts. The forces of protectionism, resting on tradition as well as immediate circumstances, were active in all European countries but seemed to have a particularly strong position in France. All these circumstances made France somewhat laggard in the liberalization of trade and payments, the main achievement of Western European economic cooperation up to the summer of 1950.

Many Frenchmen recommended measures of fuller economic union, often in the form of complete convertibility of European currencies among themselves—or possibly even the creation of a single European currency—and sometimes in the form of some sort of industrial unification (such as was frequently suggested by André Philip, among others). But the government did not press in these directions. Again British opposition made it unnecessary to test loose French support of principles by practical action. When the French government had accepted more drastic proposals for economic union, the results had been negligible. A customs union treaty between France and Italy was worked out with some difficulty over a period of years, but domestic opposition in France was allowed to kill the proposal without a major battle by the government. France had also proposed a kind of economic union with the Benelux countries, in which the currencies of members would have been more easily convertible and in which trade barriers would have been reduced. This too had died, at least in part because France opposed the Dutch view that the proposed union should include Western Germany—and this not so many months before Schuman proposed the coal and steel pool.

The Schuman Plan was a landmark in Western European economic cooperation. It proposed going, at one leap, well beyond what had already been done, yet it was linked with what had gone before, both in its aims and in some of its methods. For example, one of the chief obstacles to the removal of trade barriers was the fear of dislocation of production and unemployment. This was one reason past action had been confined to partial removal of quotas under the OEEC's liberalization measures. The Schuman Plan proposed complete and immediate removal of tariffs as well as quotas on coal and steel. It sought to eliminate the fear of dislocation by an international mechanism that would ease adjustments through subsidies and help finance the adaptation of capital and labor to the new circumstances.

The fact that the Schuman Plan was confined to coal and steel coincided with another line of thought about Western European cooperation. This was the belief that greater progress could be made in economic cooperation if one proceeded by sectors of the economy instead of by measures that dealt with all products at once. Closely related was the "functional approach," a belief that each measure of cooperation should be confined to a certain sphere and that a government's commitment should be limited to what was necessary to achieve specified purposes. The rationale of this approach lay in the difficulties of more sweeping measures and the apparent unwillingness of most Western Europeans to accept a full political union within which economic adjustments could be made in terms of the general interest rather than of a collection of supposed separate national interests. By a series of functional measures, said the proponents of this view, one would move toward full economic and political union, but the pace would be set by the practical possibilities and meanwhile there would be immediate gains, not merely the postponed hopes of more perfect union. This approach had not been adopted on any significant scale, so its strengths and weaknesses—and it had both—remained largely in the realm of argument. Looked at in this perspective, the Schuman Plan appeared as the greatest functional measure ever launched, and with a more directly political cast than most.

The Schuman Plan also provided a new approach to some problems which the OEEC's efforts had done little to solve. During late 1948 and early 1949 the OEEC had tried to harmonize the national recovery programs of its member countries. This effort had failed, partly because of its complexity, partly because of the unwillingness of countries to make drastic adaptations in their plans that would make them dependent on developments over which they had no control. In any case, few, if any, of the participating countries had kept to the programs they had outlined. A somewhat more modest effort also failed; this was an attempt to coordinate national investment programs in a number of different fields, one of them steel. The committees which the OEEC set up to deal with each industry studied national investment programs, pointed out duplication of effort, and suggested modifications to conserve resources and produce a more rational structure of production in Europe. Some countries may have made modest changes in their investment programs as a result of this work; some private enterprises may have altered plans or decided against certain investments for fear of being caught in a situation where the prospects of profits would be reduced. But by and large investments were not being coordinated, though the committees continued to meet. The Schuman Plan tackled these basic problems in a somewhat different way. A successful pooling of the heavy industry of Western Europe would ensure not only a more effective division of labor, taking advantage of the larger market, but would also provide a setting in which investment would shape the growth of heavy industry in accordance with the needs of the whole area.

Though there had been failures, there was no immobility in European economic cooperation in the winter of 1949-50, as many thought there was in political cooperation. The European Payments Union, one of the major and most successful measures in the entire process, was being actively negotiated. With it, trade liberalization advanced to a new level. The OEEC was in one of its most active periods; new plans for intensifying cooperation were being put forward and studied with considerable frequency. In the setting of European economic cooperation, the Schuman Plan rose out of ferment, not stagnation. It was different, though, from the other measures in its supranationality, in the extent of the integration it proposed, and in the apparent willingness of the French government to carry out the plan.

THE STEEL AND COAL INDUSTRIES

Since Schuman and Monnet were primarily interested in French-German relations and the unification of Europe, the choice of coal and steel for their great initiative cannot be explained in terms of the economic problems of these industries. One looks for explanations based on psychological, historical, symbolical considerations, and perhaps on the arguments about making war impossible that were used by Schuman.[2] To those thinking along these lines, coal and steel may have seemed an easy and obvious choice, but once made—and perhaps before, for all we know—the economic position of the two industries in Europe, and particularly in France, became relevant.

Monnet's Commissariat Général du Plan de Modernisation et d'Équipement had played a major role in French economic recovery since 1947. It had given special attention to the coal and steel industries as it guided measures to expand capacity and reduce costs and supplemented other sources of investment with public funds. These two industries absorbed about 30 per cent of the funds disbursed by the Monnet Plan organization in its first five years. French coal production in 1949 was above the level of the late '30s at a time when German and British production was lagging. Further expansion was planned. The progress in steel production was even more marked, and was generally regarded as one of the main achievements of the Monnet Plan. Crude steel output in 1949 was just over nine million tons, more than in any year since 1929. Further expansion was planned and in 1951 the prewar record was surpassed. The capacity of the steel industry was rising rapidly; two continuous wide-strip mills were being built, the most modern in Europe.

It looked as though France would need export markets to absorb all this steel, especially if the new wide-strip mills were to operate at their most economical level. Coal, on the other hand, was something France would have to go on importing for some time. Although production was high, equipment good, and output per manshift well above the

---

[2] Gerbet, cited, explores this matter and stresses the mass psychological response to coal and steel and the possibilities of expanding integration if it started with heavy industry. He goes a bit too far, in my opinion, in dismissing coal and steel problems as not pressing, but makes a good argument contrasting the difficulties of integrating coal and steel and the probable greater ease of doing this in newer industries.

European average, France lacked adequate supplies of coking coal. Imports came mostly from the Ruhr in a long-established pattern of French dependence. Adequate supplies of German coking coal were among France's main objectives after 1918 and again after 1945. A sliding-scale agreement with Britain and the United States assured France of a share of the Ruhr's coal output. The French had hoped that the International Ruhr Authority would continue to guarantee them access to German coal. But German independence and the rise in Ruhr steel production were putting pressure on the supply and one could foresee a time when France could get Ruhr coal only on terms that suited the Germans. Schuman's proposal promised help on both steel exports and coal imports.

While France's steel output was rising above prewar levels, that of Western Germany was lagging. During the last five years before the war, Western Germany alone (excluding the Saar and Eastern Germany) produced more than twice as much crude steel as France. But in postwar years Western Germany's output did not equal France's until 1949 (excluding the Saar). As Allied controls fell away and German recovery proceeded, the Ruhr's steel output was bound to increase rather rapidly. One could not be so sure about coal production, however. The occupying powers had fostered coal mining but productivity and production were both well below prewar levels. What had traditionally been a major German export was now sent abroad only by order of the occupying authorities, over German protests.

Western Europe's coal position was more comfortable in the spring of 1950 than at any time since the war. Increased production and the slackening of the rate of general economic growth that accompanied the 1949 recession had played a part. At the beginning of 1950, Western Europe's demand and supply for coal seemed reasonably matched though there were still some shortages. There were many who thought that the worst of the trouble was over, and that while Europe would have to work hard at increasing coal supplies and would have occasional difficul-

ties, major shortages and the need to import large quantities
of expensive American coal were things of the past.

In steel, a different outlook had attracted attention. One
of the difficulties the OEEC had encountered in trying
to coordinate investment progams was the apparent determination in almost every country to increase steelmaking
capacity or, where it did not exist, to build at least one
steel mill. The Economic Commission for Europe, survey-
ing this tendency and totting up new plants and the plans
for expansion, concluded in the fall of 1949 that if plans
were not modified Europe's steelmaking capacity in 1953
would be substantially greater than the predictable demand
for steel both for consumption and for export.[3] This report
raised in a most authoritative way the specter of over-
production and surplus capacity that had haunted the
European steel industry for decades. It could be argued
that the report was too pessimistic, or that it underestimated
the probable demand for steel for rearmament, but these
arguments made far less impact than the general conclusion. The slight recession in the United States in 1949
reinforced the effect of the report by reminding people
that the expansion of production and demand might not go
on indefinitely and that Western Europe was not fully in
control of its own economic future.

The specter of overproduction had a twin, the cartel
bogey. Conversations were already going on among Western European steel producers to see what might be done
about reviving prewar cartel agreements or negotiating new
ones. The ECE report seemed likely to strengthen the hand
of those who argued that producers must get together to
prevent the creation of excess productive capacity or, if
that proved impossible, to avoid the "cut-throat competition
amongst steel producers in 1953" that the ECE foresaw.
Those who feared the revival of a steel cartel were moved
to look around for safeguards; necessarily they looked first
to governments. The coal and steel proposal, which M.

[3] UN Economic Commission for Europe, *European Steel Trends in
the Setting of the World Market*, p. 72 (1949. II. E. 2). (Hereafter cited
as ECE, *European Steel Trends.*)

Schuman sharply distinguished from a cartel, touched both their interests. It suggested machinery that might cope with the threat of overproduction and uneconomic expansion of investment; at the same time, it presaged some kind of public control over cartel activities.

* * * * *

French foreign policy, the revival of Germany, the movement toward European integration, the condition of the coal and steel economy of Western Europe—all these help explain the Schuman Plan. The circumstances sketched so broadly here do not fully explain why the French foreign minister made precisely the proposal he did at just that time. For that one must take account of a wide range of factors. As Gerbet says: "The coal-steel pool cannot be correctly explained, in its origins or in its characteristics, except by the psychology and will of M. Monnet." [4] There are also the personality and aims of Schuman, his political and diplomatic calculations. The next chapter tells something of the long and many-stranded history of ideas about unifying French and German coal and steel, and about proposals made not long before Schuman spoke. The importance of the broad elements set out in this chapter is that they explain why it was possible to translate ideas, enthusiasms, and novel and ingenious construction into French policy. " . . . The idea of the pool . . . provided a solution to problems that had confronted France for several years, on the global level, on the European level, on the German level." [5]

On each of these levels there was a need for France to "do something" and the statement of May 9, 1950, satisfied that need. "France has acted," said Schuman, "and the consequences of her action could be immense. We hope that they will be."

[4] Gerbet, cited, p. 552.
[5] Same, p. 553. "This is why M. Robert Schuman did not hesitate to give his approval to M. Monnet's project, courageously took the entire responsibility for it through seven successive governments, and contributed in a decisive fashion to securing Parliament's ratification of the treaty."

THREE

AN OLD DREAM

For a long time it has been a textbook commonplace that the "natural" unity of the coal and steel industries of the Ruhr-Lorraine region was destroyed by "artificial" barriers. It has been taken for granted that the "natural" was good and the "artificial" bad. The picture has looked a bit different at different times and places; the offenders against nature have been sometimes the victors of 1871 and sometimes the victors of 1918; it may have been "nationalistic governments" who were blamed for the artificial barriers, and it may have been "selfish industrialists" and "cartels." But always the vision is of unity and integration, a common effort for the common weal. The dream has not been just an idle fancy. Serious, hard-working men have taken the measure of this vision and tried to make it real. Like most symbols, this ideal has sometimes been a cloak for narrower interests than the public good.

The persistence of this dream and the widespread acceptance of the intellectual arguments for it account for some of the success of the Schuman Plan. The French proposal promised unity, the public interest, and the common good. It stood in contrast to thirty, perhaps eighty, years of history. With the sanction of high diplomacy, it offered a chance to accomplish what almost everyone professed to want accomplished. Few could be found who would challenge the ideal, however much they might attack the means proposed for attaining it or question whether the Schuman Plan was not a façade for the old game. Schuman's initiative gained an unknown amount of strength from the fact that in a world where frustrations thrived and multiplied it promised fulfillment of an old dream.

BEFORE 1918

The French delegation to the Treaty negotiations expressed a general spirit when it said that thanks to the Schuman Plan, Europe was at last going to make a reality of the common market *"depuis toujours inscrit dans la géographie, mais empêché par l'histoire . . . ."* [1] The natural unity envisioned was primarily that of the great triangle comprising the Ruhr, Lorraine, a strip of northern France, Luxembourg, the Saar, most of Belgium, and the coal fields of southern Holland (see endpaper map). While the iron, steel, and coal industries of the Schuman Plan countries outside this area are not negligible, the mass of production—and thereby the main chance for success or failure of the Schuman Plan—lay in this triangular patch.

The "natural unity" of the area begins with geology. Coal fields and iron deposits run across national boundaries. But more important is the apparent complementarity of the industries that grew on this base. The coal districts needed more iron than they had locally, and the iron ore regions had to bring coal from elsewhere. Within the steel industry complex interrelations developed, with the crude or semifinished products of one country being sent to others for processing. The natural routes of transportation added to the picture of unity. The Rhine and its tributary streams, supplemented by canals, cut across several countries. Railroads were built along the river valleys. The several mouths of the Rhine provided access to overseas markets and foreign sources of supply for much of the region.

National boundaries have criss-crossed this area throughout modern times. Their effect on the industrial complex has varied according to where they ran and what governments made of them. A serious tug of war seemed to begin just before the great surge of Continental coal and steel production in the last quarter of the 19th century. At the

[1] France, Ministère des Affaires Étrangères, *Rapport de la Délégation Française sur le Traité Instituant la Communauté Européenne du Charbon et de l'Acier et la Convention Relative aux Dispositions Transitoires Signés à Paris le 18 Avril 1951,* Oct. 1951, p. 176.

end of the Franco-Prussian war, Germany took a large section of Lorraine from France. It got thereby a little under half the iron ore deposits then known and the larger share of the blast furnaces, rolling mills, and iron-fabricating plants. Acquisition of these resources was probably not Bismarck's primary motive in drawing the boundary, nor was their value as great as it later became.[2] Because of its high phosphorous content, Lorraine ore could not then be used to make good steel by the Bessemer process. Toward the end of the '70s the Gilchrist-Thomas process, invented in England, made it possible to use Lorraine *minette* to make high-grade steel. Then steel production expanded rapidly, both in France and in Germany, and much more iron was mined. Some of the German steel mills were located in the annexed part of Lorraine, because it seemed preferable to carry the coal to the iron, but there were also numerous blast furnaces in the Ruhr, working on the opposite principle. Often firms operated in both places.

The amount of coke that could be produced from the coal of Lorraine or northern France did not suffice for the growing French output of steel. Most of the imported coke or coking coal came from the Ruhr, some from Belgium and relatively little from England. Quite a bit of trade took place between the German and French parts of Lorraine and between both and Luxembourg, then part of the German customs union. In 1913, 40 per cent of the coke consumed in France and nearly 85 per cent of that consumed

[2] A recent study of the negotiations and the German discussions about them makes a convincing case for the view that although some German industrialists and experts were anxious that the new Reich should get as much of the ore as possible, Bismarck was primarily influenced by strategic considerations and the desire not to have too many Frenchmen inside Germany's boundaries. "In sum, in determining the location of the Franco-German boundary of 1871, the concern for the iron of Lorraine was about equal in importance to the concern for military cemeteries. Germany secured a major part of the iron area chiefly because strategic considerations dictated the inclusion of the cuesta overlooking the Moselle that contained a considerable part of the iron resources; it took only this part and not the whole field because the remaining area was purely French in character." Richard Hartshorne, "The Franco-German Boundary of 1871," *World Politics,* Jan. 1950, p. 250.

in German Lorraine came from the Ruhr. The Ruhr, in turn, got about 27 per cent of its iron ore from French and German Lorraine.[3]

This exchange of basic materials has been the best known symbol of the "natural unity" of the area, though there was an important, complex relation at all stages of production. The figures just cited show that the integration of the area did not rest on a balance of interest between the Ruhr and Lorraine. As a close student of the area has pointed out:

It is a mistake to imagine that Lorraine and the Ruhr were developed during the late nineteenth and the early twentieth centuries as complementary regions, exchanging iron ore for coke, forming an economic whole which was thoughtlessly and ruthlessly torn open by the Allies in 1919. While Ruhr coke was essential to Lorraine, Lorraine's iron ore was only a useful adjunct to the Ruhr's supply. Nor is it true that freight cars performed a shuttle service, carrying coke in one direction, ore in the other. This did happen to some degree, but it seems that the trucks used to export the coke from the Ruhr were not regularly allowed to delay their return journey by picking up ore, but returned empty in order to carry more coke.[4]

AFTER VERSAILLES

The peace settlement at the end of the First World War brought drastic changes to the region. France recovered Alsace-Lorraine and so acquired the bulk of Germany's iron mines, and a substantial number of its blast furnaces and steel mills. Luxembourg moved out of the German customs area into a customs union with Belgium. Germany also lost the Saar coal mines until 1935 and part of the Silesian resources. Ownership of mines and mills generally changed with the flag, and Germany lost other foreign investments as reparations.

The shift in the frontier might not have been a major source of trouble had it not become a trade and currency

[3] Guy Greer, *The Ruhr-Lorraine Industrial Problem*, 1925, pp. 69, 70.
[4] N. J. G. Pounds, *The Ruhr*, 1952, p. 172.

barrier as well. The adjustment to the change intensified difficulties. Many of the former German plants in Lorraine were sold to French firms that already carried out the same processes in other plants, whereas in German hands they had often been links in vertically integrated complexes, running from raw material to finished products. The German owners, compensated by the German government, built new plants in the Ruhr to substitute for those they had lost in Lorraine. Although France gained productive capacity by the return of Lorraine, it at the same time became more dependent on the Ruhr for coke and soon needed export outlets for its increased steel production. There were reparations deliveries in kind but they ran into opposition from French producers. Occupation of the Ruhr failed to produce the coke deliveries needed by the French steel industry. New steel plants built in Germany had the advantage of more modern equipment than those in Lorraine and northern France. In many cases, the owners were relieved of much of their capital burden by the inflation. In 1925 Germany regained its tariff autonomy and imposed duties on iron and steel from Lorraine.

The "natural unity" of the industrial triangle was seriously disturbed. "The Treaty," said Keynes, "strikes at organization, and by the destruction of organization impairs yet further the reduced wealth of the whole community." [5] His view was widely shared and many people tried to find ways to restore the links between the Ruhr and Lorraine, for political as well as economic reasons. Cabinet ministers like Rathenau and Loucheur, leaders like Stinnes and Paul Reynaud, were involved at one time or another with ideas of this sort. The French occupied the Ruhr as a means of collecting reparations, but that was clearly not a sound basis for restoring economic unity. At the height of the Ruhr crisis the *Oberbürgermeister* of Cologne, Konrad Adenauer, told the chairman of the Allied Rhineland Commission: "a lasting peace between France and Germany can

[5] J. M. Keynes, *The Economic Consequences of the Peace* (N. Y.: Harcourt, 1920), pp. 100-101.

only be attained through the establishment of a community of economic interests between the two countries." [6]

Some of the ideas of that period are clear prototypes of the Schuman Plan. Guy Greer, an American who had served as an international official of the Reparations Commission, recommended an economic entente between France and Germany that would result in "the re-establishment of the system of integration in the iron and steel industry of western Europe which existed before the war." [7] It would preferably include some kind of customs union between the two countries or at least a comprehensive commercial treaty. "But the essential task of the governments is . . . permissive action rather than positive control." To secure the advantages of vertical integration, private corporations would link mines, mills and blast furnaces in both countries. Horizontal cooperation, in the form of a steel syndicate "would in all probability be found necessary in order to control production and allocate markets."

The main obstacle to an entente, in Greer's view, was the French fear of becoming dependent on Germany, which would be economically stronger. He felt, though, that safeguards could be worked into the agreement, and that the entente itself would be the best possible assurance of international security. His closing words strike a note very close to that of statements about the Schuman Plan: "If political barriers are removed, the two principal elements of the Ruhr-Lorraine industrial system may be expected to become more closely welded together than ever before . . . . As the years pass and the emotions of the war give place to the more normal activities of life, the economic union between France and Germany will have a tendency to end the age-long feud between them. Even as the coke of the Ruhr and the iron ore of Lorraine have been a source of conflict in the past, they might become

[6] Quoted from the Stresemann Papers by Fritz Stern, "Adenauer and a Crisis in Weimar Democracy," *Political Science Quarterly*, Mar. 1958, p. 22, n. 55.

[7] Greer, cited, p. 257. The recommendations summarized here are on pp. 257-273. Quotations come from these pages.

the common basis for renewed prosperity and genuine peace."

In contrast to this emphasis on avoiding politics and letting "natural" economic forces work, C. K. Leith, an eminent American minerals expert who had participated in the peace conference, stressed the political implications of linking French and German heavy industry. He made two key points. First, "this unit is the arsenal of Europe, which should not be left to commercial control." Second, because Germany was not heavily dependent on Lorraine ore and had numerous other advantages over France, which needed Ruhr coke, any purely economic agreement would lead to German domination. Yet, "eventually, the coal and iron will be operated together . . . ." If France could not stay in the Ruhr, it should strike out on a new tack. "Having recognized Germany's ultimate ascendancy with respect to the unity, the French should move heaven and earth to unify the industry under the control of a strong external organization such as the League of Nations." [8] This is very close to the central line of Schuman's political reasoning twenty-five years later.

Nothing came of these plans for linking French and German resources. A different kind of international cooperation affecting the steel industry began in 1926 when an international cartel was formed whose principal members were the national organizations of steel producers of France, Germany, Belgium, and Luxembourg, along with those of the Saar. This, too, was to some extent a forerunner of the Schuman Plan. It was regarded as a major measure of international cooperation. Governments helped in its formation. Parliaments discussed it. Socialist parties welcomed it, while calling for more public control. Much of this attitude reflected strong elements in European thought that

[8] Typescript of a talk given to a private group in New York, March 16, 1925. A somewhat altered version published in *Engineering and Mining Journal Press*, Apr. 11, 1925, omits these passages. Leith dealt more fully with this and related questions in two articles in *Foreign Affairs* in June 1923 and June 1925, but again refrained from drawing the conclusion quoted.

regarded economic cooperation as a major contribution to peace and cartels as a significant and effective form of cooperation.

Gustav Stresemann, the German Foreign Minister, called the cartel agreement "a landmark of international economic policy the importance of which cannot be overestimated. . . . It has been the objective of my life to realize in the political field what has been accomplished in economics by this pact. . . . I hope that this great idea of collaboration will be fruitful and that other industries without regard to state boundaries will follow the example of the steel industries." [9] The cartel did not live up to these enthusiastic expectations and after a while much less was said about its sweeping political implications. So far as restoring the "natural unity" of the Ruhr-Lorraine area was concerned, the cartel proved to be an unfulfilled promise. Within its framework, national groups strongly maintained their unity and sought government support to buttress their positions. The breakdown of the cartel was due in part to its failure to limit German production and exports to the levels desired by the producers of other countries.

There were other plans and proposals between the wars that looked toward the creation of economic and possibly political unity among the industrial areas of France, Germany, and the Low Countries. Usually, though, this was incidental to a broader project, like Briand's plan for the United States of Europe and Count Coudenhove-Kalergi's Pan-European movement. The next great wave of ideas for solving political and economic problems by unifying Western European coal and steel was again the product of war.

THE SECOND WORLD WAR AND AFTER

What to do about Germany?, was the central question of much of the thought and planning about postwar problems that went on in the Allied countries during the war. What to do about the Ruhr?, was, in turn, a central ques-

[9] Quoted in Ervin Hexner, *The International Steel Cartel*, 1943, pp. 221-222.

tion in the debates over German policy. Two main aims were widely accepted: to prevent Germany from once again using the Ruhr's industrial strength to support aggression, and to employ the area's resources for the benefit of Europe as a whole.[10] How to achieve these aims was a matter of great disagreement.

There were plans for breaking up Germany into a number of small states or for separating the Ruhr and perhaps other border areas from the rest of the country. Annexation by France or other neighbors was favored by some. In one of its versions the Morgenthau plan called for the pastoralization of the whole country, including the Ruhr; control over German industrial output by types or quantities was a feature of other schemes. International control of the Ruhr, or of key industries in the Ruhr, had numerous champions, some of whom would have established international corporations to control heavy industries in all of Western Europe. A study by the United States Foreign Economic Administration recommended that a public corporation, operating under a political administration responsible to the United Nations Security Council, take over most of the Ruhr's economic activities. Another school of thought held that security controls should interfere as little as possible with the German economy; a ban on German production or use of a few key items of purely military significance seemed the most promising course, in this view, which would not have entailed any special treatment of the Ruhr.

Variations and combinations of these main themes were widely propounded and examined. Each had its own difficulties and advantages. To many who considered the matter most closely, the difficulties and weaknesses of either detaching the Ruhr from Germany or subjecting it to permanent international control were compelling. A postwar judgment reflected much of the wartime thinking in the United States:

[10] A third element, which for present purposes can be subordinated to the others, was the desire to break the power of the Ruhr magnates who were widely regarded as having played an important part in Hitler's rise to power.

The conclusion is that while Allied control of the Ruhr industries involves fewer difficulties than separation of the Ruhr from Germany, it is difficult to see how active management of those industries for the benefit of the world as a whole can be organized so as to escape the danger of subjecting the Ruhr to control by its competitors. Control for security purposes alone would be feasible but does not do away with the need for some disarmament control over the rest of Germany. It appears, therefore, that the best safeguard against the misuse of the industrial potential of the Ruhr is to be found in the elimination of certain war industries in all Germany, reinforced by continuous inspection by agents of Allied governments of the final uses of iron and steel products.[11]

After the end of the war, the drive to put the Ruhr under some form of international control came principally from France. Before V-E Day, General de Gaulle was calling for severance of the Ruhr from Germany. Thereafter authoritative French policy statements zigzagged between separation and some form of international control that would leave the territory in Germany.[12] An elaborate plan put forward by the French in February 1947 called for Allied ownership of Ruhr coal mines and steel mills, largely German management under international public

[11] Hoyt Price and C. E. Schorske, *The Problem of Germany*, 1947, pp. 64-65. This book was the Council on Foreign Relations' report to a private international conference. It drew on extensive work on the Ruhr problem done in the Council's War and Peace Studies Project.

[12] Visiting Washington after the Potsdam conference, De Gaulle and Bidault asked for internationalization. In March 1946 Félix Gouin, the Socialist premier of France, advocated international occupation and control of the Ruhr but specified that the area should remain German. The next month at a meeting of the Council of Foreign Ministers, the French delegation submitted a memorandum again calling for separation of the Ruhr and the Rhineland from Germany. In January 1947 Bidault told a newspaperman that France wanted "an international and independent Ruhr under really international supervision." *The New York Times*, Jan. 13, 1947. Léon Blum explained the wavering by saying that De Gaulle's original extreme position was a source of difficulty for France in its relations with its allies, so Bidault had the task of jockeying France into a more practicable position (i.e., like Gouin's). See a series of articles by Blum under the title "Grande Bretagne et France" in *Le Populaire* during January 1948. For a private expression of a somewhat parallel shift in attitude on the Ruhr, compare L. F. Aubert, *Sécurité de l'Occident: Ruhr-Rhin*, 1946, with the same author's essays in L. F. Aubert and others, *Contrôle de l'Allemagne*, 1949.

supervision, and a vaguely defined international political control of the Ruhr.

Plans of this sort were unacceptable to the United States, and also to Britain, in whose zone of occupation the Ruhr lay. The American position was that the Ruhr should remain German but might be placed under some kind of international control. This should not subject it "to political domination or manipulation of outside powers." [13] While the occupation lasted, no special regime was needed; anything done afterwards must take full account of German interests as well as those of other countries.[14] Just before the Conference of Foreign Ministers at London in November 1947 Secretary of State Marshall said: "The United States believes that safeguards must be set up to insure that the resources and industrial potential of the Ruhr, particularly in respect of coal and steel, should not be left under the exclusive control of any future German Government but should be used for the benefit of the European community as a whole." [15]

Conflicting forces were at work within the American government. Those responsible for running Germany favored the promotion of economic recovery and noninterference in the Ruhr. They suspected French motives and felt sure that German recovery would be hampered by a new international body. Others approached the issue differently. They had some sympathy with the French view that there was a long-run security problem. They saw that an agreement with France on the Ruhr could be used to get French acceptance of measures that would hasten

[13] Secretary of State Byrnes's speech at Stuttgart on September 6, 1946. U.S. Dept. of State *Bulletin*, Sept. 15, 1946, p. 501.

[14] Secretary of State Marshall's speech at Moscow. Same, Apr. 20, 1947, pp. 694-695.

[15] Same, Nov. 30, 1947, p. 1028. During the London conference, John Foster Dulles, one of Marshall's main advisers who had long favored giving the Ruhr a special status, traveled to Paris and apparently discussed some kind of Ruhr agreement there. Léon Blum wrote that his conversation with Dulles at this time confirmed his view that a new attitude was developing in the United States favorable to a handling of the Ruhr issue along the lines desired by France. "La Position Américaine," *Le Populaire*, Jan. 17, 1948.

German economic recovery and political rehabilitation. Increasing attention was being given to closer economic cooperation in Europe; the Ruhr might well have a special part to play. As the lines of the cold war were more sharply drawn, more steps were taken to tie Germany to the West. Until one was sure where Germany stood, international control of the Ruhr would give the Western powers a useful position, especially if the Russians began proposing some kind of German reunification with an Eastern orientation.

INTERNATIONAL CONTROL OF THE RUHR

Out of this complex of forces came the International Agreement on the Ruhr. Discussions that began formally in February and March 1948 produced agreement on principles that were published in June. The final text that was signed in April 1949 echoed words familiar since the wartime discussions. ". . . The resources of the Ruhr shall not in the future be used for the purpose of aggression but shall be used in the interests of peace. . . ." To this end, "access to the coal, coke and steel of the Ruhr [should] . . . be in the future assured on an equitable basis to the countries cooperating in the common economic good. . . ." To achieve this an Authority was created on which Germany was in a minority.[16]

The primary function of the Authority was to allocate the Ruhr's output of coal, coke, and steel between exports and domestic use, "taking into account the essential needs of Germany." The Authority had a number of other powers of supervision and collection of information and some potentially important functions bearing on German trade practices. The Agreement anticipated that as the occupying authorities relinquished some of their controls, the Authority or another international agency, with which it would work closely, might take over powers to enforce

[16] Text of Draft Agreement, U.S. Dept. of State *Bulletin*, Jan. 9, 1949, p. 46. Britain, France, the United States, and Germany were to have three votes apiece and the Benelux countries one each; until Germany had a government that took its place on the Authority (this happened in December 1949), the occupying powers were to cast Germany's votes.

German disarmament, to prevent cartelization and industrial concentration in the Ruhr, and to keep out of key
positions people who had "furthered the aggressive de-
signs" of the Nazis. In performing its major function
of allocating output between domestic consumption and
exports, the Authority was bound by agreements among the
occupying powers on the allocation of coal and by the programs of European recovery worked out through the
OEEC.

The French were not altogether satisfied with the new
agreement. They had hoped for tighter control over the
industries and perhaps their transfer to international ownership;[17] they wanted more guarantees against possible
German aggression. In assenting to the Agreement, the
French National Assembly urged the government to press
negotiations along these lines. Underlying the French
reservations was undoubtedly the realization that the working of the Ruhr Authority depended on continuing agreement among France, Britain, and the United States and
the fear that the other two occupying powers did not share
France's view that continued restraints on Ruhr production were desirable.

The Ruhr Agreement might have worked in one of
several different ways, ranging from virtual exploitation
of Germany by the victors to the exercise of a control so
light as to be negligible. In fact, it never assumed the major
role projected in the Agreement. This was partly because

[17] Between the agreement in principle of June and the completion of
the detailed document in December there was a dispute resulting from
the promulgation in November by American and British authorities of
a law creating German trustees for the iron, steel, and coal industries
pending deconcentration. The French particularly objected to a statement in the preamble to the law that "the question of the eventual
ownership . . . should be left to the determination of a representative,
freely elected German Government." They felt this closed the door on
internationalization. General Clay, the American Military Governor,
considers that "The French protest was made concurrently in order to
create an atmosphere favorable to the more rigid control [of the Ruhr]
which the French Government desired." *Decision in Germany*, 1950,
p. 337. One outcome of the dispute was French acceptance of membership in the formerly bipartite boards through which the occupying
powers controlled the steel and coal industries.

of its subordination to the decisions of the occupying powers; for example its allocation of German coal exports was largely a formal substitution for the Allied committees already doing that. For the rest, the desuetude of the Ruhr Authority resulted from the course of events that made German economic recovery and political rehabilitation more urgent in Allied eyes than the exercise of controls.

Though the International Authority for the Ruhr never became really important, it has a place in an analysis of the Schuman Plan. First, its negotiation and short history demonstrate some of the problems besetting French policy that Schuman later tried to solve by his new proposal. Second, French and German reactions to the scheme of international control helped set the stage for the Schuman Plan. The French, who had placed such hopes on the internationalization of the Ruhr, were disappointed with the only agreement their allies would accept. They do not seem to have made any major efforts to strengthen the new agency or to base their German policy on it. What was done by the American and British occupation authorities and, later, by the German government at Bonn, was more important than what was done or not done in the headquarters of the International Authority for the Ruhr at Düsseldorf. Recognition that the Ruhr Authority was a weak reed undoubtedly made Schuman's new approach to German problems more acceptable in France.

The Germans, naturally, did not like the Ruhr Authority, but they were in no position to rebel outright against it, or to undertake the passive resistance that had undermined French occupation of the Ruhr in 1923. They accepted the seat on the Authority that was offered them and took part in the international body's decisions. When in 1950 and 1951 the Ruhr Authority was allocating coal for export that the Germans felt ought to have been used at home for industrial expansion and consumers' needs, it was heavily attacked. From the first there were also strong criticisms of the Ruhr Authority on more or less straight nationalistic grounds, often with a good deal of plausibility: that it left Germany in an unequal position, subject to permanent foreign exploitation; that it was a setback on the

road to autonomy; that at the moment Germany was urged
to frame a constitution, it was deprived of control over
basic elements of its economy; that the Allies were perpe-
trating a fraud when they talked of cooperation while
imposing a one-sided control on Germany. But as background for the Schuman Plan, another phase of the German
reaction to the Ruhr Authority is more interesting.

On June 6, 1948, a statement issued from a meeting of
the Ministers-President of the *Länder* in the three Western
zones of occupation and other leading Germans. Fairly
moderate in its criticism of the proposed control of the
Ruhr, the statement stressed that if there was to be international control, it should apply to all the important centers
of heavy industry in Europe and the Germans should
participate in it. On the New Year's Day after the text of
the Ruhr agreement was published, Karl Arnold, Minister-
President of North Rhine-Westphalia, said in a radio
address: "The question arises whether the goal for which
the participating western powers are striving cannot be
reached by another path, by a path that will guarantee
honorable and voluntary cooperation by the whole Ruhr
economy, including the workers, on a basis of equality. In
place of this one-sided and therefore necessarily irritating
control of the Ruhr area, could one not erect an association
with an international legal status and a foundation of
partnership? Into this association Germany would bring the
Ruhr, France the ore resources of Lorraine, both of them
the Saar, Belgium and Luxembourg their heavy industries.
The basis of equality that modern legal thought sanctions
would mean that each of the partners would participate
according to the value of what it brought in." [18]

Arnold's voice seemed important. His *Land* included the
Ruhr, and his position on international control was endorsed
in general terms by a Landtag resolution supported by the
four major parties. Arnold was one of the leaders of the

[18] Regierung des Landes Nordrhein-Westfalen unter Mitwirkung des
Deutschen Büros für Friedensfragen in Stuttgart, *Das Abkommen über
die Errichtung einer Internationalen Ruhrbehörde* . . . (Düsseldorf,
1949), p. 5. In addition to excerpts from the speech cited, this brochure
includes parts of a speech Arnold gave to the Landtag and the resolution
of the latter referred to later in the text.

Christian Democratic Union (CDU), drawing his support especially from the groups that had formerly been part of the Catholic trade unions. Since there was no German government, the Ministers-President of other *Länder* decided to give Arnold primary responsibility for expressing German views on the Ruhr problem.

Other German political leaders, newspapers, and some business circles expressed somewhat similar ideas about a broader control of heavy industry. In fact, the reaction was so general as to be suspicious. It was hard for outsiders to believe that so many Germans had become so international-minded so suddenly. Undoubtedly many advocated this view primarily as a debating point which gained sharpness from the Allies' talk of "cooperation" while they were imposing an arrangement on the Ruhr. The proposal for general internationalization of heavy industry was often made in contexts of understandable, but nevertheless nationalist, views with which it comported ill. An idealistic proposal which Germany's neighbors were not likely to accept might also be useful in improving Germany's bargaining position in the whole process of regaining autonomy and equality.

Some Germans were sensitive to the danger that internationalist language would be abused for nationalist purposes. While agreeing that international control ought to be extended to the heavy industry of other countries, they pointed out that Germans were in no position to demand this of countries they had so recently occupied, or to challenge the good faith of the victors while expecting them to take German good faith for granted. Far better, argued these Germans, to show what could be done constructively in the Ruhr under international control and so make it an example of a method that could then spread to the rest of Europe.[19]

---

[19] For expressions of this view see "Die Ruhr ruft Europa," *Der Tagesspiegel* (Berlin), Apr. 14, 1948, and the statements of Karl Spiecker quoted in the article; RP (Rüdiger Proske), "Aufruhr um die Ruhr," *Frankfurter Hefte*, Feb. 1949, pp. 97-99; *Süddeutsche Zeitung* (Munich), Jan. 11, 1949.

The German reaction did not go altogether unnoticed abroad. *Le Monde*, in an editorial on December 31, 1948, pointed out that the International Authority for the Ruhr would not function fully until after the final decisions on security controls had been taken and noted that by then the Germans might have their wish of seeing other industrial centers under international control. André Philip, a French Socialist, had already proposed in the National Assembly that the Ruhr Authority should be given power over the coal and steel exports of other Western European countries.[20] Lewis Douglas, the chief American negotiator, had made a similar suggestion while the Agreement was being drafted.[21]

When all proper allowance has been made for ulterior motives, two things stand out about the German statements that the Ruhr Authority's power should be extended to other areas. One is the great importance to the Germans of being treated equally. The other is that the old dream of recreating the "natural unities" was still alive and functioning. Both facts were relevant to the acceptance of the Schuman Plan.

OTHER VOICES

International control of heavy industry was a theme common to many discussions of postwar Europe that were not especially linked to the arguments about the Ruhr Agreement. In some form such a cause was favored by people with a variety of political viewpoints. As a politician and as a publicist, André Philip was one of the main champions of the internationalization of Europe's heavy industry. As a Socialist he hoped this would also mean collective ownership but he was more concerned with control over the use of these resources, the division of

[20] *The New York Times*, Dec. 1, 1948. Later, referring to the German reaction to the Ruhr Authority, he said, "*Je ne demande pas que ce soit un régime d'exceptions.*" "L'Unification de l'Europe," *Cahiers du Monde Nouveau*, Mar. 1949, pp. 32-37.

[21] Clay, cited, p. 338. The suggestion "did not receive favorable consideration" and was probably just a bargaining instrument to meet the French demand for stricter controls.

scarce supplies, the rationalization of production, and public control of prices. Barbara Ward, on the staff of *The Economist*, suggested that a "public steel corporation" comprising the whole of Western European industry might be established. The prewar steel cartel had proved it was possible to organize the industry; the question was "can Western Europe create a steel industry fit to be the main-spring of an expanding Western economy . . . ?" [22]

Among the Germans interested in similar ideas was a group of intellectuals at Heidelberg, centering around the old and respected economist Alfred Weber. Rejecting the idea of cutting the Ruhr off from Germany, this group suggested a form of international holding company with authority over the basic industry of the area. To replace private ownership, the Heidelberg proposal called for a rather complex form of socialization that would avoid the difficulties of nationalization, allow for representation of the workers, and keep most managerial decisions in the hands of entities supervised by German agencies "separated from day to day politics." Although the specific recommendations applied primarily to the Ruhr, the approach was more widely applicable and the principal author of the plan aimed at using the new Ruhr organization as a basis for European political cooperation. [23]

Ending private ownership of heavy industry was one of the main aims of Socialist proposals for international control of heavy industry. In its own country each Socialist party usually advocated nationalization; in international confer-ences party spokesmen examined ideas for the international coordination of national plans and, sometimes, for the crea-tion of agencies that could exercise public international control. There were often differences of opinion along national lines; French Socialists generally favored interna-tional ownership for the Ruhr industries while German

[22] Barbara Ward, *The West at Bay*, 1948, p. 237.
[23] *Die Wandlung* (Heidelberg), Dec. 1947, pp. 768-791. This includes an exposition of the plan by Konrad Mommsen, a rather cautious endorse-ment and exploration of some of the general issues by Alfred Weber, and the text of a resolution supporting the main features of the proposal, passed by the Heidelberg Action Group in October 1947.

Socialists opposed it, having in mind ultimate nationalization by a German Socialist government.[24] Differences of this sort arose in Socialist discussions of the Ruhr that took place in Vienna in June 1948. A series of special conferences followed. In March 1950, almost on the eve of the Schuman Plan, the problems of international control of the heavy industry of all Western Europe were discussed by a study group convened by the International Socialist Conference, at Witten in the Ruhr.

Taking the desirability of socialization for granted, the Socialists had to face two basic problems: (1) Could international control be applied to countries that had not nationalized their industries? (2) How far could countries with nationalized industries go in subjecting them to international control? Neither Socialist doctrine nor international experience provided a clear answer to these questions. Opinions differed as to the soundest Socialist attitude, both in principle and in tactics. On the first point, a participant in the Witten Conference concluded from its deliberations that "international control of basic industries is possible . . . between socialist and capitalist countries . . ." provided, "first, that each country should run its economy with the objective of maintaining full employment, and second, that each country should have control over its own basic industries even though they may be in private hands."[25]

The discussion of the second question was to prove more important for Socialist attitudes toward the Schuman Plan. For effective internationalization of basic industries, said

[24] In the spring of 1950 the German Social Democratic Party recommended extension of international control from the Ruhr to the rest of European heavy industry. But, it added, these industries should be socialized, and if that were not possible, "then the idea of socialization in Western Germany will have preference over the desire for internationalization in Western Germany." SPD, *News from Germany*, Mar.-Apr. 1950.

[25] Wilfred Fienburgh, *International Control of Basic Industries* (London: British Labour Party, Apr. 1950), pp. 7, 6. This is a report based on the work of the study group, but neither an account of the proceedings nor a document agreed to by the participants at the conference.

the report on the Witten Conference, the international body would have to have extensive powers; it would also have to be subject to international political control, otherwise one of the purposes of nationalization—to secure democratic control—would be frustrated. These stipulations made it clear that the chance of true internationalization of basic industries was dim. Two possible earlier stages were discussed. In the first, the international agency would serve largely for consultation and the exchange of information. In the second, "each nation would retain full autonomy over its own industry but where unanimous agreement was reached the central authority would have power to give effect to its recommendations." The third stage, when an international authority might act by majority rule, would require "a revolutionary change in the political structure of Western Europe."

Somewhat similar discussions were going on in labor groups. In the fall of 1949, the DGB—the German trade union federation—added its voice to those Germans willing to accept the Ruhr Authority if it was to be the first step toward international control over other European industrial areas.[26] In May 1950, a few weeks after Schuman's statement, a conference sponsored by the International Confederation of Free Trade Unions met in Düsseldorf to discuss the problem of the Ruhr in the light of a report by a committee that had worked on the subject over a period of years. A major recommendation of the report was that "the governments of France, Western Germany, the Benelux Union and Sweden be urged to enter into negotiations aiming at the conclusion of an agreement for an intergovernmental organisation of the type, and in the place, of the [International Authority for the Ruhr], but with adequate trade union representation, for the entire North West European and Swedish coal, iron ore, iron and steel industries."[27]

[26] Süddeutsche Zeitung, Nov. 25, 1949.
[27] International Confederation of Free Trade Unions, *Information Bulletin*, May 17, 1950, p. 3 (mimeographed). Shortly before, American union leaders, apparently as a result of the work of the ICFTU committee, had endorsed similar recommendations to the President and the Secretary of State. *The New York Times*, Mar. 12, 1950.

Other circles, in which business leaders as well as Socialists and labor spokesmen participated, talked of somewhat
similar approaches. In April 1949 the Westminster Conference of the European Movement passed a resolution
recommending steps to coordinate the heavy industries of
Europe. In each basic industry—coal, iron and steel, electricity, and transport—three kinds of organizations should
be created. An intergovernmental body would determine
general policies concerning investment, production, and
prices.[28] A body representing employers, workers, and the
public would advise the governmental body on policies and
objectives. Organizations of employers, including nationalized industries, would carry out the policies established by
the first body; they would aim at increasing production,
raising productivity, and reducing costs; safeguards would
be adopted to ensure that they did not abuse their positions
by becoming cartels.

The cartel question, which in its own way was part of
the old dream, helped stimulate the discussion of possible
international control of European industries. Reports of
conversations between French and German industrialists,
as well as those of the Benelux countries, seemed to many
observers to be the stirrings of the *disjecta membra* of the
prewar cartel. Concern grew in some circles about the need
to prevent, or at least control, such developments. It showed
itself when the themes of the Westminster Conference
were discussed in the Consultative Assembly of the Council
of Europe in the fall of 1949. In December the economic
committee of the Assembly recommended an intergovernmental expert body for steel, assisted by an advisory body
of labor, industry, and the public, to devise policies for
establishing a balance between consumption and production. This, it was argued, would require similar action in
other fields, since the steel industry could not determine
its own level of demand. A related proposal called for the

[28] The intergovernmental body would define policy so that "it shall
always be in line with the general policy and with the economic and
social aims of a European union," thus raising the question whether this
industrial coordination was to wait until a European union was created.
General Account and Resolutions (London: European Movement),
pp. 17-19.

chartering of "European companies," conceived as international organizations for carrying on production and distribution.[29] By the time the Consultative Assembly met to consider these reports, in August 1950, the Schuman Plan had been produced and the debate about it crowded the variants off the stage.

The Germans continued to contribute to the ambiance out of which the Schuman Plan was to come. The need for some kind of better understanding with France was felt to grow as Germany gained in economic and political strength and took a more and more prominent part in European cooperative measures. During French-German trade negotiations in November 1949, Adenauer suggested that the French might invest in major coal and steel companies in the Ruhr. The Ruhr would get capital, the French would have assurances about their security, the need for decartelization would be reduced. Early in 1950 Adenauer threw out a series of suggestions along the same line, ranging from internationalization of the Saar to a complete French-German union.[30]

The French apparently looked on these statements as gestures rather than as concrete propositions. They may have felt the need to respond in kind. In April 1950, a few weeks before Schuman offered his plan, André François-Poncet, the French High Commissioner in Germany (who was once an employee of the Comité des Forges) told an audience in Berlin that the ancient antagonism of France and Germany "is now not more than a secondary factor. After two world wars we can see that, abandoned to ourselves, we could do nothing but enter into competition with one another on only one point: poverty." The antagonism that dominated world politics was that between the American bloc and the Slavic bloc. "French and German, we live in a sort of 'no man's land' and it is with the same disquiet that we observe the reactions which move both of

[29] Council of Europe, Consultative Assembly, *Documents, Working Papers*, 2d Sess. 1950, doc. 5, pp. 414-516 *passim* and appendixes K, O, P.
[30] Pierre Gerbet, "La Genèse du Plan Schuman," *Revue Française de Science Politique*, Jl.-Sept. 1956, lists a number of these.

these two colossi." To unify Europe, exchanges and the movement of goods must be liberalized, but such a course also ran the risk of economic chaos. To avoid that, the conditions of production would have to be harmonized, and "there must be added the division of markets to assure the sale of goods." This would be a kind of planning, to be sure, but it would not have to be imposed from above. Certain kinds of cartels were to be condemned, but not those agreements that were intended to regularize production.[31]

In a few words the French spokesman to Germany had struck some of the keynotes of the movement toward closer French-German cooperation and the main themes of an important body of French opinion about the risks of competition and the need for economic order. The overtones of his partial equation of the United States and the Soviet Union, and the suggestion that Europe should somehow be dissociated from their struggle also found their echoes in various segments of European opinion. Others who put more stress on the value of trans-Atlantic links could also believe that independent European strength was necessary to provide maneuverability that could break the deadlock of the cold war. This was Monnet's view. Schuman may have had the same thing in mind when, in introducing his formal statement, he said "France has acted essentially for peace. If peace is to have a chance, there must first of all be a Europe."

Meanwhile, the United States was itself actively championing the same European unity that was being advocated as a means of reducing political dependence on Washington. There had been a continuing American interest in this matter and it was one of the keynotes of the Marshall Plan. But not until Paul Hoffman's speech to the OEEC in October 1949 did "integration" become one of the dominant notes of the European recovery effort, with concrete plans being formulated to serve that end. There was nothing in the program Hoffman laid out that pointed toward the kind of pooling that Schuman later proposed;

[31] *Réalités Allemandes*, Apr. 1950, pp. 32, 33.

his emphasis was on the liberation of trade and exchanges, the broadening of markets, and the benefits of competition.

Still, there was an interest among many Americans in the possibilities of some kind of pooling of heavy industry. So far as policy was concerned, this had remained a matter of how to deal with the Ruhr. The German suggestions that the jurisdiction of the Ruhr Authority be extended to other centers of European heavy industry may never have received formal American support[32] but were undoubtedly viewed with sympathy. In the fall of 1949 John J. McCloy, the American High Commissioner in Germany, suggested some broadening of the kind of arrangement used in the Ruhr to the rest of Western Europe.[33] As President of the International Bank he had been interested in this possibility. His statement met British objections that it would have a bad influence on the negotiations with Germany then under way and might suggest that the other High Commissioners shared what was at most only an American, and possibly only a personal, point of view. Other Americans continued to pursue this interest,[34] though it took second place behind a more general concern with European integration.

Considering the degree of American involvement in Europe, Washington's interest in European integration, and the links between American officials and Adenauer, it is inevitable that some should see the United States as the real originator of the Schuman Plan. That was one of the arguments the Communists used to discredit the French proposal, but they regarded the point as virtually self-evident and adduced no allegations of any interest about specific activities. Non-Communist opponents of the Schu-

[32] The possible exception is in the position taken by the American negotiators while the Ruhr agreement was being drafted. But, as has been suggested above, n. 21, it seems unlikely that this was more than a bargaining gambit. For a less skeptical interpretation, see Stephen Raushenbush, *The Ruhr: A Better American Policy* (Public Affairs Institute, Occasional Paper Series, Dec. 1948), pp. 12-14.

[33] *Chronology of International Events and Documents,* Oct. 6-19, 1949, p. 681.

[34] For instance, Walter Reuther advocated this view. *The New York Times,* Dec. 4, 1949.

man Plan also thought they detected the American hand, operating through Adenauer and possibly Monnet. But no one has produced any real evidence and in a matter like this the absence of evidence becomes almost a positive case. It would have been to the advantage of many of the opponents of the Schuman Plan to prove it was an American device. On the American side, in the years that have passed, there would have been strong temptations to claim the Schuman Plan as a success for United States diplomacy, and that has been done only in broad terms. So the absence of leaks strongly suggests that there was nothing to leak.

Undoubtedly the idea of pooling the coal and steel of Western Europe was discussed in private by American and European officials. How could they avoid it? As this chapter has shown, all sorts of people were discussing it in public, and had been doing so in one form or another for thirty years. But of a deliberate American effort to get the French to propose what Schuman proposed, there is no trace. Most observers have regarded as very genuine indeed the surprise registered by Acheson and his advisers when they were told what Schuman was about to say.[35] When Acheson had been in Paris the day before, says the chief French student of the topic, "M. Schuman spoke of it very vaguely . . . but it does not seem that the Secretary of State realized the importance of the project." [36]

While authorship or specific initiative cannot be attributed to the United States, there was, of course, an inevitable

[35] In the week before Acheson got to Paris, Harold Callender reported that "M. Schuman would propose a new step toward the unification of Europe's basic industries in the form of a consortium embracing British coal, Ruhr steel and Lorraine iron." *The New York Times*, May 4, 1950. American officials probably thought this was only "a diplomatic maneuver," an opinion Callender had reported.

[36] Gerbet, cited, p. 546. Gerbet cites some of the French allegations about the American role and does not appear to give them credence, though he is not explicit. His statement that "no official consultation took place with the Americans," may be read as slightly guarded. However, it is obvious that Gerbet does not think that American influence was of any special significance; it would be largely irrelevant to his sound central argument that Monnet's proposals were accepted by Schuman and the Cabinet because they offered solutions for so many of France's problems.

American influence on the French decision. American policy had played a part in bringing European and German affairs to the point at which Schuman was moved to take his initiative. He knew that his bold move was bound to be welcomed in the United States and would almost certainly win strong support from the American government. But too much was involved for him to have made a genuine proposal only for that reason. American opposition might have been fatal, American support could not guarantee success. French and German interests were bound to be controlling; too much was at stake, the criss-crossing of interests too intricate, to explain the European action by trans-Atlantic opinion.

The galvanic character of Schuman's proposal did not lie in its novelty. Its central themes—though not their specific form and combination—had been public property for decades and were increasingly common currency in postwar Europe. The great thing about Schuman's statement was that these ideas were now French policy. But his words got part of their magic because they expressed an old dream.

FOUR

NEGOTIATING THE TREATY

Less than a year after Schuman's statement, a treaty embodying its main principles was signed and awaiting parliamentary ratification in six countries. This is fast work for a measure sweeping in fundamentals and highly complex in details. Not surprisingly, there are ambiguities in the Treaty, some of them probably deliberate compromises, others inevitable in an attempt to find language that will cover a variety of circumstances. There are, however, surprisingly few broad statements of principle unaccompanied by rules of application, however debatable the meaning of these rules may be. That so many technical questions could be worked out and that the negotiations proceeded fairly smoothly is a tribute not only to the competence of the negotiators but also to the seriousness and sincerity of their governments.

An accurate, detailed history of the negotiations about the Schuman Plan from the day it was announced until the Treaty was ready for parliamentary action cannot be written from the public record.[1] This chapter tells the story in broad outline and calls attention to the emergence of several issues that are examined in more detail later. A narrative of the negotiations falls naturally into three main phases: the negotiations between France and Britain that ended in the latter's decision not to participate in the drafting of the Treaty; the work of the six-power conference

[1] No *Travaux Préparatoires* have been published, apparently in order to permit the Treaty to stand on its own feet, unfettered by any additional statements about the intentions of the negotiators or the special meanings they may have come to attach to formulations.

47

that prepared most of the Treaty between June and December 1950; the overcoming of final difficulties that led to the signature of the Treaty in April 1951.

THE INVITATION TO BRITAIN

Germany was in the forefront of the minds of the French statesmen who proposed the Schuman Plan, but Britain could not be far behind. Britain was an ally, a fellow-victor, a colleague in the occupation of Western Germany. To assure British support as a counterweight to Germany was a maxim of policy in the minds of many Frenchmen. In Europe's coal and steel economy Britain was a major factor. It produced much more coal than France and West Germany together. In prewar years Britain produced more steel than France but less than Germany; in 1949 its output was well ahead of that of either Continental country. In matters of Western European cooperation, France had had a continual tug of war with Britain over the kind of steps to be taken and the pace at which to take them, but this did not remove Britain from Europe. Frenchmen might be skeptical about how Britain would react to an invitation to the bold new conference but they could not fail to find out.

It is said that René Massigli, the French Ambassador in London, reached for a chair when he learned that Schuman was about to propose a high authority to control Western European coal and steel. The British, in turn, were not only startled but reserved and not a little skeptical. "I told M. Massigli," said Ernest Bevin, the Foreign Secretary, "that when we saw the proposal in detail we would, of course, examine it with great care, but that meantime I could make no comment." [2] Two days later Prime Minister Attlee told the House of Commons that his government welcomed the French initiative which must "be regarded

[2] Great Britain, Foreign Office, *Anglo-French Discussions Regarding French Proposals for the Western European Coal, Iron and Steel Industries—May-June,* 1950 (London, 1950), doc. 1, p. 3 (Cmd. 7970). Hereafter cited as British White Paper. Subsequent quotations in this section come from the same source, which includes Attlee's statement in Parliament and the final communiqués as well as the diplomatic correspondence.

as a notable contribution towards the solution of a major European problem" because of what it did to help bring Germany into the European comity as a free nation. He promised that the British would look at the matter in a sympathetic spirit but noted that the "far-reaching implications for the future economic structure of participating countries" would have to be carefully studied.

Monnet and some of his advisers spent a working week in London talking with British officials. Echoes of these conversations produced the clichés in informed circles in London that there was no Schuman Plan, only an idea, or that Monnet and his advisers were each describing different and contradictory plans. There was some feeling, too, that the French were counting on the hard-working civil servants of Whitehall to figure out the means of putting their great ideas into practice. But during Monnet's visit something else transpired that was to play a crucial part in the negotiations. "It became clear . . . ," said a British government minute, "that the French Government felt it desirable that the acceptance by other Governments of the principles set out in the French communiqué of 9th May should precede any working out of the practical application of their proposals."

This point immediately became the central issue when governmental negotiations began in earnest about a week after Monnet left. The French presented the British with a draft communiqué already approved by the German government. It stated that the signatory governments "are resolved to carry out a common action aiming at peace, European solidarity and economic and social progress by pooling their coal and steel production and by the institution of a new higher authority whose decisions will bind" them. The British replied that they "would reluctantly be unable to accept" "a commitment to pool resources and set up an authority with certain sovereign powers as a prior condition to joining in the talks. . . ." They were willing, however, to participate in talks with countries that did accept the principles "with the hope that by obtaining a clearer picture of how the proposals would operate in detail, they would be able to join the scheme."[3]

Next day the French Ambassador called at the Foreign Office to make sure the British were not opposed to the principle of the Schuman Plan and were "prepared to enter into discussions with the object of finding a practical method of applying the principle." On being assured that this was approximately the case, Massigli said it seemed to him that the British reservations "would not in any way limit [their] . . . effective participation in the discussions." Massigli then redrafted the proposed communiqué "producing something which seemed . . . on the whole unobjectionable . . ." to Kenneth Younger, Minister of State, with whom he was negotiating. The two diplomats agreed, however, that the communiqué ought to make clear the British position.

The Quai d'Orsay, a few days later, sent a somewhat involved memorandum that seemed less sanguine than Massigli's remarks but held out some hope of agreement. First, the memorandum stressed the importance of the Schuman Plan for French-German relations, thus hinting that the French stipulations were being made primarily with the German problem in mind. Noting that the first British reply had assumed direct French-German negotiations, the memorandum then implicitly gave the British a chance to save face by changing their position on the ground that the negotiations had meanwhile become multilateral. Later paragraphs stressed the idea of creating a community of interest different from present national interests and pointed out that the powers to be given the high authority would be limited by the treaty but emphasized that, "This partial

---

[3] This offer had already been made in a message that crossed the French note containing the draft communiqué. Bevin's message had said, "I feel that the important thing is to get something started soon" to take advantage of the effect Schuman's statement had had on Franco-German relations. He urged direct conversations between France and Germany in which Britain would participate on the terms cited. When the British learned that the French had already sent the draft communiqué to the Benelux and Italian governments they repeated their offer to sit in on these broader negotiations.

fusion of sovereignty is the contribution which the French proposal makes to the solution of European problems." Another long paragraph assured the British that the high authority's work would not prejudice the results already achieved by the policy of full employment and would permit the reconciliation of full employment with rationalized production.

The core of the memorandum, however, was in three central paragraphs. The French denied that they were asking "for an undertaking to pool coal and steel resources, and to set up an authority with certain sovereign powers" ". . . as a prior condition, for full participation in the discussions. . . ." A commitment would exist only after the treaty had been signed and ratified. What they were concerned about, said the French, was that in order to overcome practical difficulties "the discussions . . . should constantly be guided by common principles. Only if the negotiations are clearly directed by agreement between participating Governments on the fundamental objectives to be reached, will it be possible to work out quickly the ways and means and the supplementary arrangements necessary for giving effect to M. Schuman's plan. . . ." It is hard to make out just what the French intended with this memorandum. They may have wished to appear less adamant without yielding the substance of their position, or they may have been trying to shade their meaning just enough to invite the British to "interpret" it as a change of position while still using words that could be read according to the original French view.

In any case, the British were not willing to see a significant change in the French position. They told the French that the memorandum still seemed to involve a prior commitment. They felt "unable to associate themselves with a communiqué which appears to take decisions prior to, rather than as a result of, intergovernmental discussions." Taking up a suggestion made by Schuman to the British Ambassador in Paris, the Foreign Office suggested that the communiqué carry an additional paragraph saying that the British government would "participate in the proposed conversation in a constructive spirit and in the hope that, as a result of the discussions, there will emerge a scheme which they will be able to join. But they cannot at this stage enter into any more precise commitment."

The French answered that the communiqué should "announce in the same terms" the participation of all governments. They had secured the consent of the other signatories to a modification of the draft communiqué. It now said that the governments "have assigned to themselves as their immediate objective" the pooling of coal and steel and the creation of a high authority which could make binding decisions. This, said the French, "expresses the unity of view which is indispensable for the successful prosecution of the negotiations." If the British could not subscribe to it, the French would go ahead and open negotiations with the other countries, while keeping the British informed in the hope that they would join later.

On June 2 the British replied that if they signed the revised draft they would still feel committed to the aim of preparing a treaty embodying the principles set out by the French "without opportunity being given for their practical application to be worked out." They suggested a meeting of ministers to see whether a better method of discussing the issues could not be found. Oral exchanges followed which showed no further change of position, and on June 3 both governments issued different communiqués reporting their positions. The six countries that had agreed to negotiate issued the revised communiqué stating their intentions.

The record of the negotiations seems arid and thin. Revolutionary changes in the political and economic scene of Western Europe were being proposed and two of the largest European powers, recently allied in victory, could not agree on a formula that would enable them to discuss the issues involved. One protests that the mind of man is not so feeble; the governments must not have wanted to discuss the question. This may be true, but another interpretation of the course of events can be found. On its face the record is fairly lucid; the one intractable issue was the acceptance of the aim of the negotiations as creation of a coal and steel pool governed by a supranational body. Winston Churchill, who criticized the British government's handling of the negotiations, admitted he was nettled by the French "making pedantic stipulations before sitting in council with their wartime comrades."[4] But the French attitude may not have been as formalistic as this suggests. If the main aim of the French proposal was to subject German coal and steel to a supranational authority as a means of diminishing Germany's independent national strength, then the importance of the stipulation is clear.

As Lord Brand explained to the House of Lords, the French view seemed to be that control of the Ruhr was the paramount issue and "that question must be settled as between France and Germany on as firm, unbreakable, and concrete a foundation as possible; and this, it seems to me, was the reason for the 'high authority' and all the paraphernalia of control. I should say that the French were more concerned to maintain their principle of the high authority in relation to Germany than to see the British taking part in the negotiations."[5] Attlee said much the same thing when he indicated that the key factor in the negotiations was the German government's acceptance of the French draft communiqué committing itself to a pool and a supranational high authority with the power to bind the participating countries. "This fact," he pointed out, "naturally determined the course of the subsequent exchanges of view between" Britain and France "and made difficult the achievement of . . . [the British] Government's desire to play an active part in the discussion of the French proposal but without commitment to the acceptance of its principles in advance. . . . [The] Government fully appreciate the reasons for the procedure adopted by the French Government. . . ."[6]

Prior commitment to a high authority seems a real enough issue and may really explain the breakdown of

[4] Weekly Hansard, Commons, no. 159, col. 2143, Je. 27, 1950.
[5] Daily Hansard, Lords, v. 167, col. 1177, Je. 28, 1950.
[6] Weekly Hansard, Commons, no. 157, col. 36, Je. 13, 1950.

negotiations. It seems even more likely, however, that it would not have become an issue if the British had really wanted to get into the negotiations or the French had wanted badly enough to have them there. The French must have known that their stipulation was almost certain to be unacceptable to the British. Did they fear that if the British were in the negotiations the central idea of the Schuman Plan would be adulterated? That would have left them the choice of either refusing to accept the outcome of something they had started with great éclat or of going into an arrangement that lacked safeguards they considered essential. If the main French aim was to start the process of federation, they may have felt sure they could not move Britain very far along that road. There were some risks in leaving Britain out of the coal and steel pool, of course. Many Frenchmen criticized Schuman's diplomacy. It seems probable, though, that his course was based on the calculation that British participation in the pool was not essential to French purposes and that it might even become a hindrance. Considering the difference in the French and British attitudes toward the basic problem, it seems likely that if the prior-commitment issue had not proved to be an insurmountable obstacle, something else would have.

If the British government wished to avoid negotiations, the prior-commitment issue was a good one in terms of British psychology and habit. Very few people in England were willing to say that they would have done otherwise in the Ministers' places, on this issue at least. Lionel Robbins, an independent liberal, put the matter pithily: "Like the public in the days of the South Sea Bubble, we are being asked to subscribe without reserve to an undertaking the nature of which shall hereafter be revealed." [7] *The Times* and *The Economist* supported the government on this point. When the matter was debated in Parliament, responsible Opposition leaders argued that the French stipulation should have been accepted with reservations like those

---

[7] Letter to *The Times* (London), Je. 16, 1950.

made by the Dutch, but the government said this was impossible.[8]

In spite of wide agreement on this issue, there still was much criticism of the government and a feeling that there could have been a different result. "As sorry a piece of diplomatic muddling as the world has ever seen" was *The Economist's* characterization of the negotiations.[9] But the leader carrying this condemnation did not suggest how another outcome could have been attained. Rather its concern was that Britain would appear to world opinion to have failed a test, to have taken a stand on a false issue— though, as Robbins pointed out, Britain was usually being criticized for apparently accepting propositions about international cooperation and then undermining them—and to have let the assessment of national interest be colored by impractical ideas of isolation and doctrinaire Socialist views.

Such concern was heightened, and the debate about Britain's attitude toward the Schuman Plan was complicated, by the appearance some ten days after the negotiations ended of *European Unity*, a statement by the National Executive Committee of the British Labour party. This was not an isolationist document—it stressed Britain's worldwide concerns and emphasized its Commonwealth connections. It did not establish rigid ideological tests for international cooperation—it spoke warmly of the progressiveness of the United States, and called for more Atlantic unity. It rejected neutralism and the concept of Europe as a third force between the United States and Russia. But there was much in the statement that seemed to put sharp limitations on how far Britain would go in international cooperation, particularly in Western Europe. The supra-

[8] As principal advocate for the government, Sir Stafford Cripps argued, first, that the Dutch formula accepted the principles and merely made reservations about the possible failure to put them into practice while Britain could not accept the principles at all. Second, Cripps argued that while France could accept such a reservation from the Netherlands, it could not accept it from Britain which was so much more important politically and as a producer of coal and steel.

[9] "Inverted Micawbers," *The Economist*, Je. 10, 1950, pp. 1257-1259.

national approach was rejected, partly on grounds that it was undemocratic but more forcefully because even a "representative" supranational authority "would have a permanent anti-Socialist majority. . . ." [10] The section of the pamphlet dealing with basic industries said that governments must take the responsibility for international planning and that this would require nationalization. Otherwise the pressure of private interests was likely to dominate and an international organization serving those ends would be worse than lack of coordination. The specific references to the Schuman Plan, presumably added to the statement at a late date, were noncommittal and relatively gentle but ended with a reiteration that "The decisive part in co-ordinating Europe's basic industries must be played by the governments, as trustees for their peoples."

There is no place here for a critique of the Labour party statement. It got a very bad press and was condemned in exaggerated terms in the United States, on the Continent, and by some in Britain. The timing was unfortunate for the government and Attlee was put in the difficult position of trying to sustain the note of his government's statements in the White Paper welcoming the Schuman Plan while discordant chords arose from what Churchill dubbed "the Dalton brown paper," after the chairman of the committee that drafted it.[11] A speech by John Strachey, Secretary of State for War, at the beginning of July added to the trouble and required explanations in the House of Commons. While denying that he had called the French proposal a capitalist plot, Strachey said ". . . I regret the tone of some of the expressions which I used. . . ." [12] He meant to caution against general dangers rather than to question the motives

[10] *European Unity*, p. 8. This generalization and prediction is a good example of the kind of flat-footed statement that helped create a bad impression. The document is examined more fully in my "Imponderables of the Schuman Plan," *Foreign Affairs*, Oct. 1950, pp. 114-129.

[11] There is some indication that Attlee gave little attention to the latter stages of drafting the paper and may not have realized that it was being released. Either there was very bad management, or a complete failure on the part of leading figures in the Labour party to appreciate the impact the statement would have on world opinion.

[12] Weekly Hansard, Commons, no. 161, col. 1156, Jl. 11, 1950.

of the French government, explained Strachey. Attlee said that Strachey had made mistakes in going beyond the government position to say that a supranational authority would certainly be unacceptable and in apparently imputing false motives, but he denied that his government had been acting on the kind of views Strachey expressed. There can be no doubt, however, that Strachey's speech reflected attitudes shared by many in the Labour party which must have influenced the government's approach.

In short, there was a good bit of feeling and some evidence that the British government disliked the idea of the Schuman Plan and was not unhappy that the French stipulation had provided a good issue for staying out of the negotiations. The fact that Bevin had been in the hospital and Attlee and Cripps out of London during much of the negotiations suggested that the government had not put its maximum effort into reaching an understanding with the French. Much of the criticism in the House of Commons went on the assumption that the French stipulation could somehow have been dealt with so that Britain could have participated in the negotiations if the Labour government had really wanted to. Naturally, arguments along this line lacked precision and tacitly assumed the French would have been receptive. Alternatively, they implied that Britain would not have been irrevocably bound to anything by accepting the French formula. "Our Government took a literal view of this condition," said Anthony Eden, "and felt it to be an insuperable obstacle. . . ." His own view was that, "If our Government had felt a profound necessity to be present at Paris in its proper role of European leadership, I am convinced that it would have found a means to satisfy M. Schuman of its sympathy with the spirit of the proposals." [13]

Much of the debate concerned general issues. Churchill, Eden, and others stressed the danger to Britain of standing aside from such important political developments on the Continent, particularly since they might, in Britain's absence, lead to German domination over France. The Labour

[13] Same, no. 159, cols. 1918, 1923, 1925, Je. 26, 1950.

government's attitude toward European cooperation in general, its relations with the French government, its alleged insularity, and—under the influence of the *European Unity* pamphlet—its supposed subordination of national interests to doctrinaire viewpoints, were all heavily criticized. The government stood firm on the impossibility of committing itself to a plan before negotiations while the Opposition's main argument was that by getting into the negotiations Britain could strongly influence the nature of the plan. Not enough was known of the Schuman Plan to discuss its merits, but only a few speakers were willing to contemplate yielding control of Britain's basic industries to a supranational authority. On that issue, Churchill said that if he were asked, " 'Would you agree to a supranational authority which has the power to tell Great Britain not to cut any more coal or make any more steel, but to grow tomatoes instead?' I should say, without hesitation, the answer is 'No.' But why not be there to give the answer?" [14]

Several months later the British Conservative party members of the Consultative Assembly of the Council of Europe offered a substitute for the Schuman Plan. Their proposal called for an international authority on which countries would have votes in proportion to their production. In the ordinary run of business decisions would be by majority rule, but on matters of fundamental importance governments could appeal to an intergovernmental ministerial council. The way was left open for national vetoes and the right of withdrawal from the whole enterprise.[15] In supporting this proposal, Harold Macmillan echoed what Churchill had said in the House of Commons, "One thing is certain, and we may as well face it. Our people will not hand over to any supra-national Authority the right to close down our pits or our steelworks. We will not allow

---

[14] Same, no. 159, col. 2149, Je. 27, 1950.

[15] The details of this proposal are of no current interest. They may be found in Council of Europe, Consultative Assembly, *Documents, Working Papers*, Ordinary Sess. 1950, doc. 25, pp. 719-724. The motion was signed by a few non-British members.

any supra-national Authority to put large numbers of our people out of work in Durham, in the Midlands, in South Wales or in Scotland." [16]

Thus the issue on which the parties divided in Britain was not identical with that on which the British and French negotiations broke down. No politically significant body of British opinion was willing to accept the French idea of a supranational agency to control coal and steel, much less the stipulation that this be accepted in advance of negotiation. The question in Britain was whether to try to find a way to get into the negotiations or whether to accept the prospect of staying out with some equanimity, as the government did.

Behind these differences was a much greater one, present in everyone's mind if not always apparent in public statements. Schuman and Monnet wanted the coal and steel pool because they believed it would lead to much more extensive economic and political integration of Western Europe, eventually to federation. This was a road the British government would not take. No important body of British opinion thought it should. A compromise formula that would bring Britain into the coal and steel negotiations would do nothing to remove the larger difference and would lay up trouble for the future, perhaps dangerous trouble. This was surely recognized on both sides and does much to explain the rigidity of the negotiating positions. No one was certain what could be made of the Schuman Plan, but it was clear that very little good could result if two major partners were to enter it with radically different objectives.

Failure to take part in the negotiations did not imply complete severance of Britain from the problems of the Schuman Plan. The French undertook to keep the British fully informed on the course of the negotiations. The British made studies of their own and drafted a counterplan, but it does not appear to have been used in negotiation

[16] Council of Europe, Consultative Assembly, *Reports*, 2d Sess., 8th Sitting, Aug. 15, 1950, p. 230.

with the Schuman Plan countries.[17] Britain's standing aside did not imply that British influence would be used to block or subvert the Schuman Plan. While such an attitude or action has often been alleged, there is little evidence. Overtly the British government maintained a "correct" position, said nothing unfriendly to the Schuman Plan idea (at least after the Strachey speech) and refrained from using its influence as an occupying power in Germany to block the coal and steel pool. In ways that were less public, there may have been some effort to encourage opposition to the Schuman Plan, but it did not in the end amount to much. As one observer put it, "They sneezed and encouraged Dutch dissidence with their eyebrows but that was about it." Others think the efforts were more serious. Some members of the Labour party undoubtedly encouraged Continental Socialists to oppose the Treaty. They were not very successful; only the German Socialists opposed the Treaty and they needed no encouragement from the British. When the Schuman idea became the fact of the European Coal and Steel Community, the British established relations with it, negotiated about common problems, and finally came to the conclusion of a treaty. In all this there was some change in British attitudes, but no real departure from the central position shared by Socialists and Tories, that British coal and steel could not be put under foreign control (see Chapter 18).

DRAFTING THE TREATY

While the negotiations with Britain were going on, France was also carrying on conversations with Germany, Italy and the Benelux governments. On June 3 these six governments announced their "determination" to work toward the "immediate objective" of pooling their coal and

---

[17] The plan was drafted by a group of civil servants under Sir Edwin Plowden, the Chief Planning Officer of the United Kingdom government, beginning right after Monnet's visit to London. The "voluminous document" that reportedly resulted was sent to the British embassy in Paris and the British delegation to the OEEC at the beginning of the six-power conference for drafting the Treaty, but then disappears from view so far as the public record is concerned.

steel under a "High Authority whose decisions will bind" the governments. Negotiations on the basis of the French proposals were to begin in a few weeks. Although the communiqué made no reference to the fact, the Dutch acceptance of the French invitation had contained a reservation that seemed to leave the way open for the Netherlands to reject the result if too much power were given to the supranational High Authority at the expense of national governments.

On June 20 delegations met in Paris for the first of a series of sessions that lasted through the summer and fall of 1950. The conferences seem to have been fairly informal and it was soon decided that the participants would act as experts without committing their governments, a decision that was probably influenced by the fall of the Bidault government a few days after the first session began.[18] This approach was made easier by the view of at least some of the delegates that the job of the conference was to work out methods of carrying through the basic political decision, already taken by the governments, to pool coal and steel under a high authority.[19] The delegations consulted their governments frequently and were in close touch with business and labor groups, but no government was formally committed until the treaty was initialed the following spring by the foreign ministers. The document that the conferees turned over to their governments in early De-

[18] Whether differences of opinion over the Schuman Plan played any important part in this cabinet crisis is unclear. It was certainly not a major, overt issue but there are some hints in the French press that it influenced the position of some groups. In talking with people in Paris at the time I could get no conclusive evidence but my impression is that if Schuman Plan issues played any role, it was a secondary one. The resolution of the crisis favored pursuit of the Schuman Plan. René Pleven formed the new government with Socialist support, Guy Mollet becoming Minister of State for Council of Europe Affairs. Schuman remained at the Foreign Ministry.

[19] H. C. Boden, "Fragestellungen des Schuman-Plans," *Der Volkswirt*, pt. I, Mar. 23, 1951, pp. 9-12; pt. II, Mar. 30, 1951, pp. 10-12. Boden was one of the German delegates. Spaak used the same formula when the first Benelux agreement was negotiated (my *Trade and Payments in Western Europe*, 1952, p. 341) and again in the drafting of the report that led to the European Economic Community.

cember 1950 had several important gaps, which will be
discussed later in this chapter, but as far as it went it largely
took the form that was finally adopted.

The French delegation reported that in these conferences, "the debates that took place did not have the traditional character of negotiations but rather that of construction in common which had as its object not to eliminate divergences but to resolve the multitude of problems
raised by the work undertaken." [20] Perhaps this goes a little
too far in putting aside differences; after all, the delegations
had some instructions. On some issues, however, the major
conflicts of views seem to have cut across national lines,
bringing into play attitudes that divided the groups from
each country. Many of the problems were quite novel;
individual responses to them undoubtedly influenced the
course of the negotiations as well. The atmosphere of
working together to solve common problems was probably
enhanced by the fact that the French did not present the
negotiators with a draft treaty at the outset, only with a
working paper elaborating some of the principles set out
in Schuman's original statement.

After an opening speech by Schuman, the conferees came
to grips at once with basic constitutional issues.[21] In a long
statement on the second day, Monnet put forth the idea that
a common assembly should meet annually to review the
work of the High Authority, with the power of voting that
body out of office. This was the French response to the
criticism that they were proposing a supranational board
above and beyond democratic control. It fitted very well
with the thought that the coal and steel pool should lead to
a federal Western Europe. And it appeared to have implications for the role of the governments in the new scheme.
Very likely it was to these points that the foreign delegates

[20] *Rapport de la Délégation Française* . . . (cited in Ch. 3, n. 1), p. 11.
[21] No record of the negotiations has been published but enough information reached journalists or appears in writing by participants, in
official matter and elsewhere, to permit an analytical summary. The
fullest narrative I have seen is in Raymond Racine, *Vers une Europe
Nouvelle par le Plan Schuman*, 1954. See Critical Bibliography for other
sources.

referred as they went away from the opening meetings saying that they had not appreciated the political audacity of the French proposal and would have to consult their governments on its full implications.[22]

At the opening of the second session, early in July, the Belgian and Dutch representatives proposed a second basic change that they regarded as essential. They wanted to subject the High Authority to some kind of review by an intergovernmental body. The French were alert to changes that would strike at the supranational element basic to their whole scheme. Out of the interplay of views came a new organ, the Council of Ministers, made up of government representatives and charged, broadly speaking, with problems in the area between the action of the High Authority and that of national governments.

The compromise on this issue was undoubtedly linked with the division of powers between the High Authority and the governments, an issue that will turn up frequently throughout this book. The extent of the High Authority's powers, the definition of the conditions under which they could be used, and assurance of the rights of firms and of governments, appear to have occupied the conferees for a large part of the summer. The whole character of the new organization was at stake. According to the French conception, protection against the High Authority's abuse of power lay primarily in the right of appeal to the supranational court of justice of the Coal and Steel Community. Provisions to this effect appear to have been in the Treaty from an early date, including not only appeal on specific legal grounds but also the right of governments to seek a review when the operation of the Community caused fundamental economic difficulties. Others preferred a larger role for governments as an additional check.

Another proposed method of partially diluting the powers of the High Authority disappeared in the course of the

[22] Racine, cited, p. 83, says it was the Germans who asked for the recess to consult their government on this matter. Paul Reuter, *La Communauté Européenne du Charbon et de l'Acier*, 1953, p. 52, says the Assembly was decided on in a French interministerial committee on June 12.

negotiations. The French working paper mentioned regional associations of producers as "intermediaries" between the High Authority and the individual firm. Regional organizations straddling national boundaries and carrying on some of the functions of the pool seem to have been looked on by some as parts of a federal structure that would limit the High Authority's power and also help to apply the Treaty's broad principles to varying situations. They were also regarded as means of spreading the burden of adjustment over more than one country. In the finished Treaty there were no regional bodies. The main explanation seems to be the discovery that by any reasonable definition some of the most important regional groupings, notably the Ruhr, did not cut across national boundaries. Any major devolution of power to national regional organizations would strengthen the old patterns, instead of weakening them. Cartels on national lines might have become harder to control. For the French, in particular, the whole point of the Schuman Plan would have been lost if the Ruhr were to any great extent taken out from under supranational control and permitted to shape its development according to autochthonous and purely German forces in a "regional" organization.

Closely related to the constitutional arrangements were questions about the kind of powers the High Authority should have. The *dirigiste* views attributed to Monnet and the men around him aroused the suspicions of many, either because they believed in liberal economic principles or because they were businessmen who wanted no governmental interference. If the High Authority had extensive powers, would this not lead to some kind of supranational socialism? But if the High Authority did not have extensive powers, how could it meet the problems involved in bringing about a common market as well as those of guiding the affairs of the coal and steel industries in difficult times?

Monnet's working paper aimed to dispel suspicion and to suggest the broad lines of compromise by stressing the "limited and specific powers" of the High Authority and making special mention of its consultative and informational work. "It would be understood," the paper said, "that certain of the powers conferred on the Authority would be of a precautionary character, and that the Authority would direct its activities so as to avoid use of these powers save in exceptional circumstances." [23] Something like this description could reasonably be applied to the finished treaty, but the process of deciding on the powers to be granted to the High Authority and the circumstances in which they could be used undoubtedly occasioned some of the greatest difficulties in the negotiations. In all probability, the main movement was away from *dirigisme*. Almost unavoidably the results include a series of compromises and uncertainties which have kept the basic issues alive throughout the life of the Community.

The negotiators' experience with some specific issues provided a foretaste of the complexities of creating a coal and steel pool. For instance, there had been much talk at an early stage about a single price for coal and steel in the common market. This proved to be an oversimplified concept which might have required extensive price-fixing and would have led to many artificialities. Similarly, statements had been made that suggested that the Treaty would call for equal wage rates throughout the Community. It soon became apparent that wages in coal and steel were more closely related to wages in other industries in the same country than to wages in the same industry in other countries. So, while containing some guarantees against competitive wage-cutting, the Treaty's provisions on wages were rather more general than many had expected them to be.

There were trade problems as well. The decision to remove tariffs and quotas on a fixed date soon after the Treaty went into effect meant that the adaptation of coal mines and steel mills to the new circumstances would come after the creation of the common market, not before. Drafting the terms of the convention containing the rules that were to apply during the five-year transitional period

[23] *Summary of the Working Document Submitted by the French Experts*, p. 3 (mimeographed).

proved to be one of the hardest tasks of the conferences. Much of the difficulty centered on coal. The Belgians felt unable to compete because of high costs and foresaw the closing of many mines. The French had somewhat similar though less acute fears. Subsidies to ease the transition seemed called for, but the Belgians said that other countries would have to share the cost. How much, how long, and who should pay, proved very troublesome questions. At one point the Germans, who were slated to make the largest contribution, seemed to prefer leaving Belgian coal outside the common market for the time being. In the end, at a very late stage in the negotiations, a compromise was reached. The trade barriers were to come down, the Germans and Dutch were to pay, the Belgians were to use the money to adapt their coal production to the new situation, the French were given assurances of help if the need arose in concrete form (see Chapter 9).

Work on the economic provisions occupied the drafters for the latter part of the summer and most of the fall. It took longer and was more difficult than the creation of the organs of the Community, as had been expected. "The difficulties in the realization of the Schuman Plan begin where the economic problems start," said Hans vom Hoff, a labor leader on the German delegation.[24] Still, most of the difficulties were dealt with one way or another, and rather expeditiously. When the drafters turned the Treaty over to their governments in December there were only two major omissions from the text (apart from the Belgian coal settlement, which was part of the transitional Convention). First, a number of questions about the organization of the High Authority and the other organs of the Community

[24] *Neue Zürcher Zeitung*, Nov. 5, 1950. At one time the French had in mind a treaty that would concentrate on "the essential principles and undertakings." The "details of their application" were to be embodied in subsequent conventions negotiated "with the help of a referee" who could make decisions in case of a deadlock. (The quotations are from Schuman's original statement.) The Benelux countries, and perhaps others, considered this too vague and said that they could not commit themselves to a treaty without having a fairly clear idea of its effect on their economies.

had been left to the governments. Second, there was a blank where the key provisions on cartels and concentrations should have been.

The first omission was deliberate; it had been intended for some time to leave these questions to politically responsible ministers. The second omission did not mean that the subject of cartels was inherently more complicated than others that the conferees had successfully handled. Certainly there had been serious disagreements; the schools of thought about how to deal with cartels cut across national lines. But the failure to agree registered a much more fundamental difficulty: doubts about German willingness to accept the Treaty at all and French insistence on certain preliminary measures as a prior condition of entering the coal and steel pool with the Germans. The decisions that had to be taken on these matters went far beyond the terms of reference of the men who were spending long hours in the drafting rooms in Paris. They called into play diplomacy on a scale greater than any previous question affecting the Treaty and provided a convincing display of the connection between the proposed steel and coal pool and major political and economic forces.

THE CHANGED SETTING

Only a few days after the Treaty negotiations began in Paris, North Korean troops invaded southern Korea. Immediately the political atmosphere changed and soon the economic climate as well. American rearmament, the beginnings of European rearmament, and above all expectations of what both these efforts would lead to, swelled demand and drove up prices. The fear of surplus steel that had preyed on the edges of people's minds a few months earlier was pushed back by the prospect of almost insatiable demand for steel. Actual demand built up rather more slowly, especially since European rearmament did not expand as rapidly as talk about it, but the market turned upwards and some steel was even exported to the United States. Insofar as fear of a steel surplus had motivated support for the Schuman Plan it should have ceased operating. But since the effort was already launched, the new market conditions may have worked the other way. So long as rearmament went on, there would be little need for anyone to think of shutting down a coal mine or a steel mill even if trade barriers were removed to form a common market. To that extent the new boom helped along the negotiations.

The opposite side of the coin was also ambiguous. Insofar as easier access to foreign markets was an attraction of the Schuman Plan—especially for France—the boom reduced urgency because more steel could be sold at home. But the attraction might still be there for the long run. Booming markets are likely to brighten the soberest man's view of the future, but in the European steel industry the set pattern of thought is that present expansion means future excess capacity. So the prospect of facing this bogey with a united front may have continued to favor the pool.

It was not, however, the new economic situation that was most important for the Treaty negotiations. It was the impact of heightened tension on Germany's position. Schuman's offer held the promise of speeding Germany's return to autonomy and equality. Allied controls over German coal and steel production, and perhaps other restrictions as well, would be removed. Barriers to the sale of German steel in major European markets would disappear and Schuman had touched an old ambition of the Germans when he mentioned Africa in his opening statement.[25] Added to this was the possibility of getting capital through the pool for the modernization and expansion of German coal and steel production. Even more important in many ways was the advance along the road to equality and independence that Schuman was offering the Germans. In the pool Germany would be a fully fledged and autonomous member of

[25] Pierre Gerbet, "La Genèse du Plan Schuman," *Revue Française de Science Politique*, Jl.-Sept. 1956, p. 545, says René Mayer suggested including Africa, which Parker calls "one of those flabby spots in German thinking where cynicism is eagerly extinguished by gullibility, and reinforced subsequently by disenchantment." N. J. G. Pounds and W. N. Parker, *Coal and Steel in Western Europe*, 1957, p. 363.

a European community. Germany was already moving in that direction, but the implied change in France's position would remove a major drag and speed the pace.

These advantages were expected to play an important part in winning German acceptance of supranational control of the coal and steel industries—the great French aim. The Korean war changed the whole equation. Improving Western European defense became an urgent policy objective. Germany, with its front position and its manpower, seemed more important than ever. Rearmament's claims on production, coupled with the desire to keep civilian consumption and investment as high as possible, made it likely that the occupying powers would move even faster to remove the remaining barriers to maximum production in one of the great "workshops of the world." The risk that Russia would make a serious bid to reunify Germany on terms that would draw the country toward the East made it important to speed up the process of integrating Germany with the West.

No great subtlety in statecraft was needed to see what was bound to happen. The process by which Germany was shedding the shackles of occupation and of the postwar settlements would be speeded. Germany's advance toward sovereignty and acceptance as an equal would be hastened by the Western powers, under American leadership, in an effort to strengthen the free world and to tie Germany to it. Increasingly one heard it said, especially in the United States, that Germany was indispensable to the defense of the West. If you are indispensable you can write your own ticket, modified only by discretion and the degree of your own unwillingness to go very far on an alternative course. In short, Germany now had a good chance to get many of the things it wanted without accepting the Schuman Plan. It might still accept the French proposal, but the calculations of German interest would be changed, and with them the bargaining about the terms of the Treaty. Adenauer and the other governmental leaders who were actively pressing for European integration would still be strong for the coal and steel pool. But they would find it harder to carry with them industrialists and others who were less interested in the broad political aim but were willing to accept the Schuman Plan for the other benefits it would bring.

The sharpest manifestation of the changed circumstances came at the meeting of the French, British, and American foreign ministers in New York in September 1950, when Acheson proposed the creation of ten German divisions in the near future. Bevin agreed, perhaps reluctantly. Schuman found the idea unacceptable. France was not ready to accept German rearmament, and certainly not before the coal and steel treaty was signed and the Ruhr was made subject to supranational control. The conference took no formal, public action on German rearmament, beyond opposing recreation of a national German army, but it emphasized the importance the West attached to Germany by a declaration that the three countries would regard an attack on the Federal Republic or West Berlin as an attack on themselves. There were other gestures as well, notably the decision that steps would be taken to pierce the ceiling on German steel production, "where this will facilitate the defense effort of the west."

About this time the Treaty negotiations became more difficult. In the months that followed, opposition to the pool increased in German industrial circles. On October 1, 1950, at a Bavarian foreign trade day in Munich, Dr. Robert Lehr, who was connected with Vereinigte Stahlwerke, called the Schuman Plan an effort to overcome the difficulties of the French steel industry. The real need, he said, was to produce more steel at the lowest possible cost and the place for that was Germany. But the French aimed to protect their high-cost steel production and to achieve, with the help of Germany, a hegemony in steel that they could not impose on Germany. If peaceful cooperation in steel was the aim, said Lehr, the methods followed by the international steel cartel of 1926 would prove a better instrument for the fair recognition of the interests of all participating countries. At first the speech did not attract much attention, but by the time its full text was published in mid-October Lehr had become Minister of the Interior.[26]

About the same time, Hermann Reusch, a spokesman of the steel industry, quit his position as an adviser to the German delegation to the Schuman Plan negotiations. The French took alarm and asked if these events meant that Germany had changed its position on the desirability of the pool. Walter Hallstein, the German Secretary for Foreign Affairs, admitted that industrial opposition to the Schuman Plan had grown—in France as well as in Germany, he noted—but declared that the Bonn government still supported the idea of the pool. In a speech to members of his party, Adenauer departed from his manuscript to deny rumors of a change in the government's position and said that the cabinet still supported the Schuman Plan and all other measures that could lead to a European *Zusammenschluss*.[27]

Despite these assurances, the French felt that the Schuman Plan and the policy toward Germany that it embodied were in grave danger. The whole logic of the new approach was threatened. Advantages for Germany that were to have helped entice it into the pool were being thrown into its lap without a *quid pro quo*. The pool was to have provided a guarantee of security that might, conceivably, make it possible for France to accept the risks of some future German rearmament. Now the risks were being invited before the guarantee was given. Not merely diplomatic strategy, but the political life of the French government was at stake. The old pattern was re-emerging: American pressure, French rejection, resulting in a compromise less satisfactory to the French than to the Americans, and with no firm obligations placed on the Germans.

The French responded in several ways. They hurriedly produced the Pleven Plan for an integrated European army in which Germans would serve in fairly small contingents

---

[26] The account of the Lehr episode and the contents of his speech are drawn from the *Neue Zürcher Zeitung*, Oct. 20 and Nov. 5, 1950. The information that follows comes from other issues of the same paper and from other sources.

[27] Same, Oct. 23, 1950.

under an international command. The plan met with a chilly reception in Washington, where military officials judged it impractical. But later the American position veered around and supported a modified version of the plan. In the end, in 1954, the tables were completely turned and in spite of strong American advocacy and acceptance by Germany and other countries the French National Assembly rejected the European Defense Community.

The French also said that they would accept German rearmament in any form only after the Schuman Plan had been signed. Feeling, not unnaturally, that the American government, which had heartily welcomed the Schuman Plan, had pulled the rug out from under the French position, the French also seem to have called on Washington to help them get the Treaty signed. On November 6, President Truman repeated his earlier endorsement of the project; other government officials also spoke up on the subject. But the most important activity was undertaken by John J. McCloy, the American High Commissioner in Germany. During the winter and spring of 1950-51 he and his staff played a key part in the final negotiations of the Schuman Plan Treaty. Along with David Bruce, the American Ambassador to France, McCloy had a hand in a number of matters, but the central issue was the organization of Ruhr industry.

From the beginning of the occupation, decartelization and deconcentration of German industry had been a goal of American policy. The official attitude on this subject had gone through a number of phases and at times it had seemed as if the policy had become so inactive that it would eventually be dropped altogether. The coal and steel industries had been among the first major targets of deconcentration and decartelization but the process had never been completed. The shares of the major steel companies were vested in a group of trustees while plans were to be worked out for the reorganization of the industry into smaller units. Coal was still marketed through a common sales agency, the Deutscher Kohlen-Verkauf (DKV), under Allied control. The French were fearful that the DKV would give the Germans too much bargaining power within the common market and hinder French access to Ruhr coke. Failure to break up the great steel concerns would, in the French view, give the Germans too strong a position in the pool. The extensive ownership of coal mines by steel firms would reduce the amount of coal that the Ruhr could export and would give German steel producers a chance to manipulate their costs so as to undersell French steel.

The Germans had all along opposed, and to some degree resisted, deconcentration and decartelization. Some Germans were prepared to see a reduction in the power of the largest steel firms, but the strongest groups to take this view—labor and the Socialists—were more interested in nationalization or co-determination than in deconcentration. Virtually all Germans opposed the elimination of the traditional arrangement for selling coal, and the destruction of *Verbundwirtschaft*, the steel industry's ownership of coal mines. That was the German attitude before there was a Schuman Plan. The French proposal sharpened the issue; the Germans saw it as a serious disadvantage to enter a common market with the handicaps they believed would result from decartelization and deconcentration. American emphasis on these policies had weakened greatly in five years, and the Germans may well have felt that the further attrition of occupation would end it altogether. The new stress on Germany's essentiality for defense and plans for the replacement of the Occupation Statute with "contractual obligations" that would take the place of a peace treaty also suggested that the matter might come to a fairly easy end.

Whatever the United States might eventually have done about these matters in other circumstances, the French insistence that there would be no Schuman Plan unless satisfactory decartelization and deconcentration measures were carried through ensured American activity. During the first two months of 1951 virtually all the negotiations of importance for the coal and steel pool were in McCloy's hands. He negotiated with the German government, the Ruhr industrialists, the French, and to some extent the British as well.[28] By the beginning of March the main lines of an agreement emerged. The steel industry would be reorganized in 28 companies (but there would be no ceiling on the amount any firm could produce, as the French had proposed). No steel firm could own coal mines producing more than 75 per cent of its needs; this put only about 16 per cent of the Ruhr coal output under control of the steel industry. The coal sales organization was to be broken up by October 1952 and replaced by several smaller bodies.

On March 14, 1951, Adenauer officially presented the agreed arrangements as his government's proposals "on the assumption that the Schuman Plan will be put into effect." [29] Two days later the negotiators met again in Paris and approved the articles of the Treaty concerning cartels and concentrations. On March 19 the delegates initialed the Treaty. Two weeks later the High Commissioners informed the German government that restrictions on the production of synthetic oil and rubber and some other products had been removed and that steel could be produced in excess of the ceiling when this contributed to Western defense. This was an implementation of the decision reached by the foreign ministers in New York the previous September, which had been held in suspense while negotiations for the Schuman Plan and other matters were completed. About the same time the Germans asked about liquidation of the International Authority for the Ruhr when the Schuman Plan came into effect; while formal assurance only came later, they must have allowed for the fact that this action would almost certainly be forthcoming.

In addition to their importance in settling a specific prob-

[28] While McCloy consulted the British, they played no major role in the negotiations and were not committed by the arrangements he made with the French and Germans. The British may have dragged their feet a bit and were not altogether satisfied with the way the decartelization provisions worked out. Legally they could have blocked action, but when presented with the negotiated arrangement they gave their assent, probably partly to avoid the charge of sabotaging the Schuman Plan.

[29] Adenauer's letter to the chairman of the Allied High Commission appears in *Die Neuordnung der Eisen und Stahlindustrie im Gebiet der Bundesrepublik Deutschland; Ein Bericht der Stahltreuhändervereinigung,* 1954, pp. 455-457.

lem that seemed crucial to the conclusion of the Schuman Plan Treaty, the negotiations over the reorganization of German industry were significant as a test of German and French intentions. If, in the new circumstances that had arisen since negotiations for the Treaty began,[30] either government had wanted to rescind its original decision to create a pool, unwillingness to compromise on these issues would have provided a plausible, if not graceful, exit. The episode was also important because it required active American assistance to bring about the realization of a project of European origin and primarily European concern. This was widely recognized and a French newspaper writer was only one of many to put the situation clearly: "After having given the Germans the hope of obtaining more advantages by rearmament than by adhering to the pool, only the United States could lead them to the necessary concessions. Without the United States, the French theses on decartelization and deconcentration in the Ruhr would have continued to be rebuffed by the Federal Republic." [31]

SIGNATURE

With the initialing of the Treaty, the delegates withdrew and their governments took over to fill in the blanks in the Treaty before presenting it to their parliaments for ratification. The blanks concerned the size of the High Authority and the method of choosing it, voting in the Council of Ministers, the allocation of seats in the Common Assembly, and a number of other organizational matters. Here the issues were principally between large and small states. Though France and Germany might often be at odds, the Benelux countries and Italy wanted to be sure that when the two major producers were in agreement they could not make the pool an instrument of joint hegemony.

[30] In addition to those already mentioned, that winter saw the threat of world war as the Chinese entered Korea and United Nations forces fell back; new Soviet overtures about German reunification; serious debate about the defense of Western Europe; the demonstration of German unwillingness to rearm; a serious German deficit in the EPU that raised questions about the role of Germany in the Western European economy.

[31] Le Monde, Mar. 16-22, 1951 (weekly edition).

The foreign ministers met in mid-April and spent several days in negotiation. The result was a series of interrelated compromises. The High Authority was to be made up of nine members, no more than two of them of one nationality; eight of the members were to be chosen by agreement of all countries, thus giving each a veto power; the ninth was to be chosen by the eight.[32] Each country was to have one vote in the Council of Ministers, which sometimes needs unanimity to act, but more often only a majority. A minority that included both France and Germany was to be sufficient to block action. In the Assembly the Benelux powers got a total of 24 seats, compared to 18 each for France, Germany, and Italy. Some changes were also made in the procedure for amending the Treaty.

Quite a different sort of question emerged briefly to trouble the final negotiations: the Saar. The complicated disputes over this area had touched the Schuman Plan at a number of points, for it was a coal- and steel-producing region of some significance. Its control by either France or Germany would affect the strength of those countries in the pool. Moreover, disagreement over the Saar was a major blemish on the good relations between the two countries that were necessary to operate the Schuman Plan successfully. At this stage of the game, the Adenauer government was willing not to press its claims on the Saar and to hold to the formula accepted earlier that final disposition would be made in a peace treaty. There was some hope, too, in France and in Germany, that the Schuman Plan would make it easier to work out some way of "Europeanizing" the Saar so that it would not have to be entirely French or German. The French put aside ideas they had had that the Saar should be a party to the Schuman Plan Treaty, or

[32] After six years somewhat different arrangements take effect and subsequent replacements are to be alternately by government choice and by cooption (Article 10). At one point France and Germany favored a five-man High Authority to be chosen by a two-thirds vote of the governments. The arrangements adopted tacitly assured each country that at least one of its nationals would sit on the High Authority. The Treaty also specified that only nationals of Community countries could sit on the High Authority, a departure from some earlier ideas when the possibility of drawing people from other countries was bruited.

should at least have its own representatives in the Common Assembly. Instead, the Treaty stipulated that the French delegation to the Assembly would include representatives of the Saar and it was taken for granted that France would speak for Saar interests in the Council of Ministers.[33] The Germans insisted on an exchange of letters, attached to the Treaty, in which the German government stated that by signing the Treaty it did not recognize the status of the Saar, or yield its position that a final decision would have to wait for a peace treaty, and, in which France acknowledged that the action on the Schuman Plan did not imply any change in the German position.

On April 18, 1951, the foreign ministers signed the Treaty, celebrating their action with appropriate speeches. Whatever reservations one might have about the future at that point, there was cause for satisfaction in the immediate past. Less than a year had passed since Schuman put forward a proposal that seemed almost incredible and probably impracticable. Instead of breaking down on any of the innumerable issues that might easily have caused a collapse or served as an occasion for a break wanted by one of the participants, the negotiations had survived a most difficult year in world politics. This proved that there was real force behind the plan and that governments either were sincere in their support of it or judged the concept attractive enough to make upsetting it disadvantageous. Of course, much more remained to be done, but the evidence of the first year was that either as *idée force* or as a practical economic and political arrangement the Schuman Plan embodied real strength.

[33] The Treaty was amended to include the Saar representatives in the German delegation when the Saar became part of that country in 1957. There was no change in the total representation of each country.

FIVE

RATIFICATION

THE DOCUMENTS signed by the foreign ministers in April 1951 were long and formidable. The Treaty itself had 100 articles.[1] It was followed by several protocols and other documents. Almost as important as the Treaty itself was the Convention concerning Transitional Provisions which was to govern the Community during its breaking-in period of five years. This was the substantial fodder now turned over to the public opinion and parliaments of the six countries.[2]

THE TERMS OF THE TREATY

The Treaty's basic stroke was to create the European Coal and Steel Community, a new and separate entity existing by virtue of the Treaty and living according to its provisions. As a constitution, the Treaty provided for the establishment of the organs of the Community, assigned their functions, and demarcated their spheres of activity. The High Authority, made up of individuals forbidden to accept the orders or influence of governments or private interests, was to be the central organ to which most of the powers were assigned. It was truly to be an *imperium in imperio*, wielding powers previously held by national governments and having some functions not previously exer-

[1] This exact century was the product of a last-minute change introduced by someone with a fine sense of order and symmetry on the decimal model. The previous draft of the Treaty, as initialed by the negotiators, had 95 articles.
[2] What follows is a very bare summary omitting important qualifications and details. Many of the provisions are more fully examined in later chapters.

cised by governments. At some points the High Authority's action required the concurrence of the Council of Ministers, made up of representatives of the participating governments; the Council also had some powers of independent action. At least once a year the Common Assembly, with representatives of all participating countries, was to meet to debate the work of the High Authority; a two-thirds vote of no confidence would throw the High Authority out of office. A high Court of Justice was to hear complaints from governments or private parties against alleged abuses of power by the High Authority, settle disputes about the interpretation of the Treaty, and pass on certain other large issues that might affect the basic welfare of a country participating in the pool. To advise the High Authority in its work, a Consultative Committee was created with representatives of coal and steel producers, workers, and users.

The mission of the Community, said the Treaty, was "to contribute to the expansion of the economy, the development of employment and the improvement of the standard of living in the participating countries through the creation, in harmony with the general economy of the member States, of a common market . . ." (Article 2). ". . . The most rational distribution of production at the highest possible level of productivity," assured supplies of coal and steel, equal treatment of all consumers, "the lowest possible prices" compatible with necessary amortization and a normal return on capital, opportunity for expansion, improved working conditions, modernization of production, and expanded international trade, all appeared among the goals of the Community. These aims were to be achieved "while safeguarding the continuity of employment and avoiding the creation of fundamental and persistent disturbances in the economies of the member States."

To achieve these purposes, the Treaty made two main kinds of provisions. It proscribed certain national practices in order to create a common market. And it provided the High Authority (and to some extent the Council of Ministers) with a wide array of powers for conducting the affairs of the Community. At the head of the list of devices proscribed within the Community were tariffs, import and export quotas, exchange restrictions, discrimination and subsidies. With a few exceptions during the transitional period, virtually the whole array of government trade controls, and subterfuges for them, were forbidden for trade in coal and steel among the six countries.

The task was not so simply done, however. Proscription alone would not solve all the economic problems. Not only the governments but the enterprises in the Community had to be subject to rules. Conditions would change so there must be flexibility if aims were to be pursued effectively while circumstances altered. Between the starting point in the six separate national economies and the goal of the common market lay a period of adjustment and, to some extent, exploration. Rules would need to be interpreted to apply to cases; art, diplomacy, and wisdom would be required to carry out professed common purposes. To be constitutional—and to be accepted—the competence of the Community organs had to be defined and their powers limited. For all these reasons, and others, the Schuman Plan Treaty could not be confined to a few simple articles creating the common market.

The longest section of the Treaty comprised its "Economic and Social Provisions" which included the principal prescriptions about the conduct of affairs within the Community and the main assignment of power to the High Authority. In financial matters, the High Authority was given power to levy a charge on the production of coal and steel within the Community, to borrow money, and to guarantee loans floated by others. Another set of articles gave the High Authority powers to influence investments in the coal and steel industries and to use its own funds to help finance some of them. With regard to production the most important articles were those authorizing the High Authority and the Council of Ministers to limit output in times of surplus and allocate supplies in times of shortage. Prices were the subject of a complicated series of rules; principal emphasis was put on equal treatment of all Community customers. The High Authority was to fix prices only in special circumstances. An important chapter of the Treaty constituted the antitrust law of the Community. Restrictive trade practices and cartel-like arrangements were banned unless the High Authority sanctioned them as meeting criteria laid down in the Treaty. Mergers and the concentration of enterprises were to be subject to the High Authority's supervision. Rules intended to prevent competitive wage-cutting, and others providing for some free movement of labor, made up another chapter. Discrimination in transportation rates was to be ended; the trade relations of member countries with others outside the Community were to some extent to be subject to common control; an important article provided for action by the High Authority if what a state did seemed likely to alter drastically the conditions of competition within the Community by means other than increasing productivity.

A final chapter of the Treaty contained articles on various matters ranging from action against members found to be in violation and the means of amending the Treaty through housekeeping details to the usual paraphernalia of provisions about the deposit of ratifications, official languages, and the like. Then there was the Convention concerning transitional provisions which provided certain special arrangements for the five years before the Treaty's provisions came fully into force. Relevant parts will be examined piecemeal in later chapters.

THE ISSUES FOR PARLIAMENTS

This, in broad summary, was the proposition put before the parliaments of the six countries. Ratification would mean a fifty-year commitment to arrangements that would greatly alter the conditions under which basic national industries operated, create new currents of interest and influence, and perhaps ultimately change the constellation of power in Western Europe. The economic and political repercussions of the new arrangements would inevitably be felt beyond the bounds of the coal and steel industries. They would affect not only the rest of each national economy, but, very likely, the position, strength, and influence of major groups within each country. Of course, the Treaty might not work. The participants might allow it to become a dead letter. Traditional patterns of national or private interest might reassert themselves through the new mechanism. It would be rash, however, for a parliamentary body to consent to ratification on the assumption that nothing would come of its action.

The issues involved were large, and rather dramatic. Governments were being asked to give up a whole array of practices that had been normal, day-in and day-out attributes of sovereignty for decades. Industries that were all to some extent beneficiaries of government help or protection were to be thrust into a common market and exposed to the direct competition of others, often their principal rivals. Defenses against dislocation were, to a considerable extent, forsworn by both governments and industry or handed over to the High Authority. Firms in coal and steel were to be subject to new rules about pricing and business practices. On top of all this, real power—possibly decisive power—over coal and steel was to be given to an entirely new body; how nine individuals applied the Treaty might make or break the new Community. In recompense for these risks and the yielding of power, the governments, industries, and peoples of the six countries were offered a chance to carry on economic activity on a new scale, at higher levels than before, and to overcome political rivalries of long standing that carried the threat of war.

Since there was now a document with concrete provisions to talk about, discussion of the Schuman Plan became more pointed. Since decisive commitments were to be made or rejected, discussion became more intense and those who thought they would be affected set out to influence the course of events. By the time the Treaty came before the Bundestag, the Assemblée Nationale, and the other legislative bodies for voting, their committees had made fairly detailed studies and the parliamentarians were also being supplied with analyses and briefs intended to persuade them to a particular view or to arm them to persuade others.

The timetable of action by the parliaments of the six countries is set out in Table 1. The detailed history of ratification in each country, the analysis of what votes were decisive and how they were won, I must leave to others. The rest of this chapter deals with the debates that took place in each country, in and out of parliament, about the Treaty. The aim is not to catalogue the arguments but to convey some sense of the issues that seemed important and of the hopes and fears attached to the proposed venture. The debate in each country comprised considerations of two kinds: those reflecting the special features of the

Table 1

PARLIAMENTARY APPROVAL OF THE TREATY

Date	Country	Body	Vote (Abstentions)
1951			
27 June	Germany	Bundesrat–First Reading	26- 17
31 Oct.	Netherlands	Second Chamber	62- 6 (1)
30 Nov.	France	Conseil Économique (Advisory)	111- 15 (29)
13 Dec.	France	Assemblée Nationale	377-233
1952			
11 Jan.	Germany	Bundestag	232-143 (3)
1 Feb.	Germany	Bundesrat–Final Reading	*unanimous*
5 Feb.	Belgium	Sénat	102- 4 (58)
19 Feb.	Netherlands	First Chamber	36- 2
17 Mar.	Italy	Senate	148- 97
1 Apr.	France	Conseil de la République	182- 32
13 May	Luxembourg	Chambre des Députés	47- 4
11 June	Belgium	Chambre des Représentants	165- 13 (13)
17 June	Italy	Chamber of Deputies	265- 98

NOTE:
Other sources contain somewhat different figures for some of these votes. There are several possible explanations and while those used here proved sound where they could be checked, they cannot be guaranteed against error. The Common Assembly's publication, *Le Traité C.E.C.A. devant les Parlements Nationaux* (February 1958), should be authoritative, but having found two cases in which the votes exceeded the membership of the parliamentary bodies, I felt unable to make use of its figures.
SOURCES:
Chronique de Politique Étrangère, Jan. 1953, pp. 7-51; *Relazioni Internazionali*, Je. 21, 1952, pp. 611-612 (for the vote in the Italian Chamber); *The New York Times*, Feb. 2, 1952 (for the Bundesrat's final approval).

national situation and those bearing on the character of the Community as judged from different points of view. Our concern is not with the balance of the arguments or the merits of each case, but with what the debates show about forces and issues that continued to play a part in shaping the Community after the Treaty was ratified.

FRENCH VIEWS

The main line-up of votes in the Assemblée Nationale became clear when the foreign affairs committee approved a report favorable to the Schuman Plan.[3] Supporting the report were members of the Mouvement Républicain Populaire (MRP, Schuman's party), Socialists, Radical Socialists, a number of Independents, and men from the smaller parties. In opposition were the Gaullists, the Communists, and some Independents. This was pretty much the pattern to be repeated in the debate and in subsequent votes in the Assembly, modified by defections in several parties. Of course, the party line-up by itself conceals differences of opinion. Participation of their party in the government, reinforced by votes of confidence, undoubtedly required some people to support the Treaty who had serious misgivings. It is likely that this was most important for some of the Socialists since in that party there was fear of a pool without England, and resistance to the idea of a "Vatican Europe." On the other side, some individual Gaullists may well have been more sympathetic to the Treaty than they appeared in the votes.

Outside the Assembly, perhaps the greatest support for the Schuman Plan came from a variety of groups interested in European unity and from those who had been looking for a new approach to Germany. Others may have shared a view probably held in Monnet's Commissariat du Plan: that the French economy must open its windows to

---

[3] The favorable vote in the foreign affairs committee was 26-18. Other committees reporting favorably were those on finance (23-8, 12 abstentions), industrial production (21-17), and labor (21-20, 2 abstentions). The military affairs committee opposed the Treaty (21-15, 1 abstention) and the committee on economic affairs asked for postponement (24-15).

the world if ancient *immobilisme* was to be displaced by the flexibility needed for a modern, dynamic economy. Or they may have been interested in the prospect of establishing some public control over the French, as well as the German, steel industry. The national labor organizations that were not under Communist domination supported the Schuman Plan as did the Confédération Générale de l'Agriculture. There was some business support and an association of steel-users was created for the occasion.[4]

For the most part, though, the official voice of organized industry spoke against the Schuman Plan or, at a minimum, pressed for amendment and more limited commitments. The steel industry led the fight, through the Chambre Syndicale de la Sidérurgie Française, and carried with it the Conseil National du Patronat Français, the top organization of French business. Their arguments were many, but the strongest notes of their campaign seemed to be concern over their competitive disadvantages compared to the Ruhr and especially the fear that industry would be submitted to the control of an international bureaucracy.[5] Since the coal industry was nationalized, whatever opposition may have come from that quarter was neutralized so far as public debate was concerned and experts were available to support the government's case.[6]

There was a general impression, however, that from another source inside the French government there emanated a series of arguments and perhaps also maneuvers

[4] This represented a split, of apparently fairly serious proportions, from the regular organization of the engineering industry which opposed the Treaty. The president of the nationalized Renault works became a leading spokesman for the interests of consuming industries. Henry W. Ehrmann, "The French Trade Associations and the Ratification of the Schuman Plan," *World Politics*, Jl. 1954, pp. 453-481, gives a valuable account of all these activities.

[5] Ehrmann notes that many of the individuals and organizations involved had supported the proposals discussed at the Westminster Conference (p. 41). That scheme gave business a greater role and, in any case, was only a proposal, not something that was on the verge of acceptance.

[6] But the representatives of the Charbonnages de France in the Conseil Économique abstained on the vote approving ratification of the Treaty.

intended to block the Schuman proposal. In the Quai d'Orsay, or at least in the offices of some of its important officials, the flame remained bright of a traditional French diplomacy based on wholly independent nationalism and directed especially against the hereditary enemy. Outside, the same view was reflected by a rather diverse group including men of the left and the right who often had little in common except a certain traditional nationalism, especially where Germany and security were concerned. Many thought that security depended on France's keeping in step with Britain, not Germany. Not long before Schuman's original statement in 1950 his prime minister, Georges Bidault, had called for stronger Atlantic unity in a speech widely regarded as rejecting European integration as a basis for security. There were individual liberals, too, who opposed the scheme because they saw it as super-state socialism, or because they did not believe it would work, or because they could not believe that such a tailor-made piece of machinery would not be captured by private interests. With such a spectrum of views, widely dispersed throughout the political life of France, one could find in almost any party, organization, or interest group, people who were for and people who were against the Schuman Plan, as well as those who would be for it if it were changed in this, that, or the other way.

Alfred Coste-Floret, rapporteur of the foreign affairs committee, began the debate with the dominant political argument: to support the Treaty was to support European unification. Out of the Coal and Steel Community would come other measures, all moving toward some kind of European unity. This was the policy of France and if the Treaty were defeated, France could not again hope to gain the leadership of this movement.

In the Assembly debate few questioned this goal—not necessarily because they believed in it. Even Communists, who played nationalist themes and called the whole enterprise an American scheme to put the Germans in charge of France, rather circled around the unity issue and directed attention elsewhere. The Gaullists professed to want a better European union than the coal and steel Treaty would provide. They wanted a controlling political organ; they wanted more countries in the pool, especially England; and, outside the Assembly, De Gaulle made it clear that he thought that only a stronger France could afford to face Germany in a unified Europe. The coal and steel industries, where France was weak, were poor starting places, in his opinion.

The new relationship with Germany that would be established by the Treaty was naturally at the core of much of the debate. The basic line of approach of the French government has already been set out (p. 11). It was not so fully articulated in the debate, either in the Assembly or outside. Not much was said about the failure of France's German policy to date. Emphasis was on the positive aspect: the links that the pool would create that would keep Germany on a Western orientation; the mingling of heavy industry and its control that would deprive Germany of warmaking power; the substitution of unity for nationalism.

In opposition, Pierre-Étienne Flandin said, "Why offer Germany what she would have imposed on us if she had conquered us?" [7] That was an extreme view, odd one might think in a man of Munich and Vichy. General Aumeran, an Independent, sounded most of the themes of those who opposed the Treaty on the ground that it gave too much to Germany. To start with, he said, the Germans could never be bound by a treaty. They could always throw aside Adenauer and his group. Their main interest was reunification. The smaller countries in the pool were too weak to enforce the Treaty so the outcome would be that France faced Germany alone and weakened (because the pool would deprive France of control of its basic industries). Moreover, as the rapporteur for the defense committee had pointed out, certain French producers of special steels needed for military purposes, especially for armor plate, should not be sacrificed to German competition simply be-

---

[7] Pierre-Étienne Flandin, "Les Aspects Politiques du Plan," *Nouvelle Revue de l'Économie Contemporaine*, nos. 16-17, 1951, p. 10.

cause their costs were high. Out of the Treaty the Germans
would get sovereignty and would not find their heavy
industry restricted. The next step would be to give Germany
a full role in defending Western Europe and that would put
it in a position to dominate the area. The only safe defense
for France was on an Atlantic basis; without England and
the United States the defense would be dominated by
Germany. Europe without England was absurd and
England had rejected the Treaty in terms that made its
refusal final and definite. France would have no protection
for its interests because all the power in the Community
would be in the hands of an "oligarchy"; after seven years
there might not even be a Frenchman on the High Authority. To clinch the argument Aumeran quoted Churchill:
"Without Britain, the coal and steel pool in Western
Europe must naturally tend to be dominated by Germany,
who will be the most powerful member." [8]

Others used economic arguments to come to the same
conclusion. With controls off and barriers down German
industry would expand. The need for coal would put the
steel industries of the rest of the Community at Germany's
mercy. Germany would have the greatest material weight
in the common market and the institutional arrangements
would not offset this. Hence France would lose the main
weapons it had for defending its interests against
Germany. The tête-à-tête with Germany was to take place
in too enclosed a space; without England, France risked
engulfment.

Here the lines were clearly drawn because it was the
essence of Schuman's argument that only by the direct
confrontation of France and Germany, coupled with the
mutual yielding of national powers to a supranational body,
could the issues between the two countries be solved. This
did not mean that France faced Germany alone in military
matters. England and the United States were still there;
there were guarantees; Germany was not yet rearmed and
before it was there would undoubtedly be more guarantees; it was repeatedly said in the debate that the acceptance

[8] Weekly Hansard, Commons, no. 159, col. 2155, Je. 27, 1950.

of the Schuman Plan did not mean acceptance of German rearmament. In Schuman's view, the changed material conditions of French-German relations that would result from pooling coal and steel were the strongest guarantees that France could have.

Opposition to the Treaty on economic grounds roughly paralleled the argument about German domination at a number of points. With no trade barriers and no subsidies French steel could not compete against German steel; that was the essence of the argument, though it was not often put so bluntly. Investment, it was argued, would flow to the Ruhr. Lower wages and other costs would enable the Germans to undersell French producers. The expansion of steel production in Germany would mean there would be less coke for export, especially since many mines were owned by steel companies. Thus the access to Ruhr coal that was held out as an advantage of the pool to France was illusory. Moreover, argued these critics, the High Authority would not really be able to prevent the organization of cartels and concentrations in German heavy industry. One way or another, secretly if necessary, the well-established and only too familiar tendencies to monopoly would reassert themselves, adding to the bargaining power of the Germans in the Community. Germany's preponderance, economic and eventually political, would mean that France could expect no lasting benefit from the pool and much damage. The immediate economic damage predicted by the critics was: unemployment, pressure on wages and prices, bankruptcies, a deterioration of France's foreign trade balance, and general economic dislocation. Over a longer period, it was argued, the iron ore of Lorraine would be more quickly exhausted because other countries would gain easy access to it. The program for turning Lorraine coal into coke would have to be abandoned because the process was plainly uneconomic in its present stage and so France's dependence on the Ruhr would be increased.

In the steel industry the complaint was frequently made that the Treaty would subject producers to *dirigisme* of a sort they were trying to escape at home. Many arguments centered on this theme: the powers given the High Authority were too great; it would be a "technocracy," not subject to political control; its powers over prices and investments were socialistic and dangerous; the rules on cartels and restrictive practices were unrealistic, dangerous, and a reflection of American ideologies instead of European experience. Two threads seem to run through all these arguments. First, the steel industry wanted to be able to regulate its own affairs in a manner to which it felt largely accustomed. As Louis Charvet, General Secretary of the Chambre Syndicale, said, "One prefers what one has negotiated oneself to what is imposed from the outside."[9] Second, to the extent that there had to be governmental regulation the industry preferred to deal with the French government. Under the Schuman Plan power over the industry would be wielded by a body that was not French, that was not subject to the known pressures and considerations of a French government, that would see French industry in a different context from that seen by any French government, and that might be much more remote from the reasoning, values, and pressures of the French industry.[10]

Concern with this problem did not always bring the spokesmen of industry to oppose the pool in all respects. Instead they sometimes called for a series of measures that would weaken the High Authority in favor of national governments and private industry. They sought more escape clauses in case a government found the common market creating unemployment and a fall in living standards; a lengthening of the transition period and its transformation into a probationary period, after which the decision to undertake the full-blown Treaty would be reexamined; a shift in the cartel provisions of the Treaty to

[9] Quoted by Ehrmann, cited, p. 461.

[10] Moreover, though this was not stated, under the existing arrangements in France, the Ministry of Industry counted on the Chambre Syndicale, which had a much larger staff of steel experts, to "implement" policies. In fact, the Ministry "withheld only seldom the seal of official approval from the decisions reached in the *Rue de Madrid*." H. W. Ehrmann, *Organized Business in France*, 1957, p. 262.

permit industrial arrangements unless the High Authority could clearly demonstrate the existence of abuses; and a greater role for business organizations in the execution of the Treaty.[11]

The proponents of the Treaty argued in part that France would have to take economic risks for a larger political gain. But they also claimed that France would get positive economic gains from the pool and that without it France would still face many of the problems and risks that opponents were attributing to the Treaty.

The immediate issue was coal. France's steelmaking depended on imported coke and coking coal. Britain was exporting little or no coal. There was American coal but it was expensive. The logical source of most of France's coal and coke was the Ruhr. France was guaranteed a supply of Ruhr coal under the occupation arrangements, but it would need more and the occupation would not last forever. Under the Treaty, French and German buyers would have equal access to Ruhr coal. Germany would no longer be able to charge higher prices for the coal it exported than for that sold at home. In times of shortage there would be an international allocation. Germany could not use its coal supply to exert pressure on France. Nor could private German interests establish a monopoly position to the detriment of French buyers. The Allied measures of deconcentration would be carried out before the Treaty took effect and reconcentration would be regulated by the High Authority.

A second argument concerning the immediate benefits of the pool to France dealt with steel exports. It received much less stress than the argument about coal, partly perhaps lest other countries be alarmed, partly because many Frenchmen would find it hard to believe. Monnet touched on it in an interview: "In steel especially, France is very well placed and the conditions created [by the Treaty]

---

[11] These are embodied in a fairly specific set of proposals put forward in the Conseil Économique by the employers' group. France, Conseil Économique, *Communaté Européenne du Charbon et de l 'Acier*, 1951, pp. 140, 166-169.

will permit her to get the benefit of her natural advantages and of the modernization effort carried out since the liberation." [12] The Monnet Plan had given France some very modern steel mills of great capacity and had improved the conditions of production in a large part of the industry. A domestic market for all this steel was not in sight. Exports could be important in enabling France to get the economies of large-scale production of which its new mills were capable. Thanks to modernization (and to some extent to the lag in investment in Germany), France was in a good position to compete in foreign markets, if it could get access to them. The removal of foreign tariffs and quotas under the Treaty could help provide that access. The removal of France's own barriers to imports was also a benefit in Monnet's view. Much had been accomplished to modernize and rationalize the French steel industry but a great deal remained to be done. The pressure of foreign competition would help. "We need German competition in order to rouse French enterprise from its slumbers," Reynaud had said some time before the Schuman Plan was proposed.[13] Inefficient firms were already a problem for the French economy. They were shielded from internal competition by a variety of cartel-like arrangements which were reinforced by import barriers. The common market would increase the pressures to choose between efficiency and going out of business; the High Authority could help in either transformation. These two arguments in favor of the Treaty were also a major part of the defense against the charge that it would damage France by opening the doors to lower-cost German competition. France needed some competition, ran Monnet's argument, and one could not say that the steel industry as a whole was inefficient. "In reality, there are as many problems as there are enterprises," wrote André Philip.[14]

Finally, the Treaty's supporters asked, What was the

---

[12] *Le Monde*, Apr. 20-26, 1951 (weekly edition).
[13] Quoted by Herbert Lüthy, "Why Five Million Frenchmen Vote Communist," *Commentary*, Sept. 1951, p. 208.
[14] Conseil Économique, cited, p. 129.

alternative to the common market? True, the pool would free Germany from certain restrictions. But without a treaty these restrictions would eventually disappear anyway and without safeguards for France and other countries. With or without the pool the German economy would grow and add to Germany's political weight. There would be advantages to having the German growth take place inside a European community; the political consequences would be less dangerous; German heavy industry would be part of a larger complex and not just the province of German nationalism. To gain these advantages, the French had to make certain concessions, opening their economy to the Germans as the German economy was to be open to them. This did not mean that France was making a sacrifice. In his report to the Conseil Économique, André Philip said that if the Schuman Plan were not adopted France would develop "systematic protectionism" which would result in "the maintenance of marginal enterprises; the development of unprofitable investments. . . . The limitation of the trade in steel." This last would result from "the exploitation of certain obsolete installations; the difficulty of the coke supply . . . . the maintenance of irrational transport . . . . the absence or insufficiency of competition between the producers, aggravating the situation of the users . . . an always more precarious adjustment of supply and demand, in coal as well as in steel. . . ." [15]

That there would be problems, the supporters of the Treaty did not deny. The government accepted the mandate of the Assembly—in a resolution joined to the approval of the Treaty—to begin negotiations for the canalization of the Moselle, to continue and expand investment programs in coal, steel, and transportation, and to improve the terms of loans made to the steel industry. The government had fended off other proposals that would have tied its hands

---

[15] Same, pp. 136-137. Original paragraphing changed. The Conseil Économique adopted this report by 111 to 15 (the CGT) with 29 abstentions (the *patronat*, the representatives of small enterprises, and some others).

in matters of domestic economic policy or required any
reopening of Treaty negotiations.

There were many other arguments but by and large
these were the main issues, particularly the economic ones,
on which the French debate centered in and out of the
Assembly. All of the discussion was influenced by two
factors. For everyone but the most doctrinaire, who were
sure what the future would bring, acceptance of the Schuman Plan was truly a leap into the unknown as it was so
often called. For that reason every argument for the Treaty
carried an invisible baggage of misgivings, except for those
who were not only dissatisfied with the way things were
but were clear that they could only lead once more to
what Pleven sardonically called *le beau temps de jadis*.[16]

The second factor was one which held in check some of
the criticisms of the Treaty, or at least made people who
might have wanted to oppose it outright take a more moderate stand, such as advocating specific changes (which in
some cases would have amounted to a disemboweling of
the original idea). This was the realization—on which the
government played heavily—that French prestige was
greatly involved in the new initiative. If the noble ideas of
May 9, 1950, were watered down too much, or if the failure
of the whole effort resulted primarily from the efforts of
Frenchmen, then France would slip downward, lose the
advantages it had gained from the bold stroke, see a further
diminution of its influence in world affairs, and perhaps
even lose the power to carry out measures favored by those
most opposed to the Treaty. "It is impossible that a French
initiative of such importance should be allowed to fail,"
said Pierre Ricard of the steel federation, who was not
favorably disposed to the Treaty.[17] His was not the only
case in which this immeasurable influence was perceptible.

However one weighs all these factors—politics, foreign
policy, sectional interests, the merits of the scheme, party

---

[16] France, Assemblée Nationale, *Journal Officiel, Débats Parlementaires,*
3e Séance du 7 Décembre 1951, p. 8969.

[17] "The French Steel Industry and the Schuman Plan," *Europe Today
and Tomorrow,* no. 17 (1952), pp. 6-8.

discipline and parliamentary tactics—they combined to produce an exceptionally large majority for the Treaty in the Assembly.[18] It was the sole triumph of the Pleven government which fell shortly after.

THE GERMAN DEBATE

As might be expected, many of the arguments used for and against the Treaty in Germany ran parallel to those used in France. Others were mirror-images, with the points just turned around. Some strange comparisons and contrasts result.

As in France, political alignments and commitments not relevant to the merits of the Schuman Plan played an important part in building support for or opposition to the Treaty. The Adenauer government was firmly committed to a "European" policy. There was no room for serious, public dissension within the CDU on so major an issue as the coal and steel Treaty. There were some stirrings within other parties in the coalition that formed the government, notably the FDP in which some of the business opposition to the Treaty made itself felt, but in the end their support was maintained. The SPD, the principal opposition, took a very strong line against the Treaty, invoking a variety of arguments, some concerning the provisions of the Treaty and others making the whole issue part of a general indictment of Adenauer's policy which—the Socialists said—was moving away from German independence and unification.[19]

[18] If the investiture of government is omitted, no other measure up to that time except the North Atlantic Treaty secured as large a favorable vote and as large a margin over opposition plus abstention, among the "principal votes" of the Assembly shown in Philip Williams, *Politics in Post-War France*, 1954, Appendix IV, pp. 438-439.

[19] At the beginning, Kurt Schumacher had been somewhat more receptive to the Schuman idea, expressing doubts mainly about its possible effect on the ownership of heavy industry. See, for example, the speech reported in the *New York Times*, May 23, 1950. *The Economist*, Jl. 1, 1950, said that Schuman's proposal was too popular in Germany for Schumacher to oppose it outright. Throughout the debate there was a group in the SPD quite favorable to the coal and steel Treaty. It included the Mayor of Berlin, Ernst Reuter, and others who tended to differ from the dominant "nationalist" and "anti-European" policy of the party. On the basis of interviews, E. B. Haas (*The Uniting of Europe*,

The SPD did not, however, have the support of the central organization of the trade unions, the DGB. The first president of the DGB, Hans Böckler, and his successor, Christian Fette, supported the Schuman Plan and the organization formally followed their lead. There was some internal opposition, however, especially from the steelworkers, which led to a somewhat reserved attitude. During the debate in the Bundesrat—the upper house of parliament—in June 1951, Viktor Agartz, head of the economic research institute of the DGB, made a strong attack on the Treaty, while Franz Leopold Grosse of I. G. Bergbau, the miners' union, supported German accession to it. Rolf Wagenführ, a member of Agartz's staff who subsequently became head of the statistical division of the High Authority, also spoke in favor of the Treaty.

The Bundesrat's passage of the first reading of the bill for German adherence to the Treaty, on June 27, 1951, was the first legislative action by any parliament. Final approval was made conditional on certain points, the most important of which concerned Allied controls. The Bundesrat wanted assurances from the occupying powers that when the Schuman Plan came into operation they would eliminate the Ruhr Authority, their control groups over coal and steel matters, and all restrictions on production of steel and the capacity of the industry. The resolution also recommended that the German government take account of the investment needs of the German steel industry and the establishment of satisfactory arrangements concerning the integration of coal and steel production and the organization of German coal sales.[20]

1958, p. 132, n. 32) believes that the SPD would have voted for the Treaty if that had been necessary to ensure its acceptance. Socialist members of the Bundesrat went along with a unanimous vote in favor of the Treaty.

[20] When the Bundesrat came to take final action on the Treaty on February 1, 1952, it noted that the government had not yet fulfilled all the conditions of the earlier resolution. Nevertheless the Bundesrat followed the Bundestag in approving the Treaty. It also passed a resolution adding to its earlier list a series of wishes, or expressions of opinion, concerning further removal of Allied controls, assurances about the right of German firms to merge and to undertake vertical integration after the Treaty came into effect, about West Berlin, the Saar, the future

These themes remained prominent throughout the German debate. While it was going on the occupying powers took a number of steps affecting controls. Some of these steps pleased the Germans. For instance, a number of coal companies were freed from Allied control in July 1951 because they had met the conditions of the deconcentration program. The Allies agreed to let those who were required to sell coal and steel holdings receive partial compensation in the form of stock in the reorganized companies. But later in the year there was German resentment when the Allied Military Security Board denied the Thyssen firm the right to rebuild certain plants that had been dismantled. Coal was short and when the Germans were required to export more than they wanted to, Franz Blücher, the Vice Chancellor and leader of the FDP, resigned from the International Authority for the Ruhr. In October 1951 the occupying powers and the Benelux governments announced that they would liquidate the International Authority for the Ruhr if the Schuman Plan came into effect. Britain, France, and the United States also stated that at the same time the ceiling on steel production would be lifted and Allied agencies would end their control of the coal and steel industries, except for the measures necessary to complete decartelization.

Adenauer argued the case for the Schuman Plan on much broader grounds than the elimination of Allied controls. In and out of the Bundestag, he, like Schuman, put the main stress on the coal and steel pool's role in creating European unity. Without it there could be no health for Europe, no future for its youth. "On your 'yes,' " he told the Bundestag, "depends whether European union will become a reality." [21] On more specifically German themes he stressed the fact that Germany would be coming into this union as an equal. "The French invitation to us to

role of the Bundesrat in discussing German policy in the Community, and about other matters. It associated itself with a somewhat shorter resolution by the Bundestag referring to Allied controls, coal sales, and investments.

[21] Germany, Bundestag [*Debates*], 182. Sitzung, Jan. 9, 1952, p. 7600 (B).

negotiate over the Schuman Plan led Germany for the first time since the end of the war out of its isolation and opened for us chances for an equal partnership with these powers—even with an occupying power—on an economically, politically, and military-politically decisive territory." [22]

Much of his opponents' attack challenged the idea that this new enterprise put Germany on an equal footing with the other countries. The High Authority would really perpetuate Allied controls in a new form, they said. Germany would always be in a minority. All the other countries were consumers of German coal and so had a strong incentive to act together against Germany. There lay the true "community of interests." [23] The Socialists compared features of the coal and steel pool with those of the International Authority for the Ruhr and argued that the new arrangements would function the same way. The Allied controls had been imposed on a defeated country; now Germany was being urged to accept the same kind of arrangements of its free will, and as an act of sovereignty (a neat counterpoint to the statement by Flandin quoted on p. 87). The fact that Germany was very vulnerable to outside pressure, especially from the United States, sharpened this issue. "We are being very specifically asked to sign something that, the others are convinced, we would not sign without force. And we are being asked to give up things that no responsible German politician dare give up without very serious misgivings and without very compelling grounds." [24]

The British would not give up control of their national economy, the Socialists said. Germany was not in a position to make this choice since it was not really free. Moreover, when Germany did regain its sovereignty, it would be

---

[22] Same, 184. Sitzung, Jan. 11, 1952, p. 7818 (A, B).

[23] Henssler, Same, 182. Sitzung, Jan. 9, 1952, p. 7613 (C).

[24] Professor Fritz Baade, an SPD member of the Bundestag, in a discussion with Walter Hallstein, secretary of state in the foreign office. *Probleme des Schuman-Plans: Eine Diskussion*, 1951, p. 22. He had just quoted *The Economist* to the effect that the United States could use Germany's dependence on food and raw material imports "to press for signature."

significantly impaired by the Treaty and there would be difficulties in managing a "torso economy." [25] The Socialists objected to the lack of democratic control over the High Authority and spoke of a "sovereignty of autocratic managers." [26] They argued, too, that adherence to the coal and steel pool would make it harder to reunify Germany. They charged that accepting the representation of Saar interests in the Coal and Steel Community by France reduced the chances of regaining the Saar.[27] Another argument was that the Allied controls would eventually be dropped anyway and that then Germany could enter a pool, if it wished, in a better bargaining position.

Such arguments, and many other criticisms of the Treaty, were not confined to Socialists, of course. On the matter of equality, opponents of the Treaty claimed that Germany did not have a fair representation in the pool. It brought by far the largest contribution to it—both in coal and in steel—but received only an equal voice with France in the High Authority and in the Common Assembly. This was not the way things had been done in cartels, some pointed out, where the size of one's production was the main determinant of one's voice in policy.[28]

Economic criticisms of the Treaty centered on the bad starting position of Germany. France and the other countries had invested heavily in the coal and steel industries. To a considerable extent they had received Marshall Plan aid in doing so. The result was that they had modern equipment and sometimes whole new plants. Germany, by contrast, had not been able to reconstruct its steel industry. In addition to the damage caused by the war, there had

[25] They could not effectively use the argument that their professed aim of socialization would be blocked since Article 83 of the Treaty said, "the establishment of the Community does not in any way prejudice the system of ownership of the enterprises subject to the provisions of this Treaty."

[26] Nölting, Bundestag [Debates], 183. Sitzung, Jan. 10, 1952, p. 7669 (D).

[27] At one point Hallstein argued that inclusion of Saar representatives in the French delegation to the Common Assembly "gives us a stronger voice than the French." Probleme des Schuman-Plans, cited, p. 33.

[28] See Lehr's speech cited on pp. 70-71.

been dismantling and a ceiling on production. As a result, Germany was about to enter into competition without a proper plant for doing so. Although coal production had been fostered by the Allies, investment had lagged in that industry, too. Coal was still short and the High Authority's power would be used, as the Allied controls had been used, to force Germany to export. This, in turn, would prevent an increase in steel production at home. Because German coal was cheap, a new tax was to be placed on it by the Treaty in order to subsidize uneconomic mines in Belgium, a rich country. Moreover, it was alleged, Germany would be deprived of its ability to trade coal for Swedish iron ore; the Swedes would not sell on other terms, or only at higher prices, and German steelmaking would suffer another disadvantage.

Deconcentration got a great deal of attention. It had been carried out in such a fashion, said the opponents of the Treaty, that German firms were deprived of the economies of vertical integration, one of the features of Ruhr organization. Complementary units had been broken apart so that each had higher costs. The economies of scale were lost by the breaking-up of large enterprises. An attack was to be made on the coal sales agency which the head of the miners' union said could not possibly be in the German interest. The supporters of the Treaty did not defend decartelization—few Germans could be found to do that. Instead they made a sharp distinction between the measures imposed by the occupying powers and the conditions that would exist when the Coal and Steel Community was created. Then German enterprises would be subject to the same rules as everybody else, not to discriminatory measures. If there was a case for reconcentration, Germans would be judged on the same basis as producers of other nationalities.

There were some complaints about the threat of imports and allegations that the common market was primarily an extension of the Monnet Plan, intended to provide outlets for expanded French steel capacity. But in spite of unemployment in Germany, fears of foreign invasion of the

market were expressed less often than in the French discussions. The main emphasis was on the handicaps
Germany would have in competing, without particular
reference to imports.

The German supporters of the Treaty did not have an
immediate economic advantage to point to (like the improvement in coal supplies expected in France). They used
more general arguments. A larger market in which there
would be no barriers to the export of German coal and
steel would be an advantage. The coal shortage seemed
unlikely to last forever; Germany was normally anxious
to find continuing markets for coal exports. Agreeing that
there was a great need for investment in German heavy
industry, the supporters of the Treaty pointed out that in
spite of the difficulties that had existed, German steel prices
were still low compared to those of France, Belgium, and
Luxembourg. This, plus the advantageous location of the
Ruhr and the traditional German efficiency in these lines
meant, they felt, that Germany had a good future in the
larger market of the Community. Just because Germany
was behind France in investment, it had a good case,
especially with low costs, to claim some kind of priority in
help from the High Authority. Few suggested—as some
Frenchmen feared and some outside observers believed—
that the Germans ought to welcome the Schuman Plan
because it would at last give free rein to their economic
abilities and put them, sooner or later, in a dominant position in Europe. A Socialist speaker caused a commotion in
the Bundestag when he accused some of the Treaty's supporters of holding this view. Some who say "yes" to the
Treaty, he said, say it with a *Dolus:* "Oh yes, now we are
signing for fifty years; in three or four years through
German *Tüchtigkeit,* through our famous thrift and our
Fleiss and I don't know what else, we will have pushed the
others against the wall." Of the French, he said, "They say
Europe but mean coal." [29]

German businessmen were even more sensitive than the

[29] Schoettle, Bundestag [*Debates*], 183. Sitzung, Jan. 10, 1952, pp. 7740
(B), 7742 (D).

French to the odor of *dirigisme* in the pool. Since the currency reform of 1948 they had been given quite a free hand by the government which believed in encouraging initiative by permitting substantial rewards in the form of profits. The German industrialists were understandably doubtful whether the Community regime would be equally "pro-business," especially if a "planner" like Monnet had a lot to do with the High Authority's policies. Moreover, they had a strong political position in Germany; would they in the larger Community?

Many of the businessmen were regarded as "pro-European" but with few exceptions their formula for economic integration was based on the removal of trade barriers, exchange controls, and reduced governmental interference.[30] They were bothered by the fact that they had not been given a direct part in the drafting of the Treaty at the outset. Like Schuman, Adenauer had emphasized the political. Although Hans Boden of the electrical firm AEG was on the delegation to the opening sessions in Paris, there were no members from the coal or steel industries. Later, industrialists had been brought in as advisers, and one of them had resigned, apparently over decartelization matters

---

[30] The champion of this policy in Germany was Ludwig Erhard, the Minister of Economics. His stand on the Schuman Plan has been quite reserved. During an election campaign in June 1950, he called the coal and steel Treaty the foundation stone of European unity. But afterwards he took no part in the debate in the Bundestag where one would have supposed him to be a key figure in explaining the government's policy on such a matter. He did, however, vote for the Treaty. Since then, although he has from time to time professed his support for the Schuman Plan, he has scarcely been one of its champions. In two books, he makes only brief mention of the Schuman Plan and stresses the importance of moving to a broader integration. In a speech in Switzerland, after the Treaty was ratified, he admitted that he had been privately very critical of it but said he now took a more positive attitude. If the liberal principle in the Schuman Plan was pushed, it could have good results. There was also a principle of *dirigisme* in the Treaty, as there had been for years in the coal and steel industries. If it triumphed, "at the worst we will not experience anything new; we will only have put the same principle on a supranational basis. . . . No one can now wager a prognosis—we can only hope that sound thought will triumph . . ." and work to encourage free competition. Ludwig Erhard, "Die deutsche Wirtschaftspolitik im Blickfeld Europäischer Politik," *Schweizer Monatshefte,* Apr. 1952, pp. 11-32. Erhard's record on the European Common Market is rather similar.

(see p. 71). Another issue that may have bothered German businessmen was the question whether membership in the pool would help or hinder them in competition with English firms, whom they were apt to regard as their really serious long-run rivals.

It is hard to discover just how all these considerations balanced out in the minds of the industrialists because the German business community—and perhaps especially its heavy industry sector—has a highly developed sense of the value of solidarity in making its influence felt. Good arrangements exist for establishing an "official" position for industry, or any particular sector of it, and then there is a strong tendency for members of the group to hew to this line, especially in public statements. The problem is further complicated by an understandable and quite politic practice of listing the disadvantages of a certain course and then "reluctantly" going along with it "for some greater aim" without revealing how much advantage they may see in it for themselves. Undoubtedly different businessmen came to different conclusions about the balance of advantage and disadvantage in the coal and steel Treaty, but a unifying factor exerting an influence on the heavy industry community as a whole was their general support for the Adenauer government (whether through the CDU or the FDP) and its "European" policy. Reporting a speech by Fritz Berg, president of the Bundesverband der deutschen Industrie, a German journalist summarized a carefully balanced conclusion frequently expressed by industrialists:

Industry has taken this position [in support of the Schuman Plan] out of the recognition that there is only this one, single, European path, fully conscious of the dangers that a supranational *dirigismus* would entail for the development in liberty of the economy and the world, but at the same time convinced that the well-grounded objections must be put in the background in order to make the Plan a reality in the near future.[31]

---

[31] Ernst Hafer, "Kanzler und Wirtschaft," *Der Volkswirt*, Je. 29, 1951, p. 3. Hafer adds that, "for the Chancellor the question of European integration . . . has such priority that he believes it possible to undertake whatever structural changes are necessary, in internal politics as well as elsewhere."

This balancing of advantages and disadvantages was part of the mood of most of the supporters of the Treaty. They admitted that there were difficulties and compromises but saw the whole as a step forward, an opportunity to remove obstacles, and a "chance" for Germany. Like the French Assembly, the Bundestag accompanied its approval of the Treaty with a resolution. This one registered the special concern of the Germans with ending Allied intervention, keeping some kind of joint sales organization for coal, securing funds for investment as soon as possible, and getting a change in the position of the Saar. But also like the French Assembly, the Bundestag took its final action by a large majority, approving the third reading of the bill on January 11, 1952, by a vote of 232 to 143, with 3 abstentions.

THE DEBATE IN OTHER COUNTRIES

Without France and Germany there could be no Coal and Steel Community. They were the largest producers; the workability of the pool depended on its overcoming issues that divided these two countries. Still, the other countries also had significant parts to play. Geographically, and to a considerable extent economically as well, it would have been awkward, to say the least, to pool the Ruhr, the Saar, Lorraine, and the coal and steel of northern France, without including Luxembourg, Belgium, and the Netherlands. Politically, these countries were also some place in between France and Germany. Like France, they had fought Germany and had been occupied; they would not willingly see a new threat arise. Unlike France, their postwar policies toward Germany had less the tone of *le temps perdu* and showed more effort at finding a new basis for living with the inescapable big neighbor. Their position had been recognized by giving them seats on the International Authority for the Ruhr; they frequently negotiated with the occupation authorities about policies that affected their interests, especially in trade; but they had few other means of participating directly in relations between Germany and the three largest Western victors.

Italy was in a somewhat different position. Economically and geographically its heavy industry was not part of the same complex. Still it had economic ties of importance.[32] Politically one of the aims of the West was to help Italy overcome its Fascist past and avoid a Communist future. As in the Benelux countries, interest in European unity was strong in Italy. For France, the cultivation of ties with Italy and the effort to bring her into many international activities (sometimes as a makeweight on France's side) was a continuing aim of diplomacy.[33]

From the beginning it seemed that if France and Germany accepted the Coal and Steel Community the other signatories would be bound to follow. Still there remained some doubt, however little, if one looked closely at the political situation in each country and the interplay of forces and opinions about the gains and losses from entering the Community. Certain broad arguments that we have already encountered in the French and German debates are to be found in each of the other countries: the businessmen's fear of *dirigisme;* others' fears of an uncontrolled businessmen's association; the desire to "build Europe" versus concern over the absence of Britain and other countries in this smaller grouping; the dislocating impact of removing trade barriers versus the advantages of getting rid of them; political control versus "technocracy"; the question whether Germany would dominate the pool; and so on. For these smaller nations there was the added concern whether they would be able to make their opinions felt against the larger powers. The voting arrangements and the role of the Council of Ministers were devised partly in the light of this worry. Without rehearsing the general debate that took place in each of the countries, the rest of this section notes some of the special problems affecting their decisions.

[32] But this was also true of Switzerland, Austria, and Denmark, for instance, whose relatively small heavy industries are about as dependent on the French-German-Benelux complex as are Italy's. See Chapters 17 and 18 on the relation of these countries to the Community.

[33] See my *Trade and Payments in Western Europe,* 1952, pp. 373-376.

The Netherlands

The lower house of the Dutch Estates General was the first parliamentary body to take final action on the Treaty. The opposition to ratification was negligible. There were still some misgivings about the absence of England but the creation of the Council of Ministers had set at rest many of the fears of an undue delegation of power to the High Authority. The Dutch seem to have had few economic worries about entering the Community. Their coal mining industry was well established and efficient. Its costs were low. While this was to make it, like the Ruhr, subject to a special levy to help adjust the high-cost Belgian mines, the Dutch probably looked on this as a reasonable price to pay for a more rational ordering of Western Europe's heavy industry. Moreover, there might be an immediate gain for them in lower prices for Belgian steel products. The Dutch steel industry is small and quite efficient, but the country is a net importer. The government stressed the advantage to the Netherlands of equal access to the Community's output of coal and steel in times of shortage. There were hopes that integration would spread to other sectors, especially transportation. The Treaty had a clearer road to ratification in Holland than anywhere else.

Belgium

In Belgium much of the debate naturally centered on the high-cost coal mines. Some thought entry into the Community was bound to cause unemployment and a drop in coal production. The industry campaigned actively against ratification. Others pointed out that with or without ratification the coal problem had to be solved. The high-cost mines were a burden to the economy for which the Community offered foreign help. All were agreed that domestic measures would have to be taken to improve the situation. Because they were not satisfied with the government's assurances and wanted a reorganization law for the coal mines before going into the Community, the Socialists in the Senate abstained from voting for the Treaty although some members of the bloc had argued strongly for it. Their colleagues in the Chamber, also split, supported the Treaty under the urging of Paul-Henri Spaak, their well-known leader whose prominence in the European movement made his position clear. Belgian labor was strong for the Treaty.

The powers of the High Authority were also a source of special concern in Belgium. Since the end of the war there had been only limited governmental interference in the Belgian economy. Businessmen did not relish the idea of now submitting to some kind of super-governmental control. There was an impressive body of opinion in the parliament that the grant of such extensive powers to an international body would be unconstitutional. Belgian business was also used to a high degree of self-organization and cartelization which seemed threatened by the Treaty. Throughout the negotiations, beginning with the introduction of the Council of Ministers to check the High Authority, Belgian negotiators had worked to ensure greater freedom for business within the Community. They were not altogether satisfied with the result but felt they must accept it. As the spokesman for the steel industry summarized the situation:

I persist in believing that it would have been possible to establish a regime that was more supple and entailed less risk of leading to a *dirigisme* that could become excessive because of the powers of decision that are entrusted to the High Authority and because initiatives that until now—at least in our country—could be taken by the heads of business to deal with certain situations are terribly restricted. . . . But this is a matter of a compromise solution and for a country of the relatively small importance of Belgium one cannot have the illusion that we could obtain one hundred per cent of all the guarantees and arrangements we would desire.[34]

[34] Pierre van der Rest, "Le Plan Schuman," in Société d'Économie Politique de Belgique, *Comptes-Rendus des Travaux*, Séance du 8 Mai 1951, Je. 1951, pp. 17, 25. In the course of the Treaty negotiations, M. van der Rest and Pierre Delville, his colleague from the Belgian coal industry, had become known to some as *les deux pierres d'achoppement*, but Max Suetens, head of the Belgian delegation, said they were, rather, *pierres de construction*. Same, p. 29.

Luxembourg

Their heavy dependence on steel made people in Luxembourg feel that they were being asked to entrust almost their whole national economy to the Community. Any adjustments at all would have much greater relative impact on Luxembourg than on other countries. Luxembourg's wages and social security charges were the highest in the Community, and though the steel industry was efficient there was concern that opening the common market might create problems. The strong business interests of the Grand Duchy were suspicious of the extensive powers given the High Authority and worried about possibly drastic measures against cartels. On the other hand, several provisions of the transitional Convention assured special treatment for Luxembourg's main problems.[35] In any case, it was clear that if its neighbors went ahead to form the Community, Luxembourg would have little choice but to join it. The only opposition to ratification came from the Communists.

Italy

The proposed Community raised a series of economic questions for Italy, and went at least part way to answer some of them. Italian steel costs were high. Would the producers suffer from competition with foreign steel? A special concession was made to Italy to permit it to reduce steel tariffs gradually instead of at one blow. A counterweight to the concern of the steel producers about prices was the interest of the important metal and machinery industry in getting steel more cheaply. De Gasperi gave assurances that the government would help if any interests were damaged.

Almost all the raw materials for Italian steelmaking are imported, so the creation of the common market promised benefits, but the steelmakers remained skeptical. Lorraine

[35] Section 10 made possible the continuation of differences between domestic and transit rates on the railroads because of the fear that equalization would result in a major loss of revenue. Section 31 provided safeguards against serious disturbances in the marketing of Luxembourg steel and for possible financial assistance.

iron ore was not of great interest to the Italian users; they were concerned with North African ore which was not covered by the Treaty. France promised, in a side deal, to supply a certain number of tons of iron ore from North Africa each year at reasonable prices. The finance committee of the Italian Senate considered this arrangement better than having the North African ore in the pool but urged that Italy try to safeguard its position still more by asking for a share in the ownership of these mines.[36] The steel industry complained that the bilateral deal was not guarantee enough.

Getting scrap was a problem for Italy; it was often costly and sometimes scarce. Its inclusion in the Treaty, perhaps especially for Italy's benefit, would keep France and Germany from using export controls to prevent scrap shipments to Italy. But again some industrialists read the Treaty differently and suspected it would lead to a continuation of national regulation and monopoly power. Italy also had to import coal and most observers saw the Treaty's provisions on equal access and nondiscriminatory prices and railroad rates as a clear Italian advantage. But again an industrial group suspected they would be left defenseless against a Ruhr sales monopoly. Then there was the perennial problem of the Italian economy, the possibility of emigration to solve problems of unemployment and overpopulation. The Treaty promised some new outlets and a freer movement of workers, but its opponents expected the result to be extensive unemployment in Italy and wanted more safeguards and the promise of more help from the High Authority.

For Italy, in short, there seemed to most to be some clear economic gains from the pool but they could only be had at the cost of some adaptation of Italian steelmaking. The grace period provided by the continuation of tariffs enabled Italy to obtain some of the benefits immediately while postponing some of the adjustment. There was, however, a good bit of opposition in the heavy industries and the Confindustria—the major industrial association—came out

[36] *Mondo Economico*, Feb. 3, 1952.

against the Treaty.[37] Offsetting this was a strong Italian interest in European cooperation. Led by De Gasperi, who seemed to the rest of the world to belong to a special club with Schuman and Adenauer, both houses of the Italian parliament approved ratification of the Treaty without major difficulty.

THE COMMUNITY COMES INTO BEING

On July 25, 1952, the Treaty came into force. A meeting of the foreign ministers of the signatory governments that would traditionally have been a largely formal occasion turned into a difficult negotiation over the seat of the Community. In the end, a compromise fixed the provisional seat of the High Authority and the Court in Luxembourg, while the Assembly was to meet in Strasbourg. A final determination of the headquarters was to wait on the outcome of French-German negotiations on the future of the Saar.[38] The foreign ministers also decided that the Community's official languages would be French, German, Italian, and Dutch and set dates for the first meetings of the various organs.

Early in August the governments announced the composition of the High Authority. Monnet, as everyone had expected, became chairman. Although the Treaty called for only one vice chairman, two were appointed. One was Franz Etzel, a lawyer from the Ruhr who, as a CDU

[37] A pamphlet summarizing the views of "Italian industrialists" (un-identified), criticized the Treaty on the grounds that: it should have included African iron ore; it did not guarantee a free market in scrap; it left too much room for sales monopolies and other special arrangements in coal; it did not require fixed steel prices and so permitted dumping; Italy should receive foreign aid for its steel adaptation, as Belgian did for coal; the foreign aid for Italian coal adaptation should extend over a longer period; special provision should be made for the Italian cokeries that were important to the chemical industry. *Il Piano Schuman: Commenti e rilievi italiani*, 1951.

[38] Schuman had proposed Saarbrücken as the seat but Adenauer disliked the implied "Europeanization" of the Saar before Germany's claims had been recognized. The compromise arrangement was criticized in Belgium and Holland as a bad precedent for tying the fate of the multilateral organization to decisions made by its two largest members, a complaint repeated later when other French-German agreements on the Saar affected coal, steel, and the Moselle.

Abgeordneter, had been chairman of the Bundestag's committee on economic affairs. The other was Albert Coppé, a former economics professor who had held several positions in the Belgian government, most recently that of Minister of Reconstruction. Five other men were appointed by the governments: Dirk Spierenburg, an official of the Dutch Ministry of Economic Affairs who had been head of his country's mission to the OEEC and of its delegation to the Schuman Plan negotiations; Albert Wehrer, Luxembourg's minister to France who had also headed his country's delegation at the Treaty negotiations and before that had represented Luxembourg in occupied Germany; Enzo Giacchero, a vice chairman of the Demo-Christian faction in the Italian parliament who had been active in various European federalist groups; Léon Daum, by training an engineer, who had been connected with a number of major French steel companies since 1929 and before that had worked for the government's *Service des mines* in Morocco and the Saar; Heinz Potthoff, a German steelworker who had had governmental and managerial jobs for some time and had represented his country on the International Authority for the Ruhr. The ninth man, coopted by these eight, was Paul Finet who had long occupied leading positions in the Belgian labor movement and was first president of the ICFTU.[39] The choice of Finet resulted from an earlier informal understanding that the High Authority would have at least one labor member, to be nominated by agreement between the two major non-Communist international union organizations, the ICFTU and the CFTC.

On August 10 the members of the High Authority took office. They set to work quickly. A month later the Council of Ministers and the Assembly held their first sessions.

[39] When Monnet resigned he was succeeded, in June 1955, by René Mayer, former premier of France. Mayer resigned in late 1957, to go into private business, and then Etzel became Finance Minister of Germany. Finet was chosen chairman of the High Authority and Spierenburg was made a vice chairman. The two new members of the High Authority were Franz Blücher, former vice chancellor of Germany and leader of the FDP, and Roger Reynaud, a French civil servant who was also an official of the Christian labor movement.

Members of the Court took oaths of office early in December. By January 1953 the High Authority had issued its first long report on the work of the Community.

And so, only a little more than two years after Foreign Minister Schuman's remarkable proposal, this radical idea had been given concrete form. Hard decisions had been taken. But more hard decisions remained. The expectations—good and bad—that had found expression in the discussion of the Treaty were now to be realized or avoided. The "leap into the unknown" was beginning to have a history.

SIX

WHAT WAS POOLED

VULCAN WAS lame and ugly but all the gods turned to him when they wanted things of great strength, ingenuity, and sometimes beauty. Perhaps much the same could be said of the great coal and steel triangle that is the heart of Schumania. If Western Europe is one of the workshops of the world, as it has so often been called, then the complex of mining and heavy industry in this central area is the workshop of the workshop. About 80 per cent of the Community's steel and over 90 per cent of its coal is produced in this triangular patch of some 27,000 square miles. Around these two basic activities has grown a great industrial complex: chemical works that use coal, coke-oven gases, and other by-products as raw materials; machine makers and other steel-users; numerous industries of all sorts that serve the needs of the mines and mills; producers of consumers' goods for the mass markets of these densely populated areas; gas works and electrical plants whose power is either used in the area or takes advantage of the relatively cheap local fuel to make power for other areas. The whole complex is tied together by an intricate transport net dominated by railroads but including important river and canal routes and a growing truck traffic.

The triangle was the core of Charlemagne's empire. The Romans were there before him; and already in Celtic times metal was worked in the area. For centuries people made iron with charcoal in the great forests; coal was mined where outcroppings betrayed its presence. By the 19th century there were important centers of ironmaking and coal mining that grew as the Continental economy expanded, often with the help of English and Scottish technicians and entrepreneurs who ventured, or were invited, to cross the water. The great period of the modern history of these industries dates from about 1880. The depressions of the '70s were over. Germany was beginning to function as a national economy. France had recovered from the Prussian war and its aftermath. In 25 years steelmaking had been revolutionized, from Bessemer's great innovation in 1856, through the work of Siemens and the Martin brothers to the moment in 1879 when Gilchrist and Thomas adapted the Bessemer process to use phosphoric iron ore, the kind to be found in Lorraine and Luxembourg.

In 1880 Britain led the world in steel production, followed rather closely by the United States. Germany and France, the third and fourth countries, produced together about as much steel as Britain.[1] By 1890 the United States had taken first place and in the middle of the decade Germany, too, passed Britain. On the eve of the First World War, in 1913, the United States produced 31.8 million tons of steel, Germany 17.7 million, Britain 7.8 million, and France 4.7 million. Together, the six countries that were later to form the Community produced 24.5 million tons of crude steel in 1913, a figure they were not to reach again until 1925. In coal the position was somewhat different. The United States produced over 40 per cent of the world's coal, more than half a billion metric tons in 1913. Britain was second with 292 million and Germany took third place

[1] In puddled iron which was quantitatively more important, Britain took second place to the United States but again equaled the combined production of Germany and France. The figures for 1880 are, in thousands of metric tons of steel (puddled iron in parentheses): Britain, 1,316 (2,600); U.S., 1,267 (2,751); Germany, 875 (1,774); France, 506 (1,256). High Authority, *Un siècle de développement de la production d'acier* (Supplement au *Bulletin Mensuel d'Information*, Jan. 1957-Feb. 1958), pp. 22-27. This is also the source of most other figures on steel production in this section. The German figures for 1880 and 1913 are for the boundaries of the period and include East German steel production of 63,000 tons in 1880 and 2.6 million tons in 1913. The Community total for 1913 includes only West Germany.

with about 190 million. Production in the rest of the Community came to about 64 million tons.[2]

The period before the First World War was a time of great expansion in Western European production of coal and steel. Between the wars the record was very different. The jagged line marking steel production in the Community countries sometimes reached crests above the 1913 level but never stayed there very long, as decline followed postwar recovery, depression followed boom, and a new war interrupted the revival of the late '30s. Although in 1929 Western Europe's coal production was 19 per cent higher than it had been in 1913, and steel output was over 40 per cent higher, this was not significant progress by prewar standards. "The continuation of a steady average annual rate of only 3 per cent"—the prewar coal rate, well under half the steel rate—"would have yielded outputs over 60 per cent above 1913 in 1929."[3]

Other countries were having trouble in this period too, of course. Britain and the United States did not register sustained growth, but had the advantage of having expanded production during the First World War instead of contracting as the Continental countries had. Outside these established centers new producers were beginning to have an impact on world production, particularly of steel.[4]

In 1913 the Community countries had produced one-third of the world's output of crude steel: by 1937 their share had fallen to one-quarter. The second war continued the process. The Community produced only 18 per cent

[2] *Die Kohlenwirtschaft der Welt in Zahlen*, 1955, p. 20. The German figure includes over 48 million tons produced in Eastern Silesia, the Saar, and Lorraine, the territories that were later lost.

[3] N.J.G. Pounds and W.N. Parker, *Coal and Steel in Western Europe*, 1957, pp. 251, 252. These figures, and all others cited from Parker, omit Italy and the minor German areas outside Rhineland-Westphalia. More detailed figures and data on sources and methods appear in W.N. Parker, "Coal and Steel Output Movements in Western Europe, 1880-1956," *Explorations in Entrepreneurial History*, Apr. 1957, pp. 214-229.

[4] By 1939 the U.S.S.R. had passed Britain in total output. Japan passed Belgium in the '30s and began to approach France. Outside the United Kingdom the British Commonwealth produced well over twice as much steel in 1939 as in 1920. The U.S.S.R. also increased coal production greatly.

of the world's steel in 1949. Output in the six countries lagged behind that of the rest of the world. In 1949, just before Schuman made his proposal, world production of steel was a third higher than it had been in 1929 and about a fifth above the level of 1937. But the output of the six was still about 20 per cent below prewar levels. By 1952, when the Community came into being, each of the countries was producing more steel than in 1929. For the Community as a whole the increase was about 18 per cent; for the world it was 75 per cent.[5] Between 1949 and 1952, Community steel production increased 46 per cent (compared to 26 per cent for the world as a whole), making 1952 output a new record.

For coal the interwar period was one of stagnation. The competition of oil, gas, and hydroelectric power plus substantial improvements in fuel economy kept coal production behind the uncertain pace of the world economy. World production of coal in 1929 was only 8 per cent more than in 1913. The United States and Britain remained the leading producers, but throughout the '30s coal was a sick industry in both countries. Germany, in contrast, managed to increase output so that by the late '30s it was producing about as much coal as it had before it lost Lorraine and Eastern Silesia. The Community countries as a whole dug about a fifth of the world's coal in the late '30s, a share roughly equal to Britain's.[6] As in steel, Community recovery lagged after the Second World War (except in France) and in 1949 the six countries were producing only 15.8 per cent of the world's coal. Their production increased 10 per cent by 1952—at roughly the same rate as the world's—and in that year France, Belgium and Holland dug more coal than in 1929 but Germany lagged well

[5] Taking 1929 as 100, the index of steel production for each Community country in 1952 was: Germany, 107; Saar, 128; Belgium, 126; France, 112; Italy, 167; Luxembourg, 111. The Netherlands had no 1929 production. High Authority, *Report*, Apr. 1958, v. 2, *Statistical Annex*, Table 27. Figures in this book for which no references are given come from standard Community statistical sources.

[6] Only Western Germany is included in these figures. All data are from *Die Kohlenwirtschaft der Welt in Zahlen*, cited.

behind, as did Britain and the United States. It is to 1952 that we now turn for a picture of what was put into the coal and steel pool.

THE COMMUNITY IN 1952

The decline in the six countries' position in the world coal and steel economy and their lag in consumption per head behind the United States and Britain helped to prod them into pooling their basic industries. But external measurements throw little light on the process of creating a common market and making the Community work. The chapters that follow examine this process in some detail but to understand the changes that took place over the transitional period one must look at the starting point. There is no "normal" postwar year that can be treated as a secure benchmark; there was too much change, at different rates, in all the countries. Yet for a broad picture, from which refined conclusions should not be drawn, 1952, the year the Community came into existence, provides a reasonable starting point.

Table 2 sets out each country's production of the major Community products in 1952. The broad features of the new entity stand out. Germany dominates the Community's fuel economy, producing more than half the coal and nearly three-fifths of the coke. The importance of Germany's position is increased by the fact that its share of the Community's production of coking coal is even greater than these figures show. France and Belgium are the other important coal producers. The Saar, which takes fourth place, appears separately because when the Community started it was attached to the French economy, but by the end of the transitional period it was in the process of being incorporated in the German economy (while retaining some temporary special links with France).

In iron ore, matters are quite different. France is the only important producer, with two-thirds of the Community's output. Production of pig iron and steel is more widely dispersed. Again Germany is the largest producer, with something like one-third of the total, followed by France,

Belgium, Italy, and Luxembourg. The chief omission is scrap, which is collected rather than produced. Much scrap arises within the steel industry, so the domestic supplies of each country were probably roughly proportionate to their production of crude steel. But as the different

Table 2

COMMUNITY PRODUCTION IN 1952

(MILLIONS OF METRIC TONS)

	Coal	Coke	Iron Ore	Pig Iron	Crude Steel	Steel Products
Germany	123.3	37.2	15.4	12.9	15.8	10.5
France	55.4	9.2	41.2	9.3	10.9	7.6
Saar	16.2	3.9	—	2.6	2.8	1.9
Belgium	30.4	6.4	.1	4.8	5.2	3.7
Luxembourg	—	—	7.2	3.1	3.0	2.2
Netherlands	12.5	3.3	—	.5	.7	.4
Italy	1.1	2.4	1.3	1.1	3.5	2.3
Total	238.9	62.4	65.3	34.7	41.9	28.6

NOTE: Here, and throughout this book unless otherwise noted:
　"coal" means hard coal, in the European sense *(Steinkohle; houille)*, not in the American sense; that is, it includes both anthracite and bituminous, but not lignite;
　"coke" means coke-oven coke;
　"iron ore" refers to the crude ore; the ferrous content would be somewhat under one-third of the figure given, say about 19 million tons for the whole Community in 1952;
　"pig iron" includes spiegeleisen and ferro-manganese and, for Germany, ferro-silicum;
　"steel products" include railroad material, heavy and light shapes, machine wire, sheets, plates, coils, and material for tubes. The contents of this category vary somewhat among sources and occasional discrepancies appear in the figures.

SOURCE:
　High Authority, *Report*, Apr. 1958, v. 2, *Statistical Annex*, various tables. Similar but not entirely identical data can be found in High Authority, *Recueil Statistique*, various tables, and in the bi-monthly *Bulletin Statistique*. Except in tables, or when there are serious discrepancies in the data, figures drawn from the last of these sources and from the statistical appendixes of annual reports will not be footnoted.

ratios of pig iron production to crude steel output suggest, scrap differed in its relative importance as a raw material for various countries (it is used in place of pig iron in some processes). Italy in particular was a disproportionately large consumer of scrap.

As the differences in the balance of the countries' production suggests, each carried on some important trade with the others and, usually, with the outside world as well. The details of these transactions in 1952 are not necessary to this general picture; but the broad pattern is easily sketched, so long as one bears in mind that even with the trade barriers of 1952, an intricate exchange of goods took place within the Community, with many crosscurrents. Thanks to differences in types and quality, geography and transportation facilities, company connections and market conditions, countries often exchanged goods against the dominant trade currents that are sketched here. A complex trade in steel products, semi-finished goods, pig iron, and even ingots had developed over the years. Differences in quality, size, price, special features, terms of delivery and other factors all made for crosscurrents in trade.

Germany was, naturally, the largest supplier of coal in trade within the Community. It shipped to all the other countries of the Community, especially to France which needed coking coal, to Italy which had almost no coal at all, and to the Netherlands which needed more than it could produce and was immediately adjacent to two major German coal fields. The trade in coke was even more concentrated, with Germany providing some 75 per cent of the exports, most of which went to France, the Saar, and Luxembourg. Though France was the second major producer of coal, it had only a modest export trade in most years and was usually a net importer. Here the link with the Saar was of particular importance. It exports most of its coal and can ship easily to France or Germany since it lies between them. Falling within the French currency zone, the Saar offered France a double advantage: "imports" that cost no foreign exchange and "exports" to Germany that produced *Deutschemarks* for France. When the trade figures are combined,[7] France and the Saar often turn out to be nearly in balance in the exchange of coal within the Community. Belgium, while importing from Germany, has usually been a net exporter of coal, selling to France, Italy, and the Netherlands.

Throughout most of the transitional period, the six countries have had to import substantial quantities of coal from suppliers outside the Community, especially from the United States. While some of the Community's traditional exports to other Continental countries have been sustained reasonably well, they have usually been outweighed by coal imports. Often enough, imports from third countries have also been larger than intra-Community trade in coal. This reversal of the historical position points to one of the Community's major problems.

For iron ore the Community as a whole has long been dependent on imports from third countries. This pattern has not altered, but imports from Sweden, the major supplier, are being increasingly supplemented with ore from Africa, Canada and South America. Inside the Community the only important iron ore exporter is France which ships largely to Belgium; but there is also some export from Luxembourg to Germany.

In steel the internal trade of the Community is quite complex. The largest exports normally come from Belgium and Luxembourg (another economic union that confuses some of the trade figures), but France has sometimes shipped substantial quantities abroad. The markets are quite varied. For Belgium, the Netherlands has always been an important outlet and a rather steady customer, but in some years Belgium's shipments to Germany have exceeded those to its Benelux partner while France has been a market of growing importance. France has found its own best market for steel exports in Germany, but has also supplied Belgium, Holland and Italy. Germany, which might be ex-

---

[7] As they are in many statistics. Throughout this book I have usually kept the Saar figures separate and called attention to departures from this practice.

pected to be the Community's largest exporter has in fact
been a net importer of steel in intra-Community trade during the transitional period. Its main suppliers have been
France, the Saar, and Belgium, but even the Netherlands, itself a net importer, has found export markets in Germany.
Even so, Germany has exported substantial quantities of
steel and has found markets throughout the Community,
beginning with the Low Countries but then spreading to
Italy and France as well.

For the Community as a whole, steel exports to third
countries are substantially more important than trade within
the Community. Belgium and Luxembourg take the lead in
this trade, followed by Germany and then France. Even
the smaller producers, Italy and the Netherlands, find foreign markets for some of their finished products. In addition
to the steel that the Community exports in the form of steel
products (or, to a small extent, ingots and semi-finished
products), all of these countries have an important foreign
trade in manufactured goods that use steel, notably machinery, automobiles and railroad rolling stock. The markets
are world-wide, ranging from neighbors in Continental
Europe to the Middle and Far East, Latin America, and,
for some products, the United States.

Exports of Treaty products accounted for about 15 per
cent of the value of total exports by members of the Community to third countries in 1952. For the most part this
was steel, but the figure does not include the steel exported
"indirectly," in the form of manufactured goods. The coal,
iron ore, and small quantities of steel that Community
countries imported from outside the area in 1952 were equal
to 7.6 per cent of the value of their total imports from third
countries. But the trade in Treaty products within the Community came to 24 per cent of the total trade (by value)
of the countries among themselves.

THE MEMBERS

Though the coal and steel industries of the six countries
have long had important connections with one another,
they have also had quite separate existences. Technology,

economics, sometimes geography, and to a certain degree
cultural heritage have imparted some common features. But
law, history, politics, social structure, and, again, economics, have also made them rather different. War and recovery
were experiences they shared, but the effects of the war and
the phase of recovery they had reached when the Community was formed differed a good bit from country to
country. The Treaty did not force uniformity; it said
nothing about the forms of ownership; a wide range of
practices could be permitted under its rules. To an important extent the national setting of each industry would continue to be a major shaping force. There would also,
however, be some pressures for conformity and every industry, indeed every country, would have to adapt itself
to a new situation. How this process took place is the theme
of much of this book; what follows is a quick characterization of the coal and steel industries of the six countries.

Germany

By common consent and statistics, Germany was the
giant of the Western European coal and steel industries.
But the postwar Bundesrepublik was something quite different from the prewar Reich. Along with its eastern territories it had lost important steel mills and major coal and
lignite mines. Beaten in the war, Germany had been first
hindered and then helped in its economic recovery by its
conquerors. Since 1948 it had been moving ahead rapidly,
but when the Community came into existence in 1952 German steel production was not as far above prewar levels as
that of the other countries in the Community. Two other
changes were probably even more important. One could
hardly say that the tradition of a protected heavy industry,
begun by Bismarck when he devised one of the basic equa-
tions of modern German history, was dead; but it was no
longer endorsed by the German government (at least so far
as steel was concerned; the position in coal was a little less
clear; it was still regarded as something of a national treas-
ure). Nor could one say that the political influence that
goes with economic strength had been abolished in Western

Germany, but it was at least the subject of surgery by the
victor powers as they worked to reorganize the structure
of the coal and steel industries. By the time the Community
came into existence, the tug of war between occupiers and
Germans was practically over and the Germans were running their own affairs, but with a somewhat different industrial structure.

The steel industry was not as concentrated as it had been
before the war. The largest company had been broken into
a number of parts; others had also undergone some partition. Less of Germany's coal production was controlled by
steel producers. Coal sales were still cartelized. On paper
there were several sales organizations but they behaved as
if they were one. While the Treaty was being debated the
Germans brought about another change that looked radical
but was not. The *Mitbestimmungsgesetz* provided that on
the boards of coal and steel companies representatives of
labor should be equal in number to the representatives of
stockholders; the tie-breaking odd man was chosen by
agreement. In the normal three-man management of these
firms, the *Arbeitsdirektor* was to be a labor nominee. Somewhat surprisingly this drastic change has not had major
effects. It has certainly not seriously altered the efficiency,
drive, or performance of German heavy industry.[8]

The Ruhr always dominated German coal and steel
production. The loss of the Soviet Zone enhanced the importance of the Ruhr. At the same time, the lag in German
recovery gave the Ruhr a slightly less important place
among the regions of the Community than it had held for
decades. It remained, though, the core of the "triangle."
Outside the Ruhr, Germany has one major coal basin: the
area around Aachen, part of a field exploited also in Holland and Belgium. Steel production outside the Ruhr is
scattered, but not negligible. The most important single
producer is the former Hermann Goering Werke, at
Salzgitter, in Lower Saxony, the property of the govern-

---

[8] There is no room in this book for an analysis of the effects of *Mitbestimmung*. The bibliographical notes to Ch. 16 indicate part of the
literature.

ment. The government also owns several of the largest coal companies in the Ruhr.

German iron ore is of poor quality and is for the most part not particularly well located in relation to the coal. Before the war, Nazi efforts to expand the use of domestic iron were regarded as good examples of the follies of autarky. The war, of course, made any accessible resource valuable. Since then the Germans have maintained a high output of iron ore, even though its transportation has to be subsidized.

Though for much of the postwar period Germany had substantial unemployment, it was always a problem to re-cruit labor for the mines. Partly this was a matter of hous-ing—expellees in Schleswig-Holstein cannot mine coal in the Ruhr—but it was also difficult to get people to go into the mines when other kinds of work seemed more attrac-tive. Partly as a result of this, the miner's wage has been kept, by convention, the highest in Germany. The Germans have a reputation for working harder, longer, and better than any one else which is not altogether borne out by statistics. For instance, output per manshift in the Ruhr coal mines in 1952 was above the Community average but below the figure for Lorraine, the Saar, and Limburg. While there is much to support the conventional picture of German efficiency and dynamism, it is also true that for decades protection, price control, sometimes subsidy, and almost always government intervention, have made it im-possible to test the validity of this reputation in altogether satisfactory ways. Nevertheless, in 1952 the Ruhr was prob-ably a relatively low-cost producer of coal and steel by Community standards. Therein lay part of the economic promise of the Community and, when coupled with the size of German production, some of the fears of people in the other five countries.

France

As a producer of coal and steel, France has long been second only to Germany among the Community countries (for a few postwar years it was ahead in steel production).

In addition, it is the only major iron ore producer in the Community. Like the Germans, the French have a tradition of external protection and domestic cartelization that goes back to the 19th century. It was only in the summer of 1952—just when the Community got under way—that the Comptoir Sidérurgique lost its monopoly position. For several decades this agency of the steel federation had allocated orders among companies and set minimum prices as it saw fit. Whether the Comptoir was reformed because the Community with its antitrust legislation was coming into effect or because of Antoine Pinay's edicts about price discrimination is not clear. In any case, even though the Comptoir gave up its powers as a formal monopoly, its "residual powers . . . are considerable," as a careful student of the matter has put it,[9] or, as a less formal observer said to me: "They still make out the bills."

The most important factor in the postwar French coal and steel industries was the large investment program. Financed to a considerable extent by government funds, the measures of modernization and expansion worked out by the industries under Jean Monnet's aegis had put France ahead of the pack in European recovery. There was much new equipment in the steelworks; two great continous strip mills were being built. Coal was nationalized under the first De Gaulle regime, and though Charbonnages de France could not escape the difficulties that nationalized industries seem heir to, it was funneling funds and putting drive into the industry and getting a very good record of production in return. Thanks partly to the new equipment, French mines were the only ones in the whole Community that registered a higher output per manshift in 1952 than in 1938.

France suffered from a difficult monetary situation and chronic inflation. Money costs were rather high when the Community was first organized. For foreign trade they were partly offset by subsidies, tax remissions, and other measures, including strict control of imports. Some of the subsidies were used to offset the cost of Ruhr coal result-

[9] H. W. Ehrmann, *Organized Business in France*, 1957, p. 377.

ing from double-pricing and discriminatory transportation rates. Coke and coking coal from the Ruhr were imports of crucial importance to France's heavy industry.

Geographically, French heavy industry was not so heavily concentrated as that of Germany. There were two main centers instead of one. Lorraine produced almost two-thirds of France's crude steel in 1952 while slightly over 31 per cent came from the Nord-Pas de Calais area. The rest was spread among a series of other centers, mostly in the southern and central parts of the country. In coal the relative importance was reversed, with the Nord producing about 55 per cent and Lorraine 22 per cent. In iron ore Lorraine was predominant, providing nearly 93 per cent of domestic production. Saar coal, substantially under French control in the early postwar period, was important for France's own needs and for export.

Because of its heavy dependence on Lorraine iron ore, which is high in phosphorous, the French steel industry makes much more use of convertors to produce Thomas steel than of open hearths to produce Martin steel. About two-thirds of French steel is produced by the Thomas method, whereas the figure for the whole Community is about half. Belgium, Luxembourg and the Saar—which are also largely based on phosphoric ore—also produce most of their steel by the Thomas process (Luxembourg almost entirely so). Germany, however, produces more of its steel in open-hearths than by the Thomas process. For Italy and the Netherlands Thomas steel is almost insignificant. This makes a difference in sales and prices. Thomas steel is generally cheaper and while the two types are interchangeable for many purposes there has been a growing preference for quality that has favored Martin and electric steel. New technology is improving some Thomas steel.

France had fewer large steel firms than Germany. Only three French firms were among the 11 Community enterprises that produced more than one million tons apiece in 1952 (while the Germans had seven). These three, however, produced about half of France's crude steel. The addition of two or three more groups would account for about two-thirds of the French output. However, in the minds of many it was not the small number of large firms but the large number of small ones that was a source of concern. Cartelization and arrangements like that of the Comptoir had helped perpetuate this condition and protected a number of inefficient operations. Some mergers had taken place since the war but Monnet had pressed for more of them when he was guiding the French recovery program.

In the eyes of the outside world, French heavy industry was apt to be looked at as not exactly inefficient, but as combining certain rigidities common to the whole French economy with an undesirable number of restrictive practices, and perhaps a certain lack of drive, in labor as well as management. This view had much to do with the early disbelief that France would ever expose itself to the competition of the touted dynamism of Germany. It seems also to have been an ingredient of the French industry's own fears about the risks of the pool. The interesting question was whether this sense of how things were was more nearly right than the more optimistic view suggested by Monnet and the statistics.

The Saar

Lying between France and Germany, the Saar is closely linked with the economies of both but has also been the object of severe political rivalry. It has changed hands several times in the last few centuries and even during the life of the Coal and Steel Community it was making one more passage, this time from France toward Germany, but on terms that preserved special links with France. Probably the most important of these was the assurance that France would be able to buy specified quantities of Saar coal over a period of some years. Small as the area is, its coal output is large, making it the fourth most important district in the Community (after the Ruhr, Nord-Pas de Calais and southern Belgium). Productivity is high and inclusion of the Saar in the French economy at the end of the war apparently benefited the area at least to the extent of permit-

ting it to share in the French drive to improve coal output.
The mines have been government-owned since the 18th
century.

Steel is also important to the Saar. Together with coal, it
employs more than half the area's working force. Six or
eight companies account for most of the Saar's steel output. Most of them are owned by German and French
interests and ARBED in Luxembourg. One of the largest,
however, belongs to a Saar-German family, the Röchlings,
who have had continuing legal and political difficulties
during the postwar period. Nevertheless, the Saar economy
does not seem to have suffered seriously, perhaps because
both the French and the Germans were anxious to woo
the area and perhaps, too, in some part, because of the
existence of the coal and steel pool.

The Saar is a true border area, not only in its history
and the two-way direction of its economic life, but very
literally and dramatically in the location of some of its
principal coal resources. The Warndt mines are sometimes
entered from the Saar and sometimes from Lorraine, while
the tunnels reach under the other country. The whole
province exemplifies the interconnections of Schumania.

Luxembourg

The Saar's neighbor, Luxembourg, is another of the Community areas that has an economic importance out of all
relation to its size. On paper Luxembourg looks like a group
of steel mills with a line around them. Actually, the steel
is produced almost entirely in one small area in the south-
west of the country and the rest is agricultural or wild,
except for the capital. Statistically, the effect is rather like
that of establishing an international frontier around several
counties in western Pennsylvania or a shire or two in the
Black Country of England. Iron and steel account for about
70 per cent of Luxembourg's exports and two-thirds of the
industrial employment (one-sixth of the labor force). Of
the iron and steel produced, 95 per cent or more is exported.
No other member of the Community is quite so highly
concentrated on Community business.

Luxembourg has iron of relatively low grade and supplements its supplies by imports of French and Swedish ore. Luxembourg also exports iron ore. It has no coal and imports coke principally from the Ruhr. The steel it exports— much of it semi-finished—goes in large part to Belgium and the Belgian Congo (over 25 per cent) and after that to Scandinavia, Holland and a number of other countries (including sometimes the United States).[10] Wages and productivity are both high.

Three companies own all the Luxembourg steel plants and a good part of the iron mines. Nearly two-thirds of the crude steel capacity is accounted for by one company— ARBED (Aciéries Réunies de Burbach-Eich-Dudelange)— which is the largest steel firm in the Community. ARBED owns coal mines in the Aachen area of Germany and has subsidiaries in the Saar and Belgium. Its head offices in the capital city of Luxembourg appear to the passer-by to be somewhat larger than the Grand Ducal Palace, as is perhaps logical.

Belgium

In 1952 Belgium was the third most important producer of coal, steel and coke in the Community. These activities were more important for its national economy than they were in France and Germany. Belgium leads the Community in sales of steel to overseas markets. Of the 288,000 tons of major steel products a month that Belgium produced in 1952, over 60 per cent was exported—52,000 tons to Community countries and 127,000 to third countries. There was also a substantial export of steel ingots.

Inside the Community, Belgian coal exports have been substantial, in spite of the fact that Belgian coal mining, as the Community's principal "sick industry," was the cause of much anxiety when the pool was formed. The sickness is,

[10] These figures are estimates since, as a result of the economic union with Belgium, Luxembourg's official export statistics are merged with those of that country. "The Luxembourg Iron and Steel Industry," reprinted from the *Monthly Statistical Bulletin* (British Iron and Steel Federation), Aug. 1952, p. 3.

however, localized. In the old mines of the south, where Belgium gets two-thirds of its coal, costs are high and the mines have been subsidized throughout the life of the Community. In the Campine, on the Dutch and German borders, Belgium produces coal from richer seams on terms comparable with the better Community producers.

Belgium had one of the most rapid economic recoveries of any Western European country. Following a rigorous monetary reform, successive governments permitted much free play to private industry, prices, and market forces. This was in contrast to some other countries and made the Belgian industrialists particularly sensitive to the possibility of the High Authority's exercising extensive control over business. It also had the effect of making Belgium a rather expensive country, in money terms at least; the price and wage discrepancies between Belgium and other Community countries were an additional source of concern.

The Belgian coal and steel industries are entirely in private hands. The country has a strong cartel tradition and there are rather extensive interlocking financial connections. Coal marketing was subjected to various regulations, compensation schemes, and price-fixing agreements related to the problems of the high-cost mines. There are a large number of coal companies and quite a few steel producers as well. When the Community began over half the Belgian steel production was accounted for by three firms. Neither of the two largest was as big as a dozen other companies in the Community until they merged.

The Netherlands

Holland is the smallest steel producer in the Community. As a coal producer it comes after the three large producers and the Saar. The coal is mostly in South Limburg, directly adjacent to the Aachen field in Germany. Much of this is produced by government-owned firms which also manufactured over two-thirds of the country's coke in 1952.[11] Gas, fertilizer and chemical works are located in the neighborhood of the cokeries. Some of the Dutch coal and coke

[11] Staatsmijnen in Limburg, *Jaarsverlag, 1952*, p. 17.

is exported but the country was a net importer in 1952. Costs were low and the Dutch mines, like those of the Ruhr, were singled out for a special levy to help subsidize the high-cost Belgian mines. Production per man was the third highest in the Community in 1952 (after Lorraine and the Saar); though thinner seams were being mined in the early '50s, the general level of productivity was maintained for some time, partly by mechanization;[12] then it began to fall.

The Netherlands had a metal-working industry long before it had a steel industry. There were difficulties in getting adequate supplies of foreign steel during the First World War when the Netherlands was neutral. At the end of the war blast furnaces were built but steelmaking was not begun until the '30s. Meanwhile, Holland became one of the world's major pig iron exporters. After the Second World War, steelmaking expanded and substantial additions were made to the plant, partly with Marshall Plan aid. Crude steel production in the Netherlands in 1952 was twelve times that of 1938 (but only about three and a half times its previous peak, in 1941 under German occupation).

All of the pig iron and most of the steel is produced by one firm—Koninklijke Nederlandsche Hoogovens en Staalfabrieken N. V.—in which the government has a large minority interest and the city of Amsterdam a smaller share. The Netherlands still exports pig iron but imports substantial quantities of semi-finished steel. Located on the sea at Ijmuiden—"the Sparrows Point of Europe," someone has called it—the Dutch steelworks uses principally high-grade iron ore imported from outside the Community and obtains other supplies by water as well.

Italy

The First World War and the autarkic policies of fascism had much to do with the development of the Italian steel industry. But the influence they exercised was not confined to stimulating expansion; they also stimulated high costs. During the depression, to bail out the banks that had large

---

[12] Same, p. 11.

interests in the steel industry, the government acquired partial ownership of most of the major firms. With some changes this has continued and at present the Istituto per la Ricostruzione Industriale (IRI)—through a special subsidiary, Finanziaria Siderugica (Finsider)—controls 50 per cent or more of the capital of four major groups that together produce over half Italy's steel and a much larger share of its pig iron.

Italy mines some iron ore in the north and on Elba and also produces iron from pyrites. Nevertheless, substantial quantities of ore have to be imported. In 1952 about 56 per cent of the iron supply came from domestic sources. The need for iron is held down by the fact that a high proportion of Italian steel is made in electric furnaces for which scrap is the principal raw material. This, too, has to be imported. Italy has little coal. Before the war, Britain was a major supplier but it has exported little since the war. In 1952 Germany and the United States each provided about one-third of Italy's coal imports; one-eighth came from England and most of the rest from Belgium and Poland.

Heavy dependence on imported raw materials, coupled with the high costs that have characterized the industry, have sometimes led to debates as to whether Italy should manufacture steel on a large scale at all. The metal-processing and machine-making industries are important to the national economy and it has been argued that it would be more economical for Italy to import the bulk of its steel from cheaper foreign sources. The Italian government took a firm decision against this view when it made reconstruction of the iron and steel industry a major part of Italy's recovery program.

Italian steel plants seriously suffered during the war, partly because of dismantling by the retreating Germans. The recovery program called not only for rebuilding but also for an expansion of capacity. Particular attention was given to the expansion of pig iron production relative to steelmaking capacity in order to reduce dependence on scrap but there was also to be an increase in steel output by about 50 per cent over the prewar peak. The largest single item in the program was the building of a new steel plant at Cornigliano, on the harbor of Genoa. Work had begun there in 1938 but the plant was dismantled and removed by the Germans just before it was to come into operation in 1943. The postwar replacement was three times as big as the earlier one. In addition to very modern equipment, the Cornigliano plant has the advantage of a seaside location so that it can import coal, ore and scrap by water; it is also well placed in relation to the main steel-using area of Italy around Milan, Turin and Genoa. Other waterside locations to the south have also been favored in the expansion program but much of the industry remains concentrated in the industrial area of Lombardy.

In 1952 the Italian steel industry (excluding iron mines and cokeries) employed some 89,000 workers. About 40 tons of crude steel was produced per worker, compared to nearly 60 tons for the Community as a whole, and 158 for Luxembourg, the highest. This cannot be taken as proof that Italian steelmaking is inefficient. Labor is cheaper in Italy and it would therefore often be economical to employ it more plentifully than in other countries. Moreover, because of persistent unemployment Italian laws made it difficult for firms to dismiss workers. This was reinforced by union and political pressure and, to some extent, a willingness of major companies (especially the government-owned ones) to carry more workers on their payrolls than were strictly necessary in the interests of "social policy."

Entering a common market seemed to threaten the high-cost Italian steel industry. But easier access to scrap, coal, and iron ore offered advantages. Italy was the only Community country permitted to keep steel tariffs during the transitional period in the hope that this would permit its industry to lower costs to a competitive level (bearing in mind the natural protection that distance affords Italy).

THE SCOPE OF THE POOL

The triangle in the northwest was the heart of the Community, but the Treaty had to draw a line around the whole of the six countries. This created new, rather undefined relations. The very high-cost coal mines at Sulcis in Sardinia were now linked with the highly productive and extraordinarily clean Dutch mines at Heerlen in South Limburg. The iron that the Germans dug in the Harz Mountains close to the Soviet Zone had to be related to the ore the French took out of the Pyrenees. Steel mills that were built in the 1880s and used hand processes were newly associated with the most modern mechanized works.

"This Treaty shall apply to the European territories of the member States," reads the opening sentence of Article 79.[13] So far as territories outside Europe are concerned, each signatory bound itself to grant to the other member states "the preferential measures which it enjoys with respect to coal and steel." This was generally taken to refer to tariff preferences.[14] The most important feature of this provision was the exclusion from the Treaty of the iron mines of French North and West Africa, fairly important secondary sources of supply that are likely to grow in importance. To meet Italian complaints, the French promised supplies outside the Treaty regime. When the Dutch expressed concern about a preferred position for Italy, M. Schuman assured them that there would be enough for all.

Inside Europe, definition of the Treaty area raised one more problem. The Germans could not accept the idea that the new Community should add to the divisions of their country created by Soviet power. A tariff barrier down the middle of Germany was unthinkable. The matter was resolved by a provision in the Convention (valid beyond the transitional period, however) that permitted trade between the two parts of Germany to be regulated by the German government in agreement with the High Authority. The other side of the question was: What would happen if Germany were reunited? Would the coal and

[13] The Treaty also applies to European territories for the foreign relations of which members are responsible. The only important area in this category was the Saar.
[14] Paul Reuter, *La Communauté Européenne du Charbon et de l'Acier*, 1953, p. 171.

steel of the east automatically be part of the pool? The prospect alarmed some Frenchmen who thought this would add to Germany's weight in the pool, which they felt was already too great. The issue was passed over in silence. Some took comfort in general, safeguarding clauses, arguing that so radical a change could not but open basic questions about the Community. Others took the realistic view that such a change was unlikely and in any case could come about only in political conditions that would automatically reopen questions of Germany's relation to the rest of Western Europe.

The scope of the Treaty also had to be defined in terms of the products to be included. The list is quite comprehensive. With regard to fuels, the Treaty covers all hard coal (in the European usage, see p. 118), patent fuels (i.e., those processed from coal, such as briquettes), lignite, brown coal briquettes, and coke "except coke for electrodes and petroleum coke." In steel the list begins with raw materials. Iron ore, scrap and manganese ore (but not iron pyrites) are covered by the Treaty. Pig iron, foundry iron and two ferro-alloys—spiegeleisen and ferro-manganese—represent the next stage of the steelmaking process. Liquid steel, ingots, and semi-finished steel products naturally make up an important part of the Treaty's coverage. In the area of finished products the lines became harder to draw. The principal products are specifically included: rails, bars, sections, beams, plates, sheets, wire rod, hoop, tinplate and other coated sheets, and strip. The blocks and cylinders from which pipes are made fall under the Treaty, but not the process of tubemaking itself, probably the most important omission. Also omitted are very narrow thin cold-rolled strips (unless used for making tinplate), wire, and iron castings.

For our purposes, such a description is sufficient. There are, however, some other minor exceptions and additions. The Treaty cautions the High Authority against using its powers over certain processes which are common to the steel industry and other industries except when steelmaking is directly concerned. Similarly the relation of coke to its by-products is a subject for special note. Scrap was recognized as a special problem. "Special steels," those having particular characteristics such as high or low carbon content or a high proportion of alloys, were also recognized as special cases subject to somewhat different rules from those applying more broadly.

*   *   *   *   *   *

Out of such disparate elements—physical, social, economic, political and technological—a Community was to be built. To build on, it also had similarities comparable to some of the disparities and outmatching them at many points. Most of all the pool rested on a recognition of mutual interests that had made the effort possible in the first place. "I go . . . to forge in the smithy of my soul the uncreated conscience of my race," said Stephen Dedalus. The Community's mission was not quite so ambitious—but it was enough.

PART II

THE COMMUNITY IN ACTION

SEVEN

OPENING THE COMMON MARKET: TRADE BARRIERS FALL

"The movement of coal and steel between member countries will immediately be freed of all customs duty." Schuman's opening statement was sweeping. It struck one of the keynotes of the common market and soon was expanded to cover the removal of quotas and other governmental trade barriers. Considering their historical importance—it was, after all, by such measures that the "natural unity" of the coal and steel area had been fractured in the first place—the process of getting rid of these barriers has been one of the quickest, simplest, and apparently least disturbing, of all the Community's activities.

THE RULES

The Treaty provisions are clear and remarkably succinct: "import and export duties, or taxes with an equivalent effect, and quantitative restrictions on the movement of coal and steel . . . are recognized to be incompatible with the common market for coal and steel, and are, therefore, abolished and prohibited within the Community. . ." (Article 4).

Not only is the rule categorical, but it neither carries with it a series of escape clauses nor limits tariff reduction and the removal of quotas to step-by-step measures spread over a period of time. In both these respects the coal and steel Treaty departs sharply from what has usually been regarded as the only practical means of getting agreement on the lowering of trade barriers. The clear and drastic provision of the Treaty was important, both practically and psychologically. Practically, it ensured that the formation of the common market should not be indefinitely postponed by the familiar method of prolonging "temporary" protective measures. Psychologically, the speedy and sweeping removal of tariffs and quotas dramatized the fact that the Coal and Steel Community really meant drastic change. The transitional arrangements for the five years before the Treaty came fully into force did not seriously detract from these provisions or their effect.

These were great gains. Would they not command a high price in dislocation and disturbance? A step-by-step approach, with reasonable safeguards, would not have been incompatible with an honest effort to create a common market. How is it that the drafters of the Schuman Plan Treaty were willing to run the risk of quick removal of tariffs and quotas?

There were two main answers. First, tariffs and quotas were less important in determining the flow of trade in coal and steel among the six countries when the Community was formed than they had been in times past and might be again. Second, the coal and steel Treaty was not just an agreement on trade barriers. It provided other means by which the flow of trade within the Community could be influenced and it made possible more or less orderly adjustment to the new circumstances. No country faced the alternatives of accepting serious, immediate dislocation or staying out of the Community. Thus there was an opportunity to make a drastic change in the structure of trade barriers without major disturbances to industry.

This does not mean that the ban on tariffs and quotas was a fraud, the effects of these restrictions being kept by other means. Nor does it mean that the elimination of trade barriers was of no effect. Quite the contrary, the removal of trade barriers has been one of the important realities of the Community, partly in terms of short-run effects, but more importantly as a lasting guarantee of the new economic situation in which the coal and steel industries of the Community were to develop.

In contrast to its sharp, clear language on tariffs and

quotas, the Treaty is less explicit about exchange controls. "As far as they are competent to do so," says Article 86, "the member States shall take any appropriate measures to guarantee the settling of international accounts arising out of trade in coal and steel within the common market; they will lend each other assistance to facilitate such settlements." This seems to leave open the possibility of blocking payments in some circumstances, but presumably would not sanction the denial of import licenses on balance of payments grounds. The size of the loophole is presumably also to be judged in the light of two general provisions immediately preceding the language just quoted from Article 86. One obligates the members "to take any appropriate general and particular measures to ensure the execution of their obligations under the decisions and recommendations of the institutions of the Community, and to facilitate the accomplishment of the Community's objectives." The other binds the members to refrain from measures incompatible with the existence of the common market. In any case, no problems have arisen. All of the countries in the Community were members of the European Payments Union which ensured the settlement of accounts among them.[1]

The Convention governing the transitional period of five years before the Treaty came fully into force made three specific exceptions to the general ban on trade barriers. First, the High Authority was empowered to permit Italy to retain duties on imports of steel and coke, provided they were reduced in a series of specified steps and eliminated at the end of the transition period (Sections 27, 30). Second, in connection with the arrangements for adapting the Belgian coal mines to the common market, the Belgian government was permitted to "retain or set up, under the

[1] An agreement on exchange control regulations was reached at the same time that formal action was taken on the removal of tariffs and quotas, to open the common market. ECSC, High Authority, *The Activities of the European Community, General Report,* Aug. 10, 1952- Apr. 12, 1953, p. 55. (Hereafter the General Reports and all other major reports of the High Authority will be cited simply as "HA, *Report*" with the date. See the Bibliography for complete identification.)

control of the High Authority, mechanisms making possible the separation of the Belgian market from the common market" (Section 26(3)). Third, if the opening of the common market produced disturbances in the steel industry that could not be dealt with by other measures, the High Authority was given power to "limit directly or indirectly the net increase in deliveries from one region to another in the common market" (Section 29).[2] Neither the second or third exception was ever used; the Italian duties are discussed below.

By these simple means the Treaty ensured that by the end of the transitional period trade among the six countries would be free of tariffs and quotas, and thus radically different from what it had been for many decades. Tariffs and quotas on imports from the rest of the world remained. As a result, the goods of each Community country had a preferred position in other Community markets compared to goods from outside the Community. Because various international agreements forbade trade discrimination, the Community countries had to get other countries to waive their rights. Because tariffs and quotas on imports from "third countries" (to use the conventional shorthand) differed from one Community country to another, additional arrangements had to be made governing trade within the Community. The Treaty looked toward the consolidation of these separate arrangements in a single tariff and quota system that would apply to the whole Community's imports of coal and steel from third countries. These matters will all be dealt with in Chapters 17 and 18 as part of the account of the Community's relations with the outside world.

THE COMMON MARKET FOR COAL, IRON ORE, AND SCRAP

The first six months after the Treaty went into force was a "preparatory period" during which the High Authority

[2] Note that this provision specifies regions, not countries. Early in 1953 the High Authority drew up a set of criteria for applying it. ECSC, *Journal Officiel*, May 4, 1953, pp. 117-118. (Hereafter cited as *JO*.) A French proposal that it be applied to special steels was turned down (pp. 147-148).

and other organs of the Community were set up, the necessary waivers on tariff treatment sought from other countries, and the groundwork laid for full operation of the Treaty. Then, on February 10, 1953, the common market for coal, iron ore, and scrap was established. This also marked the opening of the "transitional period," when the High Authority assumed powers it had not been able to exercise during the previous "preparatory period." The end of the transitional period was reckoned as five years from the opening of the common market for coal, or February 10, 1958. After that the Treaty was to be fully in operation (subject to a few exceptions).

Opening the common market for coal did not require the removal of any tariffs. Coal had been short in Europe and supplies were largely allocated by international agreement. Of the Community countries, only Italy had a tariff —15 per cent on coke—and that was to continue for the time being. However, the creation of the common market involved other kinds of action as well.[3] The elimination of double-pricing and discrimination in freight rates did much to put foreign and domestic buyers on a more nearly equal footing; these are examined in later chapters. Certain compensatory charges that had effects like those of tariffs were abolished and also some export limitations.

These measures did not suddenly free Community trade in coal from all governmental intervention. The allocations already negotiated in OEEC and ECE committees for the first quarter of 1953 remained in effect. The High Authority permitted the continuation of a number of subsidies, established maximum prices for most coal, and approved the continuation of some special pricing arrangements. Adjustment to the common market had begun. Its progress and the manipulation of these and other controls by the High Authority and the governments are the major themes of future chapters.

[3] Eliminating the coal trade barriers required a series of national actions taken in agreement, understandings on documentation and regulation bearing on coal originating outside the Community, commitments to provide the necessary foreign exchange, etc. For some account of these see HA, *Report*, Apr. 1953, pp. 54-57.

Iron ore presented almost no problems. Here again there were no tariffs. The Community as a whole was a net importer. While the pressure of demand on supply was not as great as in the case of coal, no country was seriously interested in hindering imports or protecting its producers by tariffs. The High Authority did not fix iron ore prices and the major changes resulting from the common market were the elimination of double-pricing and of some discriminations in transportation rates, the freeing of the domestic price in France, and the elimination of export controls in that country. These measures freed the movement of iron ore within the Community and benefited the Belgian buyers of French ore, but had only limited effects on the whole iron economy of the Community, in part because a large part of the French output is in mines owned by steelmakers.

The scrap situation was more involved than those of the other products that went into the initial common market. Prices varied greatly within the Community and substantial quantities of scrap were imported from the outside, often at much higher prices. Some easing in the demand for steel during late 1952 made the scrap situation less tense than it had been. Nevertheless, the High Authority provided for an initial allocation of scrap supplies that lasted until March 15, 1953.[4] For a time thereafter maximum prices were fixed according to a system of zones into which the Community was divided. These proved to be only the first steps in a complex and fairly difficult process of regulating the Community's scrap economy that continued during the whole transitional period (see Chapter 12). Private cartel activities were subjected to supervision and regulation. There were no import duties on scrap to be eliminated, but the removal of export controls was a major step toward creating a common market. It not only resulted in a great increase in trade but also precipitated a whole series of problems which could no longer be dealt with on a national basis.

[4] The principle of allocation was very simple. Each country was to keep its own scrap except that Italy was permitted to buy 5,000 tons of German and 20,000 tons of French scrap. HA, *Report*, Apr. 1953, p. 87.

THE COMMON MARKET FOR STEEL

The common market for steel was scheduled to come into effect on April 10, 1953, two months after that for coal, but the opening was delayed until May 1 to permit the solution of a tax problem that touched the fundamentals of the Community (see Chapter 10). In contrast to the situation in coal, the Community countries all had import duties on steel. Their ranges are shown in the following figures:[5]

	Benelux	France	Germany	Italy
		(per cent ad valorem)		
pig iron	0-1	5	12	11-20
crude and semi-finished steel	1-2	7-10	15-18	11-15
hot-finished steel products	1-6	10-18	15-25	15-20
finished steel products	6-8	16-22	15-28	15-23

While some of these tariffs are rather high, they do not compare with the levels of the '30s when French and German rates came to about 50 per cent of the world price. Before the common market opened the French and German duties were suspended. The Italian duties remained in force under the transitional Convention. Thus only the low Benelux duties were actually removed as the immediate result of the opening of the common market. However, the rules insured that duties would not be reimposed on trade in steel within the Community and were therefore important beyond their immediate effect. Considering that a period of slack demand, with a fall in production, lasted for a year or more after the opening of the common market, it seems likely that in the absence of the Treaty at least some of the suspended duties would have been put back in effect. Instead, the impossibility of resorting to tariff protection became one of the basic data of the steel industry of Western Europe. This was one of the fundamental changes wrought by the Treaty.

In immediate effects the elimination of quantitative restrictions was probably more important. France had a tight

[5] Horst Mendershausen, "First Tests of the Schuman Plan," *The Review of Economics and Statistics*, Nov. 1953, p. 273.

control of imports that permitted little but token quantities of steel to enter. Imports of steel products into France and the Saar jumped from 27.7 thousand tons in 1952 to 117.6 thousand in 1953—a period of low demand with trade barriers in effect for the first few months—and 454.2 thousand in 1954, during the last six months of which demand was rising. The other countries, however, imposed relatively few import quotas on steel products. Controls over exports also restrained potential trade among the Community countries and these, too, were eliminated by the Treaty.

The High Authority did not impose maximum prices for steel. Some government price-fixing was dropped at the opening of the common market and double-pricing was eliminated. The end of national discrimination in transport rates was probably somewhat less important for the trade in steel than for the trade in coal (because of the higher value per ton of steel), but the cost of producing steel was directly affected by changes in coal transportation costs. Trade among the Community countries in steel expanded more rapidly than trade in coal. For several years it also rose faster than production, faster than trade in other products among the Community countries, and faster than their steel trade with the rest of the world. Not all of this increase was the result of removing tariffs and quotas, but that action played a part, both directly and by the guarantee that they would not be reimposed. Since there is no reliable way to assign shares in the performance of the common market to each Community action, the economic impact of the Community is treated as a whole in Chapter 20.

THE COMMON MARKET FOR SPECIAL STEELS

"Special steels," as designated in the Treaty, are those containing certain alloys or especially high or low quantities of carbon or that are otherwise specially adapted for particular purposes, such as toolmaking, scientific work, and certain types of construction. Sold in relatively small quantities, often under trademarks, and frequently produced to order, they have a different kind of economy

from run-of-the-mill steel products. In quantity, the special
steel produced in the Community came to less than 10 per
cent of ordinary steel but its value per ton was more than
three times as great.[6] One result of this high value is that
transportation costs are much less important in the marketing of special steels. Thus competition is less directly related
to the location of industry and imports from third countries
can be more serious. Special steels were regarded as requiring special treatment, different from that applied to
common steel.

The Treaty distinguished between three categories of
special steels; two were to come into the common market
a year after the opening of the common market for coal
and the other two years after that. The High Authority
concluded that the distinction would be difficult to apply
and by action of the Council of Ministers (i.e., in effect,
the vote of the governments), the opening of the common
market for all three types of special steel was set for August
1, 1954, a year and a half after the common market for
coal was opened.

The tariffs on special steels applied by Community countries covered rather wide ranges. Again those of Benelux
were lowest, from 1 to 8 per cent. France's ran from 7 to
25 per cent, Germany's were 15 to 28 per cent (some of
them provisionally reduced to 8 to 10 per cent), while
Italy's ranged from 12 to 23 per cent. There were no quotas
at the time the common market was introduced, though
France had made use of them until April 1954; on removing the quotas France imposed a special tax of 15 per cent,
as it did regularly when removing quotas under the OEEC
trade liberalization program. All these duties, except the
Italian ones, were removed when the common market was
formed. For Italy, a regime was established comparable to
that for ordinary steel—a progressive scaling down of duties.
The French government expressed concern about the difficulties its special steel producers might have and asked for
action to limit imports under the safeguarding clause of
Section 29 of the Convention (see p. 142). After investiga-

[6] HA, *Report*, Nov. 1954, p. 70.

tion the High Authority concluded that these fears were not well grounded and refused to establish limitations but agreed to watch the situation closely. Some French subsidies were left in being, with provision for their reduction. No further complaints were received from Paris.[7] The rules about published prices were only partially applied to special steels. Agreements were made about tariffs on imports from third countries.

ITALIAN TARIFFS

When the common market for steel was opened, the Italian government applied to the High Authority for permission to subject steel imports to the duties established in the tariff agreements negotiated under GATT at Annecy in October 1949. These were higher than the temporary tariff rates in effect at the time.[8] The High Authority agreed to this on the ground that unemployment, Italy's disadvantageous position in relation to coal and iron ore supplies, and the program that was under way to modernize and expand the steel industry, justified some continued protection. Moreover, the end of double-pricing meant that foreign competition with Italian steel production was sharper. But an additional safeguard was provided by forbidding other producers to absorb freight charges on shipments to Italy. The High Authority added that if foreign prices rose the Italian government should lower its duties so as to provide only the original amount of protection to domestic producers. If steel from third countries were sold to Italy more cheaply than Community steel, the duty on imports from member countries was to be lowered. Nothing ever came of this last provision so far as steel was concerned, but in September 1955 the High Authority asked Italy to suspend the duty on Community pig iron because its imports from third countries were increasing

[7] The whole story is told in HA, *Report*, Nov. 1954, pp. 70-80 and in a series of decisions in *JO*, Aug. 1, 1954.

[8] "Decisioni e problemi della Comunità Carbone-Acciaio," *Mondo Economico*, May 9, 1953. Italy had undertaken a general tariff revision and was in the process of applying the new rates. My *Trade and Payments in Western Europe*, 1952, p. 223.

more rapidly than those from the Community. This was done at the beginning of December 1955 and the duty remained suspended to the end of the transitional period.

The High Authority's initial permission for Italy to maintain duties was temporary. Further study led to the conclusion that the 10 per cent cut in steel duties prescribed by the Convention for the second year of the transitional period could safely be put into effect immediately. This was done on August 1, 1953. Then in May 1955 the 25 per cent cut provided for the third year took effect. Thereafter matters proceeded according to the schedule laid out in the Convention; duties in the fourth year were 55 per cent of the level at which they started and in the fifth year 30 per cent. Thus the steel duties fell in the course of the transitional period from a range of 15-23 per cent to one of 4.5-6.9 per cent and then disappeared in February 1958. One rate, that on thin sheets, was cut more rapidly than the rest, because as the High Authority told the Italian government in December 1956, increased sales of this product at home and abroad showed that Italian producers could meet foreign competition effectively and did not need tariff protection. The Italian duty on coke was 15 per cent when the common market opened. Following the scale of reductions set out in the Convention the rate fell each year until it was 4.5 per cent for the last year of the transitional period and was then eliminated.[9]

Italy is a fairly important producer of special steels. After the common market for these products had been in operation for a year, the High Authority observed that prices in Milan and Turin were for the most part below those charged by French and German manufacturers. It noted, too, that Italian production of these quality steels was rising and took the view that the problem of unemployment was much less acute than it had been. It proposed, therefore, that the Italian duties on special steels should move according to the same schedule as the rates for ordinary steels. The Italian government accepted this proposi-

[9] Tables in HA, *Report*, Apr. 1958, v. 2, pp. 22-23, show the whole process of Italian tariff reduction.

tion for non-alloy steels but objected that the same course could not be followed for alloy steels on which the duties were somewhat lower to begin with (4 to 15.5 per cent compared with 13 to 20 per cent). The High Authority therefore agreed to a scale of reductions which left these at 3.5 to 7 per cent for the period from December 1, 1955 to the end of the transition period. Thus the higher rates were cut by more than 50 per cent, while the lower ones were cut 12.5 per cent. All were dropped in February 1958.

The handling of the Italian tariffs is of special interest because it was an exception to the Treaty's general principle of immediately eliminating tariffs. It worked and even went somewhat more rapidly than was planned. Contrary to the classic French saying, the temporary did not last. This does not mean that the same device would have worked well for the Community as a whole. If every country had been on this basis, the sum of the pressures against keeping to the schedule of reductions would have been much greater; there would have been a host of "special circumstances"; each government would have been more "understanding" of the others' problems and more likely to agree, on a reciprocal basis, to measures that postponed the day of change. In the actual situation Italy was alone. No one else stood to gain by perpetuation of the Italian tariffs; instead each had some interest, though on the whole not a very urgent one, in seeing them come down. Apart from gaining easier access to the Italian market, this interest included the added advantage of widening the margin of preference by which Community products entered the Italian market compared to products of third countries.

It is impossible to demonstrate the effects of the Italian tariffs with any certainty. The trade figures are inconclusive. Italy's coke imports from the rest of the Community expanded tremendously while the general level of Community coke trade rose only modestly; but the Italian figure was very low to start with. Italy's imports of steel from its partners increased less than those of any other country in the Community, but it is far from clear that this was due to the tariffs. Italy's steel production rose more rapidly than that of any other country so more of its needs could be met domestically; imports were higher in the middle of the transitional period than they were toward the end when duties were lower; for at least part of the period Italy's steel imports from third countries, which carried the full tariff load, increased more rapidly than its imports from the Community at lower rates of duty; during the height of the steel boom a number of factors were at work that reduced the interest of French, Belgian and German steelmakers in selling to Italy. Italian steel prices were generally the highest in the Community and the tariffs probably contributed to this, but transport rates were also important. The gap between Italian and other steel prices narrowed somewhat during the transitional period and at some times Belgian prices were higher for certain products. Around the end of the transitional period, Italian steel mills cut their prices more sharply than other Community producers. While the final elimination of tariffs may have had something to do with this, it was also a response to the fall in demand.

The most significant fact is that by the end of the transition period high tariffs were no longer necessary to the Italian steel industry. It could be formally integrated into the common market. Knowledge that the duties would be removed undoubtedly helped make this possible. The exception for temporary tapering duties for Italy seemed to have justified itself. If demand continued to decline and producers in the rest of the Community became interested in more intensive selling on the Italian market, new questions might arise. But that was true of the whole Community economy and not just of Italy.

TRADE BARRIERS AND THE COMMON MARKET

While tariffs and quotas were the main governmental trade barriers, in the narrow sense of taxes and limitations imposed directly on the process of exchanging goods, they were not the only impediments that existed at frontiers. Even after tariffs and quotas were abolished, shipments of coal and steel across national boundaries might still require licenses and usually had to go through special formalities, for purposes of exchange control, statistical records, customs procedures, or for other reasons. Even though licenses were automatically granted, these formalities, the documentation, and the possible delay they entailed, made international trade within the Community somewhat more burdensome, and to a small degree more costly, than internal trade within one of the member countries. The High Authority undertook a series of investigations and negotiations which resulted in the elimination of some requirements and the simplification of others. By the end of the transitional period it regarded the remaining features of the "invisible tariff"—to use Percy Bidwell's term—as of relatively minor importance.

Having opened the common market, the Community has to see to it that it stays open. From time to time governments have taken steps that put some sort of barrier in the way of trade or discriminated against foreign producers or sellers. For instance, the Italian government charged an "administrative duty" of one-half of one per cent on imports of Treaty products; the Belgian government made the issue of licenses for coal imports from the Ruhr subject to certain transportation regulations; French customs and maritime law combined to treat French iron and steel products shipped via Rotterdam and Antwerp as foreign goods, subject to duty, when they entered French Atlantic ports; Luxembourg refused import licenses for coal in circumstances that raised questions about the terms of the Treaty. In all these cases and others the High Authority negotiated with the governments concerned to remove the impediments. The process was apt to be fairly slow, the results varied somewhat, the barriers themselves were not of major importance. Constant policing of this sort can be regarded as a regular part of the High Authority's job of keeping open the common market.

The common market does not rest on the removal of trade barriers alone. Measures concerning price, transportation rates, and other matters to be discussed in later chapters are all part of the process. All these steps have the same immediate aim: the elimination of the old national distinction between domestic and foreign producers and consumers within the Community. This central principle of the Treaty is not the subject of a separate chapter because it is a common theme of most of them.

The complete elimination of tariffs and quotas is one of the most widely known, and even spectacular, features of the Schuman Plan. Considering this, its immediate importance was relatively small. When the common market was opened there were only a few tariffs and quotas actually in use that could be removed. Yet, this has been an important achievement. Early 1953 was just a moment in the life of the Community. Perhaps even by the end of that year governments would have used tariffs and quotas to meet the recession, if there had been no Community. Certainly, over the 50-year life of the Community, trade barriers would have played their traditional role. By removing these weapons from the arsenal, the Community changed the character of the coal and steel economy of the six countries and altered the place of governments in it. By assuring producers that tariffs and quotas would not be imposed in the future, the Community changed one of the bases of economic calculation.

EIGHT

TRANSPORT RATES:
JOURNEY WITHOUT END

". . . THE COMMON market requires the application of such transport rates for coal and steel as will make possible comparable price conditions to consumers in comparable positions." The principle of Article 70 of the Treaty seems clear, the need for it obvious. If the common market is to rest on equality, then clearly there can be no discriminatory transport rates, no special charges that have effects like those of tariffs, and no practices that give some producers or consumers unfair advantages over others in the Community. But the simplicity of the concept belies the complexity of the practice, and conceals hard questions of principle as well. What is equality? When are consumers in "comparable positions"? How are intricate, historically molded national structures of transport rates—which apply to more than coal and steel—to be altered so as to harmonize with one another in a common market?

On some matters the Community has made striking progress. Other issues have been settled by compromises that leave a rather mixed record of results. And on some questions the activity called for by the Treaty has not yet gone beyond study, talk, and the refusal to yield national positions. This is a field in which the High Authority's powers are limited. National governments retain most of their power over transportation, subject to the Treaty principles. Thus this chapter broaches the subject of "partial integration" and its consequences that will recur throughout the book.

THE CONDITION THE COMMUNITY FACED

None of the great steel-producing centers in the Community has adequate supplies of both iron ore and coal immediately adjacent to it. All sell an appreciable portion of their steel in fairly distant markets. The bulk and weight of the materials involved make transportation an important element in their costs. In 1952 the cost of transporting coal from northern France to Paris was about one-fifth the pithead price. At places like Tours and Munich transportation added some 35 per cent to the pithead price of coal. Transportation to Italy from the Ruhr or Lorraine sometimes cost more than the coal itself. The cost of carrying Lorraine iron ore to the north of France was 127 per cent of its price at the mine in 1952; for shipments to the Ruhr in 1955 the figure was over 200 per cent. Even steel, so much more valuable per ton, has high transportation costs. The Belgian steel federation calculated that in 1956 transportation accounted for about 15 per cent of the cost of steel to Belgian users. An earlier rough estimate for the whole Community put the transportation ingredient in the delivered price of rolling-mill products at 20 to 25 per cent.[1]

The cost of transportation made it important to the coal and steel economy of the six countries, but whether transportation cost too much was not a central problem for the Community. It might be, as the rapporteur of the Common Assembly's transportation committee said, that the age of the Community's railroad equipment "often rivals that of cognac of the best quality."[2] If so, the Community was

[1] These figures come, variously, from: HA, *Report*, Jan. 1953, pp. 69, 71; France, Ministère des Affaires Économiques, *Études et Conjoncture, Économie Mondiale*, May-Je. 1953, pp. 205-213; Bruno Calabi, "Piano Schuman e costo dei trasporti delle materie prime (clausole da rivedere e da inserire)," reprint of article in *Rivista di Politica Economica*, May 1952, p. 4; Ferdinand Friedensburg, *Das Erzproblem der Deutschen Eisenindustrie*, 1957, p. 21 (Deutsches Institut für Wirtschaftsforschung, Sonderhefte); Groupement des Hauts-Fourneaux et Aciéries Belges, *Rapport Annuel, 1956*, p. 41 (hereafter cited as Groupement Belge).

[2] ECSC, Common Assembly, Commission des Transports, *Rapport . . . par M. P. J. Kapteijn, Rapporteur*, doc. 14 (1953-54), p. 9 (hereafter the Common Assembly will be cited as "CA").

not in a position to do anything about it. Investment in new rolling stock and improvements in the efficiency of railroad operations were outside its jurisdiction. The great problem for the Community was to end discrimination and remove discrepancies in transport rates that "falsified competition" and "impaired the common market." It was not always easy to say what practices would satisfy the Community's needs but the direction in which it would have to move was clear. Until one looks at some examples it is hard to believe how confusing the structure of railroad freight rates was, even if road and water transportation are left out of the picture for the time being.

To start with, there were sizable differences among the countries in the money cost of transportation. The railroads of Luxembourg charged three times as much to haul coal 50 kilometers as did the railroads of Holland; for 100 kilometers the French and German rates were more than twice the Italian. On steel sheets there was also a 100 per cent spread within the Community and in iron ore the highest Community rate was 3.5 times the lowest. Over a stretch of 300 kilometers the freight rate per ton-kilometer for hauling iron ore was 3.49 francs in France and 1.40 in Germany. A ton of coke traveling that distance in Germany paid 866 francs while in France the rate was 1,069.[3]

The national railroads also differed from one another in the relation they maintained between the rates for carrying coal, steel, and iron ore. The German Bundesbahn charged 51 per cent more for carrying finished steel products 150 kilometers than for carrying coal, while in France the cost was only 11 per cent higher. In Germany coke paid the same rate as coal, while in other Community countries the coke rate was 5 to 44 per cent above the coal rate. Scrap was more expensive to transport than coal in

---

[3] Same, p. 8; Jean Chardonnet, *La Sidérurgie Française: Progrès ou Décadence?*, 1954, p. 165; Willi Scheider, *Die Tarifpolitik der Hohen Behörde und das Deutsche Verkehrswesen*, 1954, p. 51. The last of these has full tables for coal and rolled steel as of November 1955. The other examples are for different periods; this is true of many of the figures cited in this section, but does not falsify the picture.

Belgium, France, and Germany, but cheaper in Italy, Luxembourg and the Netherlands.[4] On the German stretch of the run between the Ruhr and Lorraine the rate on iron ore was 45 per cent of that for coking coal while on the much shorter French stretch it was 102 per cent.[5] There may also be national differences in the relation of rates for Treaty products to those for other commodities. It has been argued, for instance, that French railway rates penalize the transportation of coal, iron ore, and scrap for the benefit of other traffic, while Belgian and German rates do the reverse.[6] Additional divergences resulted from different national rules regarding rebates for large quantities, regular shipment, the use of whole trains, private sidings, and a host of other factors.

Of the greatest immediate importance to the Community were the freight rates applied to goods moving from one country to another which were markedly higher than those charged domestically. Examples from major segments of trade will show how things stood when the Community came into being.

Iron ore shipped from Sancy, in Lorraine, to Azincourt in the Nord-Pas de Calais steelmaking area of France cost 631 francs per ton for a trip of 284 kilometers, while a shipment from Sancy to Ougrée-Marihaye in Belgium paid 850 francs to travel 211 kilometers.

Coke moving from the Pas de Calais to Lorraine bore freight costs of 776 francs per ton over the 340 kilometers from Lens to Homécourt, while if it came to Homécourt from Gelsenkirchen in the Ruhr, 363 kilometers away, transportation cost 2,463 francs—over three times as much to move about 7 per cent farther.

But if the coke went from Gelsenkirchen to Rosenberghütte in Bavaria—a distance of 562 kilometers but all

---

[4] Scheider, cited, Table 3, p. 54. All these rates are for 150 kilometers according to the standard schedules as of November 1955, except the Luxembourg figures which are for 100 kilometers.

[5] HA, *Report*, Apr. 1954, p. 118.

[6] Chardonnet, cited, p. 165; André Armengaud, "Der Schumanplan im Ersten Stadium," *Aussenpolitik*, Nov. 1952, pp. 712-720.

inside Germany—the freight rate was 1,813 francs per ton—
25 per cent less to go more than half as far again.

Rolling-mill products coming from Athus in southern
Belgium to Antwerp, a major port for overseas exports,
paid a freight rate of 184 Belgian francs per ton to cover
254 kilometers. But if they came from a steel mill at
Rodange, only 3 kilometers farther away, they paid 230
francs, because Rodange is in Luxembourg. And if the
rolling-mill products had to be carried three kilometers
farther, from Mont-St. Martin in Lorraine, the freight rate
was 317 francs—over 70 per cent more than that for the
Belgian product.[7]

A complete array of discrepancies between the rates for
national and international hauls would show a complex
tangle involving differences according to routes, frontier
stations, ownership of freight cars, the character of their
load, its destination, and many other factors. One thing was
uniform, however: it always cost more to ship coal and
steel by rail across national boundaries than to carry them
an equal distance inside one country.

THE SOURCE OF THE DIFFICULTIES

The root of these remarkable differences was obvious
enough: each country had developed its own freight rate
structure in its own way. There are few commonly accepted methods of setting rates; cost of service, value of
goods, "what the traffic will bear" (or not bear), and a
collection of other principles all point in different directions. Probably no country followed any set of principles
rigorously, but altered practice to suit circumstance,
custom, political pressure, and specific aims. Emphasis
might be on the income of the carrier, but was more likely
to be on aims of national policy. The location of industry,
the encouragement of certain areas, the army's view of
strategic requirements, and a series of other factors shaped
national transportation practice. All the railroads of the
Community were run by governments, but practices

---

[7] HA, *Report*, Jan. 1953, p. 72; *Report*, Apr. 1953, p. 60.

differed as to their finances, and also as to the way the competition of trucks and barges should be met.

The freight rates for coal and steel and iron ore with which the Community was concerned were embedded in these divergent, complex national rate structures. These goods were also often affected by "special rates"—departures from the general rate-making practice to serve specific purposes. Low rates might be used to subsidize certain areas, to encourage their development, or to promote traffic along certain routes. Sometimes the aim was to put certain producers or consumers on an equal footing with others in the country. In Germany, for instance, coal and steel from the Ruhr moved to south Germany at especially low rates. Districts near the eastern frontier were supplied at special rates to compensate these places for their severance from the Soviet Zone. Blast furnaces outside the Ruhr got coal at special rates to put them on a more even footing with the main centers of iron and steel production. Throughout the Community goods moving to ports for sale overseas often benefited from special rates.

The apparent confusion of freight rates was not altogether the accidental result of separate national development. An important element in some of the coal and steel rates was protection of national producers and penalization of foreigners. Competing imports were apt to have to pay high rates; exports might be aided by low rates, or charged high rates to raise a foreign producer's costs; certain domestic shipments might move at low rates to offset a foreign competitor's geographical advantage. In short, freight rates were used in the same ways as tariffs and subsidies.

The difference between the cost of national and international rail transportation over equal distances was the product of many practices, some general and some limited to particular kinds of transactions. The largest part of the extra burden on international traffic was, however, due to three main factors: discriminatory rates, double (or triple) terminal charges, and the related practice of treating an international trip as if it were two (or more) national trips. The discrimination was simple and overt: foreign goods, or goods headed for a foreign destination, were often charged higher rates than domestic products. The extra terminal charges implied the fiction that when goods crossed a national frontier they were unloaded from the train they were on and reloaded on a new one. Thus the complete "terminal charge" for loading at the beginning and unloading at the end of a journey, which is a normal element in the freight rate, was paid for every country through which the shipment passed. These terminal charges are not negligible but ordinarily account for an appreciable part of the total freight bill.[8] The third extra burden had a somewhat similar basis. All Community railroads charge lower rates per kilometer on long trips than on short ones. The longer the trip the more the rate falls. But this degression stops at the national frontier. That is as far as the national railway rate schedules run. Then the other country's rates take effect and the trip is treated as a wholly new one; the distance a train has come is ignored and it starts paying the rate at the top of the schedule. Thus a 300-kilometer trip that crosses a border at mid-point benefits from degressive rates only in two 150-kilometer slices instead of getting the benefit of the greater degressivity that would apply in either country to a 300-kilometer trip.

Looked at in terms of their origins, the transport rates and practices remain complex and confusing, but a rough order seems to emerge; those which have the most direct impact on the common market seem, at least superficially, to be those that should be least difficult to deal with. Flagrant national discrimination and practices that directly burden international trade with heavier charges than domestic trade are obviously offensive to the concept of the Community and, in principle at least, should be susceptible to fairly direct treatment. But measures that either result from domestic rate-making practices or are alleged to serve some

[8] As of November 1955, on a shipment of coal over 100 kilometers, terminal charges ranged from 19 per cent of the total freight charge in Germany and Italy to 47 per cent in the Netherlands. The French and Belgian rates were 33 and 31 per cent respectively. Scheider, cited, p. 129.

domestic purpose, can only be treated more circumspectly. First there is a problem of determining whether they actually infringe the principles of the common market; second, there remains the problem of finding ways to deal with them that are compatible with the fact that the rest of each transport rate system is to remain national. The importance of trade in Treaty products made this problem more difficult rather than easier. Coal, steel, scrap and iron ore accounted for about half the total volume of transportation within the Community, by road, rail and water, and for about 40 per cent of the freight receipts.[9] Obviously, therefore, what was done about Community trade might have a major impact on the receipts and operations of the whole transportation system of each country. This in itself would increase the resistance to changes that might be acceptable if nothing but Community business were in question. Yet, as a Dutch member of the Assembly put it, the High Authority's task was to "bring forth from *l'Arlésienne, Tannhäuser,* and even *Ciribiribin* a new symphonic poem, conceived perhaps in the style of Honegger; but I should like it if they would give us an assurance as soon as possible that this will not be a matter of be-bop." [10]

THE TREATY AND ITS IMPLEMENTATION

The Treaty deals with transport in one article of five paragraphs. After stating the general principle quoted at the beginning of this chapter, Article 70 specifies that national discrimination in rates or conditions of transport is forbidden; the same rates must be applied to goods moving in foreign trade as to those in domestic trade. "Special rates" used in behalf of coal and steel producers are dealt with separately. The High Authority is to "ensure that such measures are in accordance with the principles of this Treaty; it may give a temporary or conditional agreement."

The article concludes with a paragraph explicitly recognizing the major role of governments in transportation

[9] HA, Information Service, *Transport in the Community,* Sept. 1, 1955, p. 7.
[10] CA, *Débats,* Je. 16, 1953, p. 76 (Kapteyn).

matters. Subject to the Treaty provisions, "commercial policy for transport, in particular the fixing and modification of rates and conditions of transport of any type as well as the arrangement of transport prices required to assure the financial equilibrium of the transport enterprises themselves, remains subject to the legislative or administrative provisions of each of the member States; the same is true for the measures of coordination or competition among different types of transport or among different routes."

The need that the drafters felt to include this paragraph, and the brevity of other passages specifying forbidden practices in very general terms, are the marks of partial integration. Authority for the Community's action on transport rates was being shared between governments and the High Authority and no one was quite sure where the greater power would lie in practice. The theme is continued in Section 16 of the transitional Convention which provides the means for applying the Treaty rules.[11] The initial step was for the High Authority to convene "a Commission of experts chosen by the governments" who were to study the problems and suggest arrangements which the High Authority would propose to the governments. The initiative in negotiations within the Community and with third countries is to lie with the High Authority. Throughout the section there are reminders that most matters are left to the governments to decide.

The Convention set three main tasks for the commission of experts:

[11] The Treaty also stipulates that freight rates and other transport charges should be published "or brought to the knowledge of the High Authority," a weaker provision than the Treaty's general rule about publishing prices. The explanation given was that privately negotiated rates might be needed to meet the competition of other forms of transportation. Such cases were reported in Italy, the Netherlands and France. No one seemed to attach any great importance to these instances. Later, however, there were complaints that lack of publicity made it impossible for users to make an intelligent choice of methods and routes of transportation. There was also some suspicion that private rates might conceal discrimination. In attacking the difficult problem of truck transportation, the High Authority gave first place to publication of rates.

in three months they were to propose measures to eliminate discriminatory practices, which were to come into effect at the time the common market for coal was established;

in two years they were to draw up international through-rates "which take into account the total distance and are degressive, yet do not prejudice the distribution of charges among the transport enterprises concerned";

also in two years they were to examine the problem of "harmonizing" transportation rates "as far as may be necessary for proper functioning of the common market. . . ."

The latter two sets of measures were to come into effect simultaneously when the governments accepted them. But if there was no agreement on harmonization in two and a half years, through-rates were to come into effect on a date set by the High Authority. Thus, while discrimination was dealt with as brusquely as trade barriers had been, through-rates were postponed,[12] and harmonization was treated as if it might not be achieved at all. Meanwhile, the High Authority was to establish time limits for the modification of the "special rates" that would not lead to serious economic disturbance.[13]

Clearly the application of the transport provisions would depend largely on the commission of experts. Though Dirk Spierenburg of the High Authority adjured them to act as independent experts, not as government officials,[14] one can hardly believe that the members of the commission

---

[12] Interpretations differed as to whether the High Authority could put these measures into effect if the governments did not agree on them by the end of the time limit. Agreement made the matter academic but it remains symptomatic of the difficulties and uncertainties surrounding action on transportation. D. C. Bok, *The First Three Years of the Schuman Plan*, 1955, p. 20, n. 20.

[13] Luxembourg was exempted from the transportation rules until special arrangements could be worked out. The problem was that Luxembourg's transit rates were lower than its domestic rates. To raise the former risked diverting traffic which was an important source of income; to lower the latter would be very costly to the railroads because it would affect so large a part of their business.

[14] *Bulletin des Presse- und Informationsamtes der Bundesregierung* (Bonn), Oct. 25, 1952, p. 1469.

wholly succeeded in divesting themselves of their day-to-day character and, indeed, their official responsibility. In addition to being officials they were also technicians, probably not immune to the technician's fondness for the operation of his own particular machine—and a marvelously intricate one this is. Reluctance to see the neatly arranged and equilibrated operations disturbed would be natural for men who had been in part the designers as well as the operators of these machines. These thirty men must also have carried with them to Luxembourg not only governmental instructions but their normal awareness of the outlook and interests of their national industries as well as their own concern, as transportation officials, with revenue and business.

In an important degree, then, the pattern was one that would have existed in ordinary intergovernmental negotiations. But there was another element: the Treaty with its agreed though sometimes ambiguous goals and the constant supervision and pressure of the High Authority. So far as technical competence was concerned, the High Authority had a transportation division staffed with knowledgeable men, who worked closely with the commission. Its head and his deputy were former officials of the German and French railway systems who undoubtedly knew just as many of the tricks of the trade as their former colleagues in the commission. They knew where to look for the hard problems that had to be dealt with, as well as how much "water" there might be in a particular freight rate (which they might have set themselves). No doubt the High Authority emphasized strict construction of the Treaty, and took the view that the experts' task was only to implement it. To the governments the High Authority presumably held up the mirror of failure and the charge of subterfuge if they refused to carry out the spirit of the great new enterprise they had solemnly ratified. It cannot be assumed that the governments or their experts were necessarily opposed to all the changes the Treaty seemed to require. Each nation stood to gain as well as to lose by the reforms; having cast their lot with the common market, the countries had to change their pattern of behavior to take advantage of it; sometimes there were domestic interests in favor of the changes as well as others opposing them; technicians can satisfy themselves building and working new machines as well as driving the familiar ones.

The commission did some of its work quickly, much of it more slowly. Enough has transpired from these private sessions to indicate that some of the delay stemmed, as was to be expected, from reluctance to yield a point of national transportation policy or from consideration of the views of interested parties in various countries. The conceptual problems of applying the rather simple standards of the Treaty to the rich complexity of the transportation systems troubled the experts and led to a good bit of intellectual elaboration, quite warranted in many ways but not conducive to the quickest action. One must not, however, conclude that it was only the intergovernmental or expert character of the commission that helped slow matters. The pace on the special rates, where the High Authority could act directly, was not noticeably more rapid. Whatever the technique, the problems remained complex, and effective action required the consent of governments.

THE REMOVAL OF DISCRIMINATIONS

Three months was not long for the expert commission to deal with discriminations. It accomplished something in that time but completion of the job dragged on a good bit longer. When the common market for coal was opened, the High Authority was able to announce quite an impressive list of changes. For instance, discriminations were ended on such important segments of Community trade as Saar coal moving into south Germany, Lorraine ore moving to Belgium or Germany, and the steel carried by Belgian railways from Lorraine to Antwerp. The transit trade also benefited, especially imports and exports of steel through German ports, Luxembourg steel exports through France, and the movement of coal from Belgium, the Saar, and Lorraine to Austria via the German ports on the upper Danube.

By the end of 1953, the High Authority was able to report "that the abolition of discriminations. . .is absolutely complete, so far as railway transport is concerned."[15] All the findings of the commission of experts had been endorsed by the High Authority and carried out by the governments. Thirty-two discriminations were abolished: 15 in the French rate schedules, 10 in the German, and the rest in Belgium, Italy, and Luxembourg. According to the Assembly's transport committee, some 13 to 15 per cent of the Community's traffic crossed national frontiers, and the amount affected by the elimination of discrimination was 11 to 12 per cent.[16]

The elimination of discrimination did not mean a general lowering of rates. The High Authority made recommendations which, according to the Treaty (Article 14), were binding only as to the end to be achieved, leaving the means up to the governments. Some governments lowered the discriminatory rates to the level charged on domestic trade. Others raised domestic rates toward the higher level, while lowering the discriminatory rate to meet it. In this way the revenue yielded from the traffic could be preserved, in whole or in part, but domestic costs were raised. It was estimated, for instance, that in 1953 the loss in revenue to France from lowering the rate at which iron ore exported to Belgium was carried, was exactly offset by the rise in revenue from internal ore traffic. But since the volume of the latter was so much greater—16.5 million tons compared to 5 million—a rise of only about 4 per cent (on the Sancy-Azincourt run, for instance) could offset a drop of 8 per cent on the export rate (Sancy-Ougrée).[17] The biggest absolute drop—about $2.4 million on the basis of 1953 trade—was in the rates charged on Saar and Lorraine coal entering Germany, where the regular domestic tariff for German coal was applied. On balance there was a net reduction in transportation costs of about $500,000 a year

---

[15] HA, *Report*, Apr. 1954, p. 110.
[16] CA, Commission des Transports, *Rapport . . . par M. J. Fohrmann, Rapporteur*, doc. 9 (1952-53), p. 9.
[17] HA, *Report*, Apr. 1954, p. 111, and *Report*, Apr. 1953, p. 59.

in 1953.[18] In a number of cases transportation rates were cut substantially. Coal from Reden in the Saar to Regensburg in Bavaria was shipped at 16 per cent less after the elimination of the discrimination, a saving of about $1.50 a ton. From Reden to Stuttgart the saving was 9 per cent. (Table 3, p. 171, gives other examples.) But there were also some increases. While the cost of shipping steel products from Lorraine to Antwerp fell by 8 per cent, there was a rise of 21 per cent in the cost of reaching the port from southern Belgium. Discrepancies were reduced, but they had not disappeared. To carry iron ore from Sancy to Ougrée still cost more than the longer trip from Sancy to Azincourt. The freight for coal from the Saar to Ulm fell from 117 per cent of the rate from the Ruhr to 103 per cent, that to Augsburg fell from 130 to 110 per cent—but still the rates did not reflect the fact that the Saar is closer to these south German cities than is the Ruhr.[19] Broken rates and the fictitious frontier unloading were still playing their parts.

Another important segment of Community trade, the shipment of coking coal from the Ruhr to Lorraine, caused more trouble. A year after the common market for coal had come into existence, the French railways were still charging a higher rate for most of the German coal and coke they hauled than for the French product. This arose from the fact that the large rebate normally given by the French railroads for complete trains did not apply to goods coming from abroad. The Germans, in turn, did not give special rates for complete trains. While there were technical difficulties, the bargaining probably was also related to the plan for setting through-rates, on which the Germans were holding out. Agreement was reached after extensive negotiations in which the High Authority played a part; new rates for trainloads were put into effect November 1,

[18] HA, *Report*, Apr. 1954, pp. 111, 112. These estimates are rather rough. The changes affected 45 million tons of traffic, on the basis of 1953 trade, but well over half was the internal ore and coal trade of France and Belgium on which rates were raised.

[19] Scheider, cited, p. 69. Ulm is 207 kilometers nearer the Saar than the Ruhr, and Augsburg 160 kilometers. Other figures from HA *Reports*.

1954.[20] The main result was to lower the amount of subsidies the French were paying on coal imports from the Ruhr (see Chapter 9).

No measurement of the exact effect of the rate changes is possible. As in the case of trade barriers, one cannot isolate the role of single factors in gauging the results of opening the common market. Looking for sustainable estimates, the High Authority concluded:

There is particular evidence of a clear increase in exports of iron ore from Lorraine, and it is also clear that coal trade between the countries of the Community has been considerably stimulated by the abolition of many discriminatory practices which affected it. Finally there has been an undoubted influence also on the direction taken by export flows of iron and steel products.[21]

The statement seems too strong, even though it is prefaced by a warning about the difficulty of allowing for other factors. The flow of Lorraine iron ore to Belgium was probably largely a response to the removal of French administrative impediments to exports,[22] and perhaps to price changes. The saving in freight on coal moving in and out of France and the Saar probably showed itself mainly in a reduction of the subsidies paid by the French government. A study of other movements of Community goods on the German railways showed a few increases attributable to the changes in freight rates.[23] Still, there were undoubtedly cases in which the elimination of discrimination affected volume and routing of trade as well as prices. Perhaps more important, the end of discrimination laid the groundwork for future trade development. Like the removal of trade barriers it was a change in the conditions within which the coal and steel industries of the Community were to function.

[20] HA, *Report*, Apr. 1954, pp. 117-118; *Report*, Nov. 1954, p. 92; CA, Commission des Transports, *Rapport . . . par M. Paul J. Kapteyn, Rapporteur*, doc. 15 (1954-55), May 1955, p. 23.
[21] HA, *Report*, Apr. 1954, p. 112 (italics in original omitted).
[22] Groupment Belge, cited, p. 30.
[23] Scheider, cited, pp. 71-72.

THROUGH-RATES

The governments did not sign a formal agreement on through-rates until the spring of 1955. While technical problems contributed to the delay, the main trouble was probably the resistance of groups in each country who did not want to see a lowering of the delivered price of foreign goods in areas they had formerly supplied, and the reluctance of national railway administrations to accept the loss of revenue and changes in their rate structure. One of the principal obstacles was the resistance of the German representatives to measures that would eliminate the special treatment of coal and steel sales to south Germany. Compromise on this issue seems to have cleared the way for agreement in the commission of experts. Then the governments negotiated and in January 1955 the Council of Ministers agreed on the terms of an understanding that was signed in March.

The key features of the agreement were:[24]

As of May 1, 1955, for coal, coke, and iron ore, and as of May 1, 1956, for iron and steel products and scrap, through-rates were to be applied on international shipments. Over the whole length of the trip the rate to be applied would be the average of the national rates for a trip equal to the whole distance, weighted according to the amount of the journey in each country.

When the through-rates came into effect, the terminal fee of each sending and receiving country would be reduced by one-third and that of transit countries by two-thirds. A year later the only terminal fee would be half the total fee of the sending and receiving countries; no terminal fees would be paid on goods in transit. Thus the fictitious loading and unloading at the frontier would be abolished.

The degressivity—but not the basic rate—was standardized

[24] This is a somewhat simplified account, omitting some relatively minor exceptions, procedural provisions for changing the rules, and the potential significance of certain fairly technical matters. See the text in *JO,* Apr. 10, 1955, pp. 701-713, and Scheider's discussion, cited, pp. 43-49 and elsewhere. The agreement was amended in 1956, largely to extend special treatment to Italy and to apply the through-rates to goods of third countries moving through the Community. *JO,* Apr. 30, 1956, p. 130.

for all trips, internal or international, up to 250 kilometers in the case of coal and iron ore and 200 kilometers in the case of steel. On longer trips the rate of degression had to remain within a margin fixed by international agreement. This did not require any great change in rates of degressivity. There was already a good bit of uniformity over the shorter runs. Over the longer runs the margin permitted countries to maintain their existing coefficients of degression.

The main accomplishment of this agreement was to end the penalization of international traffic. This was undoubtedly an important step in creating the common market. It opened additional possibilities for international trade and put competing sellers who were in different countries on a more nearly equal basis than before.[25] Geography made a gain over politics.

The arrangement on degression was a compromise. Within the 200-250 kilometer range in which degression was to be uniform, Community producers (and consumers) were put on an equal basis, regardless of national frontiers. Uniformity was not applied over a longer range because, in the words of the High Authority, "the standardization of the degression might lead to a disturbance of the economic structure of some member States."[26] That is to say, it would have opened wider areas to more intense competition and dislocated traditional currents of trade and national transport rate structures. The agreement left governments free to retain, or to manipulate within fairly wide limits, rates of degressivity that gave advantages to national producers. For instance, by sharply falling rates, the Germans could help the Ruhr compete in south Germany against the closer producers of Lorraine and the Saar. By adopting rates that declined only gradually, the French could give the mines of the Nord and Pas de Calais an advantage over German shipments to Paris. Low degressivity added to the natural protection which distance gave Italian steel pro-

---

[25] They were still not completely equal because the freight cost, combining two sets of rates, would vary according to the length of the journey in each country.

[26] HA, *Report*, Nov. 1954, p. 94.

ducers against imports from the Ruhr and Lorraine. The agreement enhanced this protective feature for some countries, notably Germany, by setting lower limits to the coefficient of degression that had to be applied to international traffic. In some circumstances this could have the effect of restoring the situation that would have existed without

Table 3

EFFECT OF RATE REFORMS ON COST OF TRANSPORTATION

RATE BEFORE COMMON MARKET = 100

Traffic	Rate after abolishing discrimination	Rate after introduction of through-rates	
		Partial[a]	Complete[b]
Coke—Ruhr to Lorraine (Gelsenkirchen-Homécourt)	85[c]	73	69
Coking fines—Ruhr to Saar (Alsdorf-Saarbrücken/Burbach)	91	77	74
Coal—Saar to South Germany (Reden-Regensburg)	83	76	70
Iron ore—Lorraine to Belgium (Sancy-Ougrée)	92	79	71
Semi-finished steel products— Lorraine to South Germany (Thionville-Stuttgart)	100	87	82
Finished steel products—Ruhr to Paris (Oberhausen-Paris)	98	86	82

a. May 1, 1955, for raw materials; May 1, 1956, for steel.
b. May 1, 1956, for raw materials; May 1, 1957, for steel.
c. About 5 per cent due to changes other than abolition of discrimination.

NOTE:
These rates apply to particular modes of shipment; see sources for details. Some of the rates show changes between or after these dates as well.

SOURCES:
Calculated from HA, *Report*, Apr. 1955, Table 29, pp. 108-109 (raw materials), and *Bulletin Mensuel d'Information*, Je. 1957, Annexe Statistique, Table 5 (steel).

the establishment of through-rates (except for the elimination of terminal charges).[27] However, the rule that uniform degressivity had to apply to domestic and foreign goods seemed likely to cover most Community traffic.

The agreement on through-rates also had the effect of reducing freight charges on international shipments. There were no offsetting factors such as the raising of domestic rates when discriminations were abolished. Table 3 gives a few examples of the rate reductions on major segments of Community trade resulting from both sets of reforms. The savings are substantial: in the neighborhood of 30 per cent for raw materials and 20 per cent for steel. The relative importance of ending discrimination and of applying the through-rates varies considerably—a further reminder of the difficulty of generalizing about measures in this field.[28] However, through-rates on coal and iron seem to have accounted for about two-thirds of the drop in freight changes, compared to one-third for the elimination of discriminations. On steel, the through-rates accounted for almost all of the changes. Scheider's detailed study of German freight rates yields a somewhat similar result. Applying the full introduction of through-rates and the elimination of frontier charges to 1953 trade, he estimates the total annual loss of income to the Bundesbahn would be DM 28.3 million, mostly in the coal trade. By the same method, the loss from the elimination of discrimination works out at DM 11 million.[29]

[27] Scheider, cited, p. 93. His exposition at various points in his book of the relation between German degressivities and the application of the standard rates proposed in Luxembourg is very helpful.

[28] It must also be borne in mind that these figures cannot be applied to all Community trade. Even for the traffic to which they refer differences in quantities and form of shipment (complete trains, single cars, etc.) could alter the figures. However, they are probably typical of much of the traffic. Groupement Belge, cited, p. 42, says that the changes in through-rates made in 1956 saved about 10 per cent in the cost of transporting Lorraine iron ore, a figure that fits closely with that in the table.

[29] Scheider, cited, pp. 75, 76, 95-105, especially Tables 13, 17, 19. Of course, this is not an actual loss. Trade had increased by the time the through-rates came into effect and would have made up at least part of the difference. However, when the subsidy for the Belgian railways was

Though their effects are impossible to calculate in any detail, the elimination of discrimination and the introduction of through-rates were important steps for the Community. They moved directly toward a more rational division of labor in the Community industries. They made an important contribution to the creation of a common market. They went only a limited distance, however, and had done that rather painfully. Many problems remained and the process of dealing with them was no easier.

SPECIAL RATES

Passing on special rates was the exclusive province of the High Authority, but this part of the work proved as difficult and laborious as that directly involving governments. It was not just a matter of looking at a few exceptional arrangements; a large part of the Community traffic moved under what were at least technically special rates. Even definition created problems.[30] To decide whether a rate was "special" implied some grasp of the general principles on which a country's rates were based. As the Assembly's transport committee remarked, "It is difficult to discover a fundamental concept followed consecutively to serve as the basis for a transport policy of the countries. This policy gives generally the impression of having often been built up of solutions to particular problems." [31] Once some criteria had been developed by the commission of experts, the problem still remained of deciding whether each case fell under the Treaty. Only then could the High Authority

increased by 264 million francs between 1955 and 1956, this was largely ascribed to the loss of income resulting from the Community's rate reforms. Agence Internationale d'Information pour la Presse, "Europe" (Luxembourg), Nov. 3, 1955.

[30] Scheider estimates that three-quarters of the traffic on the Bundesbahn moves under special rates. His definition is, however, broad: "The general rate includes freight charges for *all* goods and is applicable to *all* routes, while the special rates are valid only for the shipment of individual, exactly specified, goods and between specified points of shipment and receipt that are named in the schedule" (p. 114).

[31] CA, Commission des Transports, *Rapport . . . par M. P. J. Kapteijn, Rapporteur*, doc. 14 (1953-54), p. 11.

decide whether the rate was compatible with the Treaty, and, if not, how quickly it should be modified.

The ending of national discrimination removed some of the problems. The Bundesbahn had carried steel plates for shipbuilding at German ports at 30 per cent below the regular rate and steel products for export by sea at rates that fell to half the normal schedule over long distances. In these cases applying the domestic tariff to Community products largely eliminated the "special rate" problem, as it did for the importation of Saar and Lorraine coal to south Germany. In the same area steel from France and the Saar got added advantages by being permitted to share in a system of German rail rebates that sometimes gave buyers a premium for buying from foreign sources.[32] There were cases, though, in which eliminating discrimination meant little because foreign producers could not effectively take part in the business, usually for geographical reasons. Special rates for exports or for goods in transit were "particularly delicate" according to the transportation experts,[33] since they had been set by considerations of the national economy and were now to be judged by Community principles. Rates involving competition between means of transportation were held to be matters for each government, but it was not always easy to decide whether this kind of competition was really the exclusive purpose of a special rate.

[32] German steelworking industries get back the difference between the transportation cost of the steel they buy and the rate to a point 220 kilometers from Oberhausen in the Ruhr. The money comes from a fund to which all German steel-buyers (including those beyond the 220-kilometer radius) pay DM 3.25 for each ton of steel they buy. When transport discriminations were ended, the purchasers in southern Germany continued to receive the same rebates, calculated on Oberhausen, even if they bought steel from Lorraine or the Saar. Thus firms nearer Thionville than Oberhausen could have a larger part of their freight charges subsidized than before. There were even cases where buyers received more than they paid in freight charges. Harald Jürgensen, *Die Westeuropäische Montanindustrie und Ihr Gemeinsamer Markt*, 1955, pp. 170-174.

[33] CA, Commission des Transports, *Rapport . . . par M. J. Fohrmann, Rapporteur*, doc. 9 (1952-53), p. 21 (HA annex).

By the spring of 1956 the commission of experts had decided that 215 rates were "special" and indicated which it thought offended Treaty principles. The High Authority began working through this list by commodities, beginning with scrap and proceeding through steel and iron ore to coal. It made a few recommendations to the French and German governments on scrap and steel rates but delayed taking any action on the core of the problem, which lay in a series of French and German special rates for coal and iron ore. These were rather touchy matters, especially some of the German rates. The French complained increasingly about the German practice of providing a low rate for coal going to steel mills outside the Ruhr. The differences involved were substantial: shipments to Bavarian steelworks paid 21 per cent less than the regular rate, to plants in the Sieg-Lahn-Dill area 27 per cent, and those to Lower Saxony (notably to the Salzgitter works) as much as 70 per cent, partly because of the competition of canal traffic. The French argued that this practice discriminated against Lorraine and the Saar where steel mills had to pay higher charges on Ruhr coal moving over equal distances. Though the French may have felt some competition from the German steel firms outside the Ruhr, their primary aim was probably to lower the cost of Ruhr coal in Lorraine.[34] Following its usual policy of seeking agreement before acting, the High Authority apparently tried to work out compromises but was unsuccessful.[35] In February 1958, it asserted its authority and ruled that a whole series of French and German railroad rates were discriminatory and therefore violated the Treaty. For each rate it announced a formula for removal, most of them providing for gradual

[34] In 1953, Lower Saxony produced 8 per cent of Germany's rolled steel, Bavaria 3.8 per cent, and Württemberg-Baden and Hesse together .8 per cent. Figures for raw steel were lower, except for Lower Saxony, which was 9.1 per cent. The southern districts provided 3.5 per cent of the German rolled-steel exports in 1953 and Lower Saxony 10.5 per cent. Jürgensen, cited, pp. 163-164.

[35] The French may also have approached the German government directly. R. Hellmann, "Die Montanunion wird umgegangen," *Der Volkswirt*, Aug. 24, 1957, pp. 1890, 1891.

elimination of the discriminatory margin, usually over a period of two to four years.

The High Authority's decision applied to the German rates for steelworks outside the Ruhr mentioned above and also to a series of rates for the carriage of German iron ore at 16 to 45 per cent less than the rate for foreign ore. However the Germans were allowed to keep several special rates that favored districts along the frontier of the Soviet Zone. The French rates that fell under the High Authority's ban were of several sorts. The steel firms of the Centre and Midi had been getting coal at 18 to 35 per cent less than the regular freight rate; a preference of 15 to 20 per cent was given to coal from the south to enable it to compete on the Paris market. The iron mines in the west and in the Pyrenees had the advantage of low rates for various deliveries. All these were to be ended. The French were permitted to keep, for the time being at least, low rates for the shipment of coal from the Midi and the Centre to various places on the Atlantic coast south of the Loire.[36]

The decision brought on a storm. Soon a substantial number of French and German firms and the German government had challenged the High Authority's action in the Court. The firms in central and southern France were asking to be allowed to keep their special rates. In northern France and Lorraine the steel companies, with the backing of their government, were contending that the proper solution was not to raise the rates applying to areas outside the Ruhr but to extend them to France. The German government argued that there was no discrimination under their system since the companies were in unique situations not shared by others in the Community. It considered that the High Authority had not taken sufficient account of the effect of the partition of Germany on Bavaria and Lower Saxony. "In the opinion of the Federal Government, the High Authority should not make a reasoned policy on the location of industry impossible, quite apart from the fact

[36] This rate was introduced in the fall of 1954 and temporarily authorized by the High Authority on various grounds. It is to be ended on July 31, 1961. *JO*, Dec. 18, 1958, p. 670.

that it is required by explicit provision of the Treaty to take care that no interruption of employment or fundamental and continued disturbance in the economic life of the member countries occurs."[37]

The stakes were high. For the companies affected, elimination of the special rates would be important to their costs of production and their competitive position. For the Community economy, the measure might have an appreciable long-run effect on the allocation of resources. For the High Authority, the case might be a fairly serious test of its ability to make decisions stick that were widely unpopular, and to which the governments had not agreed. For the Community's transportation policy, the elimination of these major special rates seemed a significant step in the direction already taken by the action on through-rates and discriminations; some new principles would also have been enshrined in precedents. If, as the conflicts between governments and within industry suggested, a compromise solution was worked out, it would be a slight additional step toward the hazy goal of harmonization.

WATER TRANSPORTATION

Railroads were clearly in the minds of those who drafted the Treaty's provisions about transportation. But waterways are also important to the Community; they carry about one-fifth of its internal traffic in coal and steel. The Rhine carries more freight than any other route in the Community. Coal and steel are also important to inland water transport. In the early '50s, Treaty products accounted for 45 per cent of the Rhine traffic and 70 per cent of all German

[37] Statement by the German transport ministry, *Bulletin des Presse- und Informationsamtes der Bundesregierung*, Feb. 21, 1958, p. 306. There were rumors that if the first court cases failed the German government might invoke Article 37 which would lead to a full-dress re-examination of the decision by the High Authority, the Council of Ministers, and perhaps the Court, on the grounds that a fundamental and persistent disturbance in the German economy was alleged. Similarly the French government was reported to be considering action under Article 35 (involving the High Authority and the Court) on the ground that the High Authority had failed to take action required by the Treaty. *Der Volkswirt*, May 10, 1958, pp. 808, 809.

river and canal traffic. Even in Holland, where canals are more generally used than elsewhere, the carriage of coal and steel amounted to 27 per cent of the total canal business.[38]

As in the case of railroads, there was some national discrimination in water transport. Part of this was eliminated when the common market was opened; some undoubtedly remains, wrapped up in systems of national control, cabotage rules, and flag discrimination, that have been left untouched by the Treaty. The main problem, however, is a rate structure quite different from that of the railroads. Domestic water traffic is regulated by each government; rates are fixed and often cargoes are allocated among carriers. Rates for international traffic, however, are for the most part not regulated and respond to supply and demand. As a result, at one time an international shipment may cost less than a shorter domestic shipment over the same route— the reverse of the railroad problem—and at another time it may be more costly than a domestic run of equal distance— a situation analogous to that of the railways. In July 1954, for instance, steel could be shipped 719 kilometers from Liège to Heilbronn in southern Germany for DM 9.66 per ton, while steel from the Ruhr paid DM 10.78 to cover the 468 kilometers from Duisburg to Heilbronn by water.[39] In 1953 coal moving up the Rhine from Ruhrort to Mannheim paid DM 7.55 in freight, while to carry it from the mouth of the river at Rotterdam to Mannheim cost only DM 5. Later, the market shifted and international rates became higher than the domestic ones or sometimes carried the latter with them.[40]

The Rhine presents a special problem. For almost a century, Rhine navigation has been subject to some degree of

[38] CA, Commission des Transports, *Rapport . . . par M. P. J. Kapteijn, Rapporteur*, doc. 14 (1953-54), p. 10.

[39] The rate per ton-kilometer for the international trip was 1.34 pfennig, and for the purely German stretch 2.45. At the same time, internal Belgian water traffic between Antwerp and steel centers around Liège paid about 2.49 pfennig per ton-kilometer for runs in the neighborhood of 140 kilometers. Scheider, cited, p. 82.

[40] CA, Commission des Transports, *Rapport . . . par M. Paul J. Kapteyn, Rapporteur*, doc. 15 (1955-56), Je. 1956, p. 15.

international regulation. There has been a good bit of legal discussion as to the extent to which action under the Schuman Plan Treaty may be inhibited by the Act of Mannheim of 1868. The older document emphasizes freedom of navigation from Basle to the sea, but also permits each government to reserve cabotage to vessels of its own flag. What has resulted is national regulation of domestic trade and agreements among ship operators and users on international rates. Those engaged in the trade look on the Act of Mannheim as guaranteeing them against governmental interference and, *a fortiori,* supragovernmental interference.[41]

The Community has made little progress in handling the problems of water transport. The commission of experts decided at an early stage that the rate problem, though it gave rise to discrimination, would have to be treated as part of the question of "harmonization" because any solution would require the action of several governments. The High Authority was left in the position of prodding the governments, who moved slowly.

In the High Authority's view, the main issue was equality. This could be achieved either by extending to international traffic a control system like that employed internally or by freeing internal traffic from controls. As early as 1954 it was clear that neither of these drastic approaches was acceptable to the governments. As a compromise measure the High Authority suggested that international rates be subjected to some kind of international control to keep them within agreed maximum and minimum limits.

A majority of the Community governments favored the proposals made by the Conference of Transport Ministers.[42]

[41] For instance, the Rotterdam Chamber of Commerce objected on these grounds when the High Authority opened conversations within the governments of the Community and Switzerland, a party to the Act of Mannheim. *Neue Zürcher Zeitung,* Apr. 19, 1956.

[42] This body, created in 1953 and linked to the OEEC, was an attempt to pick up the pieces of—or, more charitably, to take concrete steps to implement in a realistic fashion—proposals for a European transport pool that were contemporaneous with the Schuman Plan. For a time the

For the Rhine, these called for agreements among ship operators and users to iron out disparities. For the other waterways, there would be similar action and also an intergovernmental agreement involving some funds for equalizing costs. The High Authority, with strong backing in the Assembly, regarded the Rhine proposal as unacceptable because it simply encouraged a cartel and yielded the responsibility for providing the conditions called for by the Treaty. The proposal for the other waterways seemed inadequate since it did not guarantee any steps that would effectively remove the discrepancies between international and domestic rates.

In June 1957 the Council of Ministers reached agreement on the Rhine. Reaffirming the Act of Mannheim's principle of nonintervention, the governments undertook to adjust their domestic rates to conform to international rate schedules worked out by the shipping companies and their customers. If there were difficulties, the governments would confer to adapt the new arrangements to meet these problems. The High Authority was left somewhat in the position of an observer but made it clear that the Treaty principles still applied to Rhine shipping. As agent for the governments it undertook negotiations with the Swiss who are important Rhine shippers to see if they could be brought into the new agreement.[43]

On other matters of water transportation, nothing happened. The governments continued to discuss the matter; the High Authority continued to urge them on.[44]

Community governments delayed any action on water rates to let the Conference carry on the work. Not enough was accomplished so the Council of Ministers again took up the discussion.

[43] *JO*, Feb. 1, 1958, pp. 49-52. The agreement went into effect May 1, 1958. An agreement with Switzerland was concluded in 1958.

[44] Though a basic solution eluded it, the High Authority was called on to handle several specific problems arising from water transportation. Some have been mentioned in the previous chapter. A classic example of the discrepancy of domestic and internal rates appeared in 1953. It was cheaper to ship coal to Paris by barge from Belgium than from Lille. The French government established an equalization scheme under which Belgian cargoes were to pay into a fund the difference between their transport charges and the sum of the domestic Belgian and French rates for the same distance. The High Authority ruled that this was a con-

Canalization of the Moselle

Since heavy goods can usually be carried more cheaply by water than by rail, the prospect of the common market stirred the interest of producers in the adequacy of their national waterways compared to those of other countries. This was particularly true in France where the coal and steel regions are less well served by canals and rivers than are the Ruhr and Belgium. The French steel federation subscribed as "a veritable necessity" to the slogan, "*Mettre la sidérurgie française sur l'eau.*" [45] New canals were asked for, especially between the Nord-Pas de Calais area and Lorraine and from the Nord to Paris.[46] The biggest issue, however, has been the canalization of the Moselle.

Rising on the western slope of the Vosges, the Moselle flows through the heart of the Lorraine iron and steel industry, past Nancy, Metz, and Thionville. After forming part of the border between the Saar and Luxembourg, and then between Germany and Luxembourg, it completes its course entirely in Germany, emptying into the Rhine at Koblenz. Inside France the Moselle is canalized over almost 200 kilometers and supported in part by a parallel canal; it carries important commercial traffic and gives Thionville access to Paris and Strasbourg. Between Thionville and the Rhine the Moselle is a matter of scenery, wine, and the ruins of Constantine's northern capital at Trier.

---

cealed import tax which must be ended. The French government objected that it was only correcting a distortion and a compromise solution was reached with a reduction of the payment to be made by Belgian cargoes (to 10 per cent less than the combined domestic rates). The rules applied also to imports by water from the Netherlands; the compromise proposal was extended to imports from Germany. The High Authority's description of this episode (*Report*, Apr. 1955, pp. 112-113) is slightly different from and less precise than this account which comes largely from Charbonnages de France, *Rapport de Gestion*, 1955, p. 35.

[45] Chambre Syndicale de la Sidérurgie Française, *La Sidérurgie Française en 1956*, Je. 21, 1957, p. 21.

[46] *Le Figaro*, Nov. 1, 1954, reports the demand of collieries in the Nord for better access to Paris, including increased electrification and improved railroad service. Chardonnet, cited, pp. 189-199, discusses the whole question of French waterways interestingly and at length and sketches a series of proposed new canals.

When the Assembly voted to ratify the Schuman Plan
Treaty, it called on the government to press for the canalization of the lower Moselle, and the government agreed.
It was an old ambition in Lorraine to provide a direct
water route to the Rhine that would reduce the cost of
importing Ruhr coke and of sending Lorraine steel to the
sea at Rotterdam.[47] The advantages for Germany, where
most of the canalization would take place, were less obvious. The Ruhr saw no advantage in lowering Lorraine's
raw material costs; the French had to buy Ruhr coke and
coal anyhow. The canalization would improve France's
competitive position in overseas markets and bring French
steel into the German market more cheaply. The Ruhr
showed little interest in cutting the cost of the *minette* it
bought from Lorraine. The Bundesbahn, of course,
resisted the threatened loss of traffic and suggested electrification of the line as an alternative.

There was some French opposition, too. Strasbourg,
France's largest coal port, feared for its traffic. The railways objected on the same grounds as the Bundesbahn,
fearing especially the loss of traffic overland to the Channel
and North Sea ports. Dunkerque objected and Antwerp
as well, an ancient rival of Rotterdam. The Belgians preferred other canal routes that would also help them. The
French industries outside Lorraine and those of the Saar
and Luxembourg saw in the project only an advantage for
a rival. There were also deep divisions on the financial
soundness of the project.[48]

[47] Past plans to canalize the Moselle were dropped for financial or political reasons. When the Germans controlled the whole area during
the Second World War, they built one dam 11 kilometers above Koblenz; but it is not clear how important they regarded the project; they
had done nothing about it when they controlled the whole area before
the First World War. The French government, according to Chardonnet, cited, had always discouraged the project for fear of the political
pull on Alsace-Lorraine of the German Rhine.

[48] The French argued that the canal would pay since electric power
could be sold to supplement the income from shipping. The Germans
held that the canal would lose money unless transport rates were so high
that there would be little if any saving over the use of the railroad. In
any case, too much money was involved that the Germans would
rather use elsewhere.

There were negotiations, studies, committees, an International Moselle Day. The French pressed for action—but could not press too hard because the decision lay with the Germans. The Germans dragged their feet—but not so much as to give the French grounds for accusing them of bad faith or betrayal of "the European idea." Inevitably, the Moselle question was drawn into the orbit of issues of greater gravity between Bonn and Paris. As the French gave up hope of holding the Saar, they looked for advantages that they could claim in return for accepting the loss gracefully. The more closely these advantages could be tied to the interests of French heavy industry the better, since the coal and steel producers were disturbed by the additional influence they feared the Saar would give Germany in the Coal and Steel Community. A guarantee of coal supplies from the Saar was one of these advantages. Canalization of the Moselle was another. The Germans were interested in an amicable settlement. The tone of some of the articles in the German economic press began to change. Perhaps the Ruhr would not suffer so much from the canalization of the Moselle, they said, since it could hope to compete quite successfully against Lorraine in the long run. So long as one did not have to make believe that the canalization was an economically desirable thing for Germany, it would be possible, if needs must, to pay an economic price for a political advantage. In May 1956, Adenauer and Mollet reached a series of agreements on the Saar, one of which provided for joint arrangements to canalize the Moselle. A more detailed agreement on financing, rates, and the use of power followed, after some delay to work out compensations for Luxembourg, which had rights as a riparian but saw no economic advantage in the project.

The High Authority played no part in the Moselle negotiations. For this it was criticized by some who felt it should have an active role in anything affecting the Community and who were uneasy that matters of common concern, benefiting some and not others, were being left to the decision of two governments (especially the two most powerful governments) whose motives were bound to be mixed. There is something to the argument, though it is hard to see how the High Authority, lacking both power and responsibility in the matter, could have done much more than manifest an interest and register the principle of Community concern. If the matter had been less closely tied to international and domestic politics, the High Authority might have contributed something useful by way of study or analysis. If the advantages had been less problematical and potentially more general in their incidence, it might usefully have tried to influence the course of the negotiations. But in the circumstances it was probably the part of prudence to abstain, as the High Authority did, thus protecting itself from the political by-blows of the bilateral negotiation and perhaps shielding some of its members from pressure of a sort that would have made the rest of their work more difficult.[49]

ROAD TRAFFIC

That staple among contemporary transportation problems, the competition of road and rail, has appeared in the Community and presents a series of questions for the future. Trucks do not compete seriously with trains and barges in carrying coal or iron ore, but they have begun to carry significant amounts of steel. Comprehensive statistics are lacking, but data for Germany are startling. In 1949 trucks carried 17 per cent of the finished rolled-steel products shipped by German plants to German destinations; by the first part of 1954 the figure had risen to 42 per cent. The increase was all at the expense of rail traffic, which fell from 80 to 53 per cent of the total. The amount of trade carried by trucks varied greatly among products, ranging in 1953 from under 15 per cent for large and heavy products to over 80 per cent for tin plate and gal-

---

[49] The Moselle measure may well have repercussions elsewhere. The Belgian steel industry, for instance, has called for improvement of Belgian canals and ports and a connection between the Meuse and the Rhine via Aix-la-Chapelle, to be achieved by the time the "canalized Moselle will appreciably diminish the costs of the plants in the Moselle area." Groupement Belge, cited, p. 44.

vanized material. This is not entirely a matter of local traffic, as might be expected. A breakdown of interregional trade figures shows that for many products truck transportation was as important for the Ruhr's shipments to Bavaria or Hamburg as for local traffic, and sometimes more important.[50] Data on foreign trade are not as good but between 1952 and 1953 trucks substantially increased their share in German imports of steel products, especially from Luxembourg and the Saar.[51] The experience of Germany may not be altogether typical, but there is no doubt that the share of road traffic in Community transport is rising. The High Authority's rough estimate that 10 per cent of the Community's traffic was carried in trucks may well be out of date.[52] In any case, it is not the total figure but the importance of trucking in carrying certain goods and on particular routes that is likely to raise the most problems.

The Community's work on road transport has largely been confined to drawing up plans for getting better information and requiring the publication of truckers' rates. This is certainly the first need. In Germany truck rates are regulated in relation to those of the Bundesbahn (but not so strictly adhered to, according to Scheider). Elsewhere, and for international traffic, there is little or no direct regulation of rates.[53] It seems likely, therefore, that the general belief that there is extensive discrimination is well founded. There is also the problem of the competition of road transport with railways and waterways, leading to problems of "special rates" and harmonization. The High

[50] Jürgensen, cited, pp. 165-170, has all these figures and others.

[51] Between 1952 and 1953, German imports of iron and steel products from the rest of the Community rose by 37 per cent, but imports of these products via truck rose 123 per cent. On the other hand, exports by truck did not increase as rapidly as total exports of iron and steel products to the Community. Scheider, cited, p. 89, compared with HA, *Report*, Apr. 1957, *Annex*, p. 34.

[52] HA, Information Service, *Transport in the Community*, Sept. 1, 1955, p. 6.

[53] Scheider, cited, p. 88, reports that because domestic rates are fixed, German truckers sometimes cut prices by charging almost nothing for the foreign stretch of an international run.

Authority did not actively pursue the matter of road transport until 1956; by the spring of 1958 neither publication of rates nor regulation had been achieved. There was some agreement on principles but the experts were encountering difficulties and the governments were reserved.

HARMONIZATION

By common consent, "harmonization" was put at the bottom of the Community's transport agenda, because it was recognized as the hardest problem. It has stayed there. In the minds of many it remains some kind of goal. But the Convention implied a question even about this when it spoke of harmonizing rates and conditions of transport "as far as may be necessary for the proper functioning of the common market." The Community's record shows that there is no agreement on how far this is and the Community's experience suggests that no major progress is likely to be made quickly.

To be sure, the steps the Community has taken move in the direction of harmonization. International traffic has been put on a more nearly equal basis with domestic traffic. Degressivity is uniform within limits; there is some possibility of extending them. The elimination of major special rates—if the High Authority's decisions are upheld—will remove some important discrepancies in the Community's rate structure. But this action also raises questions about the meaning of "harmonization." Is that goal achieved simply by applying the same rate to all producers or users? The High Authority itself pointed out what a limited concept this is: "It is not so much the diversity of rates as the diversity of the principles of rate-making which is at the bottom of a distortion; and still more, it is the lack of coherence in the application of the principles or the violence done to them in order to help certain users [of transport services]." [54]

What would be required to apply the same *principles* of rate-making throughout the Community? Clearly there would have to be an agreement on what principles were

[54] HA, *Report*, Apr. 1958, v. 1, p. 66.

to be used and an agency that could apply them throughout the area. No government has been willing to adhere rigorously to a simple theory of rates; it may favor "real cost" but it will depart from it to promote a pattern of industrial location or for some other purpose. It is reasonable that it should; these too are matters of public importance. Therefore the agency that applied rate principles internationally would also have to have a good deal of discretion, which would mean that governments would have to give up some significant amount of power to an international (or supranational) body. This is exactly what they have shown themselves most unwilling to do in the Coal and Steel Community. The Treaty reserved most of the power over transportation to the governments; they held onto it firmly in the negotiations that followed; the challenges to the High Authority's action in special rates were largely based on the view that it was intruding on the prerogatives of government.

It is particularly unlikely that governments would agree to thorough harmonization by international action applying only to coal and steel. Freight rates for coal and steel are embedded in rate structures that affect all other products as well. There is a double interplay. On the one hand, coal and steel are so important a part of freight traffic that major changes applying to them would have a heavy impact on the total costs and revenues of each national transport system. On the other hand, because steel and coal rates are only a part of a larger complex, governments will be reluctant to make major changes in them unless they are willing to revamp their whole transportation systems. Because of these facts, many people, including the Common Assembly's transport committee, have concluded that harmonization will have to be undertaken for transport systems as a whole and not just for coal and steel. This is very reasonable, but there is little evidence that such broad measures of harmonization are likely to be adopted soon. There has been a certain amount of cooperation on transportation matters outside the Coal and Steel Community, but it has had little or nothing to do

with rates. There have been a number of ambitious proposals, but they have had few practical results. The
Common Market treaty of 1957 calls for a common transport policy, but the principles set out and the procedures
for applying them do not seem to go beyond the coal and
steel Treaty, and fall short of it at some points. This suggests, if anything, a drop rather than a rise in the willingness of governments to undertake such measures.

If this diagnosis is correct, the Coal and Steel Community
will have to go on for some time with its present dis-
harmonies in transportation rates and policies, except to
the extent that it may prove able to generate some change
by itself. The extent of the present discrepancies is clear
enough: basic differences in national railroad rates, including different relations among Community products from
one country to another; rates for international trade that
produce weighted averages of these discrepancies; variations in degressivity beyond a certain distance; some special
rates, based on differences in national policies; lack of
almost any common rules for international water and road
transportation; different national practices in the coordination of road, rail and water.

The last two of these are matters on which the Community has done least. It has work in hand that should
make the actual situation clearer than it is and that may
make possible measures that will achieve some of the same
results that have been obtained for railroads. The publication of rates, the elimination of discrimination and the
application of more uniform principles are clearly matters
in which the Community has real interest. On the other
hand, as consumers of transportation services, the coal and
steel industries probably benefit from the maintenance of
road-rail-water competition and would suffer if "harmonization" took the form of protecting railroads against
the other forms of transit. The Belgian steel producers,
for instance, have taken a strong position against regulation
of road and water transport because they suspect that the
proponents of this kind of harmonization actually mean
"to limit, by a very rigid regulation, the competition

offered the railroads by road and water transportation
which are in many cases more flexible and economic." [55]
Certainly the growth of truck traffic at anything like the
rate shown by the German figures indicates that there are
important advantages for the steel industry (and not only
in lower rates) that would be lost if regulation of competition became primarily a protection of the position of
the railroads. To be sure, different producers and consumers of Treaty products may benefit differently from
this competition, but there is nothing to be said against
this from the point of view of Community principles
unless it leads to some kind of discrimination. This it may
do, since competition among modes of transportation tends
to produce additional "special rates" that will make a
situation that is already difficult to understand still more
opaque. [56] In all probability, whatever action the Community takes in this field, it will run up against difficulties
of the sort already encountered in the handling of railroad
rates. Road-rail-water competition has too many ramifications, and too great a bearing on a wide range of economic
and political interests, for governments to yield any large
share of their powers. Nor are they likely to find it sensible
to seek "harmonization" in these matters for coal and steel
alone.

The basic problem was set out by the High Authority
in discussing the discrepancies between France and
Germany in the relative rates for iron and coal. The differences, it said, "result from the fact that each railway
has worked out a system of rates adapted to the situation
of its own national industries, and consequently the French
National Railways and the German Federal Railways have
arrived at fundamentally different solutions." [57] As we

[55] Groupement Belge, cited, p. 43. The French steel federation also
supports free international water rates. *La Sidérurgie Française en 1956,*
cited, p. 19.

[56] To the extent that a railroad can, it may also seek to offset losses
(or low profits) on a competitive rate by higher rates on traffic where
its monopoly position is better defended, thus adding to the differential
effect.

[57] HA, *Report,* Apr. 1954, p. 118.

have seen, nothing in the Community's organization is likely to change this situation. The High Authority may be able to make some modest progress on a few points but the basic decisions remain in the province of the governments. One potentially effective force for change in practices remains. Economic pressure within the Community may alter the calculations of governments and private groups about the transportation arrangements that are best for them. There might, then, be unilateral changes in rate structures. Their direction can hardly be judged in advance. If the aim was to protect or subsidize national industries these might further complicate Community problems and hamper the development of the common market. There would be checks in the Treaty rules and in Community procedures. Probably of greater importance would be the reaction of other governments in trying to offset unilateral changes that damaged their interests. Depending on the strength of the contending parties and the seriousness of the issues, such developments might induce agreement on principles going somewhat beyond those that exist.

If it is true that institutions develop by meeting crises, there may be some advantage to the Community in sharpening the issues arising from discrepant national transport practices. It is even conceivable that the strong reaction to the High Authority's decisions on special rates should work this way, if it is not dissipated as so many have been in the past by the discovery that the damage was not as great as was feared. Having seen the results of a situation in which the High Authority "saw itself constrained to limit its action to a strict application of the Treaty provisions . . ." [58] the governments and the industries might be moved to devise more elaborate principles that could meet a greater variety of circumstances. Since these are conflicting interests, the new measures would have to be compromises and might thereby produce a further degree of "harmonization."

One of the greatest present deficiencies is the lack of any clear understanding of how, and to what extent, the

[58] HA, *Report*, Apr. 1958, v. 1, p. 70.

discrepancies between national transport systems impair the common market and hinder achievement of Community aims. Speaking of one phase of the problem, the High Authority said, "the distortions caused by the disparity between the rates for coal, iron ore and scrap may radically disturb the calculated prime-costs of the burden of the various iron and steel industries in the Community and thereby distort the rational use and distribution of the raw materials needed in that industry." [59] This is perfectly true, but it is also true that if the industries have been operating for some time with these differences in spread, a basic change would also cause disturbances. These will be the more visible and will be resisted. One of the functions of the common market is to bring change, but one of the practical problems in inducing it is to show that the gain will be worth the disturbance. Certainly rigged rates distort the allocation of resources and so impair the best possible functioning of the common market. But it is only when the consequences of a particular practice, and of a proposed change, can be clearly demonstrated that effective Community action is likely. More is involved than just showing how the achievement of the Community's purposes is hampered by existing transport practices.[60] That is important, but it is also important to show more clearly than has been done who is hurt by the present situation and who would benefit from change. That way dynamism is engendered. Its outcome cannot be predicted with any assurance. Separatist forces are still strong in the Community. But the alternative, of pursuing the lines of past practice, shows no possibility of major change.

THE COMMUNITY'S RECORD

To look at the Community's transport position only in terms of the difficulties of achieving further harmonization is to see only one side of its record. The things that have

[59] HA, *Report*, Apr. 1954, p. 116. The "burden" is the combination of raw materials going into the blast furnace.
[60] The High Authority has organized a committee of economists to make such a study.

been done are substantial. They go somewhat beyond what has been described in this chapter. The through-rate system has been extended to transit traffic through Switzerland and Austria.[61] A whole series of relatively minor measures have been taken inside the Community which cumulatively are of some importance especially as part of the general liberalization of transportation that went with the removal of discrimination and the devising of through-rates. For instance, stations on the French-Belgian frontier that had been reserved for the import of Belgian or Dutch coal were opened to coal from the Aachen fields of Germany; points on the border between France and Luxembourg were opened for the passage of steel from Luxembourg to the Saar and Germany; the French agreed to permit exceptions to the rule that French products delivered in France must be carried by French transport; there were agreements on terminology, measures, and classifications.

Outside the Community there has also been cooperation on transport matters among European governments. ECE committees did much to promote technical agreements, standardization, uniform usage and the like. International arrangements for the more efficient use of freight cars, and an international corporation to pool orders for rolling stock, were significant achievements. But so far as the opening up of international traffic is concerned, none of these measures bears comparison with what the Community achieved. Though confined to a few products, the Community's measures in fact cover a sizable fraction of the freight traffic within and among their six countries.

For the creation of a common market, the transportation reforms were obviously very important. While their effects cannot be fully appraised they are clearly among the most important steps the Community has taken. Their immediate effect may well have been more important than that of the removal of tariffs and quotas. The job remains incomplete. The discrepancies in transport rates that still

[61] The texts are in *JO*, May 29, 1957, pp. 223-229; and Feb. 20, 1958, pp. 78-85.

exist are likely to be hard to remove and may persist a long time. This does not necessarily mean that what remains to be done is more important than what has been done; the remaining problems are largely of a different sort from those already solved, though the difficulties have similar roots. These are primarily difficulties inherent in measures of partial integration. The Community demands extensive change from what has existed before, but it operates on only part of each national economy; in addition it leaves the power to bring about change distributed among a series of separate political entities. The inevitable result is delay, resistance, incongruity and incompleteness in the process of change that the Treaty set in motion.

NINE

SUBSIDIES OLD AND NEW

THE COMMUNITY has a rather mixed record on subsidies. It has been quite effective in getting rid of a number of national measures that were plainly incompatible with a common market. It has introduced new, internationally financed subsidies intended to hasten the process of adaptation. These have not altogether served their purpose. Behind this experience lie some of the Community's basic coal problems. Beyond the transitional period there are questions about the extent to which the Community should concern itself with all kinds of subsidies and to what end.

THE RULES

The Treaty forbids subsidies ("or state assistance . . . in any form whatsoever") in the same flat fashion as tariffs and quotas, indeed in the same article. The rules for the transitional period are also simple and most flexible. Governments notify the High Authority of all subsidies; the High Authority either authorizes their continuation, stipulates conditions, or sets a date for their suspension (Section 11).

The idea behind the flat ban is clear. Spokesmen for the American shipping industry have called the subsidies from which they benefit "the tariff in reverse," and this comes close to the essence of the matter. While subsidies are not trade barriers in the same sense as tariffs and quotas, they may have similar effects. They use public funds to obtain an allocation of resources, and perhaps a structure of production, different from the one that market forces alone would support. To leave governments free to use subsidies would plainly be incompatible with the basic aims of the Community.

The idea behind the flexible transitional provisions is also clear. The more important subsidies have been, the greater the adjustment when they are removed. If the adjustment came too quickly, there would be dislocations of production, sales, and employment that might better be avoided. If there had been no safeguards against dislocation, the Treaty would have been less acceptable in the first place and would have generated more opposition as its effects were felt. The flat, immediate abolition of trade barriers (except for Italy) was itself a reason for permitting a more flexible, and possibly more gradual, approach to the removal of subsidies. Their manipulation under the control of the High Authority could help to bring about a smooth transition. Subsidies could be used, if need be, to cushion the immediate effects of the removal of trade barriers, the adjustment of transportation rates, and the application of the Community's new price rules.

As if to emphasize the usefulness of subsidies as instruments for bringing about the transition, the Convention introduced a major new set of coal subsidies. Belgian and Italian mines which had high costs were to receive subsidies from the High Authority, financed by low-cost Dutch and German producers. So far as Belgium was concerned, this arrangement was one of the basic compromises that made the Treaty possible. The purpose of the new subsidies was to help the recipients get into a position in which they would not need subsidies. That proved rather hard to do.

REMOVING OLD SUBSIDIES

Governments were slow to answer the High Authority's initial inquiries about the subsidies they were paying. Through study and negotiation, however, the situation became quite clear during the preparatory period before the opening of the common market for coal. No one was subsidizing steel, the High Authority reported.[1] There were, however, a number of subsidies on coal. Those in Belgium and Italy were fitted into the arrangements for using the new funds provided by the High Authority. Of the rest, the most important were French. These were continued temporarily, subject to conditions established by the High Authority. As time passed, they were for the most part removed.

The largest of the four main sets of French subsidies was used to reduce the cost of coking coal to a number of briquetting plants on the Atlantic coast. Loss of the English coal they had used in the past increased the raw material costs of these plants and put them at a disadvantage compared to most other French briquetting plants which are near the mines. To avoid a rise in prices to local consumers and to keep the plants operating at a high level, the High Authority agreed "that these subsidies should be eliminated only gradually . . . ," but it limited their amount.[2] By 1955 the subsidy had fallen to less than half its 1953 level (in total and per ton), but then it rose again because production increased and more expensive American coal was used.[3] The basis of the subsidy was then changed. After a further rather small payment the French government stopped subsidizing Community coal at the end of the transition period. When the briquetting plants used coal imported from third countries, however, they continued to receive a subsidy.[4] The effect of this change was to link the subsidy for the briquetting plants with the

---

[1] When the time came to open the common market for special steels, it appeared that the French government was in effect subsidizing export sales by refunding social security and other taxes. After a slight delay, this was stopped for sales within the Community. *JO*, Aug. 1, 1954, p. 473.

[2] HA, *Report*, Apr. 1953, p. 75, and *JO*, Mar. 13, 1953, p. 84. The initial stipulation was that subsidies should not be more than 70 per cent of their level during the first quarter of 1953 and should fall by any increase in the price of the briquettes. An additional motive for the subsidy was to provide a market for some of the small, privately owned coal mines in France which had been selling to the briquetting plants. *JO*, May 11, 1956, p. 736.

[3] HA, *Report*, Nov. 1954, pp. 84-87; *Report*, Apr. 1956, pp. 108-111; *Report*, Apr. 1957, pp. 168-170.

[4] *JO*, Mar. 23, 1957, p. 116.

general subsidy paid on imported coal (mostly American) to bring its cost down to the French level.

The two next most important French subsidies were paid on imports of coking coal and coke, principally from Germany. Their purpose was to keep the cost of these imports, which went mostly to Lorraine, in line with domestic prices. In addition, the subsidy on coking coal was part of the French effort to produce more coke domestically. Most of the coal of Lorraine and the Saar is not easily cokefied and produces a fuel that breaks too readily in blast furnaces. There are processes that improve the product, but they increase costs.[5] The best results come from mixing Ruhr coking coal with the local product. Both Charbonnages de France and the steel companies had been expanding coke production in Lorraine and the import subsidy was intended to help in this effort. The High Authority authorized France to continue this subsidy subject to certain limitations.[6]

The amount of the subsidy declined during the next two years. Then in 1955 its basis was changed. Part was to be paid as before but the rest was to be divided among Lorraine cokeries according to the total amount of coal they processed. This put a premium on the use of a larger portion of cheaper local coal in coking charges and, in effect, subsidized the price of Lorraine coal when it was used for cokefaction. The High Authority stipulated that the new "coking bonus" should decline each quarter. It was dropped after April 1, 1957. The "residual subsidy," paid on the old basis, also declined and it was dropped entirely when through-rates came fully into effect.[7]

[5] Jean Chardonnet, *La Sidérurgie Française: Progrès ou Décadence?*, 1954, pp. 68-69, examines the matter in some detail.

[6] The average payment per ton was not to rise and a fall in the price of imported coal or a rise in the price of Lorraine coal was automatically to reduce the amount of the subsidy. The subsidy per ton in 1954 averaged 1,053 francs (about $3.00); total payments that year came to 3.2 billion francs; they had been 3.9 billion the year before.

[7] Between 1952 and 1957 French production of coke rose from 9.2 to 12.6 million tons while imports from other Community countries rose from 5.1 to 5.5 million. *Bulletin Statistique*. Charbonnages de France's output of coke and semi-coke in Lorraine rose from 430,000 tons in

The subsidy on coke imports was simpler. Its aim was to reduce the delivered price of Ruhr coke at Homécourt in Lorraine to the level of that brought from the Nord. The total cost fell sharply when the common market opened, largely as a result of the elimination of double-pricing and transport discrimination. In the spring of 1955, the subsidy was eliminated on most imports by rail and since early 1956 it has been paid, in a somewhat different form, only on imports by water via Strasbourg, to compensate for the disadvantage of using this route resulting from the reduction of rail rates.[8] On the new basis, a much smaller amount of coke was subsidized and total payments were below what they had been, but the subsidy per ton was about as high as before. The subsidy's character has changed and it primarily benefits Rhine shipping and the port of Strasbourg rather than the coke users. Therefore the High Authority decided that it could be continued beyond the end of the transitional period pending examination of transport problems after the new Rhine agreement comes into effect.

The fourth of the French coal subsidies was quite dif-

1953 to 1.4 million in 1956. Charbonnages's sales of coke to the steel industry (taking the country as a whole), rose from 2.4 million tons to 3.8 million in the same period, so Lorraine's share rose substantially. Charbonnages de France, *Rapport de Gestion*, 1955 and 1956. How much the subsidy may have contributed to this is not clear. From 1953 through 1956 French investment in cokeries amounted to $4.32 per ton of coke produced, compared to a Community average of $1.51. During 1956 the French steel industry used 12 million tons of coke, of which 4.5 million were imported. Its main concern was about the rise in importance of American coal, which provided 1.1 million tons of the coal used in the steel industry's own cokeries (compared to 1.3 of French coal, 1 from the Saar, and 1.5 from other Community countries) and about another million tons for coke that had been produced on order by the Charbonnages de France and a Dutch cokery. Chambre Syndicale de la Sidérurgie Française, *La Sidérurgie Française en 1956*, Je. 21, 1957, p. 14.

[8] Before the introduction of through-rates it cost 2,358 francs a ton to carry coke from Gelsenkirchen to Pont à Mousson by rail (in un-scheduled complete trains of 950 tons) while the freight by water to Strasbourg and then by rail to Pont à Mousson came to 2,167 francs. After May 1, 1955, the all-rail rate was 1,797 and the route via Strasbourg 2,205 francs. Willi Scheider, *Die Tarifpolitik der Hohen Behörde und das Deutsche Verkehrswesen*, 1956, p. 99.

ferent from the others; it was paid on exports. Coal prices were lower in Germany than in France. To make it possible to sell coal from Lorraine and the Saar in south Germany, the French government made up to three-quarters of the difference. Again the High Authority approved continuation of the subsidy subject to a number of conditions.[9] The subsidy fell slightly between 1953 and 1954, and then more sharply in 1955 when the amount paid per ton was less than half what it had been at the outset. Circumstances were changing. German coal prices had risen more than French. The transportation reforms gave the Lorraine and Saar producers some of the benefit of their geographical position. The High Authority's zonal pricing arrangement permitted them to absorb some of the freight charges for deliveries to south Germany (see Ch. 11). The French government decided to drop the subsidy altogether.

The Community's record in getting rid of the French coal subsidies is a good one. The sums were substantial. In 1953, over 13 billion francs were paid out in these four subsidies; the total fell to just over 5 billion in 1956, after which the subsidies diminished further and changed their form. Large amounts of coal were involved, equivalent to about 17 per cent of France's coal production and 36 per cent of its coke production in 1953. The main impact was on foreign trade; at the outset virtually all the coal and coke passing between France and Germany was subsidized.[10] At the end of the transitional period, the only intra-Community trade being subsidized was the rather small amount of water-borne coke France was importing via Strasbourg (and it was the transport route, not the coke that was the issue). To a considerable extent it was the Community itself that had made these subsidies unnecessary by eliminat-

[9] The subsidies were not to reduce the difference of 200 francs per ton between the list price of Saar and Lorraine coal and the price at which they delivered to Germany. If German prices fell, there was to be no increase in the subsidies. If changes in transportation rates or other competitive conditions increased the receipts from these sales, the subsidies were to be reduced.

[10] Figures for subsidized tonnages from HA, *Report*, Apr. 1956, p. 11.

ing double-pricing and reducing transport costs and dis-crimination. Another crucial factor was the pressure of the High Authority, which set limits to the subsidies, stipu-lated conditions, and watched for opportunities to bring them to an end.

The subsidy to the coastal briquetting plants has not, however, disappeared. It has only been transformed by linking it with the subsidies the government provides to lower the cost of the coal France imports from the United States. The French government provides another sizable sum to make up the deficits of Charbonnages de France.[11] Neither of these operations has come under Community scrutiny. The problem of financing imports of expensive American coal is one the Community has so far left to each country, but which it may have to consider on a broader basis as part of its long-run coal policy. The questions raised by the deficits of a nationalized industry are part of another broad problem of Community coal policy that, by common consent, has been left untouched for the time being. The sums involved are large compared to those spent on the subsidies that have been abolished, and the issues are of a somewhat different order. The virtual elimination of the coal subsidies bearing directly on intra-Community trade was a useful step in which the Community's methods showed to advantage. What remains is part of its unfinished business.

NEW SUBSIDIES FOR BELGIAN COAL

Belgium has long been troubled by the high cost of mining coal. Since before the First World War output per miner in Belgium has been well below that in neighboring countries (Italy is excluded from these comparisons). After the second war, Belgian coal production recovered at a good pace, but high wages and low productivity raised costs and prices. The seriousness of the problem is shown by the figures for 1949 which show how much below other

[11] The deficit of Charbonnages de France (including amortization) was about 22.5 billion francs in 1953, 8 billion in 1954, and 14.6 billion in 1955 and in 1956. Charbonnages de France, *Rapport de Gestion*, various years.

countries Belgium was in productivity and how much above in costs:[12]

Belgium as per cent of:	Output per manshift	Labor per manshift	Costs per ton produced	Total Operating Expenses per ton	Average Pithead Price
France	92	114	124	150	137
Germany	65	133	206	178	173
Saar	73	126	174	165	142
Netherlands	49	166	347	—	—

Much of Belgium's trouble came from conditions that also plagued some of the mines in almost every coal field in Europe: thin and crooked seams; deep shafts; great distances from the shaft to the face; resulting high costs for ventilation and transportation; poor and sometimes dangerous working conditions; overage equipment and installations. These difficulties were aggravated by inadequate investment between the wars; price equalization schemes and other arrangements that retarded the development of new fields and preserved many small companies that lacked resources for modernization; persistent labor shortage that led to heavy dependence on foreign workers with a low average level of mining skill. These handicaps were particularly marked in the coal fields of southern Belgium, which produced two-thirds of the country's coal. Worst of all was the Borinage, an area near the French border. On the other side of the country in the newer coal mines of the Campine conditions were generally better, output higher, and costs lower.[13]

The Belgian government had not neglected its coal problem. A decision to do something about the Borinage had been taken in 1938. From 1947 on the government had

[12] Calculated from ECE, *Economic Bulletin for Europe*, Oct. 1950, p. 25.

[13] In 1949 labor costs per ton in the Campine were $7.60 compared with $9.84 in the basin around Mons. Output per manshift was 750 kg. instead of 610. Around Liège output per manshift was only 550 kg. and labor costs were $10.98 per ton, nearly three times the German average and about 4.5 times the Dutch. However, the Liège coal is good anthracite which commands premium prices so the problems were not so great. Same, p. 27.

provided a variety of subsidies, grants-in-aid for investment, and credits for re-equipment to improve productivity. Though Belgium was not a major recipient of
American aid, Marshall Plan money had helped the process;
nearly 80 per cent of the counterpart funds had gone into
the coal industry.[14] Some marginal mines had been closed
and there had been a number of amalgamations to cut overhead and improve management. Investment per ton rose
from 37.7 francs in 1949 to 96.28 in 1952.[15] Productivity
rose, but there was no marked progress and Belgium remained in a very disadvantageous position on the eve of
the Schuman Plan.

One of the chief brakes on more rapid adjustment was
the fear of adding to the unemployment that already
plagued the country. In the isolated coal mining districts
there were few alternative occupations. Much of the economic life of such places depended on the mines. The
Campine could probably have absorbed miners from the
south, but it was hard to persuade people to move. Native
conservatism was enhanced by the fact that the Campine
is a Flemish-speaking area while the Borinage is peopled
by French-speaking Walloons of another religion; even
the Belgian school law complicated matters. Coal was
deeply involved in Belgian politics and played a key role
in the balance of forces among parties, classes, regions,
ideologies, and in the religious and cultural divisions of
the country. The pattern was complex but for the most
part inhibited drastic action.

Before there was a Coal and Steel Community, considerations of national interest could be found that might
justify policies preserving uneconomic domestic coal production. It might be wise to bear the cost if the alternative
was dependence on Ruhr coal that might some day be
diverted for German national purposes. Double-pricing

---

[14] This came to something over $24 million between April 1948 and
the end of 1956. U.S. International Cooperation Administration, *Counterpart Funds and ICA Foreign Currency Accounts, Data as of December
31, 1956*, May 1957.
[15] HA, *Report*, Apr. 1954, p. 83, where the activities of the Belgian
government are described in more detail.

prevented the Belgians from getting the full benefit of lower costs of production abroad. The hoped-for expansion of Belgian industrial production would require more coal. These considerations would carry less weight if Belgium was part of a coal and steel community where it was guaranteed equal treatment in supplies and nondiscriminatory pricing. But the domestic factors inhibiting change would not necessarily be altered.

The Treaty Regime

Not equal treatment but special treatment was what the Belgians wanted for their coal. They were willing to make adjustments, but coal was too important a part of their economy to be exposed to the competition of lower-cost producers without safeguards. These were provided in several forms. Belgian coal production was not to fall more than 3 per cent a year.[16] During the transitional period— and up to two years afterward, if the High Authority and the Council of Ministers gave their consent—"the Belgian Government may retain or set up, under the control of the High Authority, mechanisms making possible the separation of the Belgian market from the common market." That is to say, trade barriers could have been erected. This was never done. However, the most important feature of the special regime for Belgian coal was the promise that for the length of the transitional period Belgium would get international aid to pay subsidies for two purposes: to permit Belgian coal to be sold competitively, and to adapt Belgian coal production so that it would be competitive without special help by the end of the transitional period.

The international aid was to come from the High Authority, which was to get the funds from a special tax levied on the coal sold by producers "of those countries whose average costs are less than the weighted average of the Community" (Section 25). As was known when the

[16] This was the simple rule if Community production was stable or increased. If Community production decreased, the 3 per cent was to apply to Belgian production as reduced by the coefficient of the decline in total Community production.

formula was negotiated, "those countries" were Germany
and the Netherlands.[17] The rate of the levy declined from
1.1 per cent of the producers' receipts from sales of coal in
1953 to .3 per cent in 1957. Over this period the High
Authority had collected $56.2 million, more than nine-
tenths of it from the German producers. By the end of 1957,
$48.4 million had been paid to Belgium and $6.5 million to
Italy.[18]

The High Authority's grants were matched by contributions from the Belgian government. Most of the funds were
used for the general subsidy to be discussed below. Section
26 of the Convention also provided for two special-purpose
subsidies. One, to reduce the price of coal and coke delivered to the Belgian steel producers so that they would
be on an equal footing with the industries of other Community countries, was never used. The other, to permit
Belgian coal to be exported in the common market, absorbed $5.2 million of the High Authority's funds and an
equal amount provided by the Belgian government between
June 1953 and the second quarter of 1955. Then it was
dropped because market conditions made it possible for
Belgium to sell in other Community countries without
assistance or to absorb the coal at home.

[17] In June 1957 the Dutch producers were exempted from the levy
because the High Authority found that their costs had risen above the
Community average. *JO*, Je. 24, 1957, p. 264. German payments stopped
at the end of the year. France, whose costs lay somewhere in between
the German and the Dutch on the one hand and the Belgian on the other,
neither gave nor received in the international "compensation" scheme
but devoted itself to its own coal problems. There had been some
thought that France should receive Community assistance in adapting its
coal mines since it seemed certain that some pits would have to close
as a result of the common market. This idea was dropped but France
was guaranteed that its coal production would not have to fall more
than one million tons a year (plus a proportional drop if Community
production as a whole fell) and that if serious problems arose a special
tax might be put on foreign coal sales to France that exceeded earlier
levels (Section 28).

[18] A detailed accounting of rates, annual yield, payments, etc., appears
in HA, *Report*, Apr. 1958, pp. 28, 314. The Convention established a
ceiling of 1.5 per cent on the rate for the first year, declining by .3 percentage points annually, but the High Authority applied a rate of 1.1
per cent for the first two years and then used the original scale.

The export subsidies played an important part in developing Belgium's trade with the rest of the Community at a time when the demand for coal was rather slack. Nearly 60 per cent of Belgian coal exports to the rest of the Community benefited from the subsidies during the latter half of 1953 and 1954. About 70 per cent of the subsidized exports went to the Netherlands and most of the rest to Italy. Almost all the Belgian coal sent to those countries benefited from payments equal to 80 per cent of the difference between the delivered price of Belgian coal and that of other Community coal.[19] Exports to France were not subsidized. The French had already complained about the cheapening of Belgian coal by the general subsidy and had secured an adjustment in the prices fixed by the High Authority for some types.[20]

Presumably the export subsidies contributed to the fact that between 1952 and 1954 Belgian coal exports to Community countries increased about twice as fast as total intra-Community coal trade. The unsubsidized sales to France increased only moderately.[21] At the same time Belgian imports of coal from the Community increased rapidly and stocks were piling up at the Belgian mines. When the subsidies were dropped after the first quarter of 1955, Belgian exports fell sharply but for the year as a whole stayed well above those of 1954. Demand had become strong and in the nine months of 1955 during which exports were not subsidized Belgium's average monthly

[19] The other 20 per cent was met by the Belgian coal producers' organization. Subsidies were given only on shipments approved by the High Authority. Not all of the authorizations were used. Figures on the subsidized trade used in this section come from HA, *Report*, Apr. 1955, p. 95, compared with regular Community statistical sources.

[20] Charbonnages de France, *Rapport de Gestion*, 1953, p. 31. There were also Dutch charges that the export subsidies led to sales of Belgian coal in Holland at less than the established prices, but the High Authority believed these were not well founded. CA, *Débats*, May 14, 1954, p. 143; May 17, 1954, pp. 195, 196. Three-fifths of Belgium's exports to Germany were subsidized but the amounts were small.

[21] Belgian exports to third countries increased much more rapidly, without benefit of subsidy, but the starting point was very low. Most of this trade was with England, to which total Community sales increased substantially during this period.

sales to the Community were higher than in 1954 when subsidies were in effect for the whole year. The main loss was in exports to Italy which turned to the United States for supplies.

Export subsidies were a passing phase. The big problem that faced the Community throughout the transitional period and beyond was the more general subsidy intended to integrate Belgian coal in the common market. The initial question was how these payments should be used. Many people, in Belgium and elsewhere, had supposed the new international help would be used to finance a rather drastic program of readaptation. But the Belgian government and the coal industry already had a program of investment and adaptation under way and seemed averse to any serious change in its pace or character. Meanwhile there was the immediate problem of Belgian prices which were one- to two-thirds above those of the Ruhr for major types. Unless they were lowered it would be impossible to remove trade barriers and link Belgium to the common market.

To meet these problems, the High Authority set maximum prices for Belgian coal somewhat below the previous levels and then calculated what price would be needed to give producers the receipts they formerly had. The difference was provided as a subsidy, which averaged 29 Belgian francs per ton at the outset. Under this formula, the subsidies increased the income of all producers, leaving it to them and to the government to decide on the amounts and types of investments. Although all mines benefited from the subsidies, the uniform formula was modified by the Belgian government's special arrangements for giving greater aid to the mines in the worst situation. Payments under this program were included as part of the Belgian government's contribution to the joint subsidies and were supplemented by some of the High Authority's funds.

In June 1955 the High Authority altered the basis of subsidy payments to concentrate their influence on bringing about more rapid change. The methods chosen were based on the work of a mixed commission in which the officials of the High Authority and the Belgian government had been studying the situation since early 1954. Under the new arrangements[22] subsidies were no longer to be paid on the production of those kinds of coal—such as Liège anthracite—that could be sold in the common market without special assistance. This removed about one-third of the Belgian output from the subsidy scheme. Three firms carrying on mining in the Campine had their subsidies reduced on the ground that they could meet the competition of the common market with much less help than they had been getting. Four of the principal companies mining in the Borinage were to get increased aid for the re-equipment and improvement of certain pits and the definite shutting down of nine others according to a schedule running to the end of 1958. In addition to continuing the regular subsidy, the High Authority agreed to use some of the readaptation funds for retraining and, if necessary, relocating the workers thrown out of employment by the closing of the pits.[23] They were expected to number 1,100 over the whole period (not quite 0.8 per cent of the workers in the Belgian coal industry at the end of 1955; a little over one-third the number who had been added to that force between December 1954 and December 1955). Those thrown out of work by the closing of the first three pits, in 1956 and January 1957, were soon re-employed in other Borinage mines and did not require aid from the High Authority.[24] The Belgian government also concentrated its efforts and provided credits for re-equipment and the building of pithead power stations to use the poorer grades of coal (aided in the latter activity by some High Authority loans; see Ch. 13).

The Belgian coal industry was very critical of the new arrangements, and of the price cut that accompanied them.[25] The collieries whose aid was reduced complained

[22] This is a somewhat simplified account. The details appear in *JO*, May 31, 1955, pp. 753-758; Feb. 22, 1956, pp. 20-22; HA, *Reports*, Apr. 1956, pp. 114-124; Apr. 1957, pp. 179, 180; Apr. 1958, v. 2, pp. 30-32.

[23] The Council of Ministers waived the requirement that Belgium match these grants.

[24] HA, *Report*, Apr. 1957, pp. 218-219, 277.

[25] Alfred Bertrand, from the Campine, stated the full gamut of arguments. CA, *Débats*, Je. 22, 1955, p. 549 ff.

of discrimination, pointing out that they were the ones best placed to make profitable new investments and that reduction of the subsidy decreased their ability to do this. They asked the Community Court to annul the High Authority's decision but lost the case on the ground that the purpose of the subsidies was to bring about adjustments, not to finance particular investment programs or ensure the income of each firm. Selectivity, said the Court, was not discriminatory, but helped to overcome inequalities.[26]

Late in 1956 the High Authority again changed the method of granting subsidies.[27] On the basis of a study of costs of production, investment programs under way, and technical possibilities of improvement, Belgian coal mining companies were divided into three groups. Twenty-one were judged capable of making their way in the market without subsidies. The four Borinage collieries were judged incapable of adapting themselves to competitive conditions by the end of the transitional period and were cut off from Community subsidies after February 9, 1957. However, the Belgian government continued to cover their losses and the High Authority stood by to use its adaptation funds to help the workers who were discharged. Thus, all subsidy payments were concentrated on the remaining mines judged able to improve their positions sufficiently to do without subsidies, either by the end of the transitional period or in the two years after, during which the Belgian government was to be permitted to continue subsidies with no contribution from the Community. To sharpen the incentives for these firms, the subsidies were paid on a calculation of expected losses, based on performance in 1956 and prices fixed by the High Authority. By implication, if the companies did better than this they could keep the difference. The eligibility of several firms for continued subsidies was made dependent on their carrying out certain improvements, subject to inspection by the High Authority and the Belgian government.

[26] JO, Jan. 23, 1957, pp. 25-58.
[27] JO, Dec. 27, 1956, pp. 409-411; Feb. 9, 1957, pp. 81-82; HA, *Reports*, Apr. 1957, pp. 175-180; Apr. 1958, v. 2, pp. 32-35.

Behind these changes and the negotiations, studies, proposals and counterproposals they entailed, one can discern a more active struggle. Plainly the High Authority, the experts, and others were dissatisfied with the progress of Belgian adaptation. So were many Belgians. The government felt the need for caution for many reasons, not the least the political risks of pushing ahead too rapidly. "A reform must be allowed to ripen," said L.-E. Trochet, Minister of Labor in the Van Acker government. "One must meditate over it; it must be prepared for a long time. . . . Reforms made too rapidly are superficial reforms, and in the sphere with which we are concerned the reform is too important for there to be, for a second, a question of building on sand." [28] Industry and labor were also inclined to go slowly on the whole, though some groups would benefit from a more vigorous program. Strong demand for coal from 1955 through most of 1957 reduced the pressure for cutting costs. Behind the changes of 1955 and 1957 in the subsidy program lie hard argument and a series of bargains. It may well be that the resolution of internal Belgian tussles on policy and politics was made possible by the intervention of the High Authority as a source both of pressure and of supplemental resources. The revisions made the subsidy better suited to improving Belgian coal production. The market exerts more pressure on those who no longer get the subsidy but have the possibility of surviving. Those still getting the subsidy are on clearer notice that it is conditional and have added incentives that the earlier blanket method did not provide. More pits have been closed. How great the continuing drain on Belgian public funds will be is not clear. At best Belgium will continue to have a high-cost segment in its coal industry. Other countries have that too. One of the long-run coal problems of the Community is how to meet the economic, social, and political problems this situation creates.

[28] Speech at La Journée des Mineurs, Charleroi, reported in *Le Soir* (Brussels), Oct. 7, 1954.

The Results

The common market did not bring disaster for Belgian coal, as some had feared. Production declined gently (less than 5 per cent over the whole period from 1952 to 1957), but remained above the level of 1950 (27.3 million tons). Belgian exports expanded markedly, mostly to other countries in the common market. Imports rose, too, but on the whole not so rapidly. Until 1957 Belgium maintained a fairly strong export surplus in Community trade but, like its partners, had to import growing amounts of American coal from 1955 on. While the subsidies helped, the strong demand for coal during most of the transitional period was undoubtedly the most important factor enabling Belgium to hold these levels.

In addition to guarding the Belgian coal industry from damage, this condition increased the country's ability to make necessary adaptations. High prices and high demand made operations more profitable (or less unprofitable) than they would otherwise have been. Firms had more funds that might be used for investment. There were more opportunities to absorb in growing enterprises the labor displaced by shutting down others. On the other hand—and this was probably the stronger factor—high demand and high prices reduced the pressures for adjustment. Relatively inefficient operations became profitable. The urgency of reducing costs was less obvious. The whole atmosphere made it easier to postpone adaptation.

Though the transitional period is over, it is hard to make exact judgments about the extent of the Belgian coal industry's adaptation to the common market. Table 4 presents a collection of indicators that give something of a picture, albeit in broad strokes. To appraise the adaptation process thoroughly one would have to study the performance of particular companies or mines. Still, several things are clear.

The most obvious is that adaptation is far from complete. Belgium started with the disadvantage of high costs and prices. At the end of the transition period it still had these

Table 4

BELGIAN COAL IN THE COMMON MARKET, 1952-1957

	1952	1953	1954	1955	1956	1957
Belgian production (millons of tons)	30.4	30.1	29.2	30.0	29.6	29.1
Per cent of Community production	12.3	12.7	12.1	12.0	11.9	11.8
Belgian net exports (+) or imports (−)						
Total	+0.9	+2.0	+2.0	+3.5	−0.3	−1.1
In trade with the Community	+1.9	+2.6	+1.4	+2.8	+1.3	+0.8
Percentage of Belgian coal produced by:						
Campine	32.0	31.5	31.7	33.8	35.4	35.4
Southern fields	68.0	68.5	68.3	66.2	64.6	64.6
Output per manshift underground (kg)a						
Campine	1300	1307	1352	1484	1492	1450
Southern fields	965	986	1011	1028	1034	1032
Community excluding Italy	1389	1401	1447	1502	1529	1545
Rate of increase in OMS						
Campine	100	101	104	114	115	112
Southern fields	100	102	105	107	107	107
Community excluding Italy	100	101	104	108	110	111
	May	Mar.	Apr.	Nov.	Apr.	Apr.c
Belgian prices as per cent of Ruhr prices:						
Low volatileb	167	147	147	156	153	163
Semi-bituminous	148	126	126	115	111	128
Bituminous	132	118	122	115	111	129
High-volatile bituminous	161	136	138	126	122	132
	Last quarter of each year					
Cost of production						
Belgium	100.0	99.4	97.9	99.9	116.8	N.A.
Community	100.0	100.3	98.2	102.3	109.5	N.A.
Investments in the coal industry (dollars per ton of output)						
Campine	N.A.	1.33	1.45	1.27	1.64	N.A.
Southern fields	N.A.	1.08	1.23	1.15	1.27	N.A.
Community average	N.A.	1.02	1.00	1.04	1.00	N.A.

a. 1938: Campine, 1,523; South, 1,004; Community, 1,590—HA, *Report*, Apr. 1956, p. 264.

b. High Authority translations of *maigre, demi-gras, gras, flambants*. For further description and Belgian categories, see HA, *Report*, Apr. 1957, *Annexes*, p. 56, and *Bulletin Statistique*, May 1957, p. XXIV.

c. In March 1958 the figures were: low volatile 157; semi-bituminous 127; bituminous 123; high-volatile bituminous 127.

SOURCES: Production, trade and productivity, *Bulletin Statistique*. Prices, HA, *Reports*, Nov. 1955, Section I, p. 36; Apr. 1957, *Annexes*, p. 57. Cost of production, HA, *Report*, Apr. 1957, p. 125. Investment, HA, *Report*, Apr. 1958, v. 2, Table 50.

disadvantages. Costs of production, as calculated by the High Authority, held steady for several years but then, in 1956, jumped ahead twice as fast as those of the Community as a whole. At the end of 1957 Belgian costs appeared to be 40 per cent above the Community average and 50 per cent above those of the Ruhr.[29] Increases in labor costs, comprising higher wages, shorter hours, and more social security charges, were an important factor in the rise. In 1956 the High Authority approved an additional subsidy of 700 million francs by the Belgian government to offset some of these increases.[30] It was nothing new for Belgium to have difficulty in getting and keeping an adequate labor force in its coal mines, but now this problem appeared in a new guise as one of the major obstacles to adaptation, if the cost of production figures provided by the Belgian coal federation were accurate.[31]

The record on prices is more complicated, but it does not suggest marked progress toward adaptation. After the initial impact of the subsidies and maximum prices (see Table 4), there was a further improvement in the relation between Belgian and German prices for bituminous coals, due partly to a rise in Ruhr prices. At that point Belgian coal was not seriously out of line with that of some other Community countries, thanks to the subsidy. When anthracite and lean coal were taken out of the subsidy scheme their prices increased, but this was not necessarily harmful to Belgium. Community prices generally rose during 1956 and 1957 but Belgian prices—under the impact of the increased costs of production and the contraction of coal trade within the Community—rose faster so that ground that had been gained by comparison with Ruhr prices since 1953 was lost and in some cases the situation resembled that before the common market was opened.

[29] HA, *Report*, Apr. 1958, v. 2, p. 40.
[30] *JO*, Mar. 27, 1956, p. 88.
[31] These showed an increase of 26.5 per cent in wage costs per ton from 1953 to the end of 1957 (and much higher wage and social security costs per shift), and an increase in total costs of production per ton of 24.9 per cent. HA, *Report*, Apr. 1958, v. 2, p. 40. Earlier data on labor costs appear in HA, *Report*, Apr. 1957, pp. 191-201.

Toward the end of 1957 the High Authority permitted another rise in Belgian prices except for the "fat" bituminous coals of the Campine. Though the difference from the prices for the same types of coal from the southern fields was only 2 to 4 per cent (20-35 francs per ton, depending on the quality), the potentialities of the distinction were significant. They took on added meaning when the fall in demand over the winter of 1957-58 hit Belgium particularly hard. Prices were cut, and those of Campine coal fell faster than the others. In fact, the Campine mines wanted to make still greater cuts but were restrained by the government which feared that this would harm the mines of the south.

The differentiation was related to the general problem of Belgian adaptation. The division between the Campine and the south which has been used here is crude. There are good mines in the south as well as bad ones; because of the high prices their coal commands, some mines can operate soundly even though their record on productivity looks poor when compared with that of the industry as a whole. Nevertheless, a shift in emphasis toward the Campine would seem to be a necessary part of an improvement in Belgium's coal position. Table 4 shows that this has been taking place slowly. To further it, the High Authority urged the Belgian government to permit the exploitation of untapped reserves in the Campine, but the terms on which this should be done have long been a matter of great controversy in Belgium that delayed action.[32] The Belgians have, however, invested more heavily in the Campine (in relation to output) than in the south.

Taken by itself, the Campine has a much better position in the common market than does the south. Output per

[32] Concessions were granted in parts of these fields in 1911, but operations were made subject to specific legislative authorization. Several postwar efforts to get the necessary parliamentary action failed because of disagreements among Socialists, Liberals, Christian Democrats, governments, unions and the old concessionaires. There is also disagreement as to how rapidly production would proceed once the first steps were taken. Paul Haupt, "Interesse für Belgische Kohlenreserve," *Der Volkswirt*, Je. 23, 1956, p. 19.

manshift is below the Community average (and well below Lorraine, the Saar and the Ruhr), but it is well ahead of that in the neighboring basin of Aachen and compared favorably with Limburg and the Nord until it fell in 1957. Through 1956 productivity in the Campine was rising more rapidly than in all but a few Community basins, but then it fell back. Productivity in the southern fields remains the lowest in the Community outside Italy. While the rate of improvement was about average for the Community for several years, it then fell behind. The only distinction of the southern field is that its level of productivity is higher than it was before the war, while the Campine and the Community as a whole have not yet regained the levels of 1938.

The Community's record in adapting Belgian coal production to the common market is mixed. Belgium has not been hurt. The subsidies made it possible to do without trade barriers and to export Belgian coal from the outset. They did not, however, exercise much pressure for adaptation until the reforms of 1955 and 1956. High demand helped the Belgian mines but may also have inhibited adaptation. The program for closing uneconomic mines is very modest, but this is only part of the problem. Its core lies in the cost of production of those that continue to operate. Belgium suffered quite a setback in this matter at the height of the coal boom, after having made moderate progress up to 1956. The shift toward the Campine, and that area's general progress—at least through 1957—are favorable signs. The ability of a sizable part of the Belgian coal industry to command high prices for the quality of its coal also alleviates the problem. But at the end of the transition period, much of the Belgian coal industry still needed subsidies. The decline in demand set in motion pressures for adjustment that had not been felt in Belgium, or elsewhere in Western Europe, for several years. It also stimulated defensive and protective measures. By early 1959 it appeared that the balance was shifting, at least for the time being, toward adjustment and the closing of additional mines in the Borinage.

Meanwhile, the future of the coal industry continues to be a central issue of politics and economics inside Belgium. Fitting into the common market is only one aspect of the problem, operating perhaps more to force other issues than as a focus of major decisions. The resistance to drastic change is strong and comes from many sources. The possible political, economic, and social dislocations make strange bedfellows on many occasions. When any government seeks greater leverage over coal it generates opposition which accuses it of socialism. Nationalization is repeatedly mentioned but has not been strongly pushed by the Socialists or the unions in any sustained fashion. It would help solve the coal problem only if more were changed than ownership of the mines.

If at the end of the transition plus two years the Belgian coal industry really had to face a common market for coal in which effective competition based on costs of production was the dominant force, then the country's hardest period of adjustment would come at that moment unless extraordinary progress had been made in the two years. A more likely alternative, as later chapters will show, is that the whole Community is moving toward a regulated, subsidized, coal economy in which ways will be found to accommodate, more or less rationally, more or less efficiently and economically, a large number of "special" situations. The dominant notes of this economy would be that coal must be produced, that a wide range of costs can exist side by side, that improvement must not entail too great a pressure for change where change is disturbing, that the new must grow without necessarily scrapping the old, except slowly and if necessary gently, and that almost every difficulty can be handled, by spreading its cost if need be, and by avoiding the sharpest impact of market economics. In such a setting the Belgian coal industry could live and probably progress, if not too rapidly, and could carry its economic burdens in ways to which it has become accustomed. Within this system, crises may also have a place if, like the coal glut of 1958-59, they give a sudden push to the factors making for adjustment.

SUBSIDIES FOR ITALY

The mines at Sulcis in southwestern Sardinia produce about nine-tenths of Italy's coal.[33] Their output has been in the neighborhood of a million tons a year compared with Italian imports of 9 to 12 million tons. Output per worker remains the lowest in the Community in spite of sharp improvement in recent years. The quality of the coal limits its uses; about one-third is marketed in Sardinia and the rest in Sicily and on the Italian mainland. The Sulcis mines are run by a government-owned corporation, Compania Mineraria Carbonifera Sarda (Carbosarda), which has consistently lost money. It is the most important enterprise in southern Sardinia, a region of heavy unemployment, and figures in Italian plans as the main producer of energy for the island's development, which promises to be a long process.

When the coal and steel Treaty was being negotiated, the Italian government had under way a plan for new investment in the Sulcis mines, supported in part by American aid funds. The transitional Convention provided that for two years the High Authority could draw on the funds raised by the levy on Dutch and German coal production to assist the Sulcis mines "in order that they may be able, pending completion of the investment operations now under way, to face competition within the common market" (Section 27). How much aid should be given was left to the High Authority, which in March 1953 began making monthly payments based on Carbosarda's losses the year before. These became less regular when the Italian government proved dilatory about submitting a concrete plan to show what the investment program would accomplish.[34]

---

[33] The rest comes almost entirely from an anthracite mine in Val d'Aosta on the Swiss border which serves a steel firm. Domestically produced coal provides about 3 per cent of the energy Italy uses and the share is falling as oil and natural gas expand.

[34] The experience in this matter had not been good. A plan approved in March 1950 as a basis for American aid had projected a 50 per cent reduction in costs and an increase of production to 3 million tons by late 1953. Early in 1953 schedules were revised, calling for the attainment of

The High Authority seemed disposed to stop payments altogether but on the request of the Italian government it made some further grants, "making allowances for the social repercussions caused by a situation which appeared likely to go from bad to worse as time went on. . . ." [35]

The program submitted by the Italian government in the fall of 1954 was considerably revised by the High Authority's experts, and finally agreed to. Though the original two years expired, the High Authority made further payments bringing its total aid to $6.5 million, the original estimate. The High Authority also agreed to use some of its re-adaptation funds to help workers discharged from the Sulcis mines. [36]

The reorganization program approved by the High Authority called for a variety of measures, some bearing on the financial position of Carbosarda and others on the administrative and physical efficiency of its mining operations. Over a period of three or four years several pits were to be closed and all production concentrated in two. These measures led to the discharge of about 40 per cent of the workers. Production declined only slightly so output per manshift underground rose very rapidly (from 609 kg. in 1953 to 959 kg. in 1957). Obviously there was a great deal of concealed unemployment in the Sulcis mines. It follows that the statistical improvement in productivity and in the balance sheets of Carbosarda is matched by a shift of the problem to other parts of the Sardinian economy. Strikes have been frequent. Italy wanted an extension of Community subsidies for Sulcis. [37] Its request was turned down,

---

these goals by 1955, in a plan that a firm of American engineers called "without foundation and meaningless." U.S. Commission on Organization of the Executive Branch of the Government, *Task Force Report on Overseas Economic Operations* (Washington, Je. 1955), p. 273.

[35] HA, *Report*, Nov. 1954, p. 84.

[36] A total of 804 million lire of readaptation funds was set aside for Sulcis. By the middle of 1957 some 1,400 workers had benefited from this help. HA, *Report*, Apr. 1957, pp. 216, 217, and *Annexes*, p. 11; *Bulletin Mensuel*, Je. 1957, p. 12.

[37] From the beginning Italians felt it was discriminatory to limit aid to Sulcis to two years while Belgium got it for five. *Il Piano Schuman: Commenti e rilievi italiani*, 1951, p. 50.

probably because the High Authority suspected that coal mining at Sulcis could not be put on a sound basis.

Already in 1954 the High Authority had said it was "extremely doubtful whether the Sulcis mines, by using the funds advanced, will be able to face competition within the common market at the end of a period of two years." [38] A special committee of the Assembly shared this view. "In the opinion of all those concerned," said its rapporteur, "the Sulcis mines, so far as one can see ahead, will always be among the marginal basins." Even if better plans for the production and use of the coal were devised, costs would remain high and the mines would have difficulty in selling their products on the Italian market. "In these conditions, one should not expect the coal to be able to adapt itself to general conditions of competition in Europe." That being the case the committee questioned whether this was properly a matter of adaptation at all. Was it not rather a question whether Sulcis, and other marginal basins in the Community, should be kept in operation because they were of national importance, and if so at whose charge? [39]

The readaptation funds were an added subsidy, to Italy if not to Carbosarda, but they did not entail any High Authority responsibility for the continued losses of this enterprise (which fell from 4 billion lire to 1.4 billion

[38] HA, *Report*, Apr. 1954, p. 93.

[39] CA, Commission des Investissements . . . , *Rapport . . . par M. Heinrich Deist, Rapporteur*, doc. 21 (1954-55), Apr. 1955; quotations are from pp. 32, 36. The American engineers who surveyed the project had been equally gloomy a year earlier. After reviewing many of the same considerations as the Assembly committee, they concluded, "The solution or correction of the problems presented by this project are so complex and far reaching as to present no promise of accomplishment in the foreseeable future." *Task Force Report . . . ,* cited, p. 274. Daum, of the High Authority, refrained from endorsing the committee's views. While making it clear that the mines would remain marginal and unprofitable he thought that "very severe and very courageous measures" would produce costs "not too different from the probable selling price." CA, *Débats*, May 11, 1955, p. 346. Enrico Carboni, himself a Sardinian, presented a somewhat more optimistic view, emphasizing the social and development problems and criticizing some of the committee's conclusions. Same, pp. 342-346.

between 1956 and 1957).[40] It would appear that the answer
to one of the committee's questions is that if marginal
mines are to be subsidized, the governments will have to
find the funds. There remains the question whether the
High Authority would authorize continuation of Italian
subsidies. The issue is of great importance for Sulcis and
Sardinia; it is fairly important for the Italian government;
it is of little importance to the economy of the Community.
The amount of coal involved is small (less than half of one
per cent of the Community's output). If not available, it
would not be seriously missed. If subsidized, it would not
seriously distort the Community's economy. It is hard to
believe that anyone will feel very strongly that the Community should stand in the way of Italy's coping with this
one item of its multiform political and development problems. The principle involved in making such an exception
might seem more serious if it were not likely that by one
means or another exceptions will be made for many cases
in the Community's coal economy.

Unimportant as the matter is economically the Sulcis
experience seems to have been a rather sour one for the
Community. It took a good deal of pressure, including the
withholding of funds, to induce effective action by the
Italian government. The High Authority seems also to
have felt that it was not being treated as a partner in the
enterprise. The period of time set for the subsidies was
completed before effective action was taken. The suf-
ficiency of what was done seems doubtful. Although on
the face of the figures the High Authority's contribution
appears as mostly an underwriting of part of Carbosarda's
losses for several years, its real contribution was probably as
a goad, and perhaps as a supplier of expertise in the adoption
of a reorganization plan. The position of the Sulcis mines
has improved, so far as efficiency, costs, and the like are
concerned. Presumably this is a gain to the Italian economy,
even if Sardinian coal cannot do without a subsidy at the
end of the transitional period. But if that is the outcome,

[40] HA, *Report*, Apr. 1957, p. 181. The dates of the fiscal years are not
clear.

the whole exercise will have been rather futile so far as the Community is concerned. The futility results from a difference in criteria: the Community is concerned with the production of coal without artificial aid; the function of the Sulcis mines in the Italian economy is to produce coal and employment in Sardinia. The small, neat problem of Sulcis is an object lesson. It is not hard for the Community economy to accommodate the discrepancy in this case because of the negligible production. But there are elements of the Sulcis problem elsewhere in the Community, on a larger scale.

SUBSIDIES AND THE COMMUNITY

The French, Belgian, and Italian subsidies are not the only ones that exist in the European coal and steel industries. They are the overt, easily identifiable ones, which have a history because Community interest focused on them. They may well be the most important subsidies, but even that is hard to say because the rest are not so clearly defined.

"State assistance . . . in any form" is banned by the Treaty. The language is broad. Does this include the losses of nationalized enterprises, like the French coal mines, if they are met out of public funds? If government-owned railroad systems lose money, are not any practices that lead to the carriage of coal and steel below cost—or perhaps even at less than "the traffic will bear"—subsidies? If government financial agencies lend money at less than the market rate, or guarantee borrowings on these terms, is there not an element of subsidy? And what of tax laws? Is tax remittance a subsidy? What of exemptions and favorable amortization arrangements that have the effect of putting what would be public money into private investment? Equalization schemes, of which the Community has many, subsidize high-cost producers at the expense of more profitable enterprises (or the consumer). Transportation costs from the place of production to a basing point are sometimes shared equitably among all enterprises regardless of actual cost. Someone is being subsidized here, and though public funds may not

be directly involved—they are when any of the enterprises
are government-owned—the arrangements ultimately have
an effect on the fisc by cutting the taxable revenues of some
producers.

Obviously some distinctions have to be made. These are
not all the same thing, they do not all have the same economic effect. Plainly there are many kinds of subsidies, or
arrangements hard to distinguish from them, spread
through the Community economy. They cannot be treated
systematically for lack of information and because the
Community has not treated them systematically. Where
some have come to the surface, the High Authority's record
is hardly clear. The Belgian government was allowed to
subsidize coal mines to make up for the higher costs of
shorter work time. That was part of a larger scheme. The
French government was permitted to grant extra credits
to coal mines to equalize regional differences in family allowances.[41] That, it could be argued, was just a matter of
how the national accounts are kept, since coal mining and
social security are both government functions. The German government was told that it was all right for it to pay
part of the share of the coal companies' social security
taxes but that it would be an illegal subsidy to permit them
to deduct from their taxes a premium paid to encourage
steady work by miners.[42]

As the magnitude of the Community's problem of increasing coal production and obtaining the necessary labor
received added attention, as the continuing need to import
coal and scrap was more widely accepted, it began to look
as though subsidies of some sort would become more and
more common, and that the High Authority would have to
work out principles to help it determine what kinds of
state assistance it could permit (in spite of the Treaty's
flat language) and what kind it would call illegal. The
manipulation of subsidies and the decision what is a subsidy
are likely, then, to be continuing problems for the Com-

[41] HA, *Bulletin Mensuel*, Jan. 1956, p. 11. The payment is shown as a
receipt on the books of Charbonnages de France, not as part of its
deficit.

[42] Same, Je. 1956, pp. 18, 19; Nov. 1956, pp. 34, 35.

munity, and not just matters that were put behind it at the end of the transitional period. It is even conceivable that the time will come when all the complex forms of state aid mentioned above may have to be examined—not necessarily under the rubric of "subsidies"— to decide what effects they have on the Community's economy and, above all, what anyone can do about them.[43]

In the more limited sphere of the handling of overt subsidies during the transitional period, we find a mixed record. The French subsidies have in large part disappeared, partly because their aim was to offset conditions that the common market itself changed. Those that are left have been altered so that they fall into the vague area just described that the Community has not yet explored with any care. Belgian subsidies, transformed and augmented by the Treaty, have served part of their purpose but did not achieve their main aim and leave the future in doubt. Not the least significant part of this experience was the extent to which the High Authority had to reach right down into the Belgian coal economy, to the extent of distinguishing between firms as to their ability to use or do without the subsidy, in order to make its aid effective. This is an interesting example, which will bear further study, of the complex interplay between international and domestic pressures and decisions that can evolve out of a mixed entity like the Community. Finally, in the Italian case, the subsidies have probably failed to achieve their purpose, but the results do not seem serious for the Community.

Subsidies have a special place in the Community as flexible instruments for bridging the transitional period. In this role they have served moderately well but the full significance of the hardest test, Belgium, was obscured by the good times for the coal and steel industries that have helped the Community in so many ways while at the same time making its record so much harder to judge.

[43] In discussing the High Authority's need to get accurate figures on costs of production, Albert Coppé called attention to the subtleties of the subsidy problem and the difficulty of discovering what is going on merely from normal accounting arrangements. CA, *Débats*, Je. 27, 1957, pp. 726-729.

TEN

TAXES: A CRISIS PASSED

A SUPRANATIONAL tax that made the High Authority financially independent of the member countries was one of the features of the Community that warranted the claim that it was a new form of international cooperation. But of national taxes, much more important in amount and in their effect on production and sales, the Treaty said almost nothing. Governments were forbidden, naturally, to impose taxes "with an equivalent effect" to those of the abolished customs duties. The ban on discriminatory treatment had implications for tax systems, and other general principles of the Treaty could also have a bearing on taxation. Otherwise, taxation remained within each national jurisdiction. It was not even mentioned as a field in which governments should seek to harmonize their policies.

This was logical enough, given the character of the Community as a measure of partial integration. Power over taxation would reach deep into the economic and political life of each country, affecting not only the international position of the coal and steel industries but their place in the national economy as well. The touchy and complex problems of acting in this field might well have proved dangerous or insuperable for the Community authorities. No serious effort seems to have been made to extend Community powers to cover taxation, nor have the many proposals for expanding the Schuman Plan touched on this matter in any important way. Yet an argument over the rules to be applied to taxation became one of the first serious disputes within the Community. It divided France and Germany, the two countries on whose cooperation the

effective working of the new enterprise depended, and
required postponement of the opening of the common
market for steel—a potentially dangerous matter when so
much hinged on the psychology of initiating the Community by quick, effective steps. The issue was settled expeditiously, by reference to the aims of the Community
and objective, expert opinion, rather than by a test of
strength or a compromise. And then the problem—which
seemed to have so much importance—slipped out of sight
and never reappeared on the Community's agenda.

THE PROBLEM

Coal and steel traded between Community countries,
though exempt from tariffs, pass from one tax system into
another. Taxes in France, Germany, Belgium, and the
other countries are not uniform, so a ton of coal or steel
produced in one country is subject to quite different taxes
from that produced in another. This is a commonplace of
international trade and the practices for dealing with it, or
ignoring it, have become quite standardized. As a rule
nothing is done about direct taxes, those falling on the
producer and usually measured by his income or profits.
Wherever they are sold, goods simply bear the taxes applied in the country of their origin. But indirect taxes—
excise, turnover, sales taxes, for instance—are usually treated
differently. Here the common practice is for the importing
country to subject foreign goods to a special tax intended
to match the tax paid by domestic goods. Exports, in turn,
are frequently exempted from at least part of the indirect
tax that would be paid if they were consumed inside the
country.

The compensatory import taxes are not "equivalent
to tariffs," since they do not fall on imports alone but are
supposed to match the taxes paid on domestic production.
Nor is the exemption of exports from the last stage of the
domestic turnover tax—similar to a sales tax—regarded as a
subsidy or unfair trade practice. Both practices are recognized by GATT, the General Agreement on Tariffs and
Trade, as normal. The drafters of the Treaty probably took

it for granted that the same system would be applied in the Community.[1] However, when the time came for the High Authority to decide how steel prices should be quoted when the common market was opened, the Germans challenged the principle.[2] They urged that goods traded within the Community should bear the indirect taxes of the country in which they originated and should not be subject to compensating levies intended to match the taxes of the importing country.

In principle, the German argument rested on the contention that since there was now a common market there were no longer exports and imports, only trade within the Community. Rules that applied to foreign trade were therefore inappropriate. If consumers were all to be treated equally, as the Treaty prescribed, their nationality should not be the occasion for their having to pay different taxes on the same producer's goods. Whoever bought from the Ruhr, whether he was French, German, or Italian, should pay only the taxes imposed by the German government, just as he would pay the same price for Ruhr steel regardless of his nationality.

Not surprisingly, the Germans were not concerned only with establishing a principle. They were also concerned about the French. The traditional system of compensating for indirect taxes led to a much higher tax being paid when foreign steel entered France than when it entered any other Community country and a much larger tax rebate being given on exports from France than from the other countries. The effect, in the German view, was

[1] Professor Reuter, who participated in the negotiations, says, "the maintenance of the traditional system . . . was always envisaged in the course of the negotiations; in the absence of the official publication of the *travaux préparatoires* it is difficult to prove this, but the pattern of the Treaty's arrangements confirms the point." *La Communauté Européenne du Charbon et de l'Acier*, 1953, p. 183.

[2] The formal issue was whether producers' price quotations for steel could include taxes on which there might be a rebate when the goods were exported. In opening the common market for coal—on which turnover taxes were less important—the High Authority simply sanctioned existing practices. This was made easier by the fact that a ceiling price on coal was established.

to distort price relations and, in particular, to inhibit the
sale of German steel to France and encourage the sale of
French steel to Germany.

All of the countries of the Community had turnover or
transactions taxes on coal and steel, levied when the goods
changed hands at various stages of the process of production and sale. The French tax differed from the rest in two
respects. Its rates were higher, and instead of being levied
separately at each stage it was cumulative, but the share of
the tax paid at previous stages was refunded. Under the
German tax, a total of 9.8 per cent of the value of a ton
of steel billets was paid in turnover taxes, but if the goods
were exported they were exempted from 4.7 per cent,
roughly equivalent to the final stage of the tax.[3] Similar
figures applied in Belgium and Holland, while in Italy and
Luxembourg the rates were lower. In France, however, the
total turnover tax amounted to 29 per cent of the value of
steel billets, and the exemption for exports was 19.6 per
cent. Billets imported into Germany paid a compensating
tax of 4 per cent—roughly matching the last stage of the
domestic levy—while those imported into France were subject to a tax of 20 per cent.

The result of this, the Germans pointed out, was that
French steel coming to Germany paid a total turnover tax
of 13 to 14 per cent, while German steel moving to France
carried a total burden of 25 per cent, four-fifths of it made
up by the levy at the French frontier.[4] The German
objection was that to sell German steel to France one had to
pay a turnover tax nearly twice as high as that applied to

[3] Figures throughout this chapter come from the report of the Tinbergen committee (HA, *Report on the Problems Raised by the Different Turnover Tax Systems Applied within the Common Market*, Mar.
5, 1953—hereafter cited as Tinbergen Report) and differ somewhat from
those in other sources because of differences in assessing the incidence
of the taxes. The report gives data for four products, of which only
steel billets are used here for illustration. Figures are slightly different for
steel sheets and quite different for coal and coke.

[4] French steel paid 29 per cent minus 19.6 on being exported, plus 4
on being imported into Germany, for a total of 13.4. German steel paid
9.8 minus 4.7 plus 20 for a total of 25.1.

French steel sold to Germany, even though tariffs were abolished.[5] The effect of this system on price relations varied, of course, from product to product and from time to time. It could be significant. For example, at the end of 1952 the internal German price for Siemens-Martin merchant bars was 428 marks per ton, including tax, and the internal French price was equivalent to 472 marks. If the steel was traded, the effect of the tax changes alone—omitting transportation charges—was to raise the price of German steel in France to 480 marks and to lower the price of French steel in Germany to 419 marks. Thus, instead of being 9 per cent below French prices (as it was on a comparison of internal prices plus taxes) German steel became 2 per cent more expensive than French steel in both France and Germany.[6]

From the German point of view the problem was compounded by the fact that direct taxes, such as corporation income taxes, were more important in Germany than in France, where indirect taxes, particularly the turnover taxes, provided a much larger share of the government's revenue. Thus German steel was doubly burdened when it had to pay the high French turnover rates and the high German direct taxes, while French steel was doubly benefited when it paid lower direct taxes in the first place and then was exempted from much of the indirect tax on being exported, picking up only the relatively low compensatory German turnover tax in the process. The Germans did not propose to do anything about the difference in direct taxes. They apparently introduced them into the argument as a sort of makeweight to emphasize the inequities of the whole situation.[7] There was, to be sure, a

[5] However, the compensating arrangements were not altogether exact. It appeared from the Tinbergen committee's calculation that German billets moving into France paid less in taxes (25.1 per cent) than French steel sold inside France (29 per cent), while French steel moving to Germany paid rather more in taxes (13.4 per cent) than did German steel sold domestically (9.8 per cent).

[6] Horst Mendershausen, "First Tests of the Schuman Plan," *The Review of Economics and Statistics*, Nov. 1953, p. 279.

[7] They also pointed out that some German taxes could not properly be put in either category. "At least one member of the Committee felt

certain plausibility in this approach since the Germans were saying, in effect, that since no effort was made to compensate differences in national direct taxes, the same rule should be applied to indirect taxes within the Community. If the German proposal were adopted, German steel billets moving to France would pay about 10 per cent in turnover taxes instead of the 25 per cent they paid under the other system. French steel moving to Germany, on the other hand, would pay taxes of 29 per cent instead of about 14 per cent.

Thus the alternatives posed to the High Authority were: (1) to maintain the system traditionally applied in international trade, (2) to adopt the German proposal of applying only the taxes of the country of origin, or (3) to work out some new formula, presumably intermediate between the two approaches. Only indirect taxes were in question; there was no serious suggestion of doing anything about direct taxes.

THE SOLUTION

As it was to do in many later instances, the High Authority appointed a committee of economists.[8] They were asked a series of questions about existing practices and "the economic effects on the operation of the common market" of the alternative systems of handling indirect taxes. Within a month the committee had filed a report that clarified the actual situation in reasonable detail, showed the changes that would result from adopting the German proposal, and analyzed the issues in terms that contributed greatly to

---

compelled to agree with this assertion," but his emphasis was on the *irrelevance* of the distinction while the German argument implied that all taxes had to be treated in the same fashion, which did not follow. W. B. Reddaway, "The Implications of a Free Trade Area for British Taxation," *The British Tax Review*, Mar. 1958, p. 75n. Much of this article deals with the work of the Tinbergen committee of which its author was a member.

[8] Jan Tinbergen, Netherlands School of Economics, chairman; Leon Dupriez, Louvain; F. di Fenizio, Pavia; W. B. Reddaway, Cambridge. They were assisted by six experts, one from each country in the Community.

the understanding of some of the implications of partial integration.

The committee received representations, by delegation and document, from a number of interested parties. The experts had to make their own estimates of the existing tax situation. The figures presented to them varied considerably from brief to brief and a study of the practice of governments showed that existing exemptions and compensations did not fully equalize tax treatment of imported and domestic goods, partly because of differences in calculations of the incidence of the turnover taxes. Noting rather complicated arrangements for exemptions and compensations in some countries, the committee recommended simplification and a limitation of exemptions to the actual last stage of the tax. Otherwise, they pointed out, the High Authority would have no clear basis for appraising possible national manipulation of these levies. By and large, however, the existing practices could be regarded as amounting to the system of applying the indirect taxes of the country of destination. Adoption of this principle—the French alternative—would therefore cause no new disturbance when the common market was opened. On the other hand, adoption of the German alternative of levying the indirect taxes of the country of origin only would create significant changes.

While the avoidance of new disturbances was a consideration the High Authority might take into account, the committee did not base its case on this. Its aim, the committee said, was "to consider which system of taxation would produce the least distortion of the pattern of production and trade which would be established in the absence of taxes or, more exactly, in the absence of taxes which would introduce on the supply side an element which would distort the assessment of relative real costs of production." [9] The key point on which analysis rested was that the Community could deal only with taxes on coal and steel traded within the Community. What would happen if countries applied the "origin-only" principle to

[9] Tinbergen Report, cited, p. 23.

indirect taxes on coal and steel traded within the Community while applying the traditional "destination-only" system to all other trade among themselves and to their coal and steel trade outside the Community?

The key to the committee's thinking was put clearly and succinctly by one of its members: "The distinction between direct and indirect taxes is in itself irrelevant . . . : the relevant distinction is between taxes which apply uniformly (or approximately so) and the rest." [10] A nation's taxes, like other elements affecting its costs of production, enter into the determination of the exchange rate at which it can in the long run carry on its affairs with the rest of the world. But a single exchange rate cannot differentiate between products, so if there are special taxes, applicable only to certain industries or products, special treatment for their exports or imports may be suitable. General taxes, however, that apply to all products, must be treated uniformly in foreign trade, if the aim is that stipulated by the committee: to minimize, or neutralize, the effect of the tax system on the pattern of production and trade.

In practice, governments apply the origin-only system to direct taxes and the destination-only system to indirect taxes, though somewhat imperfectly. In principle they could apply either system to both sets of taxes, though administratively it would be very difficult to compensate for direct taxes in foreign trade. What they could not do without producing distortion was to apply a different system to the indirect taxes on coal and steel from that applied on all other products.[11] If the origin-only system were applied to coal and steel and not to other products, then the relation of costs within each country would be distorted by the tax system alone. The result would be false guidance as to the lines of production that should be pursued in each country. For instance, under the existing tax structure, if

[10] Reddaway, cited, p. 78.

[11] Unless all the turnover taxes within the Community were uniform, in which case application of a different system to certain products would make no difference so far as the tax burden was concerned (though there would of course be differences as to who received the revenue).

the origin-only system were applied to French coal and steel, exports of these products would bear a tax of 29 per cent while exports of other products would carry only 9.4 per cent tax. The result would be to encourage production of non-Treaty products, without regard to the real relation of costs of production within France. Imports of Treaty products would be encouraged artificially. Conversely, Germany would be encouraged to export Community products to France as a result of tax measures alone and without regard to whether Germany's real advantage might be to use the same resources to produce non-Treaty products. By a series of examples, the committee showed that a partial measure of this sort could lead to various anomalies, such as making the export of French nails to Germany cheaper than the export of the wire from which they were made, and to absurdities, such as indicating that France was a more economical place than Germany from which to export steel outside the Community while Germany was the better source of steel inside the Community. Distortion would also result from applying the origin-only system inside the Community and the conventional destination-only system to trade in coal and steel with third countries.

The effect of the Tinbergen committee's report was to support the French case. The alternatives, if economic distortion was to be avoided, were either to change the treatment of indirect taxes in all foreign trade—not only in non-Treaty products, but in trade outside the Community—or to apply the same turnover taxes in all Community countries (to all products, not just coal and steel; and this would still leave a problem regarding trade with the rest of the world). No one seriously considered these to be feasible alternatives. The High Authority accepted the committee's findings and the common market for steel was opened on May 1, 1953, with no change in the traditional system of handling indirect taxes.[12]

---

[12] The formal issue was solved by ruling that producers could not include in their quoted prices any taxes that would be refunded on export.

THE OUTCOME

Of course, the Germans were not very happy about this result. Some felt that finance had been lost in mathematics.[13] They complained that the committee had not taken full account of their "real" case, which concerned the total tax burden, direct and indirect. Agreeing that nothing could be done about direct taxes, they continued to argue that one could at least partly compensate for the situation by applying the origin-only rule to indirect taxes. The "defeat" was pointed to by some Germans as a harbinger of what was to come in the Community. With SPD support the Bundestag gave the government authority to raise the import equalization tax on steel to 12 per cent, which would have the effect of raising the price of French steel in Germany. The power was never used, perhaps because such a move, unaccompanied by a change in the domestic turnover tax, could be regarded as violating the Treaty since it would certainly appear to be a "tax equivalent to a tariff." More important, without doubt, was the Adenauer government's desire to make the Community work. An American who was officially concerned with European steel problems at the time says that when the German government announced that it would not change its tax rate, "A sigh of relief went up from the High Authority. . . . Thus passed a most significant crisis for the High Authority; a sovereign state had recognized the super-sovereignty of the new supranational organization and had agreed to abide by the latter's decision—a real milestone in European unification. . . ."[14]

The German assent was conditional. There were to be more explorations and discussions. But the strong German concern about turnover taxes died down. An increase in French prices and a drop in German prices at about the time the common market for steel was opened was looked

[13] Kurt Richebächer, "Luxemburger Hexen-Einmaleins," *Der Volks- wirt*, Apr. 25, 1953, pp. 13-14.

[14] T. C. Clark, "Inaugurating the Coal and Steel Community," in A. W. Macmahon, ed., *Federalism: Mature and Emergent*, 1955, p. 486.

on by many as an adjustment to the ruling. Since then there is little evidence of special concern with the turnover tax as a factor influencing German trade in Treaty products. Such complaints as there have been about French competition have focused on other matters. Revision of the whole domestic turnover tax structure has been under study and discussion for years but its foreign trade aspects fade into insignificance compared to its domestic complications, political and economic. German tax experts looking toward the European Economic Community have followed the reasoning of the Tinbergen committee in rejecting the idea of applying the origin-only rule to turnover taxes.[15]

On the Community agenda, turnover taxes have almost dropped out of sight. Studies go on; the High Authority has dealt with some discriminatory practices resulting from failure to apply the rules properly.[16] One issue of interest arose in late 1957, of a very different character from the first. The contending parties were the Ruhr coal industry and the German Minister of Economics. Displeased at the rise in German coal prices, Dr. Erhard was seeking ways to subject Ruhr coal to greater competitive pressure (Chapter 11). He thought of eliminating the tax on imported coal that compensated for the last stage of the German turnover tax. But the High Authority objected that this would discriminate against German coal producers.

[15] Institut "Finanzen und Steuern," *Europäische Wirtschaftsgemeinschaft und Steuerpolitik—eine Einführung*, Je. 1957. However, this report also regards the destination-only rule as unsatisfactory for the common market in the long run because it entails the maintenance of customs frontiers and because of the difficulty of matching the exemptions and compensations with the actual incidence of the tax. The report favors harmonization of taxes that would reduce discrepancies among countries and so make the border-crossing adjustments unnecessary. A similar view was expressed by an official of the German finance ministry. *Bulletin des Presse- und Informationsamtes der Bundesregierung*, Dec. 19, 1957, pp. 2170, 2171.

[16] At one time the Belgian government failed to remit the turnover tax on scrap exports. At another it exempted government purchases of Belgian and Luxembourg goods from the turnover tax and was required to extend this privilege to all Community products. In late 1955 French steel producers passed along a tax saving to domestic buyers but not foreigners and this had to be rectified. It was really a matter of price discrimination rather than of the tax rules.

If Erhard's suggestion was seriously intended, this episode is notable as probably the first instance in which Community rules that stemmed primarily from a fear of national discrimination against foreigners have been used to protect producers against their own government.

In a way it is curious that the tax issue has disappeared so completely from the list of Community difficulties. The analysis of the Tinbergen committee, cogent as it is, is pitched at a level that does not always satisfy businessmen worried about competition, politicians looking for issues to be exploited for national advantage, or journalists concerned with the part of the iceberg that shows. The committee's reasoning was close, and perhaps a bit difficult for laymen. It had to abstract from a number of features of the real world and made some assumptions about "other things," for instance exchange rates, that may not have corresponded to all of the facts.[17] That the lesson in economics had not been fully learned, or at least was not being heeded, was clear from some of what was said about related issues in the arguments over the "harmonization" of social charges when the treaty creating the European Economic Community was being discussed.

Nevertheless, in the Coal and Steel Community the original decision about turnover taxes has been accepted with no further to-do. There have been some changes in the way turnover taxes were handled, especially in France, but no Community government appears to have tried to manipulate these arrangements to its national advantage since the opening of the common market; hence, the possible conflict between tax autonomy and the conditions of competition on the common market has not caused any embarrassment. Very likely the fact that the solution maintained the *status quo* and did not make big changes helped. Prosperity and the satisfactory state of the German steel industry during the life of the Community undoubtedly contributed their share. The Germans have found them-

---

[17] The committee did not rest its whole case on exchange rate adjustment. It took account of factor prices, especially wages, as elements that normally helped in the adjustment to different tax burdens.

selves reasonably able to compete where they wanted to without worrying too much about the incidence of turnover taxes. Producers have probably come to regard taxes largely as elements in the cost of production that simply have to be reckoned with and that are not too troublesome so long as governments do not make frequent or marked changes in rates or methods of levying them. They may also have come to see the solution as "fair" since the customer always pays approximately the same sales tax, no matter from whom he buys his steel. Also, the solution may have come to seem quite normal since it follows the usual practice in international trade outside the common market.

The analysis of the Tinbergen committee and the policy the Community has followed "must not be taken as implying that 'any old set of taxes will do': unquestionably there are certain types of action in the tax field which would distort international trade very badly."[18] Neither is there an implication that the pattern of taxation existing in the Community or the system of leaving turnover tax rates to national decision is the best possible one for achieving the purposes set out in the Treaty. The argument is only that a common market is *compatible* with such a system provided certain rules are followed. This issue may come up again as the six countries develop their European Economic Community and as they consider joining with others in a larger free trade area. One of the key arguments of the Tinbergen Report will not apply, since all, or almost all, products will be involved, not just coal and steel. But it will remain true that some very odd results would be obtained by applying one system to the compensation of turnover taxes within the Common Market or Free Trade Area and another to trade with the rest of the world. The arguments of the Tinbergen committee apply generally to international trade; it is only if countries move much further toward complete monetary and fiscal fusion that major new issues arise.

The *Steuerstreit* is important for an understanding of the

[18] Reddaway, cited, p. 73.

Coal and Steel Community. First, it provided a striking demonstration, thanks to the Tinbergen committee, of the way in which the scope of "partial integration" is limited not only by the powers retained by the national governments but by the economic consequences of some measures that affect only part of an economy. Second, the outcome shows how, in spite of their apparent illogicalities, imperfect measures of partial integration can operate in a reasonably satisfactory fashion. Finally, the whole episode is significant as a reminder of how the great issues of one moment can become the nullities of another.

ELEVEN

PRICES, THE KEY TO
SEVERAL ISSUES

"CHEAPER COAL and steel," many people would have told you, was what they expected from the creation of the common market. The formulation was unsophisticated (cheaper relative to what?), but the idea was real enough. Certainly the common market was supposed to make coal and steel production in the six countries more economical. But if "cheaper" was to be translated into prices, the Treaty had to be more circumspect.

Price is not mentioned at all in the Treaty's opening statement of the Community's mission; tacitly, and quite properly, price policy is treated as a means to the ends of "the expansion of the economy, the development of employment and the improvement of the standard of living. . . ." The implication is that what the Community does about prices must be what is necessary to achieve these broad aims. But prices are specifically mentioned in the next article—and immediately tumbling after comes the spate of words qualifying, explaining, and conditioning, that accompany everything the Treaty says about prices. ". . . the institutions of the Community shall . . . seek the establishment of the lowest possible prices without involving any corresponding rise either in the prices charged by the same enterprises in other transactions or in the price-level as a whole in another period, while at the same time permitting necessary amortization and providing the possibility of normal returns on invested capital" (Article 3).

The Treaty's provisions on prices are complicated

(Articles 60-64). My summary that follows sets out only their main points, not their lush fullness. Some nuances have probably been lost, some special circumstances ignored, and perhaps some legal solecisms committed. But the exposition should suffice as a framework for the rest of the chapter which deals with the broad outlines of price formation and policy in the Community without attempting to analyze the price structure completely.

THE RULES

Equality is the basic principle of the Community's price law. Discrimination is flatly forbidden. Within the common market a seller may not price his goods so as to apply "unequal conditions to comparable transactions." He is specifically forbidden to discriminate according to nationality. Nor may he engage in "unfair competitive practices," especially temporary price reductions to gain a monopoly.

Sellers are required to publish the prices at which they will offer their goods to all comers within the Community. The prices are quoted at specified places from which buyers must pay the cost of transportation. The seller may change his prices at any time, after giving five days' notice, but while a published schedule is in force he may not depart from it except:

(1) to lower (but not raise) his price to meet competition at a different basing point from his own; that is, he may absorb part or all of the cost of transportation between his mine or mill and the other basing point in order to offer his goods as cheaply as those of a competitor selling from that basing point;

(2) to meet the competition of goods coming from a country outside the Community, subject to regulation by the High Authority;

(3) to accomplish specific purposes authorized by the High Authority.

If the Treaty had contained only these rules for "normal" times, serious questions would have arisen as to whether its price mechanism was adequate to serve the

Community's major purposes in times of difficulty. The High Authority has, therefore, been given power to establish minimum and maximum prices within the common market (and, under a different formula, for exports). Minimum prices can only be fixed if the High Authority finds that "a manifest crisis exists or is imminent." Maximum price-fixing is not subjected to these conditions, but may be used only as a means of attaining the aims set out in Article 3 and especially that quoted above. In either of these cases—as, indeed, in many other matters concerning prices—the High Authority can only act after consulting the Consultative Committee and the Council of Ministers. In times of crisis the High Authority may also establish quotas on production or allocate scarce supplies but before it does this it is expected to try to achieve results by price-fixing (which is also procedurally easier, since the direct controls require positive action by the Council of Ministers).

On paper, these provisions give the High Authority a good bit of discretion to influence, and in some circumstances control, prices in the Community. It is a testimony to the breadth and flexibility of the Treaty's provisions that the Convention governing the transitional period, which is normally a vehicle of flexibility, has no special rules concerning price policy (except for one or two points incidental to other arrangements). The range of powers and the discretion given the High Authority were necessary if the Community was to cope effectively with a variety of circumstances. The drafters also had to steer their way through conflicting views of the way coal and steel prices should be set, the functions they should perform, and the degree to which the Community should be *dirigiste* or *laisser faire*. Some of the language in the articles dealing with prices reflects compromises among these views. It is notable, too, that the Treaty carries no broad statements of principle about the role of prices. The price system neither is ensconced as *the* proper guide to the allocation of resources nor is it made subordinate to "social purposes." Instead, it is left to inference that pricing

practices are to serve the ends of the Treaty, in one way
or another.

Broadly speaking, the Treaty has conformed to the
pricing philosophy set out by Monnet and his French
colleagues in the working paper they submitted to the other
delegations at the outset of the drafting negotiations.

The objective assigned to the High Authority would be to
contribute by all means at its disposal to a policy of economic
expansion, of full employment, and of a rising standard of
living for the workers. . . . For the accomplishment of these
tasks, the High Authority would receive certain limited and
specific powers. . . . Thus in the matter of *prices* the powers
of the High Authority would be focused on the protection
of the consumer without discrimination, on the elimination of
unfair trade practices, and on the constant expansion of production and markets. The essential task of the Authority in
this field would be to set general rules designed to enable the
price system to perform its real function.[1]

As rendered in the Treaty these principles mean that
ordinarily prices will be set by producers, in accordance
with the regulations. Sometimes, the High Authority will
set maximum or minimum prices, but this will be exceptional. Prices are to be public and nondiscriminatory.
Underlying all is the tacit assumption that the Community
is concerned with prices not primarily to keep them high
or low or even at a level that satisfies a particular formula,
but rather to assure that they serve the general aims of
the Treaty. As Raymond Vernon puts it, "The normal
rule . . . is that the Community should control pricing
practices, but not prices." [2]

How the price rules have been applied is the burden of

[1] *Summary of the Working Document Submitted by the French Experts* (mimeographed). A later passage suggests that prices would be
free to move only between upper and lower levels that would be "under
constant review," presumably by the High Authority. This idea which
was fostered by some of the French experts was not incorporated in the
Treaty except in the attenuated form of emergency maximum and minimum prices.

[2] Raymond Vernon, "The Schuman Plan—Sovereign Powers of the
European Coal and Steel Community," *American Journal of International Law,* Apr. 1953, p. 198.

the rest of this chapter. After a brief account of the first impact—the end of double-pricing—coal and steel will be treated separately, for they have raised different problems and called forth action under different provisions. The final section examines some major issues about the character of Community prices and points to some unanswered questions.

DOUBLE-PRICING

The clearest, quickest, least disputable result of the application of the Treaty's price rules was the elimination of double-pricing. The whole point of double-pricing was that foreigners must pay a different price from domestic buyers—usually more[3]—and it was thus clearly incompatible with the Treaty's flat ban on discrimination according to nationality within the Community.

During much of the postwar period coal and steel were scarce in Europe. Governments were anxious to keep down the domestic cost of these basic commodities, so they fixed maximum prices for home sales, but foreigners could be charged more. The whole British coal economy was at one time geared to financing domestic losses from export profits. The Allied officials controlling the German economy charged higher prices for Ruhr coal when it was exported. France had done the same with its iron ore. Belgium, which thus had to pay higher prices for iron ore than its French competitors and higher prices for imported coke than its German competitors, resorted to double-pricing for the steel it had for export when that commodity was short in other countries.

The ECA and OEEC had worked toward the elimination of double-pricing.[4] Their limited success was probably due less to the will to cooperate than to improvement in supply and decline in demand which made it harder to

[3] In times past the reverse was often true; exports were sold more cheaply in order to meet competition while domestic prices could be kept higher thanks to tariffs or other trade barriers. This is dumping, in the technical as well as popular sense. It was frequent in the steel trade between the wars.

[4] See my *Trade and Payments in Western Europe*, 1952, Chapter 15.

command export premiums and made producers more interested in keeping their export markets. Though double-pricing declined in importance the High Authority found some significant examples. When the common market was established. German coal exports cost DM 5 a ton more than home sales; the margin for lignite was double that. Thick steel plate cost over DM 100 more when it was sold to Italy than when it was sold in Germany (plus transport, of course). French iron ore sold for 854 francs a ton to Frenchmen but cost 1,300 if the buyers were Belgian.[5]

It was up to the sellers (subject to the influence of their governments) whether to end double-pricing by cutting the export price or raising the domestic one. In practice, they often set the price halfway. For instance the export price of French iron ore was cut from 1,325 francs per ton to 1,240 while the domestic price, which had been 854, rose to meet it. In this case the change made less difference than the figures suggest because most major French steel firms owned iron mines. Taken in the large, however, the elimination of double-pricing was an important step in achieving the Treaty's aim of equality. In effect, and in method too, it was comparable to the treatment of trade barriers and national discrimination in transport rates.[6] On exports to countries outside the common market, however, double-pricing continued and became one of the important issues between the Community and the rest of the world (see Chapter 17).

COAL PRICES

Western Europe was desperately short of coal when the war ended. Large imports from the United States helped

[5] HA, *Report*, Jan. 1954, pp. 12, 13.

[6] Somewhat related to double-pricing was the system of "special prices" applying inside Germany. By law coal was sold to certain classes of customers at less than the regular prices. This practice covered households, the Bundesbahn and other railroads, inland and maritime shipping, deep-sea fishing boats, and gas and electric power stations. In a series of steps worked out by the High Authority and the German government this special treatment was ended within a year or two.

meet immediate needs and continued even after production had risen substantially. Only in early 1950 when the steady rise in European production combined with a drop in demand resulting from the recession, did the shortage seem to be over. Then in mid-1950 the Korean war set forces in motion that expanded demand for all heavy goods and raw materials and once more brought a coal shortage to Europe. By the time the common market for coal opened in February 1953, the main force of the Korean boom was spent. The pressure of demand had eased; coal production in the Western European countries was still rising; imports from the United States were falling; stocks were growing. Industrial production in France, Belgium, Luxembourg, and the Saar declined somewhat during 1952, but continued to rise in Holland and Italy, and to jump ahead in Germany. One could begin to talk of some kind of stability in Western European coal markets, especially as there had been a sharp drop in steel exports and prices.

Still governments retained their control over coal prices and the High Authority decided to be cautious and follow the same course. It wished to avoid any immediate jolts to national economies and, perhaps, to prepare the ground for a possible decline in coal prices. Sudden removal of controls might invite price rises that would temporarily disrupt the structure of other costs and prices, which would then be upset again if a decline followed. The High Authority expected, too, that there would be delays before trade found its way into the new channels formed by the creation of a single market; continued controls might make adjustments easier. Not least important among the factors influencing the High Authority's decision was the fact that most of the coal trade was still in the hands of national exporting or importing monopolies. To remove price ceilings would simply be to turn over control to these cartels, especially to the German sales organization that would control the Ruhr's output, the largest part of the Community's supply.

So the common market opened with most coal prices

fixed by the High Authority close to the prevailing level set by national action.[7] As production rose and demand fell, coal continued to become more plentiful during the first year of the common market. In the spring of 1954 the Consultative Committee advised the High Authority that it favored removing the price ceilings unless there was special temporary need for them. The Council of Ministers divided. The High Authority decided to keep the price ceilings for the two largest basins, the Ruhr and the Nord, lest the marketing organizations controlling their sales determine the level of Community prices. All other coal was freed from price fixing, except in Belgium where the subsidy arrangements established a maximum price.

The Dutch believed that the High Authority's policy inhibited a fall in coal prices, from which they would benefit. They felt that the maximum price tended to become the minimum, too. They wanted more effective action against the coal sales organizations but believed this should be taken under the cartel provisions of the Treaty and not by price controls. They took a case to the Community Court but lost.

From the later part of 1954 on, the demand for coal grew in the Community. The price ceilings continued to be an issue to which was added pressure for raising the ceiling as costs rose, particularly in the Ruhr where there were annual wage increases. Alignments on these issues in the Consultative Committee and the Council of Ministers shifted from time to time.[8] The decision, however, lay with the High Authority. In the spring of 1955 it ended maximum pricing for French coal and allowed an increase in the Ruhr. Later in the year, the Belgian coal removed from the subsidy scheme rose in price when ceilings were removed.

[7] Certain small fields were exempted on the ground that competition from the larger basins would keep their prices in line. A few price changes resulted from the introduction of basing points. The way ceilings were set permitted some flexibility. See HA, *Report*, Apr. 1953, pp. 68-69, for details. Belgian prices dropped because of the introduction of the subsidy. German and French prices remained generally where they had been.

[8] E. B. Haas, *The Uniting of Europe*, 1958, traces these, pp. 345-348, 493.

The ceiling price on Ruhr coal became the central issue of the Community coal policy. Factors of quite different sorts had to be taken into account. There was obviously danger that continuing to limit Ruhr prices would come to smack of discrimination. It risked reviving the criticism by some Germans that the Community was really a scheme to give Germany's customers control of the Ruhr coal supply. To restore price ceilings in other fields would have looked like a backward step. The High Authority wanted to avoid giving the impression that whenever things got difficult it resorted to controls. The pressure for continuing the Ruhr price ceilings was not particularly strong; a majority of the Consultative Committee favored freeing prices. For the High Authority the issue of the Ruhr price ceiling was linked with the negotiations for reforming the Ruhr coal sales organization (Ch. 14).

Formally the question of the price ceiling was a matter for the High Authority alone to decide. It had to confer with the governments, through the Council of Ministers, but it was in no way bound by their opinion. In Treaty law the German government had no special position; it could not legally impose a maximum price for coal if the High Authority removed its ceiling. In fact, however, an arrangement between Bonn and the Ruhr to limit the rise in the coal price preceded, and was probably understood to be a condition of, the action finally taken in Luxembourg.

Concerned about the effects of the boom on its economy and currency, the German government was anxious to keep down prices. It was, however, committed to a philosophy of free enterprise and a practical policy of using few direct controls. This had not prevented it from fixing coal prices in the past but it was, in a sense, relieved of a burden when the High Authority took over this job. Politically there were also difficulties, since the support of heavy industry was important to the Adenauer government. The ideal solution from Bonn's point of view would probably have been an arrangement that removed the price control without increasing the price, but this was clearly not to be.

The Ruhr mine-owners claimed that their price should

go up about DM 6 per ton (10-12 per cent for most types), to cover two wage increases and a rise in other costs.[9] Minister of Economics Erhard wanted to keep the increase smaller. After some hard bargaining a compromise provided a price increase of DM 2 per ton for most coal, but a gain in receipts to the mines of about DM 6. The gap was filled by the government's agreeing to a bonus for underground workers that could be deducted from the companies' wages tax; reduction of the mines' contribution to the workers' insurance fund, the government making up the difference; a tax concession in the form of new write-off provisions for underground installations, and some other changes.[10] After this agreement was announced in the Bundestag, the High Authority eliminated the price ceiling for Ruhr coal, as of April 1, 1956.

Thus in the course of a little over three years the Community moved from a situation in which all governments controlled coal prices through one in which the High Authority controlled most of them to a new stage in which almost all the coal was free of formal control. Only the subsidized Belgian coal was subject to High Authority ceilings.[11] The governments were supposed to have no controls at all. They continued, however, to have a crucial influence. The arrangement between Bonn and the Ruhr—called by some "the peace of Walsum" after the place at which Erhard announced its major features—was

[9] Bernd Huffschmid, "Unbefriedigende Rentabilität an der Ruhr," *Der Volkswirt,* Jan. 14, 1956, pp. 14-15, gives their calculations.

[10] Early in May 1956 the High Authority ruled that the payment of the miners' bonuses out of public funds constituted a subsidy not permitted by the Treaty. It accepted the other measures. A process of study and negotiation began which resulted in the German government's being permitted to continue the special subsidy until the spring of 1958. After that, the bonuses would continue but the employers would have to pay their full share of the insurance premiums. If prices were increased before the spring of 1958, the subsidy arrangement was to end.

[11] In Italy a governmental committee regulated the price of imported coal for some time after the High Authority called this practice illegal. It was stopped in September 1956. The High Authority also challenged an arrangement by which an import agency of the Luxembourg government manipulated coal prices.

not only the condition precedent for the High Authority's removal of price ceilings. In Erhard's view it also obliged the German producers to make no major price changes without the government's agreement.[12] In France, officials of the nationalized coal industry complained that the government would not let them raise prices as much as necessary. In the Netherlands, there were also government-owned mines and prices generally were set through consultations in which the government played a part. By the spring of 1957 the High Authority was concerned about the influence of governments on prices (in steel as well as coal).[13] Complete freedom was hardly to be expected, its language suggested, but in the absence of coordination of national economic policies governments would influence prices in different ways, resulting in distortion of production and trade.

Then, in the fall of 1957, an episode raised questions about the influence of governments and suggested new possibilities for the patterns of Community price-making. Again the focus was Germany. Prices in other countries followed the Ruhr upward in the spring and summer of 1956. With the rather reluctant consent of the German government, the Ruhr raised prices again in the fall. By the middle of 1957 coal prices throughout the Community had risen, usually some 7 to 9 per cent over the level of April 1956, but as much as 20 to 25 per cent for some Belgian coal. Demand continued to rise as industrial production increased in the first half of 1957, but the output of coal was lower than it had been the year before.

In July the Unternehmensverband Ruhrbergbau informed the German government that it would need a further price increase, principally to cover higher labor costs. The pro-

---

[12] On November 28, 1957, he told the Bundestag that in the negotiations of the previous spring, "the representatives of the coal-mining industry expressed their readiness, without infringing the competence of the High Authority, to reach agreement with me before taking decisions affecting economic policy." *Bulletin des Presse- und Informationsamtes der Bundesregierung*, Nov. 30, 1957, p. 2048.

[13] HA, *Report*, Apr. 1957, pp. 24-28, 129.

ducers were apparently persuaded to wait until after the election.[14] Immediately after the CDU victory they made clear their intention of proceeding. Costs had risen, they said, and especially social security charges as a result of measures put into effect not long before the election.[15] Wage costs were also higher; the shorter workweek meant hiring additional miners. The Unternehmensverband said that three-quarters of the Ruhr mines would lose money at the existing level of costs—a figure not widely credited outside the industry. Even with the higher price, Ruhr coal would still be the cheapest in the Community. Demand was high and there was little doubt that the traffic would bear a higher charge.

Erhard wanted the mines to wait. A price rise so soon after the election might have a bad political effect. It might also start a wave of price increases at a time when the government was fighting against inflationary forces. In answer to the charge that he was betraying his own principles of a free economy, Erhard pointed out that the coal price was still a cartel price. In any case, he was skeptical of the Ruhr's calculations. Costs ranged so widely between the best and the worst mines that general figures were always rather arbitrary. The new social security charges might not prove as burdensome as the employers alleged. Many coal mines were owned by profitable steel and chemical companies that could afford to carry them at less than maximum profit for some time if the government's *Konjunktur* policy was at stake.

Though some coal producers had misgivings—"We all know how hard it is to carry on mining if the government

[14] Interview with Alfred Wimmelmann, chairman of the Unternehmensverband, *Der Spiegel*, Oct. 23, 1957.

[15] In particular the employers alleged that more men were reporting sick because of the improved sickness benefits. Under the new arrangements sick pay started sooner and was higher than before. The employer had to make up the difference between 50 and 90 per cent of a man's wages. Erhard later confirmed the higher rate of absence (11 per cent in August and 17.3 per cent in September compared to 8.5 to 8.7 per cent in the same months of 1956) but suggested that summer heat and Asian flu accounted for most of the increase. *Bulletin* . . . , cited, p. 2046.

does not cooperate," said one[16]—the majority of the members of the Unternehmensverband voted to go ahead in spite of Erhard's opposition. They refused his plea for a month's delay; the facts would not change and meanwhile they would be losing revenue. Manners were rather brusque on both sides and before Erhard thought the negotiations were over the producers submitted their new price scales to the High Authority. Though appealed to by Erhard, the High Authority had no clear basis for ruling against the price increases so long as there was no abuse of monopoly power or violation of the rules for setting prices. No country asked for reimposition of the ceiling on Ruhr prices. On October 1 Ruhr prices rose about 6 to 8 per cent on coal and 10 per cent on coke. Noting that the increases "correspond very closely with the increases that had already been introduced by the principal basins of the Community," [17] the High Authority nevertheless agreed to study the situation in detail.

Erhard threatened countermeasures. A change in transportation rates that discriminated against imported coal would make American coal cheaper at various points in Germany. Elimination of the equalization tax on imported fuel oil and coal would bring down their price. Ending the government aid to the coal industry would be another possible sanction. The government-owned coal mines—producing about 17 per cent of the Ruhr's output—could continue to sell at the old price. There were difficulties with some of these courses; some fell afoul of the nondiscrimination rules of the High Authority or of GATT; some were not so easily put into effect; the government-owned mines had long-term contracts tying them to the Ruhr sales organization. There was political danger in threatening the whole coal industry and there would soon be elections in North Rhine-Westphalia. The political opening that the episode gave the Socialists tended to damp any impetuosity on Erhard's part. The coal miners' union called for creation of a *Kohlenwirtschaftsrat* in which

---

[16] *Der Spiegel*, October 23, 1957.
[17] HA, *Bulletin Mensuel*, Nov. 1957, p. 11.

workers and the government would participate with the employers in making major decisions.

Erhard's arguments raised questions about long-run coal policy (see Ch. 23) and also about the way responsibility was shared between governments and the High Authority. "It seems to me," he told the Bundestag, "that there is here a logical gap in the Coal and Steel Treaty. A minister of economics, who bears the responsibility for the whole national economic policy, that is for the whole sphere of the national economy, cannot be fully dismissed from responsibility for such important branches as coal and steel." [18] Once again, partial integration presented itself as a central problem of the Community.

Other members of the Council of Ministers were undoubtedly sympathetic with Erhard's views; they might—and perhaps already did—have similar problems. To the High Authority, the whole episode proved the importance of pushing ahead the work on coordination of national policies, a course it had been urging for some time without much success. (It particularly lacked support in Germany where "coordination" was looked on as only too likely to spell adulteration of a successful domestic policy and an unwelcome shouldering of the burden of other countries' inflations.) Another possible course (favored, some said, by Erhard) was to amend the Treaty so as to provide some greater check on the freedom of producers to set prices. But to whom should this power be given? The governments, was the most likely answer, for they had the political responsibility and, as Erhard said, could not exclude coal and steel from their activities. Another possible answer, which no one seemed to be advocating publicly, was to expand the High Authority's powers and responsibilities, so that it would be able to take account of the impact of price changes in broader terms than the Treaty allowed. To provide more time for working out these problems when the issue rose again, the High Authority changed the price rules to require at least a month's

[18] *Bulletin des Presse* . . . , cited, p. 2045.

notification from the Ruhr sales organizations of contemplated price changes.[19]

Not long afterwards the immediate concern of the governments changed. The drop in demand over the winter
of 1957-58, along with large imports of American coal led
to increases in stocks that became sizable by the early
spring of 1958. Though producers in some basins reported
additional increases in costs of production, none felt able to
increase prices. The Ruhr postponed the DM 2 rise that
was to compensate for the loss of government aid in April
1958. That the problems of coal surplus were likely to be
with the Community for a long time seemed doubtful,
and the questions about the proper role of governments in
pricing were not answered. For the time being, however,
they would be dealt with, not just in terms of how to
hold down the price but in a setting that required answers
to further questions about the relation of coal to other
fuels, the place of coal imports in the Community, and the
way coal production should be organized. (See Ch. 23.)

Zonal Prices

In addition to fixing maximum coal prices at the opening
of the common market, the High Authority took two other
steps to avoid immediate disturbance. It suspended the
right of coal producers to align their prices on those of
competitors at distant basing points. Rigorous adherence
to this ban would have substantially raised the price of
coal in some areas and disrupted some established trade
channels. Aachen coal, for instance, would cost more than
Ruhr coal in most parts of Germany. Southern Germany
would have to pay more for coal from the Saar and
Lorraine. On the French coast, British and perhaps other
foreign coal might displace supplies from the Saar, the
Nord, and Lorraine, if full transport costs were added to
the basic prices set in those basins. Elsewhere in southern

---

[19] This rule also applied to Cobechar, the Belgian coal sales organization. The month could be extended to two if the High Authority consulted the Consultative Committee. *JO*, Dec. 27, 1957, pp. 629-631.

and central France there would be sharp rises in price. For these and some other trades the High Authority established "zonal prices" that permitted partial absorption of transport costs by producers. From time to time others were added. The Ruhr gave concessions for sales to coastal points in Germany, the Netherlands, and Italy. Mines in Lower Saxony, the Centre-Midi, and Sardinia were all permitted some zonal pricing, usually within their own countries. Belgian coke was subject to zonal pricing when sold in Belgium, Luxembourg, and Lorraine.

As conditions changed, the margins of difference between zonal prices changed and some were abandoned altogether. By the spring of 1957 the Lorraine zonal pricing for German sales was dropped, but that for the Saar was continued for another year, presumably as part of the process of tying the Saar into the German economy and helping to overcome the difference between the area's price structure (which was close to that of France) and the lower Ruhr prices. Apart from the Saar sales, the only zonal price arrangements continued during the final year of the transitional period were those for Lower Saxony, Sulcis, and the Centre-Midi. These, said the High Authority, "represent certain permanent elements in the pattern of sales in the Common Market, and it will probably be necessary at the end of the transition period to introduce in their place an arrangement allowing price alignment," as provided by the Treaty.[20]

Shortly after the end of the transitional period the High Authority rescinded its ban on the alignment of coal prices. It was somewhat uncertain about what the effects might be and set a number of limiting conditions. Its aims, it said, were to protect small basins whose production was needed by the Community and to assure that the transportation of coal should be as regular as possible.[21] One effect of this

---

[20] HA, *Report*, Apr. 1957, p. 167.
[21] HA, *Report*, Apr. 1958, v. 2, pp. 25-27; *JO*, Mar. 29, 1958. Prices could be aligned only on those of the major producers, had to conform to their sales conditions, could not be used for road transport and had to be reported to the High Authority. Each producer could sell only a limited amount of coal in this fashion.

rule was to permit the price alignment to replace the remaining zonal price arrangements.

Zonal pricing offsets geography and favors certain consumers; it may also make it cheaper to buy from a more distant supplier than from the nearer one who would be the natural source. It is, therefore, a considerable departure from the Community's pricing principles. Perpetuation of the system would have produced a rather different structure of coal sales from that implicit in the Treaty. Some features of the system seemed likely to make for its perpetuation. Not only would producers want to hold on to privileged market positions but buyers would not have an incentive to seek out their economically "correct" supplier so long as someone else paid enough of the freight to make his coal cheaper. If the demand for coal had remained low, these measures intended to permit gradual adjustment might in fact have hindered it. But the rise in demand and the pressure on supply reduced the producers' interest in freight absorption while the transport rate reforms reduced the burden on consumers of applying the Treaty rules.[22] Seen in these terms, the end of zonal pricing is primarily a way of increasing the average return to the producer per ton of coal sold, with differential effects on buyers according to their location.

In spite of the uncertainties, the zonal prices have for the most part been used only for their professed purpose, as transitional measures. The experience with them has been somewhat comparable to that with subsidies. Except for the special case of the Saar, the zonal prices remaining

[22] Even before demand increased greatly, other factors were apparently more important than zonal prices in determining where producers would market their coal. Geographically, the Aachen Basin is well placed to sell to non-German consumers but is at a disadvantage, compared to the Ruhr, in selling to much of Germany. The zonal prices seemed intended to encourage domestic sales. But between 1953 and 1954 deliveries to Germany fell from 46.5 per cent of Aachen's sales to 40.4 per cent. Deliveries to Belgium more than doubled (from 2.5 to 5.5 per cent) and those to France rose from 19.5 to 23.2 per cent. More was also sold to Luxembourg but the proportion going to Holland fell slightly. "Livraisons de Combustibles Solides des Bassins de la Communauté en 1953 et 1954," *Informations Statistiques*, Oct.–Nov. 1955, Tableau II bis.

at the end of the transitional period were largely a means
of permitting relatively minor and poorly placed basins to
market their coal.[23]

STEEL PRICES

The Community has handled steel prices very differently
from coal prices. There have been no ceilings fixed by the
High Authority, no systems of zonal pricing. From the
beginning the issues have centered on key provisions of the
Treaty concerning publication and nondiscrimination and
on the behavior of producers. But as in coal there is a continuing question about the influence of governments on
prices.

When the Schuman Plan was first proposed, a nagging
fear of overexpansion of capacity hung over the European
steel industry. Within weeks everything changed. Steel
began to ascend the roller coaster of the Korean war boom.
Then before the common market was opened a fairly rapid
descent began; steel trade and prices fell more than production which had also reached record heights. In the year
before the common market was opened steel export prices
fell 40 per cent.[24]

New orders fell during early 1953 in most Community
countries. Some interpreted this as postponement by buyers
who expected the common market to bring lower prices.
Once the common market existed, the uncertainties of the
new situation were offered in explanation. "The first effect
of the opening of a common market in steel was almost

[23] The method can also be used on a temporary basis to meet special
marketing problems. Early in 1955 stocks of *maigre* coal in the Nord
were rather large because good rainfall had increased the amount of
hydroelectricity available and limited normal sales to thermal power
stations. There were opportunities to sell this type of coal in Germany
and the Netherlands but transportation from the Nord would make it
too expensive. Therefore the High Authority authorized a reduction in
price for a certain period of time for limited quantities of the *maigre*
coal going to specified markets.

[24] HA, *Report*, May 1953, p. 17. Domestic prices fell much less, because
to a considerable degree they had been held down by government
controls.

indescribable confusion in the marketing of steel. This has already resulted in a marked drop in output. . . ." [25]

During the Korean boom governments had worked to restrain domestic steel prices, though they usually let export prices rise. The Pinay government in France had reduced steel prices as part of its campaign against inflation in 1952. French prices rose just before the common market opened, when it became clear that the High Authority was going to accept the French position on turnover taxes. The French government, however, retained control of the steel prices. In Germany, on the other hand, the easing of the market in 1952 was taken as an opportunity to start freeing the steel price. Along with coal, food, and some other basic products steel had been kept under control when most prices were set free after the currency reform of June 1948. On August 1, 1952, the German government ended its steel price fixing. A few days later, producers, steel processors, dealers, and government representatives met and worked out an agreement setting prices for major products from 5 to 15 per cent above the previous official level.[26] In Belgium a somewhat comparable situation existed; the steel producers set prices in agreement with Fabrimetal, the trade organization of the main consuming industries, with government approval. In the Netherlands government influence on prices was strong, and in Luxembourg a somewhat similar committee system was used. In Italy the government set maximum prices, but at the time the common market was opened firms were charging less than the maximum.

The High Authority decided to forgo the caution that caused it to continue ceiling prices for coal when the common market opened. Instead it plunged right in and "decided in favor of the freedom of prices and competition

[25] Michael L. Hoffman in *The New York Times*, Je. 23, 1953.

[26] There had been a good bit of industrial opposition to freeing the price. The rise did not in all cases really mean higher prices because a black or grey market had developed with prices 60 to 80 per cent above the official level. Ernst Schröder, "Marktfreiheit für Eisen und Kohle?," *Der Volkswirt*, Dec. 20, 1952, pp. 91-93.

between the producers." [27] Firms were to set their own prices, publish them according to the regulations, and apply them equally to sales to all comers within the Community.

The High Authority made it clear that it realized that steel firms were not used to price competition or even, for 15 years—and more for some countries—to having the right to set prices. It did not expect great changes overnight. ". . . business as well as consumers will have to undergo a veritable apprenticeship in liberty," said Monnet.[28] But the High Authority warned against a danger it feared. "The High Authority . . . knows that powerful involuntary reactions and old memories may cause quite a number of people to seek protection against the effects of free competition in more or less rigid price or market agreements." It warned against one of the more likely patterns of action. "Should it be found that as a result of the establishment of the Common Market, prices which had hitherto been different were aligning themselves at a level which would mean an increase for many producers, the High Authority would have to review its position, and resort to various measures which are open to it under the Treaty." [29] It called a conference of steel-users to meet a few months after the common market opened.

The High Authority was not saying that producers should not act in concert in setting prices; it seems to have expected that they would. It was drawing the line at collusion to raise prices appreciably. If this happened, the High Authority was saying, it might use its powers to set maximum prices at the old levels and perhaps take action under the Treaty articles forbidding restrictive business practices. It announced that it had "held formal consultations with the Council of Ministers and the Consultative Committee concerning the advisability of price-fixing measures and the level of prices, so as to be able to intervene, should circumstances arise to call for such intervention." [30] In

---

[27] HA, *Report*, May 1953, p. 30.
[28] Quoted by Michael L. Hoffman, *The New York Times,* cited.
[29] HA, *Report*, May 1953, p. 31. Also previous quotation.
[30] Same, pp. 30-31.

the discussions preceding the opening of the common market the High Authority had probably made its readiness to act plain to producers.

When firms published their price schedules it was as the High Authority had expected. There was not a great variety or wide range of prices for comparable items in each country of the Community. Instead, the prices quoted for each basing point were highly uniform. This was nothing new; it was a continuation of the condition that had existed for a long time. But though the prices were set collusively they were not much higher than they had been.[31] Whether it was the High Authority's threat or an assessment of market conditions that brought this result is hard to judge. Certainly market conditions were not propitious for a general rise and events were to show that not many producers were willing to sacrifice sales in order to protect a competitor's price.

While collusive pricing was familiar to the steel industries of the six countries, published price lists that represented real prices were a novelty for many, perhaps most, steel firms. The common practice was to vary terms and prices according to circumstances and the bargaining power of buyer and seller. Now not only would base prices be the same for all comers, but the sellers also had to publish terms of sale, delivery dates, standard surcharges for special qualities, and the discounts they would allow for large purchases, "fidelity" and so on.[32] Rather elaborate rules had to be devised to cover the fine points of price quotation and a start was made on standardizing nomenclature. The aim was not just neatness and order. The great innovation of the Community's pricing system was the insistence on equal treatment. Many businessmen disagreed with this

[31] It is unclear how much international agreement there may have been on prices. They certainly came together at the outset but in subsequent developments there is little indication of continued *international* collusion.

[32] In November 1956 the High Authority exempted from the publication requirement rebates on second-grade and substandard products on the ground that few of the transactions in these goods were comparable. It substituted a monthly report of the quantities sold to ensure that false labeling was not used for surreptitious price-cutting.

principle or at least saw no real need for it. The details of the pricing provisions were important because of their bearing on equal treatment and on the policing of the rule.

The Monnet Margin

Demand continued to fall after the common market was opened, but trade among countries in the Community increased, suggesting that producers and consumers were taking advantage of their new opportunities. The decline in demand also had an effect on prices, in a way that strained the Community's rules. ". . . The price schedules of the enterprises have remained entirely unchanged," the High Authority noted in January 1954, "in spite of the fact that the actual selling prices have substantially declined in various degrees. . . . Therefore, contrary to the . . . Treaty, the prices and terms of sale published in the schedules did not correspond any longer to the real selling prices and terms of sale on the Common Market." [33]

Why did the steel firms not lower their published prices? Presumably traditional thinking was at work. Overt price competition is poorly regarded in the steel industry. If the whole level of steel prices starts falling, according to this line of thought, buyers will hold off, expecting still better prices, and a process of general decline may start. A concerted price cut might be hard to negotiate. To the extent that steel could be sold at the published price it was a gain. Each firm could hope to take advantage of the flexibility made possible by simply departing from the published schedules when that seemed useful. Another inhibition on formal reduction of price schedules may have been the producers' expectation that demand would rise again before too long and their uncertainty, in the novel common market, whether they would really be able to raise their published prices with impunity as soon as the market permitted.

Cutting prices without changing published schedules was, as the High Authority pointed out, a clear violation of the Treaty. There was probably also a violation of the rule requiring equal treatment. Discrimination seems im-

[33] HA, *Report*, Jan. 1954, p. 26.

plicit in a situation where sellers work out whatever arrangements they can with each customer. The High
Authority made no charges along these lines, perhaps because it lacked the data to prove a case and did not want
to display a further weakness in the price rules, and perhaps because in the circumstances there was no prospect of
enforcing the new rules fully. Instead of trying to force all
producers to obey the rules the High Authority revised
the rules. It made them more flexible and, apparently, in-
duced the steel firms to publish more realistic schedules.

Under the new rules sellers were permitted to depart
from their published prices by as much as 2.5 per cent (upwards or downwards) without filing new schedules. Only
if the average of prices for 60 days fell outside this limit
did the producers have to alter the published schedule.
Other revisions made it easier to change published prices
quickly. The High Authority emphasized that the increased
flexibility did not permit discrimination but it was hard to
see how equality could be strictly enforced under the more
flexible rules.[34] Effective February 1, 1954, the firms published new prices somewhat below the original schedules.
During much of 1954 prices tended to be near the lower
limit of the 2.5 per cent margin. By late summer demand
increased and the prices of many firms began to move toward the published schedule. As the market continued to
move upwards, prices moved into the upper margin and by
the end of the year, as delivery dates got longer, often
pressed against the upper limit.

Meanwhile, the "Monnet margin" was being challenged
in the Court of the Community. The governments of
France and Italy contested the High Authority's right to
permit any departure from a single published price. Behind the legal points of Treaty interpretation, lay two kinds
of issues.[35] Politically and constitutionally, there was the
principle of "strict construction" which would limit the

[34] D. C. Bok, *The First Three Years of the Schuman Plan,* 1955, pp.
38-40.
[35] It is not my intention in this book to analyze the Court's cases, the
arguments of various parties, or the reasoning on which the decisions
rest. Only the facts of suits and decisions as they bear on other issues
will come into consideration.

High Authority's freedom of action; the matter was important both because the governments wanted to protect their own powers and because they could not tell how the new agency might choose to adapt the Treaty to circumstances. Economically, the French and Italian producers were probably worried by a step that encouraged price competition and reduced the means of enforcing equal treatment. They may also have feared that if demand continued to be slow, Belgian and German steel would come into France and Italy in increasing quantities. In its first decision the Court held that the High Authority had misinterpreted the Treaty and that the margin was illegal.

The immediate practical effect of the ruling was small. It was handed down in December 1954 when the upper limits of the "Monnet margin" were being exhausted and demand was rising. Firms began handing in new schedules to the High Authority establishing higher prices. The rises were not uniform for all products and were fairly moderate. As demand continued to rise, prices were changed quite frequently.[36] The boom continued through 1955, 1956, and most of 1957. By the beginning of 1956 most steel prices were slightly above their level when the common market opened. They continued to rise, in most countries, until the spring of 1957 when they were 14-17 per cent above the May 1953 level except in France and Germany, where the rises were 4 and 7 per cent.[37] In those two countries there were increases in the fall of 1957 while elsewhere prices remained steady. At the end of the year and early in 1958, in the face of a fall in demand, prices were cut slightly. There were no major changes in the price and no serious complaints about undue rigidity or general gross violations such as led to the temporary change in the rules during 1954.

Since the beginning of 1955 Community steel pricing has been carried on essentially under the general Treaty

[36] "Since the beginning of February, enterprises have been lodging new price-schedules with the High Authority practically every day." HA, *Report,* Apr. 1955, p. 75.

[37] The index is based on a weighted average of both Thomas and Martin steels. HA, *Report,* Apr. 1957, pp. 102, 103.

principles, as expressed in the rules set out by the High
Authority. Whether this means these rules have been fully
enforced, with few departures from the published schedules and little concealed discrimination, is hard to tell. In
February 1954 the High Authority began checking the
books of individual firms in order to police the price rules.
By the end of the transition period it had imposed 16 fines,
issued 16 warnings and formally written to 16 firms explaining certain points.[38] In addition, its inspectors had informally rectified many minor or technical violations. No
one writing from the outside can have any certainty about
what proportion of the violations has been detected and
corrected. There is only negative evidence: neither the
High Authority, nor any of the interested parties, whether
producers or consumers, have complained of extensive in-
fractions of the rules.

The application of full Treaty conditions to steel prices
during most of the transitional period is in contrast with
what was done about coal prices. Only the interlude of the
steel price margin was an exception. That adaptation of
the rules to the facts was presumably dictated mostly by
the belief that the rules could not be rigidly enforced,
which was probably so. The common market was new, the
High Authority had nothing like the full equipment of an
established government, in administrative resources, quickly
effective legal sanctions, or habitual acceptance of its authority. In addition to administrative prudence the course
the High Authority took had the advantage of favoring
price competition but the disadvantage of reducing the
possibility of eliminating discriminatory pricing. How effective this approach would have proved if demand had
continued to fall, or had evened off at a low level, is a
matter too speculative to pursue. This is but one of a number of instances in which more trying tests of some aspects
of the Community arrangements have been avoided by the
favorable course of business activity during most of the
transitional period. Nor will there be a "next time" at
which this approach can be tested anew; the margin device

[38] HA, *Report*, Apr. 1958, v. 2, p. 57.

has been ruled illegal (unless the Treaty should be amended) and the High Authority is in a different position, in resources and in its acceptance by the Community, than it was when it was little more than a year old.

There was, however, a feature of the 1954 episode that can be found elsewhere in the Community experience: the delay between initiation of a course of action and its abandonment because it was contrary to the Treaty has often been long enough to provide at least temporary relief or a temporizing solution to a problem. Most often it has been a government that was given time to adjust its practices to a ruling by the High Authority; this time it was the High Authority versus the Court, but in either case the force of events has permitted adjustment outside the Treaty law without ultimate flouting of it. And, as in the case of the 1954 price margin, it has often been the fact that markets may move faster than men that has provided the reconciliation of law and practice with little violence to either.

Collusion

It is not only through application of the Treaty rules that the Community affects steel prices. The rules prescribe behavior no matter what the price may be. The existence of the Community also influences the level of prices.

Though each firm must publish its prices separately, what they will be is agreed on among the producers of each country. Almost no one denies this; "cup of coffee prices" is the usual term. (Judge Gary required dinners.) Whether there is also some kind of international understanding among producers on prices is much less clear. Some observers claim to have detected it, others are more doubtful. Evidence is obviously hard to come by. The fact that Community producers agree on export prices in the Brussels cartel has been regarded by many as likely to have its repercussions on prices within the Community, either for the reasons Adam Smith mentioned,[39] or because of the

[39] "People of the same trade seldom meet together, even for merriment and diversion, but the conversation ends in a conspiracy against the public, or in some contrivance to raise prices." *The Wealth of Nations,* ed. by Edwin Cannan (London: Methuen, 5th ed., 1930), v. 1, p. 130.

consequences of the export understandings for trade within the Community (see Ch. 17). The matter remains un-proved and since it seems possible to explain the main features of Community price developments without as-suming an international understanding on prices, it is sim-pler to proceed on that basis.

Although the Treaty forbids agreements that restrain trade and production, price collusion is not regarded with alarm in the Community, by the High Authority or others. There are several reasons for this. First, there is doubt about how much price competition is practicable or desirable in the steel industry. Price competition in steel is rare. In the United States price leadership is the accepted pattern. In Britain the price is regulated on an estimate of average costs. If the Community demonstrated true price compe-tition—in the classical pattern of grocery stores or small textile mills—it would be unique among major steel producers.

Many factors explain this general absence of competition in steel. One is the wide acceptance of a now-conventional analysis of the economics of the industry. Owing largely to the great investment required to produce steel, fixed costs are high. It is not easy to expand capacity rapidly, so if the industry is capable of meeting a large demand it will also have unused capacity much of the time. Because of the high proportion of fixed costs, each producer may find it advantageous to sell steel even at low prices so long as they cover more than direct costs and make some contribution to the heavy overhead costs. Any given firm may be in a position to expand sales by cutting prices and taking bus-iness away from a competitor. However, since the total demand for steel is not determined in any major fashion by price but by the level of activity in the major steel-consum-ing industries, price-cutting will not make it possible to expand the sales of the steel industry as a whole. Price cuts by one firm will have to be met by others, which will reduce the general level of prices and the total revenue of the industry. Therefore, runs this argument, some form of price discipline is needed to keep the industry from injuring itself. Proponents of this view could concede that the argument divorcing the demand for steel from its price might be debatable and still hold that whatever possibilities there are for selling more steel by reducing the price could be explored better by coordinated action of the producers than by competitive price-cutting which might set in motion a process that would carry past the point of maximum return for the industry.

It is not my intention to discuss the validity of this view. The point is that its wide acceptance makes it likely that any pricing rules would be in some way "adapted" to permit moving in step on matters of price. If this is so, the main things one needs to know about the collusive arrangements concern their strength, or rigidity, under the pressure of changing circumstances; the kinds of pressure that can be put on recalcitrants; the extent to which the collusive practices are likely to lead to unduly high prices and to protect the less efficient producers while restraining the more efficient ones. Our knowledge of these features of the Community pricing practices is limited; close study and especially a comparison of prices with differences in costs would be needed for a definite conclusion. Lacking this, we have to rely on some general considerations about the factors inside and outside the steel industry that limit the scope of collusive pricing.

There is undoubtedly a considerable spread in costs among steel producers within each country and within the Community as a whole. Presumably the distribution of high- and low-cost producers in each country usually overlaps that in other countries. Therefore unless there are effective international agreements setting prices or restraining trade, the existence of the common market would help to set an upper limit to the price which producers in any one country could charge without inviting foreign producers to invade their market. This consideration is likely to be stronger when demand is weak than in boom times. Its importance varies according to transport costs.

Within each national industry there is also an element of competition in reaching agreement on prices. Unless they can sell all the steel their plants will produce at an optimum rate of output, low-cost producers will not want to agree to prices high enough to satisfy the highest-cost producers. They might, however, be happy to get a somewhat higher price than they could obtain in a strictly competitive market. When low-cost plants are owned by firms that also have higher-cost plants, the former are obviously less likely to have as strong an impact on the general level of prices as if they were independent.[40]

Probably the best evidence of the limits of collusive practices in holding up prices was the price-cutting during 1953 and 1954, the only period before 1958 when demand was weak in the Community. Though the published schedules had been set by industry agreement, and in spite of the general acceptance of the rationale against price-cutting sketched earlier, the steel producers competed at that time by cutting prices. Probably the surreptitious cuts did not go very deep; there might have been collective action to check them if they had. The High Authority was in an odd position. If it had been strong enough to enforce adherence to the Community price rules, it would have been strengthening the collusive price agreements. The competition could have continued only if steelmakers had overcome their aversion to overt price competition. If the situation recurs the High Authority will not be able to use the method of compromising that it found in the margin device which is now outlawed. It may find another form of accommodation that partially encourages price competition. It may seek to check price cutting if it thinks nothing would be gained. It may not prove able to do what it wants —price policing is notoriously difficult. And perhaps it will be relieved of its problem by a new willingness of steel firms to compete overtly by reducing their published prices. But in the absence of these conditions the paradoxical al-

---

[40] The continuous wide-strip mills built under the Monnet Plan have probably had less than their maximum possible effect on the level of prices in France because the marketing of their products is controlled by a group of firms which also have older, higher-cost mills making competing products.

ternatives may be to reduce competition by enforcing the Treaty, or to permit competition by letting the Community's rules be violated (whether by will or by weakness).

While the prevalence of collusive pricing may not be as innocuous as it is usually alleged to be in Luxembourg, it may also be true that, given the history, habits, and attitude of the European steel industry, the kind of pricing arrangements that now exist may represent almost the smallest degree of collusion likely to be expected. When the steel boom was well under way, the ECE's steel experts expressed the view that "in the Community countries prices are determined basically by market forces." [41] This does not preclude collusive pricing or deny its importance, but stresses the influence both of the moderating forces already mentioned and of the extent to which steel prices are under public surveillance in the Community.

Surveillance

When the High Authority set steel prices free as soon as the common market was opened even though it knew producers would agree on prices, it was relying on surveillance backed by the threat of maximum price-fixing to prevent a sharp rise. The effectiveness of the initial approach was not really tested because of the decline of demand. Surveillance has, however, been credited with moderating Community price increases in the boom that followed.

When the market improved after the middle of 1954 prices rose, but not rapidly. At the end of the year they were still below their level when the common market was opened and a year later, at the end of 1955, an index of the prices of rolling-mill products for the Community as a whole stood only 2 per cent above the level of May 1953, though production and trade were at high levels.[42] At its peak in 1957, the index of Community prices was something more

[41] ECE, *The European Steel Market in 1955*, Je. 1956, p. 37.
[42] HA, *Report*, Apr. 1957, p. 103.

than 10 per cent above the level of May 1953.[43] It is very
hard to say what standard can be used to judge the "reason-
ableness" of price increases. Almost any comparison has
only limited meaning. The High Authority considers the
rise in Community steel prices quite moderate and compares its 10 per cent figure with 31-34 per cent for Britain
and the United States.

The Community's domestic steel prices rose much less
than its prices for exports to third countries (at least up to
mid-1957 when the latter fell at a time when the former
were still rising). On the whole steel prices rose more than
prices of basic products in general in the Community but
the curve is not very different from that of some other
goods. Such comparisons are of limited value, however, and
in any case are largely vitiated by differing conditions in
base periods, especially because of price fixing. Perhaps
the most that can be said, from such a rough reading of the
record, is that since the common market opened steel prices
within the Community have not been runaway prices and
have moved at what appears to be a moderate pace considering the boom in steel demand. This moderation, especially in the period of most rapid increase in demand during
1955, has been claimed as an important success for the
Community. This price behavior, it is said, is in sharp
contrast to the traditional practice of the Continental steel
industry of raising prices rapidly when demand increased.[44]

[43] The index reached 110 in late 1957 but would have been higher if
French prices had been counted in francs instead of being converted
into other currencies at the post-devaluation rate. This would have put
France in the group having price increases of 17-20 per cent with the
Benelux countries. Italy had declined from its 14 per cent peak to 10 by
the end of 1957. The German figure was 12 per cent. HA, *Report*, Apr.
1958, v. 2, p. 163.

[44] This generalization is not altogether easy to document, partly because
of the difficulty of comparing prices in different markets, lack of data on
real prices in some periods, governmental price-fixing, and, during parts
of the twenties and thirties, the operation of the international cartels.
Postwar experience is quite limited. There was a sharp rise in steel
export prices during the Korean boom but this was not matched on
domestic markets. There is, however, some support for the generalization
in data on the movement of domestic prices in 1926, 1928-29, and 1937,
notably in France and Belgium, but much less so in Germany and
Britain. See the graphs and statistics in Günther Kiersch, *Internationale
Eisen- und Stahlkartelle*, Feb. 1954, pp. 116, 117, 193-208.

Community surveillance—as distinguished from that practiced by the governments—has several aspects. One is formal, and linked to the High Authority's power to fix maximum prices. During most of the transitional period there has not been much risk of this power's being invoked but it remained a stick behind the door that no one was likely to forget. Another aspect of surveillance is linked to collusive pricing. Most producers would claim that collusion makes for stability and justify it partly on this ground. They have to be careful, then, not to belie their case too easily by a quick price response to a rising market. Moreover, such a reaction might endanger the process of collusion itself by bringing the High Authority's sanctions to bear.

Community surveillance also has a broader aspect which is regarded by some well-qualified observers as weightier than the threat of High Authority action. This is the focusing of attention on steel prices that results from the existence of the Community. Publication of price lists, reports by the High Authority, and discussion throughout the Community about the issues involved, all help to focus the attention of labor, consumers, governments, and the general public on prices, their changes, justification, and effects. This is bound to cramp the style of a price-raiser who might be tempted to go to extremes if unobserved. The need to make a reasonable case, to present a responsible front to the world, and to avoid generating too much opposition, all operate to moderate price rises. Those who emphasize the importance of this situation compare it, roughly, with the United States where steel prices are newsworthy, may attract the attention of a Congressional committee or a commission of the executive branch, and are always there for labor to consider in formulating wage demands. This kind of publicity and attention, we are told, is new in Europe and is largely a contribution of the Community.

The Secretariat of the ECE, which is not prejudiced in favor of the Community, accepts the importance of these developments:

There seems little doubt that the system of publishing price lists has directed public attention to prices and thus introduced a certain stability into the market. Producers now appear to hesitate to increase prices at the first signs of a hardening of the market. Moreover, producers in the different countries tend to watch one another closely and hesitate to introduce price increases which might open the door for competitors in neighboring countries.[45]

The Community's surveillance includes measures that give consumers a chance to be heard. The "users and traders" category of the Consultative Committee includes representatives of the chemical, cement, engineering, metals, and shipbuilding industries, as well as the railroads and power-production. They have had a chance to express their views on the High Authority's price policy decisions. In addition, the High Authority has had three special conferences of steel-users. That held shortly after the common market was opened could do little but say that it was too early to tell how the new rules would work. The next was held in November 1955, when the boom was on. The main concern of the 80 users who attended was the assurance of future supplies. If there was any complaint about the level of prices, it escaped observers.[46] Instead there was some expression of satisfaction with the restraint in price rises and a feeling that the rules on publication had eliminated many discriminations. The third conference was in May 1957, another period of high demand. As before, the main concern seems to have been with supplies, and this was also the emphasis of special meetings the High Authority had with the rolling mills of the Community which did not produce their own steel.

[45] ECE, *The European Steel Market in 1954*, Je. 1955, p. 51. Published in June 1955, the comment refers to the previous 18 months during which demand first fell and then rose sharply.

[46] This account is based on Leo Solari, "La CECA di fronte agli utilizzatori di acciaio," *Mondo Economico*, Dec. 19, 1955, pp. 12-14, and a report of "Europe," Agence Internationale d'Information pour la Presse (Luxembourg), Nov. 3, 1955. Solari complained that many at the conference represented commercial organizations which had no real conflict of interest with the steel producers. He recommended that the High Authority work at getting "less domesticated" consumers and establish closer and more frequent relations with them.

Surveillance is an important counterweight to price collusion. The common market, with its removal of trade barriers and its multiplication of the possibilities for both buyers and sellers, also sets some limit to what the producers in any one country can do to raise prices. Therefore, what happens in one or more major producing countries will—in some degree—influence the level of prices in the whole Community. In steel as in coal, government pressure on the price has been an important factor.

Governments

The German government has exercised an influence over the steel price by the same kind of understanding that prevailed in coal until the difficulties of the fall of 1957. The Minister of Economics expected to be consulted before prices were raised and the industry seemed to accept this arrangement with no great complaint. Price discipline is an important part of German business ideology and the steel producers probably found it natural to show a sense of the "responsibility" of their position, at least so long as they felt fairly treated. There has been no rupture of the sort that marked the coal price rise of the fall of 1957 though when steel prices were raised shortly afterwards, the government-owned plant at Salzgitter broke out of the mould and continued to charge the old prices.

In France matters were rather different. Government pressure took several forms, and the industry fought against it. Throughout the postwar period French governments struggling with inflationary pressures from time to time imposed price "freezes" of varying degrees of effectiveness, supplemented by subsidies and tax concessions. After the Schuman Plan went into effect the government lost the legal right to fix steel prices but not its desire to. Government funds which were essential to the industry's investment program provided a useful lever for holding down prices. As the industry began to raise a larger share of investment funds from the capital market or out of its own earnings, a second weapon gained in importance: fixing the prices of goods in which steel was an important element. These products were not covered by the Community Treaty so the French government was free to act. The result was a squeeze on the French industry, reinforced by measures regulating the profit margin in trade and using, the High Authority said, artificially low steel prices as the basis of its calculations.[47]

The French producers complained that by fixing the prices of the steel-using industries the government had "prevented the steel-making firms from changing their own prices to the extent and in the time that would have taken account of the requirements of the level of business activity, of the increases that occurred in costs of production and of the necessities of financing their investment programs."[48] The government had thrust the steel industry into the common market but was not prepared to abide by the rules of the game. "The public authorities have never been able to resign themselves to abandoning completely to the High Authority their prerogatives and to letting the price of steel products develop freely; they have never ceased, during three years [from the opening of the common market] to exercise on our industry a pressure intended to block the movement of its sales prices. . . ." The industry said that it recognized the importance of economic stability and was prepared to give assurances against abusing the freedom to which it was entitled. As things stood, the public authorities were taking on "grave responsibility for the future of our industry which is confronted in the common market by the redoubtable competition of steel industries which have been able to benefit without restriction from the favorable development of the market."[49]

In May 1956 the French steel producers filed with the High Authority price schedules that showed increases of from 4 to 8 per cent. Apparently the government had not

[47] HA, *Report*, Apr. 1957, p. 107.
[48] Interview with Jacques Ferry, Délégué Général of the Chambre Syndicale de la Sidérurgie Française in *Actualitiés Industrielles Lorraines* (Metz), May-Je. 1957, p. 6.
[49] Both quotations from Chambre Syndicale de la Sidérurgie Française, *La Sidérurgie Française en 1956*, Je. 21, 1957, pp. 27, 28 (hereafter cited as Chambre Syndicale).

sanctioned this move. A French political scientist denounced the Coal and Steel Community. It was intolerable,
he said, that key elements in the economy should be with-
drawn from the area of government responsibility in this
way. The "brutal fact" was that the supranational authority
was too weak to impose its will, so this process simply
meant a surrender of public authority to private interests.[50]
The government showed that it was not powerless and
withdrew a tax concession which, according to the steel
federation, "had the effect of practically nullifying the advantages which our firms had a right to expect from the
measure they had taken." [51] That fall there were extensive
negotiations between the government and the steelmakers,
centering on the industry's long-run plan for increasing
investments.[52] A 3 per cent price increase followed in April
1957 which the producers regarded as inadequate, but accepted because, they said, they wanted to show their support for the government's policy of promoting economic
stability. Steel-using industries were permitted to pass on
this increase to their customers, thus following the "simple
solution" the steel producers had been urging. This might
mean, said M. Ferry, that the government had become
"more conscious of the prejudicial consequences for the
French economy resulting from the permanent contradic-
tion between the demands of the French government's
policies and the rules of the coal and steel Community." [53]
In August 1957, the French producers raised their prices
another 4.5 per cent, suggesting that their hope might be
proving well founded. In November, after devaluation, they
rose another 7.4 per cent for Thomas steel, France's major
product, and 5 per cent for steel made by the Martin
process.

In its general concern about increased government interference with pricemaking, the High Authority in the
spring of 1957 singled out France as a particular offender.

[50] M. Duverger in *Le Monde*, Jl. 5-11, 1956 (weekly edition).

[51] Chambre Syndicale, cited, p. 30.

[52] The industry's memorandum appears in *Actualités Industrielles Lorraines*, Nov.-Dec. 1956, pp. 3-11, and Jan.-Feb. 1957, pp. 5-13.

[53] Interview, cited, p. 7.

It told Paris that indirect fixing of steel prices violated the Treaty. It also complained about the French government's effort to extract commitments from the industry about price policy in return for financial aid.[54] Acting to enforce the Treaty, the High Authority was thus, in effect, lending its support to the producers in a situation which, as the Chambre Syndicale said, "at some moments took on the appearance of a conflict." [55]

In steel as well as in coal, Community price problems had come to a point where partial integration was sharpening the issue of how the principles of the Treaty would be permitted to work, how free the producers were really to be in setting prices, and who was to take the political responsibility for their actions.

THE CHARACTER OF COMMUNITY PRICES

Different as the Community's experiences have been in coal and steel prices, they have some things in common, the most important of which is that the whole price system is in transition. What it is a transition from is easily described, what it is in transition to can hardly be judged with any assurance. About the transitional stage itself there are questions going beyond the rough description of this chapter which has dealt only with some salient features. Formal national controls have disappeared; the High Authority has moved away from using its own powers of direct control; but the governments retain a strong influence on coal and steel prices. During the transitional period they used it to check price rises in a boom. How would they use it at other times? In the steel industry collusion, surveillance, and the influence of governments, have combined to shape prices. To understand fully what has resulted requires a much more detailed study of the structure of prices (geographically and by commodities) and of their relation to costs than could be undertaken for this book. Such a study would also clarify some matters which this chapter has not examined in any detail.

[54] HA, *Report*, Apr. 1957, pp. 106-107.
[55] Chambre Syndicale, cited, p. 28.

For instance, most of the Community's coal is covered by price equalization arrangements and compensation schemes. Though costs differ, all the mines in the scheme sell at the same price. Part of the return to the more efficient mines is distributed to less efficient ones. This makes it possible to keep prices lower than they would be if they had to be remunerative to the high-cost mines, but prevents any coal being sold at the lowest price the most efficient mines could offer. In France there is a further equalization among the main coal basins operated by Charbonnages de France. In one form or another measures of this sort have been normal in the European coal industry for decades. The Treaty permits them provided they are authorized by the High Authority. Whether the main effect of price equalization arrangements is to deprive consumers of the benefits of low-cost production or to hold down coal prices by subsidizing marginal output is not an issue that can be settled by generalization. Much depends on how heavily demand pushes on supply when it reaches the point of inelasticity. The cost of imported coal also affects the equation. Much, of course, depends on the way the equalization scheme is managed and how prices are set. If the Community can expect to be chronically short of coal as it was during much of the transitional period, the equalization schemes would probably tend to hold down the cost of coal so long as no serious barriers are put in the way of imports. They entail risks of inhibiting adjustment, a matter close to the heart of the Community's long-run coal policy (Ch. 23). As instruments of the kind of managed coal economy the Community is developing they are obviously of considerable importance.

An aspect of coal and steel pricing on which the Community's influence is unclear is the practice of dealers and wholesalers. They are not fully covered by the Treaty but the High Authority may extend the rules to them by means of the requirements it puts on producers. Rebates permitted to dealers, terms of sale, and such matters provide some leverage. From the outset firms in the steel trade were required to publish their prices. The coal trade, however, was only under a general injunction about equal treatment; not until the spring of 1958 did the High Authority undertake discussions looking toward a fuller regulation. The number of dealers and the different circumstances in which they operate make this a hard field for the High Authority to supervise. Unequal treatment is particularly difficult to establish with any certainty. While there have probably not been gross distortions of the Community's principles resulting from the structure and practices of the coal and steel trades, the area remains a murky one.

Another matter on which a fuller price study could shed some light is the significance of the Community's basing points. The Treaty leaves producers free to choose the places at which their published price schedules are to apply, unless the High Authority regards them as "abnormal" and likely to make it more difficult to apply the rules, especially those about equal treatment. The result in steel is a set of 41 basing points unevenly distributed over the Community. Germany has five, only three in the Ruhr; Luxembourg in its small compass also has five while France has fourteen, half of them in the north and east; Italy has eight scattered over the country, Belgium six, Holland three, and the Saar one.[56] Some are used only by a single producer; normally they differ according to the commodity sold. Still the list suggests that the basing-point system has been used rather differently in various parts of the Community.

In the history of the United States steel industry, few subjects have been as ardently debated as basing points. Whether they promote or inhibit competition, and whether they make for or against the best allocation of resources and location of industry, have been the central issues.[57] The arguments and the literature embodying them are enough to warn against any attempt to interpret the Community system in generalities and without a detailed analysis of the price structure and practices that have accompanied it. The

[56] There is a map in *Steel Review*, Apr. 1958, p. 22.
[57] The key issues of the tremendous literature and the history of the subject have been excellently summarized in Clair Wilcox, *Public Policies toward Business* (Chicago: Richard D. Irwin, Inc., 1955), Chapter 8.

Treaty drafters were aware of the American experience and the arguments about it; there were American advisers available with specialized knowledge. The drafters wanted price rules that would make competition possible, that would bring real costs to bear in the allocation of resources, and that could be policed and supervised by the High Authority. They also had to compromise conflicting interests and provide some assurance to producers that their positions would not be radically damaged. The Community's new pricing rules had to be applied to a mature, complex economy with established practices, not all of them compatible with the aims of the Treaty. A set of forces existed that could be used, combated, diverted, or neutralized, but not ignored in building a new system.

All of these factors went into the devising of the Community's basing-point system. It would take a long examination of a series of hypothetical situations to be clear as to how it differs from one in which either all prices were to be ex-mine or mill, or full freight absorption was permitted, or the zonal pricing system used in some countries was applied, or any alternative combination of factors. A few characteristics seem reasonably clear. The rules give producers a good bit of freedom of action, subject to High Authority supervision. The use of basing points may make collusion easier but it would be quite possible under other rules as well. The main virtue claimed for the basing-point system is its relative simplicity, especially compared with the complexity of an ex-mine, ex-mill price structure. The main features of the market are made clear to the buyers. The High Authority's task of policing the market is made much easier, especially in the complicated matter of assuring equal treatment. In short, the basing-point system contributes to the "transparency of the market" and since the introduction of new pricing practices and principles was a major task of the Community, this advantage may well have been judged to be of decisive importance.

The Community's multiple basing-point system is not like "Pittsburgh-plus" with its market-wide distortions of real costs. There is still some freight absorption and some "phantom freight" but how much and with what results cannot be judged without close statistical analysis. Intimately linked with the significance of the basing-point structure is the right of alignment. Producers may absorb freight to reduce their delivered prices to the point necessary to meet competition from another basing point (or from third countries). Alignment was apparently not extensively used during the transitional period. At the outset, when demand was slack, there was some alignment, not so much because producers were seeking new business as because large consumers demanded price concessions in this form.[58] During the steel boom there was little incentive for producers to absorb freight since they could sell at full prices at home. The French devaluation in the fall of 1957 opened new possibilities since it made French steel the cheapest in the Community, in terms of the other currencies. Demand remained high in France and there was no great push to export, but buyers in Belgium and elsewhere seem to have secured price concessions from their normal suppliers on the ground that the price of the semi-fictitious French deliveries had fallen.

The fall in export demand during the latter half of 1957 and the slackening of demand within the Community that followed gave producers a new interest in the possibilities of alignment. Coal producers only obtained this right to align prices in the spring of 1958 when stocks were mounting and coal was hard to sell for the first time in years. Some prices were cut; alignment offered the possibility of more sales without changing the official lists. In Germany the private steel producers pressed for and got the agreement of the government-owned Salzgitter works (which had not gone along with the general price rise of November 1957) to raise its prices for certain products, not because of Salzgitter's competition but because French and Belgian producers could undersell the Ruhr in the German market

---

[58] ECE, *Economic Survey of Europe in 1953;* Geneva, 1954, p. 14.

by aligning on Salzgitter.[59] Extensive alignment, if it occurred, would be an important indication of the behavior of the Community in recession, for it would at the same time register a willingness of producers to "invade" markets normally supplied by someone else and would provide a degree of price-cutting not shown by changes in the published lists.

The Community's price structure is, clearly, more complicated than it looks. Its actual operation is a matter of considerable importance in judging the effects of the common market but at this stage of the game we have to be satisfied with a broad outline of its character and some understanding of the way prices are set. It is also possible to see in broad outline the kind of relations among prices of different countries that have developed over the transitional period. They raise some further questions.

THE RESULTS AND THE FUTURE

Before the Community was created, prices of coal and steel in each of the six countries were the product of national circumstances and varied widely. The opening of the common market narrowed the differences. Further progress in perfecting it might have been expected to bring the prices still closer together. In a fully functioning Community the differences in price from one center to another ought to correspond very closely to transport costs (if taxes are eliminated). Only some of these things have happened.

Figures 1, 2 and 3 give the outlines of the picture. They show the movement of prices for coal, merchant bars, and plates measured as percentages of the prices in the Ruhr.[60]

---

[59] *Der Volkswirt*, Je. 28, 1958, pp. 1183, 1184. When the High Authority established price rules at the opening of the common market for steel, it stipulated that a firm could not publish a price for something it did not produce. The purpose of this curious rule was to prevent price-cutting by collusion with an outside firm that would align on the fictitious price.

[60] There are many limitations to this kind of presentation but it seems legitimate for its specific purpose. The notes to the graphs explain what types and qualities are represented by each line. In coal the choice has

The graphs tell their own stories, each slightly different. For coal, the opening of the common market had an immediate effect (partly overstated because the 1952 prices are for domestic deliveries while those for 1953 eliminate double-pricing). Prices continued to come together until 1956. The graph dramatizes this movement by eliminating intervening years and temporary fluctuations but it does not distort the essential development. Then Belgian prices break out of the mould and create a divergence which is narrowed again by 1958. French devaluation creates another divergence.

In steel the picture is less sharp. Moreover the products shown, while of major importance, cannot be regarded as typical for all products.[61] As the difference between the two graphs shows, there was a markedly greater divergence in prices for merchant bars (35 per cent of the Community's finished rolled products in 1956) than in hot-rolled plates (16 per cent). Nevertheless, taking the three graphs together one sees that in coal convergence is marked, though there have been exceptions, while in steel dispersion has been more marked than convergence during the boom. When prices drop, however, they tend to come closer together.

At an early stage observers could say that given differences in costs, "The approach to uniformity of prices is more striking than the continuing differences." [62] After several more years of experience, the High Authority put the emphasis on the divergences.

---

been of a major type from each basin that is also produced in the Ruhr. In steel the matter is more complicated because of differences in process. Since Thomas steel predominates in France, Belgium, and Luxembourg only products made of it are shown for those countries and are compared with Thomas steel from the Ruhr, where Martin steel is more important. For the other countries the figures are all for Martin steel. It is therefore not legitimate to use these graphs to judge the relative height of prices in the different countries. Their purpose is to show the relative movement of prices. These are list prices; actual prices would carry "extras" that may differ from country to country.

[61] However, calculations for several other products show basically similar patterns.

[62] ECE, *The European Steel Market in 1954*, p. 50.

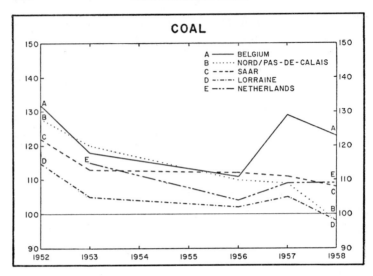

Figure 1. Movement of Coal Prices in
Relation to Ruhr Prices, 1952-1958

NOTES TO FIGURES 1, 2, AND 3

Current prices are shown as percentages of Ruhr prices at the same date, calculated at official exchange rates. The 1958 figures for France are shown at the exchange rate introduced by the devaluation of August 1957. At the old rates the figures would be about 20 per cent higher.

All coal figures refer to bituminous; for fuller description see notes in sources. The dates are May 1952, March 1953, April 1956 and 1957, March 1958. The graph shows no figures for 1954 and 1955.

In the steel graphs the data for Belgium, France, and Luxembourg compare prices for Thomas steel with Ruhr prices for Thomas steel. The data for Italy and the Netherlands compare prices for Siemens-Martin steel with Ruhr prices for Siemens-Martin steel. The dates are: May 20, 1953, February 1, 1954, March 30, 1955, 1956, 1957, 1958. Taxes are excluded. Basing points by country and product are given in sources.

For further comment see n. 60.

SOURCES:

    Coal: HA, *Report*, Apr. 1958, v. 2, Statistical Annex, Tables 12 and 14, pp. 326-328, 330.

    Steel: Calculated from *Informations Statistiques* (Jan.-Apr. 1957), pp. 24-33; HA, *Report*, Apr. 1956, Statistical Annex, Table 8, p. 259; HA, *Annexes to the Fifth General Report*, Apr. 1957, Table 25, pp. 42-43; HA, *Report*, Apr. 1958, v. 2, Statistical Annex, Table 41, p. 358.

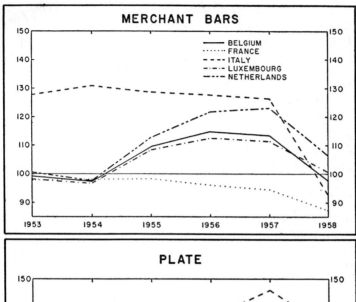

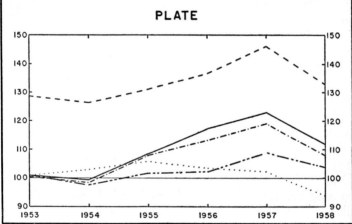

Figures 2 and 3. Movement of Prices of Steel Products
in Relation to Ruhr Prices, 1953-1958

"In a great number of cases," it noted, "the difference between the published prices of different groups of producers
is much greater than the cost of transportation between
the corresponding basing points. . . ." [63] Several factors
explain this. "The persistence of traditional links between
the producers of a single country, on the one hand, and
between buyers and sellers of the same country on the
other," limits international competition, which was further
weakened by boom conditions. "Nevertheless it seems that
it is the intervention of governments in the formation of
prices which is the principal cause of the elements of dissociation observable in the common market for steel." As
the High Authority had previously pointed out, differences
in national economic policies were bound to influence the
movements of coal and steel prices, in addition to the
direct measures taken, for instance, in France and Germany
to hold down price rises. High demand seems the crucial
factor, however. Producers had no great need to seek out
new markets; buyers were inclined to stick to traditional
sources of supply on which they felt they could depend
even if they might have obtained cheaper steel elsewhere.
Sellers could gain more by exporting at premium prices to
countries than by selling inside the Community. This is
what the Belgians did. The French and Germans could not
take advantage of the higher Belgian prices because they
had to offer their steel at the same price throughout the
Community and governments held it down at home. Thus
to a degree the price rules themselves help to explain the
divergences in prices. As a British critic pointed out, "the
non-discrimination rules hindered, rather than encouraged,
the unification of the common market." [64] Even so, a good
deal of trade took place within the Community, but without
having the equalizing effect on prices that would have been
expected. The fall in the demand from third countries and
the subsequent slackening of demand within the Com-

[63] HA, *Report*, Apr. 1958, v. 2, p. 68.
[64] "ECSC: The First Five Years," *Steel Review*, Apr. 1958, p. 25. This
article shows the increased divergence in Community prices by showing
the enlargement in the spread between the highest and the lowest for
various products from May 1953 to August 1957.

munity created different conditions which could begin to narrow the price differentials within the Community in the spring of 1958. To the extent that producers aligned on basing points in other countries, the differences would be even narrower than those shown by comparing official prices. How much they would do this would depend on a willingness to "invade" markets that were considered the province of someone else, a major question about the future of the Community.

The "dissociation" of coal prices in various parts of the Community of which the High Authority complained was a natural result of the high level of demand in the transitional period and of the divergences among the countries of the Community, in broad economic policies, in the place of the coal and steel industries in each national economy, and in the practices of governments. Much of the High Authority's attention has focused on this last point, not least because this is the most direct challenge to the spirit and letter of the Treaty. It must take a firm position that the governments have no business interfering in the pricing of coal and steel, yet it cannot escape the fact recognized by René Mayer: "We cannot prevent the governments from being concerned with prices. . . . Even if governments do not fix the prices of coal and steel, they are concerned about them. It is a human fact that the governments cannot be uninterested in this matter." [65] The High Authority's job was to limit their influence, said Mayer. This is a conflict that seems inherent in partial integration. It can only be resolved if the governments succeed in coordinating their national economic policies, a matter which goes beyond price policy and beyond matters of coal and steel as well. It is, in any case, a goal quite distant from the present state of affairs.

There is, however, more to the matter of Community price policy than the issues of partial integration that have dominated the transitional period. These will continue; the High Authority will continue its tug of war with the governments; the resolutions of the conflicts will continue to

[65] CA, *Débats*, Je. 27, 1957, p. 721.

depend on a balance of forces, not a clear-cut "victory" for either side. Indeed, there is not always a contest. When the High Authority decided to drop the ceiling price on Ruhr coal, the understanding between the German producers and their government helped make this course safe and, therefore, possible. When the High Authority decided to let the steel price go formally free at the opening of the common market, its own warning about the abuse of collusion was, as it knew, backed up by the pressure the French government was exerting on the French steel producers. Later the High Authority believed that the French government was holding the steel price too low (and perhaps it thought the same of the German government and the coal price), so it had reason to complain of government "interference" about which it could previously afford to be silent. What this means is that the High Authority is not in fact concerned only with who sets the prices but with what they are.

This may seem obvious. One can find it in the Treaty— at least in very broad terms. Yet it is not something fully admitted or clearly set out in Community discussions. It goes well beyond the formulations accepted at the outset about the limits of the Community's concern with prices. It requires that the High Authority formulate some rather basic principles about the kinds of price that are suitable for coal and steel. Up to a point it has done so. The question was fairly easy when the aim was to moderate price rises. The next phase was the decision that prices should be high enough to permit producers to meet some of their investment needs out of current earnings. This was set out fairly clearly in the strictures on the French government in the spring of 1957 (p. 273), and more fully developed in a discussion of long-run steel policy.[66] For coal the High Authority had essayed suggestions favoring some flexibility of prices that were not greeted with great approval in the industry and that may not be the last word from Luxembourg on the subject, since the Community is still working

[66] HA, *Report*, Apr. 1958, v. 1, pp. 36-37.

to develop a coherent approach to its coal problems. The
next problem will concern price policy when demand is
slack. If the High Authority adheres to the view that prices
should continue to provide the means for investment, it will
stress not competition but restraint, not a lowering of
prices but the policy followed by the American steel industry in recession, of price maintenance even though the level
of operations falls. That is explicitly the view attributed to
Léon Daum, the only member of the High Authority who
was once a steel producer. "He asserts roundly that it is a
positive and recognized interest of the ECSC to ensure
that the prices of steel products be kept up, if 1958 turns
out to be a year of declining business." [67] A more general
policy statement made in the spring of 1958 suggests a
similar conclusion by its emphasis on stable prices for
steel.[68]

The High Authority is not likely to be in a position to
impose its price policy, whatever it is; the governments
will retain an influence on prices; producers will respond
to conditions according to their own views. But it is its
view of what prices ought to be that provides the basis for
the High Authority's decision whether to throw its influence in one direction or another. The policy may prove
to be one of expediency alone; if not, it will depend in
turn on a broader view of how the coal and steel industries
of the six countries should develop and of what the Community should try to become. Just as the Treaty subordi-
nates price rules to its general purposes, the High Authority
will have to derive price policy from broader aims. Coal
prices, for instance, make sense only in terms of the relation
that coal is to have to other forms of energy.

The more fully the High Authority succeeds in imple-
menting a price policy, either directly or through its influence on the governments and industry, the more it is likely
to be drawn into detailed decisions like those a government

[67] A. Shonfield, "The Community Grows Up," *Steel Review*, Apr. 1958,
p. 29.
[68] HA, *Report*, Apr. 1958, v. 1, p. 38.

must make. This was the case when it was applying direct controls to prices.[69] There are serious disadvantages to this position since the High Authority has neither the powers nor the responsibilities of government on a sufficient scale for it to perform these functions satisfactorily. The chances are, however, that matters will not come to this point. There is no evidence in the Community's record on prices that either governments or the industry are likely to let matters go this far, nor would the High Authority welcome it. Partial integration remains the basic principle of the Community. Its development in the matter of pricing is not toward greater power for the High Authority, but toward a situation in which if the High Authority is to exercise its influence most effectively—whether through the direct use of its powers or otherwise—it must develop a policy on prices going beyond anything clearly anticipated in the Treaty or fully realized in the transition period.

[69] For instance, during the period of zonal pricing, when the collieries of the Saar and Lorraine were reducing the rebates they gave on sales to south Germany, thus raising prices in that area, the High Authority moved the region around the town of Bad Kreuznach from one zone to another, where the price would not rise as much, because the biggest coal consumers in the Bad Kreuznach area were a hospital and several municipal power stations.

TWELVE

SCRAP, A TROUBLESOME RAW MATERIAL

OLD STEEL is one of the principal ingredients in new steel. The pieces that fall by the way as ingots are rolled into sheets, bars, and plates; the material shaved, stamped, and sheared off as rolling-mill products are shaped into parts for automobiles, machines, and household goods; broken-up ships, bridges, and railroad tracks, along with the metal yielded by junk-yards and automobile dumps, all these return to the productive cycle as they are fed back into steel furnaces, and to some extent blast furnaces to make pig iron as well.

Scrap has presented the Community with a series of problems. The opening of the common market marked a radical change from the previous system of extensive national controls. Dependence on imports of American scrap has put pressure on the Community's supplies and led to the manipulation of prices in ways that made it harder to cut the consumption of scrap. Because the Community faces a scrap shortage for a period of some years, the High Authority has sought to penalize its use while expanding the output of pig iron. These efforts to deal with a major problem of raw material supply have led to a greater degree of intervention, involving a wider range of Community policies, than anything we have so far encountered in coal and steel.

COMMUNITY SCRAP SUPPLIES

The war left the Community countries well supplied with scrap. There were profitable markets in the United

States and Britain where steel production had expanded. Demand inside the Community was more restrained, especially because of the slow recovery of steel production in Germany, the largest scrap user. The occupation authorities fostered sales of German scrap abroad, especially to Britain. The Community as a whole became a major exporter.[1]

As Continental steel production expanded, the scrap situation changed. From 1952 to 1954 the Community was a small net importer of scrap. Beginning in 1954 imports increased sharply and thereafter became an important part of the Community's supply, as the following figures show:[2]

	1955	1956	1957
	(millions of tons)		
Scrap consumption	24.4	27.3	28.8
Supplies:			
from within the industry	12.6	14.7	15.6
collected in the Community	9.8	9.3	9.3
imported from third countries	3.0	3.2	4.3
Change in stocks	——	—.1	+.3

Most of the scrap went directly into steelmaking. Open-hearth furnaces producing Siemens-Martin steel consumed over three-fifths of the Community's scrap in 1956. There is much less opportunity to substitute scrap for pig iron in the converters that make Thomas steel. Though this process supplied over half the Community's steel in 1956, it used only 6.5 per cent of the scrap. Electric steel furnaces, which normally use scrap or liquid steel exclusively, consumed about one-sixth of the Community's scrap. An

[1] The peak was reached in 1949 when net exports to third countries came to nearly 3 million long tons, almost two-thirds of it to Britain and one-fifth to the United States. *World Trade in Scrap,* reprint from *Monthly Statistical Bulletin* (British Iron and Steel Federation), Oct. 1955, pp. 4, 8.

[2] HA, *Report,* Apr. 1957, p. 93; Apr. 1958, v. 2, p. 134. Discrepancies due to rounding. Exports to third countries were minor. There are some discrepancies in Community scrap statistics and fairly frequent revisions. For simplicity I have relied on these two reports rather than *Bulletin Statistique* when there are conflicts, and on the 1958 report when it differs from the year before.

equal amount was fed directly into blast furnaces to produce pig iron.[3]

Several factors have favored the use of scrap in the Community during the transitional period. It has been cheap in relation to pig iron. The pressure on coke supplies after 1954 and the need to import increasing quantities of expensive American coking coal have made it attractive to save coke by using scrap both to make pig iron and in steel furnaces. Community production of open-hearth steel has increased slightly more rapidly than production of Thomas steel; electric-steel output has grown most rapidly of all. The most important factor, however, was undoubtedly the lag in Community pig iron production. While crude steel output rose 35 per cent between 1952 and 1956, production of pig iron rose only 25 per cent. Imports of pig iron rose sharply but even so equaled less than 3 per cent of the domestic output in 1956.

Within the Community there are marked differences among countries in supply and use of scrap, as Table 5 shows. Naturally, the biggest steel producers are also the biggest scrap consumers, but there is a significant spread in the amount of scrap they use per ton of steel produced, resulting largely from differences in the structure of their industries. Nearly three-fifths of Germany's steel is made in open-hearth or electric furnaces, while in France three-fifths comes from Thomas converters. This saving of scrap in steelmaking makes supplies available for France to use in producing pig iron, thus saving on imports of coking coal.[4] Belgium and the Saar somewhat resemble France. Luxembourg, with its relatively large blast-furnace capacity and

[3] Calculated from *Bulletin Statistique*, May 1957, p. 298. The amount of scrap used per ton of steel produced was: in Thomas converters 60 kg.; in open-hearth furnaces 728 kg.; and in electric furnaces 944 kg. Because 1956 illustrates the Community's scrap problems better than 1957 when foreign supplies were more plentiful thanks to the drop in American steel production, figures for the earlier year will be used throughout this chapter.

[4] Although France is shown on the table as a net importer of scrap, it was a sizable net exporter in 1954 and 1955, and had a modest export balance in 1957.

complete lack of open-hearth furnaces, makes the smallest use of scrap in steelmaking. Italy on the other hand has little iron ore, is poor in blast furnaces, and produced 57 per cent of its steel in open-hearth furnaces and another 37 per cent in electrical furnaces in 1956. Not surprisingly, Italy used more than twice as much scrap per ton of steel produced as France and almost seven times as much as Luxembourg. Similar factors explain the Netherlands' very high rate of scrap consumption.

Table 5

COMMUNITY SCRAP IN 1956

| | Consumption | | | | |
| | Total (000 tons) | Kg. per ton of | | Ex-ports | Im-ports | "Produc-tion"c |
		steel output[a]	pig iron output[b]	(thousands of tons)		
Germany	11,351	426	74	770	593	11,528
Belgium	2,542	214	183	38	716	2,580
Luxembourg	716	113	100			
France	6,429	356	126	553	666	7,354
Saar	1,038[d]	227	92			
Italy	4,642	774	32	2	2,315	2,329
Netherlands	735	724	0	264	61	938

a. scrap consumption in steel works ÷ steel production
b. scrap charged in blast furnaces ÷ pig iron production
c. consumption + exports − imports
d. omits consumption in independent steel foundries

SOURCES: HA, *Bulletin Statistique*, Sept. 1957, pp. 323-325; Sept. 1958, pp. 194, 301, 303-304.

As these differences suggest, there is an active scrap trade within the Community. In 1956 it amounted to about 1.7 million tons, some two-thirds the level of imports from third countries. Italy was by far the largest importer in each category, but the other countries are also extensively engaged in two-way trade within the Community and in importing from the rest of the world.

MANIPULATING THE COMMUNITY SCRAP ECONOMY

Before the common market opened, governments exercised a number of controls over scrap and groups of private firms, usually steel producers, also "organized" the market. In France and Germany, the principal sources of Community scrap, there were centralized purchasing agencies for the steel industry. Both countries also limited exports. The foreign scrap on which Italy depended was mostly purchased in common and its price was equalized with that of domestic scrap. In Holland scrap prices controlled by the government were the lowest in the Community, $22 a ton. In Belgium and Luxembourg where prices moved quite freely they ranged between $45 and $48 a ton, approaching the high Italian level of $52. France and Germany were in between with $28 and $37 a ton, respectively, at the beginning of 1953.[5]

The common market seemed bound to have a great impact on this situation. Italy would turn to France and Germany for cheaper scrap to substitute for its imports from overseas. Those countries would be unable to check exports and the notoriously volatile scrap prices would rise sharply throughout the northern part of the Community. Speculation would follow; there would be a good bit of uneconomic cross-hauling; buyers' cartels would try to strengthen their grip on the market. The High Authority decided to move cautiously. Though steel production was falling and scrap prices of the Community countries had moved quite close together, it decided to maintain a ceiling at about the German level, modified by zonal pricing arrangements. It permitted temporary allocation, sanctioned price equalization agreements, and encouraged consumers to act together in buying scrap from abroad. It curbed several of the organizations that had allocated scrap but sponsored a voluntary organization of merchants and users to discuss common problems. As the demand for steel fell, the High Authority lowered the ceiling price of scrap by stages and then removed it altogether in March 1954.[6]

---

[5] *Informations Statistiques*, Feb.-Mar. 1955, p. 18.

[6] After the ceiling was removed, prices fell for another month and then leveled off. As steel production increased later in 1954, scrap prices rose and by early 1955 were generally above the level at which prices had

Voluntary cooperation that left one group or another free to exploit the system did not work very well. National administrative barriers continued to hamper trade. The High Authority began negotiations that led to the creation of a compulsory compensation scheme which, with modifications, remained in effect for the rest of the transitional period and afterward. All scrap sold within the Community was subject to a levy. The proceeds were used to reduce the price of imported scrap to the Community level. The amount of the levy was changed from time to time in accordance with price movements. The administration of the new arrangement was entrusted to the two agencies set up by the steel industry under the earlier scheme, one for price equalization, the other for joint purchasing of imports. The High Authority kept the right to intervene in their decisions when this proved necessary.

As steel production boomed, the scrap problem became more pressing. Scrap prices rose more rapidly than steel prices between the fall of 1954 and the spring of 1955. Imports increased and became more costly as the American price rose and ocean freight rates as well. There was some dissatisfaction with the compensation scheme. French steel producers, who were squeezed by the rise in scrap prices since the government held down the price of steel, urged the High Authority to declare that a scrap shortage existed and to set maximum prices and allocate supplies. Other governments objected. The Community went more deeply into its scrap problems than ever before. The Council of Ministers and the High Authority set out a series of principles as guides to price policy, which could hardly have been reconciled by any imaginable system.[7] The High Authority tightened the machinery of the compensation scheme and attempted to strengthen its own position in its administration. A more careful calculation of needs and

---

been fixed when the common market opened. Some spread among national prices reappeared when the price ceiling was removed but it has never been more than about $11 a ton, in contrast to the spread of $30 a ton at the beginning of 1953.

[7] HA, *Report*, Apr. 1955, pp. 99, 100.

resources was to be made in determining the amount of scrap that should be imported and the proper rate of compensation payments. Stocks were to be accumulated to offset "psychological factors" which were held to have played a large part in the recent price rise. This was never done, but the re-examination of the scrap problem led to a basic reassessment.

Previously the scrap problem had been looked at as essentially temporary. Stocks for emergencies plus a price equalization scheme covering a fairly stable import of about 500,000 tons were apparently thought sufficient to meet the main problems. But after the Community moved into the steel boom, the High Authority concluded that the scrap problem was structural and would last for a number of years. Since scrap supplies seemed unlikely to keep pace with steel production—at least until the time, some decades off, when the steel products made in the mid-fifties began to appear on the scrap heaps—the Community would have to economize on scrap and make greater use of pig iron where the two were interchangeable. To promote these aims, the High Authority introduced a major change in the Community's scrap regime.

Beginning on August 1, 1955, steelmakers were given a bonus for substituting pig iron for scrap. With each firm's scrap-pig ratio in the last quarter of 1954 as a base, makers of Siemens-Martin steel were to receive a grant of about $10 for every additional ton of pig iron they used to replace scrap.[8] The bonus arrangements applied only to Siemens-Martin steel because it was difficult to achieve any important substitution of pig iron for scrap in the Thomas

[8] The bonus was set at the difference between the compensation price for scrap and the lowest pig iron price in the Community on May 1, 1955. If the price of pig iron varied by more than 10 per cent from the May 1 level, or the compensation price of scrap dropped below $28 or rose above $37 per ton (which it subsequently did), the subsidy was to be modified. The bonus was payable on imported pig iron provided it was not subject to double-pricing or did not cost more (delivered) than Community pig iron. The High Authority could waive this last condition but was also given discretion to rule that it was not in the interest of the Community to pay the bonus on imported pig iron in a particular case. *JO*, Jl. 26, 1955, pp. 870-871.

and electric processes.[9] Industry views on the new system conflicted. The Germans were inclined to favor it. With their large open-hearth capacity they saw the prospect of gaining from the new payments, and thus obtaining some compensation for the penalties they felt they were paying for the benefit of Italian scrap consumers. The Italians did not care for the new proposal. They thought they could make no economies in the use of scrap and would have to pay a higher levy on their purchases within the Community. The Belgians, with their small open-hearth capacity, saw no benefits in the new scheme. No one was enthusiastic and conflicts of interest continued to plague all the scrap arrangements.

Prices continued to rise. Imports increased; as the American "composite price" rose, ocean freight rates went up as well (they ranged from 25 to 45 per cent of the price). At the end of 1955 the landed cost of American scrap was about $70 a ton while Community prices ranged between $35 and $45. A year later American scrap cost about $90 a ton with Community prices between $45 and $56. The levy on domestic scrap had to be increased to provide funds for compensation payments which still did not always make up the difference in the two prices. The High Authority had to intervene several times because the industry could not reach agreement through its Office Commun des Consommateurs de Feraille (OCCF) in Brussels. The "compensation price" in Italy had to be raised further above that of the rest of the Community lest the system work to encourage Italian imports from third countries by making them cheaper, after compensation, than Community scrap.[10] Various industry groups tried to control trade and prices; the High Authority asked the French government to act against a private body that was limiting scrap exports. Actions were lodged in the Community Court challenging some features of the scrap regime.

All this was troublesome, but the most serious difficulty

---

[9] Later the bonus was extended to the use of liquid Thomas steel as a substitute for scrap in the electrical process. *JO*, Feb. 22, 1956.

[10] *JO*, Mar. 5, 1956, p. 15.

was that the new system was not working. Steel producers were not reducing their consumption of scrap and substituting pig iron for it. When the results for the year were known it appeared that the Community producers of open-hearth steel were using more scrap to produce a ton of steel than they had before. In 1955 the Community used 720 kg. of scrap to produce a ton of Martin steel and in 1956 it used 728 kg.[11] Imports were also rising, to record levels. Already in the spring of 1956 the High Authority was preparing a new approach: if incentives to use pig iron were not enough, they should be supplemented by penalties on increased use of scrap. This conception was strongly disputed by the industry and was apparently resisted by the governments as well. A series of extensions kept the old system in effect while negotiations continued until January 1957 when new measures were finally enacted, to take effect in July.[12]

The essence of the new system was to penalize purchases of scrap exceeding a past level. In addition to the regular perequation levy, companies would have to pay an additional sum for every ton of scrap they bought beyond the amount they had purchased in a base period. Beginning at 25 per cent of the levy, the penalty payment would rise by stages until, after May 1, 1958, it equaled the levy. However, if a company used less scrap to produce a ton of steel or pig iron than it did in the base period or than the Community as a whole was currently using for the same type of furnace or process (as determined by a weighted average), then it would receive a rebate on the penalty.[13]

---

[11] *Bulletin Statistique*, May 1957, p. 299. This was, however, an improvement over 1954 when the figure was 753, but this is unlikely to have been a result of five months' operation of the scrap scheme at the end of 1955. The pattern in electric steel is similar, though less marked: 950 kg. per ton in 1954, 942 in 1955, and 944 in 1956. The use of scrap in blast furnaces also increased faster between 1955 and 1956—8 per cent—than the production of pig iron—6 per cent.

[12] *JO*, Jan. 28, 1957, pp. 61-67.

[13] The rebate is the proportion of the penalty equal to five times the percentage by which a firm's efficiency in using scrap improves over the past period or exceeds the Community average. The rebate cannot, however, be greater than the total penalty payment. The calculation of effi-

Each firm has a good bit of freedom to choose its base period, but plants brought into operation after January 31, 1958, have to pay the penalty rates on all their scrap (but are eligible for remission if their utilization is below the Community average). Additions to stocks were indefinitely exempted from penalty payments.[14]

The concessions intended to make the new scheme more acceptable to industry were not very successful. A few weeks after the High Authority made its decision (with the unanimous concurrence of the Council of Ministers), the major steel federations of France, Germany, and Belgium, along with several less important trade groups and individual producers, filed suit in the Community Court to have the action annulled. Meanwhile, as the new system came into effect, the Community's scrap position improved. The drop in economic activity in the United States made more scrap available for export and brought down its price. The composite price fell 50 per cent in the course of 1957. The freight rate fell from a peak of $27.84 a ton in January 1957 to $6.00 by February 1958. Inside the Community the weighted average of scrap prices in January 1958 was 21 per cent below what it had been in January 1957. The levy on scrap purchases was cut from its peak of $13.00 a ton in the spring of 1957 to $10.50 in May and then to $8.00 in January 1958. Between 1956 and 1957, Community scrap consumption in steelworks increased by 8.3 per cent while the output of steel rose only 5.2 per cent, so once again the amount of scrap used to produce a ton of steel increased. In this respect, the Community's position got worse. There was, however, a cut of over 9 per cent in the amount of scrap used in blast furnaces, probably because of the easing of coke and iron ore supplies. As a

---

ciency applies to all scrap used, not just to that purchased; the penalties apply only to purchased scrap. Several firms objected to the High Authority's definition of what was a firm's "own scrap" and carried the issue to the court.

[14] JO, Apr. 6, 1957, pp. 155-156. A firm may select six out of any seven consecutive months between January 1, 1953, and January 31, 1957 as a base period. There are provisions covering equipment put in service too late to use this formula.

result, the increase in Community scrap consumption of
1.5 million tons amounted to only about the same rate as
the increase in steel production. Thanks to the larger supplies, Community steel firms were able to add to their
stocks of scrap for the first time in several years, increasing
them by 300,000 tons during 1957.

PROVIDING FOR THE FUTURE

The increasingly complicated manipulation of scrap in
which the High Authority became involved was not, by
itself, likely to provide a lasting solution of the Community's difficulties. Having diagnosed a "structural
deficit," and lacking means of increasing the scrap supply
to any great extent, the High Authority had one major
course open to it: to foster the expansion of pig iron production. This it has done, adding encouragement of the
expansion of coke production and of measures to improve
the preparation of iron ore, which would help reduce the
pressure on scrap.

The High Authority had only limited means of doing
this, most of them connected with its investment policy
(Ch. 13). Some of the loans it made were for the expansion
of coke production and the beneficiation of iron ore. In
setting out long-run objectives that were intended to guide
the investment of Community enterprises, it stressed these
objectives and the construction of blast furnaces. In July
1956 it issued a general warning that unless pig iron production developed more rapidly the new steelworks that
firms were building would not be able to produce up to
capacity because of the shortage of scrap. This consideration would have to be placed at the top of the list of the
things to be taken into account when it examined the investment programs submitted to it by each company, said the
High Authority.[15] Subsequently, when firms proposed
expanding open-hearth or electric-furnace capacity the
High Authority tried to work out with them means of
avoiding the purchase of additional scrap. Where no solution could be found it issued "unfavourable opinions aimed

[15] *JO*, Jl. 19, 1956, p. 210.

at discouraging projects which would have resulted in considerably increased tightness of the scrap market." [16] The significance of the scrap issue is emphasized by the fact that these are the only unfavorable opinions on investments that the High Authority has issued.

Whether as a result of the High Authority's advice or their own analysis of the situation, the Community's producers have emphasized the expansion of pig iron production. The following figures show the share of the total investments of the Community steel industry that have gone into the production of pig iron: [17]

	per cent
1952-55	15.8
1956	22.7
Planned for 1957	29.2
Planned for 1958	34.0
Planned for 1957-60	31.1

As a result of these investments the Community's capacity for producing pig iron was expected to increase 28 per cent between 1956 and 1960, compared to an increase of 26 per cent in the previous five years. However, steel capacity was expected to increase by an equal amount, so in 1960 the Community would be capable of producing only as much pig iron in relation to steel as it had in 1956. In the meantime, as a result of the lag in blast-furnace investment in earlier years, the Community would be able to produce only 745 kg. for every ton of steel, compared with 770 kg. in 1956. The record for 1957 was better than this prediction: 754 kg. This marked more progress than

---

[16] HA, *Report*, Apr. 1957, p. 323. One of these cases involved the Société des Usines à Tubes de la Sarre which unsuccessfully challenged in the Court the High Authority's right to give such an opinion which had no legal consequences (see p. 338).

[17] Same, *Annexes*, p. 68; as modified by HA, *Report*, Apr. 1958, v. 2, p. 263. The figures for 1957 and afterwards are based on investments under way and planned on January 1, 1957, which are ordinarily not fully carried out. The statistics cover blast furnaces, cokeries owned by the steelworks, and processing of iron ore. The figures for blast furnaces alone are: 1952-55—9.5 per cent; 1956—13.8 per cent; 1957—17.2 per cent; 1958—19.5 per cent; 1957-60—18.1 per cent.

the companies' investment plans had indicated toward the High Authority's target for 1960 of 785 kg. of pig iron capacity for every ton of steel capacity. Even this was short of the ratio of 795 kg. of pig iron to a ton of steel achieved in actual production in 1952-54. At the outside this level might be attained by 1965 if the High Authority's long-range objectives were to be fulfilled.[18]

Using another perspective—that of its projections of possible development in the Community—the High Authority saw little prospect of increased scrap supplies except from the production of steel. It calculated, therefore, that the scrap used to produce a ton of steel would have to fall from 472 kg. in 1955 to somewhere between 439 and 447 in 1960 and 426-432 in 1965.[19] This could only be achieved by making use of the flexibility of open-hearth production to substitute pig iron for scrap and by emphasizing the development of steelmaking processes that used less scrap. Of this there was some indication, both in projected investments for Thomas converters and in a rather rapid increase in the use of newer processes that economized scrap. But the High Authority noted that discipline would be called for and warned that "if a balance is not achieved between the different production processes and the raw materials available, the total figure for capacity installed can easily remain no more than a figure on paper, without ever coming to represent actual production at all." [20]

Such long-run forecasts must be treated with reserve. Some are the High Authority's ideas of what ought to be done, the others estimates of what existing investment plans will achieve—if they are carried out. None, however, foreshadow any marked easing of the Community's scrap position. The gains that can reasonably be counted on are modest enough to suggest continuing strain unless there is either a drop in the demand for steel or an unexpected increase in the supplies of scrap that the Community can import at reasonable prices.

[18] HA, *Report*, Apr. 1957, pp. 288, 337-338.
[19] Same, p. 282. In the second half of 1957 the figure was 474 kg.
[20] Same, pp. 277-278.

THE ROLE OF THE UNITED STATES

There are not many points at which specific American policies directly touch Community affairs, but scrap is one. The United States has been the Community's largest outside supplier of scrap, providing, along with Canada, two-thirds or more of the Community imports from third countries.[21] Had it not been for American action, the amounts would have been still larger.

The United States is the world's largest producer and consumer of scrap. In 1956 it used more than three times as much scrap as the Community's iron and steel industries.[22] As in the Community, about half circulated within the steel industry itself. But in the United States economy at large, scrap is more easily obtained than in the Community —or indeed than in most other parts of the world—thanks to the rapid replacement of equipment and the greater use of steel in durable consumer goods, especially automobiles, which have a relatively short life. Before the war the United States normally exported scrap, partly because of the depressed state of the steel industry. The war changed that and although the United States had a small net export of scrap in the immediate postwar years it was a net importer from 1948 through 1951. Exports to countries other than Canada and Mexico were forbidden from 1949 to October 1, 1953. After that licenses were freely granted (except for shipments to Soviet bloc countries) because the fall in the demand for steel made scrap plentiful. In 1954 exports increased sharply and then rose even more rapidly as world steel production revived. The Community took 31 per cent of United States exports in 1954, 46 per cent the next year, and 35 per cent in 1956. It was the United States' largest customer until 1956 when Japan displaced it by a narrow margin.

[21] HA, *Report*, Apr. 1958, v. 2, p. 136. U.S. export figures applied to the High Authority's import totals show the U.S. share as 69.6 per cent in 1955, 62.1 per cent in 1956, and 60.4 per cent in 1957. *Bulletin Statistique* shows a higher U.S. share but this is based on smaller total imports, one of the discrepancies mentioned in n. 2.

[22] Much of this section is a digest of Percy W. Bidwell, *Raw Materials: A Study of American Policy*, 1958, Chapter 7.

From the time the decision to end export control was taken, American steel producers protested against it. When exports climbed while domestic demand resumed and scrap prices rose to new heights, they became more importunate. The Administration resisted these pressures but urged moderation on the three largest buyers—the Community, Japan, and the United Kingdom. In mid-1955 the High Authority undertook to reduce its purchases for the rest of the year to 150,000 metric tons a month.[23] During 1956 the Community gave assurances that its imports would be limited to 1,980,000 short tons. It wanted to import more in 1957, but American officials held that the 1956 level should be maintained. During part of February and March 1957 the Department of Commerce withheld export licenses and in May announced that exports would be kept to the 1956 level pending the outcome of negotiations. In June an agreement was reached by which the Community agreed to hold down imports of heavy melting scrap to 1,586,000 metric tons, 13 per cent above the 1956 level. No limits were placed on lighter material (about 40 per cent of total U. S. exports in 1955 and 1956) but the United States reserved the right to reopen the question if difficulties resulted. Instead, American demand fell with the decline in steel production, exports to the Community rose, and in 1958 the Department of Commerce announced that licenses would be issued for all exports.

This sequence of events suggests that when world steel production is high the Community will have to reckon

[23] Statement by Thorsten V. Kalijarvi, Assistant Secretary of State for Economic Affairs, *Small-Business Problems Relating to Iron and Steel Scrap*, Hearings before the House Select Committee on Small Business, 85th Cong., 1st sess., Je. 18-21, 1957, p. 389 (hereafter cited as House Hearings). Export and import figures, which do not correspond exactly with "purchases" to which the Community commitments apparently referred, indicate that the limits referred to in this paragraph were at least roughly maintained. U.S. figures, put on a metric ton basis, show average monthly shipments for the last half of 1955 as 146,500; total annual shipments in 1956, 2.0 million (above the limit set, which was in short tons), and in 1957, 2.6 million. Heavy melting scrap in the latter year came to 1.6 million, a little more than the agreed amount. *Bulletin Statistique* gives slightly higher figures for imports in 1955 and 1956.

with the likelihood that its access to American scrap will be limited by the action of the United States government. This is not inevitable. Percy Bidwell's careful study of American scrap policy concludes that the United States does not have to limit scrap exports for its own security or to avoid a shortage that would curtail steel production. The key issue appears to be the impact of high foreign demand on the price of scrap and therefore on the ultimate cost of steel. The American steel industry will press for export controls to protect its supplies and keep down their prices when demand is strong. The scrap trade, which has so far proved weaker, will presumably urge free exports, because even if relatively few firms sell abroad all will benefit from the higher price.

The Community is not gambling on an easier American export policy. Its spokesmen told the State Department that their requirements of American scrap would be "heavy" in 1958, "substantial" in 1959, but "negligible" thereafter.[24] This diminuendo of adjectives is not altogether plausible in terms of the High Authority's own projections. In stating general objectives for the Community, the High Authority proposed that imports of scrap should be 1.5 to 2 million tons a year from 1960 onwards. The United States' share of such a figure might be from 1 to 1.5 million tons, a figure one could not exactly call "negligible" but still substantially below the levels of 1955 to 1957. There was, however, no reason to suppose that this objective could be attained (except by limiting imports) so long as Community steel production was high. By the spring of 1958 the High Authority was willing to admit as much, but then there was no immediate problem.[25]

[24] Kalijarvi, cited, p. 389. Although Mr. Kalijarvi spoke of an investment program planned to double the Community's blast-furnace capacity between 1956 and 1960, there is nothing in the Community literature to justify such a figure.

[25] Though an improvement in the relation of pig iron to steel production could be expected in 1959 and 1960, "without a supplementary investment effort, it would not appear to be of a nature to permit the reduction of imports to 1.5-2 million tons, at least for a high level of steel production." HA, *Report*, Apr. 1958, v. 2, p. 139. Supplies from the rest of the world, though not negligible, are unlikely to prove expansive

The United States cannot shape its scrap export policy
in terms of the Community alone. Japan and the United
Kingdom are important buyers who will have to be treated
equitably. While a true scrap shortage in the United States
is unlikely, there will be continuing problems about price
and supply so long as the United States continues to be the
major source of scrap in international trade. While export
control may be primarily a means of influencing the
domestic price, it is not a course that can be dismissed out
of hand so long as other major steel producers have arrangements for manipulating their scrap prices. The only comprehensive solution seems to lie in the adjustment of the
world's steel industries to greater use of pig iron and to the
economizing of scrap. The means of facilitating this adaptation lie in technology, investment, and relative prices. If
the United States government is to intervene in this process
at all, the most reasonable test of policy is whether it pro-
motes adaptation on an equitable basis, in the United States
as well as abroad.

American scrap export policy has not been conceived in
these terms, but paradoxically its influence on the Community has almost certainly been in this direction. The influence has been exercised in two ways. First, the restraint
on exports has set a limit to the amount of scrap the Community could obtain and so has provided one of the material dimensions of the Community's problem. The second
form of influence has been more diffuse, mingling with the
other factors that caused the Community to adopt the
scrap policies it did. From mid-1955 on, and perhaps earlier, the Community was on notice that the more its imports
of American scrap grew, the more likely it was that the
United States would impose some kind of export control.
But there was room for maneuver in negotiations with the
United States about how much scrap the Community

---

enough to make up a substantial part of the Community's needs. The
High Authority assumed that, if anything, they would decline in the
future as new steel industries developed, especially in some of the under-
developed countries which had been exporting their relatively small
amounts of scrap since they had no domestic use for it.

would be able to buy. By encouraging the use of pig iron and the expansion of blast-furnace capacity, and later by penalizing the use of scrap, the Community could argue that it was doing its best and that its need for American scrap would be temporary. (Kalijarvi called these measures to the attention of the Congressional committee when he was explaining American policy.) While the primary reasons for taking these steps lay in the material needs of the situation, there can be little doubt that the American position had an influence. The High Authority, which would have been more acutely conscious of the negotiating problem than users who had only to place orders through the OCCF,[26] and perhaps the governments as well, undoubtedly used these arguments in pressing a reluctant industry to go along with the measures for conserving scrap. While this was not the purpose of American policy it was in some indeterminate degree one of its effects.

THE EFFECT OF COMMUNITY SCRAP POLICY

The main thing that opening the common market for scrap did was to give Italy relatively free access to French and German supplies. Intra-Community trade nearly tripled between 1952 and 1954-1957. Over two-thirds of the scrap traded among Community countries from 1954 through 1957 went to Italy. Most of this came from France and Germany. These countries in turn had to import scrap from the United States, sometimes more than they exported to Italy. There has been a certain resentment. Of

[26] Another, less important, issue between the United States and the Community concerned the exclusive purchase contracts the OCCF had made with Luria Brothers, the major American scrap exporter. These annoyed the rest of the scrap trade and after representations by the State Department in 1955 the High Authority announced that the OCCF would make no more exclusive contracts. Nevertheless, Luria and some associated firms continued to get most of the business. After further representations by the United States, the High Authority announced a series of principles that would be applied by the OCCF in negotiating new supply contracts. Their gist was that all suppliers would have a chance to bid but that ability to supply in quantity and on schedule would be taken into consideration. *Bulletin Mensuel*, Jl. 1957, pp. 7-9. After the first contracts were made under the new system, Luria got 85 per cent of the business.

course, the French and Germans benefit from the equalization fund and do not have to pay the full price for imported scrap while selling at their own lower prices to Italy. However, in the French and German steel industries the compensation levy is apt to be regarded as a burden placed on them for the benefit of Italy. As the largest consumers, the French and German industries pay the largest part of the levy. The largest payments out of the equalization fund are made to Italy which accounted for 46 per cent of the Community's imports from third countries in 1955 and 54 per cent in 1956.[27] To this is added the objection to "the price increase resulting from the purchases made on our territory by certain countries of the Community that lacked scrap. . . ."[28]

Two separate issues are involved here. There is no doubt that Italy has benefited from the common market and that the French and German steel producers have thereby been required to pay more for scrap than they would have if export controls had given them first call on domestic supplies. This was one of the principal gains Italy expected from going into the Community. There is also no doubt that Italy has benefited by having the cost of its scrap imports from third countries reduced by payments from the other members of the Community. To this extent the French and German steel producers (and perhaps those of the other countries, as well, or whoever ultimately paid the added costs) have been burdened.

It is far less clear whether the French and German pro-

[27] According to one estimate, in the last eight months of 1954 the Germans paid out $6.5 million more in levies on scrap than they received in equalization payments on imported scrap. For France, the figure was judged to be $8 million and for Holland $2 million. In contrast, Italy received $16 million more in equalization payments than it paid out, according to these figures. *Der Volkswirt*, Mar. 3, 1956, p. 7. In April 1957 an official of Assider, the Italian steel federation, said that net payments to Italy from the equalization fund had come to $58.4 million. Cited by C. Almini, "Le Tappe della CEE e le Funzioni della CECA," *Mondo Economico*, Jan. 18, 1958, pp. 16, 17.

[28] Chambre Syndicale de la Sidérurgie Française, *La Sidérurgie Française en 1956*, 1957, p. 17. On occasion specific increases in French steel prices have been blamed on rises in scrap prices.

ducers have suffered from the equalization scheme, given the common market. Money has flowed from north to south but the alternative, if nothing interfered with the common market,[29] was heavier Italian demand for French and German scrap which would, presumably, have driven the prices much higher. Whether the French and German steel industries would have paid a higher or lower total scrap bill under these circumstances is moot. If one looks at the equalization scheme from the point of view of the Community as a whole, the distribution of collections and payments among the countries has no particular importance. If Germany pays into the *caisse* because it is using domestic scrap while Italy draws out of the *caisse* because it is importing from the United States, this comes to very much the same thing as if Italy is paying into the *caisse* because it is buying German scrap and Germany, in consequence, buys American scrap and draws out of the *caisse*.[30] No doubt the equalization system is not a delicate enough mechanism to equilibrate perfectly, and there are gains and losses from the system for certain countries or certain enterprises under particular circumstances. How this may work out cannot be judged without a close analysis of its operations. But it is clear that it is the common market, rather than the price equalization scheme, that provides the advantage for Italy over the large scrap "producers" of the Community. It may even be that an unrecognized advantage of the equalization system has been to permit better functioning of the common market, for it is hard to believe that in its absence French and German producers and their governments would not have exerted

[29] There are some indications that the scrap market is to some extent "organized" or regulated, at least informally, in France and Germany. In mid-1955 there was an arrangement for price stabilization between French scrap and steel interests. *Neue Zürcher Zeitung*, Sept. 27, 1955. The German price has sometimes remained absolutely steady for periods when other Community prices were fluctuating, usually at a higher level (for instance, January to June 1955).

[30] Whether it is truly economic for one or the other of the parties to be doing these things is still another matter, but that is not the alternative posed.

even greater efforts, however doubtful their legality, to defend their home markets against the pressure of Italian buyers.

Another aspect of the Community's scrap policy is of greater importance. This is the effect of the equalization scheme and other measures on the price of scrap. The aim was to prevent the cost of imported scrap from raising the level of all scrap prices in the Community. Affecting as it does some 10 to 15 per cent of the scrap consumption, and therefore some 20 to 30 per cent of the scrap that is traded, the equalization scheme has undoubtedly done this. There is also a moderating influence on price fluctuations, which are much affected by freight rates that largely move in response to factors irrelevant to the economics of steel production. One can certainly sympathize with these purposes, especially in view of the volatile character of the scrap market.[31] Nevertheless, the question remains whether holding down the price of scrap does not interfere with a solution of the Community's scrap problem. I cannot answer this question with any certainty. What follows suggests some considerations and indicates some lines of inquiry. (Though the Community's scrap situation has changed since the following pages were written—see the Epilogue to this chapter—I have let them stand. The question they deal with is in abeyance at the moment but in some form it is almost certain to face the Community again.)

The Community's steel industry pays the whole cost of its scrap—American price plus domestic price—without outside aid. The question at issue is not the abandonment of the equalization system or complete freedom of the scrap market, but a rise in the price of scrap. A higher scrap price might serve two possible purposes: to increase the supply and to conserve the use. The former may not be possible in the Community. In the United States a

[31] Even under the voluntary equalization scheme it was alleged that the French prices were driven up simply because Italian buyers who feared a shortage would not wait for the arrival of ships from the United States. *Le Monde*, Nov. 4, 1954.

higher price will extract scrap from the economy that would otherwise be left uncollected.[32] However, the United States is a better scrap "producer" than Europe thanks to the size of the economy, the higher levels of production in wartime, the probably higher rate of replacement of equipment, and the much greater importance of durable consumer goods. The High Authority has assumed that the Community cannot increase its collection of old scrap to more than 4.5 million tons a year between 1960 and 1965. The argument is that the supply is limited by the low steel production of twenty years before. The estimate draws support from the slight increase of scrap collection during the transitional period while prices were rising. The British steel industry makes a similar assumption and an ECE study supports the conclusion.[33]

Even if it is assumed that major scrap supplies would not be forthcoming, a higher price might help the Community by encouraging scrap economies. The High Authority has been in the difficult position of trying to induce Community producers to save on scrap and use more pig iron while the price of scrap was low enough—thanks partly to the equalization scheme—to make its use attractive. For a long time this was ignored in Community discussions, but in 1957 the Belgian steel federation clearly indicated the connection between price policy and the Community's scrap difficulties. "The systematic maintenance of the perequation price at an exaggeratedly low level in spite of the rising level of business activity of 1955 and 1956 stimulated the development of consumption without relation to sup-

[32] How long this will be true is not so clear. Department of Commerce estimates of potential generation of heavy melting scrap show it to be well above actual use (including exports) for most of the postwar years. However, the situation is supposed to reverse itself in 1959. House Hearings, cited, pp. 424, 425.

[33] HA, *Report*, Apr. 1957, p. 281. *Steel Review*, Jl. 1956, pp. 33, 34. ECE, *The European Steel Market in 1956*, 1957, Ch. IV, esp. p. 117, and Appendix. While the ECE's method requires more testing, the first calculations suggest that the scrap available to most Community countries in 1955 was only slightly greater than actual collections. Subsequently the High Authority has suggested that the increased use of consumer durable goods might somewhat alter the situation. HA, *Report*, Apr. 1958, v. 1, pp. 28-29.

plies, especially in certain countries of the Community. Imports from third countries had in consequence to be increased considerably." [34] Then in 1958 the High Authority put the matter bluntly (perhaps as a warning?): "The most effective solution for keeping the consumption of scrap in proportion to resources would seem to be a free price without any intervention, whether in imports or in domestic supply." [35]

The key issue is the relation of the prices of scrap and pig iron. While a precise comparison is not possible, it seems that in the Community scrap is generally cheaper in relation to pig iron than it is in scrap-rich America. [36] Certainly the Community uses more scrap where the relative price would be expected to have an influence. In making open-hearth steel, where the greatest possibilities of substitution exist, 70 per cent of the Community's total use of pig iron and scrap was provided by scrap in 1956. The figure for the United States was 45 per cent. In charging blast furnaces the Community used about 75 per cent more scrap than the United States in proportion to the pig iron produced. [37]

[34] Groupement des Hauts-Fourneaux et Aciéries Belges, *Rapport Annuel 1956*, p. 32 (hereafter cited as Groupement Belge).

[35] HA, *Report*, Apr. 1958, v. 1, p. 25.

[36] In February 1957 the scrap price (including the equalization levy) was about 70 per cent of the pig price in France and Italy; about 75 per cent in the Benelux countries; about 80 per cent in Germany. By early 1958 the spread increased, though the price of pig iron fell in France and Italy. In the United States the scrap price was 88.8 per cent of the price of pig iron. This cannot be taken as typical, because from August 1955 to late 1957 the American scrap price varied from about 60 to over 100 per cent of the pig price, but comparison is difficult because while the scrap price fluctuates quite freely the pig iron price is stable for long periods and then moves in single jumps comparable to those of the steel price. U.S. figures calculated quarterly from *Commodity Yearbook, 1957*, p. 199; U.S. Dept. of Commerce, *Business Statistics, 1957*, p. 157; and *Survey of Current Business*. The comparison is between No. 1 heavy melting scrap at Pittsburgh and Basic pig iron at Valley Furnaces. It is not precisely comparable to that used by the High Authority.

[37] Comparisons calculated from U.S. Bureau of Mines tables in House Hearings, cited; American Iron and Steel Institute, *Annual Statistical Report*; *Bulletin Statistique*. The British figure on open-hearth production is closer to the American than to the Community's. For total steel

How much difference a rise in the scrap price would make is not altogether clear. If the Community uses all the pig iron it can get, a higher scrap price would presumably raise costs without reducing the use of scrap. (Bidwell notes that in the United States during these years the ratio of scrap to pig used in steelmaking increased while the scrap price rose.) There might be some improvement in allocation, for instance by diverting scrap from blast furnaces to steel mills. Technical factors limit flexibility in some installations, notably electric furnaces. Nevertheless, failure to explore very carefully the possible gains from a higher scrap price is a weakness of the Community's policy. The penalty system for increased scrap use moves in the direction of higher prices, but on a limited scale.[38] The high price of pig presumably stimulates investment in blast furnaces, but a higher price for scrap would do the same.

In addition to its possible practical effects, adjustment of the price ratio would strengthen the Community's hand in negotiations with the United States for scrap supplies when export controls are in effect. The American steel industry has argued that the Community's scrap scheme subsidizes steel producers and saves them the cost of investments in pig iron production. The equalization scheme is not, properly speaking, a subsidy, but it is a price manipulation that has been used in a way that encourages scrap imports. The Community's negotiating position would be improved by either a reduction of the price incentive to use scrap or a convincing demonstration that little could be accomplished by such a measure.

---

production in 1956, scrap accounted for only about 40 per cent of the charge (scrap plus pig iron) in Community furnaces, while the American figure was 50 per cent. This is due to the large share of Thomas steel in Community production.

[38] The criticism has been made that the new system gives "a monopoly of the use of scrap to the principal current users. It crystallizes the existing structures and constitutes an obstacle to adaptations that technical developments might require of certain enterprises." Groupement Belge, cited, p. 33. This is a valid objection to any device using base periods. If the penalty plan were maintained for a long period, the problem of distortions could become serious; over a short period the problem is not so great and is probably inescapable (though different bases for determining penalties might be devised).

It may be that a higher scrap price would not greatly improve the Community's position. There may be good reasons for accepting the handicap created by the contradictions in the present policy. But until this is made perfectly clear, the High Authority's scrap policy is vulnerable to the criticism that it is not using one of the principal and most obvious means of pursuing its aims. If one accepts a rather pessimistic prognosis for the Community scrap position, with chronic difficulty over a period of years, it becomes all the more important not to neglect a major, if difficult, course of action.

Whatever the future may hold, the Community's handling of its scrap problems during the transitional period has demonstrated elements of Community life not so apparent in the treatment of coal and steel. For one thing the character of the policy has been different. To a greater degree than in coal or steel, the High Authority has sought to manipulate the Community's scrap economy. It has not been willing to go so far as to use allocation and price controls. It has not been willing to withdraw to the broadly supervisory role it has played in coal and steel. No doubt these alternatives have been considered, perhaps even threatened, in negotiations about the successive scrap schemes. At times one or the other may have tempted the nine men in Luxembourg. One can guess the general character of the objections to choosing either of them. Direct control would have been difficult; it would have spotted the reputation the High Authority is trying to build of not being dirigistic; and it would have made the High Authority the butt of every complaint about scrap. Freeing the market would have risked sharp disturbances in price and supply; efforts by government or industry to control the situation might well have been harder to supervise or check than in coal and steel; the conflict of interest would have tended to follow national lines as Italians sought to get more Community scrap while French and Germans sought to put more of the burden of importing from America on the Italians. This would probably have made a caricature of the common market in scrap.

The compromise, with its successive series of incentives, penalties, exhortations, and measures to promote equity, has avoided the major disadvantages of the extremes. It has had its own weaknesses, of which the greatest is that it has not accomplished its primary purpose of economizing scrap. While recommendations about investment may have had some influence on the expansion of Community pig iron capacity, the other measures do not seem to have contributed to the process of adaptation and may have hindered it. The main achievements of Community scrap policy have probably been the debatable one of restraining the rise in scrap prices and the more clearly desirable ones of creating a reasonable approximation of a common market and spreading the burden of the cost of imported scrap throughout the Community in a way that helped to minimize—though it could not eliminate—international tensions. This is no mean achievement considering the special characteristics of the Community's scrap problems, but there is every indication that scrap problems will persist and call for new kinds of measures before a stable situation is created.

EPILOGUE

After this chapter was in type, a radical change took place in the Community's scrap regime. In ruling on the steel producers' suits in the summer of 1958, the Court rebuffed most of the attacks on the scrap control scheme but held that the High Authority had no right to delegate regulatory functions to the OCCF, a private body. The High Authority began to take over the administration of the equalization scheme. After making some changes it proposed a revised system. Grants would be made to encourage the use of pig iron. Equalization payments on imported scrap would be made only when the price was high enough to hurt the competitive position of steel producers or when the Community's production of pig iron was approaching capacity. Then the growing opposition to different elements of the scrap control scheme mobilized itself and the governments of Germany, Italy, and Luxembourg voted against the proposal in the Council of Ministers. As a result the equalization scheme fell to the ground and the Community for the first time had a free common market in scrap, beginning in December 1958.

For the moment, at least, the scrap market was not strained. Community steel production was in a slight lull; American steel plants had been operating far below capacity, so scrap for export had been plentiful; freight rates were low; increasing amounts of pig iron were available in the Community (indeed it was partly to improve demand for pig iron and coke that the Germans wanted to see the scrap price rise). It seems unlikely, however, that these conditions will go on indefinitely unless Community steel production fails to expand as expected. If the need for imported scrap rises, and the price along with it, the old problems will reappear. Will the Community let the market remain free, though prices rise toward the landed cost of imported scrap while Italian buyers "invade" the French and German markets? Will the steel companies find ways to "organize" the market? If they manage to hold down the price of domestic scrap, who will pay for the more expensive imports? Will Italy be denied the benefits of the common market by private or governmental measures that keep French and German scrap at home? Will these familiar problems again push the Community toward some kind of equalization scheme? Can it avoid the price depressing effects of the former one? Will the High Authority's powers to allocate scarce materials come into play? Because the experience of the transitional period remains relevant to these questions, I have let this chapter stand as it was before the Community made its newest leap into the unknown by freeing the scrap market.

THIRTEEN

INVESTMENT, PROBLEMS FOR
THE FUTURE?

The investment provisions are among the simplest in the Treaty. The story of what the High Authority has done is easily told. But this simplicity is deceptive. The decisions about the kinds of investment powers the High Authority should have, and then its decisions as to how to use those powers, involve crucial and contentious issues about the character of the Community.

WHAT WAS INVOLVED

When the Schuman Plan was first proposed Western Europe was still concerned with its recovery from war. Every country had plans for further expansion. Capital was scarce; government funds and American aid financed an important part of the investment in coal and steel. Many looked on the proposed Community as a source of investment funds, or as a funnel for capital attracted by the promise of the large, new, common market. There were also fears about investment. "Cut-throat competition amongst steel producers in 1953 would be the result of existing investment trends," warned the ECE.[1] The need, according to many, was for coordination of national investment programs; the implication was that coordination would mean limitation. The Schuman Plan provided a possible mechanism. There was another side to this. If the steel producers really thought surplus capacity was in the making—and that view was endemic in the industry—they

[1] ECE, *European Steel Trends in the Setting of the World Market*, 1949, p. 72.

314

might well try to get together to limit expansion. Those who feared this but admitted that there might be need for coordination saw the Schuman Plan as a means of pitting the public interest in large supplies of steel and coal at reasonable prices against industrial Malthusianism. Whatever view one took of these matters, the Treaty's investment provisions assumed major significance.

There was also an important international aspect to this matter. France had invested heavily in coal and steel since the end of the war. The recovery of German heavy industry had lagged. Would the Coal and Steel Community perpetuate the French lead or would it help the Germans to close the gap? The prospects were argued both ways in both countries. The issue was central for the French-German equation that was at the heart of the Community. The outcome depended largely on what the Treaty said about investment and how the High Authority used the powers given to it. The extent of these powers was an essential part of another basic issue concerning the Community's character. If the High Authority could direct investment, or forbid it, or disburse investment funds according to its own ideas of what was best for the coal and steel industries, it would be as strong as any government, and stronger than some. This would be *dirigisme* in a quite literal sense, and it was something most businessmen feared.

Enough of these conflicting views would have to be reconciled to secure, first, the ratification of the Treaty and, afterwards, the support that the Community would need among the many groups with whose affairs it would be concerned. But there was still another question. What arrangements about investments were necessary for the Community to achieve its aims? Some of the burning issues of 1949 and 1950 would lose their heat in the course of 50 years but investment would remain a key to "the most rational distribution of production at the highest possible level of productivity" called for by the Treaty. Indeed, investment was of special importance. One could well imagine that in the short run the opening of the common market would not greatly alter the pattern of production;

but whether it secured the best allocation of resources over the long run would largely depend on how new investment responded to changed conditions. Who was to encourage this flow or prevent its obstruction? How much power did the High Authority need? Was it to have a direct role in financing investments and if so with whose money? If opinions differed on what would result from a given investment, whose view was to prevail? Those among the Treaty drafters whose special responsibility was to keep their eyes on the future had to ponder these questions and decide how far it was safe to go in compromising with the immediate pressures without fatally damaging the Treaty.

Out of this interplay and its compromises came a settlement in which most investment decisions are left to the enterprises and the High Authority is given three kinds of power. It can provide, or help provide, funds for investment. In some circumstances it can limit a firm's access to money. It can influence—or try to influence—the course of investment in the Community by a series of measures that are not binding on firms but that may affect their decisions or those of the people who would have to provide the funds for investment. In making use of these powers, the High Authority has been influenced by the persistence of some of the attitudes that made the investment issue so touchy in the first place and by its prudent wish to create confidence throughout the whole broad and diverse constituency of the Community. It has also managed to avoid a direct confrontation of some of the sharpest issues, particularly those involving national rivalries.

THE TAX

The High Authority, like a government, has two ways of getting money: it can borrow and it can tax. Its tax may not exceed 1 per cent of the value of the coal and steel produced in the Community unless the Council of Ministers agrees to a higher rate by a two-thirds majority. Establishing the means of levying and collecting this first supranational tax was a major part of the High Authority's early activity. Enjoined by the Treaty to avoid cumulative taxation, it exempted iron ore and coke from the levy, on the assumption that their value would be taxed in the manufacture of steel or had been taxed in the mining of coal. Forms of reporting and calculation were established. Banks were designated in each country to which companies paid their taxes.

For the first six months of 1953 the tax rate was set at .5 per cent and then raised to .9 per cent, not quite the maximum permitted by the Treaty. As production increased and prices rose, the yield of the tax increased. The High Authority was able to set aside substantial reserves and began to feel pressure from the producers to lower the rate. In May 1955 the Council of Ministers recommended a reduction. The rate dropped to .7 per cent in July 1955 and .45 at the beginning of 1956. In July 1957 it was cut to .35 per cent.

Up to the end of 1957 the levy yielded $204.5 million. Interest, fines, and other items increased the income by $16.7 million. Only one-quarter of the total had been spent by the end of 1957.[2] Of the remaining $163.2 million, some was put into reserves earmarked for readaptation, research or other matters; some was held for general expenses. The larger part, $100 million, constituted a "guarantee fund" that the High Authority built up to buttress its credit when it floated loans abroad.

Like most taxes, the Community's has been the object of a certain amount of complaint. Producers said that the levy was forcing up prices; that they could make better use of the money themselves; that a lower rate would yield all the funds the Community needed. When the tax rate was reduced in 1955, contrary criticism set in. Members of the Assembly complained that it had not been consulted about this step. A high tax in good times made sense, they said, because the High Authority should ac-

---

[2] The administrative expenses of the High Authority were $21.2 million, those of other Community organs $12.3 million. Readaptation payments came to $4.5 million, research grants to $2.1 million, and financial charges and pensions to $2.1 million. Formally, the Community accounts are reckoned in EPU units of account.

cumulate resources it might need if production fell. They urged, too, that the High Authority use more funds to push research, readaptation, and other measures that would give content to the Community's "social policy" which always lagged behind what many people hoped to make of it (Ch. 16).

The most serious criticism concentrated on the accumulation of the guarantee fund. By the middle of 1955 the High Authority had set aside $75 million in this fund, about nine times as much at it had spent for all purposes. To the critics this seemed wasteful; the coal and steel firms could have put the money to good use, now it was idle. To the men on the High Authority a large reserve fund was a matter of the first priority. They felt it was essential to establish the Community's credit-worthiness and to attract foreign capital. Without a reserve, the High Authority would have no financial resources except the current yield of the tax which would fall in bad years, just when the High Authority might have to make good on a guarantee because a borrowing enterprise had difficulty paying its debts. This course seemed excessively cautious to some people. The High Authority had not in fact guaranteed any loans made to Community firms. It did not need such a large reserve fund to cover its own indebtedness to the United States Export-Import Bank. Hermann J. Abs, a leading German banker, said that it was not necessary to "hoard" several annual payments since "the security of the borrowers [from the High Authority] and other relevant domestic agencies, will be mobilized to their full extent." This was a costly way of getting credit, he pointed out.[3]

Criticism of the High Authority's fiscal practice was particularly strong among German coal and steel producers who paid the largest share of the tax (47 per cent over the whole period) and who felt themselves short of capital. What was the point, they asked, of paying money in taxes to the High Authority in order to borrow it back

[3] Reprint from *Zeitschrift für das gesamte Kreditwesen*, May 1954, p. 9.

again in some form? Moreover, they did not like to see funds accumulating in the hands of a supranational body that was likely to use it to influence the course of investment in some dirigistic fashion. The bigger the reserve fund, the bigger the risk that the men in Luxembourg would feel an urge to use it.[4]

The criticisms did not persuade the High Authority, which persisted in building up the reserve until by early 1956 it reached the goal of $100 million. As the fund neared this total, the tax was cut. The High Authority also went part of the way to meet the charge that it had taken funds out of the capital-short coal and steel industries and kept them idle. It arranged with a number of banks in which it had placed funds on time deposits to open five-year credits to Community enterprises at rates of interest somewhat lower than those prevailing in each country. By the end of 1957, some $48 million worth of credits had been advanced in this way. Just under half were in Germany. The credits are advanced on the banks' own responsibility (thus meeting another of the criticisms of those who feared *dirigisme*), but the concession on the interest rate can be ascribed to the High Authority's leverage as a large depositor.

THE HIGH AUTHORITY AS BORROWER AND LENDER

When the Schuman Plan was first proposed, the Marshall Plan was near the middle of its appointed four-year term. American aid had already played an important part in the rebuilding of the coal and steel industries of Western Europe. It was natural enough to think that if six countries pooled their coal and steel industries, further American aid or at least some of it would be given through the organs of the pool. Economically, this would seem logical.

[4] It is generally held that the proceeds of the tax cannot be used for relending. This is suggested by the enumeration of uses of tax money (Art. 50) and the clear statement that borrowed funds can only be used for relending. However, the Treaty is not explicit and Paul Reuter, *La Communauté Européenne du Charbon et de l'Acier*, 1953, p. 70, argues that it would be contrary to the spirit of the Treaty to adopt the more restrictive interpretation.

Moreover, American officials had repeatedly urged Western Europe to "integrate," some even said "unite." The Schuman Plan was the biggest step that had been taken toward complete integration. It had been welcomed by American officials from the President down. Surely the Americans would want to show their faith and approval in material ways, and perhaps even do something extra, *pour encourager les autres*. This thought appeared in capsule form in the shortest paragraph in the Treaty. After empowering the High Authority to establish the levy on production and to borrow, Article 49 eloquently concluded: "It may also receive grants."

The United States seemed receptive. The Mutual Security Act was amended in 1952 to name the Coal and Steel Community as a possible recipient of aid (along with NATO and the proposed EDC). Congress and Administration were agreed on the desirability of encouraging European integration—materially and otherwise.

The stage was set, but the performance was canceled. By the time the Community was in a position to talk seriously about obtaining foreign capital, the pattern of American aid to Europe had changed. Mutual Defense Assistance had replaced the Marshall Plan with its civilian emphasis. "Economic aid" was declining and was largely confined to special cases unless it was clearly linked with rearmament measures. There was a new administration in Washington which, while strong for European integration, was pledged to curtail foreign aid as quickly as possible. It aimed, too, at reducing the European share in a shrinking total of aid and preferred to give civilian aid in loans rather than grants. Europe's dollar position improved greatly in the post-Korean boom. The steel and coal industries had set all-time record levels of production in 1951 and 1952.

The American Loan

If there was to be American aid in these changed circumstances, it would have to be in the form of a loan. The case for it would have to combine the Community's economic prospects and the American interest in encouraging

European integration. Exploratory talks between the High Authority and the United States government began in 1953. After a visit to Washington by Monnet, Etzel, and Spierenburg, President Eisenhower said he favored an American loan to the Community.[5] In April 1954 a loan agreement was signed.

The United States lent the High Authority $100 million for 25 years at 3⅞ per cent. Repayment was to be in 22 annual installments beginning in 1958 unless the High Authority chose to repay earlier. The money came from foreign aid appropriations and was lent by the Export-Import Bank as agent for the Foreign Operations Administration. The funds were to be paid out as the High Authority asked for them and secured by the obligations of the enterprises to which the High Authority re-lent the money.[6] Although the High Authority stressed the fact that it was borrowing on its general credit, and the agreement confirmed this, the security provisions were very detailed (and some High Authority officials considered them extraordinarily heavy).

The loan agreement was also explicit as to the types of projects for which the credit was to be used: modernizing, mechanizing and expanding productive capacity in coal and iron mining and coke production, treatment of iron ore, building of pithead power stations, and providing housing for miners. These stipulations occasioned a belief in Europe that the United States steel industry was op-

[5] In a letter to the Chairmen of the Foreign Affairs Committee of the House and the Foreign Relations Committee of the Senate, Eisenhower said that the "Community does not wish to obtain grants . . . but requires loan capital. . . . It seems to me that a portion of the financing of this development program by the United States Government . . . would foster European integration in a tangible and useful way." HA Press Release, Je. 18, 1953, 7 p. (mimeographed).

[6] The High Authority negotiated an Act of Pledge with the Bank for International Settlements, at Basle, establishing a portfolio containing the obligations of the firms to which the High Authority lent money. These comprise mostly mortgages on the new installations or promises not to hypothecate them without giving the High Authority an equal mortgage. In accepting the Act of Pledge the United States altered the loan agreement to accept equal status with other lenders in place of the priority originally provided.

posed to the loan and carried enough weight to have the government insist that it not be used for steel production. This is denied by the American steel industry, the U. S. government, and the High Authority (Ch. 19). In fact, the High Authority had already decided to concentrate aid on the production of raw materials for steelmaking. This was a logical consequence of its analysis of Community needs and had the political advantage of avoiding the issue whether France or Germany should have priority in steel investment.

Two issues not directly connected with the loan were mentioned in the communiqué about the signing. The United States was pressing the Belgian and German governments to remove quotas on imports of American coal. This was a matter for the governments and the spokesmen for the High Authority said only that nothing in the Treaty prevented the removal of the quotas and that the Community was pledged to a high level of international trade. The communiqué concluded with a note that "the prospects of maintaining and increasing competition within the Community" had been discussed during the negotiations.[7] The implication is that the United States was taking all occasions to pursue its interest in this aspect of the Community, which had been clear from the outset.

Having obtained its first loan, the High Authority had to decide how to allocate it. This would not be easy. Some people thought the High Authority should not undertake the allocation at all. It would be best, said Dr. Abs, "if the responsibility for the credit and the decision about the detailed division of the credit should be taken as far as possible by private, and if necessary also by public, bodies in the participating countries."[8] Others thought the High Authority should divide the credit among countries and industries according to some formula reflecting size or output. The High Authority had no interest in such proposals. The loan was too important to it merely to be in-

---

[7] Department of State *Bulletin*, May 3, 1954, p. 672.

[8] *Zeitschrift für das gesamte Kreditwesen*, cited, p. 9. The High Authority might, he suggested, give broad directives and settle disputes.

jected into the normal credit stream. Apart from its economic aspects, the loan was an important step in building the Community. The charge of *dirigisme* was rebuffed by pointing out that Luxembourg did not intend to take the initiative in investments; it would wait for producers to come to it with their proposals.[9] Having put aside $25 million for workers' housing, the High Authority invited firms to submit applications for shares of the remainder. It set out certain principles. The projects would have to provide expansion or improvement in production, either through new investment or modernization. More emphasis was put on bettering quality and lowering costs than on expanding capacity. Results would have to become apparent in three years or sooner.

The High Authority decided to finance only a minority of each project. The would-be borrower would have to raise the larger part of what was needed from other sources (including his own funds). The usual explanation given for this policy is that some funds were almost always available but that it was often hard for a firm to mobilize quite enough to carry out a project; moreover, the marginal element might be especially costly. By this device the High Authority could help in the mobilization of large amounts of Community capital. The choice of methods was probably also influenced by the fact that the High Authority could spread its funds over a number of projects of different types in several countries, thus helping to avoid charges of unfairness or a narrow focusing of aid, and bringing Community benefits in concrete form to more people.

A more difficult decision concerned the interest to be charged. Interest rates were not the same in all the Community countries. If all borrowers were charged the same interest rates, some would be given a greater benefit than

[9] An answer undoubtedly as unsatisfactory to Dr. Abs as German neo-liberal definitions of *dirigisme* were to the High Authority. To help appraise applications, the High Authority organized boards of experts in each country who gave advisory opinions. The financial investigation of such matters as credit-worthiness was turned over to banks in each country.

others and the loans would be more attractive in one country than in another. But if the High Authority followed the market, it would either be making money on its loans or it would in effect be giving some borrowers a subsidy with funds provided by others. The High Authority decided to charge the same rate of interest on all its loans (3⅞ per cent plus financing charges, which would bring it to a maximum of 4¼ per cent). In addition to avoiding the difficulties of a more complicated formula, the High Authority may also have hoped to exercise some small downward influence on interest rates. One consequence was that there were no loan applications from the Netherlands where money could be borrowed more cheaply.

Because the American loan had to be repaid in dollars it involved an exchange rate risk. This was placed on the ultimate borrowers. It may have inhibited some of them, since they rarely needed dollars to undertake the operations for which they were borrowing. In drawing on the loan the High Authority had to present the Export-Import Bank with the guarantee of each government that, when payments became due, it would provide dollars for the High Authority's holdings of its own currencies resulting from conversion of the original loan funds. The sums involved, spread over a period of years, were not significant for the national balances of payments. The exchange risk was given as the reason for dropping the idea of using some of the American loan for workers' housing. The decision may have been influenced by the fact that applications for loans came to $157 million and offered many opportunities for improving Community production. Other means were found to finance the housing.

Almost one-third of the $100 million went into coal mining and nearly one-fifth into the mining and processing of iron ore. The heaviest concentration, 46 per cent, was on pithead power stations which made it possible to use low-grade coal without incurring transport costs. Only 3.7 per cent of the money went into cokeries, reflecting the High Authority's view—which it later revised—that enough investment was under way in that sector and that only projects that would increase the production of coke-oven gas should be assisted. The sintering and crushing of iron ore for which some of the funds were advanced would help to economize on coke. Although none of the money went into steelmaking, steel firms benefited since they owned some of the mines and ore-processing establishments.

Given Germany's importance as a coal producer it was natural that a large share of the loans should be placed in that country. Though all of the activities for which loans were made were represented, the 47 per cent of the total that Germany received was heavily concentrated in coal mining and pithead power stations. France's 22 per cent was divided between these two activities and iron mining. Belgium's 14 per cent went entirely into pithead power stations which also accounted for half of the Saar's 10.4 per cent, the rest going into coal mining. Italy got 5.2 per cent and Luxembourg 1 per cent, all for iron mining and ore processing. Thus each national group got something, except the Dutch who made no applications. The High Authority avoided any overt or simple formulas, but the French and German shares corresponded to their shares in paying the Community tax, which was probably not a coincidence.[10] About 50 enterprises received credits from the High Authority for 136 projects. They provided an additional $270.52 million (from their own funds or borrowing), so that the $100 million advanced by the High Authority came to about 27 per cent of the total cost of the projects financed.

There had been hopes that the American loan might be larger, perhaps as much as $500 million. But the money was not the only interest of the High Authority (within a year of signing the agreement with the Export-Import Bank it had set aside a reserve equal to 75 per cent of the sum it had borrowed). It was a way of saying to other

[10] There were differential rates of turn-downs. Luxembourg got all it asked for, Germany over 90 per cent, France over 80 per cent, and the others from 46 to 65 per cent. Calculated from HA, *Report*, Apr. 1956, p. 202, on the basis of the total value of the projects, not just the share financed by the High Authority. The same report gives fuller details on the disbursal of the loan.

potential lenders, but not least to the industries of the Community, "Look, the High Authority's existence in the world is acknowledged in the most pragmatic way in Washington; it borrows as any government might." There was status as well as dollars to be obtained.

The loan has often been pointed to in Luxembourg as proof of the international credit-standing of the High Authority. Monnet made the same point at the signing ceremony. Certainly the terms of the loan were businesslike enough; it was well secured; there has never been any indication that either party has had any doubts about full and prompt repayment. Still, the United States made the loan not as a good investment but as a gesture of support for the Coal and Steel Community and for European integration in general. It came at a time when EDC was being discussed and the United States was anxious to do anything it could to encourage that movement. These circumstances do not reflect on the Community's credit-worthiness, but they take the edge off the "businesslike" argument, since the transaction proves little about the attractiveness of the Community for outside investors. The particular role of the American loan was to break the ice. It helped establish status and function for the High Authority and was intended to be but the first step in a continuing process.

Other Loans

When the Export-Import Bank loan was negotiated, the Assembly's committee on investments reflected a general expectation when it said, "it should be underlined that this loan constitutes only a first stage and that negotiations continue with the government of the United States to obtain, by new means and with governmental aid, participation by private American capital in the investments of the Community." [11] In fact two years were to pass before the High Authority again borrowed outside the Community, and three before it obtained any private American funds.

[11] CA, Commission des Investissements, *Rapport . . . par M. F. de Menthon, Rapporteur*, doc. 15 (1953-54), p. 40. Substantially the same thing was said in the Joint Communiqué issued at the signing.

Another possible source of loans did not produce any: the International Bank for Reconstruction and Development. Before the Community took shape, John J. McCloy, who had formerly been President of the IBRD, had spoken of it as a possible lender to the Community. In 1952 Eugene Black, his successor as President, said that "the Bank, should it be called on, would be glad to search for feasible ways to assist" in financing the Schuman Plan. He noted, though, that new problems would arise, notably "concerning the form of guarantee needed for a loan to an international body." [12] The informal discussions may have disclosed obstacles. Two can easily be imagined. The Bank's Articles of Agreement call for governmental guarantees. These would complicate the process for the Community and would not fit well with the central role of the High Authority. Another possible obstacle may have come from the Bank's policy of lending only on specific projects. The High Authority wanted to borrow on its own credit and stand between external lenders and the borrowers within the Community. Apparently informal discussions either produced no way around these obstacles or centered on still others. In any case no formal application was forthcoming. The possibility of IBRD loans to the German coal and steel industries was also explored but none were made.

The American loan was not immediately followed by others. There have been some indications that European banks had their interest stirred by it. The coal and steel industries were booming in 1955, creating a demand for investment funds and improving prospects. But the failure of the EDC threw a shadow over the Coal and Steel Community's future, and, it seems, led to the suspension of some negotiations for new loans. Inside the Community, lenders would tend to deal directly with the enterprises concerned. With capital markets rather limited, governments have been unwilling to provide easy access to them for the High Authority. To finance the building of workers' housing, replacing the sums originally earmarked from the Ameri-

[12] IBRD, *Summary Proceedings of the Seventh Annual Meeting of the Board of Governors*, Dec. 15, 1952, p. 9.

can loan, the High Authority borrowed $17.5 million in Belgium, Germany, Luxembourg, and the Saar, during 1954 and 1955. The governments raised a somewhat larger sum to match this. In France and Italy, the High Authority arranged for the raising of about $16 million more for the same purpose without itself becoming a borrower. In 1956 a second housing program was begun for which the High Authority expected to lend $18.4 million, mostly out of its own funds, as its direct contribution to the total cost of $73.1 million.

In July 1956 the High Authority floated its second foreign loan and first public issue. Through three leading Swiss banks it borrowed 50 million Swiss francs ($11.7 million) at 4¼ per cent against 18-year notes issued to the public. Out of the proceeds, 27 million francs were re-lent to three Italian steel firms, 18 million to two German companies, and 5 million to one in the Saar.[13] Coupled with the funds these enterprises provided from other sources (equal to 121 million Swiss francs), the new investments were to be used to expand the production of pig iron and coke and improve the preparation of iron ore—all in conformity with the High Authority's diagnosis of the Community's structural deficiency in these materials. The main differences from the distribution of the Export-Import Bank loan were that all the borrowers were steel companies and that coke production was included because industrial investment plans no longer were judged sufficient.

The following April, after about a year's study and negotiation, a group of American banking houses headed by Kuhn Loeb, Lazard Frères, and The First Boston Corporation, underwrote an issue of $25 million in 18-year bonds (at 5½ per cent) and $10 million in 3-5 year notes (at 5 per cent). The High Authority devoted about two-thirds of the new funds to coal and coke, and the rest to pig iron and the preparation of iron ore; a group of leading German steel firms combined in a joint operation to pro-

[13] For the same period as the High Authority's borrowing and with the same arrangements for amortization (beginning after six years), but at 4⅞ per cent interest to cover financial charges.

duce iron directly from ore. Most of the money went to Germany and the rest to Italy where the borrower was Finsider, the government holding company, which planned to use it to help complete the iron ore processing part of a new integrated steel company.[14] The interest rate on these loans was 5⅞ per cent.

Having tapped the United States capital market, the High Authority wanted to continue the process. There had been doubt and delay before it was able to realize its long-standing ambition in the first place. In the 14 months between the first serious conversations and the launching of the issue, money had become tight in the United States and interest rates rose. The process of gaining acceptance on the American market was regarded in the Community as extraordinarily difficult.[15] However, the operation was felt to be successful; the bonds were sold quickly, largely it seems to European investors. They continued to sell above par.

In November 1957, the High Authority invited a group of 36 American bankers and industrialists to visit the Community. In a busy nine days these men went to many parts of the Community, seeing mines and mills, talking with industrialists, and receiving briefings from High Authority officials on many aspects of the Community's work. Not all the visitors were potential lenders; they included American steelmen who indicated their doubts of the desirability of exporting American capital to help their competitors. There was no immediate talk of new loans, but it is clear that the High Authority was cultivating the ground for possible future issues.

In June 1958 it again borrowed on the American market, this time $50 million, an amount exceeding all its previous

[14] A loan of $1 million was made to house Italian steelworkers. To lend a total of $35 million the High Authority had to draw on its own funds since it received from the American issue $34.1 million after underwriting discounts and commissions were deducted. *Prospectus*, issued by Kuhn, Loeb & Co., The First Boston Corp., Lazard Frères & Co., April 9, 1957.

[15] It is described and analyzed in some detail in CA, Commission des Investissements, *Rapport . . . par M. François de Menthon, Rapporteur,* doc. 32 (1956-57), Je. 1957, pp. 34-38.

borrowing by public issues. Of this, $15 million was in three- to five-year notes at 4¼ per cent and the rest in 20-year bonds at 5 per cent. The High Authority this time re-lent $28 million for coal, $19 million for steel (mostly for iron ore processing), and $3 million for iron mining. Applications totaling $300 million again came from every country but the Netherlands. In the allocation of loans, 56 per cent of the money went to German companies, 27 per cent to French, and the rest to Belgian and Italian firms.[16]

The High Authority's Debts and Investments

The new borrowing brought the High Authority's total indebtedness to just over $215 million plus interest. Of this, $185 million was owed in the United States, $11.7 million in Switzerland, and the rest inside the Community. Interest over the whole period, on all loans, comes to $110 million, bringing the total debt burden to $325.6 million. Annual amortization and interest payments on these debts will rise from about $10 million in 1958 to a peak of $21.4 million in 1962 and then decline over the next 20 years.[17] This seems well within the High Authority's capacity to pay, even if all the firms that had borrowed from it proved to be bad debtors at once.[18]

The High Authority probably hopes to increase its foreign borrowing, and these figures suggest that it is in a sound enough financial position to do so. Whether this form of borrowing is preferable to other financing is a matter on which both borrowers and lenders must decide. The advantages for the foreign lender are obvious; his risks are, in a sense, spread throughout the Community; he has something very much like double security for his funds; it is probably easier for him to assess the credit-worthiness of the High Authority than of many individual foreign com-

[16] HA, *Bulletin Mensuel d'Information*, Jl. 1958, p. 17.

[17] *Prospectus*, issued by Kuhn, Loeb & Co., The First Boston Corp., Lazard Frères & Co., June 24, 1958, p. 23.

[18] The guarantee fund alone would cover all debt payments for six years. At less than half its maximum rate the tax has produced more than twice the level of current expenditures and has provided a surplus over all payments into earmarked reserves as well.

panies. For the Community enterprises that borrow, the key questions are whether the interest rate secured by the High Authority, plus the charges resulting from passing the funds through it, work out at less than would otherwise have to be paid, and whether it is easier to obtain a loan by this means than by dealing directly. From the point of view of the Community as a whole, there is the question whether foreign borrowing is desirable. The need is for capital, not foreign exchange. While there are always balance of payments considerations to be taken into account (the responsibilities of governments, not the High Authority), the foreseeable volume of Community foreign borrowing does not seem likely to raise important difficulties on that score. Perhaps European capital markets will expand to the point at which governments will make it easier for the High Authority to approach them. Meanwhile one of the functions of the public issues in the United States, and perhaps that in Switzerland as well, has been to mobilize Community capital that for one reason or another could not be borrowed inside the Community. Apart from the mobilization of foreign and Community funds that would otherwise not have flowed into coal and steel, the High Authority's intermediary role may have two other features. High Authority lending may be particularly useful to small enterprises which would have trouble raising capital on equally good terms. The allocations of High Authority loans and their use to mobilize additional capital may influence the pattern of Community investment.[19]

By the end of 1957 the High Authority had made loans totaling $173.1 million, of which $163.9 million came from

[19] The only request the High Authority has had for a guarantee came from Phoenix-Rheinrohr, a major German steel producer, in January 1957. The company planned to build four ships to carry coal and iron ore for its own account and wanted support in borrowing DM 80 million. When in the course of a year it had not received final word from the High Authority, the company withdrew its application. One source of the delay was the High Authority's decision to refer the matter to the Council of Ministers on the ground that ship operation fell outside the Treaty; for this it was strongly criticized by the Assembly's investment committee.

borrowed funds and $9.2 million from its own resources.[20]
If the funds used for housing are eliminated, the High
Authority's contribution to Community investment came
to $145.7 million divided as follows:

Coal mining and cokeries	$59.1 million
Pithead power stations	46.3 million
Iron ore production and processing	18.6 million
Pig iron production	21.7 million

There are various ways of calculating the share of the
High Authority's loans in Community investment, none of
them altogether satisfactory. The following figures, which
are very rough, estimate how much of various segments of
Community investment may have been provided by the
High Authority from 1954 or 1955 through 1957.[21] They
show High Authority loans as a percentage of Community
investment in various activities.

Total investment	3.5-4.5
Coal mining and cokeries	4-5
Pithead power stations	10.5-14
Iron ore production and processing	6.5-7.5
Blast furnaces	7.5-8.5

[20] This includes $350,000 which had been repaid by the end of 1957
($80,000 being from one of the loans made out of the High Authority's
own resources, the rest from borrowed funds). The High Authority had
on hand $2 million of borrowed funds and $690,000 of its own resources
earmarked for lending that had not been disbursed. None of these
figures, or the calculations that follow in the text, include the 1958 public
issue in the United States. Details are in HA, Finance Division, *Financial
Report for the Year 1957.*

[21] The High Authority began making loans in 1954 but disbursal was
concentrated in 1955 to 1957. The lower figure of the ranges shown
above applies the relevant totals of the High Authority loans to Community investment for 1954-57 while the higher figure applies the same
loan totals to 1955-57. The investment figures come from, HA, *Les
Investissements dans les Industries du Charbon et de l'Acier de la Communauté, Rapport sur l'Enquête 1957,* Sept. 1957, except for the total
which is taken from a HA press release of Sept. 25, 1958. For "coal
mining and cokeries" the figures exclude the coal industry's investments
in briquetting plants and power stations. They include independent
cokeries and those owned by steel firms. Investment figures for "iron
ore production and processing" include all investments by iron mines
and also the steel industry's "*préparation des charges*" which probably
includes some expenditures in treating coke. "Blast furnaces" compares

Crude as they are, these figures strongly suggest that while the High Authority's loans have not been of decisive importance for Community investment as a whole, they have been of appreciable significance in the sectors in which they were concentrated, especially the construction of pit-head power stations and the preparation of iron ore. Considering the importance of self-financing of investment in the coal and steel industries, the loans must represent a much higher proportion of the outside resources used in these activities. If the High Authority's estimated average participation of 25 per cent in each project is taken into account, it appears that its loans may have played some part in a substantial share of the Community's investment activities. All these figures would be increased if allowance were made for the $45 million of bank loans based on the High Authority's deposits.

Compared to the hopes and fears people had of the High Authority's financial potentialities at the outset, the record is rather modest. The High Authority has not been a funnel for massive foreign funds. It has also not used its taxing and lending powers to dominate Community investment, subordinating the judgment of the industry and the capital markets to its own views. In this as in so many other matters, the significance of what the High Authority has done lies somewhere in a middle range, hard to judge exactly in words or figures. It has directly added appreciable sums to the capital available to Community industries and used its loans to help mobilize additional funds. It has concentrated on remedying deficiencies in the Community's production of raw materials for steelmaking and in enhancing the value of low-grade coal and of iron ore. Apart from the economic results of this activity, the High Authority's financial operations undoubtedly served to strengthen its position as the centerpiece of the Community.

---

the steel industry's investments under that heading with all HA loans for "pig iron production" (excluding those for "iron ore production and processing"). The results should be regarded as rough approximations.

THE DIRECTION OF INVESTMENT

Though the High Authority's direct contribution through loans is only a small part of Community investment, it has powers that affect, at least potentially, all investment. The High Authority cannot prevent a firm from making an investment. It can, however, limit a firm's access to funds if it finds that financing or carrying out a particular project "would require subsidies, assistance, protection or discrimination contrary to the . . . Treaty" (Art. 54). If a firm wishes to go ahead with such a proposal in spite of the High Authority's finding, it must use its own funds and may not borrow or otherwise obtain outside financing for this purpose. And, of course, if subsidies, protection, or other such measures should in fact turn out to be necessary to make the investment profitable, they would be illegal unless authorized by the High Authority under some provision of the Treaty.

The High Authority also has advisory powers that it can use to influence the course of investment. It can review investment plans and express opinions on them. Copies of these opinions go to the government of the country in which the enterprise planning the investment is located, but they are not published. The High Authority can also try to influence investments by more general measures. In order "to provide guidance for the action of all interested parties . . . and . . . to determine its own action," it is required by Article 46 to:

carry on a permanent study of the development of the market and price trends;

periodically draw up programmes giving forecasts, for guidance, of production, consumption, exports and imports;

periodically set out the general objectives with respect to modernization, the long-term planning of production and the expansion of productive capacity.

The Use of Specific Powers

Not until July 1955 did the High Authority require firms to submit their investment plans. Then it ruled that any projects involving expenditure of more than $500,000 for new installations or $1 million for modernization and replacement were to be submitted at least three months before any work was begun or money laid out. A year later the rule was broadened to require declaration of all investments in steel furnaces, regardless of amount, because of the High Authority's great concern with the scrap problem.

Considering the potential importance of the High Authority's powers over investment, this delay may seem remarkable. Several factors probably explain it. There may well have been administrative difficulties. It is not easy to organize a staff of adequate size and technical competence to make significant appraisals of major investment projects. There was also a question about the criteria for judging investments. Logically, one ought to have some idea of the levels of output of different products toward which the Community should be moving in order to know what investments are wise.[22] The Treaty, after all, called for an *avis motivé*. The High Authority did not feel able to produce a statement of objectives until July 1955. No doubt this consideration carried some weight but would it have been compelling if the High Authority had felt it urgent to undertake the examination of investments earlier? After all, in allocating the American loan the High Authority used criteria at least partly relevant to guiding investment. Its surveys of Community investments had made clear the lag in the production of coal, coke, iron ore, and pig iron, behind that of steel. Without a full statement of general objectives it could have applied at least these limited criteria in judging investment proposals.

The High Authority probably wished to move slowly because of the delicacy of the investment issue. National rivalry and the fear of *dirigisme* had focused on the

[22] When the High Authority, in July 1953, brought into force Art. 54 which authorized examination of investment plans and the granting of loans by the High Authority, the rapporteur of the Assembly's committee on investments expressed himself as "astonished" that this could be done before the general objectives were defined. CA, Commission des Investissements, *Rapport . . . par M. F. de Menthon, Rapporteur,* doc. 4 (1953-54), p. 8.

Treaty's investment provisions from the first. The High
Authority had been working hard to dispel these fears and
to convince businessmen, especially in Germany, that it
would not interfere unduly in their affairs. Almost at the
outset Monnet told the Assembly's investment committee:
"The determination of each enterprise's projects must be
left to the initiative of these enterprises. The High Authority has no intention of practicing, in this field, an
authoritarian *dirigisme* or of substituting itself for those
who retain the responsibility for their enterprises." [23] To
have called for the submission of all investments for High
Authority inspection, though provided by the Treaty and
not incompatible with anything Monnet had said, might
well have alarmed the Germans at least—and no doubt
others as well—and set back the High Authority's broader
campaign of establishing its position.

The High Authority might have taken this risk if it believed that much could be accomplished by reviewing investment plans. But in the early years of the Community
its main concern was with stimulating investment in coal
mining. The High Authority showed no signs of sharing
the view that there was a risk of over-investment in steel.
The scrap problem was not yet acute. Had the recession
of 1953-54 continued, there might have been difficulties.
For instance, while total Community investment in steel
was declining, Germany's was rising. French steel capacity
was not fully used. If demand had continued to fall, the
High Authority would have been under pressure to slow
the rate of German investment on the ground that it was
creating surplus capacity. But the turn of the market obviated the problem. By the time the investment rules were
introduced in mid-1955 the boom was on and the question
was whether Community investment was sufficient. An
optimistic forecast for 1958 appeared in the first statement
of general objectives. The risk of having to give restrictive

---

[23] CA, Commission des Investissements, *Rapport . . . par M. de Menthon, Rapporteur*, doc. 7 (1952-53), p. 11. The High Authority appointed
as head of its investments division a former official of the Wirtschaftsvereinigung Eisen- und Stahlindustrie.

opinions on investment proposals was substantially reduced. The High Authority had established itself more
firmly. All fear of *dirigisme* was not gone, but the chances
were improved that businessmen, in Germany and elsewhere, would be willing to reserve judgment until they
saw how the High Authority used its new powers. Moreover, the Community's structural problems were coming
to be more generally appreciated, and there was some pressure, notably in the Assembly, for the High Authority to
exercise more influence on investments.

From the time the new rules took effect, on September
1, 1955, to the end of 1957, nearly 400 projects with a
total value of about $1.5 billion were submitted to the
High Authority. Over two-thirds of these came from the
steel industry and most of the rest from the coal industry.
Though it received 264 declarations about investments, the
High Authority only felt it necessary to express formal
(though private) opinions on 77 applications. Most of
these were favorable. The High Authority gave a pat on
the back to those that promised to eliminate bottlenecks
and improve the Community's supply of coal, coke and
pig iron. It favored measures that conserved raw materials
and especially plans to use new processes that improved
the quality of steel without requiring more scrap. Proposals
that would increase scrap consumption drew the High
Authority's fire. It issued a general warning in July 1956
(see p. 297). When firms proposed to make investments that
would raise scrap consumption, the High Authority tried
to work out alternative arrangements with them. This
overcame the need for unfavorable opinions in some cases
but not all.

The High Authority has never ruled that the carrying
out of a project would result in a need for subsidy or protection and has therefore never used its power to forbid a
company to obtain outside financing for its investments.
The unfavorable opinions it has issued had no legal effect.
The companies could still go ahead with their plans, borrowing funds for them if they wished. They might have
some trouble about this, though, the High Authority

hinted. The opinions were private but the fact that they had been issued was public and this would provide the occasion for potential lenders and others to "apply to the enterprise for full details of the opinion." [24] Presumably a company that defied an unfavorable opinion might also suffer some disadavantages in its relations with the High Authority, but formal discrimination would probably have no legal basis. [25] There is little public evidence as yet about the effect on investment of unfavorable opinions by the High Authority. The Assembly's investment committee believes that "in a great number of cases the unfavorable opinions . . . seem to have been listened to, but unhappily not always." [26] The fact that the Société des Usines à Tubes de la Sarre thought it worth carrying the matter to court suggests that unfavorable opinions have consequences. In concluding its opinion on this unsuccessful challenge, the Court referred to the High Authority's *competence ordonnatrice* and said that while the company remained free to take account of the opinion or not, "it must understand that in ignoring an unfavorable opinion it accepts the risks that could develop indirectly for it from a situation that it has itself contributed to creating." [27]

This is probably as good a description as one can find of the status of the opinions given so far to guide investment. Presumably the adjustments made in programs to ensure a favorable opinion have been useful even if the effect of unfavorable opinions is more uncertain. (Companies have also sometimes discussed investment proposals with the

[24] HA, *Report*, Apr. 1957, p. 321.

[25] At one stage in the negotiations with the Société des Usines à Tubes de la Sarre, High Authority officials threatened to discriminate against the company in the equalization scheme if it persisted in its plans to build an electric furnace. This was mentioned when the company complained of the High Authority's action, but the case rested on other issues. The Court ruled that these statements did not constitute proof of a position taken by the High Authority, so it did not pass on the legality of such a measure. *JO*, Jan. 13, 1958, pp. 15, 19.

[26] CA, Commission des Investissements, *Rapport . . . par M. François de Menthon, Rapporteur*, doc. 32 (1956-57), Je. 1957, p. 21.

[27] *JO*, Jan. 13, 1958, p. 20. The case rested on legal points about the status of the opinion, not its substance, and abounds in procedural and technical questions.

High Authority before formally submitting them.) But so far investment control has been used only for this single purpose, in conjunction with other measures, and we know little about how it might work in more complicated matters.

The General Guidance of Investment

The High Authority's "role is a role of orientation," said Monnet.[28] He was explaining that the High Authority did not regard the "program" which the Treaty called on it to make as a plan into which the Community producers would have to fit. The High Authority would survey, set out the facts, and offer advice, but it would be up to each enterprise to decide what it would do.

This general framework has not been altogether easy to devise. If the High Authority is not to set goals according to some principle, whence is it to obtain a criterion for guidance? Can it deal only with projections? It is not easy to project with any soundness for coal and steel alone; the demand for them derives largely from the rest of the economy and, in the case of coal, is influenced by the competition of other fuels. Should the High Authority concentrate on the existing investment plans of industry and suggest whether they are enough or too little in the light of the projections? Or is it to confine itself to appraising the internal consistency of the investment plans, to see if enough raw materials will be produced to keep the capacity for finished products fully occupied? The High Authority has done a little of each of these things, making its way rather pragmatically, leaving a record that is not easy to evaluate, and arriving at the end of the transitional period at a position in which the facts are much better known than before but their significance is still rather shrouded.

Almost as soon as it was organized the High Authority appointed a committee of experts under Jan Tinbergen to look at the future. In fairly short order the committee submitted projections of the Community's coal and steel needs five and ten years ahead. It arrived at these figures by

[28] CA, Commission des Investissements, *Rapport . . . par M. de Menthon, Rapporteur*, doc. 7 (1952-53), p. 11.

estimating the growth of the national economies and making certain assumptions about the relation of the demand for coal and steel to the general increase in economic activity. Shortly afterwards the High Authority made its first investment survey, which seemed to indicate that the steel industry was investing on a scale that would conform to the Tinbergen committee's projections, but that production of coal and coke would not keep pace. For the next few years the High Authority's work in this field largely centered on the annual investment surveys. Only in mid-1955 did it publish its first statement of general objectives with estimates of possible Community needs in 1958. Extensive work followed that led to the publication in early 1957 of a more ambitious statement, with estimates for 1960, 1965, and 1975.[29] Beginning in April 1956 the High Authority published quarterly forecasts of demand, which because of their short-range nature ought not to have had any important influence on investment decisions. There is fortunately no need here to examine the statements and projections in detail. Their making and their results show all the vicissitudes to which this kind of work is subject, but their accuracy and usefulness can hardly be judged in the short run.

It is impossible to reach any clear conclusion about the influence of the High Authority's studies and statements on the course of Community investment. A major effort has been made to put the High Authority's analyses in the hands of producers so that they could relate their own prospects to the general state of affairs. But at that point the High Authority's work only becomes one of the myriad factors shaping investment decisions. There was nothing in the early forecasts of growth to warrant the fall in investment in 1953 and 1954 that took place under the impact of the decline in demand (except in Germany where consciousness of the lag in recovery spurred investment). Cyclical factors again seem to explain the slowing up of

---

[29] The projections of these two studies were based on techniques similar to those used by the Tinbergen committee, but more refinements and elaborations were introduced.

investment in late 1957 and 1958, in spite of the need for expansion to create the capacities the High Authority thought necessary by 1960.[30] Other developments conformed to the High Authority's recommendations. From an early stage it had urged the importance of expanding production of coal (and later of coke), and of improving the Community's iron supply. The investments carried out and planned during the transitional period show some shift in this direction; it is fairly marked for iron but much less clear for coal and coke.[31] At another stage the High Authority cautiously warned that investments in rolling mills for flat products might be running too far ahead of demand. It was therefore glad to note a greater emphasis on sections and shapes after 1956. Comparing the expansion of capacity likely to result from investments under way or planned in early 1958 with the goals it had set for the Community for 1960, the High Authority noted a sizable gap for coal and iron ore while for coke, steel, and pig iron the goals seemed likely to be achieved.[32] With regard to scrap, as we have seen (p. 298f.), the prospects were not very good; the most favorable development was the increased investment in processes that improved the quality of Thomas steel without using more scrap. One cannot ascribe all these developments to the High Authority's guidance. It was, after all, the businessmen who felt the

[30] Investment planned at the beginning of 1957 was 42 per cent higher than actual investment in 1956, but preliminary estimates indicated that actual investment in 1957 was only about 25 per cent above the 1956 level and revised forecasts suggested a drop in 1958. HA, *Report*, Apr. 1958, v. 2, pp. 259-260.

[31] All these activities together absorbed about 42 per cent of Community investments in 1952-53, but were expected to account for 48 per cent in 1957 and 53 per cent in 1958 (on the basis of producers' plans on January 1, 1957). In between they had been slightly higher than before. The sharpest increase was in investments for the preparation of iron ore, from 1.4 per cent of the total in 1953 to 3.8 per cent in 1956 and a planned 5-6 per cent in the next two years. Investment in blast furnaces was between 5 and 6 per cent in 1952 and 1953, then dropped back but rose in 1956 to 7.4 per cent and was expected to exceed 9 per cent in the next two years. Investment in coal mining and cokeries moved unevenly. Calculated from HA, *Les Investissements . . .* , 1957, cited.

[32] HA, *Report*, Apr. 1958, v. 2, p. 265.

pressures of the deficiencies the High Authority described. The coal and steel producers, and the governments who could aid or hinder their investment plans, could see for themselves what was happening—though perhaps not quite so clearly as when the men in Luxembourg laid out the issues for them.

In times past the opaqueness of the coal and steel markets, and particularly producers' lack of knowledge about the investment plans of others, have been blamed for bottlenecks, surplus capacity and crises; friendly critics of the prewar international steel cartel regard its failure to illuminate the investment situation as one of its most serious flaws.[33] One may be skeptical. Did the major producers really not know what the others were doing? Was it ignorance that caused trouble or their unwillingness to give up the advantages they saw in pursuing their own investment plans? In any case, the High Authority's reports on investments and its indications of what it thought was needed and what should be avoided, have certainly contributed to the "transparency" of the European coal and steel situation. This is a useful function, whatever its effect proves to be. If they trust the figures, steelmen will be better oriented than they might otherwise be (but the national steel federations also make their own studies). Government officials will have a new window on steel problems. Of course, neither government nor business may draw the same conclusions from the data that the High Authority does and for business investment is not just a matter of knowing what is desirable in the general interest.

SOME POSSIBLE FUTURE PROBLEMS

The limited use the High Authority has made of its powers over investments has comported reasonably well with the conditions of the transitional period. What more might have been done is hard to say—except that earlier investigation of particular investment projects might have helped to handle the scrap problem, and if the High Au-

---

[33] Henri Rieben, *Des Ententes de Maitres de Forges au Plan Schuman,* 1954, p. 246.

thority had had more funds at its disposal it could have increased its already appreciable effect on investment in coal, coke, and pig iron production. Apart from this, perhaps little needed to be done. The High Authority's cautious course probably helped to achieve a reasonable degree of acceptance of its role while setting up a mechanism that provides for a good deal of general supervision and some current influence.

The modest record over this short period tells us little about the possible role of the High Authority in influencing Community investment under different circumstances. There has been a constant, though relatively subdued, urging that the High Authority should play a greater role in the investment process. Even without these voices, the High Authority seems likely to extend its investment activities as the Community develops. In the process it will encounter new problems.

The High Authority will probably continue to borrow and re-lend. It may seek other ways of promoting investment. In early 1957 it was exploring with governments means of reducing the risk of investment in coal mining. The means are not clear, but the problem is a real one in view of the length of time it takes to develop and then amortize new coal mines. The guarantee provisions that seemed important in the Treaty have never been used. There are difficulties, some stemming from the degree of supervision or influence over an investment project that the High Authority might feel was the necessary counterpart of engaging its responsibility by a guarantee. An early suggestion that the guarantee be used to support borrowing by groups of firms which would not separately have easy access to capital markets has receded into the background, though it has some possibilities. Another means of promoting investment is through the High Authority's support of research that will help repair deficiencies in the Community's productive structure.

More difficulties arise on the side of controlling or restraining investment. So far, the High Authority has taken an optimistic view of the need for expansion. Its only cautions have been gentle ones. But the rapid expansion of investment in steel in 1956 and 1957 raised new possibilities which would be strengthened if demand dropped seriously in 1958. (The particular years do not matter; they illustrate a more general problem.) The High Authority thought there was no need to worry, since any slight recession would undoubtedly check the rate of investment (as it did in late 1957 and early 1958). Still it tentatively suggested in early 1957 that "it is conceivable that the time has now come when the expansion in steel production potential may possibly outstrip the estimated increase in demand." [34]

The Assembly's committee on investments reacted sharply: "We should regret it if the High Authority were definitely to adopt this restrictive tendency. . . ." [35] There was also another point of view in the Community. Fear of surplus capacity is deeply rooted in the steel industry. "Uncontrolled" expansion by each national industry is regarded as likely to lead to trouble. Hence the view —held most strongly it would seem in the French steel industry—that the High Authority should use its powers to "coordinate" investment in the Community. A report to the French Senate in 1955 put the case strongly: [36]

Less optimistic than the High Authority—which seems to believe that there is no longer a problem of surplus capacity— . . . we are persuaded that from now on the development of capacity without consideration for its relation to the Community as a whole will raise problems of duplication. Any further delay in the exercise of the judgment required will do nothing but make more difficulties and the High Authority

[34] HA, *Report,* Apr. 1957, p. 339.
[35] CA, Commission des Investissements, *Rapport . . . par M. F. de Menthon, Rapporteur,* doc. 32 (1956-57), Je. 1957, p. 18. In the Assembly debate Daum stressed the fact that the High Authority was only suggesting the need for careful consideration and was not issuing a warning. The full report on investments that appeared in September 1957 said nothing about capacity outrunning demand.
[36] France, Conseil de la République, *Rapport d'Information . . . sur la Situation de la Communauté Européenne du Charbon et de l'Acier par MM. Armengaud et Coudé du Foresto, Sénateurs,* 1955, pp. 60-61 (hereafter cited as Armengaud Report).

should no longer justify its abstention by the statement of a position that is as liberal as it is anachronistic. Surplus capacity, which cannot fail to accentuate itself, would bring with it in the long run competition too brutal for the producers to avoid —except possibly in periods of high demand—forming ententes that the High Authority would have to tolerate or for which it would have to substitute a regime of quotas organized by itself, such as the treaty gives it a right to do in periods of crisis. The ransom of its present liberalism in the matter of investments risks being a more accentuated *dirigisme* in the future in the matter of production or the abandonment of the anti-cartel rules.

These comments were made at the beginning of a boom in demand and investment that continued during the next few years. Though there has been no strong pressure for coordination—perhaps because the French industry has been preoccupied with the expansion of its own investment—the attitude is endemic and will appear again. Those who fear surplus capacity speak of the "euphoria" of those who act as if expansion were going to continue. They would rather see supplies tight in the short run than risk the pressure of excess capacity on the market when times get bad again, as they are sure they will.

The problem is a real one. The dilemma that Senator Armengaud presents to the High Authority—hands off now maybe requiring hands on later—expresses a real risk. How great the risk is depends largely on the depth and duration of recessions, and on the producers' reactions to the fall in demand. As an investment problem the issue is whether the Community should expand capacity so as to be able to meet peak demand and face the problem of coping with excess capacity in periods of low demand, or reverse the process and hold down on capacity so as to ease the problem in periods of low demand but intensify it when demand is high. The Assembly committee had a clear view of the answer: "It is preferable for the Community to run the risk of a productive capacity used only 80 per cent than to hurl itself anew toward an insufficient productive capacity that would hamper general economic expansion." [37] The High Authority's record since 1952 suggests that it would probably lean toward this view, but this may not always be the case. And as a practical matter it has to take account of contrary views when it steers its course.

It might, for instance, decide that it was wise to "coordinate" investment as a precaution against the steel producers' doing it for themselves. There is already some degree of investment coordination on a national basis. In France an important part of the steel industry's financing is carried on through the Groupement de l'Industrie Sidérurgique, an offshoot of the Chambre Syndicale de la Sidérurgie Française. In Germany the Wirtschaftsvereinigung Eisen- und Stahlindustrie has had an investment committee that has sought to ensure "a harmonic and balanced development of all enterprises in the framework of the 'legitimacy and predictability of economic growth.' " [38] In both countries major measures of expansion are apt to take form as "industry" programs. It would not be easy to bridge the gap between national and international action. Each industry must think primarily in terms of its home market and its own structure and capacities; industrial rivalry on a national basis is not dead; there are positions of market power to be held; the governments will have a hand. Still, one can imagine a successful effort to check the rate of investment, at least in certain activities, to serve a mutual interest in avoiding overcapacity. Should events seem likely to take this turn, the High Authority might think it wise to step in to influence the situation. It might do this for preventive purposes, to damp down excessive investment so that the private groups would not be spurred to independent action. Or it might seek to substitute its control so far as possible for that of private groups. While its ability to maneuver would be limited by the nature of its powers, it could hope to have a reasonable amount of influence, especially since it could to some degree act

[37] CA, Commission des Investissements, *Rapport . . . par M. F. de Menthon . . .*, doc. 32, cited, p. 18.
[38] Hans-Helmut Kuhnke, "Investitionskontrolle ohne Planwirtschaft," *Der Volkswirt* (Supplement), Oct. 25, 1957, p. 21.

as arbiter. It might be able to keep the cartel links weak and encourage deviations; it could hope to remove restrictions more quickly than producers' groups would, when the situation warranted. Action by the High Authority would also offer some advantages to the industries. The most obvious would be its ability to deal with the Community as a whole, whereas national rivalries would always threaten efforts of the private groups to control the level of investment, as they did in the prewar international cartel.

There are other reasons why the High Authority might want to take a more active part in influencing investment. It might be anxious to keep a reasonable flow of investment even in bad times lest an upturn create shortages. The price of that might be some control over how capacity was to be used while demand stayed low. There will always be questions of balance, comparable to those raised by the scrap problem. There may be cases when market rivalry threatens serious overcapacity in certain kinds of installations. There may be a need to channel investment toward the reduction of cost instead of the expansion of capacity, to check what the Germans call *Tonnenehrgeiz*.

All the courses of action have rather serious difficulties, and the High Authority would probably try to avoid entering on them. If it should make a greater effort to limit or direct investment, the strength of its powers will be tested as they have not yet been tested. Even the strongest specific power—the ban on outside financing—has its limitations. It can only be used in certain circumstances. Its effect also has limits. An important part of the investment of most coal and steel enterprises is provided by self-financing. Most large enterprises could probably arrange their affairs so as to borrow for another use in order to free their own funds for an investment falling under the High Authority's ban, provided those who were supplying the funds trusted the judgment of the managers of the enterprises, or if the lender were a government and wanted to foster the same purpose. How broadly the High Authority can interpret the conditions permitting it to use the power

to limit access to finance is another unknown, as is the influence that the lesser power of issuing unfavorable opinions might have if the High Authority were using it widely.

More extensive direction of investment would also be
very likely to draw the High Authority into difficulties
arising from national rivalries. Although the investment
rivalry between France and Germany was a threatening
feature in the background of the early years of the Community, the High Authority managed to escape its hazards.
Partly this was due to its manner of approach. The investment surveys pay virtually no attention to national differences and discuss problems strictly in terms of the
Community as a whole. More important, the High Authority's limited interference with the investment activities
of entrepreneurs gave few occasions for difficulty. The
policy was not restrictive, so it did not cause apprehension
among the Germans. While spokesmen for the French
steel industry have referred to the need for coordination of
investments, they have also said they did not want High
Authority *dirigisme* and have not pressed the case.

This does not mean that national rivalries have not been
influencing Community investment. Just as the Germans
stressed their need for investment to overcome the head
start of the French, the French felt that they could not
rest on past accomplishments while the Germans pushed
ahead. In June 1954, when French steel investments had
been declining for several years, while those of Germany
were rising, the Groupement de l'Industrie Sidérurgique
said: "The maintenance, indeed the acceleration, of the
present rhythm of investment is an imperious necessity for
the French steel industry. Confronted from now on, without protection of any sort, by competitors whose will to
compete is made clear from day to day, the French steel
firms have the duty of developing without relaxation their
efforts at modernization and equipment in all the areas
relevant to reinforce their competitive potential, to improve their productivity and to reduce their costs." [39]

[39] Groupement de l'Industrie Sidérurgique, [Report to] Assemblée Générale Ordinaire des Actionnaires du 28 Juin 1954, p. 5.

Concern over investments and keeping pace with other countries was at the heart of the French steel industry's case for higher prices, at least as publicly presented. When the High Authority intervened to support the French producers, it was aiding French investment. Indeed, one of the key issues of Community price policy lay in the financing of investment (p. 284f.). The French felt this particularly strongly because they had to borrow more of their investment funds than the Germans did and as a result had heavier overhead charges.[40]

Not only price policy but most other activities affect the level of investment. Directly and indirectly governments have an important role. Economic activity outside the coal and steel industries largely determines the need for investment in the Community and the prospects of any particular investment's being profitable. This is another case where the High Authority's powers are limited not only by the Treaty and by the play of forces inside the Community, but by the facts of partial integration. Even so, the High Authority retains an influence and it must have a policy. Not only is the level and direction of investment crucial for the economic life of the Community, but its deployment among the countries of the Community remains a major, if ambiguous, fact influencing the extent to which a true merger of national interests is taking place.

[40] The French government, largely through the Monnet plan, provided 38 per cent of the finance for steel investments from 1945 through 1954. Calculated from Armengaud Report, cited, p. 117. Government aid had been less important in Germany. The German producers felt that they also had a problem in self-financing resulting from the holding-down of their prices by government action. To compensate in part for this, the German government sponsored what amounted to a special loan to basic industries from other industries whose prices were not fixed. Industrial leaders had volunteered this arrangement as a substitute for a special tax proposed by the SPD. From January 1952 when the law went into effect until June 30, 1955, when it expired, DM 1,149 million were raised in this fashion. Of the billion DM paid out by March 31, 1955, 288 million had gone to 34 firms in the coal industry and 297 million to 22 steelworks. *Anlage zum Unternehmerbrief des Deutschen Industrieinstituts*, Dec. 15, 1955 (mimeographed).

FOURTEEN

CARTELS AND CONCENTRATIONS:
A BEGINNING

CARTELS AND concentrations are part and parcel of the history of Western Europe's coal and steel industries. During the last century producers have formed literally hundreds of cartels, varying greatly in form, method, and scope. Some were long-lived, others soon succumbed to internal or external pressures. Most were national or regional, some had international extensions.

The natural desire to eliminate competition has also taken the form of bringing competitive firms under a single control. Producers have sought stability and economies by "vertical integration," the linking of all stages of production, from coal and iron mines through cokeries, blast furnaces, steel furnaces, and rolling mills, to plants that make finished products using large quantities of steel. Heavy capital requirements and technological advances that increase the optimum size of installations add to the growth of large enterprises in coal and steel.

The Treaty had to provide some kind of law to govern cartels and concentrations. Otherwise the Community would have been sadly deficient; the omission would have risked stultifying the effort to create a common market, ensure equal treatment, secure the best allocation of resources, and, especially, to introduce some degree of competition. It would have done little good to abolish governmental trade barriers if private trade restrictions could take their place. Regulation of the behavior of individual firms would mean little if the firms never behaved

individually, but only as members of cartels, or if the concentration of production was so great that the behavior of
a few giant firms in fact determined the behavior of all
others. The High Authority could not hope to assert its
influence and perform its functions if there were no checks
on the private accumulation of power.

To see the problem was not to solve it. There was no
general acceptance of the idea that competition was good
and cartels and concentrations were bad. On the contrary,
people of a wide range of political opinions shared the
view that markets should be "organized" for stability and
efficiency rather than left to the "chaos" and "waste" of
"atomistic competition." Opinion differed as to how well
cartels and concentrations served their purposes, and
feelings waxed and waned about the amount of public
control that was desirable. Over the years laws and governmental policies had grown complex. Cartels were regulated but they were also sometimes fostered and strengthened. In France, for instance, steel firms had to belong to
the Chambre Syndicale, and the Comptoir Sidérurgique's
price-fixing activities had legal sanction. After the war
most of the countries of Western Europe moved toward
somewhat closer supervision of cartels and toward the
limitation of restrictive practices; but they had not proceeded very far when the coal and steel Treaty was
negotiated.

There were no full-blown international cartels in coal
and steel. National markets had been rather effectively separated from one another. Creating a common market might
stimulate the tentative efforts that had begun about 1949 to
reach some sort of private international understanding about
steel. Or it might strengthen national cartels or cartel-like arrangements. In most of the Community countries a few
large steel firms stood head and shoulders above the others
in size and market power. In coal, marketing was highly
organized. In both fields governments owned firms or
whole industries. The question whether deconcentration
in Germany would be followed by reconcentration further

complicated matters: national rivalry was added to the difficulties of creating competition in coal and steel as part of the Community's problem of regulating business practices.

THE TREATY

Against this background it was not easy to reach agreement on what the Treaty was to say about cartels and concentrations. Monnet wanted strong anticartel provisions, to keep the Community from being captured by private interests that would debase its broad political purpose. He hoped, too, that this might prove a means of increasing flexibility in the French economy. Schuman had repeatedly declared that the new Community would differ fundamentally from past cartels. The American attitude toward the Community would be affected by what was done in this sphere. Much Socialist, labor, and independent support could be held only if the prospects of controlling cartels and concentrations were reasonably good. On the other hand, business groups in all the Community countries balked at "tough" cartel provisions. Little or no restriction of the right to form cartels, minimum regulation of business practices, and little or no discretion for the High Authority, seemed to be their formula. To claim license for restrictive practices in the name of opposition to *dirigisme* was to exhibit the rather special meanings often given to that word. Once again, as in the negotiation of rules on prices and investments, the Treaty drafters had the problem of providing not only an immediate compromise but also a set of rules and procedures that would serve the Community in various market conditions.

The provisions that emerged show all these influences. They blend several European approaches to cartel questions with elements drawn from American practice and experience. They provide statements of principle, specific rules, a strong indication of direction, and a rather wide area in which the High Authority has discretion (or at least the room for judgment that goes with applying rules to cases). The approaches to cartels and concentrations differ notably. The whole was put into two articles, the longest in the Treaty.

Article 65 begins by forbidding agreements or concerted practices "tending, directly or indirectly, to prevent, restrict or distort the normal operation of competition within the common market. . . ." Price-fixing, the allocation of markets, and restrictions on production, investment, or technical development are singled out for particular mention. This is very broad and quite definite.

"However," says the second paragraph, the "High Authority shall authorize"—not "may authorize"—agreements for specialization of production or for joint buying and selling if it is satisfied that certain conditions are fulfilled. The specialization or joint trading must "contribute to a substantial improvement in the production or distributing of the products in question." The agreement must be "not more restrictive than is necessary for that purpose." It must not give the participating companies the ability to determine prices or "control or limit the production or selling of a substantial part of the products in question within the common market," and it must not protect them from the competition of other producers in the common market. When authorizing such arrangements, the High Authority may establish conditions and set time limits.

It is up to the High Authority to determine which practices are legitimate and which infringe this article. It is given power to get what information it needs to make the decisions. Agreements ruled illegitimate become void and are not enforceable in the courts of Community countries. The High Authority may fine offenders.[1] Its decisions are, of course, subject to appeal to the Court.

Article 66 approaches concentration quite differently. Nothing was to be done about the existing structure of industry. Any transaction that would bring about a new

[1] On a daily basis fines are not to exceed twice the turnover of the products involved in the offense unless the agreement was to restrict production, investment, or technical development, in which case the penalty could be up to 10 per cent of the annual turnover by the company for fines and 20 per cent of the daily turnover for daily penalties when the violation persists.

concentration is to be submitted to the High Authority.[2] The merger must be approved if it would not give the new entity the power "to determine prices, to control or restrict production or distribution, or to prevent the maintenance of effective competition in a substantial part of the market for such products; or, to evade the rules of competition as they result from the execution of this Treaty, in particular by establishing an artificially privileged position involving a substantial advantage in access to supplies or markets." In applying this article the High Authority is to take account of the size of other enterprises of the same kind in the Community and of the principle of equality.

The remaining provisions of this long article concern enforcement, penalties, arrangements for special situations in which a legal concentration was illegally effected, the gathering of information, and the right of affected companies to appeal to the Court which is explicitly given the power to review the substance of the question and to decide whether the concentration comes within the article's prohibition.

Sections 12 and 13 of the transitional Convention prescribed the steps for putting these articles into effect. So far as concentrations were concerned, this was largely a matter of details concerning timing, the issuance by the High Authority of regulations, and matters of this sort.[3] With regard to cartels the problems were more serious, since the Treaty affected those already in existence. The Convention aimed largely at granting reasonable time for the liquidation of those found to be illegal. The High Authority was to give attention to the means necessary to achieve the most efficient distribution and use of products, to avoid reduction in capacity, and to prevent the "inequitable distribution among workers of such reductions in

---

[2] The provision is broadly drawn to cover all kinds of arrangements that would bring two or more enterprises under common control. Only one of the enterprises needs to be a coal and steel firm.

[3] The High Authority could penalize concentrations taking place between the signing of the Treaty and the entry into effect of these provisions if it had "proof that these operations were carried out in order to evade" the article.

employment as might result from a decrease in demand." It was given substantial powers to work out arrangements to this end that might extend beyond the transitional period.

Monnet called this outcome "Europe's first antitrust law." He had warrant for the description. Major restrictive practices were banned, organizations making them possible might be dissolved. New measures of concentration would be supervised and could be prevented if they threatened to give any firm too much power. The High Authority was left with a good bit of discretion, in fact if not in strict law. By realistic standards the drafters had done well. But this was only the beginning.

The control of private business practices is an intricate, difficult affair. What the law came to mean would depend on how it was administered. Americans need look no further than the history of the Sherman and Clayton Acts to see how differently the same law may appear in practice at different times, and to get some idea of the vicissitudes of administration, which depend not only on the administrators but also on the circumstances in which they apply the legislation. The High Authority was a new agency applying a new law. Its full application would require some changes in the existing situation. Could the High Authority impose its will to bring about these changes? Where would it find support? It would certainly face resistance. The rules on business practices were not wholeheartedly accepted by the business community to whom they had to be applied; instead they were, in some part at least, seriously contested by that community, as to wisdom, feasibility, and justice.

The High Authority could not hope to bring about rapid change in habitual ways of conducting business. It is not surprising that the end of the transitional period leaves major issues unresolved, and that the action taken during the Community's first five years has raised new questions about the future. Both in the High Authority's approach and in the experience of the transitional period, concentrations have been sharply distinguished from cartels. Dealing with the latter has been arduous and the results have been ambiguous. So far as concentrations are concerned, the

High Authority has not felt that it faced any difficulties—
but more complicated questions may lie ahead.

CONCENTRATIONS

During its first year, the High Authority's public references to cartels and concentrations were almost perfunc-
tory. The Convention required the High Authority to
make certain regulations about the application of the rules
during the first four months of its existence. It did not do
so because "it appeared less essential to respect these formal
deadlines than to avoid any misunderstanding in the
meaning and scope of the text which the High Authority
must establish." [4] So, with the consent of the Council of
Ministers, it was going to "proceed a little more slowly."

In May 1954 the High Authority established procedures
for passing on concentrations. It defined control, described
the information it wanted, and exempted lesser mergers
from the process. If a concentration did not affect more
than 1.2 million tons of crude steel or specified quantities
of other products, no prior authorization was needed.[5] Considering that in 1952 there were only about ten firms in
the Community producing more than that much steel, this
seemed a reasonably high ceiling. On the other hand, 1.2
million tons was less than 3 per cent of the Community's
output of steel in 1954 (and a smaller share later), which
could hardly be thought to give a firm undue influence on
the market. The High Authority had proposed a lower level
of exemption; the German government wanted a higher
one; the compromise was reached in the Council of Minis-

[4] HA, *Report*, Jan. 1953, p. 62.
[5] *JO*, May 11, 1954, pp. 345-351. The ceilings for other products were:
coke, 1.2 million tons; coal agglomerates, 350,000; iron ore, 4 million;
pig iron, 1.2 million; rolled products, 900,000 (of which not more than
500,000 could be flat products); special steels, 100,000 (of which only
40,000 could be for other purposes than mechanical construction). The
various products were given weights to make possible a calculation of
general size and a ceiling was put on that as well as on each product.
For instance, if nothing but coal was produced, a merger would need
no authorization up to 7 million tons, but this figure would fall according to the volume of other things produced. There were other rules to
cover various kinds of cases.

ters.[6] *Le reglement des bagatelles* cleared the ground. What the High Authority did about mergers exceeding its limits became the test of Community policy on concentration.

In four years, the High Authority received 49 requests to approve concentrations. It approved 25 of these, found that 18 did not require approval for one reason or another, and had 6 undecided cases on April 1, 1958. On its own initiative, the High Authority examined another 55 mergers. It issued authorizations in 5 cases, found 13 to be exempt, and had taken no formal action on the remaining 37 by April 1958. Thus, in over 100 cases, the High Authority found no reason to forbid any merger or other measure of concentration.

Table 6

CONCENTRATIONS AUTHORIZED BY THE HIGH AUTHORITY
(Up to April 1958)

	Germany	France	Belgium	Luxembourg	Total
Horizontal (9):					
Coal-coal	2	—	—	—	2
Steel-steel	1	2	1	—	4
Steel-special steel	—	2	—	—	2
Trade	—	1	—	—	1
Vertical (21):					
Steel-coal	6	—	—	1[a]	7
Steel-iron ore	—	—	—	1	1
Steel-scrap	1	—	—	—	1
Steel-steel processing	8	2	2[b]	—	12
	18	7	3	2	30

a. Acquisition of a coal mine in Germany.
b. Including acquisition of a tubeworks in France.
SOURCE: HA, *Report*, Apr. 1958, v. 2, pp. 98–104.

[6] E. B. Haas, *The Uniting of Europe*, 1958, pp. 81-82. The figure chosen for crude steel roughly approximates annual output of the biggest French firms in those years.

The character of the 30 authorizations is clear from Table 6. Vertical combinations were substantially more important than horizontal ones. While the securing of coal and iron ore supplies by steel firms was an important part of the total, the largest number of cases involved "forward integration"; steel firms acquired tubeworks, shipyards, construction firms, and companies making machinery and vehicles. Not surprisingly, three-fifths of the cases were German, but horizontal concentration was more marked in France. Since the main concentration problems concerned steel, the rest of this section deals almost exclusively with that industry, leaving coal for the cartel section that follows.

While the High Authority does not publicly explain its action in any case, the broad criteria it has used are reasonably clear. The High Authority not only does not object to "useful concentrations" but "encourages them in every way it can." [7] This policy is explained by two arguments. First, combinations can make for efficiency, by providing economies of scale, creating means for new investment, permitting specialization, uniting producers who perform different operations, diversifying steel firms, linking coal and iron with steel production, and by other means. Mergers that have this result serve the Treaty's broad aims of increasing productivity. The High Authority's second argument is that only by combining can small firms offer real competition to bigger ones. Concentration thus becomes a weapon against restrictive practices.

There is a good deal to be said for these arguments, but they also have their limitations. There are many small firms in the Community and quite a few are undoubtedly inefficient. Large firms can obtain economies by integrating several stages of production. For purely physical or engineering advantages, not the size of firms but the size and character of plants provide the relevant criteria. Managerial, financial, and other advantages that go with the size of the firm are real enough, but few broad rules can be applied to them. So far as fostering competition is concerned it is

[7] HA, *Report*, Apr. 1955, p. 117.

certainly true that size may be necessary to permit a company to engage effectively in a general competitive struggle (though small firms are often quite competitive in their particular fields). But the will does not necessarily go with the ability, and the difference between price leadership by one or two firms much larger than the rest and oligopolistic competition among several sizable firms, while of interest, is not quite what the High Authority's words would suggest. Still, if these are the only kinds of competition likely to exist in steel—as many believe—there may be advantages for the High Authority in having a moderate dispersion of power among firms, rather than extreme concentration in two or three. If the High Authority had tried to apply its broad criteria in careful detail to every case, it would have been taking on a very large assignment. There seems little doubt that what really happened is that the officials in Luxembourg left it to the industrialists to decide what would be efficient or advantageous and inspected the proposals primarily with an eye to the amount of production they brought under a single control. This was made relatively easy by the fact that so much of the concentration was vertical and that even the largest mergers involved relatively small percentages of total Community production. But criteria that were adequate for the transitional period may not suffice for the long run.

When the High Authority spoke of encouraging useful concentrations, it may have had France especially in mind. The cartel pricing that had prevailed in that country under the *comptoir* system had protected some firms from market pressures that might have forced them into more efficient arrangements. When he was at the Commissariat du Plan, Monnet had encouraged mergers and reorganizations, sometimes unsuccessfully. But, he told the coal and steel Assembly, "As soon as the common market was established, operations that had been recommended for a number of years rapidly surmounted the resistances that had never ceased to block them in national markets."[8]

The High Authority's favorite example of a merger that

[8] CA, *Débats*, May 10, 1955, p. 275.

plainly made for efficiency was the formation of the Compagnie des Ateliers et Forges de la Loire. For many years four small companies had been making high-grade steel in neighboring towns on the eastern edge of the Massif Central. Some of the output was important to the French armaments industry, but costs were high and in peacetime the firms had some difficulty. They had resisted Monnet's urging to combine, but as the common market loomed, two of the companies merged in January 1953. Some workers were thrown out of jobs and opposition to further mergers grew. The High Authority offered help in readaptation (see Chapter 15) and then all the companies combined. By doing so they made major savings through concentrating production. Before, pig iron had been produced in four of the five plants, open-hearth steel in three of them, cast steel in all five, and electric steel by one process in all five, by another in three. After the merger, all the pig iron was produced in one plant, all the open-hearth steel in another, all the electric steel by the induction process in a third. Two plants made all the cast steel. One plant was shut down. Production increased and costs fell.[9]

Quite different issues were raised by the merger, in 1955, of S. A. John Cockerill and Ougrée-Marihaye, the two principal steel producers of Belgium. The combined output of these companies was over 1.8 million tons of crude steel, about one-third the national production. This was not the full measure of their importance. Each of the companies was part of a major complex of financial, industrial, and commercial interests with holdings throughout Belgium, the Congo, and many other countries as well.[10]

If one looked only at the Belgian economy, the share of

[9] Based largely on HA, "New Deal for French Steel," *Bulletin from the European Community for Coal and Steel* (London), Jan. 1955, pp. 3-6.

[10] The Cockerill company was controlled by the Société Générale de Belgique. Ougrée-Marihaye was part of the Brufina-Cofinindus group (Société Bruxelles pour la Finance et l'Industrie and Cie. Financière et Industrielle S.A.). The Comte de Launoit who administers the Donation Royale—the heritage from Leopold II—played an important part in the merger. The two complexes and their steel holdings are examined in detail in Wirtschaftsvereinigung Eisen- und Stahlindustrie, *Die Fusion Cockerill-Ougrée*, Dec. 1955 (mimeographed).

production controlled by the merged companies was very
high. But the High Authority took the view that the proper
measure was the production of the Community as a whole.
The Cockerill and Ougrée companies had produced about
4 per cent of the Community's 1954 output in their own
furnaces; other Belgian companies they controlled indirectly added about 2 per cent.[11] Since no decisions are
published in these matters it is not clear what view the High
Authority took of the full extent of the holding companies'
foreign interests which might have raised the complex's
total share of production to 8 or 10 per cent of the Community's output in 1954 and 1955.

Cockerill-Ougrée is not unique in having ramifications
of this kind. Lines of influence are not always clear, degrees
of control may be limited, conflicts of interest may arise
within the complex.[12] At some point the High Authority
will find it necessary to formulate policies on the issues
involved in situations of this sort. Both because of the
amount of steel it involved, and because of the holding-
company aspect, the Cockerill-Ougrée merger and the
High Authority's apparent reasoning about it were closely
watched by the German steel industry.

Reconcentration in the Ruhr

Before the war Vereinigte Stahlwerke produced nearly
40 per cent of Germany's steel; another third was in the
hands of five other major producers. More than half the

[11] HA, *Report*, Nov. 1955, p. I, 44, speaks of their direct and indirect
control of 2.8 million tons. It is not clear which firms were counted. As
a precaution, the High Authority stipulated that the two sales organizations should not be merged. What results by way of competition were
expected from this step is not very clear.

[12] The High Authority requires outside owners to report to the High
Authority if they have an interest in a Community enterprise that gives
them 10 per cent of the voting power and is worth more than $100,000.
JO, May 11, 1954, p. 350. Other information may have to be provided
on request. An exception is made for banks that hold shares on behalf
of clients or as trustees. This is undoubtedly logical so far as ownership
goes, but if the banks are in a position to vote those shares, the exemption undermines the attempt to learn about the locus of control. In the
history of German heavy industry this kind of control exercised by
banks voting stock they did not own has been important.

country's coal was controlled by steel firms which also had extensive holdings in various branches of the steel-processing industry. The deconcentration measures carried out before the Treaty was ratified changed this structure substantially. Vereinigte Stahlwerke was broken up into five or six major steel-producing companies and a number of smaller firms, some of them important in specialized lines. Other companies were split up so that activities formerly carried on by one were divided among several. Some firms lost substantial productive facilities through dismantling. The steel industry's ownership of coal was greatly reduced; the coal sales organizations were reformed. There was also some redistribution of the stock of coal and steel companies, partly to prevent the reappearance of unified control.

This reorganization did not mean that German steel companies had become small producers. In 1952 there were 11 firms in the Community that produced over a million tons of steel; 7 of these were German. Two of them and ARBED were the only companies producing more than 1.5 million tons.[13] In terms of plant size, the Germans also rated high. In the whole Community there were only 7 steelworks that produced over a million tons in 1952; they all were in Germany and together they produced over 9 million tons of steel, more than a fifth of the Community output. About 30 per cent more of the Community's steel came from 18 plants producing between 500,000 and a million tons each; only 3 of these were German.[14] It appeared, then, that so far as the size of steel-producing units was concerned, Germany was not handicapped at the outset of the Community. This was not the main issue so far as the Germans were concerned. They emphasized the organization of coal sales, which will be dealt with later, and the need for integrated processes of production, from coal right through to finished steel products. The Germans had a

[13] The remaining million-ton producers were French. HA, *Recueil Statistique*, Je. 1953, p. 271.

[14] Belgium and Luxembourg had 3 each, the Saar 4, and France 5. Same, p. 272.

special pride in the degree to which they had developed this *Verbundwirtschaft*. They accused the occupying powers of destroying links that were the crux of technical, managerial, and commercial efficiency, thereby laming German production and raising its costs. There were Germans who were glad to see Vereinigte Stahlwerke broken up and who hoped that the political power of the Ruhr magnates was permanently reduced, but there were very few Germans who would defend the destruction of *Verbundwirtschaft*. No one could doubt that when they got the chance the Germans would seek to reintegrate their heavy industry.

Elsewhere in the Community, especially in France, there was concern about what the Germans would do. In addition to worry about the market power provided by the Ruhr coal sales organizations, there was concern that restoration of vertical integration would reduce the amount of coal offered for sale by putting it under the control of the German steel producers. There was more than a suspicion, too, that the Germans would try to re-create giant steel firms that could dominate the market. In France many people had been encouraged to see the Coal and Steel Community's antitrust law as a check on German reconcentration. In Germany the emphasis was put on the fact that the Treaty had nothing to do with the Allied deconcentration measures. German firms would have equal rights with everyone else, including equal rights to merge. The fact remained that the High Authority had a good bit of discretion in determining what the Treaty law would mean in practice. Observers watched for a signal.

The High Authority's message to the Ruhr took the form of a speech by its Belgian vice-chairman, Albert Coppé, delivered to a group of industrialists at Duisburg on July 28, 1954.[15] Noting the doubts and suspicions that attended any governmental interference in economic processes, Coppé said that he hoped to give his hearers "a certain measure of assurance" that the action of the High Authority on concentrations "is intended to promote economic activity and in no case to hinder it." The common market was

[15] HA doc. 5196/54 f (mimeographed French translation).

to be competitive, and the organization of industry must not upset its balance, but "this does not mean that the Treaty and the policy of the High Authority that rests on it are in principle enemies of concentrations. On the contrary, so long as concentrations are suitable for increasing the productive capacity of enterprises without limiting competition, the High Authority will authorize them. . . ."

Coppé listed the various kinds of advantages that might be achieved by concentration (surely carrying coals to Duisburg). The results, he said, were not only advantageous to the enterprises concerned but "at the same time work towards the fundamental objectives of the Treaty . . . above all in realizing 'the most rational distribution of production at the highest possible level of productivity.' " There were certainly dangers to a firm in overextending itself but the decision as to what was an optimum size was up to the entrepreneur. As he concluded, Coppé expressed the hope "that the time is near when all the German, French, Italian, Dutch, Luxembourgeois, and Belgian industrialists will have the same confidence in the High Authority that they normally accord to the economic administrations of their own countries."

The High Authority had said such things before. Repeated with emphasis in the setting of Duisburg, they constituted a special assurance, almost an invitation. It was accepted. The German steelmen went ahead with their ideas for reconcentration, knowing that when they could make a good case, and when the resulting amalgamation was not too big, they would get a friendly hearing in Luxembourg.

A fairly typical example of the process that followed is the Mannesmann, A. G., the first of the major combines to be restored in essentially its prewar form. The company had been split into three parts, one mining coal, another producing steel, and the third machinery. Some ties remained among the companies. The managements and stockholders applied for and got permission to unite the three parts, thus restoring the *Verbundwirtschaft*. Meanwhile, the company had bought another large colliery from the Flick interests, so it had larger coal resources than before deconcentration.[16]

Other groups moved the same way, with the steelworks acquiring coal mines and processing companies or filling out their range of steelmaking processes. Sometimes they restored old links, occasionally they found new ones. By the end of 1957 a German economic journal could say, with only slight exaggeration: "With the exception of Vereinigte Stahlwerke, today all the major companies have returned—in more or less complete form and burdened with this or that restriction which still applies to some group as a result of the deconcentration." [17]

Among the successor companies to Vereinigte Stahlwerke there was also some reconcentration. To make pipes and tubes, Rheinische Röhrenwerke bought about 25 per cent of the semi-finished steel produced by Hüttenwerke Phoenix, A. G. Controlling shares in both companies belonged to the widow of Fritz Thyssen; the occupation authorities had permitted them to work closely together. It was, therefore, only a slight step to complete the merger. The other main part of Thyssen's interests, left to his daughter, became involved in a series of combinations that brought together the main steelworks, Germany's largest electric-steel producer, the largest wire-drawing plant, and sizable coal interests. These measures, aided by substantial investments, brought August Thyssen Hütte, A. G., with

[16] The series of Mannesmann mergers account for six of the authorizations granted by the High Authority; four in the steel-steel processing category, one steel-coal, and one coal-coal (see Table 6). A move in 1958 to combine several parts of the Mannesmann interests did not require High Authority approval because they were already under a single control.

[17] "Die neuen Stahlkonzerne an der Ruhr," *Der Volkswirt*, Dec. 7, 1957, pp. 2625-2628. In addition to Vereinigte Stahlwerke and Krupp, which are dealt with below, the major exception was Gutehoffnungshütte (the Haniel interests) which had recombined some of its coal and steel but kept important manufacturing companies in a separate holding company for tax reasons and to avoid spreading co-determination measures to the entire enterprise. "Die Gesellschaftsstruktur der Westdeutschen Montanindustrie," *Wirtschaftsdienst*, Apr. 1958, pp. 214-219. These two articles provide a good bit of the detail for this section.

its subsidiaries, to one of the leading positions in the German steel industry by the end of 1957.[18]

Though some observers thought the two sets of Thyssen heirs were developing divergent interests, the general opinion was that some kind of combination of Phoenix-Rheinrohr and August Thyssen Hütte was the logical culmination of the process that was under way. This seemed borne out when early in 1959 it was reported that ATH proposed to buy just over half the shares in Phoenix. This was a larger concentration than any that had been put before the High Authority. The combined raw-steel capacity of the firms would be between 5 and 6 million tons, probably the largest in the Community.

Meanwhile, the High Authority faced difficulties of a somewhat different sort in the case of Krupp. This was the second largest German steel firm before the war, producing some 10 per cent of the national output. The Allies divided the concern into a number of parts. The Krupp family was left with plants making machinery, ships, locomotives, and other products, and with major building enterprises. The steelworks at Rheinhausen, the third largest postwar producer in Germany, was ordered sold. But it has not been sold and no one in Germany expects it to be sold. Krupp's general manager said that he would not willingly fulfill the sale order. German industrialists made it clear that they did not propose to step forward as potential purchasers and that there would be strong opposition to a sale to foreigners.[19] The former occupying governments seemed to

---

[18] It was not the largest producer, but rapidly increased its rate of output during the year. Lack of raw material was said to hamper full use of its steelmaking capacity, which was estimated to be 3.2 million tons compared with 3 million for Dortmund Hörder Union, the largest German producer. "Die neuen Stahlkonzerne . . . ," cited, and *Der Volkswirt*, Apr. 19, 1958, p. 670.

[19] Bernd A. Huffschmid, "Kruppstahl hat Heimweh," *Der Volkswirt*, Feb. 11, 1956, pp. 12-14. Huffschmid calls one of the obstacles to domestic sale "the healthy reticence of all relevant German interests and groups that are not prepared to help in the realization of a patently unjustified measure. In Germany one rightly goes on the assumption that the acquisition of Krupp property that has been subjected to a forced sale could one day have very undesirable consequences for the new owner. The

be trying to find a way to legalize the situation without quite forcing the issue. This, the High Authority made clear, was none of its affair. The restoration to Krupp ownership of Rheinhausen would not be a merger in the sense of the Treaty.

There was, however, a concentration question involving Krupp confronting the High Authority. Rheinhausen proposed to acquire the Bochumer Verein, one of the major successors of Vereinigte Stahlwerke. Specializing in high-grade steel and "difficult" orders, the Bochumer Verein was in the old days Krupp's major competitor in these fields. It is now seen as a replacement for the Krupp quality-steel plant at Borbeck that was dismantled and shipped to the U.S.S.R. The Bochumer Verein bought some of the Krupp coal mines after deconcentration; others have been held by Rheinhausen.[20] In form the Rheinhausen-Bochumer Verein merger is another case of the sort of integration that the High Authority says it encourages. The two firms might have a crude-steel capacity of about 4 million tons, which would be large compared with others in the Community but, if fully used, would amount to less than 7 per cent of Community production in 1957.[21] On economic grounds alone it would, therefore, be rather difficult to make a per-

---

restitution that those who acquired property as a result of the Aryanization measures of the Hitler time have had to make are still too fresh in memory for any German to want to reach out his hand toward the property of a fellow citizen who has long been rehabilitated at home and is only being discriminated against by the Allies." He concludes that "Kruppstahl of Rheinhausen is homesick for Essen and wants eventually to return to the lap of the mother."

[20] At one time Axel Wenner-Gren, the Swedish capitalist, held the majority of the shares of the Bochumer Verein but then sold them to German interests. The shares are supposedly held "by banks and insurance companies and can be obtained by Krupp as soon as the deconcentration question is cleared up." "Die neuen Stahlkonzerne . . . ," cited, p. 2626. It is widely believed, however, that Krupp has effective control of the Bochumer Verein regardless of the legal situation.

[21] If the Thyssen interests merged they would have a larger capacity. The Belgian-owned complex is still larger if all its parts are considered. It should be borne in mind that these comparisons are made in crude-steel capacity alone and that a firm's market position could be much stronger in certain kinds of steel or steel products.

suasive case against reconcentration of Krupp. But the problem is not just an economic one. The history of Krupp as an armsmaker (though no arms are made now), the symbolism of the Ruhr-Reich connection provided by the linking of several generations of Krupps with Kaisers and Hitler, the conviction of Alfried Krupp for war crimes at Nuremberg (though he was later pardoned), and the unsettled legal situation, mixed with defiance of the sale orders, all combine to make this a case involving more than a decision whether amalgamation would offend Article 66 and promote the aims set out in Article 2. Still it was not surprising that in early 1959 Krupp could announce that the High Authority would permit formal acquisition of the Bochumer Verein.

While the Krupp case is especially difficult, other proposals for major new German concentrations would also raise problems for the High Authority going beyond those of previous cases. This is not just because they would involve more steel but because they would be seen as the crest of a wave which has already caused some anxiety in the rest of the Community where the suspicion exists that more waves may follow. The standards the High Authority has set dealing with past cases of concentrations would not offer complete guidance in these cases. As a German journal remarked, "The bounds of concentration can hardly be established in theory." [22] The point has not escaped French observers. "If the theoretical criterion of a serious restriction of competition is the only one to be taken into account," says an anonymous but clearly very well-informed French author, "nothing stands in the way of the view that the High Authority would look favorably on the constitution in the Ruhr of three or four great groups which would each produce four or five million tons of steel, or perhaps even more the pure and simple return to the old concerns." [23] The greater size of the common market might be used to justify even larger concentrations and if the United

---

[22] "Die neuen Stahlkonzerne . . . ," cited, p. 2626.
[23] XXX, "La Reconcentration des Industries Sidérurgiques et Minières d'Allemagne de l'Ouest dans le Cadre de la CECA," *Politique Étrangère,* Dec. 1955, p. 729.

States were taken as a standard, there would be almost no limit, said XXX. The Allies, he noted, had had broader standards when they resolved on deconcentration. They worried about power—economic and therefore political— which they did not want to see concentrated in a few hands.

Others in France sounded the same note. Frequent references were made to the statements in the French parliament at the time of ratification about the need for deconcentration in the Ruhr. Then it had been said that the High Authority's mission was "to watch that the deconcentration is maintained, since it is for the same purpose, for the same fundamental reasons that the Treaty was signed." [24] The French feeling about the need for "balance" in the Community was invoked, and linked sometimes with the Treaty injunctions to the High Authority to take account of the size of other enterprises in the Community.[25] Michel Debré, a French member of the Common Assembly who later became prime minister of the Fifth Republic, peppered the High Authority with questions about the number of reconcentrations it had permitted, and whether it had ever refused any.

The High Authority took a firm view that it was being challenged by irrelevancies. "The Treaty . . . knows nothing of notions of reconcentration and recartelization." "The existence or nonexistence of commentaries before various parliaments about the meaning of Articles 65 and 66. . . cannot serve as a criterion of interpretation. . . ." [26] Still, what was legally irrelevant was not always politically irrelevant and the High Authority finally felt itself stung into the rather remarkable statement that "a reconstitution of

[24] Statement by Felix Gaillard, as government spokesman, on April 1, 1952, quoted in the Armengaud Report (cited in Ch. 13, n. 36), p. 43 n.

[25] For instance, XXX, cited. Paragraph 2 of Article 66 first refers to the general assurance of nondiscrimination in Article 4, then instructs the High Authority—in passing on applications for mergers—to "take account of the size of enterprises of the same kind existing in the Community, as far as it finds this justified to avoid or correct the disadvantages resulting from an inequality in the conditions of competition."

[26] JO, Dec. 16, 1957, p. 613; Je. 3, 1957, p. 239. Similar statements had been made the year before, about the Phoenix-Rheinrohr case. JO, Nov. 16, 1956, pp. 319-320; Dec. 27, 1956, pp. 412-413.

the Vereinigte Stahlwerke which was deconcentrated by the Allies would not be susceptible of being authorized if a request for this were submitted. But the conclusion should not be drawn *a contrario* from this statement that an authorization will be granted for concentration that would be less important in the field of steel production; this would notably not be the case if these concentrations permitted acquisition of a dominating position on the market for a more specialized product." [27]

The statement is a symptom of Community worries rather than a guide to future action. The Germans have quite a way to go before anyone is likely to make a case for reconstituting Vereinigte Stahlwerke or its equivalent.[28] Well before that point is reached the High Authority is likely to find its loose criteria of complementarity and the technical efficiencies of size outmoded. Firms will justify mergers for financial strength, the advantages of diversification over the whole range of steelmaking activities, geographical dispersion, and perhaps managerial concentration. The obverse of these is power and market position. Faced with such claims the High Authority is likely to find it hard to develop criteria; discretion and judgment will be at a premium and they are likely to be influenced by broad considerations of "balance" and by psychological repercussions on other producers. The more familiar criteria will probably have some relevance at a different level, as the combination of vertical integration with increasingly great horizontal combinations gives some firms a larger share of Community production of certain kinds of steel and certain steel products than they have of crude steel.

These questions will not be confined to the Ruhr. They may not even arise there first. But when they do, the High Authority, while it must apply standards that know no

---

[27] *JO*, Oct. 30, 1957, p. 533.

[28] In addition to the four firms already mentioned as successors to Vereinigte Stahlwerke there is a fifth, Rheinische Stahlwerke, a holding company that has grouped a number of smaller companies and is emerging as a million-ton producer.

nationality, cannot really escape from the fact that in much of the rest of the Community what happens in the Ruhr is looked at with an especially critical eye, trained by experience. The matter is not just psychological. There are pervasive questions of the power that goes with production and there are concrete matters of coal supply. With regard to both there are some facts and some possible developments that may serve to reduce the psychological burden of old fears of the Ruhr.

Mitigating Factors

Not all the Ruhr's production is German. The biggest steel producer, Dortmund-Hörder Hüttenunion, is largely owned by Hoogovens of Ijmuiden, the Dutch steel company. When the small Dutch interest in Vereinigte Stahlwerke was concentrated in this one firm as part of the Allied reorganization of the German steel industry, it amounted to something over 40 per cent of the shares, which apparently assures control.[29] In coal there is a larger foreign interest. For many years the de Wendel interests owned coal mines in the Ruhr. In 1953, the Wendels joined with other French producers to form Sidechar, a firm that bought the Harpener Bergbau, a major Ruhr coal mine, from Friedrich Flick.[30] This raised the French interest to something like 7.5 per cent of Ruhr production. In the Aachen basin, ARBED has long owned the Eschweiler Bergwerksverein and in 1957 extended its holdings by buying Lothringen Bergbau in the Ruhr. Other foreign owners have smaller holdings. All told, foreign interests probably control one-fifth of German coal production.

[29] While a Dutch holding company is part owner of the Klöckner company, another large German steel producer, the real ownership and control appears to be German, with little or no true Dutch content.
[30] Flick had to sell Harpener Bergbau under Allied orders, but was unable to find a German buyer. At one time the Bundesbahn was interested but the sum involved was apparently too great. Flick used his franc proceeds (only part of the whole) to invest in French and Belgian steel.

This is a considerable mitigation of purely German control. While these mines participate in the usual Ruhr sales arrangements, the foreign owners have rights to their own coal which are important to their supplies. "Two thirds of the German siderurgical coal imported by France are received, under proprietary rights, by the Lorraine steelmakers who have obtained participation in certain Ruhr coal companies." [31]

The most obvious way for steel firms in the rest of the Community to cope with reconcentration in the Ruhr was to build up their own size and resources. In Belgium, Holland, and Luxembourg, single firms controlled a substantial part of the steel production and, with their foreign affiliates, were similar in size to the large Ruhr producers. No Italian firm was that big, but more than half the national production was under the control of Finsider, the government-owned holding company. The main area in which Ruhr concentration might spur additional concentration was in France, where sensitivity to what went on in the Ruhr was also greatest and was increased by the return of the Saar and its several large producers to German control.

There had been some movement toward concentration in the French steel industry after the war. The Schneider and Wendel interests had regrouped themselves for more centralized control. A substantial merger had produced the Sidelor combine. A number of companies had participated in forming the two companies operating the wide-strip mills, Sollac and Usinor. The combination of three Lorraine steelworks to form Lorraine-Escaut was one of the first mergers approved by the High Authority. In explaining the merger that produced Sidelor, the Conseil d'Administration of the Marine et Homécourt company showed the influence of the coming common market. While it had always believed that the reduction of costs depended on specialization and "increasing the power of the units of production. . . . The need for these measures now appears more obvious than ever since it is not only a matter of

[31] "Le Charbon en France," *Bulletin d'Information Économique* (Banque Nationale pour le Commerce et l'Industrie), Dec. 1957, p. 10.

maintaining the sale of our products in foreign markets but even more of preparing for competition on our own territory with foreign producers." [32]

The anonymous XXX, cited above, who sounds the note of a traditional patriotism of steel and nation coping with new problems, urges additional concentration as the French response to reconcentration in the Ruhr. Some government help, mainly along fiscal lines, might prove necessary, he suggests. The main opportunities may lie in the absorption of small firms by the larger ones, for among the big firms there is already a rather high degree of concentration. About half of France's steel is produced by four companies. The four biggest German firms produce about 40 per cent of that country's steel. While none of the biggest French firms is as large as the largest German producers, and while there are more big German companies, these four (Usinor, de Wendel, Sidelor and Lorraine-Escaut) are regularly among the top 12 to 15 producers in the Community. Whatever the future may bring, there is not, therefore, an overwhelming German predominance by any standard and the concern in France (like that about investment, p. 348) is more about the future than about the present.

The Results of Concentration

In view of everything that has been said it is somewhat surprising that there is no clear evidence of any marked increase in concentration of Community steel production over the transitional period.[33] In 1952 and in 1956, 11

[32] Quoted by Albert Wehrer, "Les Fusions et Concentrations d'Enterprises dans les Pays de la C.E.C.A.," reprinted in *Problèmes Économiques*, Sept. 11, 1956, p. 4.

[33] There are no simple indicators that are altogether satisfactory. Production of crude steel is only a very rough measure. The definition of a firm is also a more complex matter than might appear from simple listings, and sources appear to differ (without always explaining) in their practices of grouping subsidiaries with mother-companies. There is also the complication of company connections that fall short of control. Partly for these reasons the High Authority has refrained from publishing systematic company data. *JO*, Dec. 16, 1957, pp. 611-612. Therefore this section gives only a rough approximation of developments. Its statistics should be treated with reserve, since the sources probably vary in their methods of computing them. See Critical Bibliography.

companies produced 40 per cent of the Community's crude
steel. In both years the three largest firms produced 14 per
cent. The figures for 1957 appear to be similar. Of course,
the firms have grown larger. In 1952 only three firms produced more than 1.5 million tons of steel while in 1955 and
1956 there were 13, and in 1957 there were 15. In 1952 no
firms produced more than 2 million tons while in 1954
there were two, by 1955 three, and by 1956 six. Over 60
per cent of Community steel was produced by companies
turning out more than a million tons apiece in 1956 while
in 1952 firms of that size produced only 40 per cent. In
1957 over half the Community's steel came from the 15
companies producing more than 1.5 million tons each.

The largest Community producer in all of these years
has been ARBED, followed by the Dortmund-Hörder
Union. The order of the others has shifted somewhat from
year to year but between 1954 and 1957 Cockerill-Ougrée,
Phoenix-Rheinrohr, Usinor, Sidelor (with its Luxembourg
affiliate), Krupp, Klöckner, Lorraine-Escaut, Thyssen,
Hoesch, Mannesmann, and, usually, de Wendel have been
among the first 10 or 12 producers. None of these firms
has produced much more than 5 per cent of the Community's output in any one year, and most of them have
ranged around 3 per cent.

There is really a somewhat higher degree of concentration, however. The figures cited so far do not take full account of subsidiaries and virtually ignore less direct
connections through holding companies. Lacking full information, I cannot rectify this with any precision, but a
very rough approximation on the basis of 1955 figures suggests that the major concentrations in the Community
might be somewhat as follows:

	Per cent of Community Output
Belgian holding companies	over 8
Hoogovens & Dortmund-Hörder Union	over 6
Sidelor and connections	4-5
Finsider	over 5
ARBED	about 5

The Germans are missing from this list. They would soon appear if we took account of the proposed Thyssen merger and the combination of Krupp and the Bochumer Verein. If Thyssen and Phoenix-Rheinrohr merged, they would probably be the biggest steel producer in the Community with something like 8 or 9 per cent of the output. The interconnections of the French, Belgian, and Luxembourg steel companies are not easy to ascertain, nor is there any good way to take account of minority participation. It is quite possible that the figures suggested above are too low for these groups, and perhaps other French groups would rise to near the 4 or 5 per cent level. All this suggests that if the Thyssen and Krupp mergers are included, something like half the Community's steel production might be in the hands of about seven groups of five or six nationalities. How fully the ownership in each of these cases is translated into effective centralized control is still another matter. The Italian government, for instance, is generally supposed to permit considerable independence to the firms it owns. At the other end, one would assume that the German firms, ARBED, and the Hoogovens complex are effectively consolidated. In the Belgian group, a fairly complicated holding-company structure stands between several of the steel firms. The French case is also somewhat problematical. Allowing for these uncertainties, it appears that by the end of the transition period German firms were not outstanding in the Community for their size or the extent of their control. There were more large German firms, to be sure, but Germany is also the largest steel-producing country.[34]

A more marked contrast between Germany and the rest of the Community, and especially France, is in the concentration of production in large plants. In 1955 the three largest German steel firms produced 6.8 million tons of

---

[34] Another very rough calculation suggests that in 1954-57 the five largest German firms produced about one-fifth of the Community's steel, or a little less, while the five largest non-German firms produced something more than one-fifth. The share of the German firms probably increased somewhat over the period.

steel in six plants, four of them highly integrated.[35] In France the four largest firms produced a total of 6.6 million tons in 21 plants, of which 12 were highly integrated. Output per producing unit was substantially higher in Germany than in France and, usually, than in the Community as a whole.[36]

These comparisons are relevant to the High Authority's general problem mostly in showing that neither the size of firms nor the degree of concentrated control is markedly greater in Germany than in the Community as a whole. Since the High Authority cannot formally make national distinctions, the figures more germane to its decisions are those cited above about the degree of concentration in Community steel production as a whole. The High Authority's feeling that it need not worry much about concentrations is surely based on the fact that through 1957 no company produced much more than 5 per cent of the Community's steel. In 1955 there were 17 firms that produced at least 2 per cent of the total, indicating a fairly wide dispersion. If one counts the broader concentrations through affiliates and holding companies, and if the Krupp and Thyssen mergers are assumed to exist, there would still be only a few units with as much as 10 per cent of Community production, and several others in the range between 5 and 10 per cent. This is a fairly modest degree of concentration by the standards of other countries. In England five firms each produce nearly 10 per cent of the total. In the United States, U. S. Steel usually produces something

[35] For present purposes "highly integrated" means that a plant has at least three of the four major kinds of installations: cokeries, blast furnaces, steel furnaces, rolling mills. All the German and French plants are reported as getting at least some of their coal and iron from their own mines. The figures are from a study prepared by Dr. G. Gori: Associazione Industrie Siderurgiche Italiane (Assider), *Lineamenti Strutturali della Siderurgia Italiana*, Jl. 1956, p. 122 (mimeographed) (hereafter cited as *Lineamenti*).

[36] Figures based on part of the years 1954 and 1955 show German output per blast furnace, open-hearth furnace, and convertor to be above the Community average and substantially greater than French output. In no case, however, is German output per unit the highest in the Community and in electric furnaces it is well below the average and even farther below France. Same, p. 55.

like 30 per cent of the country's steel, the top three companies something over half, and eight companies together over 80 per cent. There is no reason to use the United States as a model; the Community would obviously have difficulty if it came anywhere near that degree of concentration. The interesting question is how far the process of concentration can go in the Community without causing either political or economic difficulties.

Very likely big firms will grow more important as time passes (not necessarily by mergers only; firms may grow by higher rates of investment than the average).[37] Eventually the High Authority may face concentrations of power that are troublesome to deal with. The smaller number of centers of major power may also make it harder to check cartel-like activity. Before that point is reached the High Authority will have to elaborate its present, limited criteria for passing on concentrations, if only because the questions will present themselves in more complicated forms (see p. 370). The High Authority must also try somehow to mediate among the national rivalries that are supposed to be irrelevant to its task.

Another serious question remains. By looking at the common market as a whole it is possible to take a rather comforting view of the amount of steel production controlled by one firm. But this is a questionable criterion. We may assume that the officials in Luxembourg are looking closely at the positions that companies have in more limited markets for certain kinds of steel or particular products. But it is much more difficult for them, in terms of their mandate and the outlook they aim to cultivate, to deal with the question whether the share of total Community production is really the proper criterion. Transport costs alone tend to divide the Community into regional markets. The numerous factors of other sorts that impair the development of a

[37] The High Authority can act against "public or private enterprises . . . which have or acquire . . . a dominant position which protects them from effective competition . . ." even if no merger is involved. If the High Authority's recommendations are not accepted it can fix prices or conditions of sale for the enterprise or require it to fulfill a specific production or delivery program (Art. 66, para. 7).

single market add to the likelihood that there is a considerable element of illusion in the rather simple view that has been acceptable during the transitional period (and that has been supported by some of the calculations in this chapter). In the national markets, the degree of concentration is much higher.[38] This is not merely a matter of recognizing that in steel and coal there will always be some kind of imperfect competition, but of adding the complication that two frames of reference are relevant and that the relative importance to be given to each is not only unclear at any given moment, but may—indeed should—change as time passes. This creates a very "grey area" of Community policy and uncertainty about the kind of economy that is likely to result.

CARTELS

While the High Authority found it easy to deal with concentrations during the transitional period, cartels gave it trouble. Instead of passing on changes proposed by industrialists, the High Authority had to take the initiative to bring about changes that industry did not want to make. The whole burden of acting was shifted. Moreover, while no concentration affected a very large share of Community production, the great bulk of the coal trade was dominated by a few sales organizations that were strongly entrenched, widely supported, and plainly incompatible with the Treaty's principles of competition.

When the common market for coal was opened, the High Authority observed that it was its "duty . . . to deal immediately with agreements and organizations which were in existence. . . ." But, it noted, "For the most part, such agreements and organizations have a very compre-

---

[38] Ten firms produce two-thirds of Germany's steel, four produce more than half France's, one produces a quarter of Italy's (and two nearly 40 per cent). These figures cannot be interpreted the way they would be in old-fashioned national markets because the paraphernalia of government measures to close off the market is absent. There is also a limit set by potential outside competition from other Community producers. But up to some point the degree of concentration on national lines has significance.

hensive task to perform. They have *inter alia* to safeguard supplies to consumers and to make an allocation of those products of which there has been a serious shortage during the post-war period." In order "not to jeopardize the regular flow of supplies to the market," the High Authority considered "that it should not prohibit existing agreements and organizations, where such prohibition is called for, until the work in connection with supplies [has] . . . been taken over either by new organizations conforming to the spirit and letter of the Treaty, or by already existing organizations whose structure will have undergone the necessary changes." [39]

Beginning in July 1953 the High Authority required cartels to apply for authorizations. About 60 applications were received by the beginning of 1954 and a total of 80 by the spring of 1958. Another 32 cases were investigated by the High Authority on its own initiative. More than one-third of these 112 cases proved not to fall under the Treaty rule. In several cases the agreements were dissolved without a ruling by the High Authority.[40] Some 50 cases were still on the High Authority's books in the spring of 1958. This did not necessarily mean that the papers were gathering dust. The High Authority might leave the case open as a means of holding a watching brief, with the aim of keeping the cartel activities within bounds. Over the whole period the High Authority ruled that three cartels, all concerned with scrap, violated the Treaty. It authorized 15 arrangements.[41]

Three of the 15 authorizations concerned steel marketing arrangements, principally in Belgium. Two involved co-operation among German steel firms in the importation of American coal. Fiat was allowed to contract for a fixed proportion of the hot-rolled sheets and wide strip produced by the Cornigliano plant at Genoa. This reduced the cost of the material to Fiat and enabled Cornigliano to expand

[39] HA, *Report*, Apr. 1953, pp. 96, 97.
[40] Same, Apr. 1957, p. 159.
[41] Same, Apr. 1958, v. 2, pp. 85-86. The *Report* of Apr. 1957, p. 159, gives somewhat conflicting figures.

production with an assured market; half or more of Cornigliano's output of these two products was still available for sale to others. A French firm was permitted to make another its exclusive supplier of special steels, the assured market justifying the other's expansion of capacity. The remaining eight cartel authorizations were all concerned with the organization of the coal trade, the most important part of the High Authority's cartel work.

The Ruhr Sales Organization

From 1893 on, most of the coal and coke of the Ruhr was sold through a single organization, the Rheinisch-Westfälische Kohlensyndikat (RWKS). After the First World War, this private cartel was strengthened by legal support and subjected to some degree of public control. Under the occupation following the Nazi defeat the RWKS was dissolved but soon replaced by the Deutscher Kohlen-Verkauf (DKV), through which the Allied authorities sold German coal. As part of the decartelization process, the occupying powers and the Germans negotiated a substitute for the DKV that was intended (by the Allies) to be less monopolistic. Six sales organizations were set up to which individual mining companies belonged. A central organization, Gemeinschaftsorganisation Ruhrkohle (Georg), was given certain powers judged necessary to carry on efficient marketing. The structural difference between this arrangement and the earlier coal sales organization remained structural. The activities of the six sales organizations were substantially controlled by Georg. There were some technical factors that fostered this development but mostly it resulted because this is the way Germans believe coal should be marketed. "Georg is a good substitute for the DKV," I was told in the Ruhr. The meaning of that was pretty clear.

Georg did not just sell coal. When demand fell below production, it allocated orders so that the burden of adjustment did not fall on only a few mines. This "stabilization of employment" was looked on as one of its chief functions and helped secure the wholehearted support of the unions. Georg was also at the center of an equalization scheme that compensated higher-cost mines at the expense of the more efficient ones. This helped them keep operating when demand was low, thus avoiding unemployment, the cost of closing the unremunerative mines, and the possible loss of their unmined coal through flooding or other damage. Georg also had to allocate orders, when demand was high, this time among the customers. In addition it had an important technical function with commercial consequences. Mines produce several sizes of coal ranging from almost dust to quite large pieces; they may also produce different grades or types of coal that are to a considerable extent interchangeable but that can most efficiently be used for certain purposes. Georg pooled these supplies, making it easier for buyers to place orders for just what they wanted and for the Ruhr to dispose of the poorer grades (if necessary by tie-in arrangements). Georg also had a hand in arrangements for the transportation of coal and sometimes required buyers to use carriers owned by the mines, principally Rhine barges. Other Georg functions included standardization of grades and qualities, research in more efficient coal use, and pooling of information about technical developments. But its key activities were centralized selling and the spreading of orders throughout the German industry to maintain some kind of stability in employment.

There could be little doubt that its control over the marketing of Ruhr coal—about half the Community's output—gave Georg the power "to fix or determine prices" (if the High Authority did not) and "to allocate markets, products, customers or sources of supply." Therefore it violated the Treaty. Some of its other functions were certainly compatible with the Treaty and were held by the Germans to be of great importance. In fact, the Germans liked Georg very well as it was and did not want to see any change. This was the way the Germans had marketed coal for decades; you would look far to find a single voice of importance in Germany calling for a change. Owners, managers, union leaders, Socialists, politicians could agree on this. In their eyes, the uncertainties of the common market enhanced the importance of Georg, making its stabilization functions more important than ever. The one common chord in German discussion of the Schuman Plan was the need to preserve centralized marketing arrangements for coal. William N. Parker catches the spirit very well: "A German, facing the uncertainties and dangers of free competition and a free market in the nation's only important natural resource, experiences a deep and acute sense of panic. The very national existence seems to him to depend upon careful, planned, 'scientific' exploitation of both the coal deposits and the coal consumers." [42]

The German allegiance to Georg was not only an obstacle to action by the High Authority; it also limited the results that could be expected from any action. If there was to be a substitute for Georg that did not violate the Treaty, it would have to be a substitute that the Germans would operate. The High Authority decided to move slowly. Later, Franz Etzel, vice chairman of the High Authority who was a key man in the Georg negotiations, described the alternatives.

The High Authority could have made its task easy. It could simply have decided in a wholly negative manner:

. . . What exists is incompatible with the Treaty. A period of time is fixed by virtue of paragraph 12 of the Convention concerning transitional arrangements. At the expiration of that period, the existing organization will be illegal and must be dissolved.

Such a procedure would not have permitted the interested parties—that is, the collieries, the users, the employees, and also the High Authority—to find out to what extent tasks not contrary to the Treaty that the existing central organization carries out are necessary and useful and could be carried on in the future.

The High Authority could equally follow another route. This route was more difficult. It required more work and demanded more patience from you [the Assembly] and from us. But it promised positive results. The High Authority

---

[42] "The Schuman Plan—A Preliminary Prediction," *International Organization*, Aug. 1952, p. 386.

could, in effect, itself sketch a framework within which the mining enterprises could organize their sales without contravening the Treaty.

The High Authority has followed this route. . . .[43]

The way was to be long but the High Authority was not quick to embark on it. Not the least of the reasons for circumspection was the fact that the Georg case was bound to be a test of strength for the High Authority and an indication of the direction in which it and the Community were going. But the men in Luxembourg were not altogether free to choose their own time. The Assembly's common market committee pressed for action. The Dutch government delivered an ultimatum in March 1954: if the High Authority did not act in two months, the Hague would appeal to the Court.[44] Some German and Dutch Socialists called for the transformation of the coal sales organizations into public corporations, with worker and consumer representation on the board and some kind of supranational supervision. No one argued that classical competition of the textbook type could be introduced in the coal business; "ordered competition" was the aim that most professed, a concept which, as Etzel remarked, was just as problematical as that of "perfect competition." More than legal questions were involved. The common market committee said in its report, "The psychological aspect of the question is not negligible. A part of public opinion judges that the High Authority has not succeeded in imposing its will on the cartels." [45]

In his opening speech to the Assembly in May 1954, Monnet said flatly that Georg in its existing form could not be authorized. Two days later the High Authority informed Georg of this in writing and proposed negotiations. The High Authority invited the German government and representatives of workers and consumers to the ex-

---

[43] CA, *Débats*, May 11, 1955, p. 336.

[44] In January the High Authority had already promised to take some action by May. CA, Commission du Marché Commun, *Rapport . . . par M. H. A. Korthals, Rapporteur*, doc. 13 (1953-54), p. 22.

[45] Same, p. 24.

change of views. To avoid "social and economic inconvenience" in Germany, it would be necessary to move carefully, said Etzel.[46]

By November 1954 the views of both sides had been fully set out in the negotiations. "In the opinion of the representatives of GEORG, any competition among Ruhr producers would be detrimental to the distribution of the products and the stability of employment." [47] Competition among the six selling agencies would not be feasible; it would soon become competition among all 55 collieries. Some mines would be hurt worse than others, "resulting in intolerable social tensions." Mines would close "which are absolutely essential for future supplies. . . ."

The High Authority thought the German spokesmen were unduly alarmed. It agreed that lower prices were unlikely to increase sales but thought that price fluctuations had a role to play in regulating the sales of different grades and types. The only way a cartel could introduce stability when demand fell and buyers did not want the poorest grades was "by reallocating orders, and thereby depriving the consumer of the free choice of supplier guaranteed him by the Treaty." Other coal fields were meeting this problem by compensation arrangements within the field. "There could be no question of affording a bigger coalfield a greater measure of protection, through the removal of competition, than that enjoyed by producers in the smaller coalfields competing with it." The High Authority accepted the need for the kind of stabilization activities that Georg carried out. It was trying to devise a long-run policy on coal into which the Ruhr sales arrangements would fit, and this was slow work.

    [46] CA, *Débats*, May 13, 1954, p. 193. The Dutch withdrew their notice of intention to go to court. The Assembly passed a resolution urging action on cartels.
    [47] HA, *Report*, Nov. 1954, p. 99. Subsequent quotations from p. 100. Additional points about the High Authority's position come from a working paper it submitted to the common market committee. CA, Commission du Marché Commun, *Rapport . . . sur la question des cartels sous l'angle des problèmes de la concurrence et des ventes sur le marché charbonnier par M. H. A. Korthals, Rapporteur*, doc. 2 (1954-55), Nov. 1954, Annexe.

Negotiations continued over the winter and spring. When the Assembly met in May, Etzel announced that the High Authority had decided on the outline of an acceptable reorganization of Georg. It was now up to the Germans to make detailed proposals and ask for authorization under the Treaty. The High Authority proposed to keep the six sales agencies that existed, but to make them really independent of Georg. They would sell most Ruhr coal. Some, however, would still be sold through a central agency, principally to large consumers who preferred this arrangement. Functions that did not violate the Treaty would also be carried on in common. An advisory committee with outsiders on it would meet with Ruhr producers. The High Authority would help watch over the whole.[48]

The Assembly responded to this announcement with much discussion and activity. The subject was one that had excited great interest and there was a feeling that the Assembly had played a part in getting the High Authority to act. There was not much new to be said on the issue. It was hard to give more than an initial reaction to the High Authority's plan and to urge it to get on with the job.[49] Etzel warned that the remaining steps would not be altogether easy. But, he said, "I specifically declare that I am in agreement with all my colleagues—I say *all* my colleagues—in saying that the High Authority is resolved to proceed rapidly to the modification of the organizations, not only in the Ruhr basin, but also in France, in Belgium,

[48] CA, *Débats*, May 11, 1955, pp. 336-340. Etzel set out the plan in a good bit of detail that is omitted here.

[49] There were many questions, special committee meetings, sessions with the High Authority, meetings of the political groups, etc. One senses even from the written record a kind of parliamentary activity usually lacking in Assembly business; there was a feeling that the Assembly had something to bite into. The appearance was largely deceptive. The Assembly had no direct role to play. The High Authority had already formed its plan and communicated it to Georg; it was not asking the Assembly to advise it whether this was wise. At most, the Assembly's attitude might ultimately, and perhaps indirectly, influence the Ruhr or the German government by creating support for the High Authority. Nevertheless, the episode was quite clearly stimulating to many members of the Assembly.

and in southern Germany, in a fashion that will make it possible to give to the Assembly at its next session important and decisive communications." [50]

By the fall of 1955 matters were almost settled. It looked as if Georg had bargained hard between June and October. The market for coal was expanding rapidly. This reduced the risk of competition to the producers. It may have given the High Authority concern about stability and the effects of reorganizing distribution. The High Authority had a useful bargaining counter in its power to keep the ceiling on Ruhr prices. But if the price was to be freed, Bonn and Luxembourg were concerned with how high it would go. This in turn became a bargaining counter for Georg; stronger sales organizations could give firmer assurances on price than weak ones.

The main difference between the plans of June and November was that instead of six sales agencies there were to be three, each absorbing two of the existing ones. This looked like a weakening of the High Authority's position, but Etzel claimed it was an improvement. "With a larger number of less important sales organizations, the task and influence of the proposed coordinating body would be greater than with a smaller number of larger units. . . . These three autonomous sales organizations can by themselves, each in its own domain, largely regulate the balance of employment and the division of orders among types of coal necessary in a situation of excess, as well as equalizing supplies in a situation of shortage. In other words, three more important autonomous sales organizations could each develop for itself greater independence and more autonomy than six smaller sales organizations." [51]

The central organization—a joint bureau run by the three sales organizations—could accept orders for coal from those who wished to buy more than 50,000 tons a year. It would pass these orders on to the three sales organizations to be filled at their prices and conditions of sale. Each sales organization would be balancing orders and employment

[50] CA, *Débats*, Je. 23, 1955, p. 573.
[51] CA, *Débats*, Nov. 23, 1955, pp. 26-27.

among the 15 or so collieries belonging to it; the joint
bureau would balance them among the three sales organizations when that was necessary. Arrangements for compensations throughout the Ruhr would be subject to High
Authority scrutiny, as would be the other functions conducted by the joint organization for the whole area. Exports to third countries were to be handled by a separate
joint company.[52]

Georg had had a well-organized system of sales agents
covering a number of countries. The new arrangement
required three separate sets of agents and made elaborate
rules about the terms on which wholesalers could have
access to the three sales organizations. In the course of the
first year's operation of the new scheme a number of difficulties arose, and in July 1957 the rules were again changed
to make access easier. The trouble, it appeared, stemmed
partly from the difficulties of devising and applying rules
where there had been none before, and partly from the
reluctance of both the sales organizations and the recognized Ruhr dealers to accept increased competition.

The advisory committee mentioned by Etzel in May
was retained in the November plan. Made up originally
of 27 members, it was subsequently enlarged to 36, 12 from
the management of Ruhr collieries, 12 from the unions
representing the workers in these mines, and 12 from
dealers and consumers throughout the Community.[53] Representatives of the High Authority and the German government sit with this body. It has no powers of control but
meets at least three times a year to hear from the joint

---

[52] In addition to the joint sales organization and the corporation for
exports to third countries, other bodies were set up to handle numerous
functions that the three sales agencies would carry on jointly. Pooling of
transportation costs between all mines and the basing point at Duisburg-
Ruhrort was permitted. However, buyers were to be free to take delivery f.o.b. Ruhrort if they wished, thus eliminating the German-owned
shipping companies (a point of particular interest to the Dutch).

[53] As first set up on its enlarged basis, the committee had as its con-
sumer-dealer representation seven Germans and one member from each
of the other countries in the Community. Industry, wholesalers, the
railroads, gas and electrical works were represented on the German
side and foreign trade, steel, electricity, and cokeries among the foreigners. CA, *Annuaire-Manuel, 1957*, p. 104.

organization about the measures taken in common in the Ruhr and to discuss their repercussions. Obviously the main aim of this device is ventilation. Outsiders are to get a look at the way Ruhr sales are conducted; the Ruhr bodies have to be prepared to explain themselves in terms that have some bearing on the general interest. While the committee is heavily weighted with Germans, the foreign minority has a chance to inspect Ruhr practices more closely, and, if it is not satisfied, has access to both the public and the High Authority which retains considerable reserve power, at least on paper, over the organization and practices of Ruhr coal sales.[54]

The new arrangements were put into effect on April 1, 1956.[55] Some of the High Authority's critics in the Assembly complained that nothing was really changed. In the Ruhr doubt was expressed whether the new agencies were large enough to carry on stabilization efficiently. The validity of the legal case against Georg was admitted but this was seen as a defect in the Treaty.[56] To a considerable degree, however, the controversy over Ruhr sales quieted down. This was probably due less to confidence in the new arrangements than to an acceptance of the fact that the alternatives were limited and to growing realization that the Community's coal problem is not likely to yield to formulas but will require constant management and the trying out of new methods.

[54] The Armengaud Report, cited, pp. 38-39, indicates that at an early stage the Germans themselves proposed foreign representation on the board of Georg as an alternative to decartelization. The French authors seem favorable to this idea, because "in Germany as in the other producing countries of Europe commercial competition in coal must be limited and must give way to a rational organization of distribution which recognizes costs, facilitates supplying the consumer, assures the use of poorer quality products to make the most of them."

[55] JO, March 13, 1956. Many details have been omitted from this account.

[56] Speeches by Nederhorst, Kapteijn, and Korthals, in CA, Débats, Nov. 23, 1955, pp. 48-58, 60-63. R. Hellmann, "Gemeinschaftsorganisation Ruhrkohle wird umgebaut," Der Volkswirt, Nov. 5, 1955, pp. 16, 17. The sales organizations challenged the rules about wholesalers in the Court.

There are two bases for judging the new arrangement. One can ask if it will stimulate competition. This seems very unlikely. If the old arrangement had had an important element of compulsion, and there were reasons to suppose that some of the mining companies in the Ruhr were anxious to break out of the mold and fend for themselves on the market, then one might say that the new structure, policed by the High Authority, would give them a good chance to do so. But there is no reason to believe this. To promote competition one would have to find a way to make the coal companies act more competitively than they want to. The chances of that are poor; Georg with six selling organizations produced no more competition than the monolithic DKV. "Reading the High Authority's proposal," said a Dutch Socialist, "I sometimes had the feeling that they imagined that the world was made up entirely of *braves gens*, of people animated by an ardent desire for free competition. But this is not the case. The producers who are supposed to compete in the sales organizations are, at the bottom of their hearts, opponents of competition and defenders of the system of price agreements." [57] A prolonged period of slack demand for coal might stimulate some competition if highly productive mines had to curtail sales to permit high-cost mines to go on producing. But low demand is at least as likely to strengthen allegiance to joint sales and price-fixing arrangements. The coal recession of 1958-59 set in motion the "stabilizing" elements of the Ruhr sales arrangements and showed no signs of weakening Georg. Instead, at the beginning of 1959 the High Authority expressed concern about cartel practices on the old pattern and suggested that a closer supervision of the Ruhr might be necessary.

The other basis for judging the new arrangements for

[57] Nederhorst, in CA, *Débats*, May 13, 1955, pp. 438-439. One possibility of stimulating competition is through the coal dealers. While it is hard to judge how much leverage this offers without a closer study than I have been able to make, a superficial judgment is that while loosening of the structure of distribution is useful it cannot greatly affect the basic situation.

Ruhr coal sales is that of "countervailing power," to use J. K. Galbraith's language. Past worry about the Ruhr often rested less on specific grievances than on the feeling that the Ruhr was too strong. Half the Community's coal production, three-fifths of its coke production, 40 per cent of its coal trade, 70 per cent of its coke trade, all were in the Ruhr and all monopolized. Georg, and DKV and RWKS before it, were the Ruhr incarnate to the rest of the Community. These were the greatest concentrations of power in Europe's coal economy, and everyone else was to some extent dependent on them. The Treaty's price rules, the new limits on joint action, the advisory committee, and above all the powers the High Authority holds in reserve, including the power to fix prices, all help to counterbalance the mass of the Ruhr. How effective they will be remains to be seen. They are not the strongest kinds of counterbalancing power; their strength depends to some extent on the level of demand. But they are mitigating factors. At a minimum they will make it more inconvenient for the Ruhr collieries to act as a unit in quite the old way. They may put some brake on the mobilization of Ruhr power, but they are not likely to be decisive by themselves.

The promotion of competition in the Ruhr was probably not the High Authority's main aim in the Georg decision. It probably aimed at competition at the outset, but as time passed, it gave more and more weight to two factors that put very severe limits on the possibilities of creating competition in coal. One was the "coal ideology," so prevalent in the Community, that stresses stability, order, not "wasting" coal even if it is costly to dig, and the avoidance of dislocation to employment and to coal mining localities. The other was the need for a Community coal policy that would involve extensive management of the coal economies of the six countries. When negotiations about Georg were well advanced, René Mayer told the Assembly, "It is not a matter of pretending that there will not be common sales organizations. . . . There are necessities of distribution, of social policy and of employment that require an organization of sales in common in the Rhine-Westphalian complex." [58] While the difficulty of reorganizing Georg clearly contributed to this shift of emphasis, the main factors bringing it about were broader and deeper elements that were part of a general re-evaluation of the problems and possibilities of the Community coal economy.

The demand for coal also played its part in shaping the High Authority's views and the terms of the Ruhr reorganization. When the Georg negotiations began, the Community was nearly able to meet its own coal needs. By the time they ended, imports from the United States were large and there was talk of a coal shortage in the Community. For many reasons the High Authority was reluctant to reach for the powers of allocation that the Treaty gave it if a shortage was formally recognized. Between May and November 1955 a new feature was introduced into the Georg arrangements. An in-between situation was recognized, "in which there is still no serious shortage but an excess of demand in relation to the possibilities of delivery." [59] When these circumstances existed the High Authority was prepared to see the Ruhr sales organizations agree on common terms for the equal supply of all customers, or special measures to ensure supplies to customers of special social importance, such as households, public utilities, transportation. All such measures would be subject to the veto of the High Authority, but they would also mean that the joint organization would gain in power and that the possibility of competition among the three sales organizations would become even dimmer.

As if to emphasize the difference between creating competition in the Ruhr and regulating Ruhr sales, one of the main items discussed in the advisory committee for the first two coal years of the new regime (April 1956 to April 1958) was the Ruhr's "delivery plan" for allocating coal to its customers. The High Authority, too, was involved in this, intervening at the instance of the German government to assure a somewhat greater supply for household con-

[58] CA, *Débats*, Nov. 23, 1955, pp. 65, 64. See also the working paper cited above, and later statements, for the extent to which the High Authority accepted the fundamental rationalization given for Georg.

[59] Etzel, CA, *Débats*, Nov. 23, 1955, p. 27.

sumers in Germany, presiding over negotiations that settled the amount of coal and coke to go to the French steel industry in 1956-57, helping the independent Italian cokeries to get larger supplies of coking coal than the Ruhr producers had planned to send them. As a complementary action, the High Authority also stepped in to modify the cuts Charbonnages de France proposed to make in deliveries to south Germany, which would have added to the demands on the Ruhr.

To simplify matters and reduce the danger of being charged with discrimination, the Ruhr sales organizations fell back on formulas related to past performance. In the winter of 1956-57, for instance, most markets were getting 90 per cent of the coal they had received in 1953-55, but German households received 103 per cent to allow for population growth and new houses. This course was endorsed by the advisory committee and the High Authority. With the approval of the Council of Ministers the High Authority urged other coal basins in the Community to follow the Ruhr's example and work out delivery plans. They did so, but the results were less clear-cut. The High Authority ascribed this to various special circumstances and to the lack of flexibility resulting from long-term contracts. German observers, on the other hand, criticized the programs of the other basins for being less firm than that of the Ruhr and said that the French in particular wanted to keep a free hand to supply their domestic markets. They suggested that the difference stemmed from the fact that the High Authority did not have the influence on other basins that it had on the Ruhr, thanks to the Georg decision.[60]

Thus the new regime for the Ruhr functioned quite differently, at least in its initial stages, from the way many people expected. The emphasis was not on its competitive potential, but on its ability to direct trade, not on its separate sales organizations, but on the central agency that could allocate all of the coal supply. The important differ-

[60] "Entspannung im Kommenden Kohlenjahr?" *Der Volkswirt*, Mar. 23, 1957, pp. 557-558.

ence from times past lay in the direct outside influence on what the Ruhr did, exercised in these cases by the High Authority, possibly abetted by the advisory committee. The German government, too, had an influence, which was exercised first in the direction of assuring domestic supplies of coal at reasonable prices and second, probably, in behalf of the broad principles the High Authority was asserting.[61]

Captive Mines

Though the sales organizations have been the focus of so much activity, there is a further problem about the sale of Ruhr coal. The mines themselves use a certain amount of coal to run their own installations, and for the traditional payment in kind to miners, the *Deputat*. They also sell directly to buyers in their vicinity, the *Landabsatz*. More important is the delivery of coal to the steel, gas, electrical, chemical, and other companies that own coal mines. Nearly three-quarters of the Ruhr's coal is produced in captive mines.[62] The owners have first claim on this coal, the *Werkselbstverbrauchsrecht*. They do not consume all that their mines produce, for a number of reasons; for instance, not all of the coal produced is of the sort that the owners want, some mines produce far beyond their owners' needs. Some of the owners of captive mines (notably the Stinnes company) are engaged in the coal trade; if they make full use of their *Werkselbstverbrauchsrecht* this merely alters the channels of coal supply within the Community. On the other hand, if coal consumers, such as the steelworks and railroads, take all of the output of the captive mines, this reduces the supply of coal offered for sale within the Community. Of course, if the owners of captive mines forgo

[61] In explaining its ruling that the Ruhr sales organizations were to give a month's notice on price changes instead of five days, the High Authority pointed out that the price rise in September 1957 had been concerted throughout the Ruhr instead of being decided upon separately by the three sales organizations. HA, *Report*, Apr. 1958, v. 2, pp. 89-90. This was a warning. The real reason, however, was largely to find a compromise with the German government (p. 250-251).

[62] Etzel, CA, *Débats*, Je. 27, 1957, p. 673. This includes foreign ownership.

their rights but make up their deficits by buying in the Community market, there is no diminution of demand. The use or non-use of *Werkselbstverbrauchsrecht* primarily affects the price one pays for coal and secondarily the ease of supply. To the extent that rationing within the Community, through the sales organization, provides a consumer with less than he needs, he must buy imported coal, which has usually been more expensive.[63] To reduce the impact of "autoconsumption" on the merchantable coal supply, the High Authority has urged voluntary restraint and used such pressures as it can, with some success. During the 1956-57 coal year companies owning captive mines used only 31 million tons out of the 90 million produced by their captive mines.[64] As a result something between 40 and 50 per cent of Ruhr coal and coke probably passed through the sales organizations.[65]

The tighter coal supplies become, the greater is the premium for coal-using companies to assure their own supplies. The Ruhr is not through with vertical integration.[66] Foreign firms as well have this incentive, and have, to some degree, made use of it (p. 371f.). They are especially

[63] In recession, on the other hand, more of the coal from captive mines would be thrown on the Community market, increasing the sales problems. The High Authority decision on Ruhr sales permits arrangements among the mines, subject to High Authority approval, to equalize the impact of autoconsumption on the balancing function of the different sales agencies.

[64] Etzel, CA, *Débats*, Je. 27, 1957, p. 673. How much was self-denial is not clear.

[65] *Der Volkswirt*, Mar. 23, 1957, cited, puts the figure at about 40 per cent. It estimates *Werkselbstverbrauchsrecht* plus *Landabsatz* at 48 or 49 per cent, exports to third countries at 10 per cent. Etzel's figures would suggest a higher percentage moving through the sales organizations.

[66] Even when it is not possible to acquire coal mining companies, devices may be found to assure supplies. For instance, Thyssen, Phoenix-Rheinrohr, and Dortmund-Hörder Union all worked out an arrangement with Gelsenkirchner Bergwerks, A.G. (another Vereinigte Stahlwerke successor that produced, in all its affiliates, 16 per cent of Ruhr coal in 1956) whereby they obtained the assets (but not formal ownership) of certain of its mines for a period of 20 years, solely in order to benefit from *Werkselbstverbrauchsrecht*. They had previously benefited from special contracts having the same effect, which had been approved by the occupying powers and accepted by the High Authority, which had to pass on the new arrangements.

attracted by the Ruhr but, if supply difficulties persist, they may seek to assure domestic supplies in some form, wherever coal of suitable quality exists.[67] (Or they may turn, as some have, to American sources, hoping to hold down costs by long-term contracts.)

Here again a coal supply problem on the one hand affects the meaning of domestic arrangements within the Community and on the other hand is linked to the long-run problem of coal imports. In both directions it works against competition in Community coal.

Other Coal Cartels

There were coal cartels outside the Ruhr as well, but the High Authority could not hope to deal effectively with them until Georg was reformed. How could anyone argue that what was done in the smaller basins was offensive so long as Georg was permitted to exist? Tacitly, the High Authority accepted this and, while working on the other cases, did not try to force any issues until it had settled with Georg.[68]

Almost at the outset of its cartel work the High Authority received complaints about the Oberrheinische Kohlenunion of Mannheim (OKU). This was a cartel through which the coal producers of the Ruhr, Aachen, the Saar, and Lorraine controlled their sales in southern Germany. In July 1953 the High Authority sent off a peremptory order calling on OKU to stop certain practices within two weeks. In 1955 the High Authority informed OKU that it was in violation of the Treaty. Only in July 1957 was a satisfactory agreement concluded. Then the High Authority authorized a reformed OKU, now supposedly a voluntary association of the coal dealers in southern Germany with no producers participating (though those

[67] According to Etzel, CA, *Débats*, Je. 27, 1957, p. 673, less than one-fifteenth of the Belgian coal was subject to autoconsumption and none of the Dutch coal. In France the mines are nationalized so the problem does not exist in the same form, though it may in fact be present in a different guise (for instance in relation to public utilities and the railroads).

[68] The Netherlands Rijkskolenbureau was voluntarily dissolved at an earlier date.

of Lorraine and the Saar temporarily continued membership). The new organization was permitted to buy coal
for all its members, arrange transportation, stocking, and
terms of sale. Large consumers, who were entitled to buy
directly from the sales organization in the coal basins, were
not permitted to buy through OKU, but could arrange
their transportation and some other services through it.

Cobechar, the Comptoir Belge des Charbons, was a kind
of small-scale Belgian equivalent of Georg. It marketed
half or less of the Belgian output and dealt only with large
consumers. However, the prices and terms set by Cobechar
were generally applied throughout the industry. Negotiations in 1955 and 1956 led to some change in the organization of Cobechar and its acceptance of a number of rules to
make its practices conform to the Treaty. There seem to
have been no major difficulties; Cobechar was willing to
accept conditions similar to those of the Ruhr sales organizations; the High Authority was not fearful that the
amount of coal sold through Cobechar would give the
organization too much influence on the market (it came
to about 7 per cent of Community production in 1956).
The Belgians appear to have looked on Cobechar largely
in commercial terms. It was the High Authority that stipulated that "the sale in common should serve to balance
employment and supply." [69] In short, Cobechar was to take
on the functions that had been treated as the justification
for preserving common selling arrangements in Germany.

Next to Georg, the High Authority's most difficult problem in the coal trade concerned the Association Technique
de l'Importation Charbonnière (ATIC), which controlled
French coal imports.[70] Beginning in the spring of 1954 the
High Authority negotiated at length with the French
government to eliminate the features of ATIC that it

[69] Etzel, CA, *Débats*, Nov. 23, 1955, p. 30.
[70] Though it comprised representatives of organized French coal
dealers and of the large consumers, ATIC was formally under governmental control and wielded a series of legal powers. The High Authority
has, therefore, acted under Article 86, obligating states to do what is
necessary to accomplish the Treaty's aims and to refrain from measures
incompatible with the common market, instead of under rules applying
to private cartels.

believed conflicted with the Treaty. As time passed, the French agreed to a number of changes, weakening the power of some of the trade groups and reducing ATIC's formal powers. Differences remained, however, and in the summer of 1956—after the Georg settlement had taken effect—the High Authority ruled that some of ATIC's practices violated the Treaty. The French government challenged this in the Court but dropped its suit when it reached agreement with the High Authority that ATIC should serve only as an agent for importers, with no right of veto over their contracts. Negotiations continued, with the High Authority seeking further liberalization. Convinced that there were still too many obstacles between a would-be buyer in France and a willing seller elsewhere in the Community, the High Authority ruled in December 1957 that ATIC's role would have to be further reduced over the next two years. The French government challenged this in the Court.

The French argument for ATIC took many forms. It was frequently said that only through this agency could some of the Treaty's conditions be fulfilled. It was in these terms that the French government justified the refusal to permit French importers to buy from foreign coal dealers, because there was no means of ensuring that the Treaty rules of nondiscrimination were applied by dealers. Similarly, the buyer's free choice of means of delivery could only be assured by ATIC's supervision. "It is undoubtedly here that one comes to the heart of the matter," say two French commentators, "for this sort of policing of coal transactions—which the High Authority seems not to be willing or able to undertake itself—blocks certain practices which would exclusively serve the interests of certain foreign producers. . . ." [71] Behind this difficulty stood

[71] Armengaud Report, cited, p. 39, n. 1. Originally only very large consumers and the organizations of coal dealers, which controlled their own membership, could import. Dealers also had to buy a certain amount of French coal to get the right to buy abroad. These arrangements had been much liberalized but only large buyers could deal directly with foreign producers while ATIC served as intermediary for the others and permitted no one to buy from foreign dealers.

French concern about the bargaining power of the Ruhr sales organizations. It is in the sense of providing a united front against the Ruhr that ATIC can be defended as ensuring French buyers "equal access" to the coal supplies of the Community.[72]

The final outcome of the ATIC case may, then, be to some extent an indication of how far the French believe the Georg settlement has satisfactorily cut down the bargaining power of the Ruhr. Very likely means can be found of eliminating the practices that offend the Treaty without wholly dismantling the apparatus of supervision. (ATIC will continue to control coal imports from third countries in the old way.) A reformed ATIC might well fit into the developing managed coal economy of the Community, providing the French with some of the assurance they feel they need while operating in a way that the High Authority finds compatible with the Treaty.

In a very real sense the reorganization of the lesser coal trade organizations[73] depended on the settlement of the Ruhr arrangements, not just as a matter of negotiation but in substance. And as the significance of the Ruhr settlement seems to have been altered by later developments, so the other settlements may have to be judged in different terms from those originally contemplated.

CARTELS, CONCENTRATIONS, AND THE FUTURE

The transitional period has ended without any clear-cut demonstration of what "Europe's first antitrust law" will

---

[72] Vendroux, CA, *Débats*, Nov. 30, 1954, pp. 47-50, defends ATIC as a guarantee of Treaty principles. Gilbert Mathieu, *Le Monde*, Je. 26-Jl. 4, 1956 (weekly edition), notes that there were also political considerations; the Socialist government of the time disliked exposing the nationalized French coal industry to the private groups in the Ruhr to which, it felt, the High Authority had made concessions in the Georg settlement.

[73] There were also difficulties about Luxembourg's coal imports. A price equalization scheme subsidized household coal at the expense of industry. There was also government control over coal imports that amounted to a monopoly. The latter was eliminated in 1955; the other was judged compatible with the Treaty by the High Authority and the Court ruled against an appeal by the Luxembourg steel industry to outlaw it.

mean in practice. So far as concentrations are concerned, the major problems lie just around the corner. The first to be encountered will be political, involving national fears and the distribution of power in the Community. Then an economic (as well as political) question will be posed: "How big is too big?" Nothing that the High Authority has yet done has provided clear guidance as to how substantially larger concentrations than now exist may be treated. Not just size but the resulting character of the Community's steel oligopoly will present the High Authority with a continuing series of problems.

In cartel policy, Georg was seen as the test of the High Authority's strength. The meaning of the test has, however, been obscured, partly because the High Authority changed the direction of its pressure, and partly because the development of the Community's coal economy has been such as to put a minimum of strain on the new arrangements. The idea of increasing competition in coal sales—perhaps always a mirage—has been abandoned. Progress has been made in establishing some degree of countervailing power, largely by "opening up" the Ruhr and by providing continuing High Authority surveillance. How great this power is has not yet been demonstrated.

Because the cartel issue focused on the coal sales organizations—and to a degree because no other cartel issue was recognized as a compelling challenge during the transitional period [74]—High Authority action on other kinds of cartel questions took a rather subordinate role. Decisions on minor cartels remained minor in their import; the major question of collusive pricing in steel was shunted aside; the scrap cartels were internationalized, legitimized, and on the whole strengthened, but at the price of being put under effective High Authority control; the steel export price cartel was allowed to function relatively freely, largely because of the difficulty of asserting effective High Au-

[74] One must emphasize *recognized*. It is not easy to discern the extent of cartel-like practices. The High Authority has moved cautiously in this field and with the Georg issue squarely before it has not wanted to create additional major cartel issues if it could postpone them.

thority control, but officials in Luxembourg watched it, perhaps uneasily, to see what effect it might have inside the common market (see Chapter 17). There are other indications which might reveal to a sensitive nose one or another of the many forms of restrictive practices; for instance, the "respect" producers show for the traditional markets of others; various trading arrangements; joint subsidiaries of one sort or another;[75] the implications of industry-wide investment programs, with some government influence, and so on.

The uncertainty of the situation goes beyond the possible significance of particular issues. Public supervision of business practices is always difficult. The High Authority is trying to apply a comprehensive, pioneering, international antitrust law when it is itself pioneering in establishing its status, strength, and effectiveness. There is uncertainty about what the law means and more about how effectively it can be enforced. The subjects of this law, the industries of the Community, do not believe in its principles. For many of these people, the Schuman Plan itself is an inadequate substitute for the cartel arrangements they might have worked out among themselves. French producers made this clear at the outset (p. 90). Germans, too, usually preferred cartels on the interwar model which they regarded as more flexible because they required frequent renegotiation, sounder because they had to satisfy all parties without imposing decisions, and closer to the needs of industry because political interference was avoided.[76] Even though the industries professed full acceptance of the Schuman Plan after it was enacted, they did not thereby espouse ideas about competition that they thought were

[75] Dortmund-Hörder Union, Thyssen, and Phoenix-Rheinrohr share the ownership of Handelsunion, another former division of Vereinigte Stahlwerke, through which they market some of their steel products. It is the sort of arrangement that bears looking into.

[76] The Schuman Plan arrangements "conceal many dangers that were circumvented by the old cartels. . . . 'More use was made of the method of persuasion than of outvoting.'" Carl Horst Hahn, *Der Schuman-Plan*, 1953, p. 52. The inner quote is from a report prepared by G. Kiersch for the Rheinische-Westfälisches Institut für Wirtschaftsforschung, Essen.

unsound, unrealistic, and damaging to their interests. The evidence abounds; the essence of the attitude appears in a comment on the national cartel law that was before the Bundestag: "The organization of competition is a task that must be carried out by entrepreneurial self-administration. It must not be subjected to unnecessary 'dirigistic' influence by the government." [77]

Where there were no barriers, or the difficulties could be overcome, Community producers, or their close associates, have formed cartels: in the international tube and pipe market, in the German wire-drawing industry,[78] and in the Brussels export cartel. There is nothing surprising in these facts, but they serve as reminders of how the producers think business should be conducted—when they can reach agreement among themselves. Such matters cannot be so overt within the common market, but it remains true that what comes naturally to the heavy industrialists of Europe is not an active, aggressive competition. This does not mean that the whole of the Community's steel industry is governed by a thoroughgoing, secret cartel, or that the "Steelmakers Club"—the informal association of producers for discussion of common problems—is in reality a Sanhedrin of steel. The existence of the Community, its antitrust law, and the High Authority, are themselves brakes on too much and too formal cartelization; nor should the difficulties in working out effective cartel agreements be underestimated.

The quiescence of competition in the Community does mean that the High Authority's problems are complicated ones. It is rather hard to enforce competition. If the competitive entrepreneur should appear, the High Authority can hold open the door for him. If the buyer of coal and

[77] *Schnelldienst des Deutschen Industrieinstituts*, Sept. 4, 1956. The passage quoted is a characterization or paraphrase of a joint declaration on the proposed German cartel law made by the Deutscher Industrie— und Handelstag, the Bundesverband der deutschen Industrie, the Gesamtverband des Gross— und Aussenhandels, the Hauptgemeinschaft des Einzelhandels, and the Zentralverband des deutschen Handwerks.

[78] *Wirtschaft und Wettbewerb*, May 1957, pp. 307-308; Je. 1957, pp. 361-362.

steel should be willing to complain when he cannot get an offer from a seller who is not fully booked, or finds a suspicious similarity in the terms he is offered, then the High Authority has an opening, perhaps even a goad, to look into another phase of the Community's economy. But Community consumers have not shown themselves eager to pursue this course and the aggressive entrepreneur has found other ways to assert himself.

There is a still more fundamental problem. The arguments for orderly marketing in coal, the reasoning that opposes price-cutting in steel, are not just smoke screens (though they conceal many things). These are industries to which rather sophisticated conceptions of competition properly apply and in which it may not be very realistic to expect anything that looks like the classical, textbook model. The coal problem of the Community seems to call for a high degree of management. Even if this is not so, governments will not be willing to countenance great instability of employment in this industry (for any number of reasons) and any substantial degree of real competition is likely to produce instability. In steel, technological requirements and their financial and commercial implications make large firms necessary and virtually require imperfect competition in one of its many manifestations. Both of these factors complicate the High Authority's problems (and the problem of anyone who is trying to discuss the right course for the Community). No rules are adequate, though some may help. Continuing regulation is the only possible course. This is practically difficult for the High Authority, with its limited powers and influence. It is also difficult to know what the regulation should try to achieve at every given moment. Not competition but the fruits of competition are the aims. The High Authority may be concerned with pricing practices, penetration of markets, and other matters of this sort—indeed it must be—but it has to look also at the rate of growth, the introduction of innovations, the direction investment takes, what happens to productivity and to costs. A dean of the American economists concerned with industrial organization has said, "we want the efficiency of

large-scale production and the progress stemming from applied science, including varied products to choose from
and favorable conditions for choosing. We want all this
without losing the essential protections of competitive
forces; but these essentials obviously differ from 'pure and
perfect' competitive equilibrium. . . ." [79]

The High Authority is not alone in this interest. Governments, producers, and consumers share it, but not all
governments and all producers at all times, and the consumers have yet to show their effectiveness. On these matters, the transitional period throws only a faint light. It
provides a beginning but the more important questions lie
ahead.

[79] J. M. Clark, "The Uses of Diversity: Competitive Bearings of Di-
versities in Cost and Demand Functions," *American Economic Review*,
May 1958, p. 474 (Papers and Proceedings issue).

FIFTEEN

AID TO ADAPTATION, A MODEST EXPERIMENT

SOME OF the greatest hopes attached to the Schuman Plan were based on the changes it was expected to make in the economy of Western Europe. But there were dangers as well. Destruction of old trade patterns, it was thought, would bring unemployment, bankruptcy, the decline of towns and whole regions unable to compete in the new common market. One of the fundamental compromises of the Treaty—necessary to its acceptance, wise by almost any standard—was the matching of the promise that change would take place with the assurance that it would not take place with such rapidity as to cause serious hardship. Some of the assurances were given by safeguards against dislocation, others by measures specifically intended to promote adaptation. Among these was one of the Treaty's major innovations: international readaptation aid for firms and workers affected by the opening of the common market.

For years it has been argued that opposition to the removal of trade barriers could be reduced if firms and workers who could not meet the competition of new imports were given public aid to reorganize and modernize or to take up other lines of work. Apart from the supposed political advantages of such a step, it has generally been argued that a smoothing of the transition would also be in the public interest because it would avoid dislocation and conserve human and material resources. Attractive as this approach is, it presents quite a few difficulties and has not been adopted as a general policy in any country.

The Schuman Plan Treaty broke new ground and not only provided for adaptation measures but put them on an international (or supranational) basis. This was exciting and seemed to be an important means for bringing about adaptation to the common market. It has proved to be rather unimportant, and not very exciting. There has been much less call for Community aid than was expected. The procedure has worked quite successfully in a few relatively minor cases; in one major instance it has not worked at all; and in another it has only been applied in a somewhat strained or distorted sense. But success or failure, application or non-application, do not seem to have had marked effects on the affairs of the Community.

THE FIRST MAJOR TEST

Two kinds of readaptation are recognized in the Community. The Convention provides help for changes made necessary by the opening of the common market. The Treaty has somewhat similar provisions for dealing with technological unemployment, but these have never been invoked.[1] The measures provided by the Convention apply only to the transitional period except that for two years afterwards aid can be given if the Council of Ministers agrees. A government may ask the High Authority for help "if the consequences of the introduction of the common market oblige certain enterprises or parts of enterprises to cease or to change their activities . . ." (Sec. 23). The enterprises may be given loans either for readaptation or to undertake new activities that will employ the discharged

---

[1] Article 56 applies when new methods or equipment are introduced on such a scale as to "lead to an exceptionally large reduction in labour requirements . . . making it especially difficult . . . to re-employ the workers discharged. . . ." If asked by a government, the High Authority may lend money or guarantee loans for the creation of new lines of activity that will provide employment. If the Council of Ministers agrees unanimously, these new activities may be outside the coal and steel industries. The High Authority is also to make grants to compensate workers while they are awaiting new employment, to help them resettle and to finance their retraining. Unless an exception is granted by the Council of Ministers, the High Authority's aid must be matched by the government that requested help.

workers.[2] (If the new activity is not in coal or steel, the Council of Ministers must approve.) The workers are to be helped by grants. These are to tide them over periods of temporary unemployment and adjustment to new jobs, to provide resettlement allowances if they move, and to give them technical retraining if that is necessary. The government must match the High Authority's aid unless the Council of Ministers exempts it from this obligation.

The first major request for High Authority assistance came from the French government in 1953.[3] According to the estimates of Charbonnages de France some of its mines in the Cévennes, Aquitaine, and Provence would have to discharge 5,000 workers over five years. Productivity was rising, the possibility of sales was decreasing because of increased hydroelectric competition and the importation of foreign coal along the coast. The workers, it was believed, could be absorbed in the coal mines of Lorraine. Here was a clear-cut case of adaptation to which the Community's new techniques of aid could be applied. After rather long negotiations, the High Authority and the French government agreed on a set of measures expected to help bring about the movement of 5,000 workers by 1956. Those volunteering for the transfer were to receive a special indemnity as well as their transportation and an extra day's vacation with pay, to make up for lost working time. Housing was promised and maintenance of the worker's job classification, pension rights, etc. Since the pay scale in Lorraine was higher, it was suggested that most miners

[2] There is also the exceptional case of grants to an enterprise that shuts down "provided the sole and direct cause . . . is the limitation of the single market to the coal and steel industries, and provided that this situation leads to a relative increase of production in other enterprises of the Community." The grants will be limited to payment of sums immediately due; the clause is hedged with procedural provisions and has never been used.

[3] An earlier request was turned down since it involved only the reimbursement of the French government for unemployment payments made to 150 coal miners in the Loire region. This was regarded as not a special contribution of the sort called for by the Treaty. HA, *Report*, Apr. 1954, p. 166. Several other requests were turned down later.

transferring would eventually be better paid than if they stayed in the south. Moreover, they would probably find a full week's work after having been on short time in the south. Union officials were brought into the consultations and were given a role in the transfer arrangements. Some union leaders were taken to Lorraine to see the working conditions. The problems and opportunities were explained to the miners in the south. The total cost of the operation was estimated at a billion francs, half to be paid by the High Authority and half by the French government.

The stage seemed set for an impressive demonstration of the new approach. The High Authority prepared for news stories, feature articles, and movies that would show the world, and especially European labor, what the Community could do. The agreements were signed in April 1954. The first workers arrived in Lorraine from the south at the end of May. By the end of the year 145 workers had transferred and about 100 more were waiting until housing was provided. By the end of 1955 the number of volunteers for transfer had risen to 560. The transfer stopped there, and while a few workers moved during 1956 the whole effort was shelved by the end of the year.[4]

The great demonstration of adaptation had failed. Why did only about one-tenth the expected number of workers actually go to Lorraine? Many factors contributed. Most of all, the people did not want to move. All of the ties that bind were operating, along with the fears, uncertainties, and reluctance that deter people from radical change. Most of the miners in the south had always lived there. Some were even attached to the land to the extent of having a household economy based on their own small farms or vegetable gardens. Though they were told they faced unemployment, they "could hardly understand that the activity of the basins must be reduced at the moment when the measures of modernization and expansion undertaken after the war

[4] Sources conflict as to the number who actually moved, but the order of magnitude is clear and decisive. The figures given come from High Authority reports.

had attained their full effect and increased productive capacity." [5] Remembering past periods of unemployment, they could not see why it would not be best to hang on this time as well and wait for the mines to begin hiring again. (They turned out to be right.)

The individual's reluctance to move was strongly abetted by the rallying of local forces. Officials of municipalities and *départements*, deputies and senators, protested to the national government. Paul Ramadier, a former premier and mayor of one of the towns affected, called for the introduction of new industries. Local merchants formed defense organizations and appealed to the miners not to move. Counteracting the orders of their superiors, foremen in the mines discouraged the movement for fear of losing their best workers. Though Force Ouvrière and the Catholic trade union federation (CFTC) were cooperating with the government and the High Authority in arrangements for the transfer, the local officials of these unions do not appear to have been the most enthusiastic partisans of the shift. A majority of the miners had voted for CGT delegates and the CGT had refused from the beginning to cooperate in the move. Following the Communist line of their national organization, the CGT officials denounced the transfer as a conspiracy of the supercapitalist High Authority, undertaken for the benefit of the Ruhr. This time they had good material to exploit. Others were pressing for the same results. The Bishop of Rodez wrote to the head of one of the Catholic unions: "You are right . . . when you say that you are attached to your soil, to your country, to the cemetery where your own are buried, to your living relatives. Involuntary exile has always been '*impie.*' I can only approve the fact that you feel those things which some, who dream of nothing but machines and material things, seem unable to feel any longer. You, on the contrary, grasp the higher quality of these emotions

---

[5] A. Girard and P. Meutey, *Développement Économique et Mobilité des Travailleurs*, 1956, p. 53. This survey, prepared for the High Authority, includes a case study of the Midi-Lorraine move (pp. 43-57) that is one of the main sources of this section.

which have their source and their echo in your heart. . . ." [6]

The other side of attachment to the place they were, was the miners' expectations that they would not like so different a *pays* as Lorraine. Miners had gone from the south to Lorraine before the transfer scheme was introduced and almost all of them had returned dissatisfied. Some of the first to move under the High Authority's plan had also not liked the change. A committee of the Assembly made an investigation on the spot and reported that:

The transferred workers assimilate themselves to the local population only with great difficulty. In practice there has been no, or hardly any, assimilation up to the present. One must find the cause in the difference in the kind of life in the Centre-Midi and in Lorraine, the difference in climate, the difficulties of the language, the more rigorous discipline, the more rapid rhythm of work resulting from the complete mechanization of the Lorraine mines. Moreover, the real cost of living is higher in Lorraine than in the Centre-Midi.[7]

Housing was the most frequent cause of complaint during the early months of the plan. Not all the expectations that had been created could be satisfied immediately. Some families were very pleased with what they got but others were disgruntled; some of the bachelors took a poor view of the barracks of the Lorraine miners. Later, matters seem to have improved, but the initial disappointments undoubtedly had their effects as word got back to the Midi. Wages, which were supposed to be so much better, were another source of complaint. Some of those who were transferred told the Assembly committee that for periods up to a year they had been getting only 80 per cent of their old wage.

The handling of the move gave rise to other difficulties. The unions played less of a part than they had expected to.

[6] Quoted in same, pp. 55-56.
[7] CA, Commission des Affaires Sociales, *Rapport . . . sur les problèmes de la réadaptation de la main-d'oeuvre dans les industries de la Communauté, par M. A. Bertrand, Rapporteur*, doc. 26 (1955-56), Je. 1956, p. 23. The foremen were a special problem: "their methods of giving orders, their *raideur*, surprised the men and, in addition, bilingualism was a difficulty." Girard and Meutey, cited, p. 49.

Reception was not very well managed. Social services were lacking at various times. Some observers felt that the psychological preparation for the transfer was inadequate. This was particularly important because the Community-aided scheme had been introduced against a background of bitterness. In December 1953, 125 miners in the Cévennes were told to prepare themselve to move to Lorraine in ten days. Of these, 116 went and the rest were fired. Strikes and general dissatisfaction resulted, but in February 1954, 38 more were transferred in the same way and 12 were fired.[8] Not surprisingly, the word "deportation" was frequently heard. Some North African workers were convinced that police measures lay behind the pressure to move them. The CGT said that the move to Lorraine was only a step on the way to deporting the workers to the Ruhr. This atmosphere, intensifying the inherent difficulties of the situation and buttressing the unwillingness of workers to move, gives color to an Italian observer's interpretation of the situation: "In a word, the miners seem to live in a great opaque and irrational world, in which everything combines to give them the sensation of being the object of the arbitrament of hostile powers, of changing caprices." [9]

Later, pressure was applied again, though in somewhat more favorable circumstances. When it had become apparent that only a few miners were volunteering to go to Lorraine, Charbonnages de France reported to the High Authority that it would nevertheless have to dismiss workers in the Centre-Midi mines. Arrangements were made so that only those physically approved for work in Lorraine were discharged. They were offered the same allowances as volunteers if they chose to go. Failing that, they were offered other allowances to cover retraining and relocation.

In view of the pressures on them and their greater mobility, it is not surprising that many foreign workers and bachelors should have been among those who moved to Lorraine. Although some 70 per cent of the labor force of

---

[8] I infer this last figure since it would reconcile statistics from two sources which are silent on the point.

[9] Benedetto De Cesaris, "La mobilità della manodopera nell'ambito della C.E.C.A.," *Mondo Economico*, Je. 15, 1957, p. 28.

the south were native to the area, only 83 of those who transferred came from this group. Though foreign workers made up only 17 per cent of the labor force in Aquitaine at the end of 1954, they accounted for 71 per cent of the workers who moved during the first year of the transfer scheme. For the married French workers who moved, the greatest attractions seem to have been the prospect of better housing, expectation of better future employment in an expanding rather than contracting coal field, and the chance of future employment for their children. Some of the complete families who moved found the new life satisfactory and did not regret their decision.

By early 1955 almost all parties concerned were ready to admit that the year-old scheme for transferring workers was not going to live up to its expectations. Meanwhile, a change in economic circumstances was cushioning the effect of the failure. While the declining demand for coal during the early months of the scheme made it harder to fit newcomers into the hiring program of the Lorraine mines, afterwards the demand for coal rose steadily. With some delay, the improvement touched the south as well. In the spring of 1956, the Assembly committee said, "At present there is no excess manpower." [10] Yet, employment in the mines of the Centre-Midi was still falling and did not start to rise until the last quarter of the year. Some of this loss was probably due to the call-up for service in Algeria. Between the spring of 1954 when the transfer scheme was introduced and the low point in the fall of 1956, employment in the Centre-Midi mines fell by more than 5,000, continuing a trend that had been under way since before the common market was opened.[11] Meanwhile productivity

[10] *Rapport* . . . , cited, p. 21.
[11] Underground employment in the Centre-Midi basins averaged 42,000 during 1951 and 1952. In March 1954 it was 38,000 and fell steadily (36,000 in January 1955, 34,000 in October) to a low of 32,800 in July and August 1956. Thereafter it rose and for most of 1957 was 33,800. Employment above ground fell from 16,900 in the first quarter of 1955 to 15,800 in the third quarter of 1956 and then declined to 15,600 in late 1957. These figures refer to the whole basin, while the adjustment was largely concentrated in a few areas. The reduction in employment is, of course, not necessarily a measure of increased unemployment.

continued to rise and production as well, after a low in 1954. If all this was accomplished without having any unemployed in mid-1956, and with small emigration from the area, the adjustment must have been made largely by holding down the intake of new workers so that those originally slated to go could be kept on or re-employed. In 1957 the first of the High Authority's regional studies (p. 424) spoke of surplus labor and a long-run employment problem. Whatever the explanation, these facts stand out about the first major effort to deploy the Community's resources for readaptation: the problem was far less serious than it had seemed to be, and whatever adjustment did occur took place largely without benefit of the Community's adaptation aid.

THE FRENCH STEEL INDUSTRY

A second experiment in adaptation, this time in the French steel industry, was of quite a different sort. No movement of workers was involved. The problem was to tide them over a period of temporary unemployment caused by the reorganization of production. This was the case of the small companies that combined to form the Compagnie des Ateliers et Forges de la Loire (p. 360). The reorganization was expected to put about 1,500 workers out of their jobs for two years, after which the reorganized plants expected to be able to re-employ them, though some would need retraining for different kinds of work.

Though the merger took place in 1953, it was not until July 1954 that the High Authority, the French government, and the firms, agreed on a set of measures. The firms agreed not to discharge workers and to hire enough apprentices to provide reasonably normal employment for those just coming into the local labor force. Retirement and the normal rate of job-leaving were to take up the slack. The French government and the High Authority agreed to help the companies pay the salaries of workers in three categories: those receiving training in new skills; those continuing to work but at less productive rates than before; those working on maintenance or other more or less incidental jobs. They were to be paid skilled-workers' wages; the grants made up the excess over what the companies would normally pay for these jobs. According to the Assembly committee, most workers were paid about 25 per cent less than before; some lost as much as 40 per cent.[12] The flat rate for a 40-hour week was itself a considerable cut since they had worked 48 to 56 hours. They also lost production bonuses. The committee questioned whether this could be regarded as protecting "the workers from the burden of readaptation," as the transitional Convention said. It noted, however, that in the absence of special arrangements of this sort, workers discharged as a result of such a reorganization could not hope to get more than 30 per cent of their pay in unemployment benefits and in some areas would get nothing. When some workers quit because of the reductions the unions complained of "concealed dismissals."

The readaptation plans were drawn up in 1953 during a period of slack demand. Before they were completely carried out the steel market was booming. As a result only 700 workers were affected, not the 1,500 originally estimated. Nevertheless, the reorganization was taking longer than expected and, at the French government's request, the High Authority extended the scheme for two years. In April 1956 the High Authority reported that the scheme was "going ahead satisfactorily."[13] The Assembly committee, studying it in the field at about the same time, compiled a long list of criticisms. Many of these concerned the arrangements for administering and supervising the process. According to the committee, the High Authority was doing little but pay out funds against vouchers (and the payments were somewhat delayed). A national committee and a regional committee on which the High Authority was represented had never met; the unions complained that they were not informed of the details of the agreements so they could not tell whether their interests were fully protected. They thought too few workers were receiving retraining

[12] *Rapport* . . . , cited, p. 25, gives various pay formulas.
[13] HA, *Report*, Apr. 1956, p. 216.

and objected that instead of consulting the local committee on which the unions were represented the firms were proceeding in a completely unilateral fashion.

Still another type of adaptation was shown in a series of lesser arrangements involving French steelworks outside the main centers of production, an iron mine in the eastern Pyrenees, and a coal mine in Lower Saxony. These were all cases in which shutting-down, the conversion of facilities, or other changes were expected to lead to the discharge of a number of workers. There were no general plans for re-employment, as in the Loire, nor was any organized movement of workers involved, as in the Centre-Midi coal mines.[14] The High Authority's help (matched by that of the government) took the form of tiding-over payments as envisaged in the Treaty. In the 1955 arrangements for the four French steelworks, for instance, discharged workers were to receive payments for a year on a declining scale that began at 80 per cent of their previous salary for the first month and fell to 40 to 55 per cent in the last four months. But if a worker enrolled in a training course he would receive the 80 per cent allowance for the duration of the course, and if he found another job he would receive the 80 per cent allowance for the rest of the year. Thus it was made profitable to "re-adapt" oneself. If a worker had to move to take his new job, his traveling expenses would be paid and a resettlement allowance provided.

The Assembly committee's examination of three of these cases indicated that all but a few of those discharged had received aid and that most of them had found new jobs or were re-employed by the same firms. Only a few seem to have taken retraining courses.[15] A key factor in one case

---

[14] In at least one case, however—Les Établissements J-J. Carnaud et Forges de Basse-Indre—the company worked out a system of reclassification, aided by grants from the French government and the High Authority, that helped considerably to reduce the number of discharges. An effort to transfer workers to other jobs was less successful. Girard and Meutey, cited, pp. 73-76.

[15] Of 1,100 workers discharged, all but 50 received some form of aid. Over 700 found other jobs and about 175 were rehired by the firms that

was strong pressure by the unions on local officials and the company to hold down discharges. Force Ouvrière and CFTC joined with CGT in a common action that played a significant part in making the company depend primarily on reclassification to make its adjustments.[16]

There were some complaints about the handling of the aid, but on the whole the operations seem to have gone quite smoothly. The machinery of administration was regarded as somewhat cumbersome and there were cases of workers having to wait a long while before receiving their allowances. The unions regarded their cooperation with the employers as satisfactory, but said they found it difficult to get in touch with the High Authority or to learn about its decisions. (The High Authority pointed out that its staff and members were always accessible though they could not be approached formally except through the established machinery.) Government officials apparently regarded the process as reasonably satisfactory and thought the initial difficulties of administration would be overcome. They told the Assembly committee, however, that they thought "too much publicity should not be given to the fact that Community workers benefited from an especially favorable arrangement compared to their comrades employed in industries outside the Community, considering the difficulty of explaining to the latter the reason for this state of affairs, especially during a period of unemployment."[17]

ITALIAN DIFFICULTIES

The largest request for adaptation aid differed from the other cases and proved to be one of the hardest to handle. In December 1953 the government of Italy asked for aid

---

had discharged them. Only 69 were unemployed for as long as a year. Only 40 were specifically noted as having taken retraining courses. Others were still unemployed at the time the report was made or had reached retirement age. These figures are not set up uniformly for the three firms, so they should be treated with reserve. *Rapport* . . . , cited, p. 29.

[16] Girard and Meutey, cited, pp. 75-76.

[17] *Rapport* . . . , cited, p. 31.

for 8,000 steelworkers. The High Authority committed itself "in principle" in January 1955 but no final agreement was reached until May 1956. By then the number of workers expected to benefit had risen to about 9,000; no one seemed able to set an exact figure. The main reasons for the delay seem to have been the difficulties of devising a means of using the funds that would meet the High Authority's standards and also satisfy the exigencies of the situation in which the Italian government found itself. In the end this required legislation in Italy and a waiver by the Community of the usual terms on which aid was granted.

The workers discharged when Italian steel firms speeded up their modernization to face the common market were a very small part of the 2 million or so unemployed in Italy. Could the government give them special allowances? Favoritism might have political repercussions; the government could not afford to pay allowances to everyone. It solved this problem by proposing to advance 3.5 billion lire to help industrial firms expand their activities if they would promise to take at least 50 per cent of their new workers from among those discharged by the steel industry. The High Authority was not prepared to have its funds used this way but agreed to provide an equal sum that would go entirely to workers, in various kinds of payments comparable to those made in other cases of adaptation. Anything left over it agreed to use for social purposes inside Italy, such as housing.[18]

The passage of time made it harder to work out a concrete program for distributing the funds. One could hardly talk of tiding people over a period of unemployment that had begun three years before. Some might now have other jobs. A few had taken retraining courses established by the

[18] To sanction this arrangement the Council of Ministers in July 1955 waived the Convention's requirement that the Italian government match the High Authority's contribution to the workers. The Italian government's aid was used to reimburse firms for the interest on loans contracted for new investment, to the extent of 2.5 per cent a year for ten years. These measures were expected to provide jobs for 1,750 of the steelworkers.

Italian government and had received pay while doing so.[19] Some firms had paid "extra-contractual" allowances to workers when they discharged them and asked to be reimbursed from the High Authority's grant. This, it was estimated, would take up 1.5 billion lire of the 3.5. The workers held that they had extracted these allowances by hard bargaining, sometimes by strikes, and that there was no occasion to divert money intended for workers to employers. The Italian government inclined toward the workers' side, pointing out that extra severance payments were fairly common in Italy and that the workers were already being deprived of the matching grant from the Italian government anticipated in the Treaty arrangements. The High Authority said it would have nothing to do with repayment to the employers. In the end it was decided that steelworkers who had lost their jobs between the opening of the common market and May 1, 1956 were to receive grants at degressive rates for periods up to 15 months of unemployment. Those who had had to move to take new jobs would be paid transportation expenses and a dislocation allowance.

Useful as this distribution of funds was to those receiving them, the situation had become quite different from that contemplated by the Treaty. From the start, it was not altogether clear that the discharge of workers resulted from creation of the common market. Other Italian industries were dropping supernumerary workers as some of the compulsions of the immediate postwar years gave way to more emphasis on costs and efficiency. Because of the delays, adaptation has, in its way, taken place without benefit of Community intervention. The High Authority's aid appears as a belated supplementary social security grant rather than as a means of promoting adaptation. The Italian government's share of the aid, geared to the opening of new plants in other fields, takes on the character of a measure of general expansion. So far as the psychological effect of

[19] Employers told the Assembly committee that these courses were useless and the pay just another form of compensation.

Community aid is concerned, there is undoubtedly much truth in the Italian employers' statement that "the Byzantine discussions which dragged on for three years between the government and the High Authority have reduced to nothing the psychological advantages of financial assistance." [20]

Both employers and workers told the Assembly committee that they expected further discharges of workers as modernization proceeded and Italy's tariffs continued to come down. They recommended broader measures than the application of the readaptation provisions—which is natural enough considering their experience. In fact, total employment in the Italian steel industry continued to rise until mid-1957, though not as rapidly as production. This improved the opportunities of applying Section 23 as it was originally intended. Discharged workers should have better chances to find re-employment in the steel industry though they might have to move to another part of the country to work in the new plants. In mid-1957 the High Authority provided supplementary grants for 1,700 workers who were to be dropped by five steel plants. Additional applications were presented in 1958. In contrast to the initial program these were measures of adaptation that conformed to the Treaty concept.

THE RESULTS

By the end of 1957, the High Authority had earmarked about $12 million for approved adaptation plans. More than half this sum was set aside for the Italian steel industry. The French, Belgian, and Italian coal industries accounted for another $4 million and the remainder was earmarked for French steel and iron. Actual payments, however, totaled only $4.5 million, more than 90 per cent of them in Italy and the rest in France. The unspent sums remained as part of the High Authority's reserves for adaptation, which came to almost $27 million at the end of 1957. In the course of 1958 more adaptation plans were approved and expendi-

[20] *Rapport* . . . , cited, p. 37. The employers contributed their share to this process.

tures also increased, bringing the total outlay to $8.3 million by the middle of the year.

The High Authority estimated that 18,600 workers had benefited directly from the adaptation funds by February 1958. Most of these, of course, were in Italy (13,200), the rest largely in France (3,500) but payments had also begun in Germany (1,800) and Belgium (60). The total number is equal to just over 1 per cent of the Community's labor force at the end of 1957 but only about one-third of 1 per cent outside Italy. In Italy the beneficiaries equal nearly one-fifth the number of workers in the coal, steel, and iron mining industries at the end of 1957. But, as we have seen, this cannot be taken as a measure of what the Community has done for Italy's adaptation. Additional adaptation grants approved during 1958 for French, Italian, and Belgian coal mines might increase the number of beneficiaries by more than one-third. The largest number of these would be in southern Belgium where the closing of pits was expected to put some 6,000 miners out of work—but it was thought that not all of them would need help from the adaptation fund.

While the readaptation payments were obviously useful to a number of individuals, and eased the problems of firms and governments, the process has not played an important part in the life of the Community. This is largely due to the fact that creation of the common market has not been very disturbing. If demand had remained at the levels of 1953, there might have been many more calls for adaptation aid. Instead, the level of economic activity rose so that even poorly placed firms could continue to operate (and to some extent to modernize) without outside assistance. There is even some question whether the adaptation measures actually taken were always directed at problems created by the opening of the common market. The decline in employment in the southern coal basins of France that led to the proposed move to Lorraine was under way before the Community was created. The need for aid to Italy was occasioned largely by an investment program and by measures to permit the steel industry to get rid of its concealed unemployment, which were only partly responses to the common market. Some of the lesser French cases may also have been of the same character. To be sure there was always some link to the development of a Community economy, but cause and effect have not been as clear as was probably assumed when the Convention was drafted.

Governments probably did not ask for adaptation aid in all the cases in which it might have been used. They were somewhat reluctant to give special treatment to the coal and steel workers for fear of the demands that would be made on them by others.[21] They may have disliked the idea of the High Authority's becoming involved in the administration of adaptation measures; it had no direct political responsibility that would check the voicing of high ideals and the stressing of standards a government might find embarrassing. Individual firms may also have refrained from calling for aid in adaptation to avoid intervention in their affairs, by government or the High Authority. This appears to have happened in the case of a German iron mine that closed in the spring and summer of 1954 (Eisenzecher Zug, owned by the Erzbergbau Siegerland, A. G.). The unions urged application for readaptation funds but the management thought this would bring too much control. The unions accused the German government of failing to endorse their request because it did not wish to put up its share of the money for fear of creating a precedent. The argument was also made that the case did not fit the Treaty conditions, not being a result of the common market.[22]

[21] Commenting on the effect of readaptation schemes on the attitude of workers, the High Authority said, "in some countries similar schemes for workers in industries other than coal and steel are already being planned. . . ." HA, *Report*, Apr. 1954, pp. 168-169.

[22] At the same time the High Authority said, in connection with the readaptation program: "In Germany, the employment situation in the iron-ore mines has deteriorated markedly in the last few months. It would seem that this is chiefly due to difficulties in marketing the output of the mines because of competition from ores coming [from] outside the Community." Same, p. 168. The information on the Zug case comes from a private source.

The Assembly committee criticized the High Authority for not being more active in seeking occasions to use the adaptation procedure and for playing too passive a role when it was used. The High Authority's answers stressed the Convention's requirement that governments take the initiative; they had the responsibility for conception and execution. The High Authority could, of course, check on the use made of its funds but, according to the committee, did not feel able to impose conditions or even supervise closely the administration of adaptation programs. Moreover, the High Authority took the view that it could have no official dealings with workers or employers, since adaptation arrangements were determined by its agreements with governments.

Actually, the High Authority played a more active role in some cases than these strictures suggest. It did not, however, press adaptation as hard as might have been expected or try to make it a major feature of the Community's work. While strict construction of the Treaty and lack of administrative apparatus in Luxembourg were undoubtedly real elements in the situation, they would not seem to have been insuperable difficulties. In other fields where its legal powers were limited, the High Authority played a more dynamic role. In matters affecting labor it made a special effort to be helpful. Considering the interest the High Authority could be assumed to have in the adaptation measures—as innovation, as a benefit to labor, and even just as propaganda— one must look for more compelling explanations. They are to be found in large part in the governments' reluctance to apply readaptation provisions and the High Authority's unwillingness to press them very hard. The nine men in Luxembourg put a high value on acting in concert with the governments. They were prepared to push rather hard for some things but the use of adaptation aid was not one of them. It did not seem an urgent need; other problems were of greater importance. This was not one of the cases in which the High Authority could act if the governments did not.

There is also the fact that the adaptation procedures got

off to a bad start and have not proved easy to apply effectively. The fiasco of providing elaborately for the movement of French miners who would not move and the dull delays of the Italian episode were undoubtedly taken as warnings in Luxembourg. The latter showed how hard it might be to arrive at an acceptable concrete program, the former how irrelevant such a program could be. Both showed how easily false expectations could be aroused. Lacking the power to carry out adaptation measures, the High Authority may have felt that it must make the situation perfectly clear by leaving their execution almost entirely to the governments. This is virtually what is done in the adaptation provisions of the treaty creating the European Economic Community, which officials of the High Authority helped draft. The new treaty has less detailed adaptation provisions than the coal and steel Convention but the principal difference is that payments are to take the form of reimbursal of governments for monies already laid out.[23]

Adaptation did not end with the transitional period. The high level of demand during much of the five years had cushioned the impact of the common market on some enterprises. A fall in demand might reveal some of the difficulties of adaptation *brusquement et brutalement*, Paul Finet, the new chairman of the High Authority, told the Assembly.[24] The closing of coal mines, especially in Belgium, bore out the predictions. The Council of Ministers continued to approve adaptation grants, case by case. The High Authority had funds. But the riots in the Borinage in February 1959 showed some of the difficulties of adaptation, with or without aid.

Before it faced these new problems the High Authority, prodded by the Assembly, had set out standards of payment to discharged workers but whether it would take any more initiative in the matter remained to be seen. The

[23] One of the Assembly committee's complaints was that some of the High Authority's payments virtually came to this. The new Community has the advantage that all industries are included, so the problem of special treatment for coal and steel workers can be avoided.

[24] CA, *Compte Rendu Analytique*, Feb. 25, 1958, p. 9.

governments were still in the central position. The Assembly committee had urged that good times be used to prepare for bad and warned that unless the adaptation provisions were fully applied and a re-employment program made part of each adaptation scheme, "it will become impossible to state . . . that the Treaty's provisions concerning readaptation of labor constitute one of the most important innovations and, insofar as they establish a principle, one of the happiest. One could no longer conclude that for the first time an economic revolution is taking place while taking account of the workers and not only of the conditions of the market." [25]

The possibilities of using the second kind of adaptation, which deals with technological unemployment, are more difficult to discern. Because of its wording, some have refused to interpret Article 56 as covering any changes other than those coming directly from major technological innovations, not merely from modernization. The High Authority took the view that it could not establish a "doctrine" in advance but would have to handle each case as it came up. The Assembly concluded that the language was too restricted and recommended that the Treaty be amended to include the Convention provisions and to give the High Authority the right to initiate adaptation measures. [26] These steps would certainly broaden the original concept of adaptation, which was concerned only with the initial impact of the common market. Whether these measures would in fact do much to increase the flexibility of the Community economy and avoid recourse to protectionist measures cannot be judged from the experience of the transitional period.

[25] *Rapport* . . . , cited, p. 45. Among the specific measures recommended for improving the effectiveness of readaptation were: that labor be paid its full previous wage; that applications be made in advance of discharges, not afterwards as had happened in several cases; that there be closer collaboration of all parties concerned and more publicity; that transfer of workers be only a last resort.

[26] G. Kreyssig, *Révision du Traité instituant la Communauté Européenne du Charbon et de l'Acier*, 1958, p. 22. This report, originally prepared by a working group, was endorsed by the whole Assembly at its last session.

The failure of the movement of coal miners from the
south to Lorraine stimulated a re-examination of the whole
adaptation question. The High Authority sponsored several studies[27] and came to the conclusion, shared by many,
that movement of workers on a large scale should be
avoided whenever possible. Bringing jobs to the workers
by establishing other kinds of production in the area
seemed a preferable course. This had always been the
policy in Belgium where one of the reasons given for the
slow adaptation of coal production was the difficulty of
starting new industries in the mining areas. This is also, in
the main, the approach that has been used in the British
depressed-areas program for several decades and was the
only course open to American communities deprived of
traditional employment by the movement of industry from
New England to the South. This method has obvious difficulties when only coal and steel are involved, which may
have been another factor holding back the High Authority.
It has tried to help by initiating studies of employment
trends in various regions where coal mining or steelmaking
may decline, but the matter is largely one that goes beyond
the Community.

It would be unfortunate if generalizations about the
immobility of workers led to too firm a conviction that
men are forever anchored to their hereditary abode and
that industry must always go to them. History does not
support this and there are economic dangers in the poor
location of industry from uncritical emphasis on this approach. A balance must be struck. Organized movements
of large groups can probably work only in such exceptional
circumstances that they should not ordinarily be attempted.
Smaller movements have sometimes been reasonably successful, for instance within the coal fields of the Nord.[28]
Movement by attraction is quite a different matter and

---

[27] HA, *Étude des Obstacles à la Mobilité et des Problèmes Sociaux de
Réadaptation*, Je. 1956 (mimeographed), summarizes most of them.

[28] Girard and Meutey, cited, pp. 58-69. Fewer men were involved than
in the Lorraine effort, the distance was much shorter, there was not as
great a cultural difference as between the south and Lorraine (or the
Borinage and the Campine), and the workers felt under less pressure.

need not be gradual. When Sollac, one of the new French steelworks, began operations in Lorraine, it received some 60,000 applications for jobs from all over France in two and a half years. Of 5,600 workers recruited by the spring of 1955, about 56 per cent came from Alsace-Lorraine and the rest from other areas. Only a third came from the *département* of the Moselle, and all but a few hundred of these had to move from where they lived to the new community created by Sollac.[29] Where pressure is combined with attraction there may also be movement, as among the Italians who go to the Belgian coal mines (p. 441ff.), but the results may not be altogether desirable. If Europe is to have a healthy economy, it must have flexibility, and that will require at least some degree of human mobility. But it can probably not count on a great fluidity of the labor supply except where there is substantial unemployment and a tradition of permanent or temporary emigration. As Adam Smith said, "After all that has been said of the levity and inconstancy of human nature, it appears evidently from experience that a man is of all sorts of luggage the most difficult to be transported."[30]

Moving workers from one place to another is not the main aim of adaptation, but the Community's experience in the transitional period gives only modest guidance on other issues. The Italian episode raises a question about the usability of adaptation aid in a situation of general unemployment. The action of the Italian government was inhibited; the whole process came to be largely an international subsidy to supplement Italian social security benefits (at least until 1957; information on the newer measures is inadequate to judge them). There is, of course, an element of this in all the cases, since one of the functions of the adaptation arrangements is to leave the discharged workers somewhat better off than if they were not covered

[29] Same, pp. 127-138.
[30] *The Wealth of Nations*, ed. by Edwin Cannan (London: Methuen, 5th ed., 1930), v. I, p. 77. He was discussing the variation of wages within the British Isles. My debt to Girard and Meutey, already so great in this section, extends to their having called this quotation to my attention.

by such measures. The other aspects of adaptation—shifting
excess workers to new jobs, retraining, providing alternative employment—have been of some importance in a
number of the smaller Community cases. Only in the
Loire steel mills, however, has the whole process been
encompassed by the adaptation arrangements and there the
situation was somewhat different again, the effect of the
adaptation aid being to keep intact a labor force, at better
than unemployment-insurance pay, which was to be re-
employed after a period of adjustment.

Even the Loire case, however satisfactory it was in other
respects, shows one of the weaknesses of adaptation arrangements. Though the industries involved were small and
the plans for their alteration clear-cut, it proved necessary
to double the period originally estimated for the tide-over
payments before the workers could be fully re-employed.
The effort to move coal miners out of the Cévennes and
Aquitaine was saved from becoming a much worse failure
by the fact that events belied the original estimates and
made it possible to keep on or rehire a large number of
workers originally slated for discharge. No doubt estimates
can be improved but the effect of cyclical factors cannot
be eliminated. In a recession it would be very difficult to
distinguish between true, if delayed, adaptation to the
common market and cases in which Community aid would
really be a form of supplementary social security payment.

Apart from the conditions that might exist in the years
just after the end of the transitional period, a good case
could be made for equipping the Community with the
means of assisting adjustments, whatever their cause. To
be able to do this might make it easier for the High Authority to make decisions in some difficult cases. Aid to
displaced workers is one of the rather few concrete benefits the High Authority can offer directly to labor. But such
arguments rest on rather general reasoning. There is little
in the Community's experience to make the case persuasive.
For, one of the most striking innovations of the Coal and
Steel Community has had an inconclusive history and has
been of relatively minor importance.

SIXTEEN

LABOR IN THE COMMUNITY

THIS IS a story of contrasts. Armed with fewer explicit powers and duties than it has in most matters, the High Authority has done substantial work on labor problems. Where the Treaty was most explicit, in registering a governmental agreement on the principle of the free movement of labor, action was slow and of limited effect. Organizational arrangements generally regarded as concessions to labor to help ensure ratification of the Treaty have attained enduring significance as keys to a process by which labor's originally uncertain attitude toward the Community has been transformed into active appreciation and participation. What might have been routine studies and statistical analyses have been disproportionately important to the labor movement. Where there seemed to be little, it has been parlayed into much, while where there seemed to be much the results have been rather meager.

THE TREATY

In its first report, the High Authority stressed the importance it attributed to labor and social questions:

The fundamental articles of the Treaty require that the European Coal and Steel Community take steps to ensure an increase and a rationalization of production and an increase in consumption. Such objectives, however, also imply on the part of the Community an obligation to improve the living and working conditions of the workers and to coordinate the progress in these fields.

The Community must become a concrete reality for all of its members, workers as well as producers. This will be achieved only if the standard of living in the Community is effectively increased.[1]

This sounded as though improvement in labor conditions was an important goal of the Treaty. When he read that document, an official of the International Labor Organization reached quite a different conclusion:

The Charter of the Coal and Steel Community neither authorizes nor provides for a positive policy for the improvement of wages. Similarly, it neither authorizes nor provides for an employment policy.

[The Treaty] provides for action on behalf of labor solely as a condition or a consequence of its economic policy; it has neither a true social inspiration nor a social policy of its own. The creators of the Community have not given it such a mission. According to the Schuman Plan experts it can only contribute to social development without being responsible for it, because its scope is restricted to the coal and steel industries, whereas wages and employment depend on general economic conditions in each country. The personal opinion of the author of this article is that the argument is not convincing. Production in the two basic industries concerned is just as dependent on general economic conditions; if production in these two industries can be placed under the authority of the Community, why not wages and employment as well? The reason given neither explains nor justifies the fact that the economic powers of the Community are not accompanied by the corresponding social powers.[2]

Roux's statement is a reasonable analysis of the Treaty. The significance of the High Authority's language is that it is a statement of intent, the intent to give labor and social questions a place of importance in Community affairs. Even so the High Authority's statement—which may seem stronger in retrospect than it did at the time—was not enough to satisfy the Assembly's committee on social affairs. In its first report that body strongly urged the High Authority to take a broader view of its responsibilities,

[1] HA, *Report*, Jan. 1953, p. 93.
[2] René Roux, "The Position of Labour under the Schuman Plan," *International Labour Review*, Mar. 1952, pp. 316, 319.

assert its initiative, enlarge the staff and appropriation of the Division of Labor Problems and generally become more active.[3] This inaugurated a series of exhortations which the committee kept up; even after it became better satisfied, it kept urging a fuller and more active implementation of the Treaty's social and labor provisions. As time passed the full Assembly came to support this approach and passed a series of resolutions, general in wording and broad enough to cover a number of views, as the Assembly resolutions generally were, but with a constant tenor.

One can distinguish five types of labor provisions in the Treaty: (1) general aims; (2) certain more specific but as yet unused rules about wages and competition; (3) rules for assuring the relatively free movement of labor among the six countries; (4) arrangements for labor participation in the affairs of the Community; (5) provision of special aid for workers when coal and steel enterprises are adapting themselves to the conditions of the common market. The last of these was the subject of the previous chapter; the organizational provisions are significant chiefly as they have affected labor's attitude toward the Community, the subject of the latter part of this chapter.

So far as aims are concerned, the Treaty's language is as general as on other subjects.[4] "The mission" of the Community set out in Article 2 includes "the development of employment and the improvement of the standard of living. . . ." In establishing the most rational distribution of production "at the highest possible level of productivity" the Community is to safeguard "the continuity of employment" and avoid "the creation of fundamental and persistent disturbances in the economies of the member States." Amplifying this, Article 3 says that the Community is to "promote the improvement of the living and working

[3] CA, Commission des Affaires Sociales, *Rapport . . . par M. A. Bertrand, Rapporteur,* doc. 3 (1952-53).
[4] Provisions concerning the High Authority's duty of collecting information, publishing it, and helping to foster research, are all specifically tied to the possibility of improving working conditions, living standards, and workers' safety, as well as to other aims of the Treaty (Articles 46, 55).

conditions of the labour force in each of the industries under its jurisdiction so as to harmonize those conditions in an upward direction."

All this sounds as if it would lead up to a series of measures to influence wages and social conditions. But Article 68 is firmly negative: "The methods of fixing wages and social benefits in force in the various member States shall not be affected . . . by the application of this Treaty. . . ." The rest of the article makes some exceptions, none of them ever invoked. If a firm is charging "abnormally low" prices because its wages are "abnormally low" compared with the general wage level in its region, the High Authority may make "the necessary recommendations" to it, or to a government if it is responsible.[5] Not low wages in themselves, but the low prices that may result from them, are the direct object of this provision, thus supporting Roux' interpretation that social policy in the Treaty flows from economic policy. The idea that wages below a national or regional standard lead to unfair competition has been endorsed in recent years by some people who see a problem but who wish to avoid falling into the protectionist fallacy that all wage differences justify trade barriers.[6] However, the concept is not as clear as it sounds and the formula has never been put into practice.

The second general exception to the negative rule on wages permits the High Authority to intervene in certain cases when competition is based on wage cuts.[7] The third

[5] "Recommendations shall be binding with respect to . . . objectives . . ." (Art. 14). The High Authority must consult the Consultative Committee before making them. Before making a recommendation to a government, it must negotiate with it.

[6] Notably the Randall Commission and the Ohlin Committee: Commission on Foreign Economic Policy, *Report to the President and the Congress, January 23, 1954* (Washington: GPO, 1954), p. 62; International Labour Office, *Social Aspects of European Economic Co-operation, Report by a Group of Experts* (Geneva: Author, 1956), pp. 41-44.

[7] If a wage reduction leads to "a drop in the standard of living of the labour force and at the same time is being used as a means of permanent economic adjustment by enterprises or as a means of competition. . . ," the High Authority may recommend payment of compensation to the workers. The provision does not apply to wage changes resulting from a general national economic adjustment; to sliding-scale wage contracts;

unused exception is part of the sweeping Article 67, which may be read as either a barndoor-wide escape hatch or a general-powers clause for saving the Treaty in a crisis. If a change in wages, or social security laws, or measures for dealing with unemployment "is liable to provoke a serious disequilibrium by substantially increasing differences in costs of production," the High Authority may make the necessary recommendations.

Why are the labor provisions of the Treaty so meager while its aims are so broad? Partial integration is clearly part of the answer. Wages in coal and steel could not be sharply separated from wages in the unpooled parts of the national economies. Even so, if one eschewed extremes, it would have been possible to give the High Authority a greater role in labor matters and more influence over wages. Similar things were done in other fields in spite of the handicaps of partial integration. One may surmise why they were not done with regard to labor policy.

There was, to begin with, a good bit of uncertainty about what kind of an institution the Community would prove to be. This created doubts about the results that might come from giving the High Authority significant powers in a field so delicate, politically and economically. Employers in particular, many of whom had misgivings about Schuman's proposal, would probably have resisted any important grant of authority in labor matters. Governments, too, must have had doubts about yielding substantial powers. They would be held politically responsible for the results of others' actions; the distinction between coal and steel workers and the rest of the labor force might become disturbing. The unions were divided. The French and the Belgians, with high money wages, would have liked some "coordination"; the Germans and Dutch resisted the idea. Among the supporters of the Treaty there may well have been fear that too large an assignment in labor matters would prove difficult to carry out and might hurt the Com-

---

to wage reductions resulting from a drop in the cost of living; or to corrections of abnormally high wages paid under exceptional circumstances that no longer exist.

munity by giving it an almost impossible task and at the same time arousing expectations that it could not fulfill. Among the experts the view was generally accepted that equalization of wages was not necessary to the proper functioning of the Community and that the soundest progress toward it would result from the existence of the common market. Out of such circumstances grew the limited, and not altogether unambiguous, labor provisions of the Treaty.

THE HIGH AUTHORITY'S ACTION

Starting from a rather restricted position, the High Authority has sought ways of making some impact on the labor situation of the Community. No doubt the intrinsic value of the measures taken and their usefulness in improving conditions of production had much to do with this course of action, but the wish to win labor support for the Community was a crucial factor. Most of the non-Communist labor groups in the six countries supported the Community in principle, but except for individual leaders committed to "Europe," there was little enthusiasm, much skepticism, and some opposition. This all added up to a "wait and see" attitude. The High Authority's aim was to provide something that was good to see.

In its first report the High Authority indicated three lines of activity it proposed to follow: aid to housing, research in health and safety, and the publication of data on wages and conditions of work. The choice must almost have imposed itself since the needs were clear, the propriety of Community action not very controversial, and the potential benefits to labor obvious. They have continued to be an important part of what the High Authority has done.

On the basis of an initial survey, the High Authority concluded that one-fifth of the workers in the Community lacked adequate housing.[8] It has made a substantial financial contribution to filling this need in a series of housing programs. In grants or loans the High Authority provided, or promised, something over $65 million, some borrowed

[8] HA, *Report*, Jan. 1953, p. 98.

and some from its own funds. By February 1958 more than 12,500 houses had been built and about 24,000 more were planned or under way. While all the Community countries benefited, nearly two-thirds of the building was in Germany where the need was particularly great and building costs low. As in its other loans, the High Authority used its own contribution to help mobilize larger sums of outside capital. A third housing program seemed in the offing— a remarkable development for an activity not even contemplated by the Treaty drafters, so far as one can tell.

Most of the High Authority's activity on industrial medicine and safety has been undertaken since late 1954. By the end of 1957, some $4.5 million was allocated to this work but only about one-tenth of it had been spent. Research, conferences, publications, have been financed. Medical, scientific, and industrial institutes throughout the Community have been drawn into these activities. To a large extent the High Authority has assisted work in progress. The high point was the large conference on safety in coal mines held in late 1956 and early 1957 as a direct result of the Marcinelle disaster in Belgium in which a large number of miners, mostly Italian, were killed. Drawing heavily on the ILO, which has a long history of work in this field, the High Authority brought together representatives of governments, employers, and workers of the six countries. Working with experts on a number of different aspects of the problem the conference produced a series of recommendations to improve safety conditions, called for a permanent organ to pursue the matter, and foreshadowed a possible multilateral convention. In contrast to the easily accepted support of research in medicine and health, agreement on these issues encountered difficulties as employers and governments saw how they might affect costs, legal obligations, public responsibility for supervision, and international commitments.

The High Authority's research on labor questions has covered a variety of subjects, such as the age distribution of the working population, labor turnover, apprenticeship and training. But the main attention has naturally been on the central and most controversial issues: wages, fringe benefits, paid holidays, and social security charges and benefits. Probably the most important study has been an international comparison of real wages in the Community industries. By studying the prices of a large number of goods, statisticians worked out the purchasing power of wages in each country and industry. To reflect national habits of consumption, different "market baskets" were used to show, for instance, the real value of the wage of a German miner as he lived at home and its value if he were to consume according to the French pattern. Differences between the taxes paid and benefits received by married and unmarried workers, and especially the marked effect of family allowances paid to those with children in France and some other countries, further complicated the analysis. As the studies progressed they were refined, additional factors were taken into account, and a "European market basket" was devised.

It is impossible to give an adequate summary of this work without going into more detail than there is space for here. The very broad picture is, however, of some importance, in spite of the important qualifications to which it is subject. The highest real wages for coal miners in 1954 were those paid in Belgium, Holland, and the Saar. French miners got 80 to 90 per cent as much and Germans 70 to 80 per cent, while Italy lagged with 60 to 70 per cent. For steelworkers the spread was smaller. Luxembourg was at the top of the scale, followed by Belgium where real wages were about 10 per cent lower. The figures for all the other countries clustered around 70 per cent of the Luxembourgeois level. Among workers who had no children, the Germans made out a little better than the others; but family allowances raised the incomes of Frenchmen with two children above the level of their German counterparts. The Italians were generally on the low side of the grouping. By 1956 many of the differences in both coal and steel had narrowed, except for the Italians.[9]

[9] ECSC, *Comparaison des Revenus Réels des Travailleurs des Industries de la Communauté*, 1956, pp. 142-147. This is only one of the studies; see the Critical Bibliography.

Commenting on the initial study, the High Authority said, "differences in real incomes between one country and another are not so large as had previously been supposed, and . . . they do not, in fact, exceed the disparities sometimes found within a single country between different sectors of industry or between different industrial regions." [10] Although these studies concern what workers receive and not what employers pay, it seems clear that the High Authority hoped that the findings and the emphasis on real wages would help to offset some of the rather loose talk about commercial difficulties attributable to national differences in money wages. Other studies have concentrated on total labor costs, money wages, social security, working time, holidays, and labor laws. The focus was sometimes on developments in each country and sometimes on comparisons among the six.

These studies make three major contributions to Community labor policy. First, they break new ground in discovering what the position of workers in different countries really is, and how it changes over the years. Second, the High Authority is doing something for labor. In spite of having spent 25 years in the labor movement, said Paul Finet, "it is thanks to the work of the High Authority that I know the details of the situation and conditions of life of the workers of the Community." [11] Union leaders not as well placed as this member of the High Authority have also expressed appreciation of the publications. European unions are much less well supplied with research facilities than are those in the United States. Fewer relevant data are released by employers or compiled by governments. Third, the High Authority's statistics let the unions in each country know where they stand in relation to others in the Community. This provides a basis for possible action. For those in low-wage countries, facts about what others receive—in benefits as well as wages—may provide ideas of possible goals and ammunition for argument. Those with higher wages can sometimes show that their purchasing

[10] HA, *Report*, Apr. 1956, p. 223.
[11] CA, *Débats*, Je. 26, 1957, p. 630.

power is not as great as the spread in money wages would suggest, thus partially checking a bargaining weapon of the employers. Each can consider what interest he may have in Community-wide negotiation or discussion, courses of action that are frequently urged. This whole process of establishing a picture of comparative labor conditions throughout the Community may turn out to be one of the High Authority's main steps in "social policy," the field in which the Treaty gives it so little direct power.

THE FREE MOVEMENT OF WORKERS

The member states bind themselves by Article 69 of the Treaty, "to renounce any restriction, based on nationality, on the employment in the coal and steel industries of workers of recognized qualifications" if they are nationals of one of the Community states. However, "this commitment shall be subject to the limitations imposed by the fundamental need of health and public order." In order to put this commitment into practice, definitions of skilled workers are to be agreed on, along with arrangements for bringing together offers and demands for employment. With regard to all workers, discrimination in wages and working conditions based on nationality are to be eliminated. Social security systems are to be arranged so that they do not impede the movement of labor. If production requires a larger labor force, immigration laws will be changed to admit unskilled as well as skilled workers.

This article contains a complex of commitments, none of them self-executing. None could come into effect without the action of national governments. The High Authority's role is only "to guide and facilitate the application by the member States" of these measures. Unlike goods, which were granted free movement by the Treaty, people were only given the chance of achieving it when the governments took further action.

Initial action was rapid. In March 1953 the High Authority appointed a committee of experts to propose measures for carrying out the commitments made in Article 69.

By October the experts had reported. Shortly afterwards the High Authority endorsed their findings and called for an intergovernmental conference. Then the pace slowed. The conference was held in May 1954; in December the Council of Ministers approved an agreement. Administrative details were worked out in the months that followed. Before the end of 1955 Belgium, France, Italy, and the Netherlands ratified the agreement. The Bundestag did not approve German adherence until May 1956. Only in June 1957 was action completed when Luxembourg ratified. The agreement came into effect at the beginning of September, just four and one-half years after work on it had begun.

The agreement—which took more than twice as long to complete than the Treaty itself—provides free movement within the Community for certain workers in certain circumstances. To be eligible, a man must have a particular skill in coal mining or steelmaking. In addition, unless he has had formal training for his job, he must have worked for two years in one of the industries. If he is so qualified, he may apply to his government for a "labor card." With this card he may move freely from one Community country to another in response to a specific offer of work. He needs no visa and is exempt from other restrictions applying to foreign workers, subject always to the exception made in the Treaty for rules pertaining to health and national security. The card cannot be used merely to seek work (though a cardholder might use a tourist visa for job hunting). To use the card a man must have an offer of a job passed on by a labor exchange or sent to him directly in writing by an employer. If a worker should leave a job he obtained this way and seek employment outside the coal or steel industry, he would be subject to the national laws applying to foreign workers. A technical committee of national representatives attached to the High Authority (which will provide a secretariat) is to supervise the working of the agreement. If a government believes that the operation of the agreement is creating a danger of "disequilibrium in the labor market," it may ask the High Authority to convene the signatories to take appropriate steps.

This agreement is not likely to have a great impact on the economy of the Community. While the number of workers likely to qualify for labor cards is not known with any certainty, it is estimated to be about 200,000, less than one-seventh of the employees in the Community industries.[12] Not many of these men will want to migrate to another part of the Community. They have the best jobs. If they receive offers from abroad, they have a good chance of getting a raise if they stay home; the coal and steel companies are anxious to keep their skilled workers. The prospect of settling more or less permanently in another country rarely seems very attractive to European workers. Local unemployment might stimulate some workers to go abroad, but even then many of the normal drags on emigration would still operate. Others may feel, as the miners of the Midi did, that they might as well hang on and wait for times to get better (p. 408). If unemployment were widespread, there would be little incentive for employers to seek foreign labor. The great pressures for emigration, heaviest in Italy, are not relieved by the agreement. The limitations on skills and the period of employment prevent the agreement from providing an "underground railway" for the general movement of labor. The unskilled, who might feel economic pressures more strongly, or those from outside the coal and steel industries, get no direct advantage.

All this does not mean that the agreement for the free movement of labor is useless or a fraud. It widens the market for skilled labor and this may, over a long period, influence the general level of wages and make for some greater equalization of conditions among the countries of

[12] I have this figure from Ernst Haas. A considerably higher total is suggested by the rule of thumb in Germany that 80 per cent of underground workers in coal mines are skilled and 20 per cent of the steelworkers. R. Petz and H. Zöllner, *Die Beschäftigungsfreiheit der Montanfacharbeiter*, 1956, p. 46. Not all skills are covered, only those enumerated in the agreement.

the Community. The agreement improves the position of the few who may want to move and creates the possibility of easier adjustment. But it cannot be expected to have major results. Nor does it deal with the Community's biggest labor problem, which is to get and hold coal miners when less onerous jobs are available in other industries. If the time came when the structure of the coal and steel industries within the Community was changing to the extent that the level of activity declined in one country and rose in others, then the limited common market for labor would take on a new significance and could prove of great value, not only to the workers but to the Community as a whole in helping to secure a better use of resources. But shifts in the relative importance of national industries in the Community are more likely to come slowly, showing up in relative rates of growth, so that labor adjustment would take the form of lower intake rather than dismissal.

Several factors kept the scope of the agreement limited. Governments were reluctant to give up controls on the movement of labor, especially if there was a risk of a large influx of foreigners. Bureaucracies saw reason and wisdom in each of their rules and regulations. Unions were not anxious to see a breach made in the customary arrangements of the labor market. The record of ratification suggests that there was no strong opposition to the agreement in France, Holland, Belgium, and, of course, Italy. The delay in Germany's ratification, on the other hand, reflects considerable resistance on the part of organized labor. Germany had sizable unemployment during most of the postwar decade. Only in late 1954 or early 1955 could one begin to talk about full employment there. The great influx of people from the east, though on balance it probably contributed to German recovery, created a "labor reserve" which the unions would naturally not like to see expand. To be sure, there were difficulties in getting coal miners before there was full employment in Germany, but not until a fairly late stage was there serious talk about the possibility of importing labor. The German unions showed a general reluctance—not peculiar to them—to accept foreign workers. Partly cultural and psychological, this attitude takes on concrete form in objections that in dangerous occupations, especially coal mining, risks increase if language difficulties impede quick action and cooperation, or if people of different habits and histories react differently to a crisis. Very likely the safeguards of the agreement and the general condition of full employment removed all serious fears of trouble.[13]

There was also no very strong pressure for the agreement. The High Authority took an early initiative and probably kept prodding the governments in whose hands the Treaty left the matter. But there is little indication that the labor agreement had a very high priority on Luxembourg's prodding list, perhaps because its limited scope soon became apparent. Later, the High Authority proposed adding to the list of skills making a man eligible for a labor card. The Assembly's committee on social policy asked for a more liberal agreement. It suggested that workers should be free to use their labor cards to move about even if they were not responding to definite offers of jobs.[14] The group of experts originally summoned by the High Authority would have accepted a period of employment in either industry as establishing eligibility for a card that could be used in both. Some experts also considered the arrangements too restrictive, doubting for instance whether the national labor exchanges were well organized to bring together workers and employers across national boundaries.[15] On the whole, however, the pressures for quicker or more sweeping action on the movement of labor were not strong and the struggle, like the accomplishment, was a

[13] German laws requiring adequate knowledge of the language, regulations limiting certain jobs to people of recognized skills, etc., are not altered by the agreement.

[14] After the agreement was adopted the committee continued to call for revision but agreed with the High Authority that this might well wait until after the European Economic Community took its first steps in this field. CA, Commission des Affaires Sociales, *Rapport . . . par M. A. Bertrand, Rapporteur*, doc. 21, Je. 1958, p. 13 (mimeographed).

[15] Albert Delpérée, *Politique Sociale et Intégration Européenne*, 1956, pp. 141-142.

modest one though it involved what had seemed one of the more basic and revolutionary provisions of the Treaty.

FOREIGN WORKERS

Without benefit of the new agreement there has been a significant international movement of labor within the Community. At the end of 1955 about 12 per cent of the workers in Community coal mines were foreigners. About two-thirds of these were nationals of one Community country working in another; the remaining 40-odd thousand came from outside the Community. In steel the figures were somewhat lower, foreign workers accounting for 8 per cent of the labor force, again with some two-thirds of these being Community nationals. In iron mining foreigners provided nearly one-fifth of the labor force.[16]

Of the more than 170,000 foreign workers employed by Community industries, as many as 20,000 may be frontier workers who commute across a national boundary. If these are omitted, the employment of foreign workers is of minor importance in Germany, the Saar, Italy, and the Netherlands. Only in France and Belgium are foreign workers a significant part of the labor force. In France just under one-fifth of the coal miners and steelworkers, and over one-third of the employees of iron mines, were foreigners at the end of 1955. Poles were the largest foreign group in the coal mines, as they were before the war, followed by North Africans and colonials. In steel and iron, however, Italians were the most numerous. In the Belgian steel industry 16 per cent of the workers at the end of 1955 were foreigners, 70 per cent of them Italians. The really heavy concentration of foreign workers, however, is in Belgian coal mining where they have provided more than 40 per cent of the workers throughout the transitional period and, in 1957, 46.6 per cent. While these men are drawn from a number of countries—there are many Poles among them, as in France—Italians predominate, account-

[16] Figures throughout this section are derived from HA, *Étude des Obstacles à la Mobilité et des Problèmes Sociaux*, 1956, Annexe III, Tableau A (mimeographed).

ing for seven out of ten foreign workers in the Belgian mines during most of the transitional period.

Nearly eight times as many Italians mined coal in Belgium and France as in Italy. More than one-fourth of all the Italians employed in the Community steel industry worked abroad, again mostly in France and Belgium. More Italians mined iron in France and Luxembourg than in Italy. All told, Community industries employed 76,000 Italians outside Italy at the end of 1955. Two-thirds of these mined coal, 87 per cent of them in Belgium. Of the steelmakers, three-fifths were employed in France.

This sizable employment of Italians in France and Belgium was not brought about by creation of the Coal and Steel Community, nor was it of direct concern to the High Authority or other Community bodies until the Marcinelle disaster in 1956. The movement of Italian workers is governed by bilateral agreements between their government and those of France and Belgium. There is an appreciable clandestine emigration from Italy and also some movement into the mines by Italians who originally went abroad to work in other occupations, or as tourists.

The hope that people would have a chance to go abroad to find jobs has been one of the attractions of European economic cooperation for Italy. In a parliamentary debate on the Marshall Plan, Count Sforza, the Foreign Minister, said that at the very first meeting called to discuss economic cooperation he had declared "that we could not take part in European cooperation if in addition to goods and trade it did not also take account of that element so essential to us, labor. . . ." [17] Italy has held to this position, but the practical results have been meager. The OEEC sponsored manpower conferences and an organization was set up to facilitate migration. The abortive French-Italian customs union was expected to provide for the large-scale movement of workers. Technical work in job classification, training, and other matters has been undertaken by various groups. But almost all the actual migration has been under

[17] *Relazioni Internazionali*, Jl. 17, 1948, p. 506.

bilateral agreements, and it has never reached the level the Italians once expected. By the time the Schuman Plan was negotiated, the Italians' hopes were more modest but they continued to insist that the Community must provide for the movement of men as well as goods.

The Community agreement on the movement of skilled workers is largely irrelevant to Italy's problems. Few, if any, of the Italians who go to the Belgian or French coal districts have any experience as miners. Some stay and become a part of the settled, experienced labor force. But many others go only with the intention of working a few years to accumulate some money before returning home. These men are anxious to keep the training period to a minimum so that they can begin earning full wages; they want to go underground, where the pay is higher; they are willing to work long hours; they may skimp on food; they may cut corners on rules to earn bonuses for extra production. The results are bad for health, safety, and happiness. The work is onerous, the conditions on and off the job are strange. Many workers have left their families behind. They are subject to a constant pull of the homeland and often a push of the alien surroundings. Most of them are in the poorer pits of southern Belgium where working conditions are often quite bad. Naturally there is a high turnover of such labor and in some years more go back to Italy than come out to Belgium.

Since the first migration agreement was signed in 1946, there has been almost continuous negotiation between Brussels and Rome. In the '50s much of this has been concerned with safety. Several times the Italian government suspended emigration to Belgium until reforms were made; but the bans did not altogether stop illegal or indirect emigration. There were improvements, but trouble continued. Informed Italian critics avoided blaming only the Belgians. Said one, "The employers, with their entrepreneurial egoism, and the emigrants, with their anxiety for a secure tomorrow that they can enjoy in their homeland, conspire in a paradoxical manner to maintain the inhuman wage system in the Belgian basins."[18] The Italian government was blamed, as well, for ineffectiveness, for inadequate concern with the plight of the emigrants, and for failure to reduce the pressures at home that forced Italians to take jobs abroad in bad conditions.[19]

In February 1956 the Italian government again stopped the emigration of its workers because of an unsatisfactory Belgian response to complaints about health and safety measures. The High Authority offered its good offices. Then in August came the Marcinelle disaster in which 269 miners were killed, many of them Italians. Italian reactions were emotional and bitter; blame fell on Rome as well as Brussels. Issues that had been the concern of relatively few occupied many, for a time at least. The government stopped all emigration to Community coal mines. In Belgium reaction was much weaker but still the disaster focused attention on issues that had been known and temporized with for a long time. The Community, too, entered the picture on a new scale with a conference on safety that foreshadowed the possibility of more far-reaching international arrangements for the protection of miners (p. 433). By mid-1957 the Italian government declared that it was satisfied with the safety measures in Germany, Holland, and France and lifted the ban on emigration to the coal mines of those countries. By the end of the year an agreement had been reached to reopen emigration to Belgium in the fall of 1958, by which time the Belgians would have carried out a series of safety measures. Meanwhile illegal emigration continued,[20] but the Belgians also

[18] That is to say, the incentives to production that lead to ignoring health and safety. "L'Emigrazione Italiana nel Belgio," *Relazioni Internazionali*, Aug. 25, 1956, pp. 1011-1012.

[19] Riccardo Bauer, "La Catastrofe di Marcinelle," *Bollettino Quindicinale dell'Emigrazione*, Sept. 10, 1956, pp. 237-239; "Le Responsibilità," same, pp. 239-243. The files of this journal, edited by Bauer and published by Società Umanitaria, Milan, provide a large collection of complaints about policy, analyses of the conditions of Italian workers abroad, documentary material and firsthand reportage.

[20] "There are pouring into Belgium at an increased rate Italian 'tourists' whom one can meet in the mining regions but surely not in the cities that only tourists visit." *Sole d'Italia*, a Brussels weekly, quoted by *Bollettino Quindicinale dell'Emigrazione*, Nov. 10, 1957, p. 313.

turned elsewhere for miners. By the end of 1957 they had employed 6,000 Greeks and 3,500 Spaniards. There were 15,000 new immigrant coal miners from all countries during the year. The proportion of Italians fell to 62 per cent of the foreign workers.[21]

Partly as a result of this dependence on what are essentially temporary foreign workers, labor turnover in Belgian coal mines is very high. The movement into and out of the industry came to something like one-third of the underground workers in 1955 and 1956, about twice the rate in France and Germany. In addition, about one-fifth of the miners changed jobs inside the industry, moving from one colliery to another.[22] The figures do not show how many of those who came and went were foreigners but it is reasonable to suppose that they represented a higher portion of the turnover than of their total participation in the labor force which was over 40 per cent. As the following figures show, changes in the level of total employment in the Belgian coal mines usually correspond closely with the hiring and departure of foreigners.[23]

	Change from previous year (thousands)	
	Total employment	*Foreigners employed*
1953	− 5.4	− 5.4
1954	− 7.3	− 6.3
1955	+10.5	+ 8.8
1956	− 7.1	− 3.5
1957	+ 9.6	+10.3

[21] HA, *Report*, Apr. 1958, v. 2, pp. 38, 176.

[22] During 1955 new recruits to the underground mining force equaled 40 per cent of the number of workers employed at the beginning of the year, while 26 per cent left the industry for other jobs (or to return to Italy) and 8 per cent died, retired, or were fired. The net increase in the labor force was about 5 per cent. In 1956 new entries and departures each came to about 28 per cent. Retirement, etc., accounted for 7 per cent. Movement within the industry was 19 per cent. There was a 7 per cent decline in the labor force during the year. Calculated from *JO*, Je. 3, 1957, p. 242.

[23] The figures for 1953 and 1957 show changes in monthly average employment. Those for other years show changes in year-end figures. Calculated from *Informations Statistiques*, Feb.-Mar. 1955, pp. 33, 37; *JO*, Jl. 21, 1955, p. 248, and Je. 3, 1957, p. 242; HA, *Report*, Apr. 1958, v. 2, p. 38.

When there is a decline in employment, the foreigners are the first to go; when the foreigners go, there is a decline in employment. Does this mean that if Belgium is to expand production, it will have to look for more foreign miners? Not necessarily. Mines in the Campine, where productivity is fairly high and conditions reasonably good, may be able to attract Flemish workers. The Italian miners are concentrated in the south; if pits there are closed, the net effect may be a drop in the importance of foreign workers to the Belgian industry. If foreign labor proves hard to get and stricter safety regulations increase costs, dependence on foreign labor may prove to be one of the factors helping to bring about a necessary adjustment in the Belgian coal economy.

No other country in the Community has as serious a foreign-labor problem as Belgium. Foreign workers are important in the iron mines of France and Luxembourg and to a much smaller degree in the French coal mines and steel industry. But the whole Community shares the problem that gives rise to the Belgian situation: the shortage of coal miners when demand is high.

It seems to be a law of modern economics that prosperity makes it hard to mine coal (unless the veins are rich enough to permit great mechanization, as in the United States). The miners are drawn to pleasanter jobs in other industries. Families that have lived for generations with coal dust, cave-ins, silicosis, and explosions see the chance to guide their sons to a better future above ground. Fewer youths are apprenticed. (At the end of 1957, the Community had 10,000 fewer miners' apprentices than at the end of 1954.) Even when there was substantial unemployment in Belgium, it was hard to get people to go into the mines. Not surprisingly the foreign workers are concentrated in the underground jobs and the poorer mines.

Thanks to an increase of some 10 per cent in productivity (output per manshift, omitting Italy), the Community was able to raise its production of coal by about 10 million tons between 1952 and 1956 (the peak) while underground employment fell by about 32,000. This was

not enough coal to meet Community needs. No doubt
productivity can increase more, but if there is to be a very
large increase in coal output more miners will be needed.
If prosperity persists, it will be hard to attract and hold
them. Wages, fringe benefits, social security, hours, and
conditions of work in coal mines are all being improved.
Governments are stepping in with subsidies in one form or
another (pp. 221f.). This may suffice, but there is likely to
be chronic pressure to find more foreign workers.[24] Some
come from eastern Europe; southern Europe may provide
others. The only large source of new labor inside the Community is Italy. The existence of the Community improves
the chances of using it, but only if the Community in one
way or another overcomes the obstacles that have so far
prevented a greater recruitment of Italian workers and
solves some of the problems encountered in the Belgian
experience.

The present agreement for the free movement of workers will be of no help in this matter. Governments will continue to be concerned about channeling and controlling
the movement of unskilled workers. Bilateral agreements
of the traditional sort are likely to provide the framework.
The only approach to multilateral action in the Community
has been toward setting and policing standards, especially
in matters of safety and health. This might lead to action
covering a broader area of workers' protection. The Assembly, the High Authority, and the main labor groups
are urging adoption of a "miner's statute" that would
guarantee him certain treatment and conditions of work
throughout the Community. This would raise the floor in

[24] Moved in part by a temporary sharp drop in employment in the coal
mines during the summer and fall of 1955, Germans began talking about
the use of Italian labor. They expected a further call on manpower for
the creation of an army and increased production for the supply of these
forces; the reserves of labor among the emigrés and refugees were largely
used up; the labor force was soon to feel the pinch of the low level of
wartime births. After prolonged negotiations the German and Italian
governments signed an agreement arranging for the recruitment of Italian
workers for German agriculture and industry. The number who have
moved under these arrangements has been smaller than expected and few
have gone into coal mining.

some countries and might, therefore, influence the flow of
labor across national boundaries, but it would leave the
basic decisions to the governments, where the Treaty left
them. This is, then, one more item in the catalogue of problems of partial integration. It may, however, turn out to
have one peculiar feature. If the need for foreign workers
should prove to be a spur to multilateral action, this would
be a different pattern of Community dynamics, in the interplay of "pooled and unpooled," than we have found before.

The negotiation of the treaty creating a European Economic Community—the Common Market treaty—was
marked by difficult arguments over wages and labor costs.
The treaty itself contains some specific provisions on these
matters and some general language about harmonization
as an objective of the Community. The coal and steel
Treaty has only general language. Its drafters were able to
ignore or overcome the tendency that occasionally appeared
in the negotiations to make some degree of wage equalization a condition of the opening of the common market.
This was fortunate and sound for the Coal and Steel Community. Fortunate, because to make any important degree
of equalization a condition of the opening of the common
market would have been to postpone action indefinitely;
the political and administrative ability to effect such equalization does not exist. Sound, because the equalization of
wages, or total labor costs,[25] is not only unnecessary to the
proper functioning of a common market but would have
the effect of worsening the allocation of resources instead
of improving it.

The basic economic considerations are clear. So long as
there are differences in productivity, labor costs should
reflect them or there will be an arbitrary distortion of the
allocation of resources. As a practical matter, there are
always distortions, for instance in exchange rates, but it
would be a rare case in which it would be sound to meet

[25] Including social security taxes and other payments that fall on the
employer in connection with his labor force.

these problems by deliberately equalizing labor costs. If there were no differences in costs of production, there would be no basis for international trade; to eliminate one important part of these differences by fiat would be to remove part of the rationale of creating a common market. It is true that wages are set by the interplay of many forces and may not at any given moment represent the proper solution of an economic equation. Social security taxes also have arbitrary elements in them, though they are at some point limited by what an economy can "afford." But in the long run a level of labor costs is not tenable if it does not largely reflect the real economic situation. This, at least, is the usual consensus of economists.

Even if one rejects this analysis, or feels that the qualifications are more important than its general validity, there are few practical consequences that follow. There is neither sufficient agreement on principle nor adequate political unity to treat labor costs in the Coal and Steel Community on a common basis. Moreover, so long as integration is limited to a few industries, the possibilities of equalizing wages are limited because of the links between labor costs in the integrated industries and those in the rest of each national economy. Finally, one can easily see that equal labor costs are not in fact necessary to competition or survival in a common market. Within most countries there are differences in the wages paid by different firms—not least in the American "common market." There is a tendency for these differences to be regional, but there are also significant local variations and often differences within the same locality. American firms export successfully to countries paying far lower wages.

Equalization is an extreme which few have advocated. "Harmonization" is the more common term. It can mean a number of different things, but always it implies some narrowing of the gap in wages and other labor costs among the Community countries. Three quite separate questions are involved: Is harmonization necessary to have a common market? Would the common market function better if there were some degree of harmonization? If harmonization is desired, can the Community help to bring it about? The first of these was answered in the negative by the Treaty drafters. The other two questions have been involved, in various forms, in issues that have been faced by the Community, and especially in discussions of its "social policy."

The Belgian Chamber and Senate, when they approved the Treaty, said "a satisfactory balance of wages and social charges among the industries of the member countries is indispensable to the normal functioning of the common market." [26] In Luxembourg, too, the high level of wages was a source of worry when the implications of the Treaty were examined. When the common market opened and stripped away traditional protection, employers were bound to be concerned with the effect of wage differentials. They were, of course, concerned with all factors affecting the relation of their costs and those of their competitors, but perhaps especially with labor costs, since both wages and "social charges" have a man-made element which one may hope to influence by argument or other means. Yet, the Community has not been seriously troubled by strong pressure to do something about wages. What has happened has been more in the nature of complaint or argument intended to show that a particular group was at a disadvantage, and an answer—usually somewhat indirect through the High Authority's studies of labor conditions—casting doubt on the claim.

The complaints have come largely from France. Part of the French concern undoubtedly reflected the widely shared suspicion that the franc was overvalued. In its studies of workers' incomes, the High Authority was trying to get away from the difficulties of exchange rates. Though the reports properly stressed that the purchasing-power parities calculated in them should not be taken as a commentary on the soundness of the official exchange rates, since they are derived from only a certain segment of consumption and not the whole array of activities for which the exchange

---

[26] Texts of the resolutions are in CA, *Le Traité C.E.C.A. devant les Parlements Nationaux*, 1958, pp. 7, 10.

rate is the nexus, few missed the point that in their limited sphere the studies quite consistently pointed to an over-valuation of the French franc.

The argument was sometimes made that French employers carried a special burden because the social security charges they paid were higher in relation to wages than were those of other countries. Studies by the High Authority and the ILO showed that, in general, social security charges are highest where wages are lowest. Thus in 1954 "indirect charges" in the Italian coal industry equaled almost 45 per cent of "direct charges," while in Belgium they were 22 per cent. French producers were especially concerned about Germany, of course. It was true that French social security rates were higher than those in Germany, and often wage rates as well. The widespread German practice of "voluntary social security"—benefits to workers from programs run by companies or the industry—closed part but not all of the gap. Discussion of these matters helped secure wide acceptance of the point that the most significant figures are those representing total labor costs to employers—regular wages, bonuses, premium pay and the like, fringe benefits, all social security charges, and sometimes additional taxes connected with the pay-roll. There are a number of difficulties in determining these figures and in understanding the full significance of some of them. The gist of what has been done is to show that while there is a considerable spread in labor costs through the Community, the differences are not as great as has often been assumed. Calculated at official exchange rates, hourly labor costs in coal mining in 1954 ranged from 27.8 Belgian francs in Italy to 50.8 in the Saar. France was near the top and the others paid from 40 to 43 francs. In steel the range was narrower, from 32.7 francs in Holland to 47.3 in Luxembourg. The figure for Italy was 34.1, France, Germany, and the Saar around 37.5, and Belgium 41.5.[27]

In the French-German comparison, the only sharp con-

[27] R. Wagenführ, "Comparaison des Charges Salariales dans les Indus-tries de la Communauté," *Informations Statistiques*, Jl.-Aug. 1956, pp. 1-14.

trast appears in the case of coal in which labor costs are much more important than in steel. According to the High Authority's figures, the labor cost per hour in 1954 was about 20 per cent higher in France. National averages of productivity show no such spread, but Lorraine has about twice as great an advantage in productivity over the Ruhr. ILO figures prepared on a somewhat different basis show French labor costs per hour actually worked in coal mining as 26 per cent greater than German costs in 1955.[28] In steel, on the other hand, the High Authority figures show German labor costs as slightly higher than those of France in 1954 and slightly below in 1955. The ILO figures, however, show the German cost as higher in the latter year.

Too much weight should not be given to these figures. There are some rather arbitrary elements in their compilation and careful reference to the sources and methods is necessary to know just what uses can be made of them. The devaluation of the French franc required further alterations. There is no room here for a full analysis of the wage- and labor-cost situation of the Community. Perhaps enough has been said to show that while there are significant differences in wages and labor costs from country to country, there are also modifying influences and that crude use of partial data is apt to be misleading. There are also some facts about trade that have made it harder to argue within the Community that labor costs are of decisive importance. Luxembourg, with the highest wages in the Community, lives by exporting steel. Italy, with low wages, seemed to need tariff protection. Germany, whose low labor costs the French feared, imported heavily from the rest of the Community, including France.

Though the impossibility of the Community's doing anything directly about wages has been widely accepted, there has been an effort to find ways in which it can promote some kind of harmonization of labor conditions. Hours of work, vacations with pay, holidays, and fringe benefits were

---

[28] ILO, *Wages and Related Elements of Labour Cost in European Industry, 1955, Preliminary Report*, 1957, Table 15 (mimeographed). For the High Authority's comparison of real wages, see p. 434 above.

initially at the center of this discussion. It has since broadened to include labor law, social security, and the manner of settling issues between labor and management. Unlike similar discussions concerning the European Economic Community, this effort has not stemmed primarily from French employers. There have been divided counsels among Community employers, some favoring any measures that seemed likely to reduce disparities between their costs and those of their competitors while others had, of course, the opposite concern. There has also been some fear that any steps in this field were bound to increase the pressure on them to grant greater benefits and might lead to more intervention in their affairs by governments or the High Authority. More of the demand for harmonization has come from labor spokesmen, or at least some of them. Those in high-wage countries have a common interest with their employers in the competitive position of their industry. Those in low-wage countries assume that harmonization will be "in an upward direction," as the Treaty prescribes. All can expect that if there were some degree of harmonization, the employers would have less chance to argue that additional benefits could not be given because of foreign competition. Some governments have been interested in some degree of harmonization, partly in the hope of easing domestic problems. Some of the strongest and most persistent demands have come from members of the Common Assembly who have seen harmonization as an important part of the Community's social policy.

In late 1954 and early 1955 both the Consultative Committee and the Assembly urged the High Authority to interest itself in the harmonization of working conditions. Studies followed. The general idea took on specific point when, in the summer and early fall of 1955, Belgian unions pressed hard for a five-day week. Concerned about the effect on Belgium's competitive position if industries in other Community countries continued to have longer working weeks, the Belgian government suggested that the matter be dealt with in the Community. At first the unions of other countries objected—perhaps out of a desire to help their Belgian colleagues, who were planning to strike, and on the supposition that reference to the Community could only lead to delay. Subsequently, however, the unions agreed to Community discussions, probably because the Belgian government's tentative agreement to the 45-hour week created additional pressure for action. As unions in other countries also won reductions in working time and wage increases, interest in Community-wide discussions grew. The difficult problem of getting and keeping coal miners; the increasing use of bonuses of one sort or another, some of them financed by governments, thus raising issues of subsidy policy; the agitation for a Miner's Statute; the negotiation of a social security convention to go along with the agreement on the movement of labor;[29] and the conference on mining safety that followed the Marcinelle disaster, all added some stimulus to this movement.

While there has been a great increase in discussion, concrete results of the drive for harmonization have been rather limited. The High Authority has made a series of studies comparing labor conditions in the six countries and has provided much fuller accounts of current developments in its annual reports. It was slow, however, to do anything about organizing joint committees of employers and workers, which the Consultative Committee had recommended in December 1954. This was one of the factors that led the labor members to threaten to walk out of the Consultative Committee in the fall of 1955. The High Authority's rather gingerly approach seems to have been made up of its own doubts about what could be done in these discussions, reluctance on the part of employers to engage in them, and opposition by some governments.

Separate groups for coal and steel began meeting late in

[29] The Treaty called for a coordination of social security measures to ensure that workers who moved to other countries were equitably treated. After several years of work, in which the ILO played a leading part, a convention was signed in December 1957. It would largely replace the numerous bilateral and multilateral agreements that already exist among Community countries. The new agreement, which covers most forms of social security, will apply to almost all workers, not just those in the coal and steel industries.

1956. In the steel group it was possible to get the workers and employers together during 1957, though ostensibly only to agree on facts and to examine reports prepared by experts on a variety of factors concerned with working conditions. In coal there were no joint sessions because the employers were unwilling to have them and presented a united front. They feared strong demands by the unions for something like the Miner's Statute.[30] The High Authority met separately with each group but could get no agreement on an agenda for a joint meeting. The next step was to bring in the governments; still there was reluctance. Only in October 1958, when the coal mining industry knew that it was in difficulties, did the tripartite committee have its first meeting.

One of the principal advocates of the joint committees was André Renard, a leader of the Belgian metal-workers union and a member of the Consultative Committee. Thanks largely to his initiative, the leaders of the free trade unions of all the Community countries had endorsed this approach in the spring of 1954.[31] Later that year Renard explained the idea to a Belgian audience:

Would it really be impossible that the High Authority should bring together representatives of the employers and of the workers and simply ask them to try to apply Articles 2 and 3 of the Treaty?

I think that we are all wise enough not to begin the application of these articles by looking for an agreement on wages, but we know that we could, in a committee of that sort, begin work on the famous question of the reduction in the length of working hours. We could examine the problems of vocational education, limitations on age, access to the profession and retirement. The first international convention could obviously only be a framework establishing minimum stand-

[30] E. B. Haas, *The Uniting of Europe*, 1958, p. 382. After having been initially receptive to the idea of a miner's statute, the employers, as reflected by a study group of the coal industry, became rather cool to measures of harmonization and concluded that the High Authority should not overstep the jurisdiction given it by the Treaty. "Kohlenmarktanalyse der Hohe Behörde," *Der Volkswirt*, Oct. 11, 1957, p. 2272.

[31] *Compte Rendu de la Conférence Intersyndicale C.I.S.L.-C.E.C.A.*, Luxembourg, Mar. 16-18, 1954, pp. 169-170.

ards, for we are fully in agreement that it would not be necessary to go into detail but to leave each country a certain
freedom of action in applying the provisions as is done, among
other places, in our own country in the Conseil national du
travail and in the *commissions paritaires* of industry. If we
could set this afoot—that day we would have the beginning of
harmonization.[32]

As Renard indicates, these discussions may be seen as the
first steps toward Community-wide collective bargaining.
Anything like this seems far off. The intimacy and common
interest required for comprehensive Community-wide collective bargaining do not exist among the parties on either
side of the table, let alone between them and those on the
other side. And yet, one can imagine that things will be said
and done that constitute, perhaps in small ways, "collective
bargaining" in a limited sense. Another possible product of
the *commissions paritaires*, Renard suggests, may be formal
conventions on conditions of work. Considering the complexity that would be required and the delays such a procedure is bound to entail, this might well be one of the least
useful results. Again, one can imagine that after a time certain possibilities might appear which would make a formal
convention useful, at least in minimum standards.

It would not be surprising if the international discussions
had their main influence on national collective bargaining.
Conceivably, the national groups from each side, workers
and employers, might reach some agreement on what they
would ask or grant. But even short of this, the discussions
may educate the parties to national collective bargaining
about possibilities and consequences—what one might ask
for, who else gives or gets it, what others are likely to do if
similarly situated. The omission of wages from the discussions increases the chances of agreement, but the matters

[32] André Renard, *Action Sociale au Sein de la C.E.C.A.*, Comptes
Rendus des Travaux de la Société d'Économie Politique de Belgique,
Nov. 1954. Quoted by Delpérée, cited, p. 220. Though the term *commission paritaire* is often used in the Community, the High Authority
avoids it because "enraging certain of the social partners, it could be an
obstacle to the meeting of the two interested parties." Finet, CA, *Débats*,
Je. 6, 1957, p. 630.

being discussed all affect labor costs so there will not be much room for maneuver. There are, of course, many intermediate possibilities that would assign a limited role to the international communities and leave the principal decisions to the national sphere. It is along these lines that development seems most likely.

It is difficult to judge these matters from the outside and at such an early stage of their development.[33] Much depends on whether the unions really mean to use the mixed commissions to press for harmonization. Though that is the professed aim, and the public statements are unanimous, there have also been indications that the German unions, especially the steelworkers, do not fully share this view, or at least do not hold it as strongly as some others. This may have changed when the metal workers broke out of the "quiescent" pattern of postwar German unionism and assumed a more militant stance; their main preoccupations were domestic, however, and they proved reluctant to risk dissipating their strength or hampering their tactics by coordinated actions even with the German miners' union. Even if the unions were fully agreed on the desirability of promoting harmonization through the mixed commissions, progress would depend equally on the employers. Their interests, too, are divided and may be resolved one way or the other. If the experience of the coal commission is any guide, union solidarity may make the employers unwilling to let the role of the commissions expand. Finet referred to some of these limitations in an effort to disabuse some members of the Assembly who spoke as if the High Authority had only to take the initiative to set the process of harmonization in motion. He said, "Unhappily, the experience I have had in contact with interested groups, capital and labor, requires me to say that this idea of building a social community is far from being accepted by all." [34]

On balance, the Community's record in the harmoniza-

---

[33] Ernst Haas, who has looked quite closely into the matter, attributes a number of specific results to the meetings of the mixed commissions and attaches more importance to them than my comments may suggest. Cited, p. 382.

[34] CA, *Débats*, Je. 26, 1957, p. 629.

tion of wages and labor conditions is one of little ventured, little gained. And probably this was just as well. For the immediate tasks of creating the Community there was neither an important need to venture more, nor a reasonable prospect of much success if it had been done. To have tried, or promised, more would have involved the Community in difficulties that could hardly have been happily resolved. In the long run matters may look somewhat different. The kinds of gains to be had from harmonization may seem more important; these may not be primarily economic. But the extent of harmonization is still likely to depend less on measures taken by the High Authority than on the action of other groups, stimulated by the political and economic impact of the Community.

ORGANIZED LABOR AND THE COMMUNITY

As this chapter has repeatedly shown, the Community's record in dealing with labor matters is peculiar. Working with little in the way of powers, the High Authority has made a real effort to woo labor. It seems to have had a good deal of success, even though the results of some measures are not striking, and the total effect is somewhat less clear than what the Community has done in other fields. To get a full sense of this, one must know something of the general relation of organized labor to the Community.

When the Schuman Plan was proposed there was a favorable, but somewhat guarded, reaction from the main labor organizations of the Western European countries. Many factors entered into the calculation of advantage and risk. But in retrospect, these arguments seem less significant than the fact that organized labor was active from the beginning in appraising the proposals, formulating its views, and bringing them to bear on the negotiations. At the outset, a committee of the ICFTU undertook a study of Schuman's proposals. When Treaty negotiations began, this committee (or an offshoot of it) served as a center for the discussion of the views of the labor representatives from different countries and, to some extent, as a means of coordinating their positions in the negotiations. At the same time that he accepted Schuman's invitation to negotiate, Adenauer let it be known that he would appoint a labor representative on the German delegation.[35] Other countries followed suit. Monnet encouraged this and repeatedly said that labor participation was an essential of the new organization.

Whether as the result of the initiative of the labor spokesmen or of people who were anxious to show that the workers had something to gain from the Schuman Plan, organized labor was given an important position in the Community's organization. The agreement to let the ICFTU and the Christian unions nominate a member of the High Authority was the most striking of these measures (p. 111). Equal status for labor with producers and users in the Consultative Committee was another.[36] The unions at one time urged that the ILO be permitted to name a member of the Court;[37] this was not done but a labor man was named to the Court, perhaps as the result of an agreement like that concerning the High Authority.[38] A second labor man found a place on the High Authority when Heinz Potthoff was named as one of the members of German nationality. A third was added when Roger Reynaud became the French member who succeeded René Mayer, while Finet, the unions' own choice at the outset, became chairman of the High Authority.[39] In organizing the staff of the High Authority, people

[35] *The New York Times*, May 17, 1950. This was Hans vom Hoff, a member of the executive committee of the DGB.

[36] In addition, Article 48 of the Treaty provided that the High Authority should consult producers' organizations only when they admitted labor to an equal position on their boards. At one time interpreted as likely to revolutionize producers' organization, this article has in fact proved unimportant. Separate bodies were organized to meet the Treaty requirements, and while the High Authority frequently refers questions to them, there is little to indicate that this is anything but a formality.

[37] Resolution of the ICFTU Committee on the Schuman Plan in *ICFTU Information Bulletin*, Nov. 1, 1950, p. 3.

[38] P. J. S. Serrarens, named a judge of the Court, was from 1920 to 1952 secretary-general of the International Confederation of Christian Unions.

[39] Reynaud, a member of the executive of the CFTC, was also a government official who served on the Conseil Économique and various major French economic commissions. There was some resentment in labor circles that the unions were not adequately represented in the Euratom and Common Market commissions.

suggested by the unions were considered, and although it may have been difficult to find a large number of them with the qualifications required for this supranational civil service, some were added to the staff.

To maintain its relations with the High Authority, the ICFTU organized a liaison bureau in Luxembourg. The work of the small staff is directed by a Committee of Twenty-one. On it sit representatives of the coal and steel unions of each of the six countries and of the national free trade union federations. The remaining three members represent the international trade secretariats in coal and steel and the ICFTU's European regional office. Much of the Bureau's work is, of course, a matter of keeping abreast of developments in the High Authority and letting people in the unions know what is going on. The Bureau is not able to do a great deal of research itself but may, to some extent, stimulate the research departments of member unions and national federations to work on matters of common interest.

Its most important function, however, is to see to the threshing out of issues among union representatives before they take a position in the organs of the Community. Mostly this is a matter of meetings among the labor members of the Consultative Committee before its sessions (or of the union representatives and experts on the special committees that prepare reports). At first their agreement was limited for the most part to measures directly affecting labor. Later they worked with some success to establish agreed positions on broader issues of Community policy.[40] Unanimity does not always result and sometimes it is only tactical. There have, however, been some important cases in which unions that expected to take contrary views overcame their difficulties in the sessions of the Committee of Twenty-one and presented a united front in the Consultative Committee. The French unions favored the proposed increase in the Ruhr coal price in 1955, but they were

[40] I am indebted to Ernst Haas for this simplified summary of a complicated process. Chapter 10 of his *The Uniting of Europe*, cited, goes into the matter fully.

persuaded to go along with the prevalent view of the other unions opposing the rise.

The Christian unions for some time had a much less elaborate liaison arrangement. In the spring of 1955, however, they opened a new office in Luxembourg with full-time representation. More important, the basis of this action was the creation of a new Fédération des Syndicats Chrétiens dans la C.E.C.A. in which a common position could be adopted by a two-thirds vote which would bind the representatives of all member unions, thus ensuring a greater degree of unity than the ICFTU unions could always command. The representative of the federation in Luxembourg has also been given a good bit of authority in such matters as calling on the experts of member unions to work on Community questions, and of representing the group on special committees of the Consultative Committee if spokesmen for the member unions were not available.[41]

The Christian unions and the ICFTU unions have made it a practice to exchange views before sessions of the Consultative Committee in the hope of finding common ground. But with their differing traditions, organizations, and policies they have not sought more formal arrangements. The Catholic unions are weaker than those belonging to the ICFTU. In recognition of this fact, they have normally filled only three or four seats in the Consultative Committee while the free trade unions have filled 12 or 13.[42] This roughly follows a division worked out by the two groups of unions during 1952 but never given official status. The strength of the Christian unions is in France, Belgium, the Netherlands, and Italy. In Germany they represent only

[41] Members of the Consultative Committee may send experts in their place to meetings of the various special committees but not to plenary sessions of the full body.

[42] One seat is held by the Confédération Générale des Cadres. The unions do not directly name the members of the Consultative Committee. The recognized labor organizations nominate two men for every post allotted to them. The Council of Ministers then chooses the Consultative Committee from among these nominees. In a few cases it has asked for additional nominations. There have been occasional complaints from the unions about the failure of the Council to choose certain individuals.

the white-collar workers. I. G. Metall and I. G. Bergbau, the German steel and coal unions, are among the largest and most powerful in the DGB. Because of the combination of union strength with the dominant role of Germany in the Community's production, the German unions are the most important in the ICFTU group. They pay more than half the expenses of the Committee of Twenty-one (but in votes are on the same basis as everyone else). Another source of the German unions' strength lies in the split in the labor movements in France and Italy. Only the non-Communist unions are represented in the Community. But Force Ouvrière and CFTC in France and the CISL and UIL in Italy are, on the whole, weaker than the CGT and CGIL from which they separated and which are Communist-dominated. In the coal and steel industries of these two countries the Communist unions are strong. This inevitably weakens the influence of the democratic French and Italian unions compared to the German unions who have no Communist rivals, and also limits the extent to which they can be as effective in handling Community affairs.

The Communist unions early took a stand against the Schuman Plan and, while it has not been a major target for them, they have criticized it from time to time. They have sought to blame the Community for all unemployment or other difficulties suffered by their members. They have attacked it on nationalist grounds and anticapitalist grounds and fitted it easily into their caricature of an American-dominated Europe. They have tried from time to time to impede Community activities but their main course has probably been one of ignoring the Community. In turn the Community has firmly excluded the Communist-dominated unions (and Communist parties) from its activities.

The experience of the democratic unions in the Community has been on balance quite a good one. Except for short periods, there has been little unemployment. Wages have risen appreciably in all the Community countries.[43]

---

[43] In the third quarter of 1957, hourly steel wages were from 26 to 49 per cent higher than in 1953. In coal the range was from 26 to 46. HA, *Report*, Apr. 1958, v. 2, pp. 205, 207.

Hours of work have fallen. Whether the Community is given credit for these gains is less important than the fact that labor has at least no major complaints on this score that might be blamed on the common market. Lay-offs resulting from the fall of demand in 1958 may provide a test. The unions have benefited from the studies of labor problems made by the High Authority.[44] Probably most important of all to the attitude of the unions is the fact that, as one observer put it, "doors have been open to them" in a way they did not wholly expect and to a degree that is unusual in the coal and steel industries. The Assembly, the Consultative Committee, and their committees have provided places where labor can both make its views felt and learn about issues.[45] The unions have found ears to listen when they had something to say; their opinion has been sought. They have had their people, or people they trusted, in important positions in the Community. They have had ready access to the High Authority. In short, they have been on the inside.

Of course, one never has enough influence. Things are done that do not suit labor; things are not done for which it has pressed. Nor is it politic to seem contented. Hence, it is possible to say that, "Trade unions, of course, feel that their lobbying efforts have largely gone unrewarded and that the High Authority is more receptive to producer demands than to any others." [46] But these things vary with

[44] In the spring of 1954 Walter Freitag, head of the DGB, said to a conference of unions, "I ask you again, and let each cross his heart, who can tell me the wage situation in his country? I affirm with certainty that no one of us knows it. . . ." *Compte Rendu de la Conférence Inter-syndicale* . . . , cited, p. 109. He was urging that the unions make their own studies and not depend on the High Authority, but in fact it has done the fullest work at least in making international comparisons.

[45] From the outset labor has complained about the distribution of seats in the Consultative Committee. The "users," who are equally represented with the workers and the coal and steel producers, are actually spokesmen for industries that use coal and steel, and therefore "employers," not consumers, in the eyes of labor. The unions' feeling that they are outnumbered, is one of the reasons the High Authority has indicated that it is interested in the views expressed in the Committee and not in votes unless they are unanimous.

[46] Haas, cited, p. 476.

time, issues, and tactics. Taken in the large, I think that union leaders realize that in the Community they have attained a status in the consideration of affairs, and an influence over them, that was rare in the six countries.[47] This satisfies what was in many ways the main aim of the unions in the initial negotiations: to assure themselves a place. The experience has proved to them that the Community is not dominated by employers and is not a cloak for nefarious arrangements. They have reason to believe the High Authority is impartial, as between unions and employers, though they may think it is too weak or misguided on some matters. They are themselves better able to face employers thanks to some of the things the Community has done.

It is not only in labor questions and "social policy" that the unions have gained a position. Prices, investments, and other broad economic questions are obviously of importance to them. In the Community they not only have a say in these matters but seem to feel they are learning something. Asked about the advantages of the Community to labor, Heinrich Straeter, a key figure in I. G. Metall, said:

The biggest [advantage] in comparison with past international trade union activities is that in the Community, trade unions have to provide concrete opinions on practical questions. Their work in international organizations has till now been exclusively confined to recommendations and the expression of non-committal views. Previously, the unions never studied such questions as market research or systems of pricing. Yet these are ultimately of great importance to the workers.

Now, within the Consultative Committee, labor unions have to give opinions on this kind of question. They discuss economic problems jointly with the representatives of the enterprises. In many countries such practical discussion, before important decisions are taken, had hitherto not been possible. This is a definite advance.

To the question, "What would you list as the main positive results for labor of the High Authority's work so far?", Straeter answered:

[47] One might find some exceptions, but the most obvious, German *Mitbestimmung*, has not in fact given the unions as great a voice in the coal and steel industries as they probably expected, though this is not officially admitted.

Three things. The supervisory machinery which ensures that firms publish their prices and do not discriminate between buyers. Investment policy, which influences firms in a forward direction. The support given to research, for instance, into the problems of silicosis.[48]

Whether one agrees with them or not, these are interesting choices for a labor leader with continuous Community experience. In the same vein, when the ICFTU held a conference to discuss possible changes in the Treaty, many of its recommendations dealt with the broader aspects of the Community, not just labor and social policy.[49]

The place that labor has found for itself has influenced its view of the Community. Although there was support for the Schuman Plan among the unions, there was also a certain reserve and some pockets of opposition. Uncertainty and some suspicion were fairly widespread. In Germany in particular, where the position of union leaders was influenced by the SPD's opposition to the Schuman Plan, the basic attitude was described to me by one union leader as *ziemlich ablehnend*—rather negative. "We went along with it, we accepted it as a fact." Sometime in 1954 or 1955 there came a change. If they were going along with the Community, and accepting it as a fact, perhaps the wise thing to do was to make a real effort to see what could be gotten out of it. Certain key union officials who participated in the Committee of Twenty-one and the Consultative Committee seem to have been largely responsible for this shift, with Otto Brenner, president of I. G. Metall, playing a key role. There was, too, a link with the shift in the German Socialists' attitude toward Western European integration, but how much each influenced the other is a subject for separate inquiry.

The Action Committee for a United States of Europe, organized by Jean Monnet to support the proposals for Euratom and the Common Market, provided the first occasion on which the names of major German Socialist and labor leaders appeared alongside those of men who had been

[48] HA, *Bulletin from the European Community for Coal and Steel,* Nov. 1954, pp. 4, 5.
[49] Same, Je.-Jl. 1957, p. 3.

identified for years with the "European movement." The Germans had fully aligned themselves with their colleagues of the other Schuman Plan countries. Inside the Community, the Assembly and the Consultative Committee intensified their interest in the High Authority's work on social questions. This was not entirely due to the labor members, but they have played an important part in it.

Labor seems to have decided that the Community is a useful instrument for economic progress. Some labor leaders now feel that it was a mistake not to put more social provisions in the Treaty in the first place. To rectify the situation, some urge amendment of the Treaty. Others would prefer to interpret the existing general provisions as justifying a more active "social" policy. There is, however, some difference between those who would like the High Authority to play a leading role and those who emphasize that labor's advance depends primarily on itself. In the view of the latter, wages and working conditions can best be determined by bargaining between workers and employers, with the backing of social legislation by governments and possibly some help from the High Authority. The milieu of the Community is a favorable one, they have found, and they will no doubt work to keep it that way, but they would look to it more to create openings and an ambiance than to provide decisions that would involve direct intervention in the affairs of labor. This is probably also the course preferred by the High Authority, the governments, and the employers. Finet said that those who wanted to give the High Authority greater powers in matters of wages and working conditions were asking it "to put a finger between the tree and the bark. That is never a very comfortable position. But if we were tempted to undertake that operation, capital and labor would say to us, 'Go take a walk. You have no business in this matter; it is not your problem. Watch over fines and the common market and let us discuss questions affecting wages face to face.' " [50]

If this view prevails, and there is much to be said for it, there is unlikely to be a radical change in Community labor

[50] CA, *Débats*, Je. 26, 1957, p. 631.

policy. The High Authority may well become more active in social policy, but essentially along the lines already set. This would probably increase the indirect influence of the Community on labor's position in each country. An alternative would be such an increase in the use of the mixed commissions that the High Authority (and, probably, the governments) would be drawn in to help settle disputes. If the unions of the Community find it advantageous to increase their action in common, events might take this turn. Outside this sphere, the High Authority will need to develop a labor policy for coal if it is to help meet one of the greatest needs in expanding production. Adaptation and the place of foreign workers are other points at which it may become more involved in labor questions. While the needs of production may be in the forefront in determining how active the Community is in labor matters, another force will be at work as well. Labor has already achieved what is, in a broad sense, a political gain from the Community: an increase in influence and status. If labor makes a serious effort to turn the political gain to economic advantage, the Community will inevitably be drawn into new fields.

PART III

THE COMMUNITY AND
THE REST OF THE WORLD

SEVENTEEN

THE COMMUNITY'S FOREIGN TRADE

THE GREATEST effort of the Coal and Steel Community was naturally turned inward to the process of establishing the common market. In external relations the goals were less clearly set out and the problems seemed less urgent. Still, foreign trade[1] is important to the Community and what the Community does about it is important to other countries.

To create a common market is to draw a line distinguishing it from the rest of the world. Transactions inside the line are treated differently from those that cross it. But the distinction is not exactly like the familiar one between domestic and foreign trade. Combining six national markets, the Community started with six sets of relations to the outside world. The Treaty provided only limited means of unifying them. The countries of the Community faced the rest of the world as a unit in some matters, but not in others. From the interplay between trade among the six in the common market and the trade of each with the rest of the world some problems arose that affected both kinds of trade and touched different countries differently.

Other questions arose for the rest of the world. The Schuman Plan created a great new political and economic unit. How would its power be used? Would buyers, sellers, and competitors face a new, large-sized cartel? Even if the producers of the six countries did not form a cartel, the new relations among them would have an effect on outsiders. Could

---

[1] Throughout this chapter the Community is treated as a unit. "Foreign trade," "exports" and "imports" exclude trade among Community countries. "Foreign countries" and "third countries" are used interchangeably to refer to countries outside the Community.

those who sold to Community countries meet the competition of goods that did not have to cross the external trade barriers? Could those who bought from the Community count on getting supplies if five other countries had a prior claim? The pricing practices of the Community would affect the costs of its own producers and of some outsiders as well. What influence could the rest of the world have on how the Community conducted its foreign trade?

The Treaty did not go very far in answering these questions. From the beginning, Schuman and Monnet were emphatic in saying that the Community would promote trade with the rest of the world and not hamper it. It would not be autarkic; it would lower, not raise, trade barriers. It would not function as a cartel, or in other ways hurt third countries. The Community must be concerned with the interest of other countries, Schuman told a Swiss audience. It must not replace national egoism with the egoism of the six.[2]

The Treaty bears the imprint of this approach in some general provisions (mostly in Art. 3). In seeing to it that the common market "is regularly supplied," the Community is to take "into account the needs of third countries." It is also to "foster the development of international trade and ensure that equitable limits are observed in prices charged in foreign markets." While expanding Community production is an aim, this must be done "under conditions which preclude any protection against competing industries except where justified by illegitimate action on the part of such industries or in their favour."

The specific provisions on foreign trade are less detailed and clear-cut than those concerning the internal affairs of the Community. For the most part trade policy is left in the hands of the governments who pledge each other cooperation and mutual assistance. Old trade agreements remain in effect but new ones are not to have provisions infringing the Treaty. National export commitments are to some extent safeguarded in case supplies are allocated within the Community. Governments are free to use quotas, but

[2] *Neue Zürcher Zeitung*, Feb. 13, 1953.

the High Authority may recommend a change if they are more restrictive "than is called for by the situation which justified their establishment or maintenance." Other powers given the High Authority are also not very sharply defined. It can act against imports if there is dumping or unfair competition or if, when demand is declining, coal and steel are being imported in such increased quantities as to "inflict serious damage on production, within the common market, of similar or directly competitive products." Subject to a number of qualifications it can set maximum prices on exports. Little or no use has been made of these provisions.[3] The most important of the Community's foreign trade problems have been of a different sort.

STEEL TARIFFS

The Treaty eliminated tariffs within the Community but left them standing on imports from the rest of the world. There were no duties on coal, scrap, or iron, except for coke going into Italy. The national tariff rates on steel differed substantially so it would have been possible to evade the high French rates by paying the low Benelux duties and then shipping the steel across the customs-free frontier. This is by now a familiar problem of a free trade area. There are several ways to handle it, all rather cumbersome and none quite foolproof. The Community chose a fairly simple course that provided a rough solution. In accordance with the transitional Convention (Sec. 15), the Benelux

[3] There are some others as well. Where details are relevant they appear later in connection with problems the Community faced. The provisions summarized are in Arts. 59, 61, and 71 to 75. These matters have scarcely been mentioned in the High Authority's *Reports*. The fullest survey was made by an Assembly committee which reported that the High Authority had been discussing trade agreements with governments as they were negotiated but had only found it necessary to suggest that promises to deliver coal and steel should refer to the country's obligation under the Treaty if allocations were established in times of shortage. The High Authority had found no occasion to intervene in the use of import licenses. CA, Sous-Commission de la Politique Commerciale, *Rapport . . . par M. René Pleven, Rapporteur*, doc. 1 (1957-58), Nov. 1957, pp. 18-20. The creation of this subcommittee in February 1957 (by the common market and external relations committees) was a sign of growing interest in the Community's foreign trade.

countries agreed to apply their low regular tariff to only a certain quantity of imports. The amount was agreed on from time to time by the Benelux governments and the High Authority, taking account of past imports and changing conditions of production and consumption. On additional imports the Benelux countries levied a tariff equivalent to the lowest applied by any other Community country. As a further safeguard, Benelux importers had to agree not to re-export to Community countries steel they had imported at the low tariff rate.

On paper this solution seemed fairly loose. It could have encouraged indirect shipments to any country whose tariff was above the second lowest in the Community. Enforcement might not have been easy; agreement on the size of the tariff quota could have proved troublesome. In practice, the system worked smoothly enough. The tariff quotas were fairly large and regularly increased. There have been no serious complaints and no noticeable shifts in trade. Several factors probably explain this: high transport costs limited the gain from indirect shipments; French and German tariffs were lowered, narrowing the gap; in a period of high demand the steel trade did not make strenuous efforts to find new markets; steel imports were not of great importance to the Community. The obligation of the Benelux countries to maintain tariff quotas expired at the end of the transitional period. At the same time an adjustment of Community tariff rates virtually eliminated whatever risk of indirect shipment remained.

Community tariff rates on steel were lowered substantially during the transitional period. At the outset, Benelux tariff rates ranged from 1 to 8 per cent, and those of other countries from 7 to 28 per cent (details on p. 145). When the common market opened, most of the French and German steel duties which had been suspended were put back in force. Some of the German rates were lowered to align them with the French, and a temporary tariff quota permitted some 120,000 tons of steel a month to come in at lower duties. In 1956 Germany cut its steel duties again as part of a general tariff reduction intended to help hold down internal prices.[4] At various times Community countries suspended duties on products needed to meet domestic shortages, such as certain kinds of pig iron and various steels for special purposes.

The Community also lowered tariffs by negotiation with outside countries. These began, unsuccessfully, in 1954. Austria feared that the opening of the common market for special steels would limit its traditional exports to Germany and Italy (by giving Community producers easier access to those markets). The High Authority offered special treatment for Austrian products in return for assurances about Austrian tariff rates and the prices to be charged for Austrian steel.[5] No agreement was reached until May 1956, after negotiations in the GATT tariff-bargaining session of that year. In a new departure in international relations the High Authority negotiated for the whole Community (though it was still the governments who had the legal power to change tariffs and on whom the responsibilities of GATT membership rested). The main negotiations were with the United States and Austria. As a result of the bargaining, the Americans agreed to reduce their duties on a number of products imported from the Community, including steel bars and tubes, by 15 per cent (at 5 per cent a year over three years). Austria made concessions on all the steel products it normally imported from Community countries. In return the Community made two

[4] The maximum cuts were 10 per cent, instead of 13 per cent as planned, perhaps because of pressure from the Council of Ministers. *Relazioni Internazionali*, Aug. 4, 1956, p. 953. The Germans also had to promise there would be no re-exports to Community countries.

[5] The High Authority proposed that on sales equal to those Austria had made in 1951-53 the existing duty (which was below the legal level) should apply on shipments to Germany and, on sales to Italy, a duty halfway between the rate applied to Community products and the regular third-country rate. Above these tariff quotas the full legal rate was to apply. The High Authority asked the Austrians to guarantee that the new tariff they were about to impose should bear no more heavily on Community products than the old one. It also asked that the Austrians refrain from applying dumping prices to their sales to Italy. The Austrians wanted larger quotas, refused an agreement on prices, and objected to the French import tax of 15 per cent. There were conversations with Sweden about the same time which seem to have led nowhere.

kinds of concessions. French and German duties on some special steels were reduced to 8-10 per cent. Italian duties on both ordinary and special steels were to come down in two stages from about 22-23 per cent to about 14-15 per cent. The amount that could come into Italy at these lower rates was limited by a tariff quota.[6] While the United States and Austria would presumably be the main beneficiaries of these concessions, they would be extended, as a matter of course, to all other GATT countries as well. Among Community countries it seemed likely that the main effect on imports would be in Italy, while the exporter most likely to benefit from the American reductions was Belgium. As a committee of the Assembly pointed out, this was a new kind of demonstration of Community solidarity.[7] In a side deal, outside GATT, the Community got assurances from Austria that it would not undercut Community prices by selling its special steels to Italy at less than domestic Austrian prices.

As the end of the transitional period approached, the Community engaged in a two-phased set of tariff negotiations. Among themselves, the Community countries worked on the "harmonization" of their external duties. In the Council of Association (see pp. 506-512) they negotiated a tariff agreement with Great Britain. This had been on the agenda for some time but reached final form only on November 25, 1957, when the agreement was signed by the seven governments and the High Authority. Under the agreement, Britain reduced its duties on iron and steel prod-

----

[6] An Assembly committee estimated that the Community exports to the United States benefiting from concessions came to 17 million tons, while the American goods coming to the Community had been about 10 million tons. Austria, it estimated, had made concessions on $2 million worth of Community products and received concessions on about $15 million worth of shipments to the Community ($12.5 million to Italy alone). CA, Commission des Affaires Politiques et des Relations Extérieures de la Communauté, *Rapport . . . par M. P. Struye, Rapporteur,* doc. 27 (1956-57), pp. 15, 16. However, Austria reduced its duties on some non-Treaty products exported by Italy.

[7] Same, p. 15. The committee also judged that no Community country could have secured these concessions—especially from the United States —if it had been bargaining alone.

ucts to a maximum of 10 per cent from their previous range
of 15 to 33⅓ per cent ad valorem. This was not as drastic a
step as it sounds since the duties had almost all been suspended for several years. The Community governments,
for their part, agreed to apply their new harmonized duties
to British products—a step they could not avoid under their
GATT obligations to give Britain most-favored-nation
treatment. Whatever real concessions there were to Britain
must, therefore, have been made in the formulation of the
harmonized tariff itself. The agreement also provided for
consultation if either party wished to raise its duties.

The harmonization measures played a part in reducing
steel tariffs and also helped to make the Community more
of a unit in its dealings with the rest of the world. The Community's basic instruments were a bit vague on harmonization. The Treaty envisaged the possibility of upper and
lower tariff limits set by unanimous agreement of the
governments, with individual countries free to choose
within the range (Art. 72). The Convention seemed to take
it for granted that harmonization "with the least protective
tariffs practised in the Community" was desirable but did
not treat the subject very fully. One rule, however, was
crucial. The Benelux countries were very firm about not
wanting to depart from their low-tariff policies. The Convention guaranteed that they would not have to raise duties
by more than two percentage points in the process of harmonization. Coupled with the ending of the tariff quota
system, this would establish the range of harmonization
unless governments were willing to risk indirect imports.[8]
Both the aim of harmonization and the arrangement about
the Benelux rate were incorporated in the waiver granted
to the Community by GATT (p. 525ff.) and thus took on
some of the color of an international obligation. Little was
said about these matters in the early years of the transitional
period, but toward the end the High Authority and the

---

[8] Subject to a number of limitations, the High Authority could permit
a country to check indirect imports after the tariff quotas had been
dropped; but if both France and Germany continued to do this, Benelux
would not have to raise its original duties (Sec. 15).

Council of Ministers worked intensively on the terms of harmonization.

The groundwork had been laid by the partial alignment of French and German duties in the early part of the transitional period.[9] Therefore harmonization was going to mean a substantial measure of reduction. In the agreement that was adopted, Benelux raised most of its duties by the expected two percentage points and Germany reduced its to the same level. This produced a tariff of 5 to 6 per cent ad valorem on most steel products and 8 per cent on hoop and strip. (The German rates had been 10 to 12 per cent on most of these products but ran as high as 18 to 22 on sheets and plates.) France set its duties one percentage point higher and Italy two to four points. These margins, it was said, sufficed to prevent indirect imports while leaving France and Italy with somewhat more protection against foreign competition than Germany and Benelux had. Nevertheless, they represented substantial reductions. French duties on steel products that had ranged between 10 and 22 per cent were now 6 to 9 per cent; in Italy the decline was from a general level of 22 or 23 per cent to 9 or 10. In addition, for two years France was to keep higher duties on certain qualities of pig iron and alloy steels while Italy charged higher rates on ferromanganese and rustless steels. On coke Italy maintained a 10 per cent duty though the others had none. Compared to the rates in effect at the beginning of the transitional period (p. 145), the cuts were even bigger. Nevertheless, Sweden and Austria disliked some of the new rates and began discussions that might lead to further negotiations.

This appreciable dismantling of the Community's steel tariffs was accomplished without great travail. There were, of course, some complaints from producers who worried what the effects might be, but nothing like the wave of opposition one commonly associates with major tariff

---

[9] In addition to taking the steps already mentioned, the two countries had aligned their tariffs on special steels (just before the common market opened) at an average rate of about 11 per cent, almost midway between the 8 per cent rate in effect in Germany and the French rate of 15 per cent.

reductions. Partly no doubt this is due to the factor that eased the Community's task in so many matters, at least temporarily—the high level of production and prices. Most foreign countries have offered only rather small quantities of steel for sale in the Community; Britain, the nearest major source, has restricted exports.[10] Partly, too, the acceptance of these external reductions must reflect the fact that the most important tariff barriers—those against neighbors—had already come down in the creation of the common market. The Community producers had found that this drastic action was less damaging than they had feared, so they could view milder measures in dealing with the external world with somewhat more equanimity. A recession would raise new questions, but probably not very troublesome ones. The countries retain the power to limit imports by quotas (except where other obligations prevent it) and not all of the new tariff rates are bound under GATT schedules.

IMPORTS OF RAW MATERIALS

While steel imports have been quite unimportant to the Community, foreign coal, iron ore, and scrap have been crucial to its expanding production of steel. Only scrap was the subject of an elaborate, Community-wide policy (Ch. 12). Iron ore presented no serious problems, though there were some questions about the future. Coal presented problems enough, but they were treated by a series of measures, some national or private, rather than by a general Community policy.

Iron Ore

About one-third of the Community's iron ore comes from abroad (calculated in iron content). After 1960 the

[10] At their highest point, in 1956, Community imports of finished and semi-finished steel products came to about a million tons compared to Community production of 39 million tons of finished steel products in that year, and exports to third countries of 8.7 million tons of finished and semi-finished products. Germany was the largest Community market, taking about 45 per cent of the imports. Italy followed, with the Benelux countries in third place, thanks largely to sizable Dutch imports.

proportion should increase, according to the High Authority's estimates. Assuming a substantial increase in steel production, the High Authority suggests that in 1975 iron ore imports may have to be double their 1957 level of 13.2 million tons (iron content). The situation is not very different from that of the American or British steel industries and it is there that the Community's problem lies. Iron ore is still reasonably plentiful and for the moment new sources are expanding more rapidly than demand, thanks largely to major developments in Canada, Latin America, and Africa undertaken by American firms. In a decade or two supplies may well be much tighter and a smaller share of the ore offered for sale. Some Community producers have begun to develop their own iron mines in colonies or foreign countries, often as joint enterprises in which several steel firms participate. Some have begun to build up their own ore-carrying fleets. The problem is one of forecasting and of investment; the sums required are large. Failure to maintain a proper pace of expansion would cause future difficulties and make the Community increasingly dependent on supplies of ore owned by foreign competitors.[11] A shortage of iron ore would also add to what promises to be a chronic, world-wide scrap problem. There are important technical developments that suggest major coal economies in the steelmaking of the future, but none that dispense with iron.

Another problem concerns the cost of iron ore produced inside the Community. The focus is Germany. Before the war German iron mining was regarded as a high-cost activity that expanded in Nazi times only because the government protected and fostered it. But since the war, without tariff protection, iron ore output has expanded still further until in 1957 Germany produced more than in

[11] Concern that in the long run Community demand might press increasingly on American supplies of iron ore and steel scrap was one of the factors leading the Bethlehem Steel Company to form a group, in which the steel industries of all the Community countries are represented, to undertake exploration for iron ore in French Equatorial Africa. Moving in the same direction, the High Authority in 1958 made a grant of $5 million for the study of possible iron ore development in other French African colonies.

any year since it lost Lorraine. Most of the ore has a low iron content; the geological conditions are poor; the mines are rather distant from the steel mills (except those in Lower Saxony which serve the Salzgitter works); productivity is low.[12] Yet in the mid-fifties the German mines produced 30 per cent of the iron ore used by domestic blast furnaces and delivered it at prices per unit of iron content below that of the best imported ore and Luxembourg *minette*.[13]

The mines are for the most part owned by steel companies (including the government-owned Salzgitter works); the government has been anxious to sustain the level of economic activity in the mining areas; the railroad rate for carrying the ore to the steel mills is exceptionally low. These facts, along with the strong demand for iron ore and the desire of the German government and steel industry to maintain domestic sources of supply, explain much of the postwar record. They tell nothing about the possible burden on the German economy of maintaining high-cost production. Nor has the Community concerned itself with this question. There have been no complaints from possible competitors. Lorraine tripled its shipments of iron ore to Germany during the transitional period, but in 1957 they still amounted to only 5 per cent of Germany's total imports and about 2.5 per cent of its consumption (of unrefined ore; in iron content the figure would be lower). While the canalization of the Moselle may increase this trade, limits are set to it by the iron requirements of France and its principal customer, Belgium, and by the difficulty of using Lorraine ore to make open-hearth steel which accounts for a large part of German production. The principal Community action influencing the German iron ore arrangements was the order to end the special freight

[12] It took about 33,000 men to produce 16.9 million tons of iron ore in Germany in 1956, compared to 42,500 to produce 52.7 million tons in France. Output per shift in 1956 was 4.3 tons in Germany and 11.8 in Lorraine. By mid-1957 the spread was greater. The figure for Luxembourg was 7.7.

[13] Ferdinand Friedensburg, *Das Erzproblem der Deutschen Eisenindustrie*, 1957, pp. 24, 30.

rates on German railroads (p. 175f.). If sustained by the Court this order will present the Germans with the alternatives of finding another kind of subsidy, increasing the cost of iron to the steel industry, or adding to the Bundesbahn's costs by lowering the rate on ore imported from Luxembourg and Lorraine (about 8 per cent of domestic production in 1957).

While one cannot be sure without a closer study, fragmentary evidence suggests that if purely economic considerations governed, some of the German iron mining would be stopped. The calculation would be complicated, however, by assumptions about the supply and cost of imported ore in the future and about the cost of using new processes that enhance the value of low-grade iron ore. The High Authority estimates that there will be a substantial increase in German iron ore production, partly from new mines. The rate of expansion is expected to be less than that in Lorraine and Germany will almost certainly have to import a larger share of its iron from overseas in the future. It is likely, however, to continue to foster domestic iron mining, for a number of reasons. This may be a sound course as well as a politically compelling one, but it will be of some importance to Germany and the Community to pay attention to costs as well as supplies.

Coal

In spite of early expectations that the Community might soon become self-sufficient in coal and supply some of its traditional export markets as well, the six countries were forced to import increasing amounts of coal from 1953 on. The peak was reached in 1957 when imports came to 44 million tons, more than the production of Belgium, Holland, and Italy put together. As the total increased, the share coming from the United States grew until it reached 86 per cent in 1957. American coal was cheap enough at Hampton Roads but by the time it was landed in Antwerp, Rotterdam, or Bremen the ocean freight usually made it more expensive than Community coal. The problems that resulted have come into this book in a number of places;

their implications for future policy will be considered later. Here the issue is foreign trade policy in a partially integrated Community.

For most of the transitional period the central question was: Who would import the foreign coal and who would be supplied from cheaper Community sources? In scrap a somewhat similar problem was partially dealt with by the equalization scheme. An approach of this sort was suggested for coal and will probably reappear on the agenda of long-run coal policy. But no serious effort was made to adopt it during the transitional period. Opposition was particularly strong in Germany, because such a step would add to the bureaucratization of the coal economy, increase outside interference in the Ruhr's affairs, and lead to manipulation of the coal price. There were some national equalization schemes such as that operated in France by ATIC and a Belgian arrangement for imports of American coking coal. In Germany, however, a two-price system flourished, modified in minor ways by cooperative importing arrangements among some companies. This created a certain amount of friction and some obvious commercial and economic discrepancies, while spurring the already strong drive of big coal-users to buy their own mines.

The touchier question concerned the national division of imports. Unless a shortage were officially declared and coal supplies allocated, the Community had no means of deciding that each country should import a certain amount of American coal and get the rest from Community sources. Foreign trade policy was up to the individual governments, but the countries were all part of a common market that was intended to guarantee "equal access to the sources of production." As long as the foreign coal cost more, each had an interest in buying as much of its coal as it could inside the Community; for some there were foreign exchange reasons to prefer that course as well. Had the coal trade been less highly organized, there might have been the kind of pressure on the Community market that led to the scrap equalization scheme. As it was, many Germans resented the situation. They saw their imports of foreign coal rise to more than 9 million tons in 1955 and observed that they sent just a little more than that to the Community countries in the same year. The old feeling was awakened that, thanks to the Schuman Plan, Germany was being exploited by its customers. Some Germans spoke of being "required" to sell Ruhr coal to other countries, especially France, and thereby being "forced" to buy expensive American coal.

As Table 7 shows, the situation was more complicated than that. German coal imports from third countries grew rapidly after the recession of 1953-54, but exports to the Community were about the same in the boom years of 1956 and 1957 as in the recession years. In 1957, German net exports to the Community were 9.8 per cent of production; in 1952, before the common market opened, they had been 9.4 per cent. And so on; a number of other comparisons all demonstrate the same point: while each year might have its special features, there is a remarkable stability of German exports to the other Community countries.[14]

While there is no reason to take one year or another as "normal," a comparison of 1952 with 1957 gives a reasonably good picture of the kind of adjustment that took place over the whole period.[15] Between those two years, Germany's absorption of coal increased by nearly 20 million tons. The increase in production provided just over half this amount. Net exports to the Community rose by 1.5 million tons and were exactly offset by a contraction in exports to third countries. The gap was filled by imports from third countries, principally the United States. Thus the role of the increased imports from overseas was, very broadly, to meet heavier German requirements while exports to European markets remained stable.

[14] And of the offsetting imports of coal from Community countries. Except for a sharp increase in 1955 and 1956 these were always 4.6 million tons, made up mostly of shipments from the Saar and Lorraine, to south Germany.

[15] Only 1954 and 1955 depart markedly from the pattern. The former year is exceptional because German coal production increased faster than demand, leading to an increase in exports. The drastic spurt in demand in 1955 led to increased imports from the Community as well as from third countries, and curtailed exports.

To be sure, if Germany could have turned its exports off and on at will, it could have dispensed with imports from overseas. Having a continuing interest in export markets, it would hardly have done this even in the absence of the coal and steel Treaty. It might well, however, have held down exports somewhat, thus shifting more of the burden of financing overseas imports to other countries. To the extent that this was prevented by the operation of the common market, the Community could be said to have

Table 7

GERMANY'S COAL BALANCE, 1952-1957
(millions of tons)

	1952	1953	1954	1955	1956	1957
Production	123.3	124.5	128.0	130.7	134.4	133.2
Net Exports to Community	11.6	11.9	13.7	10.3	12.0	13.1
Exports to Third Countries	7.2	6.6	8.2	7.0	6.4	5.7
Imports from Third Countries	8.0	5.1	4.0	9.4	14.0	17.3
Total Net Exports	10.8	13.4	17.9	7.9	4.4	1.5
Domestic Coal Supply	112.5	111.1	110.1	122.8	130.0	131.7

NOTES:

Production = hard coal only.

Trade figures = hard coal, coke-oven coke, and hard coal agglomerates added ton for ton. Very little coke is imported but it usually accounts for one-third to one-half the gross exports to the Community and about half to two-thirds of the exports to third countries.

"Domestic coal supply" = production minus net exports, as shown.

Gross exports to Community: 1952—15.9; 1953—16.5; 1954—18.3; 1955—17.3; 1956—17.3; 1957—17.7.

SOURCE: *Bulletin Statistique.*

served one of its purposes.[16] The mechanism by which this was largely accomplished in 1956 and 1957, the years of greatest strain,[17] was the allocation of most Ruhr deliveries on the basis of past sales and the maintenance of French deliveries to southern Germany (p. 391f.). This internal

[16] German exports to third countries were somewhat curtailed, but not sharply.

[17] In 1955, on the other hand, Germany reduced its net deliveries to other European countries as well as increasing imports from overseas. See Table 7. The reduction of 3.4 million tons in net deliveries to the Community comprised a cut of exports of 1 million tons and increased imports of 2.4 million.

Community action then virtually determined the allocation of imports from third countries (at least between Germany and the others; among the others there might still be shifts determined by the sales pattern of French and Belgian coal). During these two years, Germany bought about 38 per cent of the Community's imports of coal from third countries. In the same period it accounted for about 47 per cent of the Community's total absorption of coal.[18] The figures for the whole transitional period are similar. While there is no basis for saying that this is the most economical division of coal imports, the figures at least suggest that if we take the Community as a whole, Germany has not carried a disproportionate share of the burden of importing coal.

Two conclusions emerge. First, Germany was not exploited by the rest of the Community in this matter. Judged in strictly national (and possibly shortsighted) terms it could be said to have made sacrifices for the Community by buying expensive foreign coal and selling its own coal more cheaply. But in terms of the Community economy, Germany did not carry more than its "fair share" of the burden of importing from third countries. Second, though it lacked the means of directly establishing a foreign trade policy in the allocation of coal imports, the Community was able to formulate one indirectly by regulating the distribution of its main domestic supply.

Quite different problems faced the Community when stocks of coal began to grow in the winter of 1957-58 and large quantities remained unsold during the following winter as well. Imports contributed substantially to the surplus; some came in under long-term contracts negotiated when coal was scarce, some because freight rates fell far enough to make American coal cheaper than European at many places. The Belgians, who felt the impact first, subjected new orders to licensing in February 1958. The Germans

[18] That is, production + imports ignoring stock movements. The tonnage figures may not accurately reflect the financial burden since the proportion of American coal was higher in Germany's imports than in those of the rest of the Community.

followed that fall. In February 1959 the Germans imposed a stiff tariff. These were national measures, not concerted Community actions. The other countries were reluctant to adapt their own importing arrangements to the needs of Belgium and Germany though they had an obligation to "lend . . . the necessary assistance" in support of trade policy measures that the High Authority considered in accordance with the Treaty (Art. 71). To what extent a clear pattern of Community commercial policy action will emerge from these events cannot be judged at this writing. (The issues are discussed more fully on pp. 683-693.) The situation seemed to present new problems in the application of the parts of the Treaty dealing with foreign trade. In so doing it also brought to the fore some more familiar issues of the relation between governments and the High Authority. The frequently discussed issues of long-run coal policy took on a new urgency in the face of short-run difficulties. The recourse to old-fashioned protective measures when the psychology of surplus quickly replaced concern over scarcity was a reminder of the importance to the Six of trade with third countries and of the fact that the changes brought by the Community did not reach as far in this sphere as in internal matters.

COAL EXPORTS: THE COMMUNITY AS SUPPLIER

The small countries of Europe that lacked coal depended on the Community, and especially Germany, for an important part of their supplies. They were concerned about the implications of the Schuman Plan. Would the removal of trade barriers divert into the common market shipments of coal and coke that used to go to Austria, Switzerland, and Scandinavia? If there were a shortage and the Community allocated coal supplies, what chance would outsiders have to get the supplies they had received under the earlier allocation arrangements in which all Western European countries had participated?

These questions were raised when the Community countries applied to their fellow-signatories of the General Agreement on Tariffs and Trade for a waiver of most-

favored-nation treatment (p.525 ff.). In granting the waiver
the Contracting Parties noted that if it was to carry out
its purposes, the Community would have "to avoid placing
unreasonable barriers upon exports to third countries." [19]

Table 8 gives the Community's record in supplying coal
and coke to third countries. There was an exceptional rise
in shipments to Britain (mostly from France, Belgium, and
the Saar) from 1954 to 1956 that was roughly matched by
a rise in British shipments to the Community, an exchange
based on differences in types and transportation routes. If
these are set aside, Austria and Switzerland account for
about three-fifths of Community exports and Scandinavia
for most of the rest. Though one might argue about what
the year to year fluctuations mean, this trade shows no
marked change that can be attributed to the common
market. The expansion in 1953 and 1954 reflects the Community producers' greater interest in selling coal when the
demand was slack. The effects of the Community's coal
shortage show primarily in the change from 1955 to 1956,
when exports to third countries contracted, both absolutely
and relative to intra-Community trade (which also shrank).
The further contraction in 1957 was only in part a continuation of Community shortage. The fall in ocean freight
rates made it cheaper than it had been to get overseas coal,
especially in Scandinavia; the High Authority reported
that importers were not placing as many orders in the
Community as in previous years. While it is risky to rely
on simple indicators of this sort, the figures in Table 8
seem to lend support to the High Authority's statement
of late 1956: "The Community authorities have endeavored

[19] GATT, *Basic Instruments and Selected Documents, First Supplement*, Mar. 1953, p. 18 (hereafter cited only by supplement number).
This was not specifically made a condition of the waiver but some such
status can be imparted to it since the purpose of the Community was
taken into account in the decision. At first there were complaints about
Community restrictions on scrap exports, especially by Austria and
Sweden. As the gravity of the Community's scrap situation became
clear and its elaborate control system developed, the complaints weakened, either because of the difficulty of claiming the export ban was
"unreasonable" or because of the hopelessness of getting action when
the Community was already having such difficulty.

to maintain exports to traditional customers in spite of an exceptional pressure on supply within the Community."[20] It is also true, however, that third countries fared a little less well than the six in their access to Community coal during the shortage.

Table 8

COMMUNITY EXPORTS OF COAL AND COKE TO THIRD COUNTRIES, 1951-1957

	Amount			Relation to Intra-Community Exports	
	To United Kingdom	To Other Countries	Total	Total	Without U.K.
	(thousands of tons)			(per cent)	
1951	—	10,250	10,250	36.7	36.7
1952	—	9,635	9,635	33.5	33.5
1953	561	9,709	10,270	33.0	31.2
1954	2,373	11,033	13,406	38.9	32.0
1955	4,455	10,961	15,416	43.4	30.9
1956	1,328	9,357	10,685	33.3	29.2
1957	859	8,025	8,884	27.7	25.0

SOURCE: *Bulletin Statistique.*

Individual countries that drew heavily on Community coal and coke fared somewhat differently, as is roughly indicated by the following figures which show Community exports of coal and coke (in thousands of tons) to six countries:[21]

	Austria	Switzerland	Sweden	Denmark	Norway	Finland
1952	1,994	1,680	2,622	1,254	181	354
1956	1,419	2,519	2,659	1,441	169	178

Sweden, with its iron ore, was in a good bargaining position. Switzerland made out well by increasing its imports

[20] Same, . . . *Fifth Supplement*, Jan. 1957, p. 129.
[21] There is some disadvantage in comparing single years but the figures do not seriously distort the general movement. Coal and coke are added ton for ton. Austria and Switzerland took more coal than coke; for Scandinavia this was reversed.

from France, Belgium, and the Saar instead of relying as heavily on Germany as it had in the past. Austria was unable to do this. It needed coking coal for its rapidly expanding steel production. Its imports of coal from the Community fell from about 2 million tons a year in the early '50s to half that in 1956 and 1957. Increased coke shipments made up only part of the difference.

The Austrians carried their complaint to GATT. At the working-party session in November 1956 they pointed out that others were getting larger deliveries of coal from the Community even though Austria's geographical position made it very expensive for it to buy American coal. The High Authority spokesman explained that the increased shipments to other countries were not of coking coal which the Community was short of. He referred to recent conversations between Community producers and Austrian users "which would prevent any further deterioration . . . and which might lead to an improvement in the exports of coking coal to Austria." [22] This seems to have had some result. Trade declined less in 1957 than in previous years and no special mention was made of the Austrian supply problem at the GATT session toward the end of the year. This was a period in which issues were being discussed between Austria and the Community and all these matters were probably linked in the negotiations.[23]

Coal prices were also the subject of a number of complaints in the GATT sessions but the issues remained unresolved. For one thing, data were lacking or in dispute. For another, the Community took the view that it was reasonable to pass on some of the higher cost of American coking coal to customers in third countries, while these in turn felt that they were being charged a disproportionate share considering the small amount of coal and coke they took from the Community. The High Authority under-

[22] GATT, . . . *Fifth Supplement*, cited, p. 127.

[23] The low price of Austrian special steel was one of the matters that worried the Community. The authorities might, therefore, have felt that they need not "unduly strive" to maintain coal exports if the alternative was to force Austria to import more coking coal from the United States, thus raising costs.

took to see to it that coal and coke export prices were not raised unreasonably and in the course of 1957 they did not go up while prices within the Community did.

Roughly stable and then curtailed supplies of coal and coke from the Community did not meet the expanding needs of the importing countries. Like the Community they had to buy more expensive coal from overseas. The Scandinavian countries got more coal from Britain and Poland than they did from the Community, but the conclusion they came to was probably shared by Austria and Switzerland, which were more dependent on the Community: "In all likelihood the nordic countries will come, as the other European lands have, to grow steadily more dependent on imports of more expensive coal from the USA; this is particularly true of coking coal." [24]

STEEL EXPORT PRICES

The aspect of the Community's foreign trade policy that has caused the greatest aggravation in other countries has been the pricing of steel exports. The manner in which these prices were determined has also caused some uneasiness in the Community because it involves cartel practices that threaten to have repercussions inside the common market. Commercially, the matter is of considerable importance to the steel producers of the Community. Politically, or institutionally, the question is a delicate one because of the uncertainty of the amount of influence that the High Authority can exercise.

Exports of steel and steel products to third countries absorbed about 22 per cent of the Community's steel production in 1956.[25] Twice as much steel was exported to

[24] Scandinavian coal imports from the United States rose from 100,000 tons in 1953 and 600,000 in 1954 to 1.7 million in 1956. *Nordisk Økonomisk Samarbeid*, Rapport fra det Nordiske Økonomiske Samarbeidsutvalg, Part 2, p. 60. This report by the Nordic Economic Cooperation Committee appeared in five parts, the first four published in Oslo, 1957, by J. Chr. Gundersen and the fifth in Stockholm, 1957, by P. A. Norstedt & Söner. Part 1 was published in English as *Nordic Economic Cooperation* (Copenhagen: J. H. Schultz, 1958).

[25] Net exports calculated in crude steel equivalents, *Informations Statistiques*, Jan.-Feb. 1958, p. 12. About 4 per cent was in products not

third countries as was traded among Community countries in 1956 and 1957. The economic union of Belgium and Luxembourg is the Community's largest exporter of finished steel to third countries, followed by France (with the Saar); Germany is in third place. About 45 per cent of Belgian and Luxembourgeois finished steel production was exported in 1956, 21 per cent of production in France and the Saar, and only 12 per cent of the German output. The largest markets were in Western Europe, followed—in an order that has varied somewhat from year to year—by Asia, Latin America, North America (high in 1956 because of the steel strike in the United States), and then Eastern Europe, the colonies of Community countries, the United Kingdom, and Africa.

Early in 1953, French, Belgian, and Luxembourgeois exporters formed a price cartel for exports to third countries. The Dutch and Germans joined them in the fall. This response to a falling market seemed a bad sign for the future of the Community. One of the fears of how the six countries would use their combined power seemed about to be realized. There were objections inside and outside the Community. The United States government made representations. In the fall of 1953 the High Authority asked the producers to dissolve their cartel but was rebuffed. The export entente has remained in existence and is the focus of the concern about export prices.

Although the Treaty is not altogether clear on the status of agreements of this sort that affect only exports, the High Authority has accepted a fairly restrictive, but probably correct, interpretation of its powers. According to this view the High Authority cannot forbid an export agreement unless it curtails competition within the common market or leads to practices that would be illegal under the Treaty. It may, if it thinks necessary, impose maximum or minimum

---

covered by the Treaty, notably tubes and wire. Later figures in this section refer principally to finished products and are calculated from standard Community sources. They ignore trade in steel ingots and non-Treaty products. The substantial indirect exports of steel in the form of manufactured products are also omitted.

prices on exports. Both the Consultative Committee and the Council of Ministers recommended against imposing maximum export prices in 1953 and the High Authority has never since taken a formal step to invoke this power. With the threat of maximum prices in the background, the High Authority has from time to time cautioned the cartel against raising export prices too high and may have intervened on some other matters as well, to go some way toward satisfying the complaints of third countries.

These complaints have centered on the fact that steel products exported from the Community have often been sold at prices above those prevailing inside the six countries.[26] Monnet's original working paper had said, "For the mutual advantage of the European countries and of their clients, export prices should be the same as prices within the single market." This proposition had not been carried out in the Treaty which spoke only of keeping export prices within "equitable limits." Double-pricing was abolished within the Community but producers made use of the practice in their foreign trade. The purpose of the cartel was to keep the export price as high as the market would bear by preventing price competition among the Community exporters. As governments and buyers in third countries saw the matter, the cartel kept them from getting any of the benefits of the creation of the Community. One of the assumptions of the GATT waiver was that there would be "general" benefits from the common market. It said, "the Community has undertaken . . . to ensure that equitable prices are charged by its producers in markets outside the Community." [27] Therefore, Community price

[26] There were also objections about price discrimination. A price cut for overseas exports in December 1953 was not extended to Switzerland since American and British competition was not felt there. Henri Rieben, *Des Ententes de Maitres de Forges au Plan Schuman*, 1954, p. 477. This difficulty was overcome in a few months but afterwards sales to Canada and the United States were sometimes made at lower prices than shipments elsewhere. The differentials were abolished by the fall of 1956 for basic prices, but this left some leeway for discrimination in the prices actually charged.

[27] GATT, . . . *First Supplement*, cited, p. 18. The language is close to that of Article 3 of the Treaty.

policy became the principal item of business during the annual sessions of the GATT working party, at which the High Authority's reports were discussed. The Danish representatives became the chief spokesmen of those who had grievances.

Much of the time at the GATT sessions was spent in comparing data on the export prices set by the Brussels cartel, the prices actually paid by outside buyers, and the relation of these to prices inside the Community and to the export prices of American and British steel. Though some progress was made in removing, or at least explaining, discrepancies in the figures presented by the High Authority on the one side and the Danes on the other, it is impossible to provide a precise account of price movements. The main elements are, however, reasonably clear.[28]

During much of 1953 and 1954 export prices were at or below the level of most Community prices, but there was some variation among products. The cartel could not always enforce its fixed prices when advantageous sales could be made below them. Export prices rose with demand in late 1954 and in 1955; by late 1955 many stood slightly above the internal Belgian level, which made them as much as 10 per cent higher than French and German prices in a number of cases. As demand rose further, actual prices rose substantially above those quoted by the cartel. The margin above internal prices reached its maximum in early 1957; then domestic increases narrowed the gap slightly. In April 1957 the minimum cartel price for some major Community exports was 4-6 per cent above the Belgian price, and 18-27 per cent above French and German prices.[29] New orders from abroad declined during

[28] Comparisons are made difficult by many factors, including differences in quality and types of product, taxes, and allowance for transportation between points at which domestic prices were quoted and ports. Traders buying from several sources sometimes charged uniform prices when re-selling. The cartel set basic prices, but "extras for quality," special orders, and other items were added to this by sellers who might also simply charge higher prices if they could. The account of price movements is put together from a number of sources.

[29] ECE, *The European Steel Market in 1956*, Table 6, p. 17, has details.

1957 and late in the year export prices began to fall. As in 1953 and 1954 exporters sold below the cartel's official minimum. The cartel cut prices several times to keep pace and to try to establish a new floor. By March 1958 some of the list prices were more than 20 per cent below their level a year before, but others had been reduced much less. On a number of products the export price was below the domestic French and German level.

The complaints of the buying countries came, of course, when export prices were above internal Community prices. How, asked the representatives of these countries, could their steel-using industries compete with those of France and Germany which paid substantially less for their basic material? [30] This was not keeping prices within "equitable limits," as the GATT waiver stipulated, said the Danes. The Swiss complained that at times it cost them more to buy French steel than to buy the finished product itself, thanks to the working of the French export subsidies and the steel price differential.[31] The fact that the export prices were sometimes not very far above the Belgian level and that Belgium was the main exporter interested the buyers less than the fact that all exports carried this high price so that outsiders got no benefit from the lower prices in France and Germany. The Danes rather deprecated comparison with the export prices of Britain and the United States, suggesting that "the Community's position in the world export market for steel was so important that it could be considered as a price leader with respect to its main steel export items." [32] For the Swiss, overseas steel was bound to

[30] In addition, the Danes alleged, Community steel producers sold at cut rates to industries producing for export. The High Authority's answer was ambiguous. It did not say precisely whether this was being done but argued that the practice was justified because otherwise Community exporters would have to pay more for their steel than competitors in countries that practiced double-pricing (i.e., England). It also argued that this was entirely a question of the application of the Treaty, not of obligations to other countries.

[31] "Die Schweiz und die Preispolitik der Montanunion," *Neue Zürcher Zeitung*, Feb. 14, 1958.

[32] GATT, . . . *Sixth Supplement*, Mar. 1958, p. 144. In the course of studies of Nordic cooperation, it was discovered that even though

be more expensive than for the Scandinavians. They felt
that their long-standing, close commercial ties with the
Community meant that they should not be treated as Latin
America, the Middle East, and the Far East were treated.
A leading Swiss paper expressed annoyance and disappointment. "These price manipulations which have important repercussions on the Swiss economy, are treated lightly,
as bagatelles, by the Community, on the basis of arguments
that have little validity. The organs of the Community do
not show any willingness at present to value a 'loyal' commercial relation with Switzerland." [33]

The High Authority had several answers to these complaints. First of all, it did not accept a comparison of
domestic and export prices as the proper criterion of the
"equitable limits" within which prices were to be kept.
Comparison with world prices was a more suitable measure,
it urged. Although there were again difficulties of comparison, Community prices—or at least the Brussels list
prices—for most steel were at or below the British and
American levels, except for some flat products. It was
generally held in the Community that those whose coal
and steel were subject to the Treaty rules had a right to
better treatment than those who had no such obligations.
The High Authority also argued that buying countries
were in fact benefiting from the greater price stability that
the Community brought about; the margin between
domestic and export prices was narrower than in earlier
boom times.[34] The High Authority gave repeated assur-

Sweden had tariffs on some steel products, prices at Swedish plants were
lower than those quoted by Danish and Norwegian importers for Community steel, except during the recession of 1953-54. Reckoned on a
c.i.f. Copenhagen basis, Swedish steel prices were higher than those from
the Community except during the Korean boom and in 1957. They were
also more stable. *Nordisk Økonomisk Samarbeid*, cited, Part 2, p. 44.
[33] "Die Schweiz und die Preispolitik . . . ," cited.
[34] This historical argument seems to have validity. "It has long been
a characteristic of the steel market that export prices fluctuate far more
than domestic prices. . . . In the postwar period, particularly from 1948
to 1952, export prices have generally been higher than domestic prices,
sometimes by as much as 100 per cent." ECE, *The European Steel
Market in 1954*, Je. 1955, p. 55.

ances that it would watch over export prices and in the Assembly and elsewhere spokesmen have mentioned cases in which it intervened to prevent further price increases.

Not surprisingly, these arguments led to no agreed conclusions. At each session the debate could only be summed up by saying, in one form or another, "The Working Party considered that there was no definite method for assessing whether export prices remained within equitable limits or not." [35] The process did not, however, result in complete frustration. At a minimum, the discussions clarified the situation and led to the pooling of a certain amount of information which, even though it contained discrepancies, narrowed the issues and checked the intensification of sharp and uninformed polemics. More important, the annual review itself, the need for the High Authority to explain the situation, has undoubtedly played a part in moderating export price increases. How important a part it is impossible to say, but it would be surprising if the cautioning by the men in Luxembourg, backed by their power to impose maximum export prices, had carried no weight with the exporters. The High Authority's action, in turn, was stimulated in part by its international commitments and the needs of "foreign policy."

More than foreign relations lay behind the High Authority's interest in the Brussels cartel and in double-pricing. The premium prices for exports have been a significant source of income for Community producers during much of the transition period. They have made it easier for the steel producers to hold down domestic prices in the face of booming demand, especially in France and Germany. The fall in export orders was one of the factors cited by the German steelmakers to justify a rise in domestic prices in the fall of 1957.

Did the price differential for exports draw supplies of steel out of the Community that would otherwise have been marketed at home? It is impossible to say with certainty. There were strong pressures on the Community steel producers to supply the home market, not to desert established

[35] GATT, . . . Fifth Supplement, cited, p. 134.

customers, to show the sense of "responsibility" about the needs of the national economy that is professed by heavy industry and asked of it by governments. While supplies of steel were tight in the Community during the boom years, there was never the same pressure on supplies that existed for coal, as there might have been had producers given absolute priority to the earnings to be had from exports. The export price pressure probably did have an effect on the direction of producers' sales efforts. Between 1955 and 1956 intra-Community trade in steel contracted but exports to third countries increased. Between 1956 and 1957, when the export demand slackened, both increased. It seems almost certain that the export price advantages exercised a pull, not on domestic deliveries but on steel that a producer might sell either to another country in the Community or to third markets. It probably contributed, then, to the partial fragmentation of the common market, the price discrepancies, and the restraint which producers showed about "invading" one another's markets at the height of the boom.

The fall in export prices at the beginning of 1958 reversed the situation. Along with the fall in foreign orders, the disappearance of the export premium throws steel onto the domestic market and ought to exert pressure on internal prices as well. More active selling inside the Community might also result, but if Community demand falls as well, exports will take on still another role. To reduce the pressure on domestic prices and to maintain a high level of operation, steel producers would probably judge it desirable to export to third countries even at prices below the domestic level. Dumping occurred, at least in a small way, in late 1953 and early 1954; it is an old practice in the steel industry. No one has complained about it. The buying countries have been acting as consumers, glad to get more for less. The rub in dumping comes in competition with domestic industries, which are small enough in Denmark and Switzerland, for instance, to have their problems taken care of easily enough by other means. Britain and the United States would rely on their antidumping laws to protect home markets if the Community industries were incautious enough to attempt to sell there on a large scale. The effect on competition in third markets is less certain.[36]

These are problems of the future. In the past the High Authority has not shared the worries of the customers about the Brussels cartel's price activities. Given the practical impossibility of dissolving the cartel, the High Authority has regarded it as potentially troublesome but actually not a source of major difficulty. For this there are several reasons, in addition to those advanced in the GATT discussions and the practical advantage of making it easier to hold down prices within the Community. There is an analogy with the High Authority's attitude toward steel price-setting within the Community: collusion by itself has been regarded as inevitable and the emphasis has been on preventing the producers from setting prices too high. The High Authority has also had the comfortable feeling that the export price cartel was not really having a great influence. In the early years, sales took place below the official price. In the boom years, demand pushed prices so high that the cartel price was a superfluous floor. When export prices fell again in late 1957 they once more went right through the cartel floor. So long as this kind of thing happened, the High Authority could afford not to worry very much about the Brussels cartel.

The weaknesses of the cartel might, however, contain the seeds of greater difficulty, in the efforts the producers would make to rectify them. If, for instance, the cartel succeeded in holding up export prices when steelmaking capacity went unused in the Community, the High Authority might have cause for concern, unless it took the view that lower prices were a worse evil than a lower level of activity (p. 285). If the price agreement failed to check competition, the members of the cartel might try to extend

[36] Neither the British nor the American industry has made any public complaint about the behavior of the Brussels export cartel, though it provides a good bit more of the steel going into world markets than either of them. During the boom they had nothing to complain of. The change in the world market brings a new situation and possible concern about the export cartel in the future.

their activities. This seems to have happened at least twice. The facts are obscure. In late 1953 or early 1954, there was an effort to establish national export quotas as a means of checking competition and supporting the cartel price.[37] Whether this effort broke down or was made superfluous by the rise in demand is not clear. The second use of export quotas occurred during the winter of 1957-58. French and German exporters agreed to hold their sales down to the levels of previous months so as not to press the Belgian and Luxembourgeois producers too hard. This was supposed to be a temporary agreement, based on the French and German producers' recognition that the export market was of greater importance for their small neighbors than for themselves. The temporary sacrifice was not great, since home demand was fairly strong and export prices had fallen. But if the export quota system continued, some reasonably clear *quid pro quo* would have to be provided for the French and German producers, especially if the home market shrank. Such a development would be disturbing for the Community. It would imply the kind of feedback into competitive conditions within the Community that the High Authority regards as illegitimate. Would an agreement to restrain French and German exports to third markets in the interest of Belgian exports make sense if the French and Germans then tried to sell equal quantities in the Belgians' home market? [38] Would not any quantitative agreement on exports have some corollary inside the common market?

Of course the export cartel is not the only force at work.

[37] The Danes alleged that the French and Belgian producers wanted to establish sales quotas but that the German producers objected to this and were forced to acquiesce only by the threat of intensified Belgian and French competition within the Community. The High Authority said that it has received no information concerning this allegation and no complaints from the Germans. GATT, . . . *Third Supplement*, Je. 1955, pp. 167-168. A fundamental distinction between the Brussels agreement and the prewar international cartel was "the complete absence of any agreement on quotas," according to Rieben, cited, p. 478. Fines were imposed on those who violated the price rules.

[38] It could, given a certain set of price relations, but these did not obtain at the time the export quotas were undertaken.

Instead of an agreement on allocation of the common market flowing from an agreement to divide export markets, one could see the latter as possible only because of a tacit agreement not to invade domestic markets on a large scale. It is in the setting of collusive pricing and of the various shadowy and not so shadowy evidences of cartel-like behavior inside the common market that the export price cartel takes on significance, going beyond its bearing on the Community's foreign trade.

EIGHTEEN

THE EXTERNAL RELATIONS OF THE COMMUNITY

A FEW weeks after the High Authority took office, American and British delegations arrived to represent their governments in dealing with the new European entity. Seven other nations have since accredited missions to the Community.[1] In other ways as well the Community has demonstrated its international status. It has borrowed money abroad, negotiated international agreements covering trade and transportation, and established standing arrangements to consult with certain countries on common problems. The Community's foreign relations have been part of its development of an international personality, in more than a legal sense. Some of them have also played a part in shaping the Community's character and policies, especially the periodical examination of Community affairs in GATT.

"ASSOCIATION" WITH BRITAIN

The constitutional documents of the Community mention by name one country that is not a member, the United Kingdom. As soon as the High Authority took office, said Section 13 of the transitional Convention, it should "undertake negotiations with the governments of third countries, and particularly with the British Government. . . ." As if it accepted a similar mandate, Britain sent the first foreign ambassador to Luxembourg, Sir Cecil Weir. The British press release of August 23 announcing this intention spoke

[1] In 1952, Sweden; in 1953, Norway, Switzerland, Denmark, and Austria; in 1954, Japan; and in 1958, Greece.

of the delegation's "task of laying the foundations for an intimate and enduring association between the Community and the United Kingdom. . . ." The Community spokesmen kept a firm grip on the word "association," reserved it for descriptions of the pool's relations with Britain, and finally enshrined it in the Community's first treaty.

This special treatment of Britain was natural enough. In the immediate background were the initial negotiations that had failed to bring Britain into the Treaty-drafting sessions, but had concluded with mutual professions of interest in establishing close future relations. In the immediate foreground were a series of economic problems involved in creating the Community; it seemed certain that their solution would affect and be affected by the actions of the largest Western European coal and steel producer outside the Community. In the distant future—a few persisted in thinking it not so distant—lay the possibility that the British would throw in their lot, on some basis, with the movement toward European integration. That would be a political decision that would have direct implication for Britain's relation to the Coal and Steel Community. Meanwhile, a relation to the Community might develop that would influence Britain's political decision. For all these reasons it seemed natural to all concerned that Britain and the Community should create some special relation between them.

What was this relation to be? There was no real prospect of Britain's joining the Community. Occasional flurries led some hopeful people to think this might be in the wind. The coming to power of the Conservative government in 1951, led by Winston Churchill who had been one of the great oratorical champions of European union, suggested to some that a change might be about to take place, but it was not so. The decision of the Labour government in June 1950 not to join the Treaty negotiations had not been a snap judgment or a partisan act. It reflected basic British attitudes and considerations. It comprised many strands of thinking. The rejection of supranational arrangements and unwillingness to let basic industries pass out of national control were matters of conviction that the Conservatives did not really challenge. After years of debate British coal had been nationalized in the hope of solving an intractable problem; no one talked of returning the mines to private hands. Steel had been nationalized by Labour; the Conservatives were denationalizing it, but under a law that gave the government extensive control over the industry. Basic foreign policy was also involved. Centuries of acting on the assumption that a single strong power on the western edge of the Continent was a mortal danger had left ways of thinking that were not completely obliterated by the conviction that the postwar world called for a new kind of balance of power. To become a "European" country by merging sovereignty with the Continent seemed to threaten defense, the Commonwealth, and the special relation to the United States that so many thoughtful Britons saw as essential. Turned around, this argument became the fear that if there was only "Europe" the appearance of unity might some day serve the United States as an excuse to withdraw its vital, new, and physical commitment to the affairs of the old world.

Short of membership, what kind of association could Britain have with the Community? While the Community was inchoate there could be few highly developed ideas in Britain. But there was a great range of attitudes toward what the Community was expected to be. The government's good wishes, professions of general support, and "correct" behavior did not express a uniform national view —in or out of the Labour or Conservative parties. Strachey's indiscretion about a "capitalist conspiracy" (p. 56) gave a glimpse of one body of thought; Churchill's reference to German domination of the pool another (p. 88). There was undisguised skepticism, based on a variety of understandable grounds. There was also a certain reticent hostility in the attitudes of many, based variously on economic, political, ideological, or strategic grounds. Little Europe seemed a dangerous gambit to some. Others honestly supported it, either enthusiastically or as the best possible, if not ideal, course. Some shared the views of Schuman,

Monnet, and Adenauer, and believed that as complete a realization of the ideal as possible would impel Britain to the most constructive course, for which a way would be found. Others believed that Britain would have to play an active part to be sure that the inevitably imperfect realization of Schuman's high principles did not produce a distorted creation, harmful to Europe and Britain alike.

Once the Community took shape, what Britain would do depended on what the Community became. Monnet took his cue from the emphasis the British put on their own pragmatism.[2] "As regards the U.S.S.R.," he said in June 1953, "the main question is to know whether or not we have faith in ourselves. As regards the United States, it is necessary and sufficient to act. As regards Great Britain, we must succeed in what we have undertaken. That is all." [3] The thing to do was to make the Community work. Then the British would be confronted with a fact, and they were good at facing facts.

The problem became one of timing. The High Authority and the British mission in Luxembourg set up a Joint Committee with various working parties, but this was little more than dressing up the discussions that would normally take place. British specialists participated in some of the Community's technical work. There were exchanges of visits at various levels between London and Luxembourg. All this while the Community was coming into being, policies and actions were developing, the facts were being established. Monnet wanted much more than this marginal cooperation. A promising course was to create an institution, a continuing joint body with a mandate to consider common interests. It might only talk at first, but out of that might come something more. And politically, in terms of Britain's relation to European union, a formal association with the Coal and Steel Community would have added meaning.

In December 1953 Monnet formally invited the British

<hr>

[2] "The general British love of empirical methods," said *The Economist*, "seems to rise to the dignity of a sacred principle where experiments in European integration are concerned." (Je. 13, 1953, p. 719.)

[3] CA, *Débats*, Je. 16, 1953, p. 90.

government to open negotiations. He suggested the lines along which conversations might proceed: removal of some of the barriers between the two markets; a procedure for common action; a continuing joint body. The British indicated that they would have to consider all this very carefully and implied that their answer would not come quickly. In February 1954 a spokesman for the British steel industry said, "the common market has been in existence for too short a space of time . . . and is working in too uncertain a manner to permit of any firm judgment on the likely effects of any British association with the Community." [4]

When London came to act on Monnet's proposal it was probably not primarily because these uncertainties had been removed or a clear decision reached that Britain would benefit economically from an arrangement with the Community. The industries remained reluctant. The government may have seen more general economic advantage. The main motive, however, seems to have been one of foreign policy. When in April 1954 Monnet was invited to come to London to negotiate, the future of the EDC was in suspense until the French Assembly voted. At about the same time Britain made an agreement with the six Continental governments to associate itself with the new defense arrangements when they came into effect. It would have been odd not even to negotiate with the Coal and Steel Community. By the time a treaty associating Britain with the Coal and Steel Community was signed in December, the EDC was dead, Britain had stepped into the breach with the initiative that brought agreement on the Western European Union, backed by unprecedented British military commitments to the Continent. The step toward association with the Coal and Steel Community seemed part of the new style in Downing Street.

The House of Commons approved the treaty in February with substantial support from both sides and little dis-

[4] Sir Ellis Hunter, "The Steel Industry in 1954," *National Provincial Bank Review*, Feb. 1954, p. 7. He stressed the fact that the price rules were not being obeyed.

sent. The Community countries were slower to ratify, so the treaty did not come into effect until September 1955. Its main feature is the creation of a Standing Council of Association made up of representatives of the British government and the High Authority.[5] The Council is to provide continuous consultation and the exchange of information. The matters with which it is to deal are listed in the treaty: trade; supplies of coal and steel and of raw materials for the industries; prices and subsidies, but not "those questions which are normally the subject of negotiation between employers and employees"; market and price trends; future developments in production and trade; technical developments and research; relation of coal and steel to substitutes and other forms of energy; safety, health, and welfare of employees; general objectives of development and main lines of investment policy. If matters are to be discussed that are under the jurisdiction of national governments in the Community, there is to be a meeting between British representatives and the Council of Ministers, with the High Authority participating. Beforehand these matters are to be examined in the Council of Association.[6]

The main commitment of the treaty was to discuss.[7] There were, however, two other provisions of substance. First, the Council was to study the barriers to trade between the United Kingdom and the Community with a view to proposing reductions. Second, if new restrictions on trade between Britain and the Community are contemplated because of shortages or a decline in demand, the

[5] Up to four from each. The British have usually been represented by two ministers and the chairmen of the Iron and Steel Board and the National Coal Board. Representatives of Community governments attended during tariff discussions. The treaty is to last for the duration of the Community.

[6] The agreement is full of signs, like this one, of a certain tension between the High Authority and the governments as to their relative roles in dealing with the British government. These are interesting but cannot be examined in detail here.

[7] The Assembly's political committee thought it especially significant that the British were for the first time willing to discuss their prices with outsiders. CA, Commission des Affaires Politiques, *Rapport . . . par Mlle. M. A. M. Klompé, Rapporteur*, doc. 16 (1953-54), p. 12.

government in question (or the High Authority) is to bring the matter before the Council of Association "with a view to considering coordinated action in the markets of the Community and of the United Kingdom to meet the situation and to provide mutual assistance in dealing with it." If circumstances prevent prior consultation, the action is to be reported immediately afterwards. Neither of these provisions seriously restricts national action, but they point a direction.

The Council met six times between November 1955 and the end of 1957. The three committees it established to discuss coal, steel, and trade relations met a little more frequently and set up several working parties. Much of the time at these sessions was devoted to the joint examination of scrap problems, the structure of steel prices, the impact of the Suez crisis, various technical matters, and the long-term forecasts and objectives being worked out in Britain and the Community. There were also discussions about the exchange of coal. As the Council got under way Britain was trying to cut exports and the Community was concerned about the already declining supplies it had been getting from that country. The trade contracted further over the next two years, but British coal deliveries to the Community fell less rapidly than Community sales to Britain. How much the discussions in the Council of Association may have had to do with the matter is not clear. In its second annual report in the spring of 1958 the Council announced a study of the long-run energy position of the two parties.

Trade Relations

The most substantial accomplishment of the association between Britain and the Community was the steel tariff agreement that went into effect in early 1958 (see p. 476f.). The study that led to this agreement began after the Council decided in March 1956 that tariff negotiations should take place under GATT.[8] The circumstances differed somewhat

[8] According to the Assembly's political committee the British had been unwilling to take this step until they saw from the GATT nego-

from those normal for tariff negotiations. For their part the British knew that the Community was to harmonize its tariffs, whether the British offered a *quid pro quo* or not. To be sure, the Community might fail to do this, especially if there were no British counterpart, but in that case the Benelux tariffs, already the lowest in the Community, might not go up even the two percentage points they were expected to rise for "harmonization." Two-thirds of Britain's steel exports to the Community went to Holland and Belgium. The Community producers, for their part, knew that British steel tariffs were suspended. If the experience of the postwar years was to be any guide, they would remain suspended whenever the steel supply in Britain was tight and especially so long as foreign steel was generally more expensive than the British product.

The Community had been taking about 6 per cent of Britain's steel exports; the Commonwealth took about 60 per cent in several postwar years. British producers claim they have no great interest in pressing for larger markets on the Continent. This may be partly a show for bargaining purposes but it is largely borne out by the historical pattern of British trade, the emphasis on indirect exports of steel **in the form of** manufactured products, and the better prospects of overseas sales at higher prices than could be commanded in sales to the Community. In Britain's recent sales to the Community, tariffs do not seem to have been a major factor. From 1954 to 1957 its largest Community market was Holland, where the tariffs were low, and the next largest Italy, where the tariffs were high. There are, of course, advantages to Britain in narrowing the margin of tariff discrimination against its goods compared to those moving within the common market, but in circumstances where tariff rates were important to the movement of trade the margin would still be a serious disadvantage for British producers competing with French and Germans.

tiations just past that the Community countries were prepared to act on tariffs. CA, Commission des Affaires Politiques et des Relations Extérieures de la Communauté, *Rapport . . . par M. P. Struye, Rapporteur,* doc. 27 (1956-57), p. 11.

The Community's imports of finished steel products from the United Kingdom in 1957 were less than 10 per cent of its imports from third countries and less than 2 per cent of intra-Community trade.

For the Community, Britain is a somewhat more important market. Exports of finished steel products to the United Kingdom were regularly larger than imports from that country; in 1956 they were about 8 per cent of the Community's sales to third countries and in 1957 less than 3 per cent. There is also a moderate export of ingots and semi-finished products to Britain. The Community usually has a fairly large share of Britain's imports, about one-third in 1955 when imports were high. The main impediment to Community sales to the United Kingdom has been "the inability of European producers, save in special cases, to compete on price with the domestic product. . . . From time to time shortages in domestic capacity and long delayed delivery dates make imports of higher-priced European products . . . both possible and profitable. Normally, however, the UK import market is a tough one." [9]

While it was being negotiated the tariff agreement seemed unlikely to have any immediate material impact or to be of outstanding commercial importance to either side. But that was just at the end of the boom. By the time the agreement came into effect, demand was weaker. This raised new questions about future trade relations between Britain and the Community, but did not seem likely to make a profound change quickly. Community export prices fell faster than Britain's home prices, but Britain would only have to restore its suspended duties to get much greater protection, even at the reduced rates.[10] Moreover,

[9] The Economist Intelligence Unit, *Britain and Europe*, 1957, p. 74.

[10] It was with an eye to slack times that the British Iron and Steel Federation in 1955 proposed an end to suspending and re-imposing tariffs to meet changing market conditions. It recommended instead a stable tariff, not subject to suspension, at a somewhat lower rate than then existed, coupled with some kind of flexible protection that would apply either when imports increased or when they became cheaper. Among several alternatives, its preference was for an antidumping duty which would apply whenever foreign products were sold at less than their domestic prices and would equal the spread between the two

the tariff is not the only barrier to trade between Britain and the Community. Casual sales are handicapped by differences in specifications and standards. "Price fixing and division of the market, as for example by the Cased Tube Association and the Railway Materials Association, is operated in some divisions of the industry. These arrangements make it more difficult to sell in the UK, exactly as similar, but less well documented, arrangements inhibit UK sales in Europe."[11] There appears to be nothing in the tariff agreement to prevent governments from imposing quantitative restrictions on trade. If producers on either side began to make a major effort to sell across the Channel, there would almost certainly be efforts to regulate the trade, either by agreement or by unilateral action. Antidumping arrangements and "the structure of steel prices" are already under discussion in the Council of Association.

The approach of the British producers to such issues has been made clear in the past. At an early stage of the discussion about the terms of association, the British Iron and Steel Federation said that an agreement on:

exports between the Community and the U.K. . . . would seem a necessary counterpart to any agreement on tariffs and special protective measures in time of over-production; indeed in the inter-war discussions the two subjects were closely linked, the conclusion of the agreement limiting Continental exports to the United Kingdom being followed by a reduction in the British tariff.[12]

Noting the industry opposition to the proposed agreement of association, the London *Times* said on May 4, 1954, "The

---

prices. "The UK Steel Tariff," *Monthly Statistical Bulletin* (British Iron and Steel Federation), Mar. 1955. The assumption appears to have been that foreign prices plus transport would always make foreign steel more expensive than British in the United Kingdom if there was no dumping.

[11] The Economist Intelligence Unit, cited, pp. 72, 73.

[12] "Britain and the E.C.S.C.," *Monthly Statistical Bulletin* (British Iron and Steel Federation), Mar. 1954. The latter part of the statement refers to 1935 when the British government raised the steel tariff to improve the bargaining position of the British industry in persuading the Continental cartel to limit sales to the United Kingdom. F. C. Benham, *Great Britain Under Protection* (N. Y.: Macmillan, 1941), pp. 178-185.

steel industry has indicated that it would prefer to deal with the Community directly, as though it were an international cartel, and the Coal Board might take the same view."

The High Authority and the British government rebuffed this approach at the time, insisting on a government-to-government arrangement. They would almost certainly hold to this same position on the regulation of trade. That would give the public interest in competition more weight than it would otherwise have but would not necessarily rule out an agreement regulating trade and prices. Another possible line of approach would concern exports to third countries, where a mutual interest might be seen in checking price competition. During one of the GATT sessions, "some representatives . . . expressed the fear that the arrangement [between Britain and the Community] might well develop into a regional agreement of the producers of a very important commodity and work to the detriment of the consumers." [13] The representatives of Britain and the High Authority stressed that this was a governmental agreement and included a pledge to consider the interests of third parties.

The Future

Is there a logical next step to the process of "association" of Britain with the Community? An agreement on trade and prices to cope with recession would certainly bring the two closer together, if only temporarily. It would not involve, perhaps not even lead to, any formally closer connection. While few Britons advocate outright membership in the Community, their opinion is divided on the wisdom of accepting some of the obligations in return for some of the privileges. Speaking at about the time the agreement of association was being concluded, Sir Oliver Franks chided Britain for standing aloof and maintaining relations with the Community "through a mission as though it were a foreign Power . . . it would be to our advantage if we

[13] GATT, *Basic Instruments and Selected Documents, Fourth Supplement*, Feb. 1956, p. 88.

made an agreement for country membership." This is Franks' term for something less than full membership. "We pay our subscription and take on our obligations but not the full subscription nor all the obligations of the regular members, our Continental neighbours." [14]

Others share this opinion, but there is a wide range of views. Those who wish to see Britain play a more active part in European integration look for a formula like Franks'. Other well-informed and skeptical people ask what the Community has done that a cartel would not have done. All the political objections to joining a united Europe are likely to be aroused by suggestions of a closer tie with the Coal and Steel Community. Certainly there is no significant agitation among British political groups to change the basis of relations. The British government, for its part, has shown no signs of altering its basic opposition to firm and lasting enclosure in a pre-federal Little Europe. Proposals like the "Eden Plan" for bringing all the European agencies under a single assembly entail no great British obligation and have, understandably enough, been rejected on the Continent as a means of giving the British a position of potential influence over matters for which they have no responsibility.

The accepted view in the steel industry appears to be that there is no great gain to be had from joining the Community and considerable disadvantage in accepting the Community's obligations. Though it may complain about the governmental controls, the British industry, like the French and German before it at the time of ratification, has a preference for dealing with national authorities rather than the agencies in Luxembourg. There is skepticism about the Community's achievement and suspicion as to how well it will work in bad times. British producers envisage themselves at a competitive disadvantage if, as they suspect would be the case, the Community's anticartel measures were enforced under British law but did not in fact pre-

[14] O. S. Franks, *Britain and the Tide of World Affairs* (London: Oxford University Press, 1955), p. 47. He "suggested that August 10, 1952, was likely to be regarded by future historians as the most important date in the post-war decade of western Europe" because "it was the day on which the Schuman Plan became a reality," p. 37.

vail on the Continent. They are concerned about the effect on their position and that of their main customers, the British steel-using industries, of any interference with double-pricing, export controls, and import equalization schemes in steel, coal, and scrap.

These issues have come into a new focus in the discussions for a free trade area. Again in the interests of its customers the steel industry accepts the general proposal, since the British manufacturing industries would be at a disadvantage if they were outside the tariff wall of the common market. But for itself it may prefer a separate status. Since coal and steel have been omitted from the new European Common Market treaty because they have a treaty of their own, they would have to have some kind of special treatment in a free trade area. The British Iron and Steel Federation has said that it "would naturally wish to ensure that the rules formulated were built up in the light of the varying circumstances and experience of all the national steel industries concerned. It would seem altogether inappropriate simply to take over in whole or in part the corpus of rules which the six main Continental steel producing countries felt to be proper for their needs . . . some six to seven years ago. . . ." [15] Which leaves matters about where they stood, with the important difference that creation of a free trade area would inevitably provide an impetus that has not previously existed to see what new content might be given to Britain's "Association" with the Coal and Steel Community.

By the same token, failure to work out some kind of free trade area would be bound to have a negative effect. Sir David Eccles told a group of European industrialists, "Somehow Europe seems not fully to understand that if there were no Free Trade Area but only the European Economic Community we in the United Kingdom could not stand aside and do nothing. . . . This is not a threat. It is the logic of the age we live in. . . . But what extra friction and difficulties should we create for ourselves if the

---

[15] "Steel and the Free Trade Area," *Steel Review*, Oct. 1957, p. 6. For the relation of the Coal and Steel Community to the Free Trade Area and the European Economic Community, see Chapter 22.

Six were pulling in one direction and we were pulling in another?" [16] Thus the future of British association with the Coal and Steel Community is likely to be determined in the main by the general development of British relations with the Continental Community rather than by the special features of coal and steel.

Looking back at the more limited experience of association under the Community's first treaty with a foreign power, we find little guidance for such large issues. There have been accomplishments, of which the greatest is the still modest tariff agreement. One should not depreciate the discussions, joint studies, and exchanges of information; a discussion of long-term objectives for steel that brings together Sir Robert Shone and M. Tony Rollman is bound to be interesting. But it is also true that the Council of Association has not yet tried to cope with really difficult problems and cannot be thought to have had a major effect on the economic relations of Britain and the Community. Partly this is because the problems were not very serious; if they become so, the understanding may show its capabilities and limitations more fully. Perhaps there is political significance in the fact that the importance of association is so often exaggerated, though less among the British than in the Community and in the United States; or perhaps that is only human.

"CONSULTATION" WITH SWITZERLAND

From the beginning of the negotiations for the coal and steel pool, Switzerland has been a most interested bystander. Interested, because Switzerland imports—in large part from the Community—all its coal, most of its finished steel, and most of the semi-finished steel for its steel-working industry.[17] A bystander, because with the political cast given

---

[16] Speech to European Industrial Conference, Feb. 20, 1958 (mimeographed press release).

[17] In 1956, Switzerland produced 171,000 tons of crude steel, all by the electrical process, and 272,500 tons of finished steel, mostly hot-rolled product. It imported 120,000 tons of ingots and semi-finished products, 326,000 tons of sections, 137,000 of sheets, 125,000 of plates, and 214,000 tons of other products. ECE, *Quarterly Bulletin of Steel Statistics for Europe,* Dec. 1957 (hereafter cited as ECE, *Steel Statistics*).

the Schuman Plan from the outset there was no chance that Switzerland would feel that membership was consistent with its traditional neutrality.

Looking at the Treaty after it was drafted, and at the Community in practice, Switzerland's concern was that of the classic outsider. Would it get supplies if there were shortages? Would its steel-using industries be hurt by Community double-pricing? If the cost of producing steel in the Community fell, would the high-cost Swiss steel industry need additional protection? Switzerland had been an outsider before and had managed rather well, thanks largely to its hard currency and its ability to supply some critical goods. But how would its bargaining position be affected by the massive new combine on its borders? *Vigilance et prudence* must be their motto, said the Swiss.

Unlike other countries that had similar worries, Switzerland was not a member of GATT and so lacked that major forum for expressing its views. It could not invoke the obligations of the waiver. The Swiss could call the Community's attention to the Treaty's mandate to "foster . . . international trade and ensure . . . equitable prices" but to give weight to the words they had to fall back on their own bargaining power. This lay in money, treaty obligations, and geography. Because the negotiations have been secret and the diplomats discreet, one can only piece together an account from visible parts and obvious deductions.

At the outset, the Community countries had to ask Switzerland to waive its most-favored-nation rights under various agreements so that they could legally form the common market. Undoubtedly the Swiss used these negotiations to get assurances about supplies and fair treatment. They appear not to have formally given up their most-favored-nation rights, thus retaining some bargaining power.[18] Switzerland also had a voice in the OEEC discus-

---

[18] CA, Commission des Affaires Politiques . . . , *Rapport* . . . , doc. 27, cited, p. 17. At a stockholders' meeting of the Ludwig von Roll'schen Eisenwerke, A. G., Dr. Hanspeter Brunner, a member of the directorate, referred to the efforts officials had made to get assurances of supplies during the negotiations about most-favored-nation rights. *Neue Zürcher Zeitung*, May 27, 1953.

sions affecting the use of quotas by the Community countries (p. 524) and probably called attention to the fact that if Swiss interests were damaged by Community policies, it could withdraw liberalization measures it had taken under the OEEC program.

When German debts were settled in 1953 and the use of blocked marks agreed on, the Swiss made a loan of DM 110 million to several German iron and steel companies. The money was to be used over a period of five years for modernization and rationalization. In return the Swiss got 4 per cent plus the right to buy up to 100,000 tons of iron and steel products a year, including the assurance that when supplies were short this amount would be set aside for them.[19] Several years later, when the High Authority wished to float a loan in Switzerland (p. 328), the Swiss government had a chance to negotiate with the people who could give weightier commitments.

Concurrently, Switzerland and the High Authority were negotiating about transportation questions. More than half the coal, steel, and scrap moving between Italy and the rest of the Community by rail normally passed through Switzerland.[20] For the Community, it was desirable that the freight rates on these routes should be determined in the same way as those on routes that ran entirely through Community territory. Broken rates and discriminatory rates would either introduce arbitrary elements into costs and prices or divert trade to less economical routes through southern France. For Switzerland the choice was between the yield of higher transit rates and the risk of losing part of a grow-

[19] *Neue Zürcher Zeitung*, Aug. 28, 1953. The promise of supply was made by the firms in question and not backed up by a governmental guarantee as the Swiss had hoped. Such a commitment might be difficult for a firm to carry out if the High Authority were using its powers to make allocations. However, if the amount is small enough in relation to production, the commitment could probably be honored, though this might only mean that the quantities involved were charged against the export quota permitted for Switzerland, which would thus not get any more steel than it would without commitments.

[20] In 1954 the railroad traffic in Community products between Italy and the other Community countries moved in the following proportions: through Switzerland, 1.35 million tons; through Austria, .45 million; over the French-Italian border, .83 million. *Der Volkswirt*, Nov. 26, 1955, p. 9.

ing traffic. Negotiations about this issue began soon after Switzerland accredited its representative at the OEEC to the High Authority as well in April 1953. Out of the interplay of interests and bargaining power came two agreements. One virtually incorporated the transit routes of the Swiss railways—particularly the passage via the Simplon and St. Gotthard tunnels—into the Community's system of railroad-rate rules. The other—the Community's second treaty—gave Switzerland some assurance about supplies and provided a mechanism for dealing with issues that might arise between Switzerland and the Community. It was, essentially, an agreement to consult, and not very much more.

The High Authority had taken the view that it could not give Switzerland firm commitments about supplies in times of shortage or about prices, "for reasons of principle and for judicial reasons." [21] In the agreement it promised to consult the Swiss government before adopting any system of allocation in time of shortage, or introducing export restrictions, or setting minimum or maximum export prices. Switzerland agreed to consult before taking any action that would affect its "traditional trade" with the Community. Assuming that "traditional trade" can be defined, the reciprocity is not purely formal; the Swiss iron and steel industry is protected and the level of protection might at some time be a matter of interest to the Community.[22] But

---

[21] CA, *Annuaire-Manuel, 1957*, pp. 228, 229. Other countries might demand equal treatment; third countries were not mentioned in the Treaty as objects of the High Authority's allocations; the limited area of maneuver in times of shortage had to be kept open; the High Authority's powers over export prices were limited and contingent. After the agreement was signed on May 7, 1956, it was put into effect provisionally until it was ratified by Switzerland and came fully into effect on January 26, 1957. The text is in *JO*, Feb. 21, 1957. Since the Swiss treaty refers only to action by the High Authority, it was signed by that body alone and not by the Community governments as in the case of the British treaty. After the end of the transitional period, it was to be automatically renewed for five-year periods unless denounced.

[22] In 1957 the Swiss published a draft tariff raising duties on certain iron and steel products. It is not entirely clear whether they consulted the High Authority before doing this, but in any case the amounts involved were not such as to be of great concern to Community producers in a sellers' market.

the big gain is obviously on Switzerland's side; it is given
a chance to make its case before the High Authority takes
any of the major actions that were feared in Switzerland.
Like the British treaty, however, this one permits action in
advance of consultation when that seems necessary. Both
sides exchanged pledges of their intentions to follow liberal
commercial policies, the High Authority's being in the form
of a recital of the Treaty provisions for the protection
of third countries like that in the GATT and OEEC
waivers.

The Swiss treaty, like that with Britain, created a standing committee for the discussion of common problems.[23]
Made up of an equal number of representatives of each
side, the joint committee's only specifically assigned task
is to hold the limited kinds of consultation called for by
the Treaty. It met for the first time on February 1, 1957,
to survey trade between the Community and Switzerland,
and has not been very active since. Of course, discussions
continue even if the committee does not formally meet. A
separate body handles railroad rates; a Rhine agreement was
signed in 1958. The dissatisfaction the Swiss feel about
the way their complaints on prices were treated is symptomatic of some of the difficulties of their position (p. 496).
For the Community, consultation with Switzerland is formally and legally a matter of limited scope, just as Swiss
trade is of minor importance. For Switzerland—to whom
the trade is vastly more important—the paper guarantees
are limited, but they imply a degree of responsibility on the
substance of which, backed by their own real but limited
bargaining power, the Swiss have to depend.

NEGOTIATIONS WITH AUSTRIA AND SCANDINAVIA

Austria is, like Switzerland, a small country heavily
dependent on the Coal and Steel Community but in somewhat different ways. Austria has a sizable iron and steel
industry, producing over 2.5 million tons of crude steel in

[23] But words like "council" and "association" were not mentioned,
probably so as to reserve a special status for Britain.

1957, more than twice as much as the Netherlands.[24] Steel products accounted for one-fifth of Austria's export earnings in 1957, more than any other category of goods. Almost two-thirds of the Austrian output of special steels was exported. The government owns most of the industry, which has expanded greatly in recent years, partly with Marshall Plan assistance; production in 1957 was two and one-half times the 1952 level. The government held down the domestic steel price, under pressure from rising costs of imported coal and scrap. Therein lay, on the one hand, the Community's worries about Austrian "dumping" and, on the other, Austria's worry about getting adequate supplies of coking coal and scrap at reasonable prices.[25]

The first problems between Austria and the Community concerned trade. Rather lengthy negotiations were finally concluded in 1956 (p. 475f.), and solved part of the problem. Mostly about tariffs, the agreements also left room for understandings on prices of Austrian steel going to Italy. Austria continued to be worried about its coal supplies (p. 490). In 1957 a transportation agreement, like that with Switzerland, virtually incorporated Austria's transit trade in coal and steel in the Community's ratemaking system. A committee was set up to supervise the working of this agreement, but nowhere in the arrangements with Austria was there the machinery for continuing cooperation the Community had established with Britain or the broad assurances the Community had given Switzerland.

The special feature of relations between Austria and the

---

[24] In 1956, Austria produced 3.2 million tons of iron ore, 1.7 million tons of pig iron (importing about 400,000 tons of coke and producing over 2 million tons more, mostly from imported coal), 2.1 million tons of crude steel, and 1.5 million tons of finished steel, two-thirds of it in plate, sheets, light sections, and wire rods. Austria was a net importer of iron ore and scrap, a net exporter of pig iron and crude and semi-finished steel. It was also a substantial net exporter of finished products, especially plates and sheets, but a net importer of heavy sections. ECE, *Steel Statistics*, cited.

[25] In 1953 and 1954 half of Austria's hard-coal imports came from Germany. By 1956 the share had fallen to one-fifth (and, in absolute terms, was cut in half), the difference being made up by imports from the United States. ECE, *Quarterly Bulletin of Coal Statistics for Europe*, Feb. 1958 (hereafter cited as ECE, *Coal Statistics*).

Community has been the possibility, taken seriously on both sides, that Austria might become a member of the Community.[26] Economically, and geographically, this was a logical proposition. It was ruled out at the moment the Community was formed by the fact that Austria was occupied. After the Austrian peace treaty was signed in May 1955, the possibility was legally open and, many thought, politically as well. The prospects were carefully canvassed in Austria; many came to the conclusion that the assurance of Ruhr coking coal plus the elimination of German and Italian tariffs on Austrian special steels left a clear balance of advantage.[27] The issue was not entirely clear-cut. Joining the Community would probably require an increase in Austrian domestic steel prices, but some people thought that would be a good idea anyway. Steel and its management were also the objects of a good bit of political maneuvering which might be affected by joining the Community.

In the spring of 1957, the High Authority noted that from the outset, "There were . . . already important economic ties between Austria and the member countries, and it would have been a natural step for Austria to join the Community. Since, for various reasons, she has so far not been able to do so . . ." other arrangements were resorted to.[28] Such language has never been used about another country. Statements by the Austrian prime minister during 1957 indicated that his country's adherence to the Community might be imminent. Afterwards it appeared that these statements had been premature and the matter was scarcely discussed in public, suggesting that Moscow had indicated that joining the Community would create "foreign policy difficulties" for Austria. Discussion of a free trade area opened new prospects. While avoiding the political over-

---

[26] Article 98 of the Treaty provides for accession to the Community by any European state if the Council of Ministers agrees by unanimous vote after obtaining the opinion of the High Authority. The Council may fix the terms of accession, also by unanimous vote.

[27] For instance, "Klares Verhalten zur Montanunion Bedingung für gesicherte Stahlexporte," *Internationale Wirtschaft* (Vienna), Nov. 18, 1955.

[28] HA, *Report*, Apr. 1957, pp. 61, 62.

tures of membership in the Community, Austria might still be able to get free access to the markets of the six countries. The prospect was particularly attractive because these countries had taken 45 per cent of Austria's steel exports in 1957 and the Austrian industry was worried about the effect of the fall in prices and demand. As a bonus, in the eyes of some, the Free Trade Area might entail less disturbance of domestic Austrian arrangements than membership in the Community would have—but that depended on how some rather difficult problems were solved, mostly by people who were not Austrian.

Denmark, too, has occasionally been thought of as a potential recruit for the Community, but there has never been anything like the official hints given in the Austrian case. Of minor importance as a steel producer, Denmark's special interest has been in the supply of coke and in the price of steel for its manufacturing industries. Denmark differs from Switzerland and Austria in its easier access to British and overseas supplies which, along with a traditional trade pattern, make it less dependent on the Community. The single factor strongly pulling Denmark toward membership would be the opportunity to qualify for "domestic" prices for Community steel. Checking this, however, are all the factors that have kept Denmark out of "Little Europe," economically and politically.

Norway's trade position is rather similar to that of Denmark but the country is less highly industrialized, has its own iron ore, and expects a substantial increase in steel output. While its imports of steel products are growing, domestic production is growing even faster. Sweden has a large domestic production of steel and a sizable foreign trade in which goods move both ways; special steels and quality products are exported, some heavier products imported.[29] This, coupled with its strong export position in iron ore, puts Sweden in a rather good bargaining position vis-à-vis the Community and there has been little talk of

[29] In 1956 Sweden produced 2.4 million tons of crude steel and 1.7 million tons of finished steel. It imported 65,000 tons of steel products, especially plates and sections, and exported 39,000 tons, especially light sections and wire rods. ECE, *Steel Statistics*, cited.

closer association. There were early negotiations with Sweden about special steel, later ones about harmonized tariff rates, and continuing discussions with all three Scandinavian countries, pursued bilaterally as well as in GATT, about export prices. But the Community has reached no formal agreements with the Scandinavian countries.

Whatever may have come about in other circumstances, the combination of the Free Trade Area discussions and the intensified pursuit of Nordic cooperation have pushed direct relations with the Community into the background for the Scandinavian countries. Looking at the joint resources of these countries in iron and steel and the expectations each country had for expanding output and consumption of steel, the Nordic Economic Cooperation Committee recommended that whether or not they formed a customs union the three countries and Finland should cooperate in their steel development. Such a course would imply improved "domestic" sources of steel for Denmark, a stronger bargaining position for all the countries together against the Community, greater independence of the Brussels price cartel, and, in one way or another, joint negotiations about matters of common concern.[30] The creation of a free trade area, or the failure to create one, would open new problems for these countries, but they would be greater in other sectors than in iron and steel. If Denmark, for instance, felt forced into the Common Market by the failure to create a satisfactory free trade area it might naturally, but not inevitably, move into the Coal and Steel Community as well. But this will not be determined primarily by the policies of the Coal and Steel Community or by Denmark's position in these industries.

SUBSTANTIVE COMMITMENTS TO GATT

The external relations that have required the greatest commitments from the Community and that have probably had most to do with the policies it followed have not been with any individual country but with groups of countries

---

[30] *Nordisk Økonomisk Samarbeid* (cited in Ch. 17, n. 24), Part 1, pp. 82-84, Part 2, pp. 18-71.

joined together in international organizations. All the Community countries had signed the General Agreement on Tariffs and Trade and also the OEEC's Code on the Liberalization of Trade. Both these agreements called for equal treatment of imports from all the signatories. The Community was proposing to grant very unequal treatment: complete free trade among its members coupled with continued tariffs and in some cases quotas on imports from other countries. To do this legally, the Community had to get the other parties to each agreement to waive the rules.

The High Authority considered that there was no difficulty at all in the matter of the OEEC. Article 8 of the Code of Liberalization provided that, "Member countries forming part of a special customs or monetary system may apply to one another . . . other measures of liberalisation of trade without extending them to the other Member countries." The High Authority took the view that the six governments need simply notify the OEEC of their new venture. However, in making its decision in February 1953, the Council of the OEEC put Article 8 in the background and laid much greater stress on a series of statements about the benefits to the members of the OEEC from the successful achievement of the Community's aims and on the undertakings given by the Community about the treatment of outside countries. The waiver was generally modeled on that drafted several months earlier in GATT, which is to be discussed below.

The OEEC obtained from the High Authority the commitment that, within the limits of the powers the Treaty gave it over commercial policy, ". . . it will comply with the obligations which would be binding upon it if the Community constituted a Member of the Organization consisting of the European territories of the Member States." Even though the High Authority's powers in this field were limited, it could act for the Community if the governments agreed that it should. (The body of the waiver decision, as distinguished from the preamble, spoke of the "Member States, acting as a Community. . . .") The effect of this was twofold. In applying antidumping measures or in withholding a certain degree of liberalization because of its economic repercussions, the Community countries would have to act as a whole. Disturbances in one country (in coal and steel) would not warrant withdrawal of liberalization measures unless the problem could not be dealt with by the combined action of the whole group. The second effect is to make the Community something of an entity in its own right in OEEC activities. This was further sustained by subsequent arrangements for High Authority representatives to participate in the work of numerous OEEC committees.

While annual review of the GATT waiver has been the occasion for extended discussion of the Community's activity, I know of only one occasion on which the OEEC waiver has served the same purpose. In June 1954 the Danish delegation to the OEEC filed two complaints, both covering issues already raised in GATT. The Danish complaint was supported in the OEEC Council by the Norwegians, the Americans, the British, and perhaps others. However, when it was proposed that the High Authority be asked to make a detailed report, the observer from the High Authority said that this would be unacceptable. It was finally decided that the two organizations would jointly discuss the matter in more detail. Whether anything substantial resulted is doubtful. Most of the same countries, and some others, were discussing the same issues in GATT, where the High Authority made more detailed reports, and the Danes were discussing it directly with the High Authority, so it is probable that Paris became superfluous as a forum.

Geneva, however, remained in the forefront throughout the transitional period. No provision in the GATT agreement permitted the kind of tariff arrangements made by the Community Treaty, so long as they fell short of creating a customs union. Each of the many countries in GATT had a single vote, and a two-thirds majority was required for the waiver. Some of these were the Community's small neighbors who were already uneasy about the problems they might face if their major suppliers were to join forces.

Others were Asian or Latin American countries to whom the beauties of European integration might not be apparent and who would be suspicious of a league of big producers. But the Community had the backing of the United States. Britain was unlikely to oppose the waiver very strenuously lest it be accused of trying to block European integration, a charge it had been carefully trying to avoid. In the end, though a few votes may have been cast reluctantly, only Czechoslovakia voted against the waiver.[31]

The waiver granted on November 10, 1952, was not a simple, unconditional declaration that the six governments were entitled to depart from most-favored-nation principles in order to create a common market. It recited the aims of the Community and the provisions of the Treaty, emphasizing the removal of internal trade barriers. Then it said, "the realisation of these aims, if accompanied by appropriate trade policies on the part of the Community, could benefit other contracting parties to the General Agreement by increasing supplies of coal and steel products, and by providing increased markets for commodities used by the coal and steel industry and for other products and thereby would contribute to the objectives of the General Agreement. . . ."[32]

The waiver decision assembled the provisions of the Treaty and the Convention referring to the interests of third countries, equitable export prices, and the harmonization of tariffs at lower levels than had existed. It deduced that in order to meet its undertakings the Community would have "to avoid placing unreasonable barriers upon exports to third countries." Finally, among the preliminary considerations, the document took note of a series of understandings by which the High Authority, as well as the Community governments, is brought into GATT consultations, the Community is treated as if it were a single country for such purposes as come fully under High Authority control, and it is made clear that actions of the Community

[31] Cuba and Indonesia abstained. The delegates of Burma, Lebanon, Nicaragua, and Peru were absent. HA, *Report*, Jan. 1953, p. 28.
[32] Text in GATT, . . . *First Supplement*, Mar. 1953, pp. 17-22.

and of the governments are subject to the full GATT obligations, except as modified by the waiver.

The GATT decision not only waived most-favored-nation treatment, but authorized a number of specific departures from the rules, such as the Benelux tariff quotas, the expected 2-percentage-point increase in Benelux duties to achieve harmonization, and Belgian use of quotas on coal imports for seven years. Like the OEEC waiver it stipulated that in applying certain kinds of controls permitted by GATT in specified circumstances, the Community should be treated as a whole and adjustments made among the Six before invoking external trade controls.

The waiver also called on the governments of the Community countries to make an annual report, during the transitional period, "on the measures taken by them towards the full application of the Treaty." The discussion of these reports in a working party of GATT provided the principal occasions on which the Community was required to give an account of itself to interested parties on the outside. At these sessions, questions were asked, complaints made, explanations given, and differences of view recorded without all of them being reconciled.

Much of the discussion has concerned steel export prices (pp. 491ff.). Closely connected have been questions about the Community's measures to control cartels. Limitations on exports of scrap were the occasion for questions, mostly from Austria and Sweden. Lack of progress toward harmonization of tariff rates stimulated criticism, especially from representatives who said that their governments had agreed to the waiver only in the expectation that third countries would benefit from the Community and that this required the lowering of duties. The Italian tariff situation, especially with regard to special steels, was a particular target. As the Italian duties on imports from the rest of the Community fell, the margin of preference against which outside suppliers had to compete grew.

Each year the Contracting Parties of GATT approved the working party's finding that the Community had not violated the waiver. These reports, however, also summarized various viewpoints that had been expressed and recommended procedures for the coming year, especially with regard to getting increased data from the High Authority. The second of the reports, approved in February 1955, gave a good bit of space to the criticisms of the Community. It stressed the need to take account not only of the specific application of the rules laid down in the waiver but also of the broad statements of intentions made by the six countries when the waiver was granted and of their commitment to carry out the objectives of the Treaty. The High Authority was somewhat disturbed by this course of events. "This year," it reported to the Assembly, "questions concerning cartels and prices were much more numerous and more awkward. Although the point of the interpretation of the waiver was not discussed from the legal point of view, certain third countries clearly intimated that by granting the waiver, they considered they had a right to supervise all undertakings entered into by the member States or the High Authority under the Treaty. The delegates of the Community expressed themselves as alarmed by such an interpretation, and pointed out that, for their part, they regarded the waiver as carrying two kinds of obligation—those under the Treaty, as specified in the waiver, which are supervised by the Common Assembly, and those entered into with the contracting parties to G.A.T.T." [33]

This was obviously somewhat awkward for the High Authority. One can sympathize with the feeling that it was hard enough to apply the Treaty and to satisfy the Assembly, the governments, the interest groups, and public opinion in the Community, without having to make an annual journey to Geneva to explain and defend its record before representatives of other countries with no responsibility for the execution of the Treaty. Still, these countries had a real interest in what went on in the Community. Having been given a foothold by the waiver they were obviously going to use it to press their own interests. Whatever one might decide the legal situation was—so far as the High Authority's argument about the two kinds of com-

[33] HA, *Report*, Apr. 1955, p. 33.

mitments is concerned—it seems clear that there is a connection of relevance and substance running through the
entire range of activities.

The third year's report of the GATT working party
again referred to most of the issues that had been raised
before but avoided the recapitulation of complaints that had
given the previous year's report its special tenor. This time,
the High Authority said, it had provided the Contracting
Parties with fuller details and statistics. "This gesture was
much appreciated, and the atmosphere in which the discussions took place in Geneva, from late October to early
December, was distinctly more encouraging than in previous years." [34] In the next two years as well the terms on
which the High Authority was appearing seemed satisfactory. The High Authority made more information
available, and the complaining governments improved their
documentation; the GATT secretariat tried to draft
objective reports on the facts that were in dispute. Complaints continued and some questions remained unsettled,
but the nature of the process was better understood and
there was, perhaps, less sense of the High Authority being
the defendant in the dock. After it had filed its last report,
the High Authority said, with some relief, "From now on
the Community will face GATT in a situation comparable
to that of any other Contracting Party; it will be prepared
to discuss all the problems of common interest that could
arise in the spirit that is usual in that environment." [35] While

[34] HA, *Report*, Apr. 1956, pp. 34-35.

[35] HA, *Report*, Apr. 1958, v. 1, p. 87. It also looked on the bright side:
"the large dialogue accepted by the six member countries and the High
Authority made it possible for all the Contracting Parties to understand
the direction and bearing of the Community's development. Better
acquaintance with the action of the High Authority has helped to sup-
press a large part of the apprehension which its creation aroused." An
American observer notes: "the discussions have been least rewarding
when the High Authority has been in the position of justifying its
stewardship before an obviously suspicious body and most useful when
there has been a sense of give and take on both sides." Miriam Camps,
Trade Policy and American Leadership, Center of International Studies,
Princeton University, Mar. 1957, p. 15 (processed). The emphasis should
perhaps be on "suspicious" since the justification of stewardship is the
essence of the process.

the need to file annual reports expired with the transitional period, the obligations continued and complaints could be made in the ordinary fashion.

The relation to GATT in the waiver, in the annual discussions, and in the tariff negotiations of early 1956, had some importance in establishing the character of the Community. It was in many ways the most effective pressure from outside, under which the Community, and especially the High Authority, had to shape its policy. Some of the Treaty's professions of purpose were turned into international commitments; some of its specific promises were reinforced by being incorporated in the waiver. Foreign countries had various means of making representations to the Community when they thought their interests were affected. When they chose to use the GATT discussions, they could add weight to their case. Because it may be challenged in this broad and semi-public forum, the Community has to be concerned day in and day out with the external effects of what it does.

In another way the GATT relation is important as one of the very few external yardsticks recurrently applied to the Community. In the GATT setting the Community is looked at—imperfectly, to be sure— in terms of its place in the world economy instead of only, in the more usual manner, as a new kind of integration in which internal relations are the sole focus. Considering the importance of the Community in world production and trade in coal and steel, it is well that this measure should be employed regularly and not always subordinated to the more obvious and often more dramatic issues involved in merging the national economies.

The GATT relation also helps the Community acquire an international personality. The High Authority itself, whether acting under its own powers or as agent for the governments, appears in international negotiations on somewhat the same basis as a national government. The Community is treated, for some purposes, as a single economic area, comparable to a nation. Insofar as the governments of the Community and the High Authority appear side by side as "the Community"—as they did in the sessions of the GATT working party, for instance—not only is the mixed supranational and international character of the Community reflected in a realistic fashion, but the working-together of the parts is inevitably enhanced.

The importance of the GATT relation, then, seems to be primarily that it requires the Community to have, at least some of the time, a global focus instead of a regional one; it subjects Community action to a real instead of a nominal test of its effect on other countries. At these sessions, questions were asked, complaints made, explanations given, and differences of view recorded without all of them being reconciled. This is not entirely a matter of the Community *against* the rest of the world. There is sometimes an element of that. But, as in the foreign relations of a nation, there is an interplay with domestic forces. The interest of groups in the Community is not always unified; some want lower and some higher tariffs; some have an interest in maintaining exports while some would prefer to keep the goods at home. Ideas of policy differ, too, as between those who want a more open or a more closed economy, for instance. The balance in these matters is affected by external relations, and so is the relative strength of contending parties. The High Authority has undoubtedly had more influence over steel export prices than it would have had without the focusing of foreign complaints in the GATT sessions. Those interested in lower tariffs have had their hand strengthened. Outside GATT as well, foreign relations have had an influence on Community affairs, as in the American restriction of the scrap supply.

The external relations may not often be decisive. The foreigners rarely get all they want. But there can be little doubt that external pressures on the Community, and especially the periodical GATT reviews, have helped overcome the risks inherent in any strictly regional economic development. These are essentially the risks of achieving a compromise of internal interests by throwing the burden of adjustment outside, and of imposing a burden on the economy of the Community by tending to insulate it, as the politically easiest course in any given case, from the external competition and demand that could exercise useful controls. It is probable, as Raymond Vernon suggests, that this process has prevented the Community from having a more "trade-diverting"—as opposed to "trade-creating"—effect than it would otherwise have had.[36]

The external pressures are partly those of the market, partly the actions of foreign governments. The role of GATT has been to focus and magnify the influence of the outside world, and to register the Community's acceptance, as obligations, of aims it professed in its Treaty. Thus the GATT relation has put the Community in a world setting as no other aspect of its activities has. The interplay of the regional and supranational entity with the global and intergovernmental one has been important to the Community and has had effects on its internal character as well as its external appearance.

[36] Raymond Vernon, "Economic Aspects of the Atlantic Community," in H. Field Haviland, ed., *The United States and the Western Community* (Haverford: Haverford College Press, 1957), p. 58.

NINETEEN

THE UNITED STATES AND THE COMMUNITY

As a champion of Western European integration, the United States government has been "for" the European Coal and Steel Community from the start. Verbal and moral support have been sustained and frequent. The occasions for practical measures of support have been rather few. Several times the United States has been of material help to the Community in economic or diplomatic ways. It has never taken a position that hurt or hindered the Community in any major fashion, though at a few points American policy or influence have created problems for the Community and some Community practices have been the subject of American complaint. There has been little controversy within the United States about policy toward the Community, perhaps largely because there are relatively few points at which the immediate interests of American groups touch Community affairs. In the steel industry one can find coolness, some suspicion, and occasional hostility to the Community. In the coal and scrap industries there has been concern over trade problems. But none of these issues has presented major policy decisions for the United States.

THE TRADE BETWEEN THE COMMUNITY AND THE UNITED STATES

The trading relations of the United States and the Community are to be seen as part of the setting of American policy rather than as a central feature of it. The only serious problems have been those in the scrap trade, which have already been discussed. In coal and steel there have been relatively minor difficulties.

Coal

Not until the Second World War did bituminous coal production in the United States reach (and pass) the peak it had touched in 1918. Between the wars the industry tended to stagnate and then decline. At the depth of the depression output was less than it had been in 1905. The revival of the late '30s was extended by domestic and foreign demand during the war. Though oil, gas, and hydroelectric power, had outpaced coal as sources of energy in the American economy, bituminous production in most postwar years was well above that of the prewar decade.

Coal exports were not very important before the war, usually running around 2 to 4 per cent of production. About 90 per cent of this went to Canada and sometimes more. Shipments to Europe were large in 1920 (over 10 million metric tons) and in 1926, the year of the British general strike (almost 15 million tons). The war changed the pattern. Exports have been near or above 20 million tons a year more often than they have been far below it. In 12 years 8 per cent of the bituminous coal produced in the United States was exported. Canada continued to be the largest regular market but its share fell to less than half for the whole period. The great new, and most unstable, market was Europe. Coal shipments to Europe moved in waves: high in the first years of peace, low in the 1949-50 recession, rising again with Korea, contracting in 1953-54 and then climbing to record heights in 1957. The Community was the most important American market. Its purchases followed the general pattern, led first by France and Italy, then, after 1950, by Germany, Italy, and the Netherlands. Only under the pressure of the serious shortages of 1956 and 1957 did France and Belgium again become important.

In contrast to the sluggish coal production of Europe,

American output is quite flexible (annual fluctuations in output between 1953 and 1955 equaled the whole production of France, between 1955 and 1956 that of Belgium). Europe bought American coal to fill the gaps left whenever its demand rose rapidly. Any marked drop in demand contracted purchases from the United States. Thanks to favorable geological conditions and extensive mechanization, productivity in American coal mines is over five times the Community average. Ocean freight rates have fluctuated more than prices and largely determine whether American coal will be cheaper than Community coal when it is landed in Europe. But the landed price does not determine the volume of sales. American coal was cheaper than Community coal in 1953 and 1954, when sales were very small, and again in 1957 when they were at their peak.

Sales to Europe have been welcome to an industry hard-pressed by the competition of other fuels. American producers and exporters would like, however, to establish a less marginal position, one that will promise a more stable market and, of course, a higher minimum sale in most years. Long-run estimates of Community coal needs suggest the possibility of increased sales, but stability depends on finding some means of moderating short-term fluctuations. Here there is a dilemma. So long as American coal costs more in Europe than the Community product, its market will naturally be very vulnerable to any drop in Community demand. If the landed price of American coal is below that of Community coal, the market will also be very vulnerable because of the pressure to use protective measures of some sort. When American prices were low in 1953 and 1954, Germany and Belgium imposed quotas that were subsequently removed after negotiations in GATT.[1] When American prices were high in 1956 and part of 1957, Community buyers and American sellers negotiated sales con-

[1] There were objections in the United States to lending money to the Community when domestic producers were having difficulty in selling their output, but the matter was not pressed. Representative Byrd of West Virginia in the *Congressional Record*, 83rd Cong., 2d sess., Apr. 12, 1954, p. 5052.

tracts for several years and tried to work out transportation arrangements that would reduce freight charges.[2] Then freight rates fell and some of those who were buying on terms negotiated at the height of the market found themselves at a disadvantage compared to spot buyers. Coal shipments increased, Community demand fell. Then buyers slowed their purchasing and stretched out deliveries under the long-term contracts. American shipments to the Community fell. There were rumors of action by the American exporters to stabilize or even raise the price so as to weaken the protective push in the Community. Europe's big problem, however, was not price but a temporary surplus. Belgium limited new imports and then Germany imposed a tariff that would cause importers to cancel long-term contracts. Naturally the American industry protested and got some support from Washington. However such temporary difficulties might be met, the industry's real problem remains: how to keep the European market in the future, even if the volume of peak years cannot be maintained.

The future of American coal in European markets depends first on the level of economic activity in the Community, and then on the coal policy the Community develops. If this policy stresses maximum domestic production and not cost, American coal sales are likely to remain marginal, to fluctuate sharply, and to be checked in one way or another when Community demand falls or the landed price of coal is low. If the Community's policy should stress the cost of coal, new possibilities might open for a continuing substantial and fairly regular supply of American coal to European markets, at least until oil and atomic power fill the gap in Europe's energy needs. Between these courses are other possibilities. Community action on joint purchasing, price stabilization or equalization measures, arrangements to hold down ocean freight rates, may help provide some limited stability. They will also

[2] Some mining companies, exporting firms, and the United Mine Workers formed a shipping company to assure stable transportation costs. The subsequent sharp fall in tramp rates meant that this experiment did not have a chance to test its value.

create new problems for the American exporters, but this may be the price of their keeping a market of appreciable value. Many people in the United States laughed when a few years of large exports connected with relief and recovery produced references to the coal industry's "historic market" in Western Europe. It will be a striking and somewhat ironical example of the processes of economic change if the products of West Virginia, Pennsylvania, and Kentucky, find regular outlets in the environs of Newcastle and the Ruhr.

Steel

With nearly 40 per cent of the world's crude steel capacity, the United States usually provides less than 20 per cent of the steel going into international trade. For the whole period 1950-57, exports accounted for less than 5 per cent of American shipments of steel-mill products,[3] compared with much higher figures for the Community, Japan, and the United Kingdom. Table 9 shows the trade in broad figures. For some products export shipments are substantially more important; for instance, nearly 10 per cent of the line pipe shipped in 1956 went abroad and over one-third of the hot-dipped tin and terne plate. Flat products and particularly cold-rolled sheet and strip usually provided the largest export items, coming to more than a quarter of the total exported in some years. In 1957, however, pipes and tubes took first place. Of course, the steel industry has an important interest in indirect exports of steel. Indeed, Percy W. Bidwell concludes after a careful study: "Producers take a dim view of the possibilities of

[3] These include semi-finished products, shapes, plates, rails and accessories, bars, tool steel, pipes, tubes, wire and wire products, tin and terne plate, sheets and strip. They do not include a variety of iron and steel products which would add from 450,000 to 650,000 tons to the annual export totals, or pig iron. For full lists see the main sources of figures for this section, which are the *Annual Statistical Reports* of the American Iron and Steel Institute, and its *Foreign Trade Trends* (June 1958), standard Department of Commerce statistics, and various numbers of *International Iron and Steel*, a quarterly published by the Department of Commerce from March 1955 through March 1957. Unless otherwise noted, figures in this section refer to steel-mill products.

increasing . . . *direct* exports. . . . They see much brighter prospects for expanding *indirect* exports in the form of automobiles and other automotive products, machinery, office equipment and other commodities in which steel is an important element." [4] The increase in exports in 1956 and 1957 does not seem to have altered this expectation.

Table 9

UNITED STATES FOREIGN TRADE IN STEEL-MILL PRODUCTS, 1950-1957

	Total Shipments	Exports	Imports	Foreign Trade as per cent of Shipments Exports	Imports	Trade with Community Exports	Imports
	(million net tons)					(thousand net tons)	
1950	72.2	2.6	1.0	3.7	1.4	231.4	720.0
1951	78.9	3.1	2.2	3.9	2.8	201.5	1,841.4
1952	68.0	3.9	1.2	5.8	1.7	241.8	843.6
1953	80.2	2.9	1.7	3.6	2.1	203.0	1,269.9
1954	63.2	2.7	.8	4.2	1.2	210.6	683.2
1955	84.7	3.9	1.0	4.6	1.2	415.9	612.2
1956	83.3	4.2	1.3	5.0	1.6	291.4	1,069.9
1957	79.9	5.2	1.2	6.5	1.4	292.7	889.8

SOURCE:
1950-56, U.S. Dept. of Commerce, *International Iron and Steel*, various numbers. 1957, American Iron and Steel Institute, *Foreign Trade Trends*, Je. 1958.

Canada and Latin America are the biggest markets for United States steel exports, usually taking about 60 per cent of the total. Except for two years in which there were exceptionally large sales to Britain, shipments to Europe came to between 15 and 20 per cent of American steel exports during the '50s. The Community took about 7.5 per cent of total American exports from 1953 through 1957; in the three years before it was created, the six countries took 7 per cent. Tin plate to the Netherlands and Belgium,

[4] *What the Tariff Means to American Industries*, 1956, p. 172. Chapter 7 of this book, "Iron and Steel: An Infant Industry Grows Up," is an excellent analysis of the foreign trade interest of the industry on which I have relied heavily. For the whole period 1953-57, indirect steel exports are estimated to have been 14.9 million tons, compared to direct exports of 18.9 million. *Foreign Trade Trends*, cited, pp. 16, 18.

and cold-rolled sheets to Italy and Germany, have usually been the largest items.

There have been no striking trends in United States exports of steel products to the Community, nor any marked indications of the effect of creating the common market. The trade is after all a very small item in the steel economies of the two areas; less than half of one per cent of United States production of steel-mill products has gone to the Community, equaling perhaps one per cent of their production. American producers have not been especially concerned about their exports to Europe and no issues have arisen on this score in the relation of the United States to the Community.

Somewhat more concern was felt in the United States steel industry, when the Community was formed, about the kind of competition it might provide for American exports to third markets, especially Latin America. Here again no very revealing results can be discerned without a more detailed examination of trade and markets than seemed warranted for the purposes of this book. From the mid-twenties to the mid-thirties, Europe (principally the Community countries and Britain) supplied between 80 and 90 per cent of the steel requirements of the under-developed areas, with the United States providing the rest.[5] The American share rose to 20-30 per cent in the late thirties and in the immediate postwar years the United States naturally had a predominant position. As the European industry recovered, it regained much of its earlier position in the markets of underdeveloped countries. In Latin America, the main area of American-European competition, the United States share of the market was about 30 per cent in 1950 and 1951, a little higher than the level of the late thirties but far below the immediate postwar years. While exactly comparable data are lacking, it appears that European sellers made some further gains during the fifties.

[5] ECE, *European Steel Exports and Steel Demand in Non-European Countries*, 1953, p. 54 (mimeographed). Subsequent figures also come from this source.

Community prices have been lower than those for many American products, but the United States remains an important supplier of rolled products, tin plate, and pipe. As in other fields the strong demand and high prices of the years up to mid-1957 eased competitive pressure. While the American industry sometimes exported at a premium, it has not practiced double-pricing as extensively as the European countries. By early 1958 European producers began to sell at dumping prices because of the slackening of demand, while the American industry was producing far below its capacity. Persistence of this situation might lead American producers to raise more questions about Community policy, cartelization, and the like, than they have in the past. Not the least interesting of the questions for an outside observer will concern the way the steel industries of the United States, Britain, and the Community respond to the possibilities and hazards of competition in Latin America and other underdeveloped areas when demand, at home and abroad, is uncertain. On the Continental side this will be one of the tests of the Brussels export cartel and in Britain of the value of tariff preferences and currency links in providing sheltered markets. For the United States it may provide a test of the policy of not cutting export prices for fear of the impact on the domestic price structure.[6]

United States imports of steel raise some other questions. As Table 9 shows, imports have usually been less than half exports and rarely exceed 2 per cent of shipments from domestic steel mills. Though much larger than they were before the war, imports of steel products are still "sporadic, fluctuating in response to short-run conditions in domestic markets. Because of the high costs of inland rail transport, foreign iron and steel products can be marketed principally

---

[6] The accepted view in the American industry during the recession was that: (a) a cut in price to foreign buyers would have to be extended to the domestic market; (b) the possible expansion of export sales could not be great enough to make a major contribution to the industry's income; (c) the industry is better off with a low level of activity than with lower prices that would do little to expand sales.

in the vicinity of seaports." [7] As a result, Florida and Gulf Coast ports usually lead the country in steel imports. Imports reach their peak when there is exceptionally high demand, as during the years of the Korean war,[8] or some restraint on American production, such as the steel strike of 1956. A possible change in the pattern was suggested by the 1958 recession when imports were high while exports fell and the United States industry worked far below capacity. Some American producers suspected that more problems might lie ahead.

If the American steel industry were concerned about the volume of imports, it would have to be concerned primarily about the Community, which provided over 70 per cent of United States imports of steel-mill products between 1950 and 1957.[9] Belgium-Luxembourg is the principal supplier, usually providing something like 40 per cent of total American imports of steel-mill products. But most of the industry has not been greatly concerned about imports. Mr. Bidwell reports that "Foreign producers who want to sell to the United States customarily price their goods at 15 to 20 per cent below the American level. American producers usually make no attempt to meet these prices, but instead depend on closer touch with the domestic market and quicker service to maintain their dominant position." American tariffs—which average about 5 per cent on steel products—"with only minor exceptions . . . have little economic significance." [10] For some products, strict specifi-

---

[7] Bidwell, cited, pp. 166-167.

[8] The drop in imports in 1952 was ascribed by the Department of Commerce largely to "over-buying in 1951 by speculative importers who had bought steel for resale," and to the effect of emergency regulations of steel distribution. *International Iron and Steel*, Mar. 1955, p. 14, n. 2.

[9] The Community's share of U.S. imports of steel-mill products (with Belgium-Luxembourg in parentheses) was: 1950, 72 per cent (37); 1951, 82 (28); 1952, 70 (37); 1953, 75 (42); 1954, 86 (51); 1955, 63 (37); 1956, 80 (45); 1957, 77 (42). Canada, the United Kingdom, and Japan provide most of the rest. If all iron and steel products are included, the Canadian share rises because of a substantial United States importation of pig iron.

[10] Cited, pp. 167-168, 176.

cations geared to American standards also limit imports. Most of the products that are imported in the largest quantities, such as structural shapes, bars, pipe, and, in some years, sheet and plate, remain very small percentages of domestic production. This is not true of wire products, however.

Imports of wire nails have risen markedly from the early fifties to about 20 per cent of domestic shipments (by weight) in 1955 and 1956 and 30 per cent in 1957. Imports of barbed wire increased even more sharply until in 1957 they exceeded domestic shipments. The Community provides almost all the barbed wire and is also the leading source of wire nails, but Japan, Britain, and Austria play a significant role in the latter trade. A tariff equivalent to 2.8 per cent ad valorem is collected on the bulk of the nails imported.[11] Nineteenth century compromises between manufacturing and farming interests put barbed wire on the free list. Together, these products made up 17 per cent of United States imports in 1957. The ability of foreign producers to sell them in such quantity in the American market may largely reflect lower wages for men employed on the same machines that are used in American plants. While domestic production of nails in the mid-fifties was about two-thirds what it had been in the early part of the decade, it had not declined noticeably since 1953. The output of barbed wire continued to fall until in 1957 it was less than one-fourth its 1951 level. Big producers were not overly concerned; the two products accounted for about .63 per cent of domestic shipments (by weight) in 1957, compared with 1.5 per cent in 1950. Some smaller producers were much more seriously affected and called for protection. Their case raised no issues about the Coal and Steel Community, however. Nails and barbed wire are not Treaty products. The complaints of the American producers were directed toward traditional targets—low wages, alleged subsidies—

---

[11] Calculated on the basis of 1956 imports and values. The duty is 2/10 cent per pound on nails one inch long or longer. On shorter nails the duty is 1/2 cent per pound, equivalent to 4.6 per cent ad valorem in 1956, but imports in this category were only $74,300 compared with almost $16 million worth of longer nails.

and not toward the new conditions created when the six countries formed the European Coal and Steel Community.[12]

INDUSTRY OPINION

There have been no major trade problems between the United States and the Community, except for scrap. Worry about what might happen has not been great. The attitudes of the American coal and steel industries toward the Community naturally reflect this state of affairs.

For the coal industry there has been nothing in the Community's activity about which to complain (except for occasional trade barriers that were not, properly speaking, the responsibility of the Community). In the scrap industry the complaints have come from the smaller dealers who objected to the buying practices of the OCCF. There was little in what they said, however, that could be interpreted as objecting to the Community itself; their animus was against the American firm that had secured the exclusive contract, since its activities were affecting them in other export markets and to some extent at home as well. So far as United States policy was concerned, the scrap industry's criticism was directed against the export controls that narrowed its market. The criticism of the Community's scrap policy came from the American steel industry which objected to the pressure on supplies and felt that the European producers were artificially holding down costs by using the equalization scheme to make American scrap cheap instead of investing in more blast furnaces.

In general the American steel industry has been rather cool toward the Schuman Plan, but has not actively opposed it. Nor has the Community been a matter of primary

[12] See, for example, the testimony of Robert S. Lynch, Chairman of the Board of the Atlantic Steel Company, Atlanta, Georgia, before the Ways and Means Committee, reprinted in the *Congressional Record*, 85th Cong., 2d sess., Mar. 12, 1958, p. A2313 ff. (daily edition). The silence of large American producers about imports has given rise to some suspicion in the industry that by more or less tacit agreement they are willing to see European producers take over the American market for these products so long as others are not pushed. Industry leaders take the view that they have an interest in low trade barriers and should not ask for special treatment whenever they are hurt (at least in minor ways).

concern; the American industry has formally expressed its views on only a few occasions. When the Randall Commission was reviewing United States foreign economic policy, it received a statement from the American Iron and Steel Institute that dealt in some detail with foreign trade policy but mentioned the Coal and Steel Community only briefly. The statement noted that foreign competitors were in a stronger position than ever before, largely because of modernization that was partly financed by American aid. The Schuman Plan, said the statement, was aimed at making the principal European producers more efficient in world trade as well as at regulating the home market of this "vast supranational industry." "It remains to be seen, probably in the very near future, just what kind of competitor this potentially powerful group will become in the free export markets left in the world." [13]

A few months later a more pointed issue arose: the Export-Import Bank loan to the Community. According to officials of the industry, they were not consulted in the matter until two days before the loan agreement was signed (which implies that it was not their doing that the loan was earmarked for coal, iron ore, and housing, and not for steel facilities). A statement dated April 6, 1954, gave the position of the industry.[14] It called attention to the vigorous recovery of European steel production and to the fact that the Community was providing half the steel that entered world trade. "While we have serious reservations in respect to the Community as a political or economic experiment, we consider this primarily an European problem except where financial support from the United States Government becomes involved."

The industry said it understood the President was committed to the loan, and then went on to express its own view. "Primarily the loan is to achieve critical political and

[13] *Statement* of the American Iron and Steel Institute before the Commission on Foreign Economic Policy, Dec. 2, 1953, p. 4. In its report, the Randall Commission said nothing about the Community—or about European integration in general, for that matter.

[14] Mimeographed statement, not otherwise marked, but presumably issued by the American Iron and Steel Institute.

security objectives rather than economic ones. Under these circumstances the American Steel Industry will not oppose this loan." However, because of excess steel capacity, the industry thought the United States should not use public funds for further assistance to foreign steel and expressed the hope that it would be consulted in the future when its interests were affected.

Two points in this statement are crucial. By saying that the loan was intended for political and security purposes, the industry avoided the issue whether it would have approved this action on economic grounds. Presumably the effect of the loan would be to improve the position of the European steel industry by improving its raw material supply—either in costs or availability. The American industry might well have argued that this was not a suitable use of public funds. But it could not have made this argument only on the basis of the statement itself. For—here is the second point—its opposition to further financing of European steel is based entirely on the existence of surplus steel capacity, and the investments in coal and iron would not affect that. Nothing is said about unfair competition, which was emphasized in the statement to the Randall Commission, not with specific reference to the Community but in connection with all foreign industries in which governments played a part. Nor is there any specific argument that it is not proper to use public funds to help foreign producers who will compete with American producers, in third markets or in the United States. One is left, therefore, with the conclusion that the statement was carefully drafted to cover only a limited number of points and to leave open the industry's position if new issues should arise or the old ones be repeated in new circumstances.

Except for the loan and scrap export controls, the American steel industry has not publicly taken positions on United States policy toward the European Coal and Steel Community. The subject has apparently elicited only limited interest. The American Iron and Steel Institute—which has committees on many issues of interest to the industry—has not made a special study of the Community or set up any procedures to follow its activities closely. Of course individuals in the industry are well informed and executives of American firms visiting Europe gather impressions and reach conclusions. But the industry as a whole has not felt the need of a special apparatus of appraisal.[15]

When research workers at the University of Maryland asked spokesmen for six major American steel companies about the Community, their answers were rather reserved. Most saw it as consistent with United States foreign policy. All were skeptical of the merits of the common market and the powers of the High Authority. There was some doubt whether the Community's industry was sufficiently competitive. "Significantly," says the report, in these answers "no representative was concerned that the Community was likely to injure American exports of steel. Opinions ranged from 'not at all,' 'unable to decide,' 'hope not,' to the observation that the Community has brought few changes since it lacks control over exports."[16]

The attitude is probably still reserved. One can discover some concern over the effect of the Community on European competition and tentative worries about the possible mobilization of the full strength of the European industry into a single cartel-like unit. There is more or less articulate opposition to the use of public American funds to expand foreign steel capacity (not only in the Community). But the industry has not found occasion to take strong stands

[15] In apparent contrast, the United Steelworkers of America had a full-time representative in Luxembourg for several years. He worked closely with the Committee of Twenty-one and other labor groups and did extensive educational work in explaining how his union had faced certain problems in the United States. Initially this man, Meyer Bernstein, may have been appointed as a result of concern about what would be made of the Community and how it would affect American interests. However, it is my impression that help to the European unions rather than the recurrence of issues of direct importance to American workers was the reason for his union's keeping him there.

[16] F. R. Root, *The European Coal and Steel Community*, Part II, Bureau of Business and Economic Research of the University of Maryland, Je. 1956, p. 4 (Studies in Business and Economics). The companies were U.S. Steel, Bethlehem, National, Republic, Inland, and Jones and Laughlin.

on matters affecting the Coal and Steel Community, perhaps because nothing has happened to substantiate the
fears it expressed to the Randall Commission in 1953.

Clarence Randall

The strongest American criticisms of the Schuman Plan
to come from the steel industry or any responsible source
are those of Clarence Randall in 1952 and 1953. A lawyer
whose association with the Inland Steel Corporation began
in 1925, Randall became president of the company in 1949
and was chairman of the board from 1953 to 1956. During
ECA's first year he served in Paris as its steel consultant.
In 1953 and 1954 he was chairman of the Commission on
Foreign Economic Policy and then became a close advisor
to President Eisenhower on foreign economic policy. Between his government jobs, Randall published several statements sharply and eloquently critical of the Schuman
Plan.[17]

Schuman's proposal left Randall "torn between admiration and anxiety. . . ." France's "magnificent gesture" was
the greatest single step toward making Europe strong since
Marshall's Harvard speech. The danger was "that the Schuman Plan will weaken Europe by laying the dead hand of
socialism and bureaucracy across its basic industry. I wish
fervently that somehow some other way might be found
for advancing the political unity of Europe."

The text of the Treaty brought no comfort. "It en-
deavors to steer a suave middle course between control . . .
on the one hand, and laissez faire on the other. It reflects
compromise in every paragraph. . . . It is a political document, not a program for production." When the members
of the High Authority were appointed, Randall praised

---

[17] "A Steel Man Looks at the Schuman Plan," *Atlantic Monthly,* Oct.
1950, pp. 35-37; "European Steel: Monopoly in the Making," same, Oct.
1951, pp. 34-38; "The Schuman Plan—An American Steel Executive
Measures Its Economic Pitfalls," *Barron's,* Nov. 17, 1952, reprinted in the
Congressional Record, 83rd Cong., 1st sess., Feb. 3, 1953, pp. A445-A447;
"Steel: The World's Guinea Pig," *Atlantic Monthly,* Dec. 1952, pp. 31-34;
Freedom's Faith (Boston: Little, Brown, 1953), pp. 124, 131, 132. Quota-
tions come from these sources.

them for their ability, their awareness of their responsibility, and their "inspiring sense of dedication to the public service." But, he said, one must look to laws, not men, as a principle of government because "scheming, selfish politicians often succeed the able men who are first appointed." The Community "is a supranational state. It can become supranational socialism."

Part of the difficulty was that "the treaty is the work of men who were halfhearted in their convictions about free enterprise." But the underlying difficulty was that Monnet and his colleagues were not really interested in steel. "They seek global objectives, possibly praiseworthy in themselves, and it is only by accident that steel was chosen as the subject for experimentation instead of textiles, or wine, or agriculture." Right at the outset the Council of Ministers had discussed, not steel, but broader plans of integration. "One wonders whether the steel master is not to be the forgotten man of the Schuman Plan. . . ." It would be difficult to merge six national economies. Questions would arise and "until satisfactory answers are given, prudent private investors will wait and see. Yet production is what General Ridgway needs most urgently. Wait and see is not good enough for him, and if private ownership hesitates, politicians will raise the cry that selfish private interests have failed the public, and that government must take over, the new supranational type of government. Thus another step will be taken down the Socialist road."

While Randall was critical of the lack of competition among European steel producers, he apparently felt that government interference was a greater threat. "Steel is not rolled by a treaty, nor blast furnaces blown by bureaucrats. If the world needs high-quality steel, in great volume and at low cost, the job must be given to men who know steel." Instead, in "country by country, since the war, steel has been singled out as an amenable guinea pig. The producers of steel have invariably been harassed and coerced by bureaucracy, and in each case they have been expected to submit to some form of revolutionary social experimentation."

Randall was concerned that the United States had had too much to do with the creation of the Schuman Plan. "Brought to cherry red in the hot blast of American aid, and pounded hard on the anvil of European fears by blows struck in every capital by our embassies and economic missions, this new edifice of steel was erected in record time. . . . If by our pressures we had any part whatsoever in causing other nations to surrender sovereignty, we have done an immoral thing, for the very obvious reason that we would not surrender sovereignty ourselves." That was in the past. For the future, "one thing is certain. The United States should not finance the Schuman Plan. Not by a single dollar should we assume the moral obligation of endorsing this cosmic experiment. . . . A blank check would give synthetically to the High Authority a stature which it should earn the hard way, and would give it such power of life and death over individual enterprises that private initiative could not survive." [18] But Randall did not suggest that the United States should try to undo the Schuman Plan. "We may withhold aid from something of which we disapprove, but we may not with our dollars buy the right to dictate to other governments and peoples."

The Commission on Foreign Economic Policy over which Randall presided had nothing to say about the Coal and Steel Community or European integration generally.[19] Subsequently, as a White House adviser on trade policy, Randall has said nothing more about the matter in public. His statements of 1952 and 1953 stand as the strongest criticism of the Schuman Plan to come from a prominent American. They bear a family resemblance to the views of many European steelmen, but they are clearly the product

[18] Even the appointment of a mission to the High Authority seemed dubious. "Now on what theory could that have been done, other than that we are going to tell Europe what to do, and attach conditions to our dollars."

[19] Nor did his subsequent Walgreen Lectures, *A Foreign Economic Policy for the United States* (Chicago: University of Chicago Press, 1954), 83 p. His earlier book, *Freedom's Faith*, cited, had expressed a good deal more skepticism about the prospects of European integration and the wisdom or propriety of American efforts to promote it than was usual among leading Americans at the time.

of Mr. Randall's own analysis. His worst fears have not been realized. Some day perhaps Mr. Randall will give us his appraisal of the Community's actual performance.

Other Unofficial Opinion

Outside the industries affected, American policy toward the European Coal and Steel Community has not been the subject of general public discussion. So far as there is an American public opinion on European integration, it appears to be generally favorable and to approve American support for the Community. Certainly the leaders of both parties have agreed on this matter. Congressional support for European integration has been strongly expressed and extends to the Coal and Steel Community. At the outset there was some criticism of the Community, in and out of Congress, based on the fear that it would lead to renewed German domination of Europe. Business groups and others echoed the complaints of Europeans that the Community was too dirigistic, or suspected it would be a façade for a cartel. Less has been heard on these matters in recent years than when the pros and cons were first debated. Throughout, however, these critical notes have been an undercurrent of a main stream of approval.

Among specialists and scholars there has been a good bit of general support for the Community, with the natural caution of those who want to see how it works out. The reservation about European integration most often found among economists is the fear that regional measures will damage trading relations with the rest of the world and create a high-cost area in Europe. This is less relevant to the Coal and Steel Community than to other major arrangements. Political analysts have questioned the solidity of the "European" feeling and speculated about the fragility the integration arrangements might show under the impact of major political blows, such as a real chance of securing German reunification on the condition of neutralization, or extended political crisis in France. Suspicions about the Community's becoming a cartel or working in much the same way as a cartel have been fairly widespread. They were more common at first than in more recent times, but the general attitude of questioning persists. One is also likely to find criticism of the High Authority for not pursuing a stronger supranational policy. There is sometimes disappointment that the results of the pooling of coal and steel have not been more striking. Some believe the Community has done little or nothing of major importance and react against the strong verbal claims often made for it.[20] Though there have been relatively few American studies of the Community it seems fair to say that, while pursuing their proper business of trying to understand the Community, American scholars have generally had a favorable predisposition toward it, and a corresponding attitude toward the generally benevolent policy of the United States government in matters affecting the Community.

NATIONAL POLICY

Governmental policy has been the main element in the relations of the United States and the Community. That policy has been part of the general American support for European integration. At only a few points has it been a policy about coal or steel or a response to concrete problems. Most of the specific features of American policy have already been discussed in connection with Community problems.[21] Here they are reassembled in general terms to provide the profile of United States policy.

Before there was a Schuman Plan, the United States had made closer economic cooperation in Western Europe a condition of the Marshall Plan. The policy persisted, through the creation of the OEEC, Paul Hoffman's call in October 1949 for steps toward a "single large market," the political and military cooperation that began with the Brussels Pact and NATO, and the measures to restore Western Germany to an acceptable and useful position in Western Europe. These were not the policies of the executive branch alone. Congress not only supported them

[20] For instance, Michael T. Florinsky, *Integrated Europe?* (N.Y.: Macmillan, 1955), 182 p.

[21] See pp. 29 ff., 43-46, 67-75, 300-304, 319-326, 475-476, 492, 525.

but often went beyond the State Department and the ECA, especially in the broad formulation of principles. The preamble to its 1949 legislation on European recovery declared it "to be the policy of the people of the United States to encourage the unification of Europe. . . ."

The Schuman Plan was in the main line of American policy in Europe, but it was not an American plan. Other measures of European cooperation introduced at about the same time, such as the European Payments Union, had originated at least in part as American proposals, or were much influenced in their formulation by American officials. While ideas of the sort embodied in the Schuman Plan had been discussed by Americans and Europeans alike, few Americans appear to have thought that European governments were ready to accept anything so radical. The formulation of a definite proposal, the elaboration of its main features, the emphasis on the essential principles, and above all the acceptance of this idea as policy, were the doings of the French. A few weeks after Schuman had made his proposal, Paul Hoffman said, "He, an European, goes much further than any American would have dared propose at this time." [22]

Considering the unexpectedness of the French action, it was not surprising that Dean Acheson's first statement should have been sympathetic but slightly reserved. Schuman's announcement, said Acheson, was prompted by a desire for rapprochement between France and Germany and for progress toward economic integration, both objectives that had long been favored by the United States. While judgment had to be reserved until more details of the proposal were known, "I recognize with sympathy and approval the significance and far-reaching intent of the French initiative." [23] It was prudent not to plunge too deeply until a few soundings had been made. Acheson presumably wanted to find out about such things as: how completely the French government was committed to this

[22] P. G. Hoffman, "Toward Integration: France Points the Way," *The New York Times Magazine*, May 21, 1950.
[23] *The New York Times*, May 11, 1950.

radical idea; whether the new step was intended to divert or delay other steps being taken to restore Germany; whether the proposal was likely to produce a new steel cartel;[24] how the trade interests of outside countries would be affected; and what, if anything, the proposal implied about the future political alignment of Europe and the emergence of a "third force." By the time he was ready to leave London after several days of conferences with Schuman, Bevin, and other foreign ministers, Acheson was prepared to make a stronger statement. "We welcome the bold and imaginative proposal announced by Mr. Schuman on behalf of the French Government, which should be a very real contribution, not only to the strengthening of relations between France and Germany, but to the integration and expansion of the European economy." [25]

Since then strong endorsements of the Schuman Plan and the European Coal and Steel Community have become staples of official American statements about Western Europe. Almost without exception, Presidents Truman and Eisenhower, their secretaries of state, ambassadors, other high officials of the executive branch, and leading senators and representatives, have struck the same note. Little would be gained by cataloguing these statements. Some emphasize one thing, some another; there are differences in nuance; but in essentials they are all the same: strong support for the Community, sympathy for its aims, admiration for the fact that this was an indigenous European movement, and avoidance of comment on details.

Almost from the beginning, then, there has been no doubt that the United States favored creation of the Coal and Steel Community and wished it success in attaining its aims. Everything else that the United States has done in connection with the Community has had this as the major premise. The remaining questions therefore concern the measures the United States took to help the Community

[24] Some months before, Harold Callender had reported to the *New York Times* (Nov. 13, 1949) that "Dr. Adenauer's suggestion to pool the Ruhr with its neighboring rivals looked to experts like a revival of the former European steel cartel under a new guise."

[25] U.S. Dept. of State *Bulletin*, Je. 5, 1950, p. 883.

succeed, and the extent to which it used its influence and bargaining power for this purpose.

There is no public evidence of any American role in the talks between London and Paris about British participation in the negotiation of the Schuman Plan Treaty. Some well-informed observers believe that there was informal advice to both sides not to be too rigid. Americans could understand the French feeling that the key to the whole scheme lay in the supranational position of the High Authority and that without this there could be no effective control over the Germans. At the same time, the Americans should not have had any trouble in understanding the British unwillingness to subscribe to the principle without seeing the concrete meaning of the arrangement. Whether American advice was directed to the end of finding a formula by which Britain could participate in the talks, or whether United States officials accepted the inevitability of British abstention and sought to avoid as much suspicion or hard feeling as possible, is not clear.

When, however, the Labour party executive's statement on European cooperation was published about the same time that the decision of the British government not to participate in the negotiations became finally clear (pp. 55-57), there was a sharp reaction in the United States. American officials were testifying before Congressional committees on appropriations for the third year of the Marshall Plan. Much of their case was built on the premise of increased European cooperation as a key to recovery. The British statement was a blow. A wider significance was read into it than its words warranted—and not altogether without reason. Leading officials of the executive branch publicly criticized the statement and seemed thereby to be criticizing the British position on the Schuman Plan as well. Some of the first statements were made on the basis of misleading newspaper reports and had to be modified later.[26] Harsh as some of the initial statements by officers of the executive branch were, they were far outclassed by the remarks of

[26] See my "Imponderables of the Schuman Plan," *Foreign Affairs*, Oct. 1950, for a fuller discussion of this episode.

leading members of Congress in both Houses, which also portended more serious results. The Administration was successful in stopping a Congressional effort to eliminate aid to Britain unless that country joined the coal and steel pool. Still, quite some time had to pass before suspicion of Britain's role became less marked and American spokesmen showed a fuller understanding of the reasons for the British position on European cooperation. Perhaps the episode served to enshrine the Schuman Plan as one of the touchstones of European integration. Congress continued to take an active, if rather generalized, interest in it and to respond favorably to all mention of its accomplishments.[27]

As the Treaty negotiations began, the United States government kept very much in the background. This was both deliberate and a realistic reflection of the situation. Politically and psychologically it was of the utmost importance, to the United States as well as to the other countries, that the carrying out of the French proposal should remain truly European. Its prospects of success were far from certain. It could be destroyed if it began to look like another American idea for the unification of Europe. Too much American involvement in shaping the Treaty might also be fatal because its continuing acceptability and workability would depend on accurately expressing the balance of European forces on which its implementation would rest. This did not mean that the United States was giving up all interest in what went on; there were discreet ways of expressing American views on major issues.

In the Paris Embassy a real effort was made to avoid the appearance of too much American activity connected with the negotiations. Instead of the squads of American experts operating at all levels, as in many other discussions of European cooperation at the time, only the ambassador him-

---

[27] Monnet and several of his colleagues appeared before the Senate Foreign Relations Committee for an "informal discussion." Later American legislators visited Luxembourg from time to time and usually praised what they found. For instance, Paul Douglas (D., Ill.) said, ". . . this is one of the most heartening and encouraging movements which it has been my pleasure ever to examine." *Congressional Record*, 85th Cong., 2d sess., Feb. 3, 1958, p. 1289 (daily edition).

self and one or two assistants were regularly in touch with
the negotiators. No doubt they were bombarded from
Washington with ideas, suggestions, and arguments, but it
was largely up to them to decide how far and in what way
to use their influence. Monnet called on some of his American friends, official and unofficial, for advice and assistance.
Some played an important part in the drafting of the
Treaty, but as advisers to the negotiators (or some of them)
rather than as formal emissaries of the United States. In
Germany as well the Americans were anxious to make it
clear that this was a negotiation between the French and
the Germans, not between the French and the other occupying powers.

The character of this early stage of the negotiations was
therefore quite clear. A European initiative was to be
worked out by Europeans. They could be sure of sympathy
and support from the United States—at least so long as they
produced a treaty conforming to the spirit and principles
of Schuman's statement. American support in a more concrete sense was also expected: ECA officials had made it
clear that aid funds, perhaps particularly counterpart funds,
would probably be available to help bring about the transition to a common market. It was often said, too, that it
would be natural for American aid for coal and steel to be
funneled through the Community—but what this meant
would depend on the character of the Community and the
powers of the High Authority. Thus one of the strongest
American influences in Europe at the time, dollars, was
enlisted to help the Schuman Plan, but as auxiliary and not as
dictator, guide, or even bait. Here again there was a marked
difference between American policy toward the Schuman
Plan and toward some other measures of European cooperation.

This was a time when there were differences of view in
Washington about European cooperation. For some, almost
anything that the Europeans could get together to do was
to be welcomed, while others were more cautious. The
latter wanted to be sure that the measures taken in Europe
did not unnecessarily distort world trade and production by

creating permanent regional trading preferences without obliterating internal trade barriers. Policy was always some kind of a compromise between these views. It was not too hard to find in the case of the Schuman Plan. Monnet and Schuman were clear enough about wanting the radical removal of trade barriers. The Americans probably urged them to avoid the checks on competition likely to be concealed in *dirigisme*, national or supranational.

Americans were also suspicious about restrictive agreements among producers. These focused especially on the Schuman Plan because of the cartel background in coal and steel and because it was so much easier to believe that a restrictive agreement would emerge than that the idealistic aims professed by Schuman could be carried through the actual negotiation and drafting. Many of the initial questions that American officials asked about the French proposals, and much of whatever influence they had on the negotiations, undoubtedly reflected this concern. But it was never allowed to show in public expressions of the attitude of the American government, at least after Acheson's initial guarded remarks. Apparently accepting the statements Schuman made about the kind of arrangement he and Monnet were trying to negotiate (backed perhaps by the assurance that no other kind would be accepted), high American officials made endorsement of the Schuman Plan full and complete. For the most part they took the view that the political importance of French-German agreement on heavy industry outweighed economic features that might seem undesirable from an American point of view. Perhaps they felt sure that any troublesome economic features could be kept to a minimum without making public issues of them.

So matters went, through the negotiations of the summer and early fall of 1950, with delegates of the six countries hard at work on the Treaty in Paris while the United States government looked on benignly but unobtrusively, deliberately keeping in the background. Then in the fall of 1950 the situation changed drastically. The American proposal to rearm Germany was one of the high points of a series of events that threatened to prevent completion of the Schuman Plan negotiations. The United States had to step in, principally to ensure German acceptance of de-concentration measures that would meet the conditions the French had stipulated as essential.

The United States thus came in the end to play an important part in the negotiation of the Schuman Plan Treaty, very likely a crucial one. It is important, though, to understand the character of this part. The American government was not saying to the governments of the Community countries, "You must take this, there is no alternative; if you do not, we shall have to consider whether we belong in Europe at all." That was the position it took later on, unsuccessfully, about the EDC. Nor was the United States saying, "Why don't you adopt this solution of your problems?", as it did about some other measures. Instead the United States was lending its weight and diplomacy to help European governments complete an undertaking they had begun and which was well advanced before the changed political situation put it in jeopardy. Insofar as American action had contributed to that jeopardy, the bringing into play of American diplomacy was only an attempt to offset a consequence of another American action. Although the American activity was concerned with one segment of the Treaty—the concentration question—this was not because the United States attached special importance to these provisions. The American aim was primarily to find a basis for agreement among the negotiating governments, in a sphere where the United States had a special responsibility because of the program it had launched as an occupying authority in Germany. The American action went beyond the particulars of the concentration issue and concerned the whole question of Germany's place in Europe. It was successful largely because it was helping a European effort and not pressing for an American solution.

When the High Authority took office the American government again registered its approval of this extraordinary innovation in European affairs. A mission was sent to Luxembourg and an ambassador accredited.[28] More material support came when the Community asked for a waiver from GATT. The United States supported the request and undoubtedly helped persuade others to vote for it. American representatives played an important part in devising the terms of the waiver, particularly in stressing the correspondence of aims between the Community and GATT, provided the Community followed a liberal commercial policy. Here was a specific means of reconciling the difference in emphasis within the American government between those who favored any and all measures of European integration and those who were anxious that what was done on a regional basis should not reduce the possibilities of building a global multilateral system of trade and payments of the sort American policy had been aiming at before European integration came onto the scene. In this perspective, the GATT waiver was a confluence of the two strands in American policy.

There was also financial aid. Had the Community existed earlier, it might have served as a channel for some of the substantial sums of Marshall Plan money that went into European coal and steel production. By 1953, United States aid had tapered off and American officials felt there was no basis for the allocation of large sums to the Community. Washington wanted to show its support for this major step forward in European integration. The $100-million loan made in 1954 had elaborate businesslike paraphernalia and found some justification on economic grounds in the argument that it would make it easier for the High Authority to raise additional capital elsewhere. However, it was largely granted on what an Assistant Secretary of State said "admittedly are straight political justifications." [29]

[28] David Bruce, former Ambassador to France, who was responsible for United States relations with European regional organizations. He was succeeded in 1955 by W. Walton Butterworth who in 1958 was also accredited to Euratom and the European Economic Community.

[29] Statement by L. T. Merchant, *The Mutual Security Act of 1954*, Hearings before the House Committee on Foreign Affairs, 83rd Cong., 2d sess., Apr. 5-Je. 8, 1954, p. 683.

While the loan was significant, its financial importance has often been somewhat exaggerated—by a kind of mutual consent—perhaps because it was the most concrete and visible action of American support to which anyone could point.

Another less visible but concrete American measure was the tariff agreement with the Community made during the GATT negotiations in the spring of 1956. It is virtually impossible to judge the importance of this transaction. Trade in steel between the United States and the Community is modest; the tariff reductions were fairly small; they cannot properly be regarded as American "aid" to the Community, since there were reciprocal concessions presumably judged to be roughly equal in value as is required by United States law. Yet, the negotiations were probably intended primarily to aid the Community. They helped bring it more fully into GATT and so paved the way for later negotiations. They probably also strengthened the forces within the Community that were working to reduce trade barriers. The need to come to an agreement may have helped develop cooperation within the Community on foreign-trade matters. The High Authority made a rather remarkable statement about these negotiations: "Special mention should be made of the spirit of co-operation shown by the American delegation who by conducting the negotiations on a strictly balanced commercial basis let it be seen that they attached considerable political interest to the matter." [30]

There were some matters on which the United States complained about Community behavior or sought to influence its action in particular ways. The Brussels export cartel was the subject of American representations. German and Belgian coal import quotas—not strictly speaking within Community jurisdiction—were dealt with under GATT. The buying practices of the scrap import cartel were modified—at least in form—as a result of State Department intervention. The High Authority agreed to limit Community imports of scrap from the United States as a means

[30] HA, *Report*, Apr. 1957, p. 63.

of reducing the pressure on the American government to impose export controls. In the annual discussions of the GATT waiver the United States delegates have at various times supported the arguments of the Danes and others who were pressing the Community about steel export prices or other questions. Each of these episodes has played some small part in the shaping of the Community, but only the use of the United States' near-monopolistic position to limit the scrap supply had a clear and major influence on the Community. While conflicts of interest between the Community and the United States have been clear enough in some of these cases, they have not been grave and have been adjusted amicably within the broad framework of the United States government's benevolent interest in the Community and general support for it.

The Community seems anxious to keep relations on this footing. Faced with a clamor to restrict coal imports when stocks mounted during 1958 and 1959, the High Authority and the German government tried to avoid or postpone such measures, which would affect primarily American coal. The first steps were private negotiations to slow deliveries under long-term contracts. A mission of Ruhr businessmen visited the United States to acquaint Americans with their situation. The German government discussed its problems extensively with American officials before imposing a coal tariff in early 1959. The State Department protested the tariff action, but it seemed likely that the conduct of the dispute would continue to be colored by basic American policy toward the Community.

There has been no change in this general approach with which American policy toward the Community began a few days after Schuman made his first announcement. Only once have circumstances raised a question about the fundamentals of the policy. The United States had put great emphasis on the EDC and engaged in an active diplomacy on its behalf. The failure of this policy when the EDC collapsed left the Coal and Steel Community as the only structure of European integration of the supranational kind. The Community's future was in doubt (Chapter 22).

There was also a question about American policy. Should an effort be made to strengthen the Coal and Steel Community and perhaps make it the center of renewed activity for European integration? Or should the EDC experience be a warning that it was not wise to stake American prestige so heavily on a process over which Washington lacked effective control? It might have proved rather difficult to find means of carrying out the former policy, but the issue was resolved by the immediate shift of gears to create the Western European Union and the fundamental, burnt-fingers decision to make it clear that while the United States was still in favor of Western European integration, and would lend support where it could, the initiatives, decisions, and actions must come from the Europeans themselves. This was very much the policy already being followed toward the Coal and Steel Community. Support in principle, praise of accomplishments, occasional concrete measures of assistance—but also a willingness to demand concessions from the Community, as in the case of scrap—continued to characterize American policy. As the Europeans began to discuss Euratom and the Common Market, the favorable sounds made in Washington frequently cited the Coal and Steel Community as an example of what could be accomplished—but without getting involved in the intra-European argument about sector integration and the appropriate degree of supranationalism to be incorporated in the new measures.

United States policy toward the Community, like Monnet's original conception, was not primarily concerned with the problems of coal and steel or even with the economic consequences of pooling their production and trade. American approval of the Schuman Plan was based principally on its obvious importance as a step toward Western European integration and toward the establishment of a durable, constructive relation between France and Germany. A corollary was that the terms on which the coal and steel pool was to operate would have to be determined by the Europeans. This left the United States with a limited role comprising three overlapping elements: help, influence, and

the protection of American interests. There were not many
occasions to pursue any of them. The help had to be given
without impairing the European character of the enterprise
and within limits of general American policies and other
calls on national resources. German deconcentration, the
loan, action in GATT, and general political and moral support, fall under this heading. The influence on the shaping
of the new enterprise had to be discreet and could be effective principally when it strengthened forces already
existing within the Community. During the negotiations
the cartel issue and *dirigisme* and afterwards the reduction
of external trade barriers, the checking of the export price
cartel, and perhaps the strengthening of the High Authority, were the principal targets of this activity. The protection of United States interests was fairly simple because
there were relatively few places where American and Community affairs intersected. Scrap was the major case and
may become troublesome again when the demand for it is
high in both the United States and the Community. A coal
trade problem will continue, as the events of early 1959
made clear. Other problems may arise about steel imports
or export competition in third markets, but there is little
to suggest that they will create major difficulties in governmental policy. These are the kinds of problems that normally exist between friendly nations and need not alter basic
policy. Nor should it be thought that in protecting American interests the United States government necessarily ham-
pers the Community's pursuit of its major aims. American
pressure on scrap probably helped the Community move
toward a better adaptation to circumstances. American opposition to restrictions on coal imports may yet strengthen
the forces inside the Community making for an economically sound coal policy.

The chances are good then that United States policy toward the Community will be subject to relatively few
domestic pressures and limitations. There will continue to
be immediate interests to protect, but in the main the government is likely to be in the happy position of formulating
policy largely on the basis of broadly judged, long-run

interests and so can maintain an unusual degree of consistency between economic and political measures. So long as there is no basic change of position toward European integration, questions of American policy toward the Coal and Steel Community are likely to center on mixed means of helping and influencing its development. Opportunities for help may not be numerous and perhaps the chances for effective influence will be limited, too. It can probably only be the kind of influence the United States has exerted in the past, an urging and abetting of forces within the Community. The enterprise remains European but the United States has a strong interest in its future development. The major issues with which this book deals are of immediate concern to the countries of the Community but at only one remove to the United States as well because it is on them that the whole character of the Community depends, along with its economic effects on Western Europe and the world and its long-run political implications as well.

PART IV

THE NATURE OF THE COMMUNITY

TWENTY

THE IMPACT OF THE COMMUNITY

THERE IS no satisfactory way to measure the impact of the Community. One can form a fair idea of what its influence has been but figures can only be arbitrary or suggestive. It is easy enough to measure some of what has happened, but how much of it can be attributed to the existence of the Community? We can only guess what would have happened if the Community had not existed. Comparisons with other countries, other times, or other products are of limited value. Elaborate analysis can reduce the area of uncertainty but cannot eliminate it. This chapter sets out some salient figures that suggest something of what the impact of the Community may have been and that indicate clearly what the Community did not do.

PRODUCTION AND INVESTMENT

Tables 10 and 11 show the main features of Community production during the transitional period. After a dip in 1953 (which extended into 1954), production turned sharply upwards. Steel production rose 50 per cent in the next four years, with the biggest jump coming between 1954 and 1955, after which the annual rate of increase declined. The 43 per cent increase in steel output over the transitional period is the principal productive accomplishment of the Community's industries. It is an impressive figure but it is a smaller increase than that between 1949 and 1952 when there was no common market.[1] The index

---

[1] There were, of course, special factors influencing the increase between 1949 and 1952: the Korean war, the continuation of the first wave of recovery from a low base, the coming into production of major

of industrial production in general, and more markedly that of the output of the metal-using industries, increased faster than steel production during the transitional period. The other Community products did not match the performance of steel. The small increase in coal output has been at the root of pervasive difficulties touched on at many

Table 10

COMMUNITY PRODUCTION AND CONSUMPTION

DURING THE TRANSITIONAL PERIOD

	Production			Consumption		Index of Industrial Production	
	coal	coke	steel	coal	steel [a]	gen-eral [b]	metal-using industries
			(millions of tons)			(1953=100)	
1929	237.2	60.6	35.6				
1949	209.4	44.1	28.7	218.1	23.0	70	67
1952	238.9	62.4	41.9	246.5	33.2	95	97
1953	237.0	61.5	39.7	233.4	32.8	100	100
1954	241.7	59.8	43.8	241.8	36.5	111	113
1955	246.4	68.6	52.6	261.2	43.7	124	132
1956	249.1	74.8	56.8	218.9	46.4	135	146
1957	247.9	77.2	59.8	280.9	48.2	143	155
Percentage Increase							
1929-57	4.5	27.4	68.0				
1949-52	14.1	41.5	46.0	13.0	44.3	35.7	44.8
1952-57	3.8	23.7	42.7	14.0	45.2	50.5	59.8

a. Includes products not covered by the Treaty.
b. Not including building or the food, drink, and tobacco industries.
SOURCES: HA, *Report*, Apr. 1958, v. 2, Statistical Annex; *Bulletin Statistique; Die Kohlenwirtschaft der Welt in Zahlen, 1955.*

works provided by the first postwar investment programs. This only demonstrates the point made above about the limited value of comparisons. If 1949 is compared with 1953 and then 1953 with 1957, the increase in the index of industrial production during both periods was 43 per cent while steel output lagged slightly between 1949 and 1953 (under 40 per cent) but outpaced the rest between 1953 and 1957 (just over 50 per cent).

places in this book. The record in 1956 was a little better than in 1957 when shorter hours in several countries and, late in the year, accumulation of stocks reduced total output. The substantially greater increase in coal consumption reflects heavy importing from third countries (whereas the increase of steel consumption faster than production reflects a relative fall in exports to third countries). The lag of coal consumption behind steelmaking and other industrial production indicates both a substantial shift to other fuels and a marked improvement in coal utilization. The production of pig iron, coke, and iron ore was in an in-between position; after the 1953 dip it climbed more slowly than that of steel or coal and did not pass the 1952 level until 1955.

In the production record as a whole, nothing is identifiable as a direct result of the existence of the Community. The Community's impact on production is largely indirect. For instance, the common market gives steel producers easier access to raw materials and to markets for their products, but the effect of this is likely to be on the production of individual countries rather than of the Community as a whole. Italian steel production was undoubtedly helped by easier access to scrap from the rest of the Community and perhaps coking coal as well, though this cannot be measured separately from the impact of the large investment program. The main effect was probably on cost since the scrap and coal could have been obtained from the United States.

There are striking differences in national production records, as Table 11 shows. Germany had a substantially greater increase in steel output than France during the transitional period. In part this reflects the previous lag in German recovery. In 1952 German output of steel was 7 per cent above the 1929 peak while French production was already 12 per cent higher. By 1957, however, the Germans had more than made up the difference and were producing two-thirds more steel than in 1929 while the French output was only 45 per cent above the level of

Table 11

PERCENTAGE INCREASES IN NATIONAL PRODUCTION,

1952-1957

	Index of Industrial Production	Coal	Coke	Iron Ore	Pig Iron	Crude Steel
Belgium	23	—4.3	11.7	3.8	16.2	21.2
France	46	2.6	36.3	42.1	21.9	29.8
Germany	62	8.0	21.4	18.9	42.6	55.0
Italy	51	—6.4	56.9	97.6	87.1	91.4
Luxembourg	15	—	—	8.2	8.2	16.4
Netherlands	44	—9.2	29.2	—	30.2	70.7
Saar	28	1.4	11.2	—	22.6	22.7
Community	51	3.8	23.7	33.9	29.9	42.7

SOURCE: HA, *Report*, Apr. 1958, v. 2, Statistical Annex.

that year. The dip in 1953 was less in Germany than in France, Belgium, Luxembourg, and the Saar and was more quickly overcome; the others did not pass the 1952 level of production until 1955, but Germany's output in 1954 was already markedly higher. The really striking increase in steel production was in the Netherlands and Italy, particularly the latter. These are small producers, of course, so the percentages mean less than in the larger countries. In spite of a 70 per cent increase in production, the Netherlands remains the smallest steel producer of the six countries. Italy, however, increased output so rapidly that in 1957 it passed Belgium and became the third most important steel producer in the Community.

In coal mining one might expect signs of adjustment to the common market. Perhaps the decline of Italian and Belgian production can be so ascribed. France and Germany, where production increased,[2] also showed the largest increases in productivity. The Dutch mines, which in 1951 had enjoyed the second highest productivity in the Community (after Lorraine) slipped sharply, falling first below

[2] In 1956, however, French output was still below the 1952 level. German production dropped in 1957 while that of France rose.

the Ruhr and then below the average for the whole Community.

Investment in the Community shows a pattern related to production but somewhat different from it. Investment did not exceed the level of 1952 until a late stage in the boom when several of the major development programs had reached their peaks. Again there was a contrast between Germany and France and, to a smaller extent, the rest of the Community. Whereas France and some of the other countries had been able to carry out a major share of their investment before the common market opened, Germany, though emphasizing investment from 1948 on, did not reach a peak until about the middle of the transitional period. Taking all Community industries together, total investment and the French and German shares moved as follows:[3]

	All Countries	France	Germany	France	Germany
				(per cent of	
	(millions of dollars)			Community total)	
1952	1,079	434.9	325.6	40.3	30.2
1953	1,031	391.5	366.6	38.0	35.6
1954	933	292.3	413.3	31.3	44.3
1955	971	255.5	486.8	26.3	50.1
1956	1,046	314.5	431.6	30.1	41.3
1957 (planned)	1,482	442.7	577.0	29.9	38.9
1952-1956	5,060	1,688.7	2,023.9	33.4	40.4

There were, of course, differences according to the lines of activity. The general pattern was largely followed in steel (Figure 4). Germany had already caught up with France by 1952 in investments in steel furnaces which then soon fell while rolling-mill investment was still expanding. The boom stimulated investment activity in both countries in 1956 and 1957 (though actual outlays in 1957 were something less than the planned expenditures show). The picture in coal and coke is rather different (Figure 5).

[3] Calculated from HA, *Les Investissements dans les Industries du Charbon et de l'Acier de la Communauté, Rapport sur l'Enquête 1957*, Sept. 1957. The figures for 1957 are based on plans. Actual expenditures were $1,242 million.

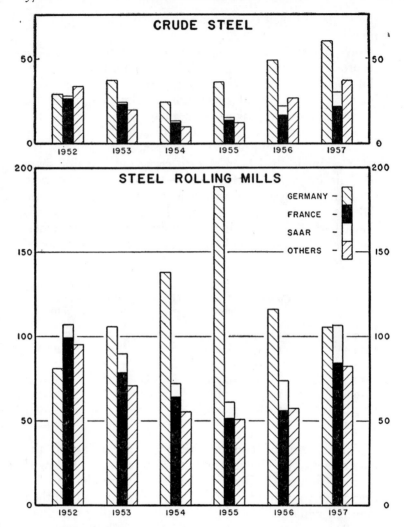

Figure 4. Community Investment in Steel, 1952-1957

Notes: Millions of dollars. 1957 figures are plans. "Crude steel" includes only steel furnaces, not blast furnaces, ore preparation, etc. Neither graph includes general services, transportation, etc.

Source: Calculated from HA, *Les Investissements dans les Industries du Charbon et de l'Acier de la Communauté, Rapport sur l'Enquête 1957* (Sept. 1957), Tables XV, XVI.

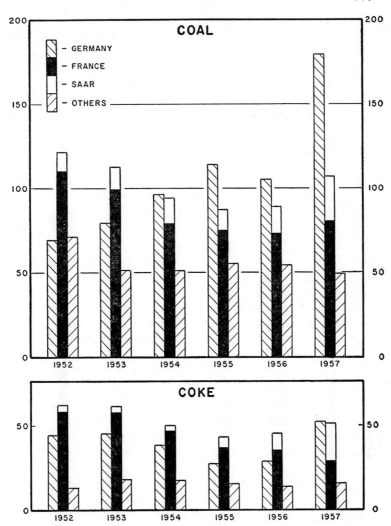

Figure 5. Community Investment in
Coal and Coke, 1952-1957

NOTES: Millions of dollars. 1957 figures are plans. "Coal" includes only
mining operations, not power plants or processing. "Coke" includes all
cokeries.
SOURCE: Calculated from HA, *Les Investissements dans les Industries du
Charbon et de l'Acier de la Communauté, Rapport sur l'Enquête 1957*
(Sept. 1957), Tables I, II, XIV.

While France had completed the major part of its steel expansion before the common market was opened, coal was a continuing problem. Though Germany was a much larger producer, its investments in coal mining did not pass France's until about the middle of the transitional period. In cokeries, French investment held its lead throughout the period thanks to the major effort being made to reduce dependence on imports.[4]

Calculated on the basis of dollars invested per ton produced over the period 1953-56, Germany's investment exceeded France's slightly in iron-ore production ($.49 to $.44), somewhat more in steel furnaces ($1.88 to $1.43), and markedly in rolling mills ($10.85 to $7.74). In the last of these, Germany's investment was the highest in the Community but in steel furnaces it took second place to the Netherlands and in iron mining it came after Italy. In coal and coke it was below the Community average. France, on the other hand, invested more per ton produced than the Community average in everything except iron mining, steel furnaces, and rolling mills. The $4.32 per ton of output invested in French cokeries was several times that of any other country and in coal only Italy, a negligible producer with special problems, invested more per ton than France.[5]

It is very hard to see any influence of the Community in the investment record. The High Authority's advice may have helped a shift toward cokeries and blast furnaces to cope with the scrap shortage. The existence of the common market was almost certainly a stimulus to modernization and perhaps to the expansion of capacity as well, though it is impossible to judge this from the figures. Initially investments in coal and steel were largely determined by each country's recovery program. They may have been adapted in pace or emphasis to the common market, but their main features were clearly national. With-

---

[4] Investment in blast furnaces and in pithead power stations and other means of using lower-grade coal largely followed the pattern of total investment.

[5] HA, *Report*, Apr. 1958, v. 2, pp. 376-386.

out a close study of costs it remains impossible to say whether the pattern of investment has responded at all to the common market in the sense of favoring the areas of lowest cost without regard to national boundaries. It is doubtful, however, whether much has been accomplished along these lines. The time has been short; the national factors determining each investment program and the inertial force of the existing pattern of production are strong. The financing of these investments is predominantly domestic; capital funds do not move freely within the Community on a scale that would shape investment programs in any major fashion. Finally, any rough judgment based on geography would be complicated by investments intended to reduce costs in mines and mills that were not currently the most efficient.

TRADE

Trade is the Community activity that could most logically be expected to show the effects of the common market. The exchange of Treaty products within the Community during the transitional period appears in Table 12. Several

Table 12

TRADE WITHIN THE COMMUNITY, 1952-1957

	Iron & Steel	Coal	Coke	Iron Ore	Scrap
		(millions of tons)			
1952	2.1	16.3	8.1	9.4	.4
1953	2.9	19.9	7.1	10.5	1.1
1954	4.2	23.6	7.0	10.8	1.2
1955	5.7	23.3	9.0	13.5	1.2
1956	5.1	19.7	9.1	14.1	1.3
1957	5.7	19.8	9.3	14.3	1.1
		Percentage Increase			
1952-55	171.4	42.9	11.1	43.6	200.0
1952-57	171.4	21.5	14.8	52.1	175.0

NOTE: Belgium and Luxembourg are treated as a unit for steel but separately for all other products. France and the Saar are combined in all figures.
SOURCE: HA, *Report*, Apr. 1958, v. 2, Statistical Annex.

things stand out: trade increased much more rapidly than production; an initial sharp rise in trade in coal, steel, and scrap coincided roughly with the opening of the common market, but in iron ore the increase was moderate while trade in coke contracted; the height of the boom in 1956 brought a contraction in coal and steel trade that was made up in steel but not in coal when demand slackened during the following year. This contraction is fairly typical of periods of high demand when the "easy" home market is provided for first, producers have fewer incentives to seek additional outlets, and there is commercial and sometimes governmental pressure to give preference to traditional customers and domestic demand. The contraction in Community coal trade was matched by a reduction in exports to third countries, but steel exports to third countries rose in both 1956 and 1957. This probably reflects in part the higher prices that could be obtained for sales to third countries.

A limited expansion or even a contraction of trade when production booms is often said to be typical of European heavy industry. Between 1950 and 1952 steel production in the Community countries rose almost 30 per cent but their exports rose less than 7 per cent. The reverse record between 1952 and 1955 (though it covered a period of slack demand as well) was frequently pointed to as a major achievement of the common market. A High Authority study covering the first six months of 1955 showed that trade in Treaty products had increased 93 per cent over 1952 (at constant prices) while trade among the six countries in products not falling under the Treaty rose only 59 per cent. Coal was laggard, showing only a 40 per cent increase, but this was higher than some other heavy non-Treaty products such as cement, limestone, clay building materials and refractory products, and ores and concentrates of nonferrous metals. Eliminating coal, Treaty products showed an increase of over 150 per cent between 1952 and 1955, a figure not approached by any other commodities.[6]

The value of coal, steel, and iron exchanged among the

[6] *Informations Statistiques*, Mar.-Apr. 1956, pp. 3-6.

Community countries (at current prices) rose from 23.97 per cent of their total trade in 1952 to 26.64 per cent in 1955 and then contracted sharply to 21.55 per cent the next year and 22.65 per cent in 1957. Coal, and to a smaller extent iron ore, acted as a drag. The value of trade in iron and steel alone increased by 126 per cent between 1952 and 1957 while trade outside the coal and steel sectors rose 97 per cent.[7]

Table 13

COMMUNITY TRADE IN STEEL COMPARED WITH
OTHER DEVELOPMENTS, 1952-1957

(1952 = 100)

	Intra-Community Trade in Steel	Crude Steel Production	Exports of Steel to Third Countries	Intra-Community Trade in Non-Treaty Products
1953	138	95	102	111
1954	200	105	102	125
1955	271	126	121	150
1956	243	136	145	179
1957	271	143	151	193

NOTES:
 Cols. 1-3 are based on quantities; col. 4 on values at current prices. Col. 1 includes pig iron, the others do not.
 Col. 3 includes ingots, semi-finished steel, and steel products falling under the Treaty.
SOURCES: Cols. 1 and 2, HA, Report, Apr. 1958, v. 2, Statistical Annex. Cols. 3 and 4, Bulletin Statistique.

There is, therefore, a good bit of evidence that trade in steel within the Community has increased with exceptional rapidity during the transitional period. Table 13 summarizes some of this evidence. Again the contraction after 1955 is marked, but it does not invalidate the generalization. This is at least prima-facie evidence of a connection between the creation of the common market and the expansion of trade in steel. There are, however, several factors that

[7] Bulletin Statistique. The steel figure includes a sizable amount for products not covered by the Treaty.

caution against too full an identification. Very few steel tariffs were actually removed when the common market was opened. There was an increase in trade between 1952 and 1953; many tariffs were suspended during the former year while the common market was in effect during only part of the latter year. Trade with third countries has also increased. Trade within the Community in steel products not covered by the Treaty has risen substantially. The contraction in trade in 1956 came when virtual completion of the transport rate reform made the common market more of a reality than it had been in previous years. Nevertheless, when all this is said, something remains that strongly suggests an impact of the common market on trade, at least in steel, and perhaps in other Treaty products as well.

One cannot be very precise about this. In scrap the evidence is quite clear. The removal of controls that checked the amount of French and German scrap going to Italy was the main factor in increasing trade (probably aided by lower demand in France and Germany during 1953 and early 1954). The modest increase in iron ore trade is largely attributable to the greater ease with which Belgians could buy the output of Lorraine. Some of the initial increase in the steel trade resulted from the elimination of the French import controls. The reduction of transport rates and the elimination of discrimination must have encouraged some international traffic. The elimination of double-pricing probably contributed to the process. One can also argue by negatives: had the governments imposed tariffs or quotas during the period when demand was low, in 1953 and 1954, trade would undoubtedly have been smaller than it was.

Trade in Steel

In one of the most interesting studies of the Community that has appeared, Harald Jürgensen casts some light on the kind of increase in steel trade that occurred during the early years.[8] Making use of transport statistics, he goes

[8] H. Jürgensen, *Die Westeuropäische Montanindustrie und Ihr Gemeinsamer Markt*, 1955; supplemented by his "Die Montanunion in den Funktionsgrenzen der Teilintegration," *Wirtschaftsdienst*, Nov. 1955, pp. 623-630.

beyond national trade figures and shows the structure of steel trade (a) within the areas where steel production is concentrated, (b) between them and the outlying areas in the same countries, (c) with the outlying areas of other countries, (d) between outlying areas in different countries, and (e) between the main centers of steel production in different countries. Southern Germany is a good example of an outlying area that would normally be supplied by the main domestic center (the Ruhr) so long as trade barriers enclosed the national economy but that is geographically well situated to draw from foreign centers (Lorraine and the Saar) if national barriers and discrimination are removed. Jürgensen found that while imports provided only 2.8 per cent of southern Germany's rolled steel in 1951, they provided nearly one-third in the first half of 1954. Conversely, the Ruhr's share of this trade fell from 60 per cent in 1951 to 41.4 per cent in the first half of 1954. Not all of this increase resulted from the opening of the common market. Between 1951 and 1952 the share of imports in the south German supply rose from 2.8 to 13.6 per cent and the Ruhr's share fell from 60 to 56 per cent.[9] But in mid-1952 Germany suspended tariffs, which could be regarded as a kind of advance installment on the common market. The composition of Germany's supply of rolled steel underwent the following changes (in percentages):[10]

	1951	1952	1954
Trade within North Rhine-Westphalia (NRW)	56.2	52.9	48.4
Deliveries from NRW to the rest of Germany	27.9	27.4	27.0
Trade within the rest of Germany	14.4	12.4	11.7
Imports to the rest of Germany	.7	3.7	9.2
Imports to NRW	.8	3.6	3.7

As Jürgensen points out, it cannot be assumed that all increases in international trade represent progress and that

---

[9] *Die Westeuropäische Montanindustrie*. . . , cited, pp. 234, 235. South Germany includes Bavaria, Württemberg-Baden, Hesse, and the Palatinate. The Ruhr stands for North Rhine-Westphalia.

[10] "Die Montanunion in den Funktionsgrenzen. . . . ," cited.

every diminution of internal trade is economically advantageous. In this case, however, the presumption of advantage is fairly strong. The figures seem to warrant the conclusion that the opening of the common market had an important effect on German steel imports and therefore on the internal structure of the German steel trade.

Lacking comparable studies of the rest of the Community's steel trade, we can only assume that much of the impact of the common market was on the reorientation of trade to conform more reasonably to geography—which is one of its basic purposes. It is possible, however, to examine the national structure of the changes in intra-Community trade in coal and steel. What results proves less about the impact of opening the common market than it does about the character of the common market that the Community has produced. Between 1952 and 1955 Community trade in steel increased by about 3.6 million tons. This was made up by the following increases in *imports* (in thousands of tons):

Germany	1,777
France and Saar	754
Netherlands	570
Belgium and Luxembourg	295
Italy	160

These were matched by the following increases in *exports*:

France and Saar	1,462
Belgium and Luxembourg	1,230
Germany	530
Netherlands	276
Italy	59

There was a net change of 1.6 million tons in trade balances, in which the dominant factor was an increase in Germany's net imports from the Community of 1.2 million tons. The Community's largest steel producer was also its largest steel importer. France, where many people feared swamping by cheap German steel, saw its exports to Germany quintuple, to the point at which they were more than seven times imports from Germany. Belgium and

Luxembourg, too, saw a great increase in steel sales to Germany, gross and net. Only Italy and the Netherlands imported more steel from Germany than they sold there. Throughout the rest of the Community it was France, Belgium, and Luxembourg who were the great providers. Obviously this was not all the result of removing trade barriers and reducing transport costs. It was the great surge of the German economy, with steel-using industries outpacing steel production, that sucked in imports from the rest of the Community. Nevertheless, it was a very different picture from that which most people had imagined would result from throwing open the main markets of Western Europe to the vaunted prowess of the Ruhr.

The sharp contraction in trade in 1956 was almost entirely accounted for by the drop in German imports from France, Belgium, and the Netherlands. The German contraction continued the next year while all other countries increased their imports; indeed, most of the increase in intra-Community trade in 1957 was accounted for by the expansion of German exports from under a million tons to nearly a million and a half for the first time since the common market had opened. France, where demand stayed high after it had begun to shrink in the rest of the Community, not only bought substantially more steel from Germany but contracted its exports as well. Still, it remained a large net exporter to Germany and retained an export surplus in its Community trade as a whole.

Some idea of what the transitional period has meant for the trade of each Community country with the others in iron and steel may be gained from the following figures which give the total trade of each country within the Community from 1952 through 1957:[11]

	Total Exports	Total Imports	Balance
		(thousands of tons)	
Belgium/Luxembourg	11,188	2,445	+8,743
France/Saar	7,995	3,468	+4,527
Germany	4,771	9,979	−5,208
Netherlands	1,465	6,934	−5,469
Italy	197	2,791	−2,594

[11] HA, *Report*, Apr. 1958, v. 2, pp. 352-353.

Trade in Coal

The coal trade showed fewer changes from year to year. The increase through 1955 was less than in steel, the contraction that followed brought trade in 1956 and 1957 below the level of 1953. All of the exporting countries played a part in this process, but in an irregular fashion. Between 1954 and 1955, German exports dropped about 2.6 million tons, and the Netherlands cut its much smaller volume of exports. In contrast France, the Saar, and Belgium increased exports in 1955 but reduced them sharply in 1956; Belgium and the Saar reduced them a little more in 1957, when Dutch and German exports were increasing. Much of the pattern of intra-Community trade depended on the shifts of German exports and imports which were examined in some detail in an earlier chapter (p.483ff.). In coke the movements of trade were even milder, a decline through 1954 being more than offset by a steady rise during the following years, owing almost entirely to the expansion of French imports.

Adding coal and coke (ton for ton) the total trade of each country with the rest of the Community from 1952 through 1957 was:[12]

	Total Exports	Total Imports	Balance
		(thousands of tons)	
Germany	102,848	29,437	+73,411
Saar	50,121	5,542	+44,579
Belgium	27,508	10,753	+16,755
Netherlands	9,909	27,278	−17,369
Luxembourg	—	22,292	−22,292
Italy	—	22,890	−22,890
France	9,098	75,117	−66,019

Apart from the great importance of Germany as a supplier to the rest of the Community and the heavy dependence of France on imports, which have always been

[12] Same, pp. 322-323; *Bulletin Statistique*.

taken for granted, two things stand out from these figures. First is the importance of the Saar, especially to France. Small as it is, the Saar provided the rest of the Community with half as much coal as Germany. Nearly half France's coal imports from the Community during the transitional period came from the Saar (excluding coke). The Saar sent almost an equal amount of coal to Germany, providing about three-quarters of that country's intra-Community imports and making a substantial contribution to France's foreign exchange earnings. The second fact concerns Belgium. In spite of high costs and high prices, Belgium was the third most important net exporter of coal and coke during the transitional period. Holland and France were the main markets while Luxembourg was of some importance in the smaller coke trade.[13] While in the period of highest demand almost any coal could be sold in the Community, Belgium's ability to keep up these exports throughout the transitional period undoubtedly shows the effect of the subsidies and, at least in the early years, of the removal of trade barriers as well.

INTERPENETRATION

While it is hard to see the effects of the Community on production, the impact on trade appears to be more marked. Putting the two sets of figures together provides still another perspective. The following figures show trade in steel as a percentage of crude steel production in the Community during the transitional period:[14]

---

[13] Luxembourg got 40 per cent of its coal and 90 per cent of its coke from Germany in 1952-57, getting only about 13 and 3 per cent, respectively, from Belgium.

[14] Calculated from *Bulletin Statistique*. The trade figures include ingots, semi-finished steel, and steel products falling under the Treaty, but not pig iron. Actual tonnages traded, not the crude steel equivalents, are compared with crude steel output. Belgium and Luxembourg, France and the Saar, are treated as units. The figures for intra-Community trade in 1952 and 1953 include estimates for Belgium and Luxembourg, for which HA, *Report*, Apr. 1958, v. 2, Statistical Annex, and ECE, *Steel Statistics* were used as well as the main source.

	Intra-Community Exports	Exports to Third Countries	Imports from Third Countries
	(per cent of Community production)		
1952	5.2	14.3	1.1
1953	6.8	15.4	1.8
1954	8.2	13.9	1.5
1955	9.2	13.7	1.7
1956	7.8	15.3	1.7
1957	8.5	15.1	1.8

Between 1952 and 1955 there was a marked increase in the relative importance of intra-Community trade which was not matched by trade with third countries. Then in 1956 there was a contraction comparable to that shown in other trade figures cited earlier. While the pressure of domestic demand was probably its main cause, these figures suggest more strongly than others the possible influence of higher profits from exports to third countries. Intra-Community trade rose again in relation to production in 1957, leaving the Community with a substantially higher "rate of interpenetration" in the steel trade at the end of the transition period than it had at the outset.[15]

Table 14 gives comparable figures for the steel trade of individual countries. While each country shows some variations, the records of all conform generally to the pattern for the Community as a whole. An added indication of

[15] The term is one used by the High Authority to cover several sets of calculations. In September 1953, Community steel producers received orders for 1.6 million tons of steel for delivery to Community buyers; 14.4 per cent of those orders crossed national boundaries. This figure, which was estimated to be about 10 per cent between 1950 and 1952, rose to a peak of 18.3 per cent in the first quarter of 1954. After that it fluctuated but by February 1955 was again down to 14.5 per cent. HA, *Report*, Apr. 1955, pp. 61, 62. Another method of calculating interpenetration takes the proportion of international deliveries of steel products within the Community to total deliveries within the Community. In 1954 this was 13.2 per cent; in 1955, 13.6 per cent; in 1956, 12.8 per cent; and in 1957, 12.9 per cent. Belgium, Luxembourg, France, and the Saar are all treated separately in this calculation. The monthly record supports the view that the contraction in trade was the result of the boom; the measure of interpenetration was generally lower from mid-1956 to mid-1957 than in the six-month periods before and after. *Bulletin Statistique*.

Table 14

TRADE IN STEEL PRODUCTS AS PERCENTAGE OF PRODUCTION
OF CRUDE STEEL, 1952-1957

		1952	1953	1954	1955	1956	1957
Germany							
Community:	Exports	1.1	2.4	3.2	2.9	3.0	4.9
	Imports	5.0	6.7	9.0	11.2	8.3	7.3
Third countries:	Exports	6.4	5.9	7.2	6.2	8.7	10.3
	Imports	0.3	1.0	0.9	1.2	1.9	2.0
Belgium-Luxembourg							
Community:	Exports	19.5[a]	19.9[a]	22.0	26.3	22.5	22.4
	Imports	1.0[a]	2.2[a]	1.8	1.9	2.1	2.5
Third countries:	Exports	38.3	38.8	31.7	30.8	35.0	34.5
	Imports	0.1	0.7	0.7	0.7	0.5	0.6
France-Saar							
Community:	Exports	2.9	6.5	8.5	9.7	7.6	7.4
	Imports	0.1	0.5	2.8	4.1	4.6	6.0
Third countries:	Exports	12.8	17.1	15.5	17.4	15.5	13.8
	Imports	0.5	0.7	0.2	0.2	0.2	0.3
Italy							
Community:	Exports	—	0.1	0.2	1.1	0.8	1.1
	Imports	6.6	10.5	8.8	4.8	4.4	5.4
Third countries:	Exports	0.6	1.9	2.1	2.6	6.4	7.2
	Imports	5.0	7.2	6.5	5.2	4.8	5.0
Netherlands							
Community:	Exports	2.0	7.8	18.9	24.0	18.2	25.1
	Imports	108.5	102.7	116.6	128.9	120.0	130.3
Third countries:	Exports	9.8	18.4	18.4	21.5	19.7	18.5
	Imports	22.8	19.3	14.1	28.2	16.0	11.4

a. Estimated, see n. 14.

SOURCE: Calculated from *Bulletin Statistique*. See n. 14 for coverage.

the extent of interpenetration in steel is the increase in
importance of both imports and exports in the intra-Community trade of France and Germany. For all three major
producers, exports to third countries are more important
than deliveries to other Community countries. For France
and Germany this trade increased in importance during

the transitional period though, on the whole, not as much as intra-Community trade.[16] For Belgium and Luxembourg, the largest exporters to the outside world, the relative importance of this trade contracted somewhat. The Netherlands, which is the smallest steel producer, showed a marked increase in Community trade in both directions and also in exports to third countries. Italy departed from the general pattern, undoubtedly because of the great rise in its steel production. After an initial increase the importance of imports from the rest of the Community fell below the 1952 level. Imports from third countries did not contract quite as much. Exports, which were tiny in 1952, came to 8.3 per cent of Italian production in 1957, going mostly to third countries.

In coal and coke the Community showed no such marked increase in "interpenetration" as occurred in steel, as the following figures show:[17]

	Intra-Community Exports		Exports to Third Countries		Imports from Third Countries	
	coal	coke	coal	coke	coal	coke
			(per cent of Community production)			
1952	8.3	14.4	1.9	8.3	9.3	0.2
1953	9.9	12.5	2.5	7.1	5.8	0.1
1954	11.1	12.7	3.3	9.3	5.8	0.2
1955	10.6	13.9	4.1	7.7	9.4	0.3
1956	8.9	13.1	2.3	6.6	15.3	0.7
1957	8.9	13.0	2.1	4.9	17.7	0.7

Against the background of the large increase in Community imports of coal from third countries that has by now become familiar, the figures in Tables 15 and 16 provide no major surprises. The stability of the intra-Community trade of Germany and the Saar in coal and the increase in importance of Belgium's Community trade have

[16] This seemed to be changing for Germany in 1956 and 1957, but the table makes it clear that annual fluctuations may not be taken to indicate trends.

[17] Calculated from *Bulletin Statistique* for hard coal and coke-oven coke. Belgium, Luxembourg, France, and the Saar are all treated as separate units.

already been examined. For France changes were relatively minor. For the Netherlands, on the other hand, coal imports from the Community more than doubled in importance between 1952 and 1954-55, but then declined part way. The Netherlands was also an exception to the general pattern in the coke trade, showing an increase in the share of its production that was exported to the rest of

Table 15

TRADE IN COAL AS A PERCENTAGE OF PRODUCTION,
1952-1957

			1952	1953	1954	1955	1956	1957
Germany								
	Community:	Exports	7.3	8.3	9.7	7.4	7.2	7.5
		Imports	3.2	3.5	3.5	5.1	3.4	3.2
	Third countries:	Exports	2.5	2.6	2.9	2.2	1.9	2.0
		Imports	6.4	4.1	3.0	7.1	10.2	12.9
Belgium								
	Community:	Exports	7.6	11.9	14.6	16.7	11.2	10.7
		Imports	1.5	3.5	9.8	7.3	6.6	7.8
	Third countries:	Exports	0.8	1.9	4.8	6.9	3.9	2.9
		Imports	3.9	3.8	2.9	4.8	9.5	9.7
France								
	Community:	Exports	1.9	2.9	2.9	4.5	2.0	2.0
		Imports	13.8	16.3	16.6	14.2	14.2	14.8
	Third countries:	Exports	1.0	1.7	2.4	6.0	2.0	1.5
		Imports	9.7	3.1	4.1	5.2	16.0	17.1
Saar								
	Community:	Exports	45.4	47.4	45.9	46.2	44.3	43.0
		Imports	6.7	5.7	5.3	5.9	5.5	6.3
	Third countries:	Exports	3.4	6.7	7.9	10.2	4.7	3.4
		Imports	—	—	—	—	—	0.5
Netherlands								
	Community:	Exports	0.03	2.0	7.7	6.4	5.6	6.4
		Imports	19.3	28.0	41.3	42.3	30.8	29.3
	Third countries:	Exports	0.1	0.4	0.9	0.9	1.3	1.3
		Imports	21.6	14.7	17.6	21.9	43.3	47.3

SOURCE: Calculated from *Bulletin Statistique*; hard coal only.

Table 16

Trade in Coke as a Percentage of Production,

1952-1957

		1952	*1953*	*1954*	*1955*	*1956*	*1957*
Germany							
Community:	Exports	17.7	15.5	15.5	17.6	16.5	15.6
	Imports	0.8	0.5	0.6	0.7	0.9	0.5
Third countries:	Exports	10.8	8.5	12.7	10.0	8.6	6.3
	Imports	0.3	0.1	0.2	0.3	0.8	0.5
Belgium							
Community:	Exports	8.5	6.1	9.1	7.5	8.6	9.6
	Imports	—	0.4	1.3	2.0	1.8	1.9
Third countries:	Exports	6.5	7.7	5.3	4.2	4.1	3.0
	Imports	—	0.1	0.1	0.2	0.1	0.8
France							
Community:	Exports	0.3	0.3	0.2	0.4	0.3	0.9
	Imports	55.4	47.8	41.4	46.6	42.6	43.8
Third countries:	Exports	0.3	0.8	1.2	1.8	0.6	0.6
	Imports	0.1	—	—	—	—	0.1
Saar							
Community:	Exports	24.2	21.6	21.8	17.0	17.4	16.5
	Imports	1.1	0.9	1.0	3.9	3.9	4.6
Third countries:	Exports	0.2	0.1	0.03	0.1	—	—
	Imports	—	—	—	—	—	—
Netherlands							
Community:	Exports	23.0	20.6	24.8	28.5	27.5	31.0
	Imports	5.4	8.3	10.5	10.8	8.2	7.3
Third countries:	Exports	19.4	17.8	18.5	19.6	19.5	14.9
	Imports	—	—	0.6	0.7	3.5	3.9

Source: Calculated from *Bulletin Statistique*; coke-oven coke only.

the Community. Belgian and German deliveries remained rather stable while those for the Saar dropped sharply as a result of increased domestic consumption. France's emphasis on coke production was reflected in the fall of its imports from the rest of the Community. Italy is omitted from the tables since it imports almost all its coal and hardly any of its coke. The importance of Italian coal imports from the Community fell as the share of imports from third countries rose. Trade in coke showed no marked trends.

Taken all together, these figures on the relation of trade to production provide some important dimensions of the Community economy. The Community coal and steel industries produce primarily for home markets. Only in coke was intra-Community trade greater than 10 per cent of production. Nevertheless, intra-Community trade was of great importance for some countries, especially the smaller ones. Trade with third countries, especially in steel exports and coal imports, is more important than intra-Community trade. Foreign trade as a whole thus assumes very significant proportions for the Community, not only for its crucial importance in certain sectors but in its size compared with production.

It is against these facts demonstrating the relative importance of trade that one should consider the substantial increase in interpenetration of Community markets in steel and in certain parts of the coal trade. There can be little doubt that the creation of the Community, and especially the opening of the common market, contributed to this expansion. The contraction in 1956 is, however, a warning about the limits within which measures directed primarily at trade barriers can have an effect, owing in part to the somewhat marginal character of much intra-Community trade.

WHAT DID NOT HAPPEN

Movements of trade and production are likely to be crude indicators of the impact of the Community. Movements of profits, costs, returns on investment, capital-output ratios, and the creation or elimination of differentials (of many sorts, among producers or buyers, or among markets and activities for each producer) ought to be more sensitive indicators of change. A careful study of them might give more definite indications of how the Community is affecting the coal and steel economies of the six countries and of future shifts in trade and production that may result. Reliable data on most of these matters are not easy to come by and it was not possible to carry out the necessary research and analysis in the course of this study. This kind of close investigation of firms and industries is most needed to advance our understanding of what the Community has done and is likely to do. Meanwhile appraisal of the impact of the Community rests on cruder observation.

What did not happen during the transition period provides a necessary supplement to an estimate based on movements of trade and production. The Community has not revolutionized the coal and steel economy of the six countries. The pattern of production and trade in 1957 bears an easily recognized relation to that of 1952. The changes that have taken place have developed at a fairly moderate pace, not convulsively. During the transitional period economic expansion put a floor under production and trade, so that changes appeared mostly in relative rates of growth, not often as contraction.

Partly for this reason none of the weak spots gave way. Belgian coal, which benefited from several props, showed only a slight contraction of production, while in the Community coal trade Belgium proved to be an important exporter. French coal production, about which there were fears, thrived. The Italian steel industry, given tariff protection because it was thought unable to stand the blasts of competition, has grown faster than any other in the Community.

The Community has not been dominated by Germany, as so many expected. True, German production has grown in importance. In 1952, 38 per cent of the Community's crude steel was produced in Germany and in 1957, 41 per cent. In coal the shift was from 51.6 to 53.7 per cent. Yet given the delayed German recovery, this is not remarkable; nor is it an indication that the common market has laid open the rest of Western Europe to an irrepressible German dynamism. In 1929 Germany produced a slightly larger share of the six countries' steel than in 1957; in 1937 and 1938, when Germany had recovered from the depression more quickly than most, its share was much higher.[18] In coal production, too, Germany's 1957 share was below the 55 per cent of 1929 and the 56-57 per cent of 1937 and 1938. France, the next largest producer, saw its share of Community steel production fall from 26 to 23.6 per cent between 1952 and 1957. In coal it virtually held its share at about 23 per cent.[19]

Specific fears—that German steel exports would sweep away weaker industries while Germany's control of coal would put the others on short rations—have also not been realized. The coal supply from Germany to the rest of the Community has held steady (with some complaint from the Germans). In steel, Germany has been a net importer from other Community countries during the transitional period. This may not last. The rapid increase in German steel exports in 1956 and 1957 may be a turning point. But after five years of the common market there is at least less ground for fear that by some inevitable logic only the Ruhr can produce efficiently and sell aggressively. The problem is not obliterated. The conditions of the transitional period will not be repeated. As the biggest country in the Community and the largest producer of coal and steel, Germany is bound to play a leading role. But there is at least less ground for people in the other Community countries to believe that this will be done at their expense and without advantage to them.

There is other negative evidence. The development of the Community's coal and steel industries has not been so radically different from that of the rest of the economic life of the six countries that one could say, "This experience proves beyond a shadow of a doubt how good (or how bad) it is to pool industries." The expansion of production may not be due to the creation of the Community

[18] 1937, 45.3 per cent; 1938, 54.6 per cent. The figures are for the present territory of West Germany.

[19] This was close to France's 1929 share in coal and well above the late '30s when French production was particularly low. In steel, however, France's 1929 share was 27.3 per cent, more than in 1952 or 1957. The fall resulted from the expansion of production elsewhere in the Community rather than in Germany.

but it certainly demonstrates the error of those who expected the Community to subordinate production to "social" or political aims or to let some form of *dirigisme* interfere with economic performance. There is little in the Community's record to suggest that it is mere façade and has made no real changes in the conditions under which coal and steel are produced and traded in the six countries.

What the Community *has* done cannot be expressed in quantitative terms. There has been a discernible, but not altogether indisputable, impact of the Community, notably on trade. It is not surprising that a more precise conclusion eludes one. The time has been short, multiple causes are at work, cyclical influences have been strong, the coal and steel industries of the six countries have not been sharply severed from the rest of the Western European economy. While the conditions in which these industries exist have been altered by the Community, they have not been radically altered in all respects. The Schuman Plan is a measure of partial integration. It provides a new area of operations and a new framework within which public policy about coal and steel is determined, but the new features are still partly embedded in the old, familiar arrangements. The kind of change that has taken place can be appraised better in qualitative terms than by statistical analysis.

TWENTY-ONE

THE CHARACTER OF THE COMMUNITY

THE CHAPTERS that have gone before show how little a simple description of the Community tells. Yet the details, complex as they are, add up to a reasonably clear picture of what the Community is and how it differs from a national economy or from old-fashioned international economic cooperation. That some questions should remain unanswered is inherent in the Community's present character, for it is a process just begun that is enmeshed with the changing economies of coal and steel and the evolving political conditions of Western Europe.

The structure of production and trade set out in the last chapter tells something of the Community's character. For more, one turns naturally to its great innovations: the common market and the establishment of international public supervision and control of the coal and steel industries. How real the common market is, and to what extent conditions of production and trade are in fact determined by supranational action, are crucial questions about the character of the Community. But the novel elements are only part of its essence. The quiddity of the Community lies in the way it mixes governmental and supranational powers and blends national markets and the common market to create a new kind of public control of business in a new "economic space."

HOW MUCH SUPRANATIONAL POWER?

From the very beginning the "supranational" element has been crucial to opinions about the Schuman Plan, favorable and unfavorable. The kind of analysis pursued in this book does not produce precise definitions of "supranational" or tests that will tell whether a given action was truly supranational or only formally so. Nor do our purposes require pursuit of these issues. The crude distinction between power wielded by the High Authority and that employed by the governments, separately or together, will suffice. Previous chapters have provided a good bit of evidence about what was done by each and about the interaction between them.

The High Authority

The relation is complex. The High Authority is made up of men forbidden to accept instructions from governments and protected against ouster by governments. Its members have what is virtually a mandate to work as trustees of a Community interest and are given specific powers which they alone can exercise. But the High Authority is dealing with matters that continue to be of great interest to the governments, not least because they may have to bear the political consequences. The governments, too, have powers over coal and steel, some specifically assigned to them and denied to the High Authority by the Treaty, others theirs because they are governments and the Treaty is silent. Matters are further complicated by the governments' Treaty commitments to principles that can only be applied by further intergovernmental agreement or by continuing governmental action. There are also matters on which the governments and the High Authority share power and responsibility.

It would not have been surprising if these arrangements had not worked. The members of the High Authority might have acted as if they were really governmental representatives, as many people in Europe thought they would. Alternatively, they might have exercised their independent power in ways that would create serious friction with the governments, ruling out cooperation and perhaps even leading to national subversion of the supranational measures. Instead, the Treaty arrangement has worked. It has not produced a simple pattern, with clear distinctions between the exercise of supranational power by the High Authority and national power by the governments, while the Council of Ministers neatly "coordinated" in between. The more complex process that has emerged has been influenced both by the kinds of problems the Community has had to deal with and by the general political climate. Not everyone has been pleased with the result but its unmistakable affinity with the normal processes of government indicates that the Community has taken on political as well as legal life.

Much of the development is due to the policies followed by the High Authority. No one who has studied the Community closely has charged the members of the High Authority with acting in a predominantly "national" manner, incompatible with their mandate. To be sure, they must be well thought of by their governments or they could not work effectively and would not have been chosen in the first place. But they must be generally trusted by the other governments as well or the same things would be true.[1] The nine members of the High Authority have to work closely together to accomplish anything and this is a brake on nationalistic behavior, along with the quality and responsibility of the men who have the Treaty's mandate to discharge. The High Authority's proceedings are treated with great secrecy but close students generally agree that a broad and, in some sense, "supranational" outlook has developed, not only in the High Authority itself but among most of its staff members as well.[2]

The members of the High Authority have not, of course, uprooted themselves from their national societies. While

---

[1] Monnet's resignation in 1955 may well have been connected with the lack of confidence between him and the government of Pierre Mendès-France; but in nominating his successor the French government had to find a man acceptable to the others, who turned down some of those first suggested.

[2] " . . . I could count on my fingers the number of decisions on which we were not unanimous. . . ," said Albert Coppé toward the end of the second year of the High Authority's life. *Potentiel du Plan Schuman*, a speech delivered in Hamburg on June 18, 1954.

persistence in a strictly national viewpoint would corrupt the Treaty structure, a certain amount of national pre-dilection, and even prejudice, is quite compatible with the proper functioning of the Community. The federative process does not ignore conflicting attitudes, it reconciles them. By keeping alive their national ties the members of the High Authority enhance their political sense of a situation, their feel of the importance of certain problems. Nor is the development of a "supranational" outlook psychologically strange. The members of the High Authority probably shared the "sense of Europe"; they had a commitment to the Community; moreover, men have always considered themselves true patriots while arguing that the real interests of their countries, seen in enlightened and long-run terms, were being damaged, not advanced, by the way governments were pursuing what they called the national interest.

To say that the High Authority has acted supranationally does not mean that the nine men sat in Luxembourg and issued edicts after consulting their consciences, their texts, and their experts. To start with, on very many issues the Treaty required the High Authority to consult governments and interest groups before it acted, even when the power of decision was its alone.[3] As a matter of policy, the High Authority went further. It tried to get as wide an area of agreement as possible before it acted, even when it had legal authority to move without the assent of the others. Private groups, the Consultative Committee, and the Assembly have all been brought into this process, but the most important partner in the dialogue has been the Council of Ministers. Looking back over the transitional period, the High Authority said, "The role of the special Council of Ministers has developed considerably . . . as the High Authority has acquired the habit of consulting

---

[3] An early and still valuable analysis of the High Authority's powers shows how many different combinations of consultation or approval are called for under the Treaty. *La Communauté Européenne du Charbon et de l'Acier*, L'Institut des Relations Internationales (Brussels), 1953, pp. 36-53.

it more and more, even when not dealing with specific cases requiring its agreement." [4] Partly by this means the High Authority has avoided the continuing duel with the intergovernmental organ that many thought was inherent in the structure of the Community.

On some important issues the High Authority has acted without full agreement among the governments or willing acceptance by the interest groups affected. But it has usually negotiated first. At the outset, the High Authority acted briskly to open the common market. This was important in getting the Community off to a quick start and helped establish the supranational agency's authority. Later steps such as the removal of ceilings on Ruhr coal prices, the order for changes in ATIC, and the elimination of special railroad rates, were all taken over the objection of one or more governments. When it could, however, the High Authority tried to find courses of action that commanded wide assent. Negotiation and discussion probably led in many cases to agreement among several governments and support from some private groups that made it easier for the High Authority to act even if some opposition remained. The advantages of this course are obvious; its price was sometimes compromise and delay.

The reasons the High Authority adopted this policy are fairly clear. Power was dispersed in the Community and there were advantages in securing as much common direction and action as possible. On many matters the governments had the power of decision; the High Authority was unlikely to carry much influence with them if, in its own sphere, it ignored their interests and views. The High Authority was new and not as powerful as it appeared in Treaty law; to the extent that it could work by persuasion instead of by fiat and attempted enforcement, it could strengthen its position and better achieve its purposes. Most of all, the members of the High Authority were conscious of the need to build the Community; that could be done better by "bringing along" the governments and private

[4] HA, *Report*, Apr. 1958, v. 2, p. 15.

groups than by setting off the High Authority against the others. Had the early idea of moving rapidly from the Community to the organization of a federal Europe persisted, the alternative course of emphasizing the High Authority's independence and making maximum use of supranational powers might have commended itself. But the defeat of the EDC showed that what could be accomplished in European integration would continue for some time to depend on governments. When René Mayer replaced Monnet as chairman of the High Authority, he said that he had not been appointed to "kill supranationalism," and his record shows that.[5] But there is little doubt that the shift comported well with the need to carry on a policy that emphasized negotiation and persuasion.

The Council of Ministers

While the High Authority's approach emphasized the importance of the governments, their role was bound to be great, partly because they were already on the scene and partly because of the powers reserved to them under the Treaty. Acting individually, each within its own jurisdiction, governments have played a great part in shaping the Community during the transitional period. This is not just a matter of the influence on the coal and steel industries of general economic policies and legislation. Probably even more important have been measures dealing directly with the pooled industries, for instance the French and German actions affecting coal and steel prices, the Belgian government's unwillingness to take drastic action to reorganize coal mining, and the role of various governments in aiding or contributing directly to investments. They also worked together. By their agreements on the Saar and the canalization of the Moselle, Germany and France seemed, to some

---

[5] E. B. Haas, *The Uniting of Europe*, 1958, p. 457. "Neither Mayer nor the other eight members of the High Authority shared Monnet's convictions with respect to the role of planning, the function of technicians in forcing the hands of governments, or the almost mystical immanent federalism of ECSC. Their interpretation of the Treaty is far more modest and their doctrine of consensus a great deal more mechanical" (pp. 456-457).

people, "to let the High Authority know who the political masters of the Coal and Steel Treaty are, indeed even to challenge the Community's specific field of action in iron and steel." [6] Acting as a group, in the Council of Ministers, the governments have been directly involved in Community business. Sometimes they have been responsible for delays and failure to act. The special task assigned to the Council by the Treaty—the coordination of national and Community policy—remains undone except for study and discussion and action on specific questions. But the Council also has accomplishments. The agreements on through-rates, the Rhine agreement, and the arrangements on limited labor mobility were intergovernmental agreements. The negotiation of the treaty of association with Britain and the tariff concessions under GATT have been matters in which the governments played essential parts. In less formal ways, through the process of consultation and otherwise, the Council of Ministers and the individual governments have had an important influence on what the High Authority has done.

The Council of Ministers is no monolith. The issues with which it deals are not often cast in terms of, "Shall there be more or less supranational power?" They are more immediate problems of advising one course or another, of taking or not taking certain action. The interests of the governments conflict and no doubt the High Authority can often take advantage of that, though it must be guided by the importance of each government's cooperation for the question in hand.[7] It is often important for the governments to reach agreement, either because they have to act or in order to carry greater weight with the High Au-

[6] Rainer Hellmann, "Die Montanunion wird Umgegangen," *Der Volkswirt*, Aug. 24, 1957, pp. 1890-1891.

[7] Haas, cited, p. 493, traces the positions of the governments in the Council of Ministers on the High Authority's ceiling price on Ruhr coal. In 1954 Germany, France, and Luxembourg were for maintaining the price ceiling, with the other three countries opposed. In 1955 only Belgium took a clear-cut position in favor of removing the ceiling, while the Luxembourgeois position was qualified. In 1956 only Germany and Luxembourg were for removing the ceiling (with the Belgians abstaining). It was then that the High Authority ended price-fixing.

thority. Ernst Haas, who has looked closely into the matter, says the governments put great stress on getting agreement in the Council. "While the ministers frequently arrive with firm instructions, it is the essence of the Council's code that these may eventually be changed or even disregarded under the pressure of other views. National interests are always compromised; they are never maintained in the face of the 'atmosphere of co-operation' which prevails." [8]

Like the High Authority, the governments have an interest in negotiation and persuasion. They are not, after all, enemies of integration. They created the Community; they have an interest in its success; they have obligations under the Treaty. The French worked with the High Authority to eliminate subsidies; the Germans accepted a tax decision they felt was adverse; no government has seriously tried to introduce important surreptitious trade barriers. What each government wants is to maintain its independent influence on the development of the Community and to settle specific issues in certain ways. Each has to allow for the fact that it may be outvoted in the Council and that sometimes the High Authority can act if the governments do not. While it may take a strong and stubborn stand on issues of great importance, each government has an interest in being reasonable and, if possible, in shaping its policies so as to avoid being the one who for "nationalistic" reasons appears to prevent action that would benefit the Community. Such a position would draw discomforting criticism, not only from the High Authority and the remaining governments but from some political and economic groups throughout the Community, and not least from the Assembly. Only rarely will domestic opinion be solidly on one side of an issue. Coal producers may oppose a railroad rate change that reduces the delivered price of foreign coke, but coal-users are likely to favor it. A rule on prices that seems too rigid to a big producer may be welcomed by others just because it puts their competitors on a common footing with them and reduces the buyer's bargaining power. One of the important features of the Community is that it provides new channels through which such conflicts of interest may influence action. Their reconciliation is no longer a strictly national matter; they enter into a political process that is played out in part in an international setting where new combinations of interest and political strength and therefore new results become possible.

The Assembly

The Treaty seemed to make the Assembly of minor importance. Its one real power, to oust the High Authority, was so drastic as to leave it almost powerless. Annual debate of the High Authority's report seemed unlikely to give members of the Assembly a detailed knowledge of Community affairs. But then Monnet, who had not even included an assembly in his original plan, apparently saw a likely source of support for the High Authority and an important means of "building Europe." He began a process the High Authority has continued, of encouraging the development of the Assembly, supplying information to it, explaining problems and policies, and answering the criticisms of its members. The work of its committees has kept the Assembly in close and continuing touch with Community affairs. Since its members are parliamentarians they have tried to make the Assembly more like a parliament. While there have been no formal changes in its powers, practices have developed, somewhat imperfectly, which have almost certainly increased its influence. This has largely been a matter of giving the Assembly a chance to discuss issues before action is taken, instead of only reviewing the record afterwards. One of its prominent members has described the process: "The High Authority, which at the outset hardly dared count on the Council of Ministers or even on the Consultative Committee, looked to the Common Assembly for support. The latter provided it without hesitation but profited from this collaboration to get recognition of the prerogatives which are implicit in the Treaty and which are also based on parliamentary common law, but which have been confirmed by constitutional practice in a rapid and progressive evolution." [9]

Monnet's calculation was right. Opinions in the Assembly differ, of course, but when its resolutions criticize the High Authority it is usually for not doing enough rather than for going too far. Members have championed the development of the High Authority and called for a stronger line toward governments. When it was clear that the High Authority had reached the limits of its own authority, the Assembly recommended broader integration, for instance to make possible more effective action on transportation and to provide a fuller "social policy." It has also been a center of activity in efforts at extending integration to other fields, both before and after the collapse of the EDC.[10] It emphasizes a "European" or Community approach in its own practices. Members are organized not in national delegations but in three party groups; to a considerable extent they carry on their business on that basis. The strongest concerted criticism of the High Authority came not from a national delegation but from the Socialist group which in a formal statement condemned the failure to pursue a more active social policy.

How much influence the Assembly has had on Com-

---

[9] Pierre Wigny, *Un Témoignage sur la Communauté des Six*, 1957, p. 36. Another member has traced the developments of parliamentary practice in an interesting fashion, pointing out, for instance, that the practice of new chairmen of the High Authority (three in all) in appearing before the Assembly to give a statement of their philosophy and the broad lines of their programs has a certain resemblance to the procedure of investiture of a new government as it exists in most European parliaments. M. van der Goes van Naters, "De Huidige Staat van her Europese Parlementarisme," *Internationale Spectator*, Mar. 8, 1958, p. 129.

[10] It meets annually in joint session with the Consultative Assembly of the Council of Europe. Some of its members belong to other European assemblies. With some additions of membership, it served as the constituent body for the EDC and the European Political Community. It created a working group that played a part in the *relance européenne* that began at Messina. In early 1958 it provided the seasoned core of members for the new European Parliamentary Assembly.

munity affairs is hard to judge, but the direction of its efforts has always been clear. Its emphasis on greater integration and the strengthening of the Community has provided support the High Authority wanted and sometimes pressure on the High Authority to act.[11] The Assembly has sought and obtained more direct contact with the Council of Ministers, including the participation of ministers in some of its sessions. What influence the Assembly may have on the action of governments remains rather obscure. There is no doubt, however, that the Assembly has added to the forces that make for decisions on a Community rather than a national basis.

The Court

Less can be said about the Court. It is a supranational body with powers that can have important effects on the character of the Community. Some of its decisions have already done so, notably the outlawing of the "Monnet margin" on prices, the ruling that subsidies could be paid to some Belgian collieries without being paid to all, the judgment upholding the High Authority's right to give an unfavorable opinion on an investment plan even though it had no legal force, and the decisions that in effect confirmed the reorganization of the Ruhr sales organization. However, only a legal study would enable one to say what construction the Court is putting on the supranational powers provided by the Treaty. While the Court can in some circumstances make economic appraisals, its decisions so far have been expressed entirely in legal and procedural terms, giving no hint of what kind of economic or political analysis the Court would be likely to support.

Resort to the Court has been used to influence the course of events in the Community. The Dutch government filed a suit to hasten High Authority action on Georg; the French government's appeal of the ATIC case to the

11 Haas, cited, pp. 477-478, believes that the Assembly has influenced the High Authority on investment policy, the formulation of general objectives and other long-run forecasts, and on the cartel issue.

Court and the German government's suit concerning the shift bonus in coal mining were both undertaken as part of a bargaining process with the High Authority; German steel producers contemplated a suit demanding action on road transportation because they felt at a disadvantage in competing with producers in countries where trucking rates were not regulated. Probably the most important function of the Court has been to establish decisions as final, whether they are supranational or intergovernmental. No one has yet sought to defy or challenge an unfavorable Court decision. Nor has any government invoked the procedure of Article 37 that could lead to an extensive Court review of a situation on the basis that the High Authority's action, or inaction, had caused a fundamental disturbance of its economy. This would virtually require the Court to substitute itself for the High Authority in passing on the facts, the law, and the economics of the case—a situation all parties might prefer to avoid.

A Mixed System

While the Court and the Assembly have played parts in the development of the Community, it is the High Authority and the governments who have the crucial roles. Their power, wielded separately or together, in the same or in different directions, largely establishes the circumstances in which the Community's coal and steel economy operates. The issue of national vs. supranational power is a real one, but it is not the only issue; it could become crucial, but during the transitional period it has not been dominant. The main question has been how the governments and the High Authority could work out methods of combining their forces to produce a sensible governance of the Community economy, to promote the common market, and to handle transitional problems. The substance and consequences of the actions are considerably more important than their form. The High Authority's policy of seeking a broad area of agreement, which can be criticized on other grounds,[12] greatly helped in this process (aside from the question whether in any given instance the High Authority should have taken a stronger line or moved in a different direction). The basic fact is that the governments have political responsibility of a sort the High Authority escapes. This establishes limits to what can be done that may not correspond to the legal dispositions of the Treaty. In law and in political fact the Community is a mixed system. No single formula, even one derived from the practice of the transitional period, will stand as an adequate description of how public power is organized in the Community. The system is evolving; change and shifting balances are of its present essence. The continuing importance of governmental action is clear, but the supranational power is also real. Without it the character of the Community cannot be understood. But the character of the supranational power cannot be understood if it is read only in the words of the Treaty, apart from the experience of the Community.

HOW COMMON A MARKET?

At the core of the Schuman Plan, along with the idea of a supranational authority, was the idea of a "common market." Barriers to trade in coal and steel were to be removed, equality was to replace national or private discrimination, uniform rules were to apply throughout the Community. This would be quite different from the previous arrangement in which their were five or six national markets linked to each other and the rest of the

---

[12] ". . . the High Authority is unwilling to risk opposition and unpopularity by giving an energetic federal interpretation to the powers which is does possess, and thus disapppoints numerous groups and some governments who expect a positive federal policy." Same, p. 472. Haas seems to share this disappointment and says that in some fields, ". . . the High Authority . . . has refused to follow up on openings provided by the Council of Ministers" (p. 472). This suggests a further complication of the national-supranational pattern that has not been explored here. It also emphasizes that the form of power employed does not necessarily determine whether the action makes for or against integration.

world only by trade and some other economic ties. The common market would not, however, be a single market comparable to that existing within each country, with common money, common laws, no serious legal barriers to the movement of capital and labor, and a government capable of applying general and specific policies to the whole area.

By its nature the common market is imperfect. It applies to only a few industries, each of them still closely linked with economic activities that remain national in the old sense. The common conditions to be established for the pooled industries are also limited. Moreover, like the distribution of power between the governments and the High Authority, the creation of the common market was bound to be much less clear-cut in reality than on paper. The next chapter will deal with the problems arising from these facts of partial integration. Here the aim is only to characterize the unit, or units, to which the Community's mixed system of governmental and supranational public supervision applies.

It is caricature to think of the national economies as *separate* at the outset. They were subject to separate jurisdictions but none was cut off from the others or from the rest of the world. Each imported significant amounts of coal, steel, or scrap; most had important exports. Ownership ran across national frontiers. What happened in one country, by way of rising or falling demand, increases in costs or prices, or expansion of productive capacity, had some effect on the others. Even the traditional trade barriers had been to some extent laid aside, as a temporary measure, before the common market was opened. Subsidies were as apt to be for the purpose of encouraging imports as for protecting domestic producers. There was, therefore, an appreciable degree of interconnection and interdependence among the coal and steel industries of the six countries before the Community was created. Nevertheless the common market, imperfect as it is, made a real change. It has created new and closer relations among the six countries and provided some assurance that these and some of the older relations would continue beyond the point at which, under the old scheme of things, one of the countries might have ended them.

The sharpest change was in trade barriers. Even more important than their immediate removal has been the assurance that they would not be reimposed to meet domestic problems. While continuous policing is a normal necessity to keep the common market open, imperfections in this sphere seem minor. Governments must find other means of solving problems than the traditional resort to protective devices. Businessmen must make their calculations on the assumption that they are living in a new "economic space" which cannot be closed off from the rest of the Community. The end of double-pricing and the elimination of national discrimination in most transport rates are closely related steps which have some effects similar to those of ending tariffs and quotas and also put buyers and sellers in different Community countries on a more nearly equal basis. Other transport matters are somewhat more complex. Over a sizable area, within which much of the Community's trade takes place, railroad rates are largely on a common basis for domestic and international shipments. Some discrepancies remain even within this area; outside it there is room for national manipulation; nothing major has been done about road and water transportation.

The extent to which these measures create a real, though imperfect, common market is emphasized by the difference between transactions within the common market and those with third countries. There are barriers to the latter which do not exist for internal transactions; the assurances that new barriers will not be raised are fewer and less firm. There is also less uniformity in external than in internal transactions. The Community countries do not have a common tariff on imports from the rest of the world, but they have very similar tariffs. It would be difficult to make major changes except by common action. Scrap is imported for the whole Community on a common basis and steel exports are to some extent cartelized. Beyond this, however, foreign trade policies and practices differ among the countries and are subject to different influences.

In matters other than trade and transportation it is much harder to define the sense in which there is a common market. Many rules apply generally but work out differently for different countries. Prices provide a clear and important example. During the transitional period, discrepancies arose in the Community's price structure that seemed incompatible with a true common market. Some of the causes could be expected to disappear with changes in business conditions. Others reflected government policies; these too might change, but not necessarily in ways that would permit the common market to function more effectively. The failure of buyers and sellers to depart from traditional commercial relations and habitual practices has also played its part in maintaining the separation of national markets. Although the creation of the common market has increased the amount of potential competition, only some of this potential has been realized. There has been increased interpenetration of the national economies but the growth of the common market has also been limited by a certain "respect" that the producers of one country seem to accord to the markets of others, coupled with some degree of collusion and cartelization.

Other differences within the Community result from special treatment, allowed in some cases by agreement. The Italian tariffs up to the end of the transitional period and the continuing Belgian coal subsidies are the most important examples. Other matters remain entirely within national jurisdictions, such as taxes, wages, and labor conditions. While the resulting differences need not impair the functioning of the common market, they put producers in different positions, as do other ties to their national economies. Closely related are the factors that shape each national industry separately. Investment, for instance, though governed by broad rules that apply equally throughout the Community, is in fact determined primarily by conditions peculiar to each country, influenced to some extent by what happens in the others. Linked with the other factors that make for separate national responses is the primary importance of the domestic market for most national industries. This does not mean that the common market can be ignored, but its influence is often not determining. The flow of capital and labor in the coal and steel industries is also subject to almost entirely national control.

What emerges from this rough summary is a delineation of the Community's "economic space" that is at least as complicated as the distribution of power traced in the previous section. The home market exerts the force of economic gravity on each national industry; not only tradition but transport costs, the advantages of an established position, and the inertia of the existing structure of production, explain this. A modifying factor is foreign trade, based on the physical need for certain supplies, the economic advantage of importing, and the possibilities of finding profitable export markets. Within the common market some of these trade links are particularly strong; on the supply side, the most notable cases are French dependence on German coke, Belgian dependence on French iron ore, and Italian dependence on French and German scrap; on the export side, the key factor is easier access to markets in the rest of the Community. The possibilities of trade have been increased by the common market and this alters the dimensions of the market with which producers, buyers, and sellers must reckon. It cannot be assumed that time will necessarily eliminate or weaken all the forces separating national economies.[13] Nevertheless, the conditions for perpetuating this separation are less good than they are between countries not joined in the Community.

The experience of the transitional period cannot be taken as a permanent description of the Community. At the same time, that experience makes it impossible to accept the simple picture of a common market projected by the

---

[13] The High Authority speaks of governmental intervention in pricing as "becoming more and more frequent and indeed taken for granted." HA, *Report*, Apr. 1958, v. 2, p. 68. Though overt subsidies have largely been eliminated, the variety of near-subsidies being used to support coal mining seems to be increasing.

broad terms of the Treaty or the usual explanations of how it would work and what it was intended to do. The industries of the Community are in a new economic space, different from that of a single economy and from those of national economies separated in the usual fashion. The characteristics of this new relation are only partly clear. There are factors making for greater unity and others that help maintain national differences. These are intimately related to but are not identical with the power and influence of the High Authority and of the governments on the affairs of the Community industries.

WHAT KIND OF PUBLIC CONTROL?

When the Treaty was being drafted, concern on the part of businessmen that the High Authority would be given too much power was matched by the worry of others that the High Authority would be too weak to control the businessmen, who might even make it a front for a cartel. The latter fear was met by the Treaty rules on cartels and concentrations and by giving labor a place on Community organs. The businessmen's fears were met by checks on the High Authority's power and by general but clear indications of intent. For instance, "The Community shall accomplish its mission . . . with limited intervention," and "In the field of production, the High Authority shall give preference to the indirect means of action at its disposal . . ." (Articles 5 and 57).

This was not the end of the matter, however. Along with these orientations, the High Authority had different powers for different circumstances. The businessmen waited to see how they might be used. The High Authority's fullest array of regulatory powers would come into play in times of surplus or scarcity; conscious of the traditional feast-or-famine character of their industries, some coal and steel producers wondered whether every year might not seem abnormal. The industrialists also felt that they could move more quickly and flexibly to cope with temporary difficulties than the High Authority which had to go through rather elaborate procedures and consult extensively before using some of its powers. Nor were they altogether happy about the elevation of labor representatives to points of vantage and influence over the coal and steel industries, but on this they were rather discreet.

The High Authority set out to show that it was neither *dirigiste* nor power-hungry. Frequent statements emphasized the Treaty mandate to keep direct intervention to a minimum. Explanation, consultation, and persuasion preceded most actions. The decision not to put a ceiling price on steel when the common market was opened expressed a certain degree of confidence in the industry, and even in its collusive practices. The record on investments is probably the best example of the High Authority's restraint in using its powers and of the accompanying emphasis on letting the industrialists make the key decisions. The policy on concentrations had a similar tenor. Repeatedly the High Authority showed that it was not trying to stretch its powers to the utmost and that it was prepared to leave business decisions to businessmen. At no time did it seem to be suppressing a desire for the powers that went with shortage or surplus and, in fact, it resisted pressure to decree that such states existed.

Restraint by the High Authority and the emphasis on nonintervention were not entirely the result of a wish to inspire the confidence of the business community. The High Authority's first task was to establish the common market. That was onerous enough to make it want to avoid the difficulties of more extensive regulation whenever possible. It is hard to govern complex industries. The High Authority was new, administratively and politically. It could not afford to issue a large number of orders that were not obeyed. It needed to be well prepared for what it did. The wise course seemed to be to develop knowledge, administrative capacity, and above all acceptance of its authority, before becoming involved in the complications of extensive regulation. It might have been particularly dangerous to assume the responsibility for the full management of the Community's economy implied in official recognition of a shortage. Moreover, the High Authority wanted to encourage the development of entrepreneurial attitudes that would take advantage of the common market and the new possibilities for competition. Flexibility and a sense of freedom were necessary if the coal and steel producers were to get away from decades of government control and cartelization; it would be hard enough to encourage people to behave this way; the chances of cultivating this attitude were better if the High Authority kept its own controls to a minimum and stressed the fact that so long as they stayed within the rules businessmen could pursue their affairs with little interference from it. This came to have little meaning for coal, but remained a reasonable consideration in dealing with the steel industry.

The High Authority did not carry restraint to the point of doing nothing. It established ceiling prices on coal and engaged in rather detailed regulation when it set zonal prices. The Belgian coal subsidy began on a rather broad basis but the modifications of it drew the High Authority quite far into the Belgian economy. The most extensive regulation came in the handling of scrap. Partly because its two purposes to some extent conflicted—cutting down on the use of scrap and keeping its price low—the High Authority was led from one regulatory measure to another until the structure became quite elaborate. This was an exception, however. For the most part the High Authority kept direct intervention and restrictions on industry to a minimum. It concentrated on setting and policing the rules according to which businessmen were to conduct themselves. On some matters it saw no need for close regulation since events were moving in directions it thought desirable. On others it relied on the self-regulation of industry, with the threat of High Authority action in the background. Sometimes it could follow a hands-off policy because governments were using their influence to produce results to which it did not object. A striking example of this was the removal of the ceiling on Ruhr coal prices. The High Authority could safely take this step because it knew that the German government was anxious to keep down the coal price and had reached an understanding with the producers. Later, when the producers defied the government, the High Authority felt that it could not interfere but took steps that seemed to assure that future price changes would be considered in three-cornered talks.

Understandings of this sort between government and industry were only part of "the network of tacit and official influences" that bound them together. "The governments need these industries; these industries need the governments. Intervention and 'unofficial' groupings are the rule. . . ." [14] For decades it had been so. The relation was accepted on both sides. There had been formal controls, too, but these were largely dropped or taken over by the High Authority when the Community was formed. But the governments kept many means of influencing the industries and could not avoid being held politically responsible for major developments. To shape the course of the coal and steel industries the governments sometimes used means as overt as the French government's fixing of the prices that could be charged by the steel-using industries. Government ownership took care of the problem in some areas: French, Saar, and some Dutch coal mining, half the Italian steel industry, and part of the German output of both products. The investment funds they supplied gave some governments direct leverage on the industries; tax laws that favored investment depended also on the government's general approval of the industry's performance. Sometimes special freight rates could be used to aid certain kinds of industrial development. With these and many other possible measures in the background, much of the governmental influence has probably been exercised through consultation and discussion in which the words of the government weigh heavily with the industry, while the industry's needs lead to compromises that commit the government to certain kinds of action (or inaction).

The aims of government policy toward the coal and steel industry vary from time to time. Over long periods the emphasis may be simply on expansion, full employment, and reasonable efficiency, matters that raise no serious

[14] François Perroux, *L'Europe sans Rivages*, 1954, p. 562.

differences between the government and the industry or between national policies and the pursuit of Community aims. During the boom years of the transitional period, the French and German governments, at least, were anxious to keep down coal and steel prices, which caused some difficulties. Governments were also anxious to assure supplies for the home market when demand was high. The industry would not ordinarily have any objection to this; the High Authority would be concerned, however, to be sure that the supplies of other countries were not too greatly curtailed. The Belgian government retained control of coal adaptation, which was one of the factors slowing that process. In recession a new set of problems would appear: the maintenance of employment and investment, the level of prices, and competition from third countries. Not all of these are matters on which the governments and the High Authority would necessarily differ, much less the industries and the governments, but additional questions would arise about the relative importance of the supranational and national powers within the Community and about the aims of public control. The experience of the transitional period provides no clear suggestion of answers to such questions but a strong presumption that, within the broad framework of Community principles, there would be negotiation and compromise as well as the direct assertion of authority.

In addition to the parts played by the governments and the High Authority, the third ingredient in the exercise of public control of business in the Community is the role of business itself. Except in the nationalized enterprises, decisions remain largely in the hands of businessmen. Public control can forbid, encourage, or aid, but it is the businessman who carries on business. Effective regulation depends on what he does as well as on what he is prevented from doing. The administration of controls over business can also be complicated and difficult. It has been customary in Europe to work through business organizations and to count on the self-government of industry to accomplish certain results. The Community's regulation of business has reflected these considerations.

Between the industries of each of the Community countries and their governments there were well-established working relations. The High Authority had to create wholly new relations with industry. It sought to do so by the combination of restraint, explanation, and negotiation already described. Through formal Community channels and otherwise the High Authority discussed problems with businessmen, explained alternative courses of action, showed what it thought was their interest and the Community's, and stressed its aim to keep intervention to a minimum. Backed by the power to act, the High Authority tried to persuade businessmen to follow policies that would make intervention unnecessary, as when it warned about the consequences of raising prices too high when the common market for steel was first opened.

While it sometimes imposed settlements over substantial industrial opposition, as in some of the scrap measures, the High Authority has also been willing, up to a point, to negotiate settlements with the industry. The most extreme example is undoubtedly the Georg settlement which in the end was rather different from what the High Authority originally intended. One of the factors contributing to that result was the need to find a mechanism that the German coal companies could be expected to operate. That required bargaining and compromise. In this case the German government and the unions, who were drawn into the negotiations, largely supported the industry, thus reducing the High Authority's area of maneuver, which gains from conflicts of interest. The other industries and governments in the Community were less interested in establishing competitive selling in the Ruhr than in some assurance of a fair share of the coal supply and of the maintenance of outside influence on the sales arrangements. This they largely got.

At a later stage the coal sales arrangements demonstrated the mingling of public control and the "self-government" of business. Because the Ruhr sales organizations could control distribution of an important share of Community coal, the High Authority relied on them to secure an equitable division of supplies instead of resorting to formal allocations and official declaration of a shortage. It approved the distribution, intervened in some of the negotiations about shares, and persuaded owners to limit their consumption from captive mines so that more coal could be channeled through the sales organizations. In the administration of scrap regulations the High Authority also made use of a business organization, subject to its control, until the Court held that it had illegally delegated too much power to this body. In these and other matters it seemed advantageous to the businessmen to comply as much as necessary with the High Authority's ideas, and to accept a certain degree of constraint. This still left them more freedom of action and provided better opportunities to influence the High Authority's policies than if full-blown regulations were applied. By conforming they also avoided pressure from governments, labor, and public opinion that might have gone with defiance.

The Treaty had anticipated close collaboration between the High Authority and business, at least to the extent of requiring consultation on a wide range of issues with the Consultative Committee where industry was represented. Having labor representatives as well, this body seemed to have the potential of becoming a "parliament of industry" of the sort that champions of functional representation have sought for many years. It has not turned out that way. In contrast to its approach to the Assembly, the High Authority has not encouraged the development of the Consultative Committee. It has instead stressed the fact that the Committee's role is only advisory and has even somewhat diverted attention from its deliberations.[15] It merely

---

[15] The Committee meets in private; its proceedings and reports are not published; the High Authority refused to transmit all its records to the Assembly. The *Journal Officiel* lists only the questions the High Authority has referred to the Committee and reports its assents. The Assembly's *Annuaire-Manuel* lists the meetings of the Committee and

puts questions to the Committee and encourages no initiative. To a degree it discouraged voting, stressing that its interest was in the views expressed by different groups.[16]

This limited role probably explains much of the evolution of employer attitudes toward the Committee summarized by Ernst Haas after a careful study of its work. At first business groups gave a lot of attention to the Consultative Committee because they thought it might be an important means of influencing the High Authority. But, "By 1955, this pattern had changed. Instead of bitter debate and careful votes, the bulk of the Committee's resolutions were being adopted by unanimity even though nothing like complete agreement prevailed in reality. Reports were unclear, resolutions tended to skirt the issue and absenteeism was rife. Interest lagged in direct proportion as the business representatives realized that they could gain access to the High Authority through orthodox lobbying channels and that the High Authority was not disposed to pay close attention to their deliberations in any case." [17]

Since April 1956 the High Authority has presented to the Consultative Committee its provisional forecasts of coal and steel production and needs for each quarter. Discussing these and the long-run policy statements which have been submitted from time to time might give the Committee a chance to influence the High Authority's outlook. There are no clear signs of this as yet. While the Consultative Committee's deliberations may remain valuable to the High Authority as occasions for explaining its own views to industry and labor, it appears that both industry and the High Authority find other channels more satisfactory means of coming to an understanding.

---

its main items of business but does not give votes or the tenor of recommendations. However, the Committee's transactions are widely known in industry and labor circles and quite a few copies of its documents seem to circulate around Europe.

[16] This also reduced the force of the complaint that labor is outnumbered on the Committee since the user representatives are also industrialists.

[17] Haas, cited, p. 340. For labor, in contrast, the Committee became "the major arena . . . in its fight for recognition and respectability" (p. 369).

The industries have not, of course, given up their close relations with governments which are still in a position to control many of their actions and to which they sometimes look for support in Community affairs. But they have found it advantageous to establish close relations with the High Authority as well, for on some matters they must increasingly look to Luxembourg instead of to Bonn, Paris, or Brussels. This in itself is a sign that the Community has reality and importance, that the supranational power is significant as well as the national powers. The initial suspicions of the businessmen have to some degree been overcome. For instance, the Delegate General of the Chambre Syndicale de la Sidérurgie Française told an Italian audience that there had been fewer conflicts of principle with the High Authority than might have been expected because "our epoch is strongly impregnated with pragmatism, from the economic point of view" and "the High Authority was very prudent in using the powers conferred on it." [18] There are also direct benefits for business in the division of power between governments and the High Authority. The same French industrialists who were opposed to giving "supranational technocrats" power that had always rested in familiar offices in Paris found themselves helped by the High Authority against their own government when they felt they needed higher prices. The Ruhr coal producers, who had thought the *dirigisme* they detected in the Treaty structure contrasted so unfavorably with German neo-liberalism, found they could escape domestic restraint on prices by appealing to the Treaty and its custodians in Luxembourg.

The other side of the equation, the ability of the High Authority to exercise effective control over industry, is not so clearly established. When Community producers resorted to illegal price-cutting in the recession of 1953-54, they virtually escaped from High Authority control. On the key cartel questions compromises have produced workable arrangements. In some matters the High Authority has

[18] Jacques Ferry, "L'Economia Francese sotto la Prova della CECA," *Mondo Economico*, Apr. 14, 1956, pp. 25-26.

been able to impose its will. It has been able to accomplish some things by persuasion. It has had the advantage of the Community's focusing of public and political attention on some coal and steel issues, and of an enhanced position for labor. By putting industry under broader surveillance, these factors have probably influenced business behavior. Through extensive negotiation and consultation, governments and industry have all become in part responsible for the success of compromise solutions and cannot treat them as alien and hostile arrangements.

For the most part, the transitional period did not severely test the possibilities of public control of business in the Community. Policy and mutual interest provided a wide area in which governments and the High Authority wanted industry to do substantially what it was doing. Compromise, self-restraint, and some direct regulation took care of most other problems. Direct challenges were largely avoided by both sides. When the High Authority and the governments were substantially in agreement, as on prices in the boom, they were able to influence results quite effectively. When they diverged and a government largely agreed with industry, as on the pace of Belgian coal adaptation, the High Authority was apt to be at a considerable disadvantage.

Again, as in other matters, what the transitional period shows about the public control of business in the Community is not a clear-cut formula but a complex and changing pattern of forces from which only a mixed result can be anticipated.

IN LIEU OF DEFINITION

To force the character of the Community as it has emerged in the transitional period into a formal definition is pointless. A series of changes have been set in motion but they are far from completed and need not continue to move at the pace, or even in the direction, they have shown so far. Real supranational power exists in the Community but national and private power also persist and play an important part in shaping its activity. They operate in a new "economic space" that comprises a common market, effective and reasonably durable, at least in terms of basic trading conditions, but also inherently imperfect. A substantial degree of public control of the coal and steel industries is an important feature of the Community. This is exercised by the High Authority, the governments acting in cooperation, and some of the governments acting separately. To a degree they work through and with business organizations. To a degree they pursue policies that leave business free to regulate itself within certain limits. Both courses stress the importance of private economic power, partly concentrated, partly divided along national and other lines. There are important aspects of the Community economy that are managed; in coal the extent of management is growing; if there is a definite development in steel it is not clear. But in both there are a series of managers, public and private, national and supranational.

The Community is crisscrossed by lines that divide interests and powers which coalesce in ways that change with time and purpose. Because the Community is a measure of partial integration, a certain tension between governments and the High Authority is built into it. But sometimes the governments and the High Authority move closely together. Private groups may be brakes on integration or they may have an interest in pushing it. Public control sometimes encourages private initiative and sometimes checks it. Such patterns as have emerged are for the moment and cannot be projected for the future. The novelty of the High Authority and the common market; the state of business activity; the dual position of the governments; and the limited application of the Treaty during the transitional period, all warrant the prediction of change but little else. More important guides to the future are to be found in the nature of some of the problems the Community faces, the interplay of forces on which it is built, and its general character as a far more mixed and complicated set of relations than is conventionally described. The transitional period shows that the existence of the Community has brought a change in the rules, in the distribution of power, in the conditions in which the coal and steel industries operate, and therefore in the nature of some of the problems and in the ways of dealing with any of them.

TWENTY-TWO

PARTIAL INTEGRATION AND ITS CONSEQUENCES

ALONG WITH the common market and supranationality, one of the essential attributes of the Schuman Plan was its character as a measure of partial integration. Only six countries took part, not the whole of Western Europe; only coal and steel were involved, not the complete array of raw materials, manufactured goods, farm products, and services that result from national economic activity; only certain practices in or affecting the pooled industries, not everything that concerned them, were covered by the Treaty. This was not because negotiation and compromise had cut the Schuman Plan down to size from a more grandiose design. Here and there, in certain matters affecting powers and functions, this had happened. These modifications were rather secondary, however. In its essentials the Community was true to the principles the French Foreign Minister set out in his original statement. From the beginning the Schuman Plan was conceived as a measure of partial integration.

This was not because anyone thought that limited integration of heavy industry was all that Europe needed to solve its major problems. Nor were there many who felt that pooling coal and steel was the ideal way to bring about broader integration. The justification was pragmatic. It was clear that the people of Europe were not willing to have their countries completely integrated, economically or politically. They might be prepared to accept some lesser measures of integration. For a number of reasons, some of them examined in the early chapters of this book, proponents of integration thought that coal and steel offered special possibilities; France and Germany, with different motives, might be prevailed on to agree to some kind of pooling; such a step would have repercussions in other fields. This calculation proved correct and so the Schuman Plan was adopted. The inevitable result was a series of problems that could never be completely solved in the terms of the coal and steel Treaty alone.

Many of these have been discussed in earlier chapters, as they affected prices, labor, transportation, and other matters. This chapter is concerned with the broader picture that emerges and with some basic questions about the effect of partial integration on the Community and of the Community's partial integration on other developments in Western European integration. A basic question seemed inherent in the Community's structure: Would the difficulties arising from partial integration be fatal flaws that must ultimately cause the failure of the Community, or would they prove to be points of fruitful friction leading to solutions that both strengthened the Community and broadened the area of integration? As might be expected, the transitional period has not established either of these clear-cut alternatives as the correct one; instead, it casts some doubt on the reality of the sharp alternatives.

THE POOLED AND THE UNPOOLED

There is a certain absurdity in drawing a line through an economic process and treating similar things differently because they are on opposite sides of it. This is the normal condition of international economic relations. To some extent, therefore, partial integration is also the usual state of affairs and its problems are familiar. They take on a special cast when relations are changed in basic ways as they are in the Coal and Steel Community. The Community goes far beyond conventional measures of cooperation in breaching the walls between national economies but it does not completely remove them; it is expected to produce greater results than those expected of the general run of international economic cooperation, but it does not fully merge the national economies. As a result, questions arise about how well this mechanism will work since it leaves the coal and steel industries of the six countries in the anomalous position of operating both in a pooled international economy and in an unpooled national economy. And even if the scheme does not fail, how much can be accomplished by pooling only two industries, basic as they are?

The Mechanism of Adjustment

Some of the main problems of partial integration concern national adjustment to the conditions of the common market. Ordinarily a nation can adjust its economy to international changes by manipulating trade barriers, by monetary measures that may include alterations of exchange rates, and by adaptation of domestic costs, prices, and the level and structure of production. The Community eliminates the first possibility (for transactions among the six countries), so it throws the entire adjustment on the other two. Domestic measures are to some extent regulated by Community rules about what governments or business enterprises can do. Monetary measures, however, escape Community rules almost entirely. The absence of any provisions about exchange rates was regarded from the first as the clearest illustration of the deficiencies of partial integration.

The reasoning was very clear. The High Authority had no jurisdiction over exchange rates; the subject was not likely to appear on the agenda of the Council of Ministers; the Treaty imposed no obligations. The six countries were all members of the International Monetary Fund and this required them to follow certain procedures in altering their exchange rates, but these rules had not in the past proved to be serious limitations to national action. Therefore, the Community might one day be faced with the fact that a member country had devalued its currency by an appreciable amount, say 20 or 30 per cent, perhaps for reasons that had nothing to do with coal and steel. The results seemed bound to be disturbing. What was dear would become cheap; coal and steel would presumably flow from the devaluing country to the others at an accelerated pace; imports, having become more costly, would presumably shrink. "The price changes might not reflect long-run changes in real costs but would upset competitive conditions and thereby the structure of production that was taking shape in response to the single market. Calculations the High Authority had made for the guidance of investments would be askew. . . ." [1] Governments could not defend themselves in the traditional manner, by imposing trade barriers, unless they resorted to the Treaty's escape clause for fundamental disequilibrium or the High Authority found emergency powers that could mitigate the impact of the devaluation. In either case there would be a setback to integration.

Then in the fall of 1957 France devalued its currency by 20 per cent and scarcely a ripple was perceptible in the Community. No one suggested resort to emergency clauses. No sharp shifts in trade took place. There was no hesitant pause as entrepreneurs and investors waited for the dust to settle. There were minor changes, as in the calculation of French payments of the Community tax. Arithmetic changed; French prices became generally the lowest in the Community in terms of other currencies; comparison of wages, labor costs, and investment totals were altered. But over the first year at least, no marked effects appeared in the Community's economy. How is this to be explained? Partly, it seems, by some features of the immediate situation, partly by mitigating factors likely to be present in most cases of devaluation, and partly, perhaps, by postponement or temporary obscuration of the results.

For years the common opinion had been that the franc was overvalued. Through a series of devices France had been making adjustments that permitted something like the real value of the money to make itself felt even though there was no formal change in the rate. It was what Ray-

[1] W. Diebold, Jr., "The Relevance of Federalism to Western European Economic Integration," in A. W. Macmahon, ed., *Federalism: Mature and Emergent* (Garden City, N.Y.: Doubleday, 1955), p. 445. I cite myself only to avoid being invidious; the literature is full of such passages.

mond Aron called *un système de dévaluation qui ne dit pas son nom*.[2] No doubt businessmen in France and other Community countries had been making allowances for the weak state of the franc and for the probability of its devaluation; thus devaluation had largely been discounted in advance. When it did come, the state of the market minimized its effect on prices. French prices had just risen. Demand in the Community was still high and was particularly strong in France. Devaluation was not accompanied by domestic measures permitting it to have its full impact on costs and demand. There was no increase in incentives for French producers to export nor were buyers in the rest of the Community able to get much steel at the lower French prices, though they may have gained some price advantage in negotiating with domestic suppliers.[3] It is not clear how much effect the devaluation had on the prices actually paid by French importers of coal and steel, but it is unlikely that the increase led to any appreciable reduction of imports. Subsequently, when demand for coal and steel slackened elsewhere in the Community, it stayed high in France so the shift in trade, if any, was likely to be in the opposite direction from that which the devaluation would tend to induce.

Largely in this manner the Community was cushioned against the shock of devaluation which, in principle, had seemed likely to be so disturbing to the common market. Then at the end of 1958 France again devalued, partly because the earlier step had had so little effect. Whether

[2] "L'Union Française et l'Europe," in R. Aron and others, *L'Unification Économique de l'Europe*, 1957, p. 27. This view is borne out by a careful study that concluded that the French government's purpose was largely "to regularize an existing situation, by incorporating in the exchange rate the effect of measures to aid exports and taxes on imports which had been the object of sharp complaints by our trading partners." A. Néel, "Les Premiers Effets, sur le Commerce Extérieur, de l'Operation 20%," *Études et Conjoncture*, Dec. 1958, p. 1163. The export subsidies and import taxes did not apply to coal and steel traded within the Community, but the main line of argument still applies.

[3] Some observers believe that since the nominal delivered price of French steel in other Community countries fell, large consumers were able to demand some measure of "alignment" from their domestic suppliers.

the new measures will have any marked effect on the common market cannot be judged as this book goes to press. The experience of 1957 does not refute the argument that the aims of partial integration are endangered by the fact that devaluation remains under national control. This rather easy transit of a dangerous situation is, however, an important piece of evidence that the Community may be able to accommodate itself to such limitations without major damage. It is also a reminder that the changes that may come about outside the Community process are not necessarily harmful to it; a more realistic French exchange rate, for instance, can only promote Community aims in the long run, not hinder them.

Another problem that seemed likely to result from partial integration was difficulty in national trade adjustments resulting from the fact that only coal and steel were pooled. Again the worry was based largely on impeccable, but general, reasoning. One of the main aims of removing trade barriers is to permit each country to expand production of those goods in which it has a comparative advantage while contracting output of those which it could more advantageously import. Each country has a better chance to make this adjustment without a net fall in production if trade barriers are removed on a wide range of goods. Then if production in one industry is cut, a compensating expansion in another may be made easier by improved access to foregin markets.[4] In spite of the limited common market, no problem of this sort seems to have arisen. Because of the general economic expansion, any shift of resources away from coal and steel that may have taken place led to differential rates of growth rather than severe contractions in production. Since total trade among the six countries was increasing and there was a substantial

[4] This argument was made in connection with the Stikker Plan; my *Trade and Payments in Western Europe*, 1952, pp. 208, 209. The argument concerns risks, not necessary consequences. A country would not necessarily have difficulty because it shifted resources from a pooled to an unpooled industry, even in terms of its foreign trade balance alone. The Treaty's adaptation provisions allowed for the possibility of developing activities outside the coal and steel industries.

degree of general trade liberalization, compensating exports
—if they were needed—were easier to find.

Still another element in the mechanism by which a
country may adjust its international position partly escapes
Community control. This is the regulation of trade with
third countries, particularly the control of imports. The
six countries have roughly coordinated their tariffs and
there are arrangements for a certain degree of Community
intervention in each country's trading practices. For the
most part, however, it is up to each government whether
it will restrict or promote imports from third countries.
One can easily imagine repercussions on the Community
economy. To conserve foreign exchange, a country may
use quotas or an import monopoly to cut off imports it has
ordinarily received from a third country, shifting its demand to Community suppliers who may already have difficulty meeting orders. Another country may encourge
imports of temporarily cheap foreign supplies, thereby
contributing to the accumulation of unsold stocks in another Community country. Suppose Germany had had a
difficult balance of payments position so that heavy coal
imports from the United States were a serious financial
strain; would Ruhr coal have continued to flow as freely
as it did to the other Community countries? Many variants
of the question are possible. In the transitional period no
serious difficulties arose, at least until the accumulation of
coal stocks in 1958 when the inability to get coordinated
action on imports added to the Community's difficulties.
Again, the imperfections stemming from partial integration
are very clear, but this time the seriousness of the problem
remains to be discovered.

Limited Powers

A second aspect of partial integration is the limit on the
powers the Community can exercise because national
governments retain jurisdiction over matters with which it
is concerned.[5] The best example, transportation, has been

[5] Throughout this section references to the Community are general,
and concern Treaty provisions and the jurisdiction of the Council of
Ministers as well as the powers of the High Authority.

fully examined in Chapter 8. The exclusion of taxes from the Community's jurisdiction caused fewer difficulties than might have been expected, partly because the Community was willing to adopt a rather sophisticated view of the proper standards to be applied in reconciling national practice and Community principle, and partly because established practices already conformed to this principle. The exclusion of wage rates and working conditions from Community jurisdiction raised still other questions. National differences in these matters are, within limits, quite compatible with a common market that functions properly.[6] It was reasonable, as well as politic, to exclude labor costs from the Community agenda because they are inevitably more closely tied to the rest of each unpooled national economy than to the practices of the pooled industries of other countries. Yet the fact that legislation affecting wages, working conditions, and the process of collective bargaining is all strictly national can create obstacles to Community action. The arrangements for the free movement of labor are rather restrictive largely because they had to be made by national action.

Each of these specific difficulties has its importance, but their broader significance lies in the fact that they are examples of limitations inherent in partial integration. Two basic industries are pried part way out of each national economy and subjected to different rules from those applying to the rest of the economy. Inevitably discrepancies result that create difficulties in the operation of the new rules and uncertainty about the effect of the combination. The Community's coal problems demonstrate the number and scope of these difficulties. Labor costs, transport rates, imports, marketing, and the elimination of high-cost production are all elements in the coal problem that are complicated by national links. The chances of dealing with them satisfactorily would be improved if the Community could devise a long-run coal policy. But the efforts to do

[6] This is, of course, also true of transport costs but, as Chapter 8 made clear, more is involved here than national differences in the money costs of transport services.

that have been studded with obvious, but significant, snags resulting from another aspect of partial integration. Coal is only one of the forms of the energy that moves modern economies. Its relation to the others is not a fact to be discovered; it is a matter that depends on governmental policies and private activities. Lacking power over other forms of energy the Community cannot formulate a reasonable coal policy unless governments coordinate their activities over a wider field.

National Influences

The coal problem shows clearly not only the difficulties that arise from the limits of Community power, but also those stemming from the influence of national economic developments on the Community industries. Domestic demand is of major importance for each national coal or steel industry. Most of that demand originates in industries that are not pooled, that are primarily influenced by national economic conditions and policies, and that may be cut off from the other countries of the Community by barriers to trade and payments. Through this demand, as well as directly, the Community industries are affected by the general economic policies of governments.

These policies respond to national pressures and predilections; they aim to solve national problems; they escape the control of Community organs or procedures. The Council of Ministers is supposed to coordinate national and Community action. What it has done about specific issues often fits this description, but efforts to work out comprehensive and continuing coordination have had few results. The aim would have to be a certain coherence among the national policies as well as between each of them and the Community's course of action. Resolutions and the organization of committees to do this began as early as 1953. Discussions have continued but during some periods they do not seem to have been taken very seriously. Somewhat greater interest appeared when in late 1957 and early 1958 it seemed possible that governments might have to take action to check a recession, but still nothing definite was accomplished.

It is hardly surprising that the effort at coordination should have produced meager results. It was never central to the Community's work; the national commitments were few and general; the urgent business in Luxembourg concerned coal, steel, and the transmutation of the Community from a thing of law into a reality; it would have been foolish of the High Authority, the main Community-builder, to make a major test of something over which it had no real control, which was inherently most difficult, and which was not one of the identifying marks of the Community. The whole idea of partial integration (or the functional approach) is that you can do something significant without solving the logically prior problem. The whole strategy of those who were interested in the Schuman Plan as a step toward uniting Europe was that it would force or encourage action on a broader scale, but it could not do that until it was itself first a reality and a going concern. Had a greater effort been made to get a coordination of national economic policies, it would probably have failed. In the treaty establishing the European Economic Community, the coordination of national economic policies has a more prominent place than in the coal and steel Treaty, but it remains an objective for the future. For all that has been said about the contemporary inadequacy of the old-fashioned nation-state, it remains the basis on which most political power is organized. As the bearer of political responsibility, each government must respond to a different set of requirements from those that would shape a common economic policy. To overcome the divergences would require major and continuous efforts at negotiation based on conviction of the advantages to be gained or, more likely, on pressure.

One form of pressure is the existence of measures of partial integration. The common market for coal and steel should, in principle at least, make for some degree of similarity in national policies because it partially molds some section of each national economy to a common market form, increases the exposure of each economy to the others, and sets some limits to what can be done by national action. How this might work is clear enough. The common market is a loophole in each national economic system. It takes on special importance if one country's economy moves in a way markedly different from the others. Let a country inflate so that its producers' costs rise; coal and steel can flow in from the rest of the Community, perhaps at lower prices, while neither import barriers nor subsidies may be freely used to protect domestic producers. Let a country deflate or hold down costs; foreign buyers may rush for its lower-priced goods, either driving up the prices it had sought to hold down or diverting to exports goods for which there is also a domestic need. One can easily think of a whole array of comparable examples affecting investment and other activities. Whether the consequences of these developments are good or bad for a country is not the question. The point is that the process escapes national control and may counteract national aims and measures. It tends, therefore, to limit the margins within which a national economy may move and so to establish a certain degree of similarity among the national economies.[7]

Whether, in fact, the Community has exercised noticeable pressure of this sort is not easy to tell. On matters affecting only coal and steel it may have had an influence, because the immediate effects on competitive positions could be foreseen. On economic policy in general, the common market probably did not have a major influence. Coal and steel do not seem to have decisive leverage in this

[7] The other side of this, of course, is the benefit a country may draw from the common market's service as a channel between national economies. A slackening of domestic demand may be compensated by a rise elsewhere, which producers have a chance to satisfy in the absence of trade barriers. Alternatively, pressure on supplies and prices in a country where demand is high may be eased by access to the coal and steel produced in the rest of the Community. As we have seen, the flow of supply and demand across national frontiers is not as easy as this ideal pattern suggests, but it does occur.

respect. As the High Authority says, ". . . experience has shown that governments do not base their general economic policies on the competitive position of two of their industries, however important they may be." [8] Perhaps just because coal and steel are such large and basic industries, ways can often be found of subjecting them to special treatment that may diverge, for the time being at least, from the course of general policy. There are also times when adjustments take the form of pressure by national policy on the common market, rather than vice versa, as we have seen in the episodes concerning prices.

Except when there is a direct impediment of this sort to the operation of the common market, it is not easy to trace the effect of national divergences on the Community. Many of the differences, as the Tinbergen committee's report argued, ought in principle to be taken care of by exchange rates and the relative factor costs in each country. Others undoubtedly alter the competitive position of producers of some countries. This by itself proves nothing about what they do to promote or hinder the Community's pursuit of its aims. The achievement of equal conditions for producers and consumers throughout the Community—which the national differences hinder—is an aim of the Treaty; it is also a means of moving toward a better allocation of resources throughout the six countries. How much can be achieved in the latter respect by a measure of partial integration is a most difficult question; uncertainty about it weakens the basis for appraising the effect of the national divergences on the Community. Not only the impediments in the common market but also the extent to which coal and steel move across national boundaries more easily than other goods raise questions about the allocation of resources.[9] In some respects movement of

[8] HA, *Report*, Apr. 1958, v. 1, p. 15.
[9] It could be argued that the common market may distort the allocation of resources. For instance, access to it might make the production of steel in one country more profitable than production of something else in which the country had a greater comparative advantage and that would be produced in larger quantity if its export market were not limited by trade barriers.

goods in the common market differs from conventional international trade; in other respects—as in the lack of movement of labor and capital—the pattern is familiar. And if the Community perpetuates distortions in the allocation of resources, or creates new ones, this is the usual state of affairs in international economic relations; likely alternatives, not ideal patterns, provide the basis for judging the influence of the Community.

All these issues need much more thorough investigation than I have been able to give them. The problem of determining the effect of national differences on the Community could be pursued by rigorous analysis of theory and principle, but it is questionable how much can be learned about the Community that way, because of the abstractions that would have to be made. The alternative process, of tracing the effect through close analysis of the Community industries, offers great difficulties. Refined statistical work might cast light on some of these problems, especially if sound data on costs and profit margins could be found. Even then I suspect the period has been too short and the other influences too numerous to permit the drawing of any reasonably sure conclusions about the effect of partial integration on the allocation of resources. Boom conditions over much of the transitional period plus a broad similarity of economic policy among the six countries, with the possible exception of France, also help to obscure the effects of the common market and the Treaty rules.

Uncertainty and Dynamics

This summary sketch of the economics of partial integration presents a regrettably indefinite picture. In part this results from the limits of the analysis I have undertaken which leaves many questions unanswered. In part the lack of certainty results from the changing circumstances that are inherent in the Community, not only because it is in an early stage, but because it is a dynamic factor, exerting pressure on economic policies and processes. Certain things are clear enough. Limiting integration to two major commodities and to certain activities concerning them checks what can be accomplished by the coal and steel pool. At most it can create a "common market" that is still something less than the "single market" that exists within each country. Even the common market is not likely to be perfect. Not all the essentials have been pooled, as the experience in transport and labor shows. Where the necessary elements are provided on paper, they may not be achieved in practice. Shortcomings in one field limit what can be done in others.[10] Yet, while imperfections abound, there is no basis in the experience of the transitional period for saying that the Community cannot function reasonably well or cannot have a significant effect because of "partial integration." It is not true that it must "expand or die." The Community functioned imperfectly. It had flaws. They were not fatal.

The opposite aspect of partial integration—its pressure for greater integration—is much more difficult to generalize about. The direct economic aspects of this process are far from clear, as we have seen. The experience in coal played a part in promoting wider cooperation on energy problems. The measures necessary to create the common market and its consequences for trade among the six countries undoubtedly had an effect on the unpooled parts of their economies, but how much this made for additional measures of cooperation or for harmonization of national actions without formal steps is hard to tell. The dynamic claimed for partial integration is not just economic. Part of it takes the form of pressure on the interests of groups and governments, causing them to move toward greater integration. It would require an intimate knowledge of policymaking in the six countries to assess what influence these considerations may have had on the further steps that were eventually taken. The experience of the Community undoubtedly played a part in the adoption of the treaties for the Common Market and Euratom, as we shall see. It did not do so,

---

[10] For instance, failure to act on water transportation led to maintenance of a greatly reduced French import subsidy on coal; failure to act on road transport led German steel producers to complain that the price rules did not perform their proper function.

however, as an economic dynamo, compelling action because of the problems it created and the forces it set in motion. Its influence was primarily that of example, demonstration, and, less directly, in providing a focus of discussion and agitation for broader integration, notably in the Assembly.

The pooling of two basic industries while other economic activity was left under varying degrees of national control had many irrational elements. It was logical to suppose that more would have to be done to permit the Community to operate effectively, or that it would be so hampered as to fail or shrink to minor importance. There have been slight tendencies in both directions, those hampering the Community being more marked. Yet this book's examination of the Community in the transitional period does not demonstrate that one or the other of these alternatives is the more likely. Instead it is a portrayal of the possibility of illogical coexistence.

THE SCHUMAN PLAN AND OTHER POOLS

When it began, the Schuman Plan was the "farthest north" of European integration. It was a salient into new territory, extending well forward from the established line of intergovernmental cooperation; Benelux had reconnoitered some of the same ground but without the range and complexity of the Schuman Plan. Almost no one doubted that the fate of the coal and steel pool was a key to the future course of European integration. In a dozen languages and a hundred ways people said: "If one is well-disposed toward European integration, then one point is absolutely dominant, namely, that the Schuman Plan must become a success. If the Schuman Plan fails, we can write off European integration; if the Schuman Plan succeeds, we have moved a significant step forward." [11]

If the Schuman Plan was part of a process, what was to be its relation to the other measures of European cooperation? Conscious of the unique character of the Coal and

[11] Geert Ruygers, "Gemeenschap voor Kolen en Staal," *Internationale Spectator*, Oct. 15, 1952, p. 2.

Steel Community, its builders took considerable pains to keep it markedly distinct, particularly from the inter-governmental agencies. "If one tries to link the Schuman organization directly in an organic fashion with all kinds of other agencies . . . then the great danger threatens of altering the special character, the special sovereignty, of the Schuman organization." [12] At the same time the Coal and Steel Community could not live in isolation. Other organizations would be dealing with matters bearing on the Community's business. More important, the "making of Europe" of which the Schuman Plan was to be a part could not proceed without creating more organizations to which it would have to be linked in one fashion or another. Where it stood in relation to the other European organizations became, therefore, one of the significant marks of the character and meaning of the Community.

The Existing Organizations

The Council of Europe originally seemed to some to be the embryo of European federation. When the Community Assembly was organized it turned out to include a number of parliamentarians who were also members of the Council of Europe's Consultative Assembly. A protocol to the Schuman Plan Treaty called for cooperation with that Assembly (significantly not with the Council of Europe as a whole, which was already having difficulty because its intergovernmental Committee of Ministers was paying little attention to what the Assembly wanted). As worked out in practice this cooperation had two main elements. Reports by the High Authority and the Common Assembly were sent to the Council of Europe. The two assemblies held an annual joint session at which the Community's record was debated. The Consultative Assembly wanted to go further. At one time it proposed that the joint sessions should vote after their debate; at another it sought joint meetings of committees. These overtures were rebuffed by the Common Assembly. Partly this was simply because of the obvious need to keep representatives of non-

[12] Same.

member countries out of Community affairs. Partly it stemmed from the feeling of the members of the Common Assembly that their body would lose its reason for existing if it permitted "the powers to become confused and the independent and sovereign element [of the Community] to become caught in the quicksands of consultative procedures and actions for which there was no political responsibility." [13]

From the point of view of the Coal and Steel Community this was a simple issue. There was no advantage in diluting the strength of the new effort by mixing it too freely with the weak potion that had resulted from an earlier, rather disappointing, effort. That was not a sensible way to move toward more European integration or to strengthen the supranational principle and the Community. For the Consultative Assembly, on the other hand, the effort to tie more closely to the Schuman Plan was an obvious way to seek greater influence than it had been able to achieve under its own statute. Having failed to break through the barrier of the Council of Europe's Committee of Ministers, the Consultative Assembly aspired to "coordinate" other measures of European cooperation. The Coal and Steel Community was a special object of this endeavor, not only because it was the most advanced stage of integration but also because there was a feeling—not borne out by the facts—that the Council of Europe had fathered the Coal and Steel Community.

There was no such question about the relation of the Coal and Steel Community to the OEEC, the main operating agency of Western European cooperation, or to the broader ECE. These were intergovernmental bodies; they dealt with some matters of interest to the Community but there could be no thought of a mingling of powers. The waiver of equal treatment in quantitative restrictions in coal and steel established the Community's position under the OEEC's Code of Liberalization. Representatives of the High Authority sat on many OEEC committees and the Community benefited from the older organization's activi-

[13] Jean Lyon, *L'Assemblée Commune de la C.E.C.A.* [1958], p. 63.

ties affecting trade and payments, but the relation was rather indirect. The fact that intra-European trade in many products was being liberalized through the OEEC helped the Community. The creation of the common market went ahead of, not against, the current. General liberalization reduced the risks that one of the six countries would have difficult trade adjustments because the common market was confined to two industries. More important, the fluidity in the financing of intra-European trade provided by the EPU relieved the Community of any serious concern over problems of payments and exchange controls, with which it was not well equipped to deal. "If the system of the European Payments Union . . . had not existed," said the High Authority's financial director, "I do not know how the ECSC could have worked properly."[14]

For the most part, the Community's relations with the OEEC and ECE consisted of participation in technical studies, economic analyses, and examinations of the market and long-run prospects. The detailed work on transportation problems done by the ECE was of some interest to the Community; had the OEEC and the Conference of Transportation Ministers made more headway in dealing with water transport, their activity would have been more significant for Community problems. As attention broadened from the coal problem to Europe's whole energy situation, cooperation was accompanied by a certain rivalry between the Community and the OEEC akin to the difference between the six-country approach that led to Euratom and the looser arrangements, including more countries, worked out under the OEEC.

The EDC Episode

All these relations were secondary, however, to the role that the designers of the Coal and Steel Community expected it to play in bringing about greater European integration. Two sets of forces would be at work, they

[14] Paul Delouvrier, "European Integration: Problems and Possibilities," in C. G. Haines, ed., *European Integration* (Baltimore: Johns Hopkins Press, 1957), p. 117.

thought. One was largely economic, the outward push of partial integration, creating problems requiring further measures of integration. The other was primarily political, the continued institution-building of the sort that had produced the Coal and Steel Community. The first we have already examined. The second showed itself rather soon, probably sooner than the designers of the Schuman Plan expected. The pace was forced by the Korean war and the discussion of German rearmament. Before work on the coal and steel Treaty was completed, governments were discussing the Pleven Plan which then took shape as the proposal for a European Defense Community, something like a military equivalent of the Schuman Plan. With two such agencies, the need for common guidance and political responsibility seemed obvious. This, and the opportunity to ride what appeared to be a tide of integration, produced proposals for a European Political Community. While falling far short of federation, the proposed political arrangements were more like the outlines of a federal Europe than any of the "functional" measures that had gone before.

The Coal and Steel Community was closely allied to the new proposals. The EDC was in many ways similar in structure; it was to have an assembly based on that of the Coal and Steel Community with certain additions. This assembly was supposed to draft the constitution for the EPC, but to speed the process the governments called on the Common Assembly to turn itself into the constituent body by adding the necessary members and becoming an Ad Hoc Assembly. The draft constitution that resulted linked the three agencies and looked toward the creation of a common market for the six countries going beyond coal and steel. This, and some of the economic implications of EDC, looked like the progress toward broader economic integration that was widely regarded as the natural development of the Coal and Steel Community. Most important of all, EDC and EPC seemed to mean that the drive for integration, the political will to create a larger Europe, the willingness of governments to work together and to give up the purely national use of some powers, had all grown since the first tentative step of the Schuman Plan was taken.

The failure of the EDC was, therefore, a serious blow to the Coal and Steel Community. The French Assembly's rejection of the EDC treaty in August 1954, though anticipated by many, left a certain numbness in Luxembourg that was soon followed by a cautious reassessment of possibilities. The legal position of the Community and its Treaty was unchanged. The High Authority's supranational powers were technically intact. The problems of pooling coal and steel remained the first order of business and had not altered. Yet the situation of the Community was changed. It was no longer the advance guard of a strong movement toward integration; it was more like an isolated outpost, the main army having been thrown far back and, at least temporarily, disorganized and confused. Assumptions about the milieu in which the Coal and Steel Community would be working had to be changed. One could no longer count on major steps toward integration in closely related matters. Most important of all, there was doubt about the willingness of governments to permit major issues to be settled by Community, instead of national, action. To be sure, it was only France that had rejected the EDC, but France was crucial to the Community and it could not be assumed that other governments would continue to adhere to the supranational principles of the Community if France did not.

Three lines of development seemed possible. The impetus to unify Europe broken, the Community might lose its drive and contract its activities to the point at which it would be doing largely technical work, coupled with a defense of as much of the common market as had been created. It might, too, have helped reach and supervise agreements among the governments or industries of the six countries. Such work would be useful, but it would make governments and industries the chief arbiters of what was done. The Community would have given up all claim to bring about radical change in Europe's heavy industry, much less to move rapidly toward broader integration. Had the defeat of EDC led to complete French rejection of a "European" policy, or had the other countries given up their interest in integration because of the French action, this would have been the consequence for the Coal and Steel Community.

The second and opposite alternative was for the Community to become a more active engine of integration than before. With other proposals temporarily dead and the Community threatened, the forces making for integration might have responded to the EDC defeat by gathering themselves for a renewed effort concentrating on the Coal and Steel Community as the only going concern in the field. They might have sought to build its strength and enhance its dynamic possibilities, counting heavily on the "spillover" of partial integration. Such an effort might have used many forms and channels; it could work through the Community organs, through national parliaments and governments, and by the mobilization of private and political influence.

Neither of these developments took place. Suggestions of each appeared as time passed, but in the main events and the Community followed a third course. The Community continued to do much of its work as it had before. The men in Luxembourg approached their problems soberly and rather cautiously. They stressed the tasks pertaining to coal, steel, and the common market rather than those making directly for broader measures of integration. Building the Community, not building Europe, was clearly the first order of business. The course already adopted of getting the agreement of governments and industry rather than stressing the High Authority's independent power became more clearly marked. The mixture of national and supranational elements probably made it easier for the Community to accommodate itself to the changed atmosphere after the EDC defeat than if everything had rested on the new supranational power. The accommodation did not require a sharp change in direction or method; it was a matter of emphasis. Since Western Europe no longer seemed on the verge of unifying itself, pressure to behave in an old-fashioned national manner was stronger and the rationale for it greater. This inevitably affected the balance of national and supranational elements in the Coal and Steel Community. For the time being at least the Community had to solve its problems in terms of its own treaty aided by cooperation among the governments without counting on the creation of other pools to resolve the contradictions of partial integration.

Two events illustrated the new state of affairs. Almost immediately after the EDC defeat the six countries and Britain provided a substitute, Western European Union. Like EDC, this provided for combined defense, but it called only for intergovernmental cooperation and established no important supranational power. This seemed to express the political reality of the time. The second event seemed almost a response. Monnet announced in November 1954 that he would leave the High Authority in order to work for further integration in a private capacity. In short, the Coal and Steel Community no longer seemed to provide the best driver's seat. [15]

The Messina Conference

The atmosphere had changed, but the Community remained. It had its champions and so did European integration. Some of them were not displeased at the defeat of EDC. Integrating armies was, in their view, a step that should be taken only after a solid economic and political foundation had been laid. But how were the supporters of integration to fit the Coal and Steel Community into the new scheme of things? What part could it play in advancing integration? First of all, it had to carry out its own mandate and establish its position. In this it was helped by the improved market for coal and steel. There was also a possibility of using the

[15] Of course, Monnet's decision was also based on his relation to the government of Pierre Mendès-France and its policies. The issues were, however, connected. As the Messina conference approached and the French government changed, Monnet indicated a willingness to reconsider his resignation, but it was too late.

Community as a center to agitate for additional steps. This the Assembly did, for instance, in May 1955 when it called on the foreign ministers of the six countries to organize a conference looking toward further measures of integration. This coincided roughly with a similar initiative by the Benelux governments. Out of the winter of reconsiderations and regrouping came the conference of Messina, at the beginning of June 1955. This marked the re-launching of the effort to integrate Europe which led to the creation of the Common Market and Euratom.

This is hindsight. At the time it was far from clear that Messina would have such consequences. The conference expressed intentions, established machinery for studying problems and devising new proposals, and kept alive the "European" issues, but Messina produced no sharp electric shock signaling a new determination to resume the process of uniting Europe.[16] Nevertheless, from Messina came the beginning of a new process that followed a different course from that of EDC and EPC and that succeeded where those had failed. This was not because striking new ideas were put forward at Messina or because a new dynamism was discovered there, but because the six governments gave a small group of men who wanted to take a big step in integration a chance to devise and promote workable plans and established a procedure that enabled them to take advantage of changing circumstances.

The period before and after Messina was marked by a revival of the debate about the ways and means of integration that had been partially stilled while the EDC and EPC discussions held the center of attention. The range of possibilities was broad. The existence of the Coal and Steel

[16] For instance, a well-informed Italian journal noted, right after the conference, that in the face of French uncertainties the other governments were gingerly in their approach, did not press for hard decisions, and showed no determination to push ahead. "The Ministers met to establish the status quo of the French political situation and to ascertain that nothing could be proposed that was not later to be nipped in the bud by the government at Paris and to decide, in short, that the Council [of Ministers] had nothing to decide." "La CECA e l'Europa dopo Messina," *Mondo Economico*, Je. 11, 1955.

Community was, up to a point, a recommendation for "sector integration," but not much else had been done that showed the possibilities of this approach. The Stikker Plan, roughly contemporary with Schuman's original proposal, had not been actively pursued. The effort to create a "green pool" in agriculture had largely foundered, ending as a loose arrangement for discussing agricultural problems in a special committee of the OEEC. Still, some form of functional or industry integration appealed to many. Energy and transport were the sectors that attracted the most attention. In part this reflected some of the experience of the Coal and Steel Community; interest in both fields, however, went back to an earlier time. Some thought it would be best to extend the High Authority's powers over transportation and energy; others favored separate new agencies with greater or less elaborate machinery for co-ordination with the Coal and Steel Community.

There were other people who strongly opposed the sector approach. For some the objection was to the extension of supranational powers and the risks of *dirigisme* which they associated with measures modeled on the Schuman Plan. Others believed that a multiplication of measures of partial integration, with separate communities for different products and functions, could only lead to disintegration of the European economy. The contradictions that could result from a series of measures of partial integration were clear enough. The risk that each would become the citadel of a special producer interest was obvious.

Those who rejected the sector approach and still wanted integration had a choice of advocating extensive political integration, which was generally regarded as most unlikely, or of pressing for economic integration that would cover a wide range of products and activities. Some form of customs union or common market was apt to be at the core of these proposals. The Benelux governments, which had been partisans of sector integration, shifted their support to the broader approach sometime before Messina.

There were others who believed that no major measures of economic integration could succeed if they were confined either to particular industries or to trade alone. The crucial requirement, according to this view, was for monetary integration without which, it was argued, there could be no check to the disturbing effects of inflation, balance of payments distortions, and the like. While there were a number of plans for a European currency commission, a Federal Reserve System, even a common currency, the main drive of this approach was toward adoption of similar national policies, easier financial transactions across national frontiers, and a revival of the cooperation and independence of central banks that formed part of the traditional liberal economic view of economic policy. Running through all the differences about the best kind of integration were questions about how much power should be retained by governments and the extent to which new agreements should rely on intergovernmental cooperation rather than the delegation of power to new agencies, however wide their jurisdiction.

Out of these conflicting and competing views the foreign ministers meeting at Messina produced a rather general formula combining several elements. Committees of experts working under the chairmanship of a political personality (Paul-Henri Spaak, as it turned out) were to report what would have to be done both to create a common market and to bring about "sector integration," especially in transport, nuclear energy, and conventional energy.[17] Despite this lack of clarity, despite the uncertainty whether the

[17] A key Belgian official, Baron Snoy, reported that in preparing for Messina the Benelux foreign ministers were primarily concerned with proposing a method of work (the committee of experts) and put less emphasis on the type of integration to be pursued, setting out several alternatives. Since no one else had given great attention to the method, the Benelux proposal was adopted, but "to our great astonishment we emerged from the conference at Messina with the joint adoption of all four of the alternative ways of re-launching integration that had been proposed." *Les Projets de Marché Commun, d'Euratom et d'Association des Territoires d'Outremer*, Conférence donnée le 12 Mars 1957 au Ministère des Affaires Économiques, Annexe au *Bulletin Mensuel de la Direction Générale des Études et de la Documentation*, no. 3 (Brussels: Ministère des Affaires Économiques, 1957). Quoted in *Chronique de Politique Étrangère*, Jl.–Nov. 1957, p. 419.

governments really meant to press very hard for major new measures of integration, despite the uncertainties of French politics, the work that began under Spaak made real progress. As time passed it became clear that, for a wide variety of reasons, the governments of the Six were prepared to make a serious effort to advance integration.

Lasting over the better half of two years, the negotiations had their ups and downs; rapid progress followed slow preparation; toilsome delay followed rapid progress. Several times negotiations seemed about to break down, sometimes on rather technical points, sometimes on questions of the highest political import. Economic issues and political issues, questions of national defense and domestic political disputes, emerged at one time or another as crucial elements in the work that was being done. Algeria, the Saar, Suez, Hungary, all played their parts. When the treaties were finally signed at Rome in March 1957 and ratified later that year so that they could come into effect at the beginning of 1958, it was apparent that the six countries had arrived at a new stage of integration. The partial integration of the Coal and Steel Community was henceforth to operate in a new setting.

The Community and the New Treaties

The Community played a part in the process by which integration reached a new stage. Formally, the meetings of the foreign ministers and heads of governments to decide the key issues were designated as meetings of "the countries belonging to the Coal and Steel Community." More important, members of the High Authority and its staff played an active part in the negotiations and especially in the work of the preparatory groups presided over by Spaak.[18] They had a good bit of expert knowledge and could draw on the experience of the Community on some matters. They were also concerned with the central issues,

[18] Formal participation ended when the governments took over the negotiations from Spaak's committee in May 1956, but informal activity continued.

believing that "full integration is the real point of the venture in which the Schuman Plan is the first stage." [19] At the same time, a working group of the Common Assembly kept in close touch with the negotiations. Committee discussions and debates in the Assembly, in some of which Spaak gave reports about the work of the preparatory groups, were part of the general European exploration of the new effort and may have had an influence in national parliaments.

The simple fact that the Coal and Steel Community existed made the creation of the new communities less of a leap into the unknown than the Schuman Plan had been in its time. A common market for coal and steel had been opened without disastrous results for anyone. Dislocation, unemployment, and bankruptcy had not followed the removal of old protection. There was less room for fear about what might result from the new treaties, less opportunity to use arguments invoking those fears. There was more understanding of the flexibility and compromise that were likely in the new entities, even though their constitutions assigned specific powers to supranational agencies and subjected industry to unfamiliar rules. More concretely, the drafters and negotiators were consciously looking at the "lessons" to be drawn from the experience of the Coal and Steel Community. It would be a mistake, however, to think of the Common Market and Euratom treaties as essentially revised versions of the Schuman Plan Treaty. They are similar in important ways and there are some provisions of the new treaties that differ from their older counterparts because of the experience of the Coal and Steel Community.[20] But there are also major differences that reflect not the Schuman Plan experience but the different problems the drafters of the new treaties faced and

---

[19] HA, Economics Division, *Memorandum on General Economic Integration in Europe*, Doc. 5579/55e (mimeographed English translation).
[20] For instance, the arrangements on adaptation aid, described on p. 422. I have made no effort in this section to discuss all the similarities and differences.

the difference between the aims, assumptions, and political climate of 1956-57 and those of 1950-51.

Of the two new communities, that concerned with atomic energy—Euratom—had the greater general similarity to the Coal and Steel Community. It was a measure of sector integration aimed particularly at pooling the resources of the six countries for the development of energy. It provided for the rather prompt creation of a common market in nuclear raw materials and equipment. The Euratom treaty did not, however, cover anything like the array of economic activities dealt with in the Coal and Steel Community. The focus of the new community was on development of peaceful uses of nuclear power and on control of fissile material. For development it emphasized joint enterprises and a common program that would permit the six countries to move ahead faster and more economically than if each were to make its way separately. While there was here a certain similarity with the Coal and Steel Community, the emphasis was different. Still greater was the difference inherent in the new community's monopoly of fissile materials, a measure based not on economic aims but on the political need to control dangerous materials and on concern for safety. While Euratom has a structure similar to that of the Coal and Steel Community in form, with Court, Assembly, Council of Ministers, and a supranational commission, the relative powers of the last two are quite different, with the supranational body having fewer powers and less discretion than the High Authority.

The European Economic Community—created by the Common Market treaty—is quite different again. This is not sector integration but a broad "horizontal" arrangement covering all trade (though agricultural products are put in a special category). To create the Common Market the new treaty reverses the approach of the Coal and Steel Community; not a quick removal of trade barriers followed by safeguarding measures to prevent disturbance and bring about adjustment, but a step-by-step removal of tariffs and quotas over a period of years was the method chosen. The transitional period, five years for the Coal and Steel Community, is extended to fifteen years or a little less in the new community, subdivided into stages in each of which certain steps are to be taken. Like its older counterpart, the new treaty contains provisions covering a wide range of economic activities. To compare them in detail with those of the coal and steel Treaty would require a lengthy analysis that would still leave many points unresolved because of uncertainty about the interpretation of the new treaty, which is still largely on paper. Broadly speaking, provisions of the economic union treaty are not as detailed as those in the coal and steel Treaty; the carrying out of many of them depends on further agreements among the governments and the elaboration of rules and methods by the European Economic Commission (the supranational body). In some matters, such as prices, the new treaty has little to say, in contrast to the detailed rules of the older document. In social policy, on the other hand, the new treaty, while lacking details, calls for a higher degree of "coordination" or harmonization than the coal and steel Treaty.

It will have to be left to the historian of the negotiations, or to some of the participants, to say to what extent any of these differences resulted from a study of the "lessons" of the Coal and Steel Community. For an outside observer it seems likely that most resulted from the circumstances of the negotiations, the difficulties of reaching concrete agreement on details of complex issues involving a wide range of products and circumstances, and the conflicting pressures of those who wanted to assure themselves of certain points and those unwilling to see too much power given to the new agencies.

If there were any general lessons to be learned from the Coal and Steel Community's experience they were two. The first was that without fairly explicit rules and commitments governments would only slowly agree to further measures of integration and might not for a considerable period of years take effective action, for instance, to free the movement of labor and capital or to coordinate transport rates and policies. The second lesson would be that even with apparently explicit provisions it was not always possible to do what the treaty seemed to say, because of changing circumstances and the impossibility of encompassing all the complications in a series of formulas. The choice made in negotiating these treaties—if it was a choice —was compatible with the general character of the new effort: the conditions for creating a customs union were made explicit, everything else was left in large part to continuing intergovernmental negotiation within the framework of more or less clearly defined objectives and principles. In large part the main accomplishment of the European Economic Community is not so much the specific provision that certain steps toward economic integration will be taken, but the provision of machinery and a framework within which further steps can be taken, partly under the pressure of the scheduled reduction of trade barriers among the six countries and the adoption of a common tariff in dealing with the rest of the world. Like the Euratom treaty the Common Market treaty provides for a distribution of powers in which the supranational body appears to have a less important position than the High Authority has in the Coal and Steel Community while the intergovernmental body is more important.

The New Communities and Partial Integration

Once in an advanced position as the only major measure of economic integration among the six countries, the Coal and Steel Community is now one part of a broad effort at integration. How the changed circumstances will affect the problems of partial integration remains a matter for speculation. Though the new measures greatly broaden the area of integration, they do relatively little to make good the specific inadequacies of the Coal and Steel Community.

Euratom comes closest. By extending integration to a potentially important source of energy it improves the chances of devising a general energy policy for the six countries and so promises help in meeting the Community's coal problems. However, Euratom and the Coal and Steel Community remain separate entities with different statutes, so there are problems in formulating a common energy policy.[21] Even perfect coordination would leave a gap. Between coal and nuclear energy lie oil, gas, and hydro-electricity, the sources of energy that for some time to come will be the real alternatives to coal. In an effort to remedy these weaknesses the foreign ministers, at the time the Euratom treaty was signed, asked the High Authority to take the lead in developing a common energy policy for the six countries. This may turn out to be one of the means of significantly advancing integration, but the promise lies in the future and for the time being the process is one of intergovernmental negotiation coupled with a certain leadership by supranational agencies and the work of experts.

Outside of energy, it is to the European Economic Community that one has to look for arrangements that could supplement the Coal and Steel Community's partial integration. One finds relatively little. The common market is greatly extended to include all trade (except in farm products) and not just that in coal and steel. This reduces the risk of difficulties in adjustment and of potential balance of payments disturbances that could result from a common market limited to a few products, but as we have seen these have not been troublesome issues. A more important benefit from broadening the common market could be the inclusion of the steel-using industries, most notably the automobile industry. However, the effects of such measures on the demand for steel, the allocation of orders and other matters, will be felt only gradually because in the new Common Market trade barriers will be removed only step by step. There does not appear to be anything in the new treaty that would directly affect the practice of govern-

---

[21] The possibility of entrusting the High Authority with the administration of the atomic energy agreement was seriously considered but had to be dropped when in the course of the negotiations the French government felt it necessary to promise the National Assembly that the new agencies would be separate from the Coal and Steel Community.

mental price-fixing in steel-using industries as a means of influencing steel prices.

The new community does little to extend integration at the points at which the Coal and Steel Community ran into obstacles because its treaty did not cover certain issues or because the key powers were left in governmental hands. For instance, the new treaty calls for common transport policies and establishes a series of procedures by which the Commission (the supranational body) is to propose measures to the governments. Except for a ban on national discrimination similar to that in the coal and steel Treaty, however, the new treaty is less explicit than the old in laying down rules for transport. With regard to the free movement of labor, the new treaty is more ambitious, calling for achievement of this goal by the end of the transitional period (twelve to fifteen years). Like the agreement reached under the coal and steel Treaty, the new treaty refers only to "free movement" in response to offers of jobs; it would apply, however, to all workers, not only those having special skills. It also provides for the possibility of working out procedures for moving to jobs in other industries. Wages and social policy are set out in the new treaty as matters on which the six countries will seek to coordinate their policies, but apart from a few specific provisions of relatively minor importance, this too is a matter for future action.

Always the picture is the same. By profession and procedure the new treaty provides the possibility of overcoming the limitations of partial integration. By itself it does not do so, either by detailed prescription or by assuring future performance. If additional evidence were needed of the fact that the creation of the Common Market and Euratom was not primarily a result of the *economic* dynamics set in motion by the imperfections of the Coal and Steel Community, this would seem to be it. There is, however, another sense in which the new treaty does something to overcome the deficiencies of partial integration. The most important aspect of the European Economic Community may not be the creation of a customs union but the setting in motion of a process making for broader measures of integration. It is significant in this respect that one of the first major sequels to the creation of the new community was an unofficial attack on the problems of coordinating national monetary policies, with the intention of preparing measures that could be urged on the governments as they moved ahead to create the economic community to which they were pledged; the coordinated action increasing currency convertibility in late 1958 fits the same pattern. To this process, the Coal and Steel Community is inevitably linked. But whether the result will in fact be to close the gaps in partial integration, or even to fulfill the promise of the new treaties, depends on more than what is written in these documents.

Organizational Links

The same Court and the same Assembly are to serve all three economic communities.[22] These two bodies have essentially the same roles in the new communities as in the Coal and Steel Community. The Assembly has been somewhat enlarged and is to work on proposals for its popular election (which will require governmental approval). Falling short of the proto-federal structure of the EPC, the new arrangements lend a certain measure of unity to the new stage of integration. Though the Court will be interpreting three separate treaties, the same judges will be at work, which must make for a certain uniformity of concepts and criteria. The same representative body will be debating the reports of all three "executives," the same committees examining their work.

The effect of linking the courts probably will be discernible only over a long period. The result of merging the assemblies should be apparent sooner and will undoubtedly be to increase the homogeneity of the three communities. Indeed, it seems quite likely that the focusing of discussion in the Assembly and its committees, with the

---

[22] Euratom and the EEC also share an advisory Economic and Social Commission which has some resemblance to the Consultative Committee.

corresponding work of the officials of the communities in preparing for these sessions, may serve as a significant force making for coordination and such uniformity as is compatible with the different problems, tasks, and rules of the three. A second reasonable possibility is that the new Assembly will work in much the same way that the Common Assembly has worked. There is a good bit of continuity. Members of the old Assembly form the core of the new body. While some new committees were added, the old ones provided the basic skeleton. A series of reports and statements made in the closing days of the Common Assembly were intended as messages to the new body, summarizing the experience of the transitional period and, in effect, recommending that the newcomers build on it. The new treaties give the Assembly a somewhat greater place than the Schuman Plan Treaty provided, but largely in ways that codify practices that have developed in the Coal and Steel Community.[23] There can be little doubt that the Assembly will make the formal advance a new platform from which to work for a further increase in influence. As one of its leading members pointed out: "One could hardly imagine the Council [of Ministers of the European Economic Community or of Euratom] putting questions to the Assembly in the abstract. Or that it would not set forth its problems, the solutions it envisaged, the advantages of each, and its own preferences. Or that it would not try to convince the Assembly and win its democratic support or, finally, that it would not make a point of justifying itself if, in the end, its decision did not conform to the opinions of the representatives of the people of the member states." [24]

It is a reasonable deduction from the natural history of political institutions that the European Parliamentary As-

[23] In the new treaties the Assembly can depose the executive by a vote of no confidence at any time, not just when debating the annual report. It also has to be consulted on a number of issues, is to debate the annual budget before it takes effect and can propose changes, and has a somewhat greater role if the treaties are revised.

[24] Pierre Wigny, *L'Assemblée Parlementaire dans l'Europe des Six*, 1958, p. 70.

sembly, as it is now called, will try to increase its influence by projecting the line established by the Common Assembly. But will it be equally adept at suppressing internal dissension and will it throw its weight so clearly on the side of speedier action, greater integration, and support for the supranational agencies? Here there is more uncertainty than in the other matters. Two differences between the old and the new communities may have some bearing on the outcome.

In the Coal and Steel Community the Assembly dealt primarily with the High Authority. In the EEC and Euratom it will be dealing both with the Commissions and with the Council of Ministers. It will have the power to depose the former but the decisions it will want to influence will often be those of the intergovernmental bodies. As members of national parliaments and national political parties the members of the European Assembly either support or oppose at home the ministers they will be meeting in another setting at Strasbourg. Considerations and pressures that were kept fairly far in the background in the Common Assembly may, therefore, be more important in shaping the character and work of the new Assembly where the political confrontation may be more direct.

The second difference concerns the constitution of the new Assembly. A salient feature of its predecessor was the conscious suppression of national alignments and the strenuous effort to find broad areas of agreement so that, as often as possible, there was an Assembly position, even if it had to be stated in rather general terms. No doubt a serious effort will be made to continue these practices. The success of that effort will be influenced not only by the larger direct role of governments in the new communities but also by possible changes in the Assembly resulting from the contrast between the breadth of the EEC and the relative narrowness of the Coal and Steel Community. Only a minority of the members of the Common Assembly spoke for groups directly involved in the coal and steel industries. There was probably a tendency for the parliamentarians who came to the Common Assembly to be chosen from those who were well disposed to the aims of the Community, at least after the German Socialists dropped their opposition. Both factors made it easier to create the corporate sense that prevailed and to get assent to positions favoring integration. In the new Assembly there may be more difficulties. Many more interests are affected by the Common Market and they are likely to find spokesmen in the Assembly. More parliamentarians may want to take part in the sessions of the new body. More agricultural spokesmen, for instance, are likely to make their way to Strasbourg; traditionally protectionist in most countries, they can hardly be counted on to be strong integrationists even though their own interests are largely safeguarded in the new community. It would not be surprising if the new Assembly had stronger "opposition" groups than the old. It is also possible, however, that part of the coal and steel Assembly's experience will be repeated and that service in the European Parliamentary Assembly will "educate" some of the opposition and influence their views.

Interaction between the new communities and the old one is likely to produce a series of problems. The EEC treaty specifically provides that nothing in it shall affect the coal and steel Treaty or the obligations of governments under it. Over an important range of issues this separation is meaningful enough. The Coal and Steel Community can continue to carry out many of its functions even though the EEC has not reached an equal state of integration. The six countries can carry out the scheduled removal of trade barriers under the EEC treaty with no major impact on the coal and steel pool. But over another wide range of issues, what is done in the new communities will affect what can be done in the old one.

While the EEC treaty provides in detail for the removal of trade barriers, in other matters "it confines itself to stating general principles of direction and to establishing procedures. . . ." [25] Some of these matters—transport, labor, national economic policies—are directly relevant to

[25] Wigny, cited, p. 62.

the working of the Coal and Steel Community and are also issues on which the specific arrangements called for by the older treaty have been completed so that the next steps depend on what the governments are willing to do. The governments, in turn, may find it awkward to move at one pace when action bears on coal and steel and at another when they are dealing with the rest of their economies. Simply as operating problems these overlapping interests will provide many occasions when committees, groups, and experts cannot reasonably be expected to confine themselves to one community or another if they are to be effective. Even in the staff work of the two new commissions and the High Authority these questions will arise. There will be a constant tendency to work through single bodies. In such matters as translation, communication, statistics, and printing, the only problems that arise are administrative. But different questions arise where work of greater substance is involved.

It might seem plausible, for instance, for the High Authority and the European Economic Commission to set up a single office to deal with cartels, concentrations, and restrictive business practices. The High Authority has experience and a staff; the new treaty extends jurisdiction. Close cooperation seems obviously desirable; unification has the appeal of efficiency. But there are difficulties. The new treaty's rules are not as explicit as those of the Coal and Steel Community. The regulation of business practices depends greatly on how the law is used and on the attitude of those charged with its administration. It is doubtful if the spirit animating the cartel provisions of the new treaty is the same as that which was behind "Europe's first antitrust law." [26] The key decisions on delicate issues will

[26] "It seems quite evident from the [Common Market] Treaty that the antitrust provisions are not regarded as priority business. . . . The substance of these articles is that the six nations have agreed to adopt regulations, sometime in the future, to enforce the antitrust prohibitions. Whether these regulations will be drafted in a spirit of strict enforcement remains to be seen. But it is important to note that these articles are not as stringent as the antitrust provisions of the European Coal and Steel Community. . . ." G. W. Ball. "The European Economic Community," in *The European Common Market* (American Management Association), 1958, pp. 52, 53.

be made by different bodies—the High Authority and the European Economic Commission—and the influence of governments may be thrown differently in each case. At best it will take the new community time to break in its people and procedures. Meanwhile, the High Authority may be standing on the verge of major decisions. It would be very reasonable, therefore, in spite of administrative appearances, for the High Authority to pursue its own course and to postpone any close linking of the staffs until it sees how the new community attacks its cartel problems.

Behind such administrative decisions, of which this is only an example, lie greater issues. Is it likely that the six governments and their supranational commissions will pursue a rigorous anticartel policy in one industry and not in others? Can they accept very different principles of pricing for various commodities? These things are possible but, unless circumstances differ greatly, they are not too likely. Thus a new sense appears in which partial integration not only continues to exist but becomes more complicated.

The Free Trade Area

Another set of complications arises from the possible extension of European economic integration beyond the six countries of the Community. Britain met the move to create a European Economic Community by proposing formation of a free trade area linking the EEC with other OEEC countries. Trade within the area would be free of tariffs and quotas, as in the Common Market, but each country could make its own arrangements for regulating trade with the outside world. It soon became apparent that an agreement on trade alone would not be acceptable to the Six who put great stock by the more comprehensive measures they had taken in the EEC treaty and were unwilling to give Britain, Scandinavia, Austria, Switzerland, and the others access to the commercial benefits of the customs union unless they would pay a higher price in policy commitments. As this passage is written (December 1958) it remains unclear what kind of agreement will emerge from the negotiations but it seems reasonably certain that either it will fall short of eliminating internal trade barriers or it will go beyond the grant of reciprocal trading advantages. In the process of reaching a compromise the negotiating governments may limit the broad measures of liberalization to certain sectors of trade while providing special arrangements to regulate the exchange of a number of major products (just as farm products are separately treated in the Common Market treaty).

Whatever relation is established between a free trade area and the general Common Market, questions will remain about the place of coal and steel. For most products there would be twelve to fifteen years in which to eliminate trade barriers, but for coal and steel a common market already exists. Four broad alternatives present themselves: (1) to include coal and steel in the Free Trade Area treaty, relying on the gradual reduction of the trade barriers between the Six and the others (and among the others) to provide for adjustments; (2) to include them in the treaty and remove duties immediately; (3) to exclude coal and steel from the Free Trade Area treaty, relying on separate trade negotiations and arrangements for consultation of the sort already used in the Community's external relations to bring about future changes; or, (4) to negotiate a coal and steel agreement linked to the Free Trade Area arrangements but providing special treatment for these products. The first two alternatives run into the objection of Community steel firms that they would be at a disadvantage in competing with British and Austrian producers not subject to the same rules of competition and pricing. The third alternative offers flexibility, the advantage of continuing an established course, and the avoidance of new complications. It has the disadvantage, however, of perpetuating differences between the Coal and Steel Community and the other measures of integration and risks losing for coal and steel the impetus to further removal of trade barriers that lies behind the Free Trade Area. (That is, of course, just the reason it appeals to some.) The fourth alternative provides means of compromising some of these issues but might do little to link the development of the Coal and Steel Community with that of other measures of integration. In particular, it seems likely to exclude coal and steel from the development of coordinated external relations.

Features of these alternatives could be combined in various ways. It seems quite likely that some sort of special treatment for coal and steel will be chosen, both to take account of the advanced stage of integration already reached in the Coal and Steel Community and to satisfy the resistance from several quarters in and out of the Community to more complete removal of trade barriers. This choice is made more likely by the fact that the probable economic gains from further removal of trade barriers between the Coal and Steel Community and the Free Trade Area do not seem great in the short run and would probably accrue principally to some of the smaller countries of the Free Trade Area rather than to the Community. Hence the pressure for linking the two measures is less a matter of economic advantage than of a general desire to press ahead with integration and to establish a certain degree of harmony among the numerous measures. There is, too, a very reasonable argument that since the Community involves so much more than the removal of trade barriers its extension to a free trade area must also involve more.[27] If the general Free Trade Area negotiations move in the same direction, special treatment for coal and steel may prove to be quite compatible with the more general arrangement.

Whatever course is chosen will raise some economic problems for the Community and for the "outer" countries of the Free Trade Area. For instance, the British, the

[27] For instance, a committee of the European Parliamentary Assembly judged it essential to have an agreement on pricing rules, governmental subsidies, and the application of the Community's rules for dealing with serious surpluses or shortages. This last might involve either application of similar rules over the whole Free Trade Area or an arrangement for temporarily isolating the Community market to the extent necessary to prevent trade from frustrating these regulations. APE, Commission de la Politique Commerciale et de Cooperation Économique avec les Pays Tiers. . . , *Rapport . . . par M. P. A. Blaisse, Rapporteur*, doc. 18, Je. 1958, p. 20 (mimeographed).

largest producers outside the Community, are worried about the effect of rules that would end their double-pricing of exports and raise the cost of domestic coal, steel, and scrap. Against easier access to Continental markets for their steel-using industries they weigh the effect of higher raw material costs on the much larger overseas sales of these industries. The Austrians, who are interested in access to Community markets, are also concerned about rules that would end their very low domestic price and perhaps about Community competition in certain products. Switzerland divides its attention between the problems its domestic steelworks might encounter without protection and its desire to let them buy raw materials and semi-finished products at the same prices as French and German producers. In Scandinavia the great interest is in lower prices. For the Community the question is whether the gains from removing trade barriers will be matched by the uncertainties of linking Community markets with those in which quite different rules apply to the conduct of business. None of these problems seems insuperable so long as the relation between the Community and the Free Trade Area countries is not a simple one limited only to the removal of trade barriers.

This arrangement, whatever it turns out to be, will open another chapter in the story of partial integration. Though changing the conditions of trade between the Community and Britain and the others will probably not have a major immediate effect, as time passes its influence will be felt not only in the pattern of purchases and sales but, probably, in the forces shaping the issues with which the Community must deal and the pressures influencing its decisions.

The Future of Integration

As a result of the steps the six governments have taken, the Coal and Steel Community is no longer an isolated measure of integration. It remains well in advance of what has been done in other fields. The new treaties do not specifically make good the deficiencies of the coal and steel Treaty but they provide a setting in which some of the irrationality resulting from partial integration may be removed, provided the new arrangements actually lead to a higher degree of economic integration in more than trade. The process of forming the Common Market is a rather slow one, as scheduled; if accompanying measures of integration in other fields move no more rapidly, the Coal and Steel Community's illogical coexistence will have to continue for some time. Since so much of what is done even in the Coal and Steel Community depends on what governments and private entrepreneurs are willing to do, and since that in turn is much influenced by the ambiance, the pace of integration under the new arrangements seems bound to have a major effect on the development of the Coal and Steel Community. There may be a reciprocal effect as well, but in the nature of things coal and steel cannot set the pace. The one respect in which the new situation may provide the High Authority with somewhat greater leverage in widening the area of partial integration is that there now exist both machinery and a set of obligations, or at least professions of purpose, which *may* make it easier to overcome some of the obstacles that have limited action in the past. Equally well the problem may be one of maintaining the position already achieved in the Coal and Steel Community if the pace of other measures of integration proves to be slow.

Twenty, perhaps even ten, years from now, the development from the partial integration of the Coal and Steel Community to a broader economic integration of Western Europe may seem clear. Interacting influences, some speeding the pace and some slowing it, may be apparent. Or the checks that held integration to a lower level than was expected may have showed themselves. In our short perspective, however, no such clear sequence can be established with certainty. Instead we can see only a complex of interrelated factors and the questions they raise.

PARTIAL INTEGRATION AND POLITICS

It is commonly said that the Schuman Plan is primarily a political measure and only secondarily an economic one.

Certainly in its origins broad political aims played the key role, first those of France, then those of Germany and the other countries. The modality of the Community, however, is economic and therefore it must also be examined in those terms, as it has been in this book. Inevitably it continues to have political consequences, both directly and through its economic effects, and it continues to be shaped by broad political forces. Since this study has not examined the political issues in detail it is impossible to draw firm conclusions about them, but a few general observations may suggest the main lines of development. These too can be thought of as problems of partial integration, because the Community is only part of a broad process of European integration and because the limitations on it are as much political as economic in their causes and expected consequences.

About the most ambitious of the political purposes, little can be said. The coal and steel pool, Schuman announced, would lay the foundations for Western European federation and make war between France and Germany "materially impossible." As to federation, it is clear that if there is some day a United States of Europe, the Coal and Steel Community will appear as one of the first stages by which it was achieved. Probably it will be the institution-building aspect of the Community rather than its economic foundation-laying that will seem most important. The Community has federal elements; its ability to function and survive provides a partial answer to doubts about whether sovereign nations can ever work in these ways. But whether the Community has done much to strengthen the political drive for a United States of Europe is a much harder question that must remain unanswered here in the absence of close analysis of the factors making for and against such a proposition. As to reducing the risk of war between France and Germany, the issue has happily seemed irrelevant in the postwar world. It is doubtful if anything done by the Community has made it "materially impossible" for the two countries to go to war against one another, but to examine that issue would require too many strained hypotheses to be fruitful. The improvement in relations between France and Germany has been one of the major political developments of postwar Europe. That the Coal and Steel Community contributed something to this can hardly be doubted, but to show how much and by what means would require a separate investigation.

There is also a reverse flow of influence. The good relations between the two countries and the willingness both governments have shown to cooperate with one another have done much to make the Coal and Steel Community workable. The wish to find amicable solutions of new and old troubles has helped prevent some Community problems from becoming more troublesome just as the transformation of some issues from bilateral questions into Community problems reduced direct points of friction between the two countries. For the Adenauer government and most French governments the collapse of the Coal and Steel Community would have been a major political failure. The survival of the Community in the difficult days after the collapse of the EDC and the avoidance of any basic challenge to its purposes or activities undoubtedly reflect the fact that its failure would have had repercussions going well beyond the immediate issues of coal and steel.

The day-to-day business of the Coal and Steel Community involves a continuing interplay of political forces within countries and in the relations between governments. Personalities, too, are important, not only to the character of compromises and courses of action, but also for the absorption of the Community into the political blood stream of Europe. A former member of the High Authority becomes finance minister; a man who has been a leading figure in the Common Assembly becomes foreign minister; a cabinet member who has looked askance at the Community finds that the chance of getting one of his policies adopted at home is improved by rallying support from other governments in the Council of Ministers; a union official finds that cooperation with foreign labor leaders reduces the force of an argument employers at home had used to refuse his demands; in such ways the

Community influences national politics. National considerations also influence the Community; some benefits must visibly accrue to all the participating countries if acceptance of the Community is to grow and the willingness to compromise is to be kept alive. The earlier chapters of this book are full of examples of action, inaction, haste, delay, and neat balancing of advantages and disadvantages that reflect the political life of the six countries as much as they do the economic problems of the Community. A judicious mixture of political adroitness and a position somewhat removed from the immediate pressures of politics, fortified by appeals to the legal requirements of the Treaty and the economic needs of the Community, provides the High Authority and the governments alike with a method of conducting Community affairs that is politically realistic and responsive but that escapes some of the exigencies of intergovernmental cooperation. So far this effort to blend the novelty of supranationalism with the familiarity of national and international politics has proved viable. It contains at least the promise of developing in ways that will make the Community and its processes an integral part of the Western European political and economic system, not an insecurely fixed capsule outside the main body.

There is here something like the political equivalent of the pattern of partial economic integration. The Community was created by a series of national decisions. It was based on the assumption, however, that certain enduring interests of the six nations could best be served by abridging the ability of each government to pursue what it considered to be the best national policy at any given moment. The right to voice national interests was not given up, and in some matters the right to act on them was also preserved. National power and policy continue to have a major influence on the course of affairs in the Community. At the same time there are real Community decisions that go beyond the reconciliation or compromising of national interests by negotiation—though these traditional processes usually have an important part as well. The fact that each government does not have to assent specifically to each decision is important not only in getting action but, in some cases at least, in enabling a government to pursue a course that it might prefer but could not have adopted independently for domestic political reasons. Limits to this process are set by the fact that the political responsibility of the High Authority—or one might say of the Community as a whole—is diffuse and very indirect.[28] The governments, on the other hand, may stand or fall on matters for which they have no legal responsibility under the Treaty. It is in this margin that the political implications of partial integration must play themselves out.

The Community introduces new elements into Europe's political processes. Conflicts of interest that used to be settled nationally, with the compromise or synthesis becoming governmental policy, may now continue as conflicts in different areas throughout the Community. The result must often be a different final constellation of forces, and some difference in the action taken. One would have to look very closely at many cases to form an opinion as to how much this happened in the course of the transitional period, but that it did occur seems clear. From it flows a related change in the political process, whereby interests that cut across national lines may find expression in different ways and with different political force than if each has to operate primarily on a national basis. The change is not total and perhaps not yet radical, for the national forum remains of vital importance, both for Community issues and for others. But by a natural law of politics the fact that decisions can be made by a given process must cause power and influence to be organized in ways that bear on that process. In the Community this means that

[28] But it is real even though the High Authority can only be discharged by a large adverse vote of the Assembly on the annual report. If the High Authority relied only on legal powers to determine something against the will of all the interested parties, it would almost certainly fail. The High Authority's policy of persuading the governments and sometimes the private interests as well to courses of action, though it rested in the first instance on the need to build a community of interest, also reflected a kind of political responsibility.

Luxembourg has been added to the national capitals as a relevant focus of political action.[29]

The kind of study I have conducted throws only a little light on the political consequences of partial economic integration. There is at least as much evidence that political desires for continued integration helped ensure the operation of the economic measures as that the economic processes increased the willingness for political cooperation, in accordance with the "functionalist" theory of partial integration. There can be no doubt, however, that the Community has had political consequences. Although national influences remain of major importance, there has also been set in motion a process by which a certain degree of political integration is being achieved. Perhaps the salient political fact is the continued existence of the Community, reflecting the continued will of the governments to maintain this form of economic integration (or at a minimum their unwillingness to see it fail). This has been accompanied by the apparent acceptance of the Community as an established part of the scene in Western Europe. These are among the facts that warrant concluding this survey of the Community's first years with a chapter looking toward the future.

[29] "The 'good Europeans' are not the main creators of the regional community that is growing up; the process of community formation is dominated by nationally constituted groups with specific interests and aims, willing and able to adjust their aspirations by turning to supranational means when this course appears profitable." E. B. Haas, *The Uniting of Europe*, 1958, p. xiv. Much of Haas' study is devoted to an examination of these issues.

TWENTY-THREE

THE FUTURE OF THE COMMUNITY

NOT PREDICTION but the need to look at some long-run problems justifies such a title. From the beginning, the long-run future has been central to serious thought about the Community. The Treaty was signed for fifty years, a kind of forever in economics, and perhaps these days in politics too. The Community's long-run development and continuing influence were regarded as more important for the European economy than its immediate impact. The major political results expected from the Community lay in such evolutionary changes as the creation of common interests that would eliminate the hereditary conflicts of France and Germany and in the emergence of some kind of European federation. While the immediate impact of the common market and of the creation of the High Authority was the subject of many hopes and fears, the *posse* of the Community was always more momentous than its *esse*.

The short history of the transitional period is itself a warning against prediction, and especially against the acceptance of logically plausible expositions of the lines of development the Community *must* follow. Still, the experience of these five years suggests some probable features of the Community's future and indicates rather clearly several of the questions that will have to be faced in the years to come. This chapter does not pretend to answer these questions, only to clarify some of them and to post a few markers by which the future course of the Community may be gauged.

HAS THE COMMUNITY A FUTURE?

The transitional period warrants the belief that it has. The Community survived its time of testing and overcame some rather serious obstacles. It maintained its essential character, emerging from the transitional period still recognizably the product of Schuman's proposal of May 9, 1950. Meanwhile the Community had demonstrated a higher degree of flexibility in method and greater adaptability to changing circumstances than might have been imagined by a reader of the Treaty or a listener to the ratification debates.

Contrary to a widely held view the Community was not simply borne along through the transitional period by economic expansion and a high demand for coal and steel. At the beginning and end of the period there were recessions. In between, the boom, while it eased many problems, also created some difficulties for the Community. Politically the Community had an uncertain start. It commanded sizable majorities in all the parliaments and had the support of the six governments, but this backing was shot through with hesitation and reserve. Among the economic groups with which the Community had to deal, support was much less general, skepticism was marked, and a good deal of opposition was overt or only slightly veiled. In these matters the Community substantially improved its position during the transitional period, disarming some opposition, dispelling some worries, and generating additional support. One of the principal sources of strength of Schuman's original initiative was a broad, rather diffuse, desire for European integration. But this wave, which was supposed to waft the Coal and Steel Community over the difficulties of partial integration, broke on the EDC. The Community weathered this trouble and by the end of the transitional period the wave of integration had gathered new strength. However it had also taken on a somewhat different form; the new measures did not promise to solve many of the Coal and Steel Community's problems and involved at least

the risk of slowing some of its efforts to strengthen supranational powers.

The Coal and Steel Community has not only survived,
it appears to have established itself as an accepted part of
the political and economic life of Western Europe. Little
is heard of the old debates whether it is a desirable or an
undesirable thing, though many words are exchanged as
to how it could be made better. Opposition has given way
to acceptance, either because the Community has brought
positive advantage or because it is only realistic to "face
facts" and find the best way of working under the new
arrangements. No significant group in the six countries
devotes itself to the undoing of the Community or the
abrogation of the Treaty. Only occasionally does someone
in a position of importance say, in private, that he honestly
would prefer that the Community did not exist. Though
mixed emotions lie behind this rather general acceptance
of the Community, it remains a political fact of considerable importance. To be taken for granted, to be part
of the social scenery, is humdrum but it is the stuff
of durability. The efforts of interest groups to get as
much out of the Community for themselves as they can are
further evidence that it is putting down political roots.
These efforts, and those that governments make to manipulate the Community, may entail dangers to its proper
functioning and raise questions about what it is accom-
plishing, but they are signs that it is real. If the Community could be ignored, its durability would be in doubt.

The Community is likely not only to continue, but to
maintain something like the form it has established. Though
the Convention governing the transitional period provided
a number of safeguards, special treatment for certain cases,
and a step-by-step approach in the introduction of some
measures, the regime actually in effect approximated that
of the Treaty rather closely. This was partly because the
strong demand for coal and steel made it possible to dispense with some of the safeguards that might have been
needed in less buoyant times. One result, as we have seen,

is that some of the adjustments expected in the transitional period remain to be faced by the Community under the full Treaty regime. This strengthens the supposition that the flexibility the Community demonstrated during its first five years will continue to be needed. Flexibility will also be called for by the need to accommodate the Community and the new measures of Western European integration to one another. Though flexibility remains necessary to durability it also has its risks, principally those of compromises carried to the point of jeopardizing the Community's purposes. The firmness required to prevent flexibility's becoming total malleability may well be linked to the persistence of the initial conception and drive of the Community in the minds of leading figures of the six countries. Later, preservation of the essence of the Community may depend on calculations of long-run interests, public and private, and on the effect on the pace and character of integration of broader forces than those inside the Coal and Steel Community.

To say that the Community appears to have staying power is not to say that it is so firmly riveted to the basic structure of Western Europe that it cannot be destroyed or twisted out of shape. Its founders conceived of the pool's eventually creating such an intermingling of interests, such a blurring of familiar national calculations of advantage, such a creation of political crosscurrents, that ultimately there would emerge a new structure of interests that would make reversion to the old order impossible. There is no reason to believe the Community has reached this state. It is, in fact, very doubtful that by itself alone it ever could, because for all their importance as basic industries, coal and steel do not carry enough weight to determine the whole course of a nation's policy. It is hard to conceive of circumstances in which a country that wanted to break out of the mold of integration would refrain from doing so solely to avoid sacrificing the advantages it obtained from the coal and steel pool. Of course, the more fully integration develops, the harder it would be for a country to disengage and the higher the price it might have to pay.

Even now there is a good bit of tenacity in the Coal and Steel Community, but there is no reason to believe that the common market, the organs of the Community, or the will among the Six to order their affairs in this way are established beyond the possibility of destruction.

The Community weathered enough difficulties to show that it is not fragile. It was not, however, subjected to heavy adverse pressure. Three kinds of danger could threaten it. Strong and persistent opposition within the Community, by governments or interest groups, has not developed. The diplomacy of the High Authority aimed to avoid it, seeking compromise and consent even at the price of delay and less drastic action than could legally have been taken. In addition the Community, by design and by accident, has promoted at least some of the interests of each country and every major group. While strong opposition may still appear, the risk seems smaller and the building of the Community may have proceeded to a point at which strong internal opposition would not be fatal.

Of the Community in recession we know something, but about its reaction to a serious depression, the second kind of heavy adverse pressure, we can only speculate. It is common form to assume that few if any measures of international economic cooperation can resist the buffeting of a major depression. Exposed to the political, economic, and social pressures of a great fall in demand, runs the argument, governments will seize every opportunity to act where they can act quickly, letting international commitments and agreed rules of behavior go by the board. This may well be so, but perhaps it ought not to be taken for granted. Obviously, a serious fall in demand would put great strain on the Community. None of the six governments would be likely to stand by, refusing to try to cut off imports, if coal or steel from one of the others was coming into its depressed markets in amounts that added seriously to the troubles of its domestic producers. A Community government would surely try to get around Treaty rules that stood in the way of action it thought would be effective in holding up prices. Producers might well try to dump on foreign markets coal and steel that were unsaleable at home, without much regard to Community rules about fair competition. Such a set of events might break up the Community, or at least cancel it as an effective entity for some period of time.

There is an alternative, however. The Treaty drafters tried to anticipate the problems of depression. In times of "manifest crisis" the High Authority and the governments may act to limit production and hold up prices. Other powers might also be invoked to deal with the difficulties of depression. There is a reasonable possibility, then, that before they resorted to purely national measures governments and producers would try the recourse provided by the Treaty. None of the six national economies is well situated to cope with a serious, world-wide depression by independent action. Community action also has its limits but offers at least a prospect of coherent policies covering a larger area. The willingness of governments to try to follow this course may well depend on the indications the High Authority gives of the speed with which it may take exceptional measures (plus, perhaps, its toleration of some national steps not wholly in accord with the ideals of the Community). Whether measures are national or joint, a period of depression would undoubtedly lead to virtual suspension of free trade, to a reduction of competition, and perhaps to severe tests of the High Authority's strength if it tried to enforce measures opposed by governments and industry. It would, however, be jumping to conclusions to assume that the Schuman Plan cannot survive a depression. It has cohesive as well as divisive elements, and this new kind of international economic cooperation may respond to familiar dangers in new ways.

A third kind of major danger to the Community would come from a basic political change in one of the member countries. Obviously the Community can be torn apart by the people who put it together. If the governments of the six countries, or of only one or two of the larger ones, were to abandon Western European integration as a major aim, the Community would collapse or, at least, grind to some kind of stop. At present none of the groups likely to come to power in any of the six countries professes a wish to dismantle the Community. The German Socialists, once its main opponents, have now become supporters of European integration in general. There are, however, groups in all the countries—and in virtually all the parties as well— that are not strongly attached to European integration or that definitely dislike the Schuman Plan approach. A growth in their influence, which might well result from developments having nothing to do with their views on this issue, might be reflected in governmental behavior in coal and steel matters. Without attempting to dissolve the Community a reluctant government could do much to impair it. This, some thought, might be the policy followed by France when De Gaulle came to power. By early 1959 there was no sign of it. Instead, a policy of support for European integration largely silenced critics of the Community among the General's supporters, at least for the time being.

Another kind of political change could affect the Community's future. A certain equation of force and power among the participating countries, imprecise but real, underlies the Community as it does any major set of relations among nations. Changes in the terms of this equation that are not too abrupt are compatible with stability; one of the primary political aims of the Community was to absorb some of the impact of the growth of German power. But there are also limits to the magnitude and speed of the shifts which can be tolerated without driving one or more members of the Community to the conclusion that it will lose from continuing in the pool.

Many Frenchmen believed—or said they believed—that return of the Saar to Germany would cause that kind of an upset. The demonstration was largely mathematical. If the production of the Saar was added to that of France, the combination approached the German totals, at least in steel during the early years; but if instead the Saar was added to the German production, the total was so much larger than France's that the "balance" of the Community was destroyed, according to this line of reasoning.[1] Applied to the formal operation of the Community, this calculation had little meaning; as a factor bearing on the actual working of the Community, the importance of the potential shift was exaggerated; as a symptom of the fears of some Frenchmen about the relation of forces on which the Community rested, it was important. Often enough French spokesmen, particularly those from heavy industry, spoke as if France could not go on in the Community if the Saar returned to Germany. They were establishing a negotiating position, of course, but there was more to it than that. When the shift actually took place and it was agreed that the Saar should move by stages out of the French economic area to political union with Germany, the impact proved not so marked, the French outcry not so great. Several factors contributed. The process was slow enough for its inevitable result to become obvious well before the final steps were taken, so the French had time to accommodate themselves to it. The guarantees the French received about coal supplies and access to the Saar market helped, along with the agreement on canalizing the Moselle. So did the German government's willingness, at an earlier stage, to accept a "European" status for the Saar, until that was rejected by the Saarlanders. The development of the Community itself played a part; it blunted the edge of purely national calculations and showed that the shift was unlikely to have as great an effect on the operation of the pool as the French had feared. The transfer was agreed on by Bonn and Paris; it was not an item of Community business. But the Community's ability to absorb the change—which undoubtedly affected the balance of forces within the pool—was one more sign of its staying power.

[1] For instance, in 1953 the Saar made the following differences to the percentage of Community production provided by France and Germany:

	France plus Saar	Germany	France	Germany plus Saar
Coal	29	53	22	59
Steel	32	39	25	46

The reunification of Germany is another potential shift in the relative strength of countries that could affect the Community. At one stroke Germany would increase its share of the Community's territory, population, and gross national product, as well as its output of coal and steel. Like the Saar issue, this possibility has been of some concern to people in the other countries, not only because of its effect on the Coal and Steel Community. But the concern seems to have grown less acute, presumably because the possibility has grown more remote. Sometimes emphasis is put on the fact that the addition to German size and strength on paper would be accompanied by a complex of internal German problems (and very likely heavy calls on German resources and effort) arising from the difficulty of putting the two, now disparate, parts of the country together. Perhaps the main factors subduing discussion of the impact of German reunification on the Community are the number of assumptions that have to be made about the circumstances in which reunification could come about and the fact that they raise far more fundamental questions about Western European integration than those concerning the relative importance of Germany as a coal and steel producer.

Depression or broad political changes in the member countries could undo the Community, though it cannot be taken for granted that they would. Short of these, however, there is every reason to believe that the Community has both the durability and the flexibility necessary to enable it to go on for some time, in recognizable though possibly changing form, developing or altering the structure that has emerged from the transitional period.

A REVISION OF THE TREATY?

Unprecedented measures were being tried out during the transitional period. It was natural to think that the lessons of that experience might be used to revise the Treaty when it came fully into force. The drafters did not, however, provide for a general review at the end of the transitional period, as might have seemed logical and as has sometimes been done in complex international arrangements. Not oversight but high policy probably explains the omission. One of the great aims of the Schuman Plan's backers was to give it continuity and long life; they had to fight off those who wanted a tentative commitment for a few years, to be reaffirmed if the early experience was satisfactory. The plausible pragmatism of the latter approach was rebutted by the persuasive argument that a temporary commitment could not possibly serve as the basis for creating a community. If engagements were tentative, each government would have to hedge and no real pooling of the industries would result. If commitments were open to renegotiation after five years, the transitional period would be a time of political maneuver and jockeying, within each country and internationally among the governments. It followed that even the lesser provision, to review the Treaty at the end of the transitional period for the purpose of amending and revising it, had dangers. One might want to do that, but a firm stipulation might plunge the Community into something very like renegotiation at a most disadvantageous moment. The conference would surely become a target for those who wanted to weaken the Treaty. Instead of having to face facts and accept the Community, interested parties would be given another chance to change it.

In the end, the Treaty left open the possibility of amendment after the end of the transitional period, but did not impose a definite obligation to review and revise.[2] The

---

[2] Article 96 provides for a conventional amending process: propositions by governments or the High Authority are considered by the Council of Ministers which by a two-thirds majority may call a conference to modify the Treaty; amendments must be ratified by all the states to become effective. Article 95 permits a different process to be used if "unforeseen difficulties" or "a profound change" in economic or technical factors bearing on the common market require a change in the rules for the exercise of the High Authority's powers. The proposals must not affect the stated purposes of the Treaty or the relationship of the High Authority's powers to those of the other Treaty organs. Amendments are proposed jointly by the High Authority and a five-sixths majority of the Council. If the Court agrees that the amendments meet the stipulations summarized above, they are submitted to the Assembly which can bring them into force by a three-fourths majority of the votes cast, provided this is two-thirds of the total membership.

possibility of amending the Treaty had no prominent place in the arguments of the early part of the transitional period. Later, however, those who objected to the way the Community was working began speaking of possible changes in the Treaty. Those interested in extending the Assembly's powers thought of possible amendments. The view that integration should be broadened by giving the High Authority more power or by extending its jurisdiction over energy and transportation involved amendments. Erhard was said to be considering an amendment when he saw his influence over the German coal price wane. The champions of a broader social policy thought of changes in Treaty language that would encourage, or even force, the High Authority to do more. Businessmen who disliked the Community tax and parliamentarians who wanted to see its proceeds used more widely both considered the possibilities of amendment. The rather disappointing experience with adaptation aid stimulated study of ways of simplifying the procedure and giving the High Authority more initiative.

As the transitional period drew to a close, Assembly committees examined the proposals for amendment in considerable detail. A working group report suggesting more than a dozen changes in the Treaty won the approval of a sizable majority of the Assembly.[3] A number of the changes, verbal or substantive, were intended to give labor and social questions a larger place in the High Authority's work. A more active role for the High Authority in coordinating national economic policies, a direct attack on problems of labor shortage, specific authority to use the Community tax to finance workers' housing, simplification of the adaptation rules, and clear authorization for the High Authority to negotiate with third countries on behalf of the whole Community, were the objects of some of the suggestions. The Treaty provisions on cartels, concentrations, and the rules for publishing prices ought to be reviewed, said the Assembly, but it made no specific suggestions about what should be done. A major innovation was the suggestion that the Treaty ban on subsidies be made

[3] Gerhard Kreyssig, *Révision du Traité instituant la Communauté Européenne du Charbon et de l'Acier*, 1958.

less flat in order to make possible the formulation of a long-run coal policy. Though this was the fullest official review of the possibilities of amendment, the list was shorter than it would probably have been two years before. There did not seem to be any great pressure behind the drive for revision.

Several reasons explain this. The Common Market and Euratom treaties had changed the situation. The area of integration was broadened, the possibilities of expanding the High Authority's role had to be put aside, either because the need was obviated or because it was plainly not politic to expect innovations in the old community at a moment when the features of the new ones were just taking shape. The Assembly now served all three communities. The provisions of the new treaties were somewhat different from those of the old but did not provide the full status the coal and steel Assembly had obtained in practice. This made formal alteration of the old treaty a bit tricky and perhaps something to be avoided. More problems concerning the relations among the communities were bound to arise; amending the coal and steel Treaty did not seem the best way to approach them. Before the new treaties were in operation it would be premature; even afterwards it might entail a weakening of the coal and steel Treaty, for instance in the cartel and concentration provisions. More than specific issues were involved. The supranational commissions of the new communities were weaker than the High Authority. If the coal and steel Treaty were opened to revision, was it not likely that a good bit of pressure would appear, perhaps from governments, to reduce the High Authority's powers and cut its role down to that of the newer bodies? Very likely it was this sort of thing that Finet had in mind when he cautioned the Assembly about "the difficulties and dangers of this matter." [4]

Inside the Coal and Steel Community there were similar risks. If the amending process were set in motion, changes would be proposed that would not advance the cause of

[4] CA, *Compte Rendu Analytique*, Feb. 25, 1958, p. 9 (mimeographed).

integration as the Assembly and the High Authority wished. To propose that the proceeds of the levy be used more widely, for instance, risked raising the whole principle of independent financing for the Community, something the newer communities lacked. To get support for amendments that broadened integration might well require bargaining away other powers. The High Authority thought the risk unnecessary. Much could be done by interpretation. The Community had shown itself capable of moving in unforeseen ways, for instance in the growth of the Assembly's importance or in the High Authority's financial aid to workers' housing. To many this method seemed politically healthier, as well as more expedient. Answering the Assembly's debate on revision, Wehrer remarked that he and his colleagues accepted the principle of many of the amendments but thought that it was unnecessary to change the Treaty in all these respects. They feared "that too much precision would deprive the Treaty of a suppleness that has proved itself very valuable. The dangers of perfectionism in this matter leap to the eye." [5]

The caution that had marked the High Authority's use of some of its supranational powers was now being applied to the idea of extending that power or giving specific legal status to practices that had developed. The nine men agreed that adaptation aid should be offered more freely— but there was a breathing space that could be obtained by extending the transitional Convention's provision for two years. They wanted it made clear that they could negotiate with third countries on behalf of the whole Community, but that might take some time to arrange and meanwhile close cooperation with the governments could serve the purpose. If the High Authority did not press these matters, perhaps no other serious efforts at revising the Treaty would be made. The Community would, then, go into the new phase in much the same shape it had started, at least until the new communities had developed to a point at which new problems were posed that had to be solved

[5] CA, *Compte Rendu Analytique*, Feb. 27, 1958, p. 44 (mimeographed).

either by formal changes or, perhaps, by new demonstrations of constitutional flexibility.

THE COMMUNITY IN RECESSION

The high level of economic activity from 1954 to 1957 did much to shape the Community's operating record. But the recessions that began and ended the transitional period also played their parts. The one at the outset helped establish the combination of surveillance and collusion that has governed the setting of Community steel prices and demonstrated the possibility of price competition when demand was low. It probably contributed to misconceptions of the Community's coal position by encouraging the view that imports from third countries were abnormal and by putting internal marketing problems in a different light from that which later appeared most important.

The recession at the end of the transitional period raised three broad questions: Could the Community stand the unaccustomed strains of a fall in demand? Would adjustments that had been postponed by prosperity now be made under forced draft? Would the new situation demonstrate elements of the Community's character that had been concealed by the ever-increasing demand of earlier years? As this is written, only tentative and partial answers are possible.

Recession is almost too strong a word for what happened in steel. Early in 1957 orders from third countries began falling off. In the last half of the year they were two-thirds those of the same period in 1956. Exports in that period were 9 per cent below 1956. Export prices fell and by early 1958 they were at or below the domestic level of most Community countries. Community production, which had been growing, stayed at about the 1957 level during most of 1958. Output fell in Germany, Belgium, Luxembourg, and Italy and rose in France and the Netherlands. The easing of supply encouraged trade inside the Community, which was nearly 25 per cent higher in the last half of 1957 than in the same period the year before. There were few reductions in published prices inside the Community until the spring of 1958, but prices actually paid may have fallen somewhat as more use was made of the right of alignment. Belgian and Italian prices were cut in the spring of 1958 while those of France and Germany were raised. By the summer of 1958 a spotty revival appeared, helped by a rise in export orders to record heights but held back by slack domestic demand.

The temporary easing of demand for steel in 1957 and 1958 was not marked or long enough to create any serious problems for the Community. The full order books from the previous period of high demand provided a substantial cushion. The advantage of the larger market created by the Community showed in the expansion of internal trade.[6] There was probably an increase in competition. Certainly the spread in prices among countries narrowed. The export cartel showed its weakness. The scrap problem was made easier, at least for the time being. On the whole, the slight recession made the common market for steel work better. It was not deep enough to cause serious trouble or to bring to the surface problems of adjustment that might have been submerged by the boom years.

In coal things were very different. During late 1957 and 1958 the Community accumulated growing amounts of unsold coal—a surplus to replace the chronic shortage or near-shortage that had been the plague of the years just past. A mild winter reduced the consumption of household coal. Some slowness in economic activity held down industrial purchases. The shift to oil continued and was sometimes accelerated, notably in Germany. Imports of American coal increased. Some came in under two- or three-year contracts negotiated as part of the effort of previous years to increase and regularize imports. The fall in ocean freight rates stimulated spot purchases of American coal as well

[6] The "rate of interpenetration" for steel products calculated by the High Authority which averaged 12.3 per cent for the last quarter of 1956 and the first quarter of 1957 rose to 13 per cent for the six months ending March 1958. The figure represents the share of deliveries from one country to another in the total of intra-Community deliveries (i.e., excluding imports from third countries). France and the Saar are treated as a unit. *Bulletin Statistique*.

and brought its landed price below that for German or Belgian coal in many areas. Anyone who had contracted for imports at the higher rates of the past wanted to buy at the cheaper current prices to reduce average costs. Coal-users who had been rationed by German sellers welcomed the alternative sources. German coal producers themselves were often major importers since they had marketing facilities; some got into the oil business as well. As imports rose, exports to third countries fell. Production remained fairly steady.[7]

Naturally coal stocks accumulated, first in the hands of users who were glad to assure their requirements and then, at an accelerating pace, at the mines, as the following figures show:

End of:	Consumers' Stocks	Stocks at the Mines (thousands of tons)	Total
December 1956	15,041	5,793	20,834
June 1957	18,860	5,960	24,820
December 1957	19,808	7,273	27,081
March 1958	20,570	12,294	32,864
June 1958	21,578	18,235	39,813
September 1958	22,488	22,594	45,082

Previous highs were 12.4 million tons at the mines at the end of 1954 and 12 million tons in the hands of users at the end of 1955. The 47 million tons of coal in stocks by the end of November 1958 equaled more than nine weeks' production. The burden was not uniformly distributed. Belgium was the first to accumulate large stocks and by

[7] Community coal imports in 1957 were 44 million tons compared to 38 million the year before; exports to third countries fell from 5.7 million tons to 5.1 million. From August 1957 through January 1958 Community coal producers' deliveries to all groups of consumers averaged nearly a million tons a month less than in the same period a year before. Then the gap grew greater; from February through May deliveries were about 41 million tons compared to over 51 million in the same period of 1957. The Community's apparent consumption (including the accumulation of stocks by coal-users) dropped from 284 million tons in the year ending June 1957 to 264 million in the next twelve months.

the end of November 1958, 6.7 million tons had piled up at the pits, nearly three months' production. In Germany stocks at the mines grew less rapidly at first, but quintupled during the first half of 1958 and by the end of November came to 8.6 million tons, more than three weeks' production. Though French stocks at the same date came to more than six weeks' production, the rate of accumulation had been much slower since the French mines regularly held the largest stocks in the Community, including a high proportion of low-grade coal.[8] At the same time, stocks of coke at Community cokeries rose from 578,000 tons at the end of 1956 to 1,653,000 tons a year later and almost 7 million tons by the end of 1958.

Long before the coal surplus reached its late 1958 levels, producers in Belgium and Germany were sounding the alarm and calling for protection. At first they met a certain reserve in the governments. A few weeks' supply of coal above ground seemed no national disaster, especially after the struggles to keep users adequately supplied during the years just past. In Belgium any major change in the coal situation raised the fundamental problems of the high-cost mines in the south, the coal price, and the subsidy. In Germany, Erhard's liberal principles made him reluctant to take protective action, either against foreign coal or the competition of oil. His past arguments with the coal producers gave him no reason to rush to protect their price. The Ruhr spokesmen were quick to point out that they were now being told that a market economy had downs as well as ups, but that when demand was strong they had

[8] Stocks at the mines, in thousands of tons, were:

	Belgium	France	Germany	Saar
End of				
1956	179	4,524	700	102
1957	1,413	4,583	735	181
June 1958	5,000	6,310	5,569	627
November 1958	6,740	7,678	8,604	923

Most figures in this paragraph came from the High Authority's *Notes Rapides*; some are provisional. In all countries but Belgium stocks fell in December.

been prevented from raising prices to a level that would have permitted them to accumulate financial reserves to meet a more difficult period.

With or without government help, familiar remedies could not easily be used. Though a number of mines cut working time, they did not wish to curtail production sharply for fear of losing workers who would be hard to attract back into the industry when times improved. Treaty rules prevented barriers being put on imports from other Community countries. Imports from third countries could be checked, but only within limits; contractual obligations, the provisions of GATT, and the probable need for future imports from outside the Community inhibited rapid and drastic action.[9]

As the problem grew, and after some negotiation to persuade producers to help themselves, the German and Belgian governments took a series of measures. In Belgium the price of Campine coal was reduced and alignment on foreign prices permitted. In the fall of 1958, 10 per cent rebates were offered to industrial consumers who took more than 80 per cent of the coal they had bought the year before. In February 1958 restrictions were imposed on imports from third countries not covered by contracts. The other governments of the Community were asked to co-operate by preventing coal from reaching Belgium indirectly. When a new government took office in Brussels, it announced the intention of doing something to shut down high-cost pits in the south that were adding to the surplus and increasing the costs of the industry as a whole.

In Germany, negotiations between the government and the Ruhr led to what Erhard called "a broad-gauged entrepreneurial gesture" on the part of the producers and some concessions by him as well.[10] Industrial users were

[9] During the first half of 1958 stocks in the Community increased 12.6 million tons while coal imports from third countries totaled 16.4 million tons. Of these imports, 6.5 million went to Germany, where stocks at the mines increased by 4.8 million, and 1.1 million tons of imports went to Belgium where stocks at the mines rose 1.5 million.

[10] Bulletin des Presse- und Informationsamtes der Bundesregierung, Sept. 4, 1958, p. 1643.

offered a 10 per cent price cut if they increased their coal purchases (an offer that had to be extended to all Community buyers to be consistent with the Treaty's price rules). A temporary reduction in the coke price was linked with efforts to check the use of oil in the steel industry and with an attempt to persuade steel producers to use more iron ore and less scrap so as to increase their coke consumption. Appealing to one of the escape clauses of GATT, the government embargoed new imports. Contractual obligations would be honored but efforts would continue to get American suppliers to reduce or postpone deliveries.[11]

Once they had taken these steps the Belgians and Germans could turn to Luxembourg for help. Before, there had been a certain reluctance on the part of other governments, and perhaps of the High Authority as well, to set Community procedures in motion to handle what was, for the time being at least, essentially a difficulty affecting only two countries. The High Authority had not been ignored, however. Some coal producers blamed it for their troubles, arguing that false estimates of the Community's coal needs, encouragement of importing, and recommendations that long-term contracts be placed, were the main causes of the surplus. Ruhr producers complained that they had been made to share their coal with the rest of the Community when it was scarce and now were trapped between imports that had been forced on them and customers who were free to take their trade elsewhere.[12] In Belgium, too, there was a feeling that the common market did not work well; though surpluses were piling up in Belgium, Italy could reduce its imports from that country (and Germany)

[11] The government also intended to examine the contracts to see if the German parties to them were actually obligated to buy. Future contracts, it was announced, would be limited to 18 months. A new rule was introduced to permit re-export of dollar coal. Neither of these latter measures could be expected to contribute significantly to the solution of the immediate problem.

[12] In the first half of 1958 German coal sales to the rest of the Community were 13 per cent below those of the first half of 1957. Domestic apparent consumption fell by 11 per cent and exports to third countries by 38 per cent.

while keeping up its purchases of American coal. From Italy's point of view the Community would have become a burden if it meant that Italy could not take advantage of the low freight rate and buy cheaper American coal. In this way the surpluses tacitly raised new questions about the solidarity of the Community and the relation of national and common interests. Before, the question had been the consumer's access to Community supplies when they were cheaper than imports; now the problem was whether Community producers were to have a preferred position in the common market even at some cost to the user.

The suggestion that the High Authority should invoke the emergency provisions of the Treaty for dealing with "a period of manifest crisis" got little support. The men in Luxembourg were probably unwilling to take the drastic and extensive regulatory measures this would entail to deal with what might well be a temporary glut. They could probably not have obtained the approval of the Council of Ministers. Holland and Italy had no interest in measures that would cut supplies and raise prices. The prospect of ceilings on production would not command much support in France or Germany. For some time the High Authority had been recommending that the Community work out a plan for financing coal stocks, as a measure of long-run policy to promote stability. The governments were slow to respond to this idea until the accumulation of stocks forced it on them. Even then they were reluctant to share in the financing. A compromise solution reached in November 1958 provided that the High Authority should devote $7 million of its own funds to help producers meet the cost of carrying large coal and coke stocks. If governments provided matching sums the money could be given to producers; otherwise it would be loaned.[13] The High Authority also undertook the presenta-

[13] To be eligible for aid a company had to have stocks exceeding 35 days' production and to have produced over 12,000 tons in the previous coal year. It could receive loans or grants covering additions to stock made after October 31, 1958. Loans could amount to 16⅔ cents per ton per month (if guaranteed by governments), grants or unguaranteed loans to half that. Aid would be given only if the High Authority approved

tion of the Community's coal problems to the United States government and American exporters. Governments were called on to import Community coal in the same proportion as in past boom periods. The High Authority also recommended a series of measures intended to avoid unemployment in the coal industry, encourage consumption, and lead to a close look at the conditions under which oil and other forms of energy competed with coal.

The Germans moved in the latter sphere by subjecting heavy fuel oil produced from imported crude to a turnover tax like that levied on coal. Then Erhard approved a cartel agreement between coal and heavy oil producers. For two years the price of heavy fuel oil inside Germany was not to fall below the world price plus certain costs. How effective this measure would be remained to be seen since users or dealers who were not parties to the cartel were still free to import any fuel oil they could get at lower prices. Producers, the miners' union, the SPD called for stronger action. In February 1959 the government introduced a tariff of DM 20 per ton on coal imported from outside the Community. Erhard had obtained assurances from the German producers that they would not raise their prices. The tariff, it was thought, would keep out American coal by making it cheaper for importers to pay the penalties for cancelling contracts than to pay the duty. To take care of the needs of regions that normally depended on foreign supplies, 5 million tons of coal could be imported duty-free; the coal already imported in 1959 would be charged against this sum. The tariff's initial life was to the end of 1959.

The German action caused some disturbance. Discussions with the High Authority were not completed when the German government introduced its tariff bill, perhaps timing

the company's program of self-help; various conditions were aimed at excluding the highest-cost Belgian mines and firms not participating in governmental programs of adjustment. Enactment of the aid program involved the first use of the first paragraph of Article 95 by which the unanimous agreement of the Council makes it possible for the High Authority to act in "cases not expressly provided for" in the Treaty if such action is necessary to achieve the objectives of the Community. *JO*, Nov. 14, 1958, pp. 486-489.

the announcement to take the wind out of the sails of the
miners' union which was about to make new demands. The
High Authority remonstrated that the German action
should have waited on a proposal from the supranational
body (under Article 74). The Dutch were worried that the
fall in coal imports would hurt Rotterdam which might be
discriminated against in favor of German ports. The Dutch,
French, and Belgians would have to cooperate if no indirect
imports of coal were to reach Germany. The British had
grounds for claiming that the issue should have been discussed first in the Council of Association. The tariff issue
was likely to be raised in GATT, perhaps by the Americans who were the hardest hit. The German action raised
new problems about the conduct of Community foreign
trade policy and old problems about the relation of national, supranational, and intergovernmental action. Like
the other recession measures it touched key issues of long-
run coal policy. Coming from the largest coal producer in
the Community, it raised anew the possibility of declaring
that a "manifest crisis" existed, a step that would endow
the High Authority and the Council of Ministers with
major additional powers over the coal supply.

Though it is too early, as this is written, to judge the
effectiveness of the corrective measures, one can see that
the appearance of a coal surplus raised issues touching the
Community's long-run coal problem. The stocks are large
by the conventional standards of the six countries, but are
these standards appropriate for an economy that only a
little while ago was virtually allocating scarce coal? Stocks
amounting to a little more than two months' production,
held nearly equally by producers and users, can hardly
be regarded as an intolerable surplus. Should the stocks not
be looked on as a useful reserve for future periods of
shortage? Nearly as much coal was imported during 1957
and not a great deal less during 1956. There is little reason
to expect a chronic surplus. Sizable stocks, properly
handled, could become an asset for the Community; there
would be advantages in a regularly easier supply position
than has often existed in the past. How large stocks should

be for this purpose is, of course, debatable, but the issue is as much a matter of custom and psychology as it is of more objective criteria.[14]

One of the crucial problems is finance. How great the burden of holding sizable coal stocks is cannot be judged without close study, both of waste in storage and of the cost of tying up capital in this fashion. The High Authority's aid program is principally a measure of supplementing the working capital of the companies holding the largest stocks. Another approach would be to shift some of the stocks to other accounts.[15] There are many ways of achieving either aim; the key point is that if larger stocks are judged useful for the Community, means must be found of spreading their cost among all those who benefit. This presents the Community with a set of problems involving relations among its member states and between producers and consumers that were not directly faced during the transitional period. Their obverse could be found, however, in such matters as assuring "equal" access to Community coal supplies in times of shortage and in the resulting sharing of the burden of paying for imported coal when it was more expensive.

One of the immediate results of the coal surplus was a change in the relative bargaining strength of the coal producers and the coal users. From Germany one heard reports that for the first time in a long while buyers felt they were being treated as customers by the Ruhr—because they had the option of buying American coal at more or less competitive prices. The successors to Georg became, for the first time, selling organizations and not just allocation agencies. The German government found its hand greatly strengthened in dealing with the coal producers who not so long before had defied it on prices. Thanks to the measures made necessary by the surplus, "I have . . .

[14] In the United States, where coal production is much more elastic than in Europe, stocks have been equal to between six and eight weeks' production during most of the '50s. They exceeded two months' production throughout 1958.

[15] Steps in this direction were taken in Germany through advance purchasing by the defense ministry and the Bundesbahn.

finally restored my peace with the coal industry," said Erhard.[16] In Belgium the argument that a high-cost mine should be kept running because every ton of coal was needed lost its plausibility. The cost of coal and not only its price began to be seriously considered. The period was too short and the change too quick to draw any conclusions about how the coal marketing arrangements of the Community, which had largely been shaped by shortage, would work in a period of relative plenty; but that question, too, was posed by the appearance of surpluses.

It seems paradoxical to argue that so unsettling an episode as the unexpected accumulation of coal surpluses may be transformed into an element of stability. One of its most striking features was the speed with which attitudes and behavior that assumed chronic shortage gave way to the defensive reactions of a psychology of surplus. Some of this was the exaggeration that so often seems necessary to evoke action, some the natural reaction to unexpected disturbance. But the roots were in the Community's continuing coal problems and the lack of any clear approach to solving them.

Imports had been necessary to meet the Community's coal shortage. The steps taken to regularize them and reduce their cost were now contributing to a surplus. No one knew how well the Community would stand the change. Gains and losses were unevenly distributed; the problem might grow much worse; there was a clear threat to the steps that had been taken to expand Community production and hold labor in the mines.

The measures taken to cope with the glut were largely palliatives; except for the long-delayed closing of Belgian mines they did nothing to ensure useful adjustments or to set a lasting Community coal policy. But they pointed to the need for fundamental measures more sharply than any number of analyses and exhortations. The temporary trouble might, therefore, precipitate the long-standing mixture of ideas, interests, and resistance that had kept a long-run coal policy in suspension. The unequal impact of the

[16] *Bulletin. . .* , cited, p. 1644.

short-run problem on different countries, the difficulty of dealing with it by Community action, and the primary reliance on governmental measures, also pointed to the complexity of the task of formulating a long-run policy that would be not only reasonable but acceptable.

POLICY FOR THE FUTURE

The Community has been given a long legal life. Its economic objectives cannot be achieved in a few years. Naturally enough there has been a feeling that the High Authority should formulate long-run policies to guide the Community. Numerous reports, committees, and debates have dealt with "general objectives" with quite uneven results. The difficulties are fairly clear. The Treaty not only sets goals but also goes far toward defining the policies by which they are to be pursued. To elaborate on these in general terms is unlikely in most cases to offer benefits commensurate with the risk of prejudicing the Community's regular practice of applying rules to concrete cases by a combination of persuasion, compromise, the mobilization of interests, and the judicious exercise of authority. To interpret policy in advance could embarrass the High Authority. A statement of Community objectives that commanded broad assent would probably be so general as to offer no guidance. One that took a firm stand on difficult issues would evoke contention without promising clear gain.

Perhaps for these reasons discussions of "general objectives" have usually focused on goals for Community production. Here the difficulty is that the Community cannot be autonomous in these matters. The demand for coal and steel comes principally from outside the Community; it is largely a function of the level of general economic activity, and especially of the activity of a number of key industries.[17] What the Community must do,

---

[17] There is, of course, some interaction between what happens in coal and steel and the general level of economic activity. These are basic industries, using many products of other industries, employing a sizable number of men, and accounting for much of the demand for transporta-

therefore, is to estimate future economic growth, derive from it the demand for coal and steel, judge what problems the Community will face in meeting the demand, and then consider the policies that offer the best chance of solving these problems and of encouraging adequate production. Such assessments have an immediate relevance as broad guides to the investment needs and raw material requirements of the Community. They have further implications, however, for the size of the Community's coal and steel production and therefore for the problems that producers, governments, and the High Authority will face. For coal, in particular, major issues of Community policy depend largely on the level of demand and on the competition of other fuels.

To assess the forecasts of demand for Community products would require an unwarranted digression. Not a study of the Community, such as this has been, but an analysis of the economics of the coal and steel industries of the six countries is the proper foundation for appraising these estimates. Here it is sufficient to work from their general character, ignoring details and most statistics. Assuming a substantial rate of economic expansion for the six countries, the projections call for a sizable increase in coal and steel production—or at least capacity. The estimates made by the High Authority in the spring of 1957, for instance, put Community steel requirements in 1965 (for home consumption and export) at least 50 per cent above the level of 1955. The estimate for 1975 called for more than double the production of 1955. For coal, in contrast, the High Authority put 1965 requirements at less than 20 per cent above those of 1955 and thought that in 1975 only about 30 per cent more coal would be needed than in 1955.[18] The contrast between the coal and steel figures

tion. Their expansion has a buoyant effect on the rest of the economy, but except for short periods their growth depends on general growth. Cyclically the two industries are also important. Depression in coal and steel would do much to pull down the rest of the economy, but it is unlikely that by themselves they have the motor force to pull national economies out of a general depression. A possible exception is a strong export demand for steel.

[18] HA, *Report*, Apr. 1957, pp. 249-263.

reflects the substantial differences in the problems the Community faces in these two fields.

LONG-RUN COAL PROBLEMS

There is little doubt that coal will provide the Community with its most difficult long-run problems. The transitional period has already shown the salient features. While the Community's production of steel—and the general level of economic activity in the six countries— increased substantially, the output of coal went up only a few per cent. This is nothing new. In 1952, when the Community started, the index of industrial production of the six countries was 36 per cent above 1929 while the production of coal was only 1 per cent above the 1929 level (and at the level of 1937).[19] Nor was the difference due principally to the use of imports; coal consumption in 1952 was at the same level it had been in 1929. The consumption of all forms of energy, however, was 19 per cent higher.[20] The proportion of the energy supplied by coal had fallen from 83 per cent to 70 per cent.

The relative importance of coal has continued to fall, as oil, natural gas, and hydroelectric power have provided increasing amounts of Europe's energy. At the same time, Community coal consumption has increased much more rapidly than production, with imports filling the gap. No doubt the shift toward oil and gas will continue, for all the reasons that make it a general world-wide development. Coal for import will continue to be available for the indefinite future, since surplus capacity and relatively flexible production are features of the present-day American bituminous mines. How large these imports will be depends on the size of Europe's demand and on the policies the Community follows. In the offing is nuclear power, but it will probably not add its complications to the Community's energy problems for at least a decade. The Community's coal problem comes partly from these shifts

[19] Same, p. 294.
[20] The discrepancy between energy consumption and industrial production is accounted for by more efficient use of power and of fuel in the production of power.

in energy sources and partly from the special position of the coal industry.

Forecasts of the Community's energy position have become quite controversial. Up to a point this is due to the difficulty of deciding how to handle the interaction of the key variables—not only the availability of the several fuels but their relative prices, the investment they require, and their technical advantages. For the rest, the controversy stems from the implications each projection seems to have for energy policies and for the interests of the several industries involved, especially coal. Without getting involved in these questions, one can work from certain broad features common to all the estimates. If the six countries maintain a reasonable rate of economic expansion over the next ten to fifteen years, Europe's energy needs will grow faster than its coal production. Oil, gas, and, to a lesser extent, hydroelectric power will increase in importance. Nuclear power may not be of economic significance before the middle or late '60s and for some time is unlikely to satisfy more than Europe's annual increase in energy consumption. Within this framework it will be possible, and perhaps mandatory, for the Community to increase its coal consumption substantially. Coal will remain the major source of Europe's energy during these decades. While coal production in the Community can increase, it is likely to lag behind coal consumption and will certainly not be flexible enough to meet peak demands. Fluctuations considerably complicate the problem. Whether freight rates are high or low makes a great difference to the cost of American coal in the Community. A fall in domestic demand or a sharp increase in imports can quickly create serious difficulties for Community production. The *economic* part of the Community's coal problem is how to maintain the most advantageous relation between coal and other fuels and between domestic and imported coal.

The condition in which the Community's coal economy faces this somewhat uncertain future complicates the economic problem and raises other issues as well. Previous chapters have delineated the situation. The whole emphasis of postwar policy has been on increasing production. The high demand during the boom years of the transitional period lent color to the view long deeply ingrained in the industry that high-cost mines should be operated until they are virtually exhausted because coal is needed and if it is not mined it is wasted. A fairly wide range of production costs seems to exist within each national coal industry. To provide a uniform price and to keep poorer pits in operation each national industry relies on various kinds of equalization schemes that spread some of the burden of high-cost production throughout the industry. Labor accounts for a high proportion of coal mining costs. To attract and keep miners it has proved necessary to pay relatively high wages; to maintain their margin they tend to rise at least as fast as the general level of wages. Productivity has increased but the scope for major labor-saving measures is widely believed to be limited by geological barriers to extensive mechanization. While coal prices have risen, governments have generally been concerned to hold them down and have used a number of measures to achieve this. Direct and indirect subsidies play an important part in the industry. Coal marketing arrangements limit competition; traditional relations hinder it; in times of high demand allocations and "loyalty" between buyer and seller eliminate it. Investment has been substantial but has probably done more to modernize production and to provide uses for poor grades of coal than to expand production. There are undoubtedly possibilities for increasing Community coal production, but the size of the expansion that is feasible and above all its pace are disputed.[21] Reserves exist equal to a century or two of cur-

[21] For instance, the German coal industry suggested that between 1960 and 1980 German production might rise by 40 million tons. (Production in 1957 was 133 million.) Mechanization was expected to contribute 10 million tons to output, improvement and expansion of existing mines 20 million, new mines and the exploitation of new fields another 20 million. Closing uneconomic pits and the decline in output of older mines were expected to reduce production by 10 million tons. A commentator suggested that doubt about the availability of labor and capital, as well as uncertainty in other matters, made these forecasts *Zukunftsmusik*. *Neue Zürcher Zeitung*, Aug. 24, 1957.

rent production, but much of the coal lies very deep or would be costly to mine for other reasons. Unless new beds can be worked from existing mines their exploitation cannot be rapid and, because of the heavy initial cost and slow amortization, will only be undertaken if the future seems fairly secure.

For a number of years it was possible to carry on Community coal production with primary emphasis on the expansion of output, leaving concern for costs in second place. Imported coal was more expensive than that produced inside the Community. The price competition offered by oil and other forms of energy was limited and in any case demand was rising fast enough to absorb the larger supplies. The main coal-producing countries had policies that through fiscal measures or otherwise penalized oil, protected coal, or "regulated" competition between them. Coal costs continued to rise. The other fuels became increasingly attractive. While the low freight rates of 1957-58 that made American coal cheap in Europe and the reduction of oil prices in Germany may prove to be temporary factors, there seems little doubt that the price gap that favored the Community coal industry is being filled. Inevitably Community coal policy must pay more attention to costs. Traditional coal mining attitudes are being challenged. If labor is the bottleneck, people are saying, then waste lies in not employing it on the richest seams instead of in exploiting the dregs of old mines. Equalization arrangements and marketing methods that prevent the most efficient mines from either charging less or making higher profits are jeopardizing the coal industry, not stabilizing it. Tie-in sales that dispose of lower grades of coal by passing them to good customers may lose their economy if they add to the attractions of other fuels or imported coal.

There are answers, of course. The burden of the high-cost mines is exaggerated, say the German and Belgian producers. To close the ten poorest mines in the Ruhr would lower the coal price only 80 pfennig per ton, according to the German producers, and would lose 6 or 7 million tons of coal a year.[22] The "valorization" of the poor grades, mostly through use for local power, represents a major economy. Prices are already too low to provide the profit margin necessary for adequate investment from the coal companies' own resources, say the industry's spokesmen. The closing of uneconomic mines and the reorganization of marginal pits are going ahead as fast as is practical, they add, because this is to the interest of the producers.

All these points are somewhat obscure. One of the most useful contributions the High Authority could make to the formulation of a sensible Community coal policy would be to discover and set out the facts, not only about the economics of these issues, but about the risk of total loss from closing mines and the cost of keeping them in stand-by condition; about the real limits of mechanization or other measures of increasing productivity and saving labor; and about the availability of rich, unmined deposits and the cost of exploiting them. Such an inquiry might be resisted, or met with the claim that the facts are known, but as matters stand these are facts of the sort a lawyer's brief contains, not those of an impartial finding. It may be that the situation will turn out to be much as it is represented, and then the question will be whether coal mining on this basis is a paying proposition for the Community, or whether a substantial loss of output would be worth a saving in costs, or whether means could be found—they would have to be subsidy or protection, for all or part of the industry—to keep coal costs at a level that would permit the industry to hold its own against imports and other fuels. Alternatively, it may turn out that with the deadest wood removed—at a loss to someone—the industry would have more flexibility and a greater economic margin than its champions now admit.[23]

[22] Statement by Unternehmensverband Ruhrbergbau, *Der Volkswirt*, Sept. 28, 1957, pp. 2171, 2172.

[23] Some observers estimate that the difference in production costs between the best and the worst mines in Germany in 1957 was DM 30 per ton and that about 10 per cent of the output was from unprofitable mines. Bernd Huffschmid, "Ruhrbergbau in der Zange," *Der Volkswirt*, Jl. 27, 1957, pp. 1603, 1604.

Even if high-cost mines were closed and conditions of production improved, some features of Community coal mining would continue to make the formulation of long-run policy difficult. Production will probably remain fairly inflexible. Growth in output is likely to be rather slow except for possible occasional spurts if major new fields are tapped. The need to keep employment high and steady in order to hold the labor force will inhibit cuts in production when demand falls. Unless marked progress is made in discovering ways to increase labor productivity, the need to hold miners and pay them well is likely to keep the industry's labor costs under constant pressure. At the same time the competition of other fuels (and perhaps of imported coal, depending on the Community's policy) will put a ceiling on price increases. Even when other circumstances would permit a rise, governments are likely to try to hold down coal prices. Since a wide range of costs will remain even if the worst mines are closed, equalization arrangements are likely to continue. The result of all these factors is almost certain to be considerable pressure for safeguarding arrangements and price stability, accompanying rather stable production.

Western Europe's coal-producing economy thus appears as a rather static, slow-moving mass, ill-adapted to satisfying a fluctuating or rapidly changing demand. Bridging the gap will remain a central issue of Community coal policy. The transitional period and its immediate sequel have shown the difficulties of relying on imported coal. Importing only when Community production falls below demand is likely to involve high costs and differential prices. Regularizing the flow of imports entails the risk of having to bring in coal when not all the domestic production can be marketed. To put no barrier in the way of imports is to permit foreign coal to be sold more cheaply than Community coal at some times and places. There are obvious advantages to this for coal-users, but it clearly presents difficulties for producers who lack flexibility. To balance these interests is one of the central problems of coal policy for the six countries. A more supple import policy, providing room for substantial variation while also giving some protection against having to pay peak prices, can almost certainly be devised, but it is unlikely to suffice unless there is also an internal stabilizing mechanism which would probably have to include means of absorbing coal in stockpiles when supply was large.

Coupled with the problem of maintaining stability within the coal economy is the relation of coal to other forms of fuel. These cannot be put in the marginal position of American coal, to be called on when needed. It is of importance to the Community to get energy as cheaply and conveniently as possible. Free competition of all forms of energy might be the best way to obtain this. But so long as coal is still counted on for an important part of the supply, some assurance of stability in the coal industry will be needed, and this seems bound to entail some limitation on competition from other forms of energy, especially oil, that are more flexible in supply and price. There is no longer serious doubt that the Community needs an energy policy, not just a coal policy, but its achievement remains something for the future. The High Authority can deal only with coal; Euratom deals only with nuclear energy, a problem of the future; the great issues concern oil and, to some extent, natural gas and hydroelectric power. The governments can, of course, act together on these matters, without a single community being given jurisdiction, but it will not be easy for them to agree on a program.

One can hardly even speak of *national* energy policies. Certainly the practices and measures of each country add up to a determination of how the various forms of energy shall be used. These are mostly, however, combinations of partial measures, remnants of past arrangements, and steps taken to deal with particular problems. Only rarely do they appear to be comprehensive, forward-looking programs. If there were clearly defined national policies, they would point in different directions. Italy, with almost no coal, naturally wants freedom to import from whatever source is cheapest, has few inhibitions about shifting to oil, and pushes expansion of domestic oil and gas. The Netherlands, lacking these last, has domestic coal production to worry about but also has a substantial stake in the international oil business and is likely to behave primarily as a consumer and net importer of energy, putting main emphasis on keeping down costs. The big coal-producing countries have a harder problem. Nationally each of them faces problems like those sketched for the Community as a whole. Belgium has already demonstrated the difficulty of adjusting coal production; it has the added domestic political conflict over the extent to which the government should control coal mining and the use of subsidies. In France the importation and marketing of oil are closely controlled but its use has expanded in recent years along with increased production of coal in the nationalized mines. Germany lags behind the rest of the Community in its use of oil, largely because of the dominant role coal has had for so long; now the pressure for a more rapid shift may be rising. Out of these differences in national interests and in the political strength of coal producers in each country come fundamental difficulties for the devising of a Community energy policy. If, however, reasonable compromises can be worked out on a Community basis, they may help to shift the balance in coal-producing countries toward the most economical solutions.[24]

The political strength of producers, labor, and other groups with a stake in coal will do much to shape national or Community policies. Their influence will certainly be exerted to resist rapid change (or perhaps any change) and to require special measures for easing adjustments. Any realistic policy will have to take account of these forces and seek compromises with them that will permit economic advance without incurring dangerous political and social strain. Behind the crude political strength of these interest groups are real "social rigidities" connected with the coal

[24] For instance, if Italy were to surrender part of its freedom to buy American coal whenever it was cheapest, it could reasonably ask for some assurance that Ruhr coal will not be markedly more expensive, thus adding to the emphasis on cost considerations in German policy.

industry. The immobility of labor, the dependence of localities on coal mining, and the large investment required to open new coal mines or to provide alternative sources of employment, are all major matters that governments must take into account. The experience with Belgian coal mines shows how serious these difficulties are and how reluctant a government is likely to be to take drastic, or even moderate, measures. There was, after all, widespread understanding of the need to promote adaptation; substantial resources were put into national and international efforts to bring this about; the results were rather meager, at least until the decline in demand virtually forced action. The rigidities throughout the coal-producing areas are real enough but some difficulties seem exaggerated. There are some isolated communities wholly dependent on high-cost coal mining, but often the uneconomic mines are in heavily populated areas where commutation across relatively short distances would suffice to permit a shift of employment from poor to good workings. Nor can almost total immobility of miners be accepted as inevitable unless the Community is willing to pay a very high price for it. At least some of the Community's difficulties in dealing with the social rigidities stem from an unwillingness of most of those involved to accept the need for adaptation. Governments, even if they accept this need, which is not altogether clear, have proved unwilling or unable to press adaptation very strongly against the will of capital and labor in the coal industry.

Political and social resistance to change are not the only factors that make for the maintenance of Community coal production at a higher level than would be justified by purely economic considerations. Security of supply is an important factor in formulating energy policy. Coal is Western Europe's great domestic raw material. Domestic oil, gas, and hydroelectric power are important but far from adequate. The great alternative to coal is imported oil. Most of this comes from the Middle East. The Suez crisis dramatized the danger: Could Western Europe afford to become dependent for its energy on supplies of oil that could be cut off by others, either by measures directed against Europe or as an incidental effect of a dispute or some other matter not directly involving Europe and escaping its control? The Suez crisis was overcome; the shift to oil continued. But the problem remained. The coal producers have not been behindhand in using the security argument, especially in Germany. Imports of coal, coming principally from the United States, do not present the same problem, but still they are outside resources, lying under non-European control and costing foreign exchange.

If the aim is total security, the problem is intractable. Unless its economy stagnates or users are strictly rationed, Western Europe cannot in the immediate future supply the energy it needs from domestic sources no matter how much protection is given to coal. Unless North American demand lags or there is an emergency that makes the whole Western world willing to go on rations, Europe must get much of its oil from the Middle East. Saharan oil may come to provide an important share of Europe's needs, but it remains to be seen who controls this supply. Eventually nuclear power may make possible a greater degree of self-sufficiency, but before then conventional energy needs will grow greatly. (Even with nuclear power, there may still be a raw material problem, but it will be smaller and will concern different suppliers.) For short-run difficulties, or to meet limited pressures, various measures can be devised to improve Europe's bargaining position in relation to the Middle East.[25] A major threat to Europe's oil supplies could be met only with American help which would surely be forthcoming if European security were threatened. Reliance on the always-available American coal would provide more security but less economy than reliance on oil. A shift to coal when oil is threatened is only feasible on a rather small scale because of limited short-run convertibility of equipment. Therefore some degree of dependence on an

[25] Some of them are discussed in J. C. Campbell, *Defense of the Middle East* (N.Y.: Harper, for the Council on Foreign Relations, 1958), pp. 226-244, 337-344.

uncertain oil supply remains an essential feature of Europe's energy position.

How high a price should Europe pay to minimize this dependence? How great a political risk should the six countries run to keep down fuel costs? There is no doubt that coal will remain the principal source of Europe's energy for years to come. It can be supplemented by indigenous oil, gas, and water power, but the security argument concerns the relative importance of imported energy. How important imports will be will depend largely on whether coal production is at the economically most advantageous level or the highest practicable level. Whether security can be found in this margin is uncertain, but it is only that moving margin which is in question.

Security, social rigidities, and the political strength of the coal-producing interest (including labor) all tend to work against allowing coal policy to be determined primarily by consideration of the relative cost of producing coal inside the Community and of importing it or using other forms of energy. Favoring such a policy are economic considerations, but even if they prevailed it would not be easy to devise clear-cut measures. Competition, the best-known method of both putting cost under discipline and guiding the allocation of resources, cannot easily be applied to coal, considering the fluctuations in the price and supply of other fuels, the need for continuity in coal production, and the economics of extractive industries. For other reasons as well, competition is not likely to play a major part in the Community coal economy, except in the form of continuing pressure on coal from the potential competition from other fuels.

A debate is on in Europe about these matters, especially in Germany where the clash between the relative freedom of the rest of the economy and the traditional special position of coal is particularly marked. "We are not for 'Coal at any price,' " say the producers; they say only that the complex economics, difficult social problems, and position of national importance of coal should be recognized. "The time has come," say the critics, "to get rid of the mythos of *national heiligentum* that has come to surround coal." [26] The same issues are debated in one form or another in the other countries. France has the easiest administrative task, because its mines are nationalized and because coking coal is mostly imported, but it does not thereby escape the economic, political, and social problems already sketched. Belgium has one of the hardest problems, because of its high-cost mines and the weight of coal in its national economy. Whether all these factors and forces can be put together in a comprehensive, agreed and clear Community coal policy may seem doubtful. Still, the Community and the countries will have to deal with coal problems and the series of measures they take will add up to something that can be called a coal policy, even if it proves to be an inconsistent one.

The experience of the transitional period suggests lines along which the Community's coal policies are likely to proceed. To hold down prices to avoid disturbance and dislocation, more and more special measures are likely to be adopted. Subsidies, in a variety of forms, will be used to meet high labor costs, to assist investment for improved production or housing, and to reduce the burden of high-cost mines on the more efficient ones. Not a free flow of trade but a regulated, managed, adjusted exchange is likely to continue; sometimes the aim will be to share supplies when there are shortages, sometimes to share the cost of holding stocks when supplies are too plentiful, always to assure a distribution of business among the better and the poorer producers. The adjustment of imports to moderate their cost and to control their volume is also likely. The list could be lengthened but its gist is clear. The Community coal economy will be increasingly "managed," by a combination of public and private forces. Increasingly

[26] The first quotation is from Theo Keyser, "Kohlenpolitik und Sicherheit der Versorgung," *Der Volkswirt*, Apr. 20, 1957, pp. 743-745. Keyser is a spokesman for the Unternehmensverband Ruhrbergbau, and his statement is only one of many examples of a similar approach. The second is from the article by B. Huffschmid cited in n. 23, and represents a much less frequently expressed view.

THE FUTURE OF THE COMMUNITY

coal will be treated not as a commodity but as a public utility.

This is not unreasonable. Probably it provides the best means of meeting the difficult and rather complicated problems of coal. There are two crucial issues in terms of which one can judge this evolution. The first is whether coal is in fact treated as a public utility and not a public ward. Will the broad public economic and security interests be put ahead of the more limited interests of the coal producers, including labor? With all the moderation and palliatives that are probably inevitable, will the basic emphasis of policy be on the Community's economic needs even if this requires a considerable adjustment of the level and conditions of coal production?

The second criterion is the extent to which coal problems are handled as Community problems, rather than as six national problems. The disintegrative possibilities are obvious. They rise from the different coal interests of the various countries, the organization of the coal industry on national lines, and the political pressures on each government. The difficulties in treating coal problems on a Community-wide basis are also clear. Some measures can best be taken nationally; many will have to be carried out nationally in any case. The governments retain key powers. The crucial question will be whether the national measures are taken in a framework of Community aims and efforts or primarily in terms of what each government separately judges to be the best course. This is not principally a matter of having an elaborate Community "policy" but of making the determination of what shall be done in ways that permit the effective interplay of the interests of all the groups affected and that respect the kind of check on national action that is inherent in the concept of the Community. If this is done, it will increase the influence of economic considerations in the shaping of coal policy, because the expression of producer interests will be more diluted. In fact, action on a Community-wide basis may be necessary to the economical solution of the coal problems;

it may also be essential to the survival of the Community. The mark of this development may turn out to be the role and influence of the High Authority, but there can be little doubt that much will be done by intergovernmental measures, if it is done at all.

Steel presents the Community with nothing like the difficulties that exist in coal. Production has increased rapidly, capacity has expanded in response to rising demand, and there is generally a greater flexibility in the steel economy than in coal. This is a relative matter, of course. Steel is not shoes or textiles; fixed costs are high, investment great, and competition limited. A recession causes problems. But there are none of the fundamental structural difficulties that beset coal. There is, for instance, nothing comparable to the pressure on coal from other forms of energy. Though aluminum, timber, concrete, and plastics offer competition that steel producers cannot ignore, they do not present the fundamental challenge with which oil faces coal.[27] So long as economic expansion continues, there is no reason to doubt that the demand for steel will expand about as rapidly as the rest of the economy.

[27] Aluminum competes in automobiles, railroad cars, building, the superstructure of ships, containers, and small pipes. Concrete competes in building, railroad ties, and large pipes. Timber is an alternative to steel in many uses, but on the whole it is steel that seems to be making headway against wood. Plastics offer slight competition in some of the same fields as aluminum and will probably grow more important. Very rough approximations worked out by the ECE secretariat suggest that in 1955 the maximum possible displacement of steel by aluminum and plastic may have amounted to 3 per cent of the steel supply in Europe. Addition of concrete and timber might raise the total to 6 per cent, but this is an even more dubious calculation. By 1960 the maximum steel-competing use of these materials might be 10 per cent of the steel supply. ECE, *Steel and Its Alternatives*, 1956, various pages. This does not mean that steel will lose this much of its market to these products but only that these products are being used to that extent for purposes for which steel might also be used. Over a long period the competition of aluminum, plastics, and light metals (and, perhaps, of glass in some of its new forms) may well be a matter of some seriousness to steel.

Over the long run, changes in steel technology are likely
to have major economic effects. Innovations in design and
process are a continuing part of steel production. A number of substantial developments have been tried out on a
sufficient scale to ensure their introduction over the next
decade. Some of the principal ones move in the direction
of economizing coal and coke, introducing oil into more
parts of the steelmaking process, making more effective
use of low-grade iron ore, and improving control over
quality, especially of Thomas steel. It would take a close
study of the industry to assess the effects of such developments on production costs, the changing market possibilities
of each producer, and eventually the location of industry.
The relevance of these measures in improving the raw
material position of the industry is clear. The reduction in
scrap use bears most directly on the problems that were
acute in the transitional period and that are likely to continue to present difficulties. Improvements in the Thomas
process bear not only on scrap needs but on the structure
of Community production and the strength of the French
and Belgian industries. Raw material problems are likely
to continue in various forms, but there is little in them
that threatens, or even challenges, the concept of the Community or that involves much more than Community
assistance to steel producers in overcoming their problems
plus encouragement of the financial commitments necessary to assure iron ore supplies far enough ahead. The
unfinished business of the Community in this field lies in
scrap policy. The High Authority struggled for years with
a complex mechanism that had certain short-run advantages
but also inherent contradictions. Its value in bringing about
a solution of the long-run problems remained unproved
up to the moment at which government opposition ended
the system and began a new approach based, at least initially, on reversion to some of the conditions that led to
Community intervention in the first place.

So long as demand is strong and profits good, investment
in the steel industry is likely to be adequate for future
needs. The amount of capital needed for a ton of output

rises, but the High Authority's estimates at the end of the transitional period were that planned investments would adequately expand the Community's steelmaking capacity. There are problems of balance within the industry among types of steel and kinds of steel products. There are pressures for investment that probably do not correspond entirely to the most economical allocation of resources; shifts in national positions resulting from the rate of investment may manifest themselves. How effective the High Authority is in influencing the pattern of investment is not clear, but there does not appear to be any major difficulty calling for a radical revision in the kind of investment guidance the High Authority has been offering. Not the least of the inhibitions that would hold back a shift to a more drastic policy—even if this were feasible under Treaty law and acceptable to the governments and industry, two issues that are far from clear—is the uncertainty that centralized investment decisions would be any better than the present diffusion of investment decisions.

There is still some agitation for a firmly guided Community investment policy.[28] Usually this is linked with the old fear of the European steel industry that capacity will become too great, demand will fall, producers with large overhead will try to sell at almost any price, resulting in cutthroat competition and serious losses in investment. Even if the Community never tries to achieve elaborate coordination of investment, it will continue to face the alternatives of an expansive or a cautious policy. If the High Authority assumes that overcapacity is a very real threat, it will sound warning notes. Firms will probably be slow to make investments even though they are free to do so. If the High Authority sounds the opposite note, that too is likely to have an influence on what businessmen do.

[28] "What is needed above all is the establishment of a rational co-ordination of investments in all the European countries taken together, to avoid duplication of facilities, the waste of none-too-plentiful capital, the risk of social difficulties in times of recession and an imperfect use of Europe's raw materials. . . ." André Armengaud, "L'Avenir de l'Économie Européenne: Organisation Raisonnée ou Décadence," *Politique Étrangère*, no. 2, Summer 1957, p. 163.

However, if the industrialists do not share this optimism investment will lag behind the rate the High Authority thinks desirable, but that is likely to be true under a policy of "coordination" as well as in the less ambitious practices used so far.

The choice between an expansive approach and a more cautious one is a continuing problem for the Community. The broad public interest seems to favor the assumption that demand for steel will grow at a rate warranting considerable expansion of capacity even though there is a risk of temporary surplus capacity during cyclical downturns. If this assumption proved false, the industry would suffer the burden of fixed costs for unused capacity; failures and bankruptcies would be likely. There would be problems for the Community affecting prices, cartel practices, trade, and adjustment. If more pessimistic assumptions were made, the Community would have a stronger position for meeting depression. But if the pessimistic assumptions were wrong there would be shortages and bottlenecks and steel would be a drag on the economic expansion of Western Europe.

If the expansionist course is chosen what can the Community do to encourage investment? The psychological influence of the High Authority's investment guidance is probably its main asset. It could be buttressed by indications that if production fell short of demand, prices would be held down and imports encouraged, which would decrease the temptations of a Malthusian attitude toward investment. Confidence that in recession or depression the Community could effectively help prevent major disasters would reduce the fear of excess capacity. Vigilance to ensure that agreed restrictionism did not prevail might also be important, for if the more enterprising producer is free to back up his judgment by expanding capacity the pessimism of others is likely to be affected.

This relates closely to one of the largest items of the Community's unfinished business, the maintenance of an effective anticartel policy, and its counterpart, the effective solution of the problems that will arise regarding concentrations. To date the High Authority has pursued a mixed policy on cartel practices in which the dominant note was the surveillance of collusion rather than its prevention. Part of the relative success stems from the absence of serious challenge in the form of efforts to extend collusion from prices to such matters as the division of markets. In dealing with concentrations, the High Authority has had good ground for the view that no mergers were being proposed that would dominate the market. It cannot be assumed that the rather comfortable conditions of the transitional period will always exist. More serious difficulties seem likely to arise.

This leads inevitably to the questions clustering around the reality of the common market. Governmental practices are involved and also the willingness of producers to compete with one another and to invade the national markets of other countries. Earlier chapters have explored the difficulties of these issues and their implications. Many of the problems existed in the transitional period, and there was progress in solving some, but the Community will continue to face these issues with no certainty that the formulas found in the first five years will serve for the future. Having come to substitute for governments in many matters, the High Authority and the other organs of the Community will be forced to formulate policies (or take decisions implying policies) over a wider range than in the past. Not just the principles of pricing but the level of prices will be an issue for the Community. The Treaty's simple rules on subsidies cover only some of the issues. The decisions on concentrations and cartels that lie ahead are harder than those made in the past five years. There is also unfinished business in transportation, adaptation, and labor matters.

All these questions exist in both the coal and the steel industries, but with different importance and sometimes in different forms, as we have seen. In coal, they must all be fitted into the framework of basic problems of the level and cost of coal production that go beyond any that were solved by the Community in the transitional period. The competition of other fuels carries the questions beyond the legal competence of the Coal and Steel Community. The noneconomic factors that are thoroughly enmeshed in coal policy and the economic difficulties themselves point to the evolution of a managed Community coal economy in which the course of policy itself will be depend to some extent on who does the managing. The existence of the Community provides the possibility, but not the assurance, that Europe's coal problems will be handled better than if each country approached them on a strictly national basis.

In coal matters, the Community will either have to become something quite different from what was envisaged or it will become of secondary importance. In steel, on the other hand, the Community's problems seem likely to be largely those it has already faced, supplemented by unfinished business. Investment, cartels, concentrations, competition, the kind of public control the Community provides, and the reality of the common market are matters on which the Community has already left its mark. One cannot believe, however, that the action taken during the transitional period has disposed of the core of each problem or even that the course of development has been unalterably set. Nevertheless, what the Community can accomplish in these matters depends to a considerable degree on the conditions it has already established and the new settings it has provided in which interests and forces can contest and combine.

HOPES, FEARS, AND RESULTS

The Coal and Steel Community has changed Europe simply by existing. By surviving through its transitional period the Community proved itself something more than a good idea, a new hope, the latest expression of an ideal to which many had long paid homage. That so old a dream should have taken on institutional form, with organization, procedures, a daily routine of problems and activities, is itself the main fact about the Schuman Plan and a major statement about Europe of the 1950s. The Community is now a part of the political and social furniture of Western Europe, one of the realities of its coal and steel economy. This is the starting place for appraisal.

The existence of the Community reflects some of the changes that are taking place in Europe and also influences those changes. To discriminate between its specific influence and that of other elements of European development is, as the last few chapters have shown, a difficult and probably an impossible task. The main *direction* of its influence is clear, however. The Community makes for the organization of economic activity on a broader basis than that of national markets; it limits the effectiveness of purely national policies affecting coal and steel; it tends toward a certain degree of harmony in the conditions of production and marketing; it alters the conditions of competition, encourages the exchange of goods, and thereby improves the chances for more economical production and a better allocation of resources. How far the Community goes in all of these matters is not something that can be simply stated, as the analysis of this book has shown. In every case there are contradictory forces. There are obstacles inherent in the situation and difficulties arising from conflicting private and public interests. There are limits on the Community's power stemming from the grant of authority under its Treaty, from the way its affairs have been conducted, and, perhaps most important of all, from its character as a measure of partial economic integration.

Partly as a result of these limitations, partly for other reasons, none of the vast changes expected from the creation of the Community have occurred. There have been none of the serious, almost convulsive, dislocations feared by some, none of the drastic declines in the position of one or another national industry or radical shifts in the direction of trade. Correspondingly, the improvement in production and living standards has been less than was hoped for by others when they imagined what a coal-steel pool would mean, though the common market has contributed to the expansion of trade. The coal and steel economies of the six countries have not been revolutionized, for good or ill. But they have been changed, for the most part fairly slowly but in a perceptible fashion. Most important of all, processes have been set in motion that seem likely to move—slowly and with setbacks, no doubt—in the direction already established.

Only a very preliminary interim balance of the Community can be drawn as yet, and that is not a model of clarity. But there can be no disputing that a new process has been begun. This is not just a matter of economic influences on coal and steel production. It involves more than the problematical interplay of the pooled and unpooled that gives the Community a certain influence over the rest of the Western European economy while it is itself subjected to outside pressures. The essence of the process lies in the creation of new elements: the new economic space created by the common market and the application of some common rules throughout the Community; the drawing of a line between the Community and the rest of the world; the establishment of new forms of public control over business. The Treaty rules and the Community procedures have established new bases for making decisions affecting the coal and steel industries. The new processes change the constellation of old and new forces and presage different results from the interplay that took place within the old framework.

There is nothing inevitable about the future of the Community. It can be destroyed, though that does not seem very likely at present. It can be perverted from its high purposes. It can be shrunk and allowed to fall into performing largely technical functions or serving to register decisions made by old national and private forces. It can be by-passed or absorbed in broader movements. What the people and governments of the six countries do will decide what is to become of the Community but their action will be influenced, and up to a point determined, by what the Community accomplishes and what it promises, by the problems which it makes Europe face, and by the forces it has set in motion, as well as by the inertia of institutions. If the political and economic integration of Western Europe goes on, the Community will continue to have a place in that process. No longer the sole practical realization of the aspirations for unity, it may lose some of its symbolic significance. For some time, however, integration in coal and steel will be more advanced than in other fields of economic activity.

Certainly the Community will continue to have its own work to do. It faces a long agenda of unfinished business. The common market is far from perfect. The adaptation of coal and steel production to it is incomplete. The effectiveness of the new forms of public control over business is not fully demonstrated. To cope with some of its future problems the Community will need policies that are more comprehensive and more precise than those of the transitional period. In supervising cartels and concentrations, for instance, the High Authority will have to apply standards going beyond any developed in the transitional period; enforcement will present new difficulties and tests of strength. In dealing with prices and investments, the High Authority and the Council of Ministers will have to concern themselves with issues that could be largely ignored in the first five years. The intractable coal economy of the six countries will have to be fitted into Europe's changing energy needs. In steel as well as coal more attention will almost certainly have to be given to the management of the Community's relations with the rest of the world. In all these matters the Community will face the difficulty of reconciling policies based on long-run aims with the exigencies of cyclical fluctuations, not just on paper but in the harsher atmosphere of jobs, profits, markets, and urgent political pressures. The tests to which the coal surplus is submitting the Community as these words are written suggest some of the problems that are almost certain to arise again. Running through all these issues is the fundamental political problem of the Community: who will exercise how much power—public or private, national or supranational—and how? The Community is by nature a mixed system but the proportions of the mixture can vary and with them the results. A fundamental political tension between old and new ways of exercising power is inherent in the Community. Its progress in integration depends on the development of the new forms of asserting authority and defining the public interest. Against this there is a constant pressure, that grows when times are hard and problems urgent, for the exercise of power in the familiar and established patterns, which are also those in which political responsibility still largely runs. The constant play of conflicting forces and the continual appearance of new problems in coal and steel make it certain that the Community will continue to change, and that too is part of its essence.

Present perspectives on the Coal and Steel Community are very different from those of May 9, 1950, when the French Foreign Minister put forth his startling proposal. The vast vistas remain, but they are fewer because we can see more clearly what can and cannot be done by the pooling of coal and steel. The distant goals that attracted all eyes in 1950 are to some extent obscured by more immediate problems and possibilities. The obstacles that loomed in the mind's eye when the Community was first proposed are, some of them, behind us, while others appear in sharper focus, their details clearly revealed. The transitional period has proved many things, most immediately about the ability of the Community to function and exist, more generally about the ability of sovereign nations and established private interests to find new ways of carrying on their affairs when some of the basic assumptions are changed. The main result, however, has been to begin a process. Robert Schuman's words of 1950 have become the reality of 1959. The process that was begun may have no end, not even a certain direction, but it has changed Europe.

CRITICAL BIBLIOGRAPHY

THE COMMUNITY had hardly been established when a German bibliography appeared listing over 1,300 items. Since then thousands of additional articles, books, and reports have been published. Though I have undoubtedly failed to use much good material, it has proved impracticable to give a complete list of my sources. Instead this bibliography provides a brief guide through the Community documents, indicates some general works that have been useful throughout the book, and notes items of particular relevance to certain chapters. I apologize for thus acknowledging only such a small part of my debt to other writers and especially to the authors of so many articles that have been my daily provender for several years. To save space I have usually not repeated references made in the footnotes to the text. For further references the student must turn to the following bibliographies (I omit several dealing with Euratom, the Common Market, and the Free Trade Area published by the Common Assembly and the European Parliamentary Assembly in 1957 and 1958).

Institut für Europäische Politik und Wirtschaft. *Bibliographie zum Schumanplan, 1950-1952*. Frankfurt: Author, 1953. 151 p.
European Coal and Steel Community. Common Assembly. *Bibliographie Analytique du Plan Schuman et de la C.E.C.A.* Luxembourg: Author, 1955. v. 1, 131 p.
————. ————. *Bulletin Mensuel de Bibliographie* (1953-1955); *Bibliographie Méthodique Trimestrielle* (1956-1957); European Parliamentary Assembly, *Bibliographie Méthodique Trimestrielle* (1958-).
————. ————. *Catalogue Analytique du Fonds Plan Schuman – CECA*. Luxembourg: Author, 1955, 1957. v. 1, 218 p.; v. 2, 240 p.
————. High Authority. *Articles Sélectionnés* (1956-). Irregular; about 70 issues published through 1958.
————. ————. *Bibliographies de la Haute Autorité*. In the years 1955-1958 bibliographies of varying lengths were published on specific subjects—nuclear energy, navigation, automation, the Common Market, the Free Trade Area, Euratom, the economic situation in Eastern Europe, problems of the recession, regional studies.

COMMUNITY DOCUMENTS

This book is largely written from published Community documents. What follows is not a complete list but a guide to the principal general sources. Additional specific studies are mentioned in the sections on separate chapters. Community documents usually appear in several official languages, some also in English. The titles indicate the editions I have used. In quoting from English language editions I have sometimes altered the translations while retaining the original page references.

Other organs

Court decisions appear in the *J.O.* and after some delay in *Recueil de la Jurisprudence de la Cour* (Luxembourg: Author, 1955-1957, v. 1-3) which also includes analytical summaries and the opinions of the *Avocat général*. Fuller documentation on some cases, including briefs of the contending parties, is sometimes available mimeographed.

The Council of Ministers has no regular publications. The results of some of its transactions appear in the texts of intergovernmental agreements or other instruments appearing in *J.O.* which also notes the occasions on which the Council gives assent to proposals by the High Authority. *Annuaire-Manuel* notes the meetings of the Council and has some other data.

The proceedings of the Consultative Committee are not public. The papers circulate rather widely in the Community however and it is not difficult to gain access to them. I have been able to consult a large number of Consultative Committee reports and accounts of its sessions and those of its subcommittees but because of their status they are not quoted or cited.

The Council of Association in which British representatives meet those of the Community has published annual reports since December 1956. Mimeographed press releases also give an account of the meetings of this body and its committees.

GENERAL STUDIES OF THE SCHUMAN PLAN

The list below comprises those books known to me that deal generally with the Community, and a few selected pamphlets. I have omitted legal works except for Valentine's useful guide to the Court. Reuter's treatise has substantial legal elements but is especially valuable as an authoritative and thorough exegesis of the Treaty. To a degree, Prieur, an official of the Court, supplements this, drawing on several years of Community activities. Though parts of some of the earlier volumes are dated, there is much of value in them, for instance Hahn's work on costs and economic conditions, some of the analyses in the Belgian institute's book, parts of Mason's account. (I have reviewed several of these books in the *American Economic Review*, September 1953, pp. 688-692.) Bok's analyses have been helpful and I have often doubted whether my more exhaustive treatment of some issues added to what he had already said. Jürgensen's study, which traces the development and trade of the European steel industry from the '20s on, is one of the most interesting pieces of work that has been done on Community problems. In making a case study of the "integrative process," Haas has produced a major contribution to our understanding of how the Community operates. He has collected published and unpublished material of great value on the attitudes and activities of interest groups and bases his analysis on an intimate knowledge of the workings of the Community organs. My own work was too far advanced to make as full use as I should have liked of Haas' book, which he was kind enough to let me read in galley proof, but I have benefited from it at many points. The seven volumes of the Centro Italiano contain a number of interesting papers. I was unable to consult the full text until after my work was done but had the benefit

Treaty Establishing the European Coal and Steel Community (no date, probably 1953, issued by HA) is the text I have used. The document also includes the Convention containing the Transitional Provisions, four protocols, and the exchange of letters concerning the Saar. A large paper edition entitled *Treaty Constituting . . . .* but otherwise unidentified has a somewhat different text.

Journal Officiel de la Communauté Européenne du Charbon et de l'Acier—since April 1958 *Journal Officiel des Communautés Européennes* —is the official gazette of the Community and a basic source (indexed; issued from time to time since December 30, 1952). *J. O.* publishes the text of High Authority decisions, some of its letters to governments, Court decisions and notices of cases, agreements with foreign countries, questions by members of the Assembly and the answers given by the High Authority, quarterly HA forecasts, various announcements and a number of other Community documents.

High Authority

Each spring the HA publishes a general report on Community activities over the past year. From 1953 to 1955 additional reports appeared in the autumn or on special occasions. All these (called *Reports*, followed by the date, but fully identified below) have been major sources for this book. The April 1958 *Report* provides a good review of the whole transitional period. (Quotations from this report differ more than usual from the official English version to which page references refer because I worked from a French text.) All the reports were published in Luxembourg by the High Authority.

Report on the Situation of the Community. January 1953. 142 p.
The Activities of the European Community: General Report. April 1953. 116 p.
The Establishment of the Common Market for Steel: Special Report. May 1953. 57 p. Supplement to the *Report* of April 1953.
Report on the Situation of the Community at the Beginning of 1954. January 1954. 61 p.
Second General Report on the Activities of the Community. April 1954. 187 p.
Report on the Situation of the Community Laid before the Extraordinary Session of the Common Assembly. November 1954. 149 p.
Third General Report on the Activities of the Community. April 1955. 186 p.
Report on the Activities of the High Authority To Be Laid before the Extraordinary Session of the Common Assembly. November 1955. [68 p.]
Fourth General Report on the Activities of the Community. April 1956. 277 p.
Fifth General Report on the Activities of the Community. April 1957. 358 p.; also *Annexes,* 74 p.
Sixth General Report on the Activities of the Community. April 1958. v. 1, 102 p.; v. 2, 391 p.

From October 1953 to the end of 1955 the High Authority published a *Rapport Mensuel* (some issues also appeared in English) providing current information of the sort contained in the annual reports. Technically documents for internal use, most issues were generally available. These were replaced in January 1956 by a *Bulletin Mensuel d'Information* (some issues covering more than one month). A *Bulletin from the European Community for Coal and Steel* (monthly or bi-monthly since the fall of 1954; indexed) published by the Community's information office in Washington, D.C. summarizes Community developments and documents and also carries original articles and interviews. (The words "for Coal and Steel" were dropped from the title in May-June 1958.) Another periodical of the same title issued in London differs in numbering and contents.

The HA also issues mimeographed press releases. Background papers dealing with labor, Belgian coal, French steel, transportation, and cartels appeared in 1955, but the series was apparently not continued. The Service d'Information at one time prepared a valuable *Revue de Presse* culling opinions about the Community, but whether this has been continued is not clear. Speeches by members of the High Authority and occasionally officials of the staff are frequently available in mimeographed form and sometimes appear as printed pamphlets. A number of the principal speeches by the first chairman appear in Jean Monnet, *Les États-Unis d'Europe Ont Commencé* (Paris: Laffont, 1955. 171 p.).

The use of HA documents is complicated by the fact that a number have circulated in mimeographed form without clear indications as to whether they were to be regarded as publications; this is particularly true of certain policy statements that were submitted to the Assembly or other Community organs for debate with the intention—not always carried out—of putting them into printed form later. To some extent one must judge by the method of distribution and by public reference to these papers. Where this was clear I have listed or cited documents. Other papers were provided to me with freedom to use their contents without citation or quotation.

Bulletin Statistique, a bi-monthly, is the most comprehensive regular source of Community statistics, but it is supplemented at many points by the annual, monthly, and special reports. *Informations Statistiques* (bi-monthly, indexed) provides extensive additional data, often in the form of special studies, and sometimes discusses statistical problems. *Recueil Statistique* (1953, 293 p.) is valuable for the situation when the Community began although there are gaps in the data. For a longer perspective in steel a High Authority brochure is very useful: *Un Siècle de Développement de la Production d'Acier* (1957, 29 p.), a supplement to the *Bulletin Mensuel d'Information*, January 1957-February 1958.

Common Assembly

The verbatim account of debates appears as *Débats de l'Assemblée Commune, Compte Rendu in Extenso des Séances* (indexed). Pending its preparation a *Compte Rendu Analytique* (mimeographed) appears, using précis and paraphrase. A *procès-verbal* noting subjects discussed, speakers, and the texts of Assembly resolutions appears in the *J.O.* which also carries Assembly agenda in advance. Some HA speeches made in the Assembly are separately issued as pamphlets.

The Assembly committees (eight in 1958, plus three subcommittee[s,] a working group) normally lay one or more reports apiece before [the] Assembly at each session. These appear in either printed or mi[meo]graphed form, usually carry descriptive titles, and are numbered for [each] session. Some of the reports are largely formal (drafts of resoluti[ons,] etc.) and some from the early years say little, but over most of [the] period they are valuable guides to Assembly opinion and sometimes p[ro]vide expositions of problems unobtainable elsewhere. A few also cont[ain] information not to be found in other sources. Some committee repor[ts] of special interest are noted in the chapter sections or in footnotes; [a] full list appears in *Annuaire-Manuel de l'Assemblée Commune*.

This document (three issues, 1956, 1957, 1958, appearing early in th[e] year mentioned) is a valuable reference work. It lists the members an[d] principal officials of Community bodies, closely related agencies, foreign delegations, representatives of interest groups, etc. The organization of the Assembly, its party groups, committees, and similar matters are given special attention; each volume carries the texts of resolutions, questions to the HA, and a list of committee reports. A very valuable section provides an extended summary of Community activities over the previous calendar year (from the beginning to the end of 1955 for the first *Annuaire-Manuel*). Though it is drawn largely from other published material, the chronological and subject organization of these accounts makes them very useful for reviewing Community activity, finding relevant documents, etc. Before *Annuaire-Manuel* appeared, the Assembly's Service d'Études et de Documentation provided similar chronicles covering six-month periods under the title *Rapport sur l'Application du Traité . . .* (processed). A consolidated review of the first five years, which looks very valuable but arrived too late for me to use, is Assemblée Parlementaire Européenne, *L'Application du Traité Instituant la C.E.C.A. au Cours de la Période Transitoire* (Luxembourg: Author, 1958; 294 p.). The Assembly published one annual report but did not continue the practice: *Premier Rapport Annuel*, Sept. 1952-Sept. 1953 (Luxembourg: Author, 1953; 94 p.).

The Assembly's five joint meetings with the Consultative Assembly of the Council of Europe are recorded in documents marked "Official Report of the Debate." The report of the first session held June 1953 was titled: *Joint Meeting of the Members of the Consultative Assembly of the Council of Europe and of the Members of the Common Assembly of the European Community of Coal and Steel*. Later reports are called *Second Joint Meeting . . .*, etc., and were held in May 1954, and October 1955, 1956, and 1957.

The Assembly's Division des Études, Information, et Documentation produces *Informations Mensuelles* (formerly bi-monthly), a pamphlet recording Community activities and often including excerpts from publications, company reports, statements by interest groups, etc. For some time the series has covered other developments in European integration as well and some issues have been wholly devoted to Euratom and the Common Market.

At the end of February 1958 the Common Assembly was replaced by the Assemblée Parlementaire Européenne. Titles of documents therefore change; some committees were added.

of a summary that appeared as a supplement to *Mondo Economico* (June 22, 1957).

The pamphlets listed here have been chosen from many to provide a short course on the Community. Less generally available, but outstanding for their clarity and conciseness are the accounts of the Community's work appearing in the two prospectuses issued for the American loans (Kuhn, Loeb & Co., The First Boston Corporation, Lazard Frères & Co.; April 9, 1957 and June 24, 1958).

Bok, Derek Curtis. *The First Three Years of the Schuman Plan*. Studies in International Finance, no. 5. Princeton: Princeton University Press, 1955. 79 p.

Centro Italiano di Studi Giuridici. *Actes Officiels du Congrès International d'Études sur la Communauté Européenne du Charbon et de l'Acier*. Milan: Author, 1957-1958. 7 v.

Goormaghtigh, John. "European Coal and Steel Community," *International Conciliation* (May 1955). 65 p.

Haas, Ernst B. *The Uniting of Europe*. Stanford: Stanford University Press, 1958. 552 p.

Hahn, C. H. *Der Schuman-Plan*. Munich: Pflaum, 1953. 158 p.

Haussmann, Frederick. *Der Schuman-Plan im Europäischen Zwielicht*. Munich: Beck, 1952. 266 p.

Institut des Relations Internationales. *La Communauté Européenne du Charbon et de l'Acier*. Brussels: Author, 1953. 338 p. (Also Paris: Colin, 1953.)

Jürgensen, Harald. *Die Westeuropäische Montanindustrie und Ihr Gemeinsamer Markt*. Göttingen: Vandenhoeck & Ruprecht, 1955. 264 p. + statistical appendix.

Kövér, J. F. *Le Plan Schuman*. Paris: Nouvelles Éditions Latines, 1952. 232 p.

Maryland, University of. Bureau of Business and Economic Research. *The European Coal and Steel Community*. College Park: Author, 1955-1956. Pt. 1, 20 p.; pt. 2, 16 p.

Mason, Henry L. *The European Coal and Steel Community: Experiment in Supranationalism*. The Hague: Nijhoff, 1955. 153 p.

Philip, André. *The Schuman Plan: Nucleus of a European Community*. [Brussels]: European Movement, 1951. 46 p.

Prieur, Raymond. *Les Relations Internes et Externes de la Communauté Européenne du Charbon et de l'Acier*. Paris: Montchrestien, 1958. 311 p.

Racine, Raymond. *Vers une Europe Nouvelle par le Plan Schuman*. Neuchâtel: La Baconnière, 1954. 242 p.

Reuter, Paul. *La Communauté Européenne du Charbon et de l'Acier*. Paris: Librairie Générale de Droit et de Jurisprudence, 1953. 320 p.

de Soto, Jean. *La Communauté Européenne du Charbon et de l'Acier*. Paris: Presses Universitaires de France, 1958. 124 p.

Valentine, D. C. *The Court of Justice of the European Coal and Steel Community*. The Hague: Nijhoff, 1955. 273 p.

Vignes, Daniel. *La Communauté Européenne du Charbon et de l'Acier: Un Exemple d'Administration Économique Internationale*. Paris: Librairie Générale de Droit et de Jurisprudence, 1956. 196 p.

Wigny, Pierre. *Un Témoignage sur la Communauté des Six.* Luxembourg: ECSC, 1957. 121 p.

Having omitted so many good articles from this bibliography, it seems invidious to cite a few in this general section. I thought, however, that a few, in English, might be helpful to those who want a quick review of Community matters. I have often found myself turning to these in the course of my work. Sanderson's appeared too late for that but strikes me as a very balanced and perceptive survey of more recent Community developments.

Mendershausen, Horst. "First Tests of the Schuman Plan," *Review of Economics and Statistics* (November 1953), pp. 269-288.

Parker, William N. "The Schuman Plan—A Preliminary Prediction," *International Organization* (August 1952), pp. 381-395.

Sanderson, Fred H. "The Five-Year Experience of the European Coal and Steel Community," *International Organization* (Spring 1958), pp. 193-200.

Vernon, Raymond. "The Schuman Plan," *American Journal of International Law* (April 1953), pp. 183-202.

Zawadzki, K. K. F. "The Economics of the Schuman Plan," *Oxford Economic Papers* (June 1953), pp. 157-189.

For anyone interested in inspecting the hostages I gave to fortune before writing this book, I should say that in addition to two papers referred to in the sections on Chs. 4 and 22, I committed myself to paper on Community problems in "Where Is the Schuman Plan Heading?" *European Union* (American Committee on United Europe, New York), (August 1953), pp. 8-15, and "Some Crucial Problems Facing the European Community for Coal and Steel," *Bulletin from the European Community for Coal and Steel* (Washington, D. C.), (June 1955), pp. 4-6.

BACKGROUND STUDIES AND CURRENT SOURCES

Anyone who tries to see the European steel industry in perspective is in the debt of D. L. Burn for his brilliant study, *The Economic History of Steel-Making, 1867-1939: A Study in Competition* (Cambridge: Cambridge University Press, 1940; 548 p.). One can only hope that the long-talked-of sequel may soon appear. Another useful book is *Coal and Steel in Western Europe* by Norman J. G. Pounds and William N. Parker (Bloomington: Indiana University Press, 1957; 381 p.)—in which Part Three, by Parker, is particularly interesting for the subjects treated in this book. The chapters on coal and steel in Ingvar Svennilson's *Growth and Stagnation in the European Economy* (Geneva: UN Economic Commission for Europe, 1954; 342 p.) are also valuable and stimulating. Through the kindness of Professor Adolph Lowe of the New School for Social Research I have had the advantage of reading an interesting unpublished study of the international steel industry prepared by Ernest Hamburger for the Institute of World Affairs in the early '50s. Other books and pamphlets of the same general sort that I have found useful (in addition to many articles) are:

Ferry, Jacques, and René Chatel. *L'Acier*. Paris: Presses Universitaires de France, 1953. 135 p.

Fontaine, Maurice. *L'Industrie Sidérurgique dans le Monde et Son Évolution Économique depuis la Seconde Guerre Mondiale*. Paris: Presses Universitaires de France, 1950. 398 p.

Friedensburg, Ferdinand. *Die Bergwirtschaft der Erde*. 5th ed. Stuttgart: Enke, 1956. 562 p.

Hellwig, Fritz. *Westeuropas Montanwirtschaft*. Cologne: Deutsche Industrieverlags, 1953. 86 p.

Kunze, Hanns-Jürgen. *Die Lagerungsordnung der Westeuropäischen Eisen- und Stahlindustrie im Lichte Ihrer Kostenstruktur*. Kiel: Institut für Weltwirtschaft, 1954. 100 p.

Rassmann, Richard. *Die Europäische Steinkohlenwirtschaft zwischen den Beiden Weltkriegen*. Oberursel: Europa-Archiv, 1947. 35 p. + statistical appendix.

U. S. Tariff Commission. *Iron and Steel*. Report no. 128, Second Series. Washington: GPO, 1938. 527 p.

Publications of the OEEC and the ECE have been useful at every turn, for instance the OEEC's annual reports, the annual *Economic Survey of Europe* by the ECE, the extensive statistical publications of the OEEC, and the ECE's *Quarterly Bulletin of Steel Statistics* and *Quarterly Bulletin of Coal Statistics*. The ECE's key place in the development of European cooperation in coal and steel is well summarized in *ECE: The Frst Ten Years, 1947-1957* (Geneva: Author, 1957; [112 p.]), Chs. IV and IX. Some of the major reports of these two organizations bearing directly on the problems of this book are:

ECE. *European Steel Trends in the Setting of the World Market*. 1949.II.E.2. Geneva, 1949. 148 p. A 37-page revision with statistical appendix, was published under the same title in 1951 (E/ECE/123).

————. *The European Steel Market in 1956*. 1957.II.E/Mim.14. Geneva, 1957. 119 p. Earlier issues of this annual survey covered 1953 (E/ECE/183, published in January 1954), 1954 (E/ECE/207, in June 1955), and 1955 (E/ECE/239, in June 1956). A longer-run survey is in preparation.

————. *The European Steel Industry and the Wide-Strip Mill: A Study of Production and Consumption Trends in Flat Products*. 1953.II.E.6. Geneva, 1953. 100 p. + statistical appendix.

————. *European Steel Exports and Steel Demand in Non-European Countries*. E/ECE/163. Geneva, 1953. 242 p. + statistical annex.

————. *The European Steel Pipe and Tube Industry*. E/ECE/208. Geneva, 1955. 103 p.

————. "The Coal and Steel Industries of Western Europe," *Economic Bulletin for Europe*, v. 2., no. 2 (1950), pp. 17-51.

OEEC. *Coal and European Economic Expansion*. Paris: Author, 1952. 68 p.

————. *The Coal Industry in Europe*. Studies by the Coal Committee. Paris: Author, annual since 1954.

————. *The Iron and Steel Industry in Europe*. Studies by the Iron and Steel Committee. Paris: Author, annual since 1955.

Two privately issued statistical works that I have found of value are: Ufficio Studi delle Acciaierie e Ferriere Lombarde Falck. *Profilo Statistico delle Siderurgie Comprese nel Piano Schuman.* Milan: Author, 1951-1952. 2 v.
Unternehmensverband Ruhrbergbau. *Die Kohlenwirtschaft der Welt in Zahlen, 1955.* Essen: Glückauf, 1955. 223 p.

The many periodicals that regularly cross my desk have all fed this book along with the publications of economic research organizations, bank bulletins, business reports, and statements by pressure groups, all too numerous to list. For a constant stream of information bearing directly on coal, steel, and the Community, I have leaned heavily on: *International Financial News Survey* (IMF), *International Trade News Bulletin* (GATT), *Neue Zürcher Zeitung, Le Monde, Mondo Economico, The Economist, The New York Times, Der Volkswirt, Problèmes Économiques, Nouvelles de l'Europe, Relazioni Internazionali,* and the various mimeographed series of the Deutsches Industrieinstitut. *Steel Review,* published by the British Iron and Steel Federation, has had a number of pertinent articles and devoted most of its issue of April 1958 to the Community. (Before the *Steel Review* appeared, the Federation's *Monthly Statistical Bulletin* frequently carried articles on these subjects.) From March 1955 through March 1957 the U. S. Department of Commerce published a quarterly industry report, *International Iron and Steel.* I have made less use than I intended of business journals such as *Stahl und Eisen, Glückauf,* and *L'Usine Nouvelle.* Company reports have helped me and also such annual reports by national industrial federations as have been published. A number of periodicals have devoted whole issues to the Community, such as *Droit Social* (Paris) for October 1954.

Many publications dealing primarily with national or regional industries supplement the more general ones already cited; for instance, annual supplements to *Der Volkswirt* on the German coal and steel industries, and an excellent series of short surveys of the steel industry of each Community country in the *Monthly Statistical Bulletin* of the British Iron and Steel Federation. Those that follow are listed more by way of illustration than to provide a complete catalogue. Others are cited in footnotes.

Associazione Industrie Siderurgiche Italiane. *Lineamenti Strutturali della Siderurgia Italiana.* Milan: Author, 1956. 123 p.
Banque Nationale pour le Commerce et l'Industrie. "Le Charbon en France," *Bulletin d'Information Économique* (December 1957), pp. 1-22.
Cairncross, John. "The Future of Italy's Steel Industry," *Quarterly Review* (Banca Nazionale del Lavoro), (September 1957), pp. 352-368.
Calabi, Bruno. "L'Industria Siderurgica," *Atti della Commissione Parlamentare d'Inchiesta sulla Disoccupazione,* no. 3 (1953), pp. 111-125.
Chardonnet, Jean. *La Sidérurgie Française: Progrès ou Décadence?* Paris: Colin, 1954. 238 p.
Della Porta, Glauco. "Origins, Evolution, Structure and Prospects of 'Finsider'," *Review of Economic Conditions in Italy* (Banco di Roma), (November 1955), pp. 553-565.
France. Conseil de la République. *Avis* (v. 2, *Sidérurgie*), by Jean

Bousch, presented in the name of the Commission on Industrial Production. Paris: Author, 1956. 123 p. (Annexe au procès-verbal, 6 mars 1956.)

————. ————. *Rapport d'Information*, by Jean Bousch, made in the name of the Commission on Industrial Production. Paris: Author, 1957. 96 p. (Annexe au procès-verbal, 11 juillet 1957.)

————. Ministère de l'Économie Nationale. *L'Économie de la Ruhr*. Series D-1, Études et Documents. Paris: Presses Universitaires de France, 1947. 82 p.

————. ————. *L'Économie de la Sarre*. Series D-2, Études et Documents. Paris: Presses Universitaires de France, 1947. 147 p.

Friedensburg, Ferdinand. *Das Erzproblem der Deutschen Eisenindustrie*. Deutsches Institut für Wirtschaftsforschung, Sonderhefte, Neue Folge no. 39. Berlin: Duncker & Humblot, 1957. 100 p.

Pounds, Norman J. G. *The Ruhr: A Study in Historical and Economic Geography*. Bloomington: Indiana University Press, 1952. 283 p.

For data on companies, products, organizations, and the like, the following are useful:

ECSC. HA. *Répertoire des Produits Sidérurgiques et des Entreprises du Marché Commun de l'Acier*. Luxembourg: Author, 1955. 238 p.

Gebhardt, Gerhard. *Ruhrbergbau: Geschichte, Aufbau und Verflechtung Seiner Gesellschaften und Organisationen*. Essen: Glückauf, 1957. 580 p.

UN. ECE. *Répertoire des Organisations Nationales d'Europe et des États-Unis d'Amérique et des Organisations Internationales S'Occupant de Sidérurgie*. 1957.II.E./Mim. 17. Geneva: Author, 1957. 104 p.

Wolf-Rodé, Karl, comp. (with the assistance of the Wirtschaftsvereinigung Eisen- und Stahlindustrie). *Handbuch für den Gemeinsamen Markt der Europäischen Montan-Union*. Frankfurt: Montan- und Wirtschaftsverlag K. Wolf-Rodé, 1955. [811 p.]

CHAPTER NOTES

The selected references, by chapters, supplement the Community documents and general works which in the absence of specific references can be assumed to be the main sources, along with those cited in footnotes. ("Cited in n. ——" means a footnote of the chapter being discussed.)

Chapter 1

The French text of Schuman's statement of May 9, 1950 appears in *L'Année Politique, 1950* (Paris: Éditions du Grand Siècle, 1951), pp. 306-307. I have sometimes made my own translation and sometimes borrowed from one of three differing English versions in: *The New York Times* (May 10, 1950), the British White Paper (cited in Ch. 4), and a processed release of the French Embassy's information service in New York (May 10, 1950). The latter includes some informal opening remarks which are given in French in Gerbet's article cited in Ch. 2.

Chapter 2

Gerbet's article cited in n. 1 is the best single source. For the general setting see the annual volumes of *The United States in World Affairs* (New York: Harper, for the Council on Foreign Relations). My *Trade and Payments in Western Europe* (New York: Harper, for the Council on Foreign Relations, 1952; 488 p.) deals with the developments in European economic cooperation out of which the Schuman Plan arose.

Chapter 3

Many kinds of material contributed to this chapter. For a full analysis of the effects of the First World War see Ferdinand Friedensburg, *Kohle und Eisen im Weltkriege und in den Friedensschlüssen* (Munich: Oldenbourg, 1934; 332 p.). Guy Greer, *The Ruhr-Lorraine Industrial Problem* (New York: Macmillan, 1925; 328 p.), stands as the fullest expression of the integration proposals of its era. For criticisms see Pounds' book on the Ruhr (cited on p. 727), some passages in Pounds and Parker (cited on p. 724), and Pounds' "Lorraine and the Ruhr," *Economic Geography* (April 1957), pp. 149-162.

My discussion of the Ruhr question during and after the Second World War rests on extensive work I did on the subject at the time. I benefited greatly from numerous discussions at the Council on Foreign Relations; see the chapter in Price & Schorske cited in n. 11 and my papers in Aubert's *Contrôle de l'Allemagne* (cited in n. 12), in *Foreign Affairs* (October 1948) and in *Økonomi og Politik* (Copenhagen; April-June 1950). Space makes it impossible to provide an adequate bibliography of Ruhr materials to supplement the footnotes.

Chapter 4

My account of the British negotiations is drawn largely from the white paper (cited in n. 2) and current comment. The Commons debate took place on June 26 and 27, 1950, and that in the Lords on June 28. Strachey's speech was discussed on July 11. I was in England and France during part of this period and recorded some impressions in "Imponderables of the Schuman Plan," *Foreign Affairs* (October 1950), pp. 114-129.

The mimeographed English version of the French working paper that I have used was given to me in Paris at the time. A slightly different version was distributed in the United States by the French Embassy's information service (Doc. no. 16, July 5, 1950). A French text appears in *L'Année Politique, 1950*, pp. 314-316. No full account of the negotiations among the Six exists. I am glad to say that Pierre Gerbet is preparing one. Most of my account was put together before I saw Racine. In addition to much fragmentary evidence and the *Rapport* of the French delegation cited in n. 20, I have found Reuter's book helpful and H. C. Boden's two articles in *Der Volkswirt* (March 23 and 30, 1951). (Racine and Reuter are cited on p. 723.) Some of the material referred to in the ratification chapter also bears on these matters. The closing part of the chapter draws on a variety of material.

Chapter 5

One of my major sources was *Chronique de Politique Étrangère*. (Institut des Relations Internationales, Brussels), (January 1953), pp. 7-51, which provides excellent summaries of party positions and parliamentary action on ratification. The CA study, *Le Traité C.E.C.A. devant les Parlements Nationaux* (Luxembourg: Author, 1958; 187 p., mimeographed), arrived too late for me to do anything but check the account I had already written against it. It organizes the material according to subjects as well as countries and thus provides a useful summary of conflicting views. It gives the texts of resolutions passed by the various parliamentary bodies and has other reference material. Unfortunately there appear to be errors in some of the figures on votes. Georges Goriely, "L'Opinion Publique et le Plan Schuman," *Revue Française de Science Politique* (July-September 1953), pp. 585-611, is the only critical survey of the whole process that I know. I believe Goriely prepared another paper on the action of the parliaments, but I have not seen it. Racine's book (cited on p. 723) also discusses ratification.

Among national sources I must again plead a surfeit of material as a reason for indicating only a few leading documents. The European press of the time is full of useful material and one can frequently find helpful surveys, for instance: "The Schuman Union," *The Economist* (July 22, 1950), pp. 181-183; "Schuman-Plan und Europa-Handel," *Wirtschaftsdienst* (December 1951), pp. 3-6; "Die Neuordnung der Westeuropäischen Montanindustrie," *Monatsberichte* (Creditanstalt-Bankverein, Vienna), (July 1950), pp. 3-5. An interesting sample of parliamentary opinion from a number of countries is displayed in the Council of Europe's debates on the Schuman Plan, but very few real critics spoke up. Council of Europe, Consultative Assembly, 2d sess., *Reports*, 4th, 7th, 8th, 18th, and 19th Sittings (August 1950), 23rd Sitting (November 1950).

For France, the full range of opinions can be found in Assemblée Nationale, *Journal Officiel, Débats Parlementaires* (December 6, 7, 11, and 13, 1951) and Conseil Économique, *Communauté Européenne du Charbon et de l'Acier*, Études et Travaux no. 21 (Paris: Presses Universitaires de France, [1951]; 169 p.).

A compendium of critical views appears in *Nouvelle Revue de l'Économie Contemporaine*, nos. 16/17 (1951). A more fully developed attack is Bernard Lavergne, *Le Plan Schuman: Exposé et Critique de sa Portée Économique et Politique* (2d ed. Paris: L'Année Politique et Économique, 1952; 117 p.). The only outside study of the French ratification process that I know is Henry W. Ehrmann's excellent article cited in n. 4.

My German account is largely based on the Bundestag debates (July 12, 1951, January 9-11, 1952). The first Bundesrat debate is summarized in *Europa-Archiv* (September 5, 1951), pp. 4305-4331. A convenient statement of the official view is Walter Hallstein's *Der Schuman-Plan*, Frankfurter Universitätsreden, Heft 5 (Frankfurt: Klostermann, 1951; 29 p.). A rather extreme statement of SPD criticism is *Götterdämmerung beim Schumanplan* (Hannoversche Druck- und Verlagsgesellschaft, [1953]; 46 p.). A very useful statement of differences of opinion appears in *Probleme des Schuman-Plans: Eine Diskussion zwischen Walter Hallstein und Andreas Predöhl und Fritz Baade* (Kiel: Institut für Weltwirtschaft, 1951; 34 p.).

For the other countries I have read only summaries of parliamentary debates plus a number of statements of position. In addition to material already mentioned or cited in the footnotes, see:

B.C. "Il Dibattito al Senato Italiano sul Piano Schuman," *Relazioni Internazionali* (March 22, 1952), pp. 301, 306-308. The Chamber debates are covered in the issues of June 7, 1952 (pp. 574-575) and June 21, 1952 (pp. 599-600, 611-612).

Falck, Enrico. *Tendenze Europee nella Costituzione dei Grandi Pools delle Materie Prime.* Conferenza tenuta al Politecnico di Milano il 16 Aprile 1951 per invito dell'Associazione Studenti Universitari. 23 p.
Metzler, Léon. *Le Plan Schuman dans la Perspective Luxembourgeoise.* Luxembourg: Beffort, 1951. 98 p.

Chapter 7

On tariff rates, quota provisions, etc. the *International Trade News Bulletin* published by GATT is a useful additional source to Community documents. A supplement to its issue of October 1954 provides texts and tariff schedules covering everything done up to that point.

Chapter 8

The High Authority is improving its statistics and will soon be in a position to show regional flows, the carriage of different goods, and related matters more fully than in the past. The Assembly transport committee's reports are often useful and that of November 1957 (Doc. no. 6, 1957-1958, P. J. Kapteyn, Rapporteur) is a good survey of basic problems that makes the case for broader transport integration.

Willi Scheider, *Die Tarifpolitik der Hohen Behörde und das Deutsche Verkehrswesen* (Göttingen: Vandenhoeck & Ruprecht, 1956; 166 p.), is the best critique of Community transport policy and includes much original material. It reflects the views of German transport specialists, which can be partly offset by the approach taken in Chardonnet (cited on p. 726) who is also useful on French problems. Bok's sections on this problem are helpful and Jürgensen has a good bit to say on the role of transport in trade in steel. (Bok and Jürgensen are cited on p. 723. Other selected items that I have found useful are:

Calabi, Bruno. "Piano Schuman e Costo dei Trasporti delle Materie Prime," *Rivista di Politica Economica* (May 1952), pp. 1-15.
Fortuin, H. "De Cabotage op de Rijn," *Internationale Spectator* (June 8, 1957), pp. 338-348.
Heeckt, Hugo. *Der Verkehr als Integrationsfaktor der Europawirtschaft.* Kiel: Institut für Weltwirtschaft, 1956. 106 p.
Hutter, R. "The Transport Problems within the European Coal and Steel Community," *Transport and Communication Review* (UN), (July-September 1953), pp. 21-30.
"Le Prix du Transport par Fer par Rapport aux Prix à la Production et aux Prix de Détail," *Études et Conjoncture, Économie Mondiale* (May-June 1953), pp. 205-213.
Predöhl, Andreas. "Harmonisierung der Europäischen Eisenbahntarife," *Der Volkswirt* (March 29, 1958), pp. 514-516.

The canalization of the Moselle has a sizable literature of its own and is dealt with in many places, for instance Chardonnet. Two useful, short statements of the issues are: "The Moselle Canal," *The World Today* (London), (January 1958), pp. 8-10; "Die Schiffbarmachung der Mosel," *Wirtschaftsdienst* (April 1957), pp. 222-224. The text of the agreement on canalization appears in French, German, and English in *Journal du Droit International*, no. 1 (1958), pp. 264-319.

Chapter 9

Belgian Coal in the European Coal and Steel Community, a background paper released by the HA in 1955, is a useful summary statement, but too optimistic. Later discussions in the Assembly, HA *Reports* (where the subject occupies much space), and the press are more critical. There is a good account of some Belgian reactions to HA decisions in *Chronique de Politique Étrangère* (September 1955). For sharp analyses from outside Belgium the *Neue Zürcher Zeitung* seems to me to be very good.

The material on Sulcis is sparse. HA *Reports* are essential but rather skimpy; there was some improvement in the April 1958 coverage. The best single source is the report by Heinrich Deist for the Assembly's Commission des Investissements (Doc. no. 21, 1954-1955), April 1955.

Chapter 10

The essentials are all in the Tinbergen committee's report to the HA, *Report on the Problems Raised by the Different Turnover Tax Systems Applied within the Common Market* (Luxembourg: HA, 1953; 38 p.). Reactions to the HA decision were numerous but short-lived; some examples are mentioned in footnotes. Reddaway's article (cited in n. 7) is an excellent gloss that clarifies some points. Other good discussions are in Hahn (pp. 79-82), Reuter (pp. 181-186), and Mendershausen (pp. 278-282), cited on pp. 723 and 724. A more extended discussion, that begins with the Tinbergen report but goes on to other questions, appears in Rolf Sannwald and Jacques Stohler, *Wirtschaftliche Integration: Theoretische Voraussetzungen und Folgen eines Europäischen Zusammenschlusses* (Tübingen: Mohr, 1958), pp. 174-194. The basic issues are concisely set out in Bertil Ohlin's "Taxation and Foreign Trade," an appendix to the ILO report, *Social Aspects of European Economic Co-operation,* cited more fully in Ch. 16.

Chapter 11

Almost all questions lead to prices and prices lead to almost all other questions, so it is natural that this chapter should be based on a great conglomeration of material. The articles mentioned in footnotes provide an almost random sample of a much more extensive literature. Episodes like that of the Ruhr coal price rise can be treated rather successfully through periodicals and newspapers.

Most people who have written about the Community have had something to say on prices and I have benefited from all their comments though I know of no full-scale study of Community pricing. *Preispolitik im Teilintegrierten Markt* (Tübingen: Mohr, 1958; 228 p.) by Gottfried Erb and Peter Rogge arrived too late for me to use it. We need comprehensive data on the structure of actual prices, far more information on pricing practices, and, of course, analyses of the relation of prices to costs and profits. Conversations with businessmen, officials, and those who have studied the Community, which have helped me in all my work, were particularly important for this chapter.

Chapter 12

Points of view are reflected in industry statements (some of which are cited) and in several periodical articles. On the American side, the best analysis I know of the scrap position is Percy W. Bidwell's *Raw Materials: A Study of American Policy* (New York: Harper, for the Council on Foreign Relations, 1958), Ch. 7. The hearings and report of the House Committee on Small Business, though they are particularly concerned with monopolistic tendencies in the scrap trade, are useful sources for the whole story of United States policy on scrap exports.

U. S. House. Select Committee on Small Business. *Small-Business Problems Relating to Iron and Steel Scrap.* Hearings, 85th Cong., 1st sess., pursuant to H. Res. 56. Washington: GPO, 1957. 2 v.

————. ————. *Final Report.* Report no. 2718, 85th Cong., 2d sess. Washington: GPO, 1959. 225 p.

Chapter 13

Convenient annual summaries of the financial affairs of the Community are published in English under the title *Financial Report for the Year.* . . . by HA's Finance Division. (The first covered 1953-1955.)

In discussing the American loan I have worked from a mimeographed copy of the agreement. The communiqué at the time of signing is cited in n. 7. Also of interest are:

Memorandum submitted by the High Authority of the European Coal and Steel Community to the Government of the United States of America. Luxembourg: HA, 1954. 25 p.

U. S. Comptroller General. *Examination of 100 Million Dollar Loan to European Coal and Steel Community*, Report to Congress. Washington: Author, 1957. (Mimeographed.) 12 p.

The Loans of the European Coal and Steel Community by Jean L. Blondeel and Henri Vander Eycken (Doc. no. 5821/55e; [HA], mimeographed, 1955) is an interesting analysis of the legal and administrative arrangements. On the private loans floated in the United States the best sources are the two prospectuses (cited on p. 723). On loans in other countries I have relied on Community documents and the financial press.

My discussion of the considerations that lay behind the HA's investment policy and the interplay of views about what the Community's role in investments should be rests on many sources and numerous conversations. The writings of Dr. Hermann J. Abs have been helpful to me in understanding the banking point of view, those of Senator Armengaud for the approach favoring "coordination." Parker's *International Organization* article (cited on p. 724) is good on the difficulty of applying "objective" criteria in a situation of partial integration. Two good reviews of the whole problem are Rainer Hellmann's "Montanvertrag und Investitionspolitik" in *Der Volkswirt* (March 9, 1957), pp. 438-441; and Bruno Calabi's "Devoirs d'Intervention de la Haute Autorité de la C.E.C.A. pour Développer et Équilibrer les Investissements" in v. 5 (pp. 79-113) of the *Actes Officiels du Congrès International d'Études* . . . (cited on p. 723).

This chapter and Ch. 20 retain only the residue of a much longer draft on the course of investment for which useful sources were the Monnet Plan reports, the annual reports to the Assemblée Générale Ordinaire des Actionnaires of the GIS (Groupement de l'Industrie

Sidérurgique), the ECE reports on the steel market, the publications of a number of German economic research organizations, notably the *Vierteljahrshefte zur Wirtschaftsforschung* and the *Wochenbericht* of the Deutsches Institut für Wirtschaftsforschung (Berlin), and annual reports of trade associations, companies, and Charbonnages de France. There are many problems on the comparability of statistics concerning investment and that is one reason I have in the end relied almost entirely on the HA's annual survey, *Les Investissements dans les Industries du Charbon et de l'Acier de la Communauté*. Unfortunately the *Rapport sur l'Enquête 1957* was the latest available to me when most of this writing was done. It covers 1957 and 1958 only in terms of plans. Results of the 1958 survey are foreshadowed in the HA *Report* of April 1958; partial figures appeared in a press release of September 25, 1958.

The long-run forecasts and objectives are reported in the annual HA *Reports* and some statements noted in Ch. 23.

Chapter 14

Ervin Hexner's *The International Steel Cartel* (Chapel Hill: University of North Carolina Press, 1943; 339 p.) remains the best general source on its subject. Additional data and especially statistics can be found in Günther Kiersch, *Internationale Eisen- und Stahlkartelle* (Essen: Rheinisch-Westfälisches Institut für Wirtschaftsforschung, 1954; 224 p.). A good short critical account is George W. Stocking and Myron W. Watkins, *Cartels in Action* (New York: Twentieth Century Fund, 1946; Ch. 5). The largest work directed specifically toward the Community's cartel problem is Henri Rieben, *Des Ententes de Maîtres de Forges au Plan Schuman* (Ambilly-Annemass: Presses de Savoie, 1954; 556 p.). His account of the rise and activities of national and international organizations and their efforts to control the market is valuable; the line of argument often provides helpful statements of the cartel case and insights into the cartel mentality; the thesis that the Community can provide what was missing in the international steel cartel—public control, fuller knowledge, and direct influence on production—is interesting. (See my review in *American Economic Review*, March 1956, pp. 224-226.)

On deconcentration in German steel, the most authoritative source, with many documents, is the report of the trustees appointed by the occupation authorities: *Die Neuordnung der Eisen- und Stahlindustrie im Gebiet der Bundesrepublik Deutschland* (Munich: Beck, 1954; 870 p.). The background and some of the issues in coal are examined in Frederick Haussmann, *Der Neuaufbau der Deutschen Kohlenwirtschaft im Internationalen Rahmen* (Munich: Beck, 1950; 182 p.). See also Paul Wiel, "Wirtschafts- und Organisationspolitik im Westeuropäischen Kohlenbergbau bis zur Errichtung der Montanunion," *Europa-Archiv* (July 5, 1953), pp. 5803-5813; and Franz Grosse, "Das Ringen um die Absatzorganisation des Ruhrbergbaus," *Wirtschaftsdienst* (September 1955), pp. 513-516. A very handy account, with details on companies, is K. H. Herchenröder et al., *Die Nachfolger der Ruhrkonzerne* (Düsseldorf: Econ-Verlag, 1953; 368 p.). There is also useful company material and a short history of coal decartelization in *Ruhrbergbau . . .* by Gerhard Gebhardt (cited on p. 727).

On the structure of the coal and steel industries in various countries, the merger movements, etc., see the general works already cited, the country studies, company reports, and sources cited in footnotes 13, 17, 23, and 32. It would be most helpful if studies of other Community industries were made along the lines of G. Gori's valuable *Lineamenti Strutturali* . . . cited in n. 35. In addition I have been helped by:

"La Sidérurgie Allemande," *Problèmes Économiques* (Paris), (January 14, 1958), pp. 12-16.

Lauersen, Walther. *Ausmass und Formen Vertikaler Verflechtung in der Eisen- und Stahlindustrie der Vereinigten Staaten, Grossbritanniens, Frankreichs, Belgiens und Luxemburgs.* Kiel: Institut für Weltwirtschaft, 1951. 197 p.

Rieben, Henri. "ECSC and Cartels," *Cartel* (London), (January 1957), pp. 6-14; (April 1957), pp. 42-49.

Steiner, Herbert. *Grössenordnung und Horizontale Verflechtung in der Eisen- und Stahlindustrie der Vereinigten Staaten, Grossbritanniens, Frankreichs, Belgiens, Luxemburgs und Deutschlands.* Kiel: Institut für Weltwirtschaft, 1952. 119 p.

The sources referred to in n. 33 are the HA's *Recueil Statistique* (1952), *Handbuch* . . . (cited on p. 727), the two Prospectuses (cited on p. 723), Wehrer's article cited in n. 32, *Lineamenti Strutturali*, and Henri Fayat's *Rapport* . . . *sur les Concentrations d'Entreprises dans la Communauté*, prepared for the Common Assembly's Commission du Marché Commun in May 1957 (Doc. no. 26, 1956-1957).

Wirtschaft und Wettbewerb, a monthly published in Düsseldorf, covers cartel problems very well and comments on related legal problems of the Community. Ernst Coenen's article in this journal, "Das Verhältnis des Entflechtungsrechts in Deutschland zum Montanunionvertrag" (February 1956, pp. 89-100), can be regarded as the German answer to the XXX article cited in n. 23.

There is a good summary of the ATIC case in the HA's *Bulletin Mensuel d'Information* (January-February 1958), pp. 23-25.

Chapter 15

On previous proposals for adaptation aid see P. W. Bidwell, *What the Tariff Means to American Industries* (New York: Harper, for the Council on Foreign Relations, 1956), pp. 267-276, and my *Trade and Payments in Western Europe* (cited on p. 727), pp. 204-215, 456, and the material cited in these places.

Community documentation on the adaptation programs is not very satisfactory. The most interesting of the Community documents is the Bertrand Report of June 1956 for the Assembly's social affairs committee (Doc. no. 26, 1955-1956). The HA *Report* of April 1958 is better than previous ones on this subject.

As my references make clear Alain Girard and Pierre Meutey, *Développement Économique et Mobilité des Travailleurs* (Paris: L'Institut National d'Études Démographiques, 1956; 158 p.), has been my best source; my debt is great. The summary volume, *Étude des Obstacles à la Mobilité* . . . (cited in n. 27), is a bit too general to be very enlightening and I have not been in a position to examine the underlying case studies, some of which sound interesting from their summaries. *Readaptation and Re-Employment of Workers*, Studies and Documents series (Luxembourg: ECSC, 1956; 149 p.); this report of a visit to the United States of a group of trade union representatives has some interesting points.

Chapter 16

Labor conditions. A great deal of information appears in regular Community publications, notably the HA *Reports, Bulletin Mensuel* (and its predecessor) and *Informations Statistiques*. In addition the HA has produced a number of special studies, some of the principal ones of which are listed below.

Tableau Comparatif des Conditions de Travail dans les Industries de la Communauté. 1953. 31 p. (Annex to the *Recueil Statistique*.)
Documentation sur les Problèmes du Travail dans les Industries de la Communauté. 1954. 115 p.
Consumers' Purchasing Power Parities in the Community Countries, special issue of *Statistical Information* published in the four Community languages and English. August-September 1955. 77 p.
Les Salaires et les Charges Sociales dans les Industries de la Communauté. Pt. 1, *Dépenses en Salaires et en Charges Patronales, Année 1954.* 1956. 122 p.
Comparaison des Revenus Réels des Travailleurs des Industries de la Communauté: Analyse Statistique, Études et Documents. 1956. 151 p.

These subjects can be pursued further through *Informations Statistiques* (indexed) which continues many of the statistical series, reports annual surveys, and devotes articles or whole issues to labor questions. There are additional HA studies on housing, mine safety, social security systems, apprentice training, and other labor questions which can be found in the bibliographies. Among a number of Assembly reports on labor questions the fullest is probably *Rapport Intérimaire . . . sur l'Évolution des Salaires et la Politique Salariale dans les Industries de la Communauté*, prepared by G. M. Nederhorst, Rapporteur, for the Assembly's committee on social affairs (Doc. no. 19, 1957-1958; 43 p.). Naturally the great mass of ILO material is valuable on a whole array of Community labor questions.

Movement of workers. Rudolph Petz and Helmut Zöllner, *Die Beschäftigungsfreiheit der Montanfacharbeiter* (Berlin: Vahlen, 1956; 198 p.), is a helpful commentary on the agreement. Some of the material cited in Ch. 15 is relevant here. There is a good general review in *Rapport . . . sur la Migration et la Libre Circulation des Travailleurs dans la Communauté*, prepared by A. Bertrand, Rapporteur, for the Common Assembly's committee on social affairs (Doc. no. 5, 1957-1958; 49 p.). A starting point for additional work that appeared too late for me to use is *Bibliographie Relative à la Mobilité Interne et aux Migrations Internationales des Travailleurs* (Luxembourg: HA, 1958; 373 p.).
On Italian workers abroad I have relied on a number of sources, especially *Bollettino Quindicinale dell'Emigrazione* (Milan) and *Relazioni Internazionali* (Milan). In addition to the statistics in Community docu-

ments there are frequent figures in ILO publications, especially *Industry and Labour*. A good summary of the conference on safety in coal mines appears in *International Labour Review* (August 1957), pp. 188-193.

Industry and Labour for October 15, 1957, pp. 314-322, summarizes the convention on social security for migrant workers. The text appears in *JO,* December 16, 1958, on the occasion of its being adopted for the European Economic Community.

"Social Policy" in general. CA documents provide extensive discussion, including important statements by HA members. The issues involved go back into a broad literature, of which the following items are worth special note, in addition to the Roux article cited in n. 2.

Delpérée, Albert. *Politique Sociale et Intégration Européenne.* Paris: Librairie Générale de Droit et de Jurisprudence, 1956. 293 p.

ILO. *Social Aspects of European Economic Co-operation.* Geneva: Author, 1956. 179 p. See the exchange of views on this report in the articles by Michael Heilperin and André Philip in the *International Labour Review* for March and September 1957, respectively, and the comment by Maurice Byé, a member of the original group of experts, in the same journal for January 1958.

Labor attitudes. My interpretations rest on many conversations, quite a few published and unpublished documents, and a large volume of scattered bits of evidence in speeches, articles, interviews, etc. A few are cited in footnotes. The fullest treatment is in Haas' book cited on p. 723; he has also been helpful to me privately. I have had the advantage of reading three unpublished papers by Louis Kriesberg, an American sociologist who, as a Fulbright Research Scholar in Germany in 1956-57, made a study of German attitudes toward the Schuman Plan and gave special attention to the views of labor and management.

Codetermination in Germany. A sample of the large literature follows. The ICFTU provides a good summary with bibliography. I found Spiro very interesting. Blumenthal is especially valuable for the testimony of participants; he considers codetermination as more satisfying to labor than I have depicted it.

Blumenthal, W. Michael. *Codetermination in the German Steel Industry: A Report of Experience.* Princeton: Princeton University Press, 1956. 114 p.

International Confederation of Free Trade Unions. *Workers' Participation in Industry.* Brussels: Author, 1954. 116 p.

Potthoff, Erich. *Der Kampf um die Montan-Mitbestimmung.* Köln-Deutz: Bund-Verlag, 1957. 150 p.

Shuchman, Abraham. *Codetermination: Labor's Middle Way in Germany.* Washington: Public Affairs Press, 1957. 247 p.

Spiro, Herbert J. *The Politics of German Codetermination.* Cambridge: Harvard University Press, 1958. 180 p.

Chapter 17

The Community's foreign trade is a rather neglected subject, except statistically. There is a good bit of information in HA *Reports,* some

CA documents (of which the Pleven report cited in n. *5* is the most notable), special articles in *Informations Statistiques,* and regular statistical sources. There is also a special statistical bulletin which, unfortunately, I did not see until my work was done: HA, *Commerce Extérieur de la Communauté: Résultats Trimestriels par États Membres.*

Such matters as export pricing, the Brussels cartel, and negotiations with other countries are repeatedly referred to in newspapers, magazines, bank bulletins, ECE publications, etc., but there is no adequate systematic documentation and no useful general studies. I have not seen the published version of Martin J. Rosen's *The Brussels Entente: Export Combination in the World Steel Market,* 106 U. Pa. L. Rev. 1079 (June 1958) but I had the privilege of examining an earlier draft, an excellent history put together from many sources emphasizing legal rather than economic issues.

The best source on the trade issues that rose between the Community and other countries is the annual discussion in GATT, reported in GATT, *Basic Instruments and Selected Documents,* First through Sixth Supplement, annually 1953-1958 (Geneva: Author).

Chapter 18

Newspapers, periodicals, country studies already cited on p. 726 f., and the GATT reports just mentioned are major sources for this chapter. British attitudes can be seen in *The Economist, The Manchester Guardian Weekly, The Times* (London), and *Hansard. Neue Zürcher Zeitung* covers the Swiss position very thoroughly; *Aussenwirtschaft,* published by the Handelshochschule of St. Gallen, is also useful (see for instance the comments by Hans Bachmann in the issue of December 1952, pp. 203-209). A good general statement made at an early stage is Carlo Meylan, "Der Schuman-Plan und die Schweiz," *Schweizer Monatshefte* (February 1952), pp. 647-657. Among other Austrian sources a number of articles in *Internationale Wirtschaft* (Vienna) have been useful to me along with Erhard Angermann, "Österreich und die Europäische Montanunion," *Der Volkswirt* (July 11, 1953), pp. 14-15. On Scandinavia I have used sources already cited along with the study of a Nordic common market cited in n. 24 of Ch. 17.

Chapter 19

There is little to add to the items quoted in the footnotes, material in the sections on Chs. 12 and 13, and some of the general works. Once again I worked from a variety of sources, from conversations, and from the feel of a subject that one absorbs over a period of close association. I had the advantage of seeing at a late stage an unpublished summary of American views prepared for Leonard Tennyson. The appearance of Monnet and his colleagues before the Senate Foreign Relations Committee is reported in "European Coal and Steel Community," Hearings, 83rd Cong., 1st sess. (Washington: GPO, 1953; 37 p.). An account of the press conference given by the American businessmen who toured the Community in late 1957 is in *Der Volkswirt* (November 23, 1957), p. 2517. For statistics I have relied on the Department of Commerce, its *International Iron and Steel,* Quarterly Industry Report, the *Annual Statistical Report* of the American Iron and Steel Institute, *Foreign*

Trade Trends, a convenient pamphlet published by the Institute, and the usual sources.

Chapter 20

By far the most enlightening studies are those of Jürgensen cited in n. 8. Understanding of the Community would be helped greatly by more work along these lines. I hope that here and elsewhere the text has made clear the desirability of much more statistical work on subjects subtler than those covered by the data published so far.

Chapter 21

This and the remaining chapters draw so extensively on the book as a whole that I have largely confined my bibliographical notes to a few points on which little literature has been cited.

Haas' book (cited on p. 723) is by far the best thing we have on the operation of the Community organs. I was very glad to find that his careful analysis, based on much more material than was available to me, supported at so many points the conclusions I had drawn from my quite different kind of study.

The only part of this subject that is at all well documented in public material is the role of the Assembly which was often discussed in full sessions of the Assembly and in committee reports. Among the works I have found especially helpful—in addition to those cited in n. 9—are Pierre Wigny's *L'Assemblée Parlementaire dans l'Europe des Six* (Luxembourg: ECSC, 1958; 110 p.) and T. E. Westerterp's "Europese Fractievorming: Een Eerste Experiment," *Internationale Spectator* (July 8, 1958), pp. 359-378. A convenient account of the Assembly's law and practice, which does not however push analysis very far, is Jean Lyon, *L'Assemblée Commune de la C.E.C.A.* (Paris: Librairies-Imprimeries Réunies, n.d.; 67 p.). On broader questions of the European Assemblies, I have found Kenneth Lindsay, *Towards a European Parliament* (Strasbourg: Council of Europe, 1958; 164 p.) interesting.

Chapter 22

A comprehensive, rigorous, and realistic examination of the economics of partial integration would be very valuable. Much literature on the Community and many more general works have something to say about this, but I know of no comprehensive treatment. There is a good beginning in Tibor Scitovsky, *Economic Theory and Western European Integration* (Stanford: Stanford University Press, 1958), pp. 136-151.

The literature on the "other pools" is much too large to be considered here. My *Trade and Payments in Western Europe* deals with some of them, while my paper, cited in n. 1, tries to distinguish the special features of the Schuman Plan and considers some of the issues of partial integration. The place of the Community in the more general process of political integration is reasonably well covered by two books reflecting rather different views of the process: Michael T. Florinsky, *Integrated Europe?* (New York: Macmillan, 1955; 182 p.) and Arnold J. Zurcher, *The Struggle to Unite Europe, 1940-1958* (New York: New York University Press, 1958; 254 p.). The literature on the new Communities is already very large (some of it is covered by bibliographies listed earlier). A good, comprehensive source is *Chronique de Politique Étrangère* (July-November 1957). For steel industry views on the free trade area see:

Ferry, Jacques. "La Création d'une Zone de Libre Échange Serait-Elle Conciliable avec l'Éxistence de la Communauté Européenne du Charbon et de l'Acier?" *Politique Étrangère*, no. 2 (1958), pp. 181-195.

Hellmann, Rainer. "Kohle und Stahl Schwierige Freihandelsanwärter," *Der Volkswirt* (December 13, 1958), pp. 2475-2476.

"Steel and the Free Trade Area," *Steel Review* (October 1957), pp. 1-6.

An excellent discussion of political and economic integration, its relation to Europe's place in the world, and the resulting problems for United States policy is provided by Ben T. Moore, *NATO and the Future of Europe* (New York: Harper, for the Council on Foreign Relations, 1958; 263 p.). For a critical examination of European economic integration see François Perroux, *L'Europe sans Rivages* (Paris: Presses Universitaires de France, 1954); pp. 530-584 deal specifically with the Community. An interesting *Memorandum on General Economic Integration in Europe* was prepared for the HA by Pierre Uri (Doc. no. 5579/55e; mimeographed, 30 p.).

Chapter 23

The revision of the Treaty is best followed in the Assembly debates and Kreyssig's report cited in n. 3. A good analysis of the general situation is Rainer Hellmann, "Keine Überstürzte Revision des Montanvertrages," *Der Volkswirt* (March 22, 1958), pp. 470-471.

On the piling up of coal stocks and the immediate and basic questions that arise, I have found *Der Volkswirt* and *Neue Zürcher Zeitung* very helpful. Good summaries of the relation of coal to other forms of energy are in Konrad Ebert, "Die Lage des Steinkohlenbergbaus im Energiewirtschaftlichen Gesamtbild," *Wirtschaftsdienst* (September 1958), pp. 491-496; and "Coal and Oil Competition in Western Europe," *Petroleum Press Service* (June 1958), pp. 203-207. The latter journal has been helpful on a number of other issues as well.

The High Authority's work on long-run problems is usually covered by the *Reports*. A *Mémorandum sur la Définition des Objectifs Généraux de la Communauté* appeared in *JO*, May 20, 1957. I have also been able to use some mimeographed documents, such as an earlier version of the paper just cited and a *Mémorandum de la Haute Autorité sur la Politique Charbonnière* of February 1, 1955. Assembly debates and reports also deal with these questions.

On Europe's energy needs the key reports are:

A Target for Euratom, Report submitted by Louis Armand, Franz Etzel and Francesco Giordani. [Luxembourg: ECSC], 1957. 104 p.

Étude sur la Structure et les Tendances de l'Économie Énergétique, a report of a joint committee of the Council of Ministers and the High Authority. Luxembourg: ECSC, 1957. 113 p.

Europe's Growing Needs of Energy: How Can They Be Met? Report prepared by a group of experts. Paris: OEEC, 1956. 120 p.

LIST OF ABBREVIATIONS

APE	Assemblée Parlementaire Européenne
ARBED	Aciéries Réunies de Burbach-Eich-Dudelange (Luxembourg)
Assider	Associazione Industrie Siderurgiche Italiane
ATIC	Association Technique de l'Importation Charbonnière (France)
CA	Common Assembly
Carbosarda	Compania Mineraria Carbonifera Sarda
CDU	Christlich-Demokratische Union
CECA	Communauté Européenne du Charbon et de l'Acier
CFTC	Confédération Française des Travailleurs Chrétiens
CGIL	Confederazione Generale Italiana del Lavoro
CGT	Confédération Générale du Travail (France)
CISL	Confederazione Italiana di Sindicati di Lavoro
Cobechar	Comptoir Belge des Charbons
Confindustria	Confederazione Generale dell'Industria Italiana
DGB	Deutscher Gewerkschaftsbund
DKV	Deutscher Kohlen-Verkauf
ECA	Economic Cooperation Administration (U.S.)
ECE	Economic Commission for Europe (U.N.)
ECSC	European Coal and Steel Community
EDC	European Defense Community
EEC	European Economic Community
EPA	European Parliamentary Assembly
EPC	European Political Community
EPU	European Payments Union
Euratom	European Atomic Energy Community
FDP	Freie Deutsche Partei
Finsider	Finanziaria Siderugica
GATT	General Agreement on Tariffs and Trade
Georg	Gemeinschaftsorganisation Ruhrkohle

GIS	Groupement de l'Industrie Sidérurgique (France)
HA	High Authority
IBRD	International Bank for Reconstruction and Development
ICFTU	International Confederation of Free Trade Unions
ILO	International Labor Organization
IMF	International Monetary Fund
JO	*Journal Officiel*
MRP	Mouvement Républicain Populaire (France)
NATO	North Atlantic Treaty Organization
OCCF	Office Commun des Consommateurs de Feraille
OEEC	Organization for European Economic Cooperation
OKU	Oberrheinische Kohlenunion
RWKS	Rheinisch-Westfälische Kohlensyndikat
Sidechar	Société Sidérurgique de Participation et d'Approvisionnement en Charbons (France)
Sidelor	Union Sidérurgique Lorraine
Sollac	Société Lorraine de Laminage Continu
SPD	Sozialdemokratische Partei Deutschlands
UIL	Unione Italiana di Lavoro
Usinor	Union Sidérurgique du Nord de la France

INDEX

Entries are selective, not exhaustive. The most important listings are those of countries, commodities, fields of Community activity, "partial integration" and "European economic integration." Since cross references among these have mostly been omitted, users should bear in mind their interconnection. References to subjects that run all through the book (e.g., Treaty, High Authority) have been held to a minimum; summaries of treaty provisions that begin many chapters are not indexed, nor are all actions by Community organs. Companies are not separately indexed; most of the information about them can be found under "organization of industry" in each country. Political parties are also omitted. Other organizations are not listed when they appear as authors or publishers of reports. The index should be used in conjunction with the Table of Contents and List of Tables; entries do not cover tables, graphs, preface, or bibliography. "C." stands for Community.